The Theory and Practice of Group Psychotherapy

FIFTH EDITION

The Theory and Practice of

GROUP PSYCHOTHERAPY

FIFTH EDITION

IRVIN D. YALOM

WITH

MOLYN LESZCZ

BASIC BOOKS

A Member of the Perseus Books Group
New York

Designed by Brent Wilcox
Text set in 11-point Sabon MT

Library of Congress Cataloging-in-Publication Data
Yalom, Irvin D., 1931–
    The theory and practice of group psychotherapy / Irvin D. Yalom with Molyn Leszcz.—5th ed.
        p.   cm.
    Includes bibliographical references and index.
    ISBN-13 978-0-465-09284-0
    ISBN 0-465-09284-5 (hardcover : alk. paper)
1. Group psychotherapy.   I. Leszcz, Molyn, 1952–   II. Title.
RC488.Y3   2005
616.89'152—dc22

                                                                    2005000056

    06 07 / 10 9 8 7 6 5 4 3

To the memory of my mother and father,
RUTH YALOM *and* BENJAMIN YALOM

To the memory of my mother and father,
CLARA LESZCZ *and* SAUL LESZCZ

Contents

Preface to the Fifth Edition

For this fifth edition of *The Theory and Practice of Group Psychotherapy* I have had the good fortune of having Molyn Leszcz as my collaborator. Dr. Leszcz, whom I first met in 1980 when he spent a yearlong fellowship in group therapy with me at Stanford University, has been a major contributor to research and clinical innovation in group therapy. For the past twelve years, he has directed one of the largest group therapy training programs in the world in the Department of Psychiatry at the University of Toronto, where he is an associate professor. His broad knowledge of contemporary group practice and his exhaustive review of the research and clinical literature were invaluable to the preparation of this volume. We worked diligently, like co-therapists, to make this edition a seamless integration of new and old material. Although for stylistic integrity we opted to retain the first-person singular in this text, behind the "I" there is always a collaborative "we."

Our task in this new edition was to incorporate the many new changes in the field and to jettison outmoded ideas and methods. But we had a dilemma: What if some of the changes in the field do not represent advances but, instead, retrogression? What if marketplace considerations demanding quicker, cheaper, more efficient methods act against the best interests of the client? And what if "efficiency" is but a euphemism for shedding clients from the fiscal rolls as quickly as possible? And what if these diverse market factors force therapists to offer less than they are capable of offering their clients?

If these suppositions are true, then the requirements of this revision become far more complex because we have a dual task: not only to present current methods and prepare student therapists for the contemporary workplace, but also to preserve the accumulated wisdom and techniques of our field even if some young therapists will not have immediate opportunities to apply them.

Since group therapy was first introduced in the 1940s, it has undergone a series of adaptations to meet the changing face of clinical practice. As new clinical syndromes, settings, and theoretical approaches have emerged, so have corresponding variants of group therapy. The multiplicity of forms is so evident today that it makes more sense to speak of "group therapies" than of "group therapy." Groups for panic disorder, groups for acute and chronic depression, groups to prevent depression relapse, groups for eating disorders, medical support groups for patients with cancer, HIV/AIDS, rheumatoid arthritis, multiple sclerosis, irritable bowel syndrome, obesity, myocardial infarction, paraplegia, diabetic blindness, renal failure, bone marrow transplant, Parkinson's, groups for healthy men and women who carry genetic mutations that predispose them to develop cancer, groups for victims of sexual abuse, for the confused elderly and for their caregivers, for clients with obsessive-compulsive disorder, first-episode schizophrenia, for chronic schizophrenia, for adult children of alcoholics, for parents of sexually abused children, for male batterers, for self-mutilators, for the divorced, for the bereaved, for disturbed families, for married couples—all of these, and many more, are forms of group therapy.

The clinical settings of group therapy are also diverse: a rapid turnover group for chronically or acutely psychotic patients on a stark hospital ward is group therapy, and so are groups for imprisoned sex offenders, groups for residents of a shelter for battered women, and open-ended groups of relatively well functioning individuals with neurotic or personality disorders meeting in the well-appointed private office of a psychotherapist.

And the technical approaches are bewilderingly different: cognitive-behavioral, psychoeducational, interpersonal, gestalt, supportive-expressive, psychoanalytic, dynamic-interactional, psychodrama—all of these, and many more, are used in group therapy.

This family gathering of group therapies is swollen even more by the presence of distant cousins to therapy groups entering the room: experiential classroom training groups (or process groups) and the numerous self-help (or mutual support) groups like Alcoholics Anonymous and other twelve-step recovery groups, Adult Survivors of Incest, Sex Addicts Anonymous, Parents of Murdered Children, Overeaters Anonymous, and Recovery, Inc. Although these groups are not formal therapy groups, they are very often *therapeutic* and straddle the blurred borders between personal growth, support, education, and therapy (see chapter 16 for a detailed discussion of this topic). And we must also consider the youngest, most rambunctious, and most unpredictable of the cousins: the Internet support groups, offered in a rainbow of flavors.

How, then, to write a single book that addresses *all* these group therapies? The strategy I chose thirty-five years ago when I wrote the first edition of this book seems sound to me still. My first step was to separate "front" from "core" in each of the group therapies. The *front* consists of the trappings, the form, the techniques, the specialized language, and the aura surrounding each of the ideological schools; the *core* consists of those aspects of the experience that are intrinsic to the therapeutic process—that is, the *bare-boned mechanisms of change.*

If you disregard the "front" and consider only the actual mechanisms of effecting change in the client, you will find that the change mechanisms are limited in number and are remarkably similar across groups. Therapy groups with similar goals that appear wildly different in external form may rely on identical mechanisms of change.

In the first two editions of this book, caught up in the positivistic zeitgeist surrounding the developing psychotherapies, I referred to these mechanisms of change as "curative factors." Educated and humbled by the passing years, I know now that the harvest of psychotherapy is not *cure*—surely, in our field, that is an illusion—but instead change or growth. Hence, yielding to the dictates of reality, I now refer to the mechanisms of change as "therapeutic factors" rather than "curative factors."

The therapeutic factors constitute the central organizing principle of this book. I begin with a detailed discussion of eleven therapeutic factors and then describe a psychotherapeutic approach that is based on them.

But which types of groups to discuss? The array of group therapies is now so vast that it is impossible for a text to address each type of group separately. How then to proceed? I have chosen in this book to center my discussion around a prototypic type of group therapy and *then to offer a set of principles that will enable the therapist to modify this fundamental group model to fit any specialized clinical situation.*

The prototypical model is the intensive, heterogeneously composed outpatient psychotherapy group, meeting for at least several months, with the ambitious goals of both symptomatic relief and personality change. Why focus on this particular form of group therapy when the contemporary therapy scene, driven by economic factors, is dominated by another type of group—a homogeneous, symptom-oriented group that meets for briefer periods and has more limited goals?

The answer is that long-term group therapy has been around for many decades and has accumulated a vast body of knowledge from both empirical research and thoughtful clinical observation. Earlier I alluded to contemporary therapists not often having the clinical opportunities to do their best work; I believe that the prototypical group we describe in this book is the setting in which therapists can offer maximum benefit to their clients. It is an intensive, ambitious form of therapy that demands much from both client and therapist. The therapeutic strategies and techniques required to lead such a group are sophisticated and complex. However, *once students master them and understand how to modify them to fit specialized therapy situations, they will be in a position to fashion a group therapy that will be effective for any clinical population in any setting.* Trainees should aspire to be creative and compassionate therapists with conceptual depth, not laborers with little vision and less morale. Managed care emphatically views group therapy as the treatment modality of the future. Group therapists must be as prepared as possible for this opportunity.

Because most readers of this book are clinicians, the text is intended to have immediate clinical relevance. I also believe, however, that it is imperative for clinicians to remain conversant with the world of research. *Even if therapists do not personally engage in research, they must know how to evaluate the research of others.* Accordingly, the text relies heavily on relevant clinical, social, and psychological research.

While searching through library stacks during the writing of early editions of this book, I often found myself browsing in antiquated psychiatric texts. How unsettling it is to realize that the devotees of such therapy endeavors as hydrotherapy, rest cures, lobotomy, and insulin coma were obviously clinicians of high intelligence, dedication, and integrity. The same may be said of earlier generations of therapists who advocated venesection, starvation, purgation, and trephination. Their texts are as well written, their optimism as unbridled, and their reported results as impressive as those of contemporary practitioners.

Question: why have other health-care fields left treatment of psychological disturbance so far behind? *Answer:* because they have applied the principles of the scientific method. Without a rigorous research base, the psychotherapists of today who are enthusiastic about current treatments are tragically similar to the hydrotherapists and lobotomists of yesteryear. As long as we do not test basic principles and treatment outcomes with scientific rigor, our field remains at the mercy of passing fads and fashions. Therefore, whenever possible, the approach presented in this text is based on rigorous, relevant research, and attention is called to areas in which further research seems especially necessary and feasible. Some areas (for example, preparation for group therapy and the reasons for group dropouts) have been widely and competently studied, while other areas (for example, "working through" or countertransference) have only recently been touched by research. Naturally, this distribution of research emphasis is reflected in the text: some chapters may appear, to clinicians, to stress research too heavily, while other chapters may appear, to research-minded colleagues, to lack rigor.

Let us not expect more of psychotherapy research than it can deliver. Will the findings of psychotherapy research affect a rapid major change in therapy practice? Probably not. Why? "Resistance" is one reason. Complex systems of therapy with adherents who have spent many years in training and apprenticeship and cling stubbornly to tradition will change slowly and only in the face of very substantial evidence. Furthermore, front-line therapists faced with suffering clients obviously cannot wait for science. Also, keep in mind the economics of research. The marketplace controls the focus of research. When managed-care economics dictated a massive swing to brief, symptom-oriented therapy, reports from a multitude of well-funded research projects on brief therapy began to appear in the literature. At the same time, the bottom dropped out of funding sources for research on longer-term therapy, despite a strong clinical consensus about the importance of such research. In time we expect that this trend will be reversed and that more investigation of the effectiveness of psychotherapy in the real world of practice will be undertaken to supplement the knowledge accruing from randomized controlled trials of brief therapy. Another consideration is that, unlike in the physical sciences, many aspects of psychotherapy inherently defy quantification. Psychotherapy is both art and science; research findings may ultimately shape the broad contours of practice, but the human encounter at the center of therapy will always be a deeply subjective, nonquantifiable experience.

One of the most important underlying assumptions in this text is that interpersonal interaction within the here-and-now is crucial to effective group therapy. The truly potent therapy group first provides an arena in which clients can interact freely with others, then helps them identify and understand what goes wrong in their interactions, and ultimately enables them to change those maladaptive patterns. We believe that groups based *solely* on other assumptions, such as psychoeducational or cognitive-behavioral principles, fail to reap the full therapeutic harvest. Each of these forms of group therapy can be made even more effective by incorporating an awareness of interpersonal process.

This point needs emphasis: It has great relevance for the future of clinical practice. The advent of managed care will ultimately result in increased use of therapy groups. But, in their quest for efficiency, brevity, and accountability, managed-care decision makers may make the mistake of decreeing that some distinct orientations (brief, cognitive-behavioral, symptom-focused) are more desirable because their approach encompasses a series of steps consistent with other efficient medical approaches: the setting of explicit, limited goals; the measuring of goal attainment at regular, frequent intervals; a highly specific treatment plan; and a replicable, uniform, manual-driven, highly structured therapy with a precise protocol for each session. But do not mistake the *appearance* of efficiency for true effectiveness.

In this text we discuss, in depth, the extent and nature of the interactional focus and its potency in bringing about significant character and interpersonal change. *The interactional focus is the engine of group therapy,* and therapists who are able to harness it are much better equipped to do all forms of group therapy, even if the group model does not emphasize or acknowledge the centrality of interaction.

Initially I was not eager to undertake the considerable task of revising this text. The theoretical foundations and technical approach to group therapy described in the fourth edition remain sound and useful. But a book in an evolving field is bound to age sooner than later, and the last edition was losing some of its currency. Not only did it contain dated or anachronistic allusions, but also the field has changed. Managed care has settled in by now, DSM-IV has undergone a text revision (DSM-IV-TR), and a decade of clinical and research literature needed to be reviewed and assimilated into the text. Furthermore, new types of groups have sprung up and others have faded away. Cognitive-behavioral, psychoeducational, and problem-specific brief therapy groups are becoming more common, so in this revision we have made a special effort throughout to address the particular issues germane to these groups.

The first four chapters of this text discuss eleven therapeutic factors. Chapter 1 covers instillation of hope, universality, imparting information, altruism, the corrective recapitulation of the primary family group, the development of socializing techniques, and imitative behavior. Chapters 2 and 3 present the more complex and powerful factors of interpersonal learning and cohesiveness. Recent advances in our understanding of interpersonal theory and the therapeutic alliance that can strengthen therapist effectiveness have influenced our approach to these two chapters.

Chapter 4 discusses catharsis and existential factors and then attempts a synthesis by addressing the comparative importance and the interdependence of all eleven therapeutic factors.

The next two chapters address the work of the therapist. Chapter 5 discusses the tasks of the group therapist—especially those germane to shaping a therapeutic group culture and harnessing the group interaction for therapeutic benefit. Chapter 6 describes how the therapist must first activate the here-and-now (that is, plunge the group into its own experience) and then illuminate the meaning of the here-and-now experience. In this edition we deemphasize certain models that rely on the elucidation of group-as-a-whole dynamics (for example, the Tavistock approach)— models that have since proven ineffective in the therapy process. (Some omitted material that may still interest some readers will remain available at www.yalom.com.)

While chapters 5 and 6 address what the therapist must *do*, chapter 7 addresses how the therapist must *be*. It explicates the therapist's role and the therapist's use of self by focusing on two fundamental issues: transference and transparency. In previous editions, I felt compelled to encourage therapist restraint: Many therapists were still so influenced by the encounter group movement that they, too frequently and too extensively, "let it all hang out." Times have changed; more conservative forces have taken hold, and now we feel compelled to discourage therapists from practicing too defensively. Many contemporary therapists, threatened by the encroachment of the legal profession into the field (a result of the irresponsibility and misconduct of some therapists, coupled with a reckless and greedy malpractice industry), have grown too cautious and impersonal. Hence we give much attention to the use of the therapist's self in psychotherapy.

Chapters 8 through 14 present a chronological view of the therapy group and emphasize group phenomena and techniques that are relevant to each stage. Chapters 8 and 9, on client selection and group composition, include new research data on group therapy attendance, dropouts, and outcomes. Chapter 10, which describes the practical realities of beginning a group, includes a lengthy new section on brief group therapy, presents much new research on the preparation of the client for group therapy. The appendix contains a document to distribute to new members to help prepare them for their work in the therapy group.

Chapter 11 addresses the early stages of the therapy group and includes new material on dealing with the therapy dropout. Chapter 12 deals with phenomena encountered in the mature phase of the group therapy work: subgrouping, conflict, self-disclosure, and termination.

Chapter 13, on problem members in group therapy, adds new material to reflect advances in interpersonal theory. It discusses the contributions of intersubjectivity, attachment theory, and self psychology. Chapter 14 discusses specialized techniques of the therapist, including concurrent individual and group therapy (both combined and conjoint), co-therapy, leaderless meetings, dreams, videotaping, and structured exercises, the use of the written summary in group therapy, and the integration of group therapy and twelve-step programs.

Chapter 15, on specialized therapy groups, addresses the many new groups that have emerged to deal with specific clinical syndromes or clinical situations. It presents the critically important principles used to modify traditional group therapy technique in order to design a group to meet the needs of other specialized clinical situations and populations, and describes the adaptation of cognitive-behavioral and interpersonal therapy to groups. These principles are illustrated by in-depth discussions of various groups, such as the acute psychiatric inpatient group and groups for the medically ill (with a detailed illustration of a group for patients with cancer). Chapter 15 also discusses self-help groups and the youngest member of the group therapy family—the Internet support group.

Chapter 16, on the encounter group, presented the single greatest challenge for this revision. Because the encounter group *qua* encounter group has faded from contemporary culture, we considered omitting the chapter entirely. However, several factors argue against an early burial: the important role played by the encounter movement groups in developing research technology and the use of encounter groups (also known as process groups, T-groups (for "training"), or experiential training groups) in group psychotherapy education. Our compromise was to shorten the chapter considerably and to make the entire fourth edition chapter available at www.yalom.com for readers who are interested in the history and evolution of the encounter movement.

Chapter 17, on the training of group therapists, includes new approaches to the supervision process and on the use of process groups in the educational curriculum.

During the four years of preparing this revision I was also engaged in writing a novel, *The Schopenhauer Cure,* which may serve as a companion volume to this text: It is set in a therapy group and illustrates many of the principles of group process and therapist technique offered in this text. Hence, at several points in this fifth edition, I refer the reader to particular pages in *The Schopenhauer Cure* that offer fictionalized portrayals of therapist techniques.

Excessively overweight volumes tend to gravitate to the "reference book" shelves. To avoid that fate we have resisted lengthening this text. The addition of much new material has mandated the painful task of cutting older sections and citations. (I left my writing desk daily with fingers stained by the blood of many condemned passages.) To increase readability, we consigned almost all details and critiques of research method to footnotes or to notes at the end of the book. The review of the last ten years of group therapy literature has been exhaustive.

Most chapters contain 50–100 new references. In several locations throughout the book, we have placed a dagger (†) to indicate that corroborative observations or data exist for suggested current readings for students interested in that particular area. *This list of references and suggested readings has been placed on my website, www.yalom.com.*

Acknowledgments

(Irvin Yalom)

I am grateful to Stanford University for providing the academic freedom, library facilities, and administrative staff necessary to accomplish this work. To a masterful mentor, Jerome Frank (who died just before the publication of this edition), my thanks for having introduced me to group therapy and for having offered a model of integrity, curiosity, and dedication. Several have assisted in this revision: Stephanie Brown, Ph.D. (on twelve-step groups), Morton Lieberman, Ph.D. (on Internet groups), Ruthellen Josselson, Ph.D. (on group-as-a-whole interventions), David Spiegel (on medical groups), and my son Ben Yalom, who edited several chapters.

(Molyn Leszcz)

I am grateful to the University of Toronto Department of Psychiatry for its support in this project. Toronto colleagues who have made comments on drafts of this edition and facilitated its completion include Joel Sadavoy, M.D., Don Wasylenki, M.D., Danny Silver, M.D., Paula Ravitz, M.D., Zindel Segal, Ph.D., Paul Westlind, M.D., Ellen Margolese, M.D., Jan Malat, M.D., and Jon Hunter, M.D. Liz Konigshaus handled the painstaking task of word-processing, with enormous efficiency and unyielding good nature. Benjamin, Talia, and Noah Leszcz, my children, and Bonny Leszcz, my wife, contributed insight and encouragement throughout.

Chapter 1

THE THERAPEUTIC
FACTORS

D oes group therapy help clients? Indeed it does. A persuasive body of
outcome research has demonstrated unequivocally that group therapy is a highly effective form of psychotherapy and that it is at least equal
to individual psychotherapy in its power to provide meaningful benefit.[1]

How does group therapy help clients? A naive question, perhaps. But if
we can answer it with some measure of precision and certainty, we will
have at our disposal a central organizing principle with which to approach the most vexing and controversial problems of psychotherapy.
Once identified, the crucial aspects of the process of change will constitute a rational basis for the therapist's selection of tactics and strategies to
shape the group experience to maximize its potency with different clients
and in different settings.

I suggest that therapeutic change is an enormously complex process
that occurs through an intricate interplay of human experiences, which I
will refer to as "therapeutic factors." There is considerable advantage in
approaching the complex through the simple, the total phenomenon
through its basic component processes. Accordingly, I begin by describing
and discussing these elemental factors.

From my perspective, natural lines of cleavage divide the therapeutic
experience into eleven primary factors:

1. Instillation of hope
2. Universality
3. Imparting information
4. Altruism
5. The corrective recapitulation of the primary family group
6. Development of socializing techniques

1

   7. Imitative behavior
   8. Interpersonal learning
   9. Group cohesiveness
  10. Catharsis
  11. Existential factors

In the rest of this chapter, I discuss the first seven factors. I consider interpersonal learning and group cohesiveness so important and complex that I have treated them separately, in the next two chapters. Existential factors are discussed in chapter 4, where they are best understood in the context of other material presented there. Catharsis is intricately interwoven with other therapeutic factors and will also be discussed in chapter 4.

The distinctions among these factors are arbitrary. Although I discuss them singly, they are interdependent and neither occur nor function separately. Moreover, these factors may represent different parts of the change process: some factors (for example, self-understanding) act at the level of cognition; some (for example, development of socializing techniques) act at the level of behavioral change; some (for example, catharsis) act at the level of emotion; and some (for example, cohesiveness) may be more accurately described as preconditions for change.† Although the same therapeutic factors operate in every type of therapy group, their interplay and differential importance can vary widely from group to group. Furthermore, because of individual differences, participants in the same group benefit from widely different clusters of therapeutic factors.†

Keeping in mind that the therapeutic factors are arbitrary constructs, we can view them as providing a cognitive map for the student-reader. This grouping of the therapeutic factors is not set in concrete; other clinicians and researchers have arrived at a different, and also arbitrary, clusters of factors.[2] No explanatory system can encompass all of therapy. At its core, the therapy process is infinitely complex, and there is no end to the number of pathways through the experience. (I will discuss all of these issues more fully in chapter 4.)

The inventory of therapeutic factors I propose issues from my clinical experience, from the experience of other therapists, from the views of the successfully treated group patient, and from relevant systematic research. None of these sources is beyond doubt, however; neither group members nor group leaders are entirely objective, and our research methodology is often crude and inapplicable.

From the group therapists we obtain a variegated and internally inconsistent inventory of therapeutic factors (see chapter 4). Therapists, by no means disinterested or unbiased observers, have invested considerable time and energy in mastering a certain therapeutic approach. Their answers will be determined largely by their particular school of conviction.

Even among therapists who share the same ideology and speak the same language, there may be no consensus about the reasons clients improve. In research on encounter groups, my colleagues and I learned that many successful group leaders attributed their success to factors that were irrelevant to the therapy process: for example, the hot-seat technique, or nonverbal exercises, or the direct impact of a therapist's own person (see chapter 16).[3] But that does not surprise us. The history of psychotherapy abounds in healers who were effective, but not for the reasons they supposed. At other times we therapists throw up our hands in bewilderment. Who has not had a client who made vast improvement for entirely obscure reasons?

Group members at the end of a course of group therapy can supply data about the therapeutic factors they considered most and least helpful. Yet we know that such evaluations will be incomplete and their accuracy limited. Will the group members not, perhaps, focus primarily on superficial factors and neglect some profound healing forces that may be beyond their awareness? Will their responses not be influenced by a variety of factors difficult to control? It is entirely possible, for example, that their views may be distorted by the nature of their relationship to the therapist or to the group. (One team of researchers demonstrated that when patients were interviewed four years after the conclusion of therapy, they were far more apt to comment on unhelpful or harmful aspects of their group experience than when interviewed immediately at its conclusion.)[4] Research has also shown, for example, that the therapeutic factors valued by group members may differ greatly from those cited by their therapists or by group observers,[5] an observation also made in individual psychotherapy. Furthermore, many confounding factors influence the client's evaluation of the therapeutic factors: for example, the length of time in treatment and the level of a client's functioning,[6] the type of group (that is, whether outpatient, inpatient, day hospital, brief therapy),[7] the age and the diagnosis of a client,[8] and the ideology of the group leader.[9] Another factor that complicates the search for common therapeutic factors is the extent to which different group members perceive and experience the same event in different ways.† Any given experience may be important or helpful to some and inconsequential or even harmful to others.

Despite these limitations, clients' reports are a rich and relatively untapped source of information. After all, it is *their* experience, *theirs* alone, and the farther we move from the clients' experience, the more inferential are our conclusions. To be sure, there are aspects of the process of change that operate outside a client's awareness, but it does not follow that we should disregard what clients do say.

There is an art to obtaining clients' reports. Paper-and-pencil or sorting questionnaires provide easy data but often miss the nuances and the richness of the clients' experience. The more the questioner can enter into the experiential world of the client, the more lucid and meaningful the report of the therapy experience becomes. To the degree that the therapist is able to suppress personal bias and avoid influencing the client's responses, he or she becomes the ideal questioner: the therapist is trusted and understands more than anyone else the inner world of the client.

In addition to therapists' views and clients' reports, there is a third important method of evaluating the therapeutic factors: the systematic research approach. The most common research strategy by far is to correlate in-therapy variables with outcome in therapy. By discovering which variables are significantly related to successful outcomes, one can establish a reasonable base from which to begin to delineate the therapeutic factors. However, there are many inherent problems in this approach: the measurement of outcome is itself a methodological morass, and the selection and measurement of the in-therapy variables are equally problematic.*[10]

I have drawn from all these methods to derive the therapeutic factors discussed in this book. Still, I do not consider these conclusions definitive; rather, I offer them as provisional guidelines that may be tested and deepened by other clinical researchers. For my part, I am satisfied that they derive from the best available evidence at this time and that they constitute the basis of an effective approach to therapy.

INSTILLATION OF HOPE

The instillation and maintenance of hope is crucial in any psychotherapy. Not only is hope required to keep the client in therapy so that other therapeutic factors may take effect, but faith in a treatment mode can in itself be therapeutically effective. Several studies have demonstrated that a high expectation of help before the start of therapy is significantly correlated with a positive therapy outcome.[11] Consider also the massive data documenting the efficacy of faith healing and placebo treatment—therapies mediated entirely through hope and conviction. A positive outcome in psychotherapy is more likely when the client and the therapist have similar expectations of the treatment.[12] The power of expectations extends beyond imagination alone. Recent brain imaging studies demonstrate that the placebo is not inactive but can have a direct physiological effect on the brain.[13]

---

*We are better able to evaluate therapy outcome in general than we are able to measure the relationships between these process variables and outcomes. Kivlighan and colleagues have developed a promising scale, the Group Helpful Impacts Scale, that tries to capture the entirety of the group therapeutic process in a multidimensional fashion that encompasses therapy tasks and therapy relationships as well as group process, client, and leader variables.

Group therapists can capitalize on this factor by doing whatever we can to increase clients' belief and confidence in the efficacy of the group mode. This task begins before the group starts, in the pregroup orientation, in which the therapist reinforces positive expectations, corrects negative preconceptions, and presents a lucid and powerful explanation of the group's healing properties. (See chapter 10 for a full discussion of the pregroup preparation procedure.)

Group therapy not only draws from the general ameliorative effects of positive expectations but also benefits from a source of hope that is unique to the group format. Therapy groups invariably contain individuals who are at different points along a coping-collapse continuum. Each member thus has considerable contact with others—often individuals with similar problems—who have improved as a result of therapy. I have often heard clients remark at the end of their group therapy how important it was for them to have observed the improvement of others. Remarkably, hope can be a powerful force even in groups of individuals combating advanced cancer who lose cherished group members to the disease. Hope is flexible—it redefines itself to fit the immediate parameters, becoming hope for comfort, for dignity, for connection with others, or for minimum physical discomfort.[14]

Group therapists should by no means be above exploiting this factor by periodically calling attention to the improvement that members have made. If I happen to receive notes from recently terminated members informing me of their continued improvement, I make a point of sharing this with the current group. Senior group members often assume this function by offering spontaneous testimonials to new, skeptical members.

Research has shown that it is also vitally important that therapists believe in themselves and in the efficacy of their group.[15] I sincerely believe that I am able to help every motivated client who is willing to work in the group for at least six months. In my initial meetings with clients individually, I share this conviction with them and attempt to imbue them with my optimism.

Many of the self-help groups—for example, Compassionate Friends (for bereaved parents), Men Overcoming Violence (men who batter), Survivors of Incest, and Mended Heart (heart surgery patients)—place heavy emphasis on the instillation of hope.[16] A major part of Recovery, Inc. (for current and former psychiatric patients) and Alcoholics Anonymous meetings is dedicated to testimonials. At each meeting, members of Recovery, Inc. give accounts of potentially stressful incidents in which they avoided tension by the application of Recovery, Inc. methods, and successful Alcoholics Anonymous members tell their stories of downfall and then rescue by AA. One of the great strengths of Alcoholics Anonymous is the fact that the leaders are all alcoholics—living inspirations to the others.

Substance abuse treatment programs commonly mobilize hope in participants by using recovered drug addicts as group leaders. Members are inspired and expectations raised by contact with those who have trod the same path and found the way back. A similar approach is used for individuals with chronic medical illnesses such as arthritis and heart disease. These self-management groups use trained peers to encourage members to cope actively with their medical conditions.[17] The inspiration provided to participants by their peers results in substantial improvements in medical outcomes, reduces health care costs, promotes the individual's sense of self-efficacy, and often makes group interventions superior to individual therapies.[18]

UNIVERSALITY

Many individuals enter therapy with the disquieting thought that they are unique in their wretchedness, that they alone have certain frightening or unacceptable problems, thoughts, impulses, and fantasies. Of course, there is a core of truth to this notion, since most clients have had an unusual constellation of severe life stresses and are periodically flooded by frightening material that has leaked from their unconscious.

To some extent this is true for all of us, but many clients, because of their extreme social isolation, have a heightened sense of uniqueness. Their interpersonal difficulties preclude the possibility of deep intimacy. In everyday life they neither learn about others' analogous feelings and experiences nor avail themselves of the opportunity to confide in, and ultimately to be validated and accepted by, others.

In the therapy group, especially in the early stages, the disconfirmation of a client's feelings of uniqueness is a powerful source of relief. After hearing other members disclose concerns similar to their own, clients report feeling more in touch with the world and describe the process as a "welcome to the human race" experience. Simply put, the phenomenon finds expression in the cliché "We're all in the same boat"—or perhaps more cynically, "Misery loves company."

There is no human deed or thought that lies fully outside the experience of other people. I have heard group members reveal such acts as incest, torture, burglary, embezzlement, murder, attempted suicide, and fantasies of an even more desperate nature. Invariably, I have observed other group members reach out and embrace these very acts as within the realm of their own possibilities, often following through the door of disclosure opened by one group member's trust or courage. Long ago Freud noted that the staunchest taboos (against incest and patricide) were constructed precisely because these very impulses are part of the human being's deepest nature.

Nor is this form of aid limited to group therapy. Universality plays a role in individual therapy also, although in that format there is less opportunity for consensual validation, as therapists choose to restrict their degree of personal transparency.

During my own 600-hour analysis I had a striking personal encounter with the therapeutic factor of universality. It happened when I was in the midst of describing my extremely ambivalent feelings toward my mother. I was very much troubled by the fact that, despite my strong positive sentiments, I was also beset with death wishes for her, as I stood to inherit part of her estate. My analyst responded simply, "That seems to be the way we're built." That artless statement not only offered me considerable relief but enabled me to explore my ambivalence in great depth.

Despite the complexity of human problems, certain common denominators between individuals are clearly evident, and the members of a therapy group soon perceive their similarities to one another. An example is illustrative: For many years I asked members of T-groups (these are nonclients—primarily medical students, psychiatric residents, nurses, psychiatric technicians, and Peace Corps volunteers; see chapter 16) to engage in a "top-secret" task in which they were asked to write, anonymously, on a slip of paper the one thing they would be most disinclined to share with the group. The secrets prove to be startlingly similar, with a couple of major themes predominating. The most common secret is a deep conviction of basic inadequacy—a feeling that one is basically incompetent, that one bluffs one's way through life. Next in frequency is a deep sense of interpersonal alienation—that, despite appearances, one really does not, or cannot, care for or love another person. The third most frequent category is some variety of sexual secret. These chief concerns of nonclients are qualitatively the same in individuals seeking professional help. Almost invariably, our clients experience deep concern about their sense of worth and their ability to relate to others.*

Some specialized groups composed of individuals for whom secrecy has been an especially important and isolating factor place a particularly great emphasis on universality. For example, short-term structured groups for bulimic clients build into their protocol a strong requirement for self-disclosure, especially disclosure about attitudes toward body image and detailed accounts of each member's eating rituals and purging practices. With rare exceptions, patients express great relief at discovering that they are not alone, that others share the same dilemmas and life experiences.[19]

---

*There are several methods of using such information in the work of the group. One effective technique is to redistribute the anonymous secrets to the members, each one receiving another's secret. Each member is then asked to read the secret aloud and reveal how he or she would feel if harboring such a secret. This method usually proves to be a valuable demonstration of universality, empathy, and the ability of others to understand.

Members of sexual abuse groups, too, profit enormously from the experience of universality.[20] An integral part of these groups is the intimate sharing, often for the first time in each member's life, of the details of the abuse and the ensuing internal devastation they suffered. Members in such groups can encounter others who have suffered similar violations as children, who were not responsible for what happened to them, and who have also suffered deep feelings of shame, guilt, rage, and uncleanness. A feeling of universality is often a fundamental step in the therapy of clients burdened with shame, stigma, and self-blame, for example, clients with HIV/AIDS or those dealing with the aftermath of a suicide.[21]

Members of homogeneous groups can speak to one another with a powerful authenticity that comes from their firsthand experience in ways that therapists may not be able to do. For instance, I once supervised a thirty-five-year-old therapist who was leading a group of depressed men in their seventies and eighties. At one point a seventy-seven-year-old man who had recently lost his wife expressed suicidal thoughts. The therapist hesitated, fearing that anything he might say would come across as naive. Then a ninety-one-year-old group member spoke up and described how he had lost his wife of sixty years, had plunged into a suicidal despair, and had ultimately recovered and returned to life. That statement resonated deeply and was not easily dismissed.

In multicultural groups, therapists may need to pay particular attention to the clinical factor of universality. Cultural minorities in a predominantly Caucasian group may feel excluded because of different cultural attitudes toward disclosure, interaction, and affective expression. Therapists must help the group move past a focus on concrete cultural differences to transcultural—that is, universal—responses to human situations and tragedies.[22] At the same time, therapists must be keenly aware of the cultural factors at play. Mental health professionals are often sorely lacking in knowledge of the cultural facts of life required to work effectively with culturally diverse members. It is imperative that therapists learn as much as possible about their clients' cultures as well as their attachment to or alienation from their culture.[23]

Universality, like the other therapeutic factors, does not have sharp borders; it merges with other therapeutic factors. As clients perceive their similarity to others and share their deepest concerns, they benefit further from the accompanying catharsis and from their ultimate acceptance by other members (see chapter 3 on group cohesiveness).

IMPARTING INFORMATION

Under the general rubric of imparting information, I include didactic instruction about mental health, mental illness, and general psychodynamics given by the therapists as well as advice, suggestions, or direct guidance from either the therapist or other group members.

Didactic Instruction

Most participants, at the conclusion of successful interactional group therapy, have learned a great deal about psychic functioning, the meaning of symptoms, interpersonal and group dynamics, and the process of psychotherapy. Generally, the educational process is implicit; most group therapists do not offer explicit didactic instruction in interactional group therapy. Over the past decade, however, many group therapy approaches have made formal instruction, or psychoeducation, an important part of the program.

One of the more powerful historical precedents for psychoeducation can be found in the work of Maxwell Jones, who in his work with large groups in the 1940s lectured to his patients three hours a week about the nervous system's structure, function, and relevance to psychiatric symptoms and disability.[24]

Marsh, writing in the 1930s, also believed in the importance of psychoeducation and organized classes for his patients, complete with lectures, homework, and grades.[25]

Recovery, Inc., the nation's oldest and largest self-help program for current and former psychiatric patients, is basically organized along didactic lines.[26] Founded in 1937 by Abraham Low, this organization has over 700 operating groups today.[27] Membership is voluntary, and the leaders spring from the membership. Although there is no formal professional guidance, the conduct of the meetings has been highly structured by Dr. Low; parts of his textbook, *Mental Health Through Will Training*,[28] are read aloud and discussed at every meeting. Psychological illness is explained on the basis of a few simple principles, which the members memorize—for example, the value of "spotting" troublesome and self-undermining behaviors; that neurotic symptoms are distressing but not dangerous; that tension intensifies and sustains the symptom and should be avoided; that the use of one's free will is the solution to the nervous patient's dilemmas.

Many other self-help groups strongly emphasize the imparting of information. Groups such as Adult Survivors of Incest, Parents Anonymous, Gamblers Anonymous, Make Today Count (for cancer patients), Parents Without Partners, and Mended Hearts encourage the exchange of information among members and often invite experts to address the group.[29] The group environment in which learning takes place is important. The ideal context is one of partnership and collaboration, rather than prescription and subordination.

Recent group therapy literature abounds with descriptions of specialized groups for individuals who have some specific disorder or face some definitive life crisis—for example, panic disorder,[30] obesity,[31] bulimia,[32] adjustment after divorce,[33] herpes,[34] coronary heart disease,[35] parents of sexually abused children,[36] male batterers,[37] bereavement,[38] HIV/AIDS,[39] sexual dysfunction,[40] rape,[41] self-image adjustment after mastectomy,[42] chronic pain,[43] organ transplant,[44] and prevention of depression relapse.[45]

In addition to offering mutual support, these groups generally build in a psychoeducational component approach offering explicit instruction about the nature of a client's illness or life situation and examining clients' misconceptions and self-defeating responses to their illness. For example, the leaders of a group for clients with panic disorder describe the physiological cause of panic attacks, explaining that heightened stress and arousal increase the flow of adrenaline, which may result in hyperventilation, shortness of breath, and dizziness; the client misinterprets the symptoms in ways that only exacerbate them ("I'm dying" or "I'm going crazy"), thus perpetuating a vicious circle. The therapists discuss the benign nature of panic attacks and offer instruction first on how to bring on a mild attack and then on how to prevent it. They provide detailed instruction on proper breathing techniques and progressive muscular relaxation.

Groups are often the setting in which new mindfulness- and meditation-based stress reduction approaches are taught. By applying disciplined focus, members learn to become clear, accepting, and nonjudgmental observers of their thoughts and feelings and to reduce stress, anxiety, and vulnerability to depression.[46]

Leaders of groups for HIV-positive clients frequently offer considerable illness-related medical information and help correct members' irrational fears and misconceptions about infectiousness. They may also advise members about methods of informing others of their condition and fashioning a less guilt-provoking lifestyle.

Leaders of bereavement groups may provide information about the natural cycle of bereavement to help members realize that there is a sequence of pain through which they are progressing and there will be a natural, almost inevitable, lessening of their distress as they move through the stages of this sequence. Leaders may help clients anticipate, for example, the acute anguish they will feel with each significant date (holidays, anniversaries, and birthdays) during the first year of bereavement. Psychoeducational groups for women with primary breast cancer provide members with information about their illness, treatment options, and future risks as well as recommendations for a healthier lifestyle. Evaluation of the outcome of these groups shows that participants demonstrate significant and enduring psychosocial benefits.[47]

Most group therapists use some form of anticipatory guidance for clients about to enter the frightening situation of the psychotherapy group, such as a preparatory session intended to clarify important reasons for psychological dysfunction and to provide instruction in methods of self-exploration.[48] By predicting clients' fears, by providing them with a cognitive structure, we help them cope more effectively with the culture shock they may encounter when they enter the group therapy (see chapter 10).

Didactic instruction has thus been employed in a variety of fashions in group therapy: to transfer information, to alter sabotaging thought patterns, to structure the group, to explain the process of illness. Often such instruction functions as the initial binding force in the group, until other therapeutic factors become operative. In part, however, explanation and clarification function as effective therapeutic agents in their own right. Human beings have always abhorred uncertainty and through the ages have sought to order the universe by providing explanations, primarily religious or scientific. The explanation of a phenomenon is the first step toward its control. If a volcanic eruption is caused by a displeased god, then at least there is hope of pleasing the god.

Frieda Fromm-Reichman underscores the role of uncertainty in producing anxiety. The awareness that one is not one's own helmsman, she points out, that one's perceptions and behavior are controlled by irrational forces, is itself a common and fundamental source of anxiety.[49]

Our contemporary world is one in which we are forced to confront fear and anxiety often. In particular, the events of September 11, 2001, have brought these troubling emotions more clearly to the forefront of people's lives. Confronting traumatic anxieties with active coping (for instance, engaging in life, speaking openly, and providing mutual support), as opposed to withdrawing in demoralized avoidance, is enormously helpful. These responses not only appeal to our common sense but, as contemporary neurobiological research demonstrates, these forms of active coping activate important neural circuits in the brain that help regulate the body's stress reactions.[50]

And so it is with psychotherapy clients: fear and anxiety that stem from uncertainty of the source, meaning, and seriousness of psychiatric symptoms may so compound the total dysphoria that effective exploration becomes vastly more difficult. Didactic instruction, through its provision of structure and explanation, has intrinsic value and deserves a place in our repertoire of therapeutic instruments (see chapter 5).

Direct Advice

Unlike explicit didactic instruction from the therapist, direct advice from the members occurs without exception in every therapy group. In dynamic interactional therapy groups, it is invariably part of the early life of the group and occurs with such regularity that it can be used to estimate a group's age. If I observe or hear a tape of a group in which the clients with some regularity say things like, "I think you ought to . . ." or "What you should do is . . ." or "Why don't you . . . ?" then I can be reasonably certain either that the group is young or that it is an older group facing some difficulty that has impeded its development or effected temporary regression. In other words, advice-giving may reflect a resistance to more intimate engagement in which the group members attempt to manage relationships rather than to connect. Although advice-giving is common in early interactional group therapy, it is rare that specific advice will directly benefit any client. Indirectly, however, advice-giving serves a purpose; the process of giving it, rather than the content of the advice, may be beneficial, implying and conveying, as it does, mutual interest and caring.

Advice-giving or advice-seeking behavior is often an important clue in the elucidation of interpersonal pathology. The client who, for example, continuously pulls advice and suggestions from others, ultimately only to reject them and frustrate others, is well known to group therapists as the "help-rejecting complainer" or the "yes . . . but" client (see chapter 13).[51] Some group members may bid for attention and nurturance by asking for suggestions about a problem that either is insoluble or has already been solved. Others soak up advice with an unquenchable thirst, yet never reciprocate to others who are equally needy. Some group members are so intent on preserving a high-status role in the group or a facade of cool self-sufficiency that they never ask directly for help; some are so anxious to please that they never ask for anything for themselves; some are excessively effusive in their gratitude; others never acknowledge the gift but take it home, like a bone, to gnaw on privately.

Other types of more structured groups that do not focus on member interaction make explicit and effective use of direct suggestions and guidance. For example, behavior-shaping groups, hospital discharge planning and transition groups, life skills groups, communicational skills groups, Recovery, Inc., and Alcoholics Anonymous all proffer considerable direct advice. One communicational skills group for clients who have chronic psychiatric illnesses reports excellent results with a structured group program that includes focused feedback, videotape playback, and problem-solving projects.[52] AA makes use of guidance and slogans: for example, members are asked to remain abstinent for only the next twenty-four hours—"One day at a time." Recovery, Inc. teaches members how to spot neurotic symptoms, how to erase and retrace, how to rehearse and reverse, and how to apply willpower effectively.

Is some advice better than others? Researchers who studied a behavior-shaping group of male sex offenders noted that advice was common and was useful to different members to different extents. The least effective form of advice was a direct suggestion; most effective was a series of alternative suggestions about how to achieve a desired goal.[53] Psychoeducation about the impact of depression on family relationships is much more effective when participants examine, on a direct, emotional level, the way depression is affecting their own lives and family relationships. The same information presented in an intellectualized and detached manner is far less valuable.[54]

ALTRUISM

There is an old Hasidic story of a rabbi who had a conversation with the Lord about Heaven and Hell. "I will show you Hell," said the Lord, and led the rabbi into a room containing a group of famished, desperate people sitting around a large, circular table. In the center of the table rested an enormous pot of stew, more than enough for everyone. The smell of the stew was delicious and made the rabbi's mouth water. Yet no one ate. Each diner at the table held a very long-handled spoon—long enough to reach the pot and scoop up a spoonful of stew, but too long to get the food into one's mouth. The rabbi saw that their suffering was indeed terrible and bowed his head in compassion. "Now I will show you Heaven," said the Lord, and they entered another room, identical to the first—same large, round table, same enormous pot of stew, same long-handled spoons. Yet there was gaiety in the air; everyone appeared well nourished, plump, and exuberant. The rabbi could not understand and looked to the Lord. "It is simple," said the Lord, "but it requires a certain skill. You see, the people in this room have learned to feed each other!"*

In therapy groups, as well as in the story's imagined Heaven and Hell, members gain through giving, not only in receiving help as part of the reciprocal giving-receiving sequence, but also in profiting from something intrinsic to the act of giving. Many psychiatric patients beginning therapy are demoralized and possess a deep sense of having nothing of value to offer others. They have long considered themselves as burdens, and the experience of finding that they can be of importance to others is refreshing and boosts self-esteem. Group therapy is unique in being the only therapy that offers clients the opportunity to be of benefit to others. It also encourages role versatility, requiring clients to shift between roles of help receivers and help providers.[55]

---

*In 1973, a member opened the first meeting of the first group ever offered for advanced cancer patients by distributing this parable to the other members of the group. This woman (whom I've written about elsewhere, referring to her as Paula West; see I. Yalom, *Momma and the Meaning of Life* [New York: Basic Books, 1999]) had been involved with me from the beginning in conceptualizing and organizing this group (see also chapter 15). Her parable proved to be prescient, since many members were to benefit from the therapeutic factor of altruism.

And, of course, clients are enormously helpful to one another in the group therapeutic process. They offer support, reassurance, suggestions, insight; they share similar problems with one another. Not infrequently group members will accept observations from another member far more readily than from the group therapist. For many clients, the therapist remains the paid professional; the other members represent the real world and can be counted on for spontaneous and truthful reactions and feedback. Looking back over the course of therapy, almost all group members credit other members as having been important in their improvement. Sometimes they cite their explicit support and advice, sometimes their simply having been present and allowing their fellow members to grow as a result of a facilitative, sustaining relationship. Through the experience of altruism, group members learn firsthand that they have obligations to those from whom they wish to receive care.

An interaction between two group members is illustrative. Derek, a chronically anxious and isolated man in his forties who had recently joined the group, exasperated the other members by consistently dismissing their feedback and concern. In response, Kathy, a thirty-five-year-old woman with chronic depression and substance abuse problems, shared with him a pivotal lesson in her own group experience. For months she had rebuffed the concern others offered because she felt she did not merit it. Later, after others informed her that her rebuffs were hurtful to them, she made a conscious decision to be more receptive to gifts offered her and soon observed, to her surprise, that she began to feel much better. In other words, she benefited not only from the support received but also in her ability to help others feel they had something of value to offer. She hoped that Derek could consider those possibilities for himself.

Altruism is a venerable therapeutic factor in other systems of healing. In primitive cultures, for example, a troubled person is often given the task of preparing a feast or performing some type of service for the community.[56] Altruism plays an important part in the healing process at Catholic shrines, such as Lourdes, where the sick pray not only for themselves but also for one another. People need to feel they are needed and useful. It is commonplace for alcoholics to continue their AA contacts for years after achieving complete sobriety; many members have related their cautionary story of downfall and subsequent reclamation at least a thousand times and continually enjoy the satisfaction of offering help to others.

Neophyte group members do not at first appreciate the healing impact of other members. In fact, many prospective candidates resist the suggestion of group therapy with the question "How can the blind lead the blind?" or "What can I possibly get from others who are as confused as I am? We'll end up pulling one another down." Such resistance is best worked through by exploring a client's critical self-evaluation. Generally, an individual who deplores the prospect of getting help from other group members is really saying, "I have nothing of value to offer anyone."

There is another, more subtle benefit inherent in the altruistic act. Many clients who complain of meaninglessness are immersed in a morbid self-absorption, which takes the form of obsessive introspection or a teeth-gritting effort to actualize oneself. I agree with Victor Frankl that a sense of life meaning ensues but cannot be deliberately pursued: life meaning is always a derivative phenomenon that materializes when we have transcended ourselves, when we have forgotten ourselves and become absorbed in someone (or something) outside ourselves.[57] A focus on life meaning and altruism are particularly important components of the group psychotherapies provided to patients coping with life-threatening medical illnesses such as cancer and AIDS.†[58]

THE CORRECTIVE RECAPITULATION OF THE PRIMARY FAMILY GROUP

The great majority of clients who enter groups—with the exception of those suffering from posttraumatic stress disorder or from some medical or environmental stress—have a background of a highly unsatisfactory experience in their first and most important group: the primary family. The therapy group resembles a family in many aspects: there are authority/parental figures, peer/sibling figures, deep personal revelations, strong emotions, and deep intimacy as well as hostile, competitive feelings. In fact, therapy groups are often led by a male and female therapy team in a deliberate effort to simulate the parental configuration as closely as possible. Once the initial discomfort is overcome, it is inevitable that, sooner or later, the members will interact with leaders and other members in modes reminiscent of the way they once interacted with parents and siblings.

If the group leaders are seen as parental figures, then they will draw reactions associated with parental/authority figures: some members become helplessly dependent on the leaders, whom they imbue with unrealistic knowledge and power; other blindly defy the leaders, who are perceived as infantilizing and controlling; others are wary of the leaders, who they believe attempt to strip members of their individuality; some members try to split the co-therapists in an attempt to incite parental disagreements and rivalry; some disclose most deeply when one of the co-therapists is away; some compete bitterly with other members, hoping to accumulate units of attention and caring from the therapists; some are enveloped in envy when the leader's attention is focused on others: others expend energy in a search for allies among the other members, in order to topple the therapists; still others neglect their own interests in a seemingly selfless effort to appease the leaders and the other members.

Obviously, similar phenomena occur in individual therapy, but the group provides a vastly greater number and variety of recapitulative possibilities. In one of my groups, Betty, a member who had been silently pouting for a couple of meetings, bemoaned the fact that she was not in one-to-one therapy. She claimed she was inhibited because she knew the group could not satisfy her needs. She knew she could speak freely of herself in a private conversation with the therapist or with any one of the members. When pressed, Betty expressed her irritation that others were favored over her in the group. For example, the group had recently welcomed another member who had returned from a vacation, whereas her return from a vacation went largely unnoticed by the group. Furthermore, another group member was praised for offering an important interpretation to a member, whereas she had made a similar statement weeks ago that had gone unnoticed. For some time, too, she had noticed her growing resentment at sharing the group time; she was impatient while waiting for the floor and irritated whenever attention was shifted away from her.

Was Betty right? Was group therapy the wrong treatment for her? Absolutely not! These very criticisms—which had roots stretching down into her early relationships with her siblings—did not constitute valid objections to group therapy. Quite the contrary: the group format was particularly valuable for her, since it allowed her envy and her craving for attention to surface. In individual therapy—where the therapist attends to the client's every word and concern, and the individual is expected to use up all the allotted time—these particular conflicts might emerge belatedly, if at all.

What is important, though, is not only that early familial conflicts are relived but that they are relived *correctively*. Reexposure without repair only makes a bad situation worse. Growth-inhibiting relationship patterns must not be permitted to freeze into the rigid, impenetrable system that characterizes many family structures. Instead, fixed roles must be constantly explored and challenged, and ground rules that encourage the investigation of relationships and the testing of new behavior must be established. For many group members, then, working out problems with therapists and other members is also working through unfinished business from long ago. (How explicit the working in the past need be is a complex and controversial issue, which I will address in chapter 5.)

DEVELOPMENT OF SOCIALIZING TECHNIQUES

Social learning—the development of basic social skills—is a therapeutic factor that operates in all therapy groups, although the nature of the skills taught and the explicitness of the process vary greatly, depending on the type of group therapy. There may be explicit emphasis on the development of social skills in, for example, groups preparing hospitalized patients for discharge or adolescent groups. Group members may be asked to role-play approaching a prospective employer or asking someone out on a date.

In other groups, social learning is more indirect. Members of dynamic therapy groups, which have ground rules encouraging open feedback, may obtain considerable information about maladaptive social behavior. A member may, for example, learn about a disconcerting tendency to avoid looking at the person with whom he or she is conversing; about others' impressions of his or her haughty, regal attitude; or about a variety of other social habits that, unbeknownst to the group member, have been undermining social relationships. For individuals lacking intimate relationships, the group often represents the first opportunity for accurate interpersonal feedback. Many lament their inexplicable loneliness: group therapy provides a rich opportunity for members to learn how they contribute to their own isolation and loneliness.[59]

One man, for example, who had been aware for years that others avoided social contact with him, learned in the therapy group that his obsessive inclusion of minute, irrelevant details in his social conversation was exceedingly off-putting. Years later he told me that one of the most important events of his life was when a group member (whose name he had long since forgotten) told him, "When you talk about your feelings, I like you and want to get closer; but when you start talking about facts and details, I want to get the hell out of the room!"

I do not mean to oversimplify; therapy is a complex process and obviously involves far more than the simple recognition and conscious, deliberate alteration of social behavior. But, as I will show in chapter 3, these gains are more than fringe benefits; they are often instrumental in the initial phases of therapeutic change. They permit the clients to understand that there is a huge discrepancy between their intent and their actual impact on others.†

Frequently senior members of a therapy group acquire highly sophisticated social skills: they are attuned to process (see chapter 6); they have learned how to be helpfully responsive to others; they have acquired methods of conflict resolution; they are less likely to be judgmental and are more capable of experiencing and expressing accurate empathy. These skills cannot but help to serve these clients well in future social interactions, and they constitute the cornerstones of emotional intelligence.[60]

IMITATIVE BEHAVIOR

Clients during individual psychotherapy may, in time, sit, walk, talk, and even think like their therapists. There is considerable evidence that group therapists influence the communicational patterns in their groups by modeling certain behaviors, for example, self-disclosure or support.[61] In groups the imitative process is more diffuse: clients may model themselves on aspects of the other group members as well as of the therapist.[62] Group members learn from watching one another tackle problems. This may be particularly potent in homogeneous groups that focus on shared problems—for example, a cognitive-behavior group that teaches psychotic patients strategies to reduce the intensity of auditory hallucinations.[63]

The importance of imitative behavior in the therapeutic process is difficult to gauge, but social-psychological research suggests that therapists may have underestimated it. Bandura, who has long claimed that social learning cannot be adequately explained on the basis of direct reinforcement, has experimentally demonstrated that imitation is an effective therapeutic force.†[64] In group therapy it is not uncommon for a member to benefit by observing the therapy of another member with a similar problem constellation—a phenomenon generally referred to as vicarious or spectator therapy.[65]

Imitative behavior generally plays a more important role in the early stages of a group, as members identify with more senior members or therapists.[66] Even if imitative behavior is, in itself, short-lived, it may help to unfreeze the individual enough to experiment with new behavior, which in turn can launch an adaptive spiral (see chapter 4). In fact, it is not uncommon for clients throughout therapy to "try on," as it were, bits and pieces of other people and then relinquish them as ill fitting. This process may have solid therapeutic impact; finding out what we are not is progress toward finding out what we are.

Chapter 2

INTERPERSONAL LEARNING

Interpersonal learning, as I define it, is a broad and complex therapeutic factor. It is the group therapy analogue of important therapeutic factors in individual therapy such as insight, working through the transference, and the corrective emotional experience. But it also represents processes unique to the group setting that unfold only as a result of specific work on the part of the therapist. To define the concept of interpersonal learning and to describe the mechanism whereby it mediates therapeutic change in the individual, I first need to discuss three other concepts:

1. The importance of interpersonal relationships
2. The corrective emotional experience
3. The group as social microcosm

THE IMPORTANCE OF INTERPERSONAL RELATIONSHIPS

From whatever perspective we study human society—whether we scan humanity's broad evolutionary history or scrutinize the development of the single individual—we are at all times obliged to consider the human being in the matrix of his or her interpersonal relationships. There is convincing data from the study of nonhuman primates, primitive human cultures, and contemporary society that human beings have always lived in groups that have been characterized by intense and persistent relationships among members and that the need to belong is a powerful, fundamental, and pervasive motivation.[1] Interpersonal relatedness has clearly been adaptive in an evolutionary sense: without deep, positive, reciprocal interpersonal bonds, neither individual nor species survival would have been possible.

John Bowlby, from his studies of the early mother-child relationship, concludes not only that attachment behavior is necessary for survival but also that it is core, intrinsic, and genetically built in.[2] If mother and infant are separated, both experience marked anxiety concomitant with their search for the lost object. If the separation is prolonged, the consequences for the infant will be profound. Winnicott similarly noted, "There is no such thing as a baby. There exists a mother-infant pair."[3] We live in a "relational matrix," according to Mitchell: "The person is comprehensible only within this tapestry of relationships, past and present."[4]

Similarly, a century ago the great American psychologist-philosopher William James said:

We are not only gregarious animals liking to be in sight of our fellows, but we have an innate propensity to get ourselves noticed, and noticed favorably, by our kind. No more fiendish punishment could be devised, were such a thing physically possible, than that one should be turned loose in society and remain absolutely unnoticed by all the members thereof.[5]

Indeed, James's speculations have been substantiated time and again by contemporary research that documents the pain and the adverse consequences of loneliness. There is, for example, persuasive evidence that the rate for virtually every major cause of death is significantly higher for the lonely, the single, the divorced, and the widowed.[6] Social isolation is as much a risk factor for early mortality as obvious physical risk factors such as smoking and obesity.[7] The inverse is also true: social connection and integration have a positive impact on the course of serious illnesses such as cancer and AIDS.[8]

Recognizing the primacy of relatedness and attachment, contemporary models of dynamic psychotherapy have evolved from a drive-based, one-person Freudian psychology to a two-person relational psychology that places the client's interpersonal experience at the center of effective psychotherapy.†[9] Contemporary psychotherapy employs "a relational model in which mind is envisioned as built out of interactional configurations of self in relation to others."[10]

Building on the earlier contributions of Harry Stack Sullivan and his interpersonal theory of psychiatry,[11] interpersonal models of psychotherapy have become prominent.[12] Although Sullivan's work was seminally important, contemporary generations of therapists rarely read him. For one thing, his language is often obscure (though there are excellent renderings of his work into plain English);[13] for another, his work has so pervaded contemporary psychotherapeutic thought that his original writings seem overly familiar or obvious. However, with the recent focus on integrating cognitive and interpersonal approaches in individual therapy and in group therapy, interest in his contributions have resurged.[14] Kiesler argues in fact that the interpersonal frame is the most appropriate model within which therapists can meaningfully synthesize cognitive, behavioral, and psychodynamic approaches—it is the most comprehensive of the integrative psychotherapies.†[15]

Sullivan's formulations are exceedingly helpful for understanding the group therapeutic process. Although a comprehensive discussion of interpersonal theory is beyond the scope of this book, I will describe a few key concepts here. Sullivan contends that the personality is almost entirely the product of interaction with other significant human beings. The need to be closely related to others is as basic as any biological need and is, in the light of the prolonged period of helpless infancy, equally necessary to survival. The developing child, in the quest for security, tends to cultivate and to emphasize those traits and aspects of the self that meet with approval and to squelch or deny those that meet with disapproval. Eventually the individual develops a concept of the self based on these perceived appraisals of significant others.

> The self may be said to be made up of reflected appraisals. If these were chiefly derogatory, as in the case of an unwanted child who was never loved, of a child who has fallen into the hands of foster parents who have no real interest in him as a child; as I say, if the self-dynamism is made up of experience which is chiefly derogatory, it will facilitate hostile, disparaging appraisals of other people and it will entertain disparaging and hostile appraisals of itself.[16]

This process of constructing our self-regard on the basis of reflected appraisals that we read in the eyes of important others continues, of course, through the developmental cycle. Grunebaum and Solomon, in their study of adolescents, have stressed that satisfying peer relationships and self-esteem are inseparable concepts.[17] The same is true for the elderly—we never outgrow the need for meaningful relatedness.[18]

Sullivan used the term "parataxic distortions" to describe individuals' proclivity to distort their perceptions of others. A parataxic distortion occurs in an interpersonal situation when one person relates to another not on the basis of the realistic attributes of the other but on the basis of a personification existing chiefly in the former's own fantasy. Although parataxic distortion is similar to the concept of transference, it differs in two important ways. First, the scope is broader: it refers not only to an individual's distorted view of the therapist but to all interpersonal relationships (including, of course, distorted relationships among group members). Second, the theory of origin is broader: parataxic distortion is constituted not only of the simple transferring onto contemporary relationships of attitudes toward real-life figures of the past but also of the distortion of interpersonal reality in response to intrapersonal needs. I will generally use the two terms interchangeably; despite the imputed difference in origins, transference and parataxic distortion may be considered operationally identical. Furthermore, many therapists today use the term transference to refer to all interpersonal distortions rather than confining its use to the client-therapist relationship (see chapter 7).

The transference distortions emerge from a set of deeply stored memories of early interactional experiences.[19] These memories contribute to the construction of an internal working model that shapes the individual's attachment patterns throughout life.[20] This internal working model also known as a schema[21] consists of the individual's beliefs about himself, the way he makes sense of relationship cues, and the ensuing interpersonal behavior—not only his own but the type of behavior he draws from others.[22] For instance, a young woman who grows up with depressed and overburdened parents is likely to feel that if she is to stay connected and attached to others, she must make no demands, suppress her independence, and subordinate herself to the emotional needs of others.† Psychotherapy may present her first opportunity to disconfirm her rigid and limiting interpersonal road map.

Interpersonal (that is, parataxic) distortions tend to be self-perpetuating. For example, an individual with a derogatory, debased self-image may, through selective inattention or projection, incorrectly perceive another to be harsh and rejecting. Moreover, the process compounds itself because that individual may then gradually develop mannerisms and behavioral traits—for example, servility, defensive antagonism, or condescension—that eventually will cause others to become, in reality, harsh and rejecting. This sequence is commonly referred to as a "self-fulfilling prophecy"—the individual anticipates that others will respond in a certain manner and then unwittingly behaves in a manner that brings that to pass. In other words, causality in relationships is circular and not linear. Interpersonal research supports this thesis by demonstrating that one's interpersonal beliefs express themselves in behaviors that have a predictable impact on others.[23]

Interpersonal distortions, in Sullivan's view, are modifiable primarily through consensual validation—that is, through comparing one's interpersonal evaluations with those of others. Consensual validation is a particularly important concept in group therapy. Not infrequently a group member alters distortions after checking out the other members' views of some important incident.

This brings us to Sullivan's view of the therapeutic process. He suggests that the proper focus of research in mental health is the study of processes that involve or go on between people.[24] Mental disorder, or psychiatric symptomatology in all its varied manifestations, should be translated into interpersonal terms and treated accordingly.[25] Current psychotherapies for many disorders emphasize this principle.† "Mental disorder" also consists of interpersonal processes that are either inadequate to the social situation or excessively complex because the individual is relating to others not only as they are but also in terms of distorted images based on who they represent from the past. Maladaptive interpersonal behavior can be further defined by its rigidity, extremism, distortion, circularity, and its seeming inescapability.[26]

Accordingly, psychiatric treatment should be directed toward the correction of interpersonal distortions, thus enabling the individual to lead a more abundant life, to participate collaboratively with others, to obtain interpersonal satisfactions in the context of realistic, mutually satisfying interpersonal relationships: "One achieves mental health to the extent that one becomes aware of one's interpersonal relationships."[27] Psychiatric cure is the "expanding of the self to such final effect that the patient as known to himself is much the same person as the patient behaving to others."[28] Although core negative beliefs about oneself do not disappear totally with treatment, effective treatment generates a capacity for interpersonal mastery[29] such that the client can respond with a broadened, flexible, empathetic, and more adaptive repertoire of behaviors, replacing vicious cycles with constructive ones.

Improving interpersonal communication is the focus of a range of parent and child group psychotherapy interventions that address childhood conduct disorders and antisocial behavior. Poor communication of children's needs and of parental expectations generates feelings of personal helplessness and ineffectiveness in both children and parents. These lead to the children's acting-out behaviors as well as to parental responses that are often hostile, devaluing, and inadvertently inflammatory.[30] In these groups, parents and children learn to recognize and correct maladaptive interpersonal cycles through the use of psychoeducation, problem solving, interpersonal skills training, role-playing, and feedback.

These ideas—that therapy is broadly interpersonal, both in its goals and in its means—are exceedingly germane to group therapy. That does not mean that all, or even most, clients entering group therapy ask *explicitly* for help in their interpersonal relationships. Yet I have observed that the therapeutic goals of clients often undergo a shift after a number of sessions. Their initial goal, relief of suffering, is modified and eventually replaced by new goals, usually interpersonal in nature. For example, goals may change from wanting relief from anxiety or depression to wanting to learn to communicate with others, to be more trusting and honest with others, to learn to love. In the brief group therapies, this translation of client concerns and aspirations into interpersonal ones may need to take place earlier, at the assessment and preparation phase (see chapter 10).[31]

The goal shift from relief of suffering to change in interpersonal functioning is an essential early step in the dynamic therapeutic process. It is important in the thinking of the therapist as well. Therapists cannot, for example, treat depression per se: depression offers no effective therapeutic handhold, no rationale for examining interpersonal relationships, which, as I hope to demonstrate, is the key to the therapeutic power of the therapy group. *It is necessary, first, to translate depression into interpersonal terms and then to treat the underlying interpersonal pathology.* Thus, the therapist translates depression into its interpersonal issues—for example, passive dependency, isolation, obsequiousness, inability to express anger, hypersensitivity to separation—and then addresses those interpersonal issues in therapy.

Sullivan's statement of the overall process and goals of individual therapy is deeply consistent with those of interactional group therapy. This interpersonal and relational focus is a defining strength of group therapy.†
The emphasis on the client's understanding of the past, of the genetic development of those maladaptive interpersonal stances, may be less crucial in group therapy than in the individual setting where Sullivan worked (see chapter 6).

The theory of interpersonal relationships has become so much an integral part of the fabric of psychiatric thought that it needs no further underscoring. People need people—for initial and continued survival, for socialization, for the pursuit of satisfaction. No one—not the dying, not the outcast, not the mighty—transcends the need for human contact.

During my many years of leading groups of individuals who all had some advanced form of cancer,[32] I was repeatedly struck by the realization that, in the face of death, we dread not so much nonbeing or nothingness but the accompanying utter loneliness. Dying patients may be haunted by interpersonal concerns—about being abandoned, for example, even shunned, by the world of the living. One woman, for example, had planned to give a large evening social function and learned that very morning that her cancer, heretofore believed contained, had metastasized. She kept the information secret and gave the party, all the while dwelling on the horrible thought that the pain from her disease would eventually grow so unbearable that she would become less human and, finally, unacceptable to others.

The isolation of the dying is often double-edged. Patients themselves often avoid those they most cherish, fearing that they will drag their family and friends into the quagmire of their despair. Thus they avoid morbid talk, develop an airy, cheery facade, and keep their fears to themselves. Their friends and family contribute to the isolation by pulling back, by not knowing how to speak to the dying, by not wanting to upset them or themselves. I agree with Elisabeth Kübler-Ross that the question is not whether but *how* to tell a patient openly and honestly about a fatal illness. The patient is always informed covertly that he or she is dying by the demeanor, by the shrinking away, of the living.[33]

Physicians often add to the isolation by keeping patients with advanced cancer at a considerable psychological distance—perhaps to avoid their sense of failure and futility, perhaps also to avoid dread of their own death. They make the mistake of concluding that, after all, there is nothing more they can do. Yet from the patient's standpoint, this is the very time when the physician is needed the most, not for technical aid but for sheer human presence. What the patient needs is to make contact, to be able to touch others, to voice concerns openly, to be reminded that he or she is not only apart from but also a part of. Psychotherapeutic approaches are beginning to address these specific concerns of the terminally ill—their fear of isolation and their desire to retain dignity within their relationships.† Consider the outcasts—those individuals thought to be so inured to rejection that their interpersonal needs have become heavily calloused. The outcasts, too, have compelling social needs. I once had an experience in a prison that provided me with a forceful reminder of the ubiquitous nature of this human need. An untrained psychiatric technician consulted me about his therapy group, composed of twelve inmates. The members of the group were all hardened recidivists, whose offenses ranged from aggressive sexual violation of a minor to murder. The group, he complained, was sluggish and persisted in focusing on extraneous, extragroup material. I agreed to observe his group and suggested that first he obtain some sociometric information by asking each member privately to rank-order everyone in the group for general popularity. (I had hoped that the discussion of this task would induce the group to turn its attention upon itself.) Although we had planned to discuss these results before the next group session, unexpected circumstances forced us to cancel our presession consultation.

During the next group meeting, the therapist, enthusiastic but professionally inexperienced and insensitive to interpersonal needs, announced that he would read aloud the results of the popularity poll. Hearing this, the group members grew agitated and fearful. They made it clear that they did not wish to know the results. Several members spoke so vehemently of the devastating possibility that they might appear at the bottom of the list that the therapist quickly and permanently abandoned his plan of reading the list aloud.

I suggested an alternative plan for the next meeting: each member would indicate whose vote he cared about most and then explain his choice. This device, also, was too threatening, and only one-third of the members ventured a choice. Nevertheless, the group shifted to an interactional level and developed a degree of tension, involvement, and exhilaration previously unknown. These men had received the ultimate message of rejection from society at large: they were imprisoned, segregated, and explicitly labeled as outcasts. To the casual observer, they seemed hardened, indifferent to the subtleties of interpersonal approval and disapproval. Yet they cared, and cared deeply.

The need for acceptance by and interaction with others is no different among people at the opposite pole of human fortunes—those who occupy the ultimate realms of power, renown, or wealth. I once worked with an enormously wealthy client for three years. The major issues revolved about the wedge that money created between herself and others. Did anyone value her for herself rather than her money? Was she continually being exploited by others? To whom could she complain of the burdens of a ninety-million-dollar fortune? The secret of her wealth kept her isolated from others. And gifts! How could she possibly give appropriate gifts without having others feel either disappointed or awed? There is no need to belabor the point; the loneliness of the very privileged is common knowledge. (Loneliness is, incidentally, not irrelevant to the group therapist; in chapter 7, I will discuss the loneliness inherent in the role of group leader.)

Every group therapist has, I am sure, encountered group members who profess indifference to or detachment from the group. They proclaim, "I don't care what they say or think or feel about me; they're nothing to me; I have no respect for the other members," or words to that effect. My experience has been that if I can keep such clients in the group long enough, their wishes for contact inevitably surface. They are concerned at a very deep level about the group. One member who maintained her indifferent posture for many months was once invited to ask the group her secret question, the one question she would like most of all to place before the group. To everyone's astonishment, this seemingly aloof, detached woman posed this question: "How can you put up with me?"

Many clients anticipate meetings with great eagerness or with anxiety; some feel too shaken afterward to drive home or to sleep that night; many have imaginary conversations with the group during the week. Moreover, this engagement with other members is often long-lived; I have known many clients who think and dream about the group members months, even years, after the group has ended.

In short, people do not feel indifferent toward others in their group for long. And clients do not quit the therapy group because of boredom. Believe scorn, contempt, fear, discouragement, shame, panic, hatred! Believe any of these! But never believe indifference!

In summary, then, I have reviewed some aspects of personality development, mature functioning, psychopathology, and psychiatric treatment from the point of view of interpersonal theory. Many of the issues that I have raised have a vital bearing on the therapeutic process in group therapy: the concept that mental illness emanates from disturbed interpersonal relationships, the role of consensual validation in the modification of interpersonal distortions, the definition of the therapeutic process as an adaptive modification of interpersonal relationships, and the enduring nature and potency of the human being's social needs. Let us now turn to the corrective emotional experience, the second of the three concepts necessary to understand the therapeutic factor of interpersonal learning.

THE CORRECTIVE EMOTIONAL EXPERIENCE

In 1946, Franz Alexander, when describing the mechanism of psychoanalytic cure, introduced the concept of the "corrective emotional experience." The basic principle of treatment, he stated, "is to expose the patient, under more favorable circumstances, to emotional situations that he could not handle in the past. The patient, in order to be helped, must undergo a corrective emotional experience suitable to repair the traumatic influence of previous experience."[34] Alexander insisted that intellectual insight alone is insufficient: there must be an emotional component and systematic reality testing as well. Patients, while affectively interacting with their therapist in a distorted fashion because of transference, gradually must become aware of the fact that "these reactions are not appropriate to the analyst's reactions, not only because he (the analyst) is objective, but also because he is what he is, a person in his own right. They are not suited to the situation between patient and therapist, and they are equally unsuited to the patient's current interpersonal relationships in his daily life."[35]

Although the idea of the corrective emotional experience was criticized over the years because it was misconstrued as contrived, inauthentic, or manipulative, contemporary psychotherapies view it as a cornerstone of therapeutic effectiveness. Change both at the behavioral level and at the deeper level of internalized images of past relationships does not occur primarily through interpretation and insight but through meaningful here-and-now relational experience that disconfirms the client's pathogenic beliefs.[36] When such discomfirmation occurs, change can be dramatic: clients express more emotion, recall more personally relevant and formative experiences, and show evidence of more boldness and a greater sense of self.[37]

These basic principles—the importance of the emotional experience in therapy and the client's discovery, through reality testing, of the inappropriateness of his or her interpersonal reactions—are as crucial in group therapy as in individual therapy, and possibly more so because the group setting offers far more opportunities for the generation of corrective emotional experiences. In the individual setting, the corrective emotional experience, valuable as it is, may be harder to come by, because the client-therapist relationship is more insular and the client is more able to dispute the spontaneity, scope, and authenticity of that relationship. (I believe Alexander was aware of that, because at one point he suggested that the analyst may have to be an actor, may have to play a role in order to create the desired emotional atmosphere.)[38]

No such simulation is necessary in the therapy group, which contains many built-in tensions—tensions whose roots reach deep into primeval layers: sibling rivalry, competition for leaders'/parents' attention, the struggle for dominance and status, sexual tensions, parataxic distortions, and differences in social class, education, and values among the members. *But the evocation and expression of raw affect is not sufficient*: it has to be transformed into a corrective emotional experience. For that to occur two conditions are required: (1) the members must experience the group as sufficiently safe and supportive so that these tensions may be openly expressed; (2) there must be sufficient engagement and honest feedback to permit effective reality testing.

Over many years of clinical work, I have made it a practice to interview clients after they have completed group therapy. I always inquire about some critical incident, a turning point, or the most helpful single event in therapy. Although "critical incident" is not synonymous with therapeutic factor, the two are not unrelated, and much may be learned from an examination of single important events. My clients almost invariably cite an incident that is highly laden emotionally and involves some other group member, rarely the therapist.

The most common type of incident my clients report (as did clients described by Frank and Ascher)[39] involves a sudden expression of strong dislike or anger toward another member. In each instance, communication was maintained, the storm was weathered, and the client experienced a sense of liberation from inner restraints as well as an enhanced ability to explore more deeply his or her interpersonal relationships.

The important characteristics of such critical incidents were:

1. The client expressed strong negative affect.
2. This expression was a unique or novel experience for the client.
3. The client had always dreaded the expression of anger. Yet no catastrophe ensued: no one left or died; the roof did not collapse.
4. Reality testing ensued. The client realized either that the anger expressed was inappropriate in intensity or direction or that prior avoidance of affect expression had been irrational. The client may or may not have gained some insight, that is, learned the reasons accounting either for the inappropriate affect or for the prior avoidance of affect experience or expression.

5. The client was enabled to interact more freely and to explore inter-personal relationships more deeply.

Thus, when I see two group members in conflict with one another, I believe there is an excellent chance that they will be particularly important to one another in the course of therapy. In fact, if the conflict is particularly uncomfortable, I may attempt to ameliorate some of the discomfort by expressing that hunch aloud.

The second most common type of critical incident my clients describe also involves strong affect—but, in these instances, positive affect. For example, a schizoid client described an incident in which he ran after and comforted a distressed group member who had bolted from the room; later he spoke of how profoundly he was affected by learning that he could care for and help someone else. Others spoke of discovering their aliveness or of feeling in touch with themselves. These incidents had in common the following characteristics:

1. The client expressed strong positive affect—an unusual occurrence.
2. The feared catastrophe did not occur—derision, rejection, engulf-ment, the destruction of others.
3. The client discovered a previously unknown part of the self and thus was enabled to relate to others in a new fashion.

The third most common category of critical incident is similar to the second. Clients recall an incident, usually involving self-disclosure, that plunged them into greater involvement with the group. For example, a previously withdrawn, reticent man who had missed a couple of meetings disclosed to the group how desperately he wanted to hear the group members say that they had missed him during his absence. Others, too, in one fashion or another, openly asked the group for help.

To summarize, the corrective emotional experience in group therapy has several components:

1. A strong expression of emotion, which is interpersonally directed and constitutes a risk taken by the client.
2. A group supportive enough to permit this risk taking.
3. Reality testing, which allows the individual to examine the incident with the aid of consensual validation from the other members.
4. A recognition of the inappropriateness of certain interpersonal feelings and behavior or of the inappropriateness of avoiding certain interpersonal behavior.
5. The ultimate facilitation of the individual's ability to interact with others more deeply and honestly.

Therapy is an emotional *and* a corrective experience. This dual nature of the therapeutic process is of elemental significance, and I will return to it again and again in this text. We must experience something strongly; but we must also, through our faculty of reason, understand the implications of that emotional experience.† Over time, the client's deeply held beliefs will change—and these changes will be reinforced if the client's new interpersonal behaviors evoke constructive interpersonal responses. Even subtle interpersonal shifts can reflect a profound change and need to be acknowledged and reinforced by the therapist and group members.

Barbara, a depressed young woman, vividly described her isolation and alienation to the group and then turned to Alice, who had been silent. Barbara and Alice had often sparred because Barbara would accuse Alice of ignoring and rejecting her. In this meeting, however, Barbara used a more gentle tone and asked Alice about the meaning of her silence. Alice responded that she was listening carefully and thinking about how much they had in common. She then added that Barbara's more gentle inquiry allowed her to give voice to her thoughts rather than defend herself against the charge of not caring, a sequence that had ended badly for them both in earlier sessions. The seemingly small but vitally important shift in Barbara's capacity to approach Alice empathically created an opportunity for repair rather than repetition.

This formulation has direct relevance to a key concept of group therapy, the here-and-now, which I will discuss in depth in chapter 6. Here I will state only this basic premise: *When the therapy group focuses on the here-and-now, it increases in power and effectiveness.*

But if the here-and-now focus (that is, a focus on what is happening in this room in the immediate present) is to be therapeutic, it must have two components: the group members must experience one another with as much spontaneity and honesty as possible, and they must also reflect back on that experience. This reflecting back, this *self-reflective loop,* is crucial if an emotional experience is to be transformed into a therapeutic one. As we shall see in the discussion of the therapist's tasks in chapter 5, most groups have little difficulty in entering the emotional stream of the here-and-now; but generally it is the therapist's job to keep directing the group toward the self-reflective aspect of that process.

The mistaken assumption that a strong emotional experience is in itself a sufficient force for change is seductive as well as venerable. Modern psychotherapy was conceived in that very error: the first description of dynamic psychotherapy (Freud and Breuer's 1895 *Studies on Hysteria*)[40] described a method of cathartic treatment based on the conviction that hysteria is caused by a traumatic event to which the individual has never fully responded emotionally. Since illness was supposed to be caused by strangulated affect, treatment was directed toward giving a voice to the stillborn emotion. It was not long before Freud recognized the error: emotional expression, though necessary, is not a sufficient condition for change. Freud's discarded ideas have refused to die and have been the seed for a continuous fringe of therapeutic ideologies. The Viennese fin-de-siècle cathartic treatment still lives today in the approaches of primal scream, bioenergetics, and the many group leaders who place an exaggerated emphasis on emotional catharsis.

My colleagues and I conducted an intensive investigation of the process and outcome of many of the encounter techniques popular in the 1970s (see chapter 16), and our findings provide much support for the dual emotional-intellectual components of the psychotherapeutic process.[41]

We explored, in a number of ways, the relationship between each member's experience in the group and his or her outcome. For example, we asked the members after the conclusion of the group to reflect on those aspects of the group experience they deemed most pertinent to their change. We also asked them during the course of the group, at the end of each meeting, to describe which event at that meeting had the most personal significance. When we correlated the type of event with outcome, we obtained surprising results that disconfirmed many of the contemporary stereotypes about the prime ingredients of the successful encounter group experience. Although emotional experiences (expression and experiencing of strong affect, self-disclosure, giving and receiving feedback) were considered extremely important, they did not distinguish successful from unsuccessful group members. In other words, the members who were unchanged or even had a destructive experience were as likely as successful members to value highly the emotional incidents of the group.

What types of experiences *did* differentiate the successful from the unsuccessful members? There was clear evidence that a *cognitive component* was essential; some type of cognitive map was needed, some intellectual system that framed the experience and made sense of the emotions evoked in the group. (See chapter 16 for a full discussion of this result.) That these findings occurred in groups led by leaders who did not attach much importance to the intellectual component speaks strongly for its being part of the foundation, not the facade, of the change process.[42]

THE GROUP AS SOCIAL MICROCOSM

A freely interactive group, with few structural restrictions, will, in time, develop into a social microcosm of the participant members. Given enough time, group members will begin to be themselves: they will inter-act with the group members as they interact with others in their social sphere, will create in the group the same interpersonal universe they have always inhabited. In other words, clients will, over time, automatically and inevitably begin to display their maladaptive interpersonal behavior in the therapy group. There is no need for them to describe or give a de-tailed history of their pathology: *they will sooner or later enact it before the other group members' eyes.* Furthermore, their behavior serves as ac-curate data and lacks the unwitting but inevitable blind spots of self-report. Character pathology is often hard for the individual to report because it is so well assimilated into the fabric of the self and outside of conscious and explicit awareness. As a result, group therapy, with its emphasis on feedback, is a particularly effective treatment for individuals with charac-ter pathology.[43]

This concept is of paramount importance in group therapy and is a keystone of the entire approach to group therapy. Each member's inter-personal style will eventually appear in his or her transactions in the group. Some styles result in interpersonal friction that will be manifest early in the course of the group. Individuals who are, for example, angry, vindictive, harshly judgmental, self-effacing, or grandly coquettish will generate considerable interpersonal static even in the first few meetings. Their maladaptive social patterns will quickly elicit the group's attention. Others may require more time in therapy before their difficulties manifest themselves in the here-and-now of the group. This includes clients who may be equally or more severely troubled but whose interpersonal diffi-culties are more subtle, such as individuals who quietly exploit others, those who achieve intimacy to a point but then, becoming frightened, dis-engage themselves, or those who pseudo-engage, maintaining a subordi-nate, compliant position.

The initial business of a group usually consists of dealing with the members whose pathology is most interpersonally blatant. Some inter-personal styles become crystal-clear from a single transaction, some from a single group meeting, and others require many sessions of observation to understand. The development of the ability to identify and put to ther-apeutic advantage maladaptive interpersonal behavior as seen in the so-cial microcosm of the small group is one of the chief tasks of a training program for group psychotherapists. Some clinical examples may make these principles more graphic.*

---

*In the following clinical examples, as elsewhere in this text, I have protected clients' privacy by altering certain facts, such as name, occupation, and age. Also, the interaction described in the text is not reproduced verbatim but has been reconstructed from detailed clinical notes taken after each therapy meeting.

The Grand Dame

Valerie, a twenty-seven-year-old musician, sought therapy with me primarily because of severe marital discord of several years' standing. She had had considerable, unrewarding individual and hypnotic uncovering therapy. Her husband, she reported, was an alcoholic who was reluctant to engage her socially, intellectually, or sexually. Now the group could have, as some groups do, investigated her marriage interminably. The members might have taken a complete history of the courtship, of the evolution of the discord, of her husband's pathology, of her reasons for marrying him, of her role in the conflict. They might have followed up this collection of information with advice for changing the marital interaction or perhaps suggestions for a trial or permanent separation.

But all this historical, problem-solving activity would have been in vain: this entire line of inquiry not only disregards the unique potential of therapy groups but also is based on the highly questionable premise that a client's account of a marriage is even reasonably accurate. Groups that function in this manner fail to help the protagonist and also suffer demoralization because of the ineffectiveness of a problem-solving, historical group therapy approach. Let us instead observe Valerie's behavior as it unfolded in the here-and-now of the group.

Valerie's group behavior was flamboyant. First, there was her grand entrance, always five or ten minutes late. Bedecked in fashionable but flashy garb, she would sweep in, sometimes throwing kisses, and immediately begin talking, oblivious to whether another member was in the middle of a sentence. Here was narcissism in the raw! Her worldview was so solipsistic that it did not take in the possibility that life could have been going on in the group before her arrival.

After very few meetings, Valerie began to give gifts: to an obese female member, a copy of a new diet book; to a woman with strabismus, the name of a good ophthalmologist; to an effeminate gay client, a subscription to *Field and Stream* magazine (intended, no doubt, to masculinize him); to a twenty-four-year-old virginal male, an introduction to a promiscuous divorced friend of hers. Gradually it became apparent that the gifts were not duty-free. For example, she pried into the relationship that developed between the young man and her divorced friend and insisted on serving as confidante and go-between, thus exerting considerable control over both individuals.

Her efforts to dominate soon colored all of her interactions in the group. I became a challenge to her, and she made various efforts to control me. By sheer chance, a few months previously I had seen her sister in consultation and referred her to a competent therapist, a clinical psychologist. In the group Valerie congratulated me for the brilliant tactic of sending her sister to a psychologist; I must have divined her deep-seated aversion to psychiatrists. Similarly, on another occasion, she responded to a comment from me, "How perceptive you were to have noticed my hands trembling."

The trap was set! In fact, I had neither "divined" her sister's alleged aversion to psychiatrists (I had simply referred her to the best therapist I knew) nor noted Valerie's trembling hands. If I silently accepted her undeserved tribute, then I would enter into a dishonest collusion with Valerie; if, on the other hand, I admitted my insensitivity either to the trembling of the hands or to the sister's aversion, then, by acknowledging my lack of perceptivity, I would have also been bested. She would control me either way! In such situations, the therapist has only one real option: to change the frame and to comment on the process—the nature and the meaning of the entrapment. (I will have a great deal more to say about relevant therapist technique in chapter 6.)

Valerie vied with me in many other ways. Intuitive and intellectually gifted, she became the group expert on dream and fantasy interpretation. On one occasion she saw me between group sessions to ask whether she could use my name to take a book out of the medical library. On one level the request was reasonable: the book (on music therapy) was related to her profession; furthermore, having no university affiliation, she was not permitted to use the library. However, in the context of the group process, the request was complex in that she was testing limits; granting her request would have signaled to the group that she had a special and unique relationship with me. I clarified these considerations to her and suggested further discussion in the next session. Following this perceived rebuttal, however, she called the three male members of the group at home and, after swearing them to secrecy, arranged to see them. She engaged in sexual relations with two; the third, a gay man, was not interested in her sexual advances but she launched a formidable seduction attempt nonetheless.

The following group meeting was horrific. Extraordinarily tense and unproductive, it demonstrated the axiom (to be discussed later) that if something important in the group is being actively avoided, then nothing else of import gets talked about either. Two days later Valerie, overcome with anxiety and guilt, asked for an individual session with me and made a full confession. It was agreed that the whole matter should be discussed in the next group meeting.

Valerie opened the next meeting with the words: "This is confession day! Go ahead, Charles!" and then later, "Your turn, Louis," deftly manipulating the situation so that the confessed transgressions became the sole responsibilities of the men in question, and not herself. Each man performed as she bade him and, later in the meeting, received from her a critical evaluation of his sexual performance. A few weeks later, Valerie let her estranged husband know what had happened, and he sent threatening messages to all three men. That was the last straw! The members decided they could no longer trust her and, in the only such instance I have known, voted her out of the group. (She continued her therapy by joining another group.) The saga does not end here, but perhaps I have recounted enough to illustrate the concept of the group as social microcosm.

Let me summarize. The first step was that Valerie clearly displayed her interpersonal pathology in the group. Her narcissism, her need for adulation, her need to control, her sadistic relationship with men—the entire tragic behavioral scroll—unrolled in the here-and-now of therapy. The next step was reaction and feedback. The men expressed their deep humiliation and anger at having to "jump through a hoop" for her and at receiving "grades" for their sexual performance. They drew away from her. They began to reflect: "I don't want a report card every time I have sex. It's controlling, like sleeping with my mother! I'm beginning to understand more about your husband moving out!" and so on. The others in the group, the female members and the therapists, shared the men's feelings about the wantonly destructive course of Valerie's behavior—destructive for the group as well as for herself.

Most important of all, she had to deal with this fact: she had joined a group of troubled individuals who were eager to help each other and whom she grew to like and respect; yet, in the course of several weeks, she had so poisoned her own environment that, against her conscious wishes, she became a pariah, an outcast from a group that could have been very helpful to her. Facing and working through these issues in her subsequent therapy group enabled her to make substantial personal changes and to employ much of her considerable potential constructively in her later relationships and endeavors.

The Man Who Liked Robin Hood

Ron, a forty-eight-year-old attorney who was separated from his wife, entered therapy because of depression, anxiety, and intense feelings of loneliness. His relationships with both men and women were highly problematic. He yearned for a close male friend but had not had one since high school. His current relationships with men assumed one of two forms: either he and the other man related in a highly competitive, antagonistic fashion, which veered dangerously close to combativeness, or he assumed an exceedingly dominant role and soon found the relationship empty and dull.

His relationships with women had always followed a predictable sequence: instant attraction, a crescendo of passion, a rapid loss of interest. His love for his wife had withered years ago and he was currently in the midst of a painful divorce.

Intelligent and highly articulate, Ron immediately assumed a position of great influence in the group. He offered a continuous stream of useful and thoughtful observations to the other members, yet kept his own pain and his own needs well concealed. He requested nothing and accepted nothing from me or my co-therapist. In fact, each time I set out to interact with Ron, I felt myself bracing for battle. His antagonistic resistance was so great that for months my major interaction with him consisted of repeatedly requesting him to examine his reluctance to experience me as someone who could offer help.

"Ron," I suggested, giving it my best shot, "let's understand what's happening. You have many areas of unhappiness in your life. I'm an experienced therapist, and you come to me for help. You come regularly, you never miss a meeting, you pay me for my services, yet you systematically prevent me from helping you. Either you so hide your pain that I find little to offer you, or when I do extend some help, you reject it in one fashion or another. Reason dictates that we should be allies. Shouldn't we be working together to help you? Tell me, how does it come about that we are adversaries?"

But even that failed to alter our relationship. Ron seemed bemused and skillfully and convincingly speculated that I might be identifying one of my problems rather than his. His relationship with the other group members was characterized by his insistence on seeing them outside the group. He systematically arranged for some extragroup activity with each of the members. He was a pilot and took some members flying, others sailing, others to lavish dinners; he gave legal advice to some and became romantically involved with one of the female members; and (the final straw) he invited my co-therapist, a female psychiatric resident, for a skiing weekend.

Furthermore, he refused to examine his behavior or to discuss these extragroup meetings in the group, even though the pregroup preparation (see chapter 12) had emphasized to all the members that such unexamined, undiscussed extragroup meetings generally sabotage therapy.

After one meeting when we pressured him unbearably to examine the meaning of the extragroup invitations, especially the skiing invitation to my co-therapist, he left the session confused and shaken. On his way home, Ron unaccountably began to think of Robin Hood, his favorite childhood story but something he had not thought about for decades.

Following an impulse, he went directly to the children's section of the nearest public library to sit in a small child's chair and read the story one more time. In a flash, the meaning of his behavior was illuminated! Why had the Robin Hood legend always fascinated and delighted him? Because Robin Hood rescued people, especially women, from tyrants!

That motif had played a powerful role in his interior life, beginning with the Oedipal struggles in his own family. Later, in early adulthood, he built up a successful law firm by first assisting in a partnership and then enticing his boss's employees to work for him. He had often been most attracted to women who were attached to some powerful man. Even his motives for marrying were blurred: he could not distinguish between love for his wife and desire to rescue her from a tyrannical father.

The first stage of interpersonal learning is pathology display. Ron's characteristic modes of relating to both men and women unfolded vividly in the microcosm of the group. His major interpersonal motif was to struggle with and to vanquish other men. He competed openly and, because of his intelligence and his great verbal skills, soon procured the dominant role in the group. He then began to mobilize the other members in the final conspiracy: the unseating of the therapist. He formed close alliances through extragroup meetings and by placing other members in his debt by offering favors. Next he endeavored to capture "my women"—first the most attractive female member and then my co-therapist.

Not only was Ron's interpersonal pathology displayed in the group, but so were its adverse, self-defeating consequences. His struggles with men resulted in the undermining of the very reason he had come to therapy: to obtain help. In fact, the competitive struggle was so powerful that any help I extended him was experienced not as help but as defeat, a sign of weakness.

Furthermore, the microcosm of the group revealed the consequences of his actions on the texture of his relationships with his peers. In time the other members became aware that Ron did not really relate to them. He only appeared to relate but, in actuality, was using them as a way of relating to me, the powerful and feared male in the group. The others soon felt used, felt the absence of a genuine desire in Ron to know them, and gradually began to distance themselves from him. Only after Ron was able to understand and to alter his intense and distorted ways of relating to me was he able to turn to and relate in good faith to the other members of the group.

"Those Damn Men"

Linda, forty-six years old and thrice divorced, entered the group because of anxiety and severe functional gastrointestinal distress. Her major interpersonal issue was her tormented, self-destructive relationship with her current boyfriend. In fact, throughout her life she had encountered a long series of men (father, brothers, bosses, lovers, and husbands) who had abused her both physically and psychologically. Her account of the abuse that she had suffered, and suffered still, at the hands of men was harrowing.

The group could do little to help her, aside from applying balm to her wounds and listening empathically to her accounts of continuing mistreatment by her current boss and boyfriend. Then one day an unusual incident occurred that graphically illuminated her dynamics. She called me one morning in great distress. She had had an extremely unsettling altercation with her boyfriend and felt panicky and suicidal. She felt she could not possibly wait for the next group meeting, still four days off, and pleaded for an immediate individual session. Although it was greatly inconvenient, I rearranged my appointments that afternoon and scheduled time to meet her. Approximately thirty minutes before our meeting, she called and left word with my secretary that she would not be coming in after all.

In the next group meeting, when I inquired what had happened, Linda said that she had decided to cancel the emergency session because she was feeling slightly better by the afternoon, and that she knew I had a rule that I would see a client only one time in an emergency during the whole course of group therapy. She therefore thought it might be best to save that option for a time when she might be even more in crisis.

I found her response bewildering. I had never made such a rule; I never refuse to see someone in real crisis. Nor did any of the other members of the group recall my having issued such a dictum. But Linda stuck to her guns: she insisted that she had heard me say it, and she was dissuaded neither by my denial nor by the unanimous consensus of the other group members. Nor did she seem concerned in any way about the inconvenience she had caused me. In the group discussion she grew defensive and acrimonious.

This incident, unfolding in the social microcosm of the group, was highly informative and allowed us to obtain an important perspective on Linda's responsibility for some of her problematic relationships with men. Up until that point, the group had to rely entirely on her portrayal of these relationships. Linda's accounts were convincing, and the group had come to accept her vision of herself as victim of "all those damn men out there." An examination of the here-and-now incident indicated that Linda had distorted her perceptions of at least one important man in her life: her therapist. Moreover—and this is extremely important—she had distorted the incident in a highly predictable fashion: she experienced me as far more uncaring, insensitive, and authoritarian than I really was.

This was new data, and it was convincing data—and it was displayed before the eyes of all the members. For the first time, the group began to wonder about the accuracy of Linda's accounts of her relationships with men. Undoubtedly, she faithfully portrayed her feelings, but it became apparent that there were perceptual distortions at work: because of her expectations of men and her highly conflicted relationships with them, she misperceived their actions toward her.

But there was more yet to be learned from the social microcosm. An important piece of data was the tone of the discussion: the defensiveness, the irritation, the anger. In time I, too, became irritated by the thankless inconvenience I had suffered by changing my schedule to meet with Linda. I was further irritated by her insistence that I had proclaimed a certain insensitive rule when I (and the rest of the group) knew I had not. I fell into a reverie in which I asked myself, "What would it be like to live with Linda all the time instead of an hour and a half a week?" If there were many such incidents, I could imagine myself often becoming angry, exasperated, and uncaring toward her. This is a particularly clear example of the concept of the self-fulfilling prophecy described on page 22. Linda predicted that men would behave toward her in a certain way and then, unconsciously, operated so as to bring this prediction to pass.

Men Who Could Not Feel

Allen, a thirty-year-old unmarried scientist, sought therapy for a single, sharply delineated problem: he wanted to be able to feel sexually stimulated by a woman. Intrigued by this conundrum, the group searched for an answer. They investigated his early life, sexual habits, and fantasies. Finally, baffled, they turned to other issues in the group. As the sessions continued, Allen seemed impassive and insensitive to his own and others' pain. On one occasion, for example, an unmarried member in great distress announced in sobs that she was pregnant and was planning to have an abortion. During her account she also mentioned that she had had a bad PCP trip. Allen, seemingly unmoved by her tears, persisted in posing intellectual questions about the effects of "angel dust" and was puzzled when the group commented on his insensitivity.

So many similar incidents occurred that the group came to expect no emotion from him. When directly queried about his feelings, he responded as if he had been addressed in Sanskrit or Aramaic. After some months the group formulated an answer to his oft-repeated question, "Why can't I have sexual feelings toward a woman?" They asked him to consider instead why he couldn't have any feelings toward anybody.

Changes in his behavior occurred very gradually. He learned to spot and identify feelings by pursuing telltale autonomic signs: facial flushing, gastric tightness, sweating palms. On one occasion a volatile woman in the group threatened to leave the group because she was exasperated trying to relate to "a psychologically deaf and dumb goddamned robot." Allen again remained impassive, responding only, "I'm not going to get down to your level."

However, the next week when he was asked about the feelings he had taken home from the group, he said that after the meeting he had gone home and cried like a baby. (When he left the group a year later and looked back at the course of his therapy, he identified this incident as a critical turning point.) Over the ensuing months he was more able to feel and to express his feelings to the other members. His role within the group changed from that of tolerated mascot to that of accepted com-peer, and his self-esteem rose in accordance with his awareness of the members' increased respect for him.

In another group Ed, a forty-seven-year-old engineer, sought therapy be-cause of loneliness and his inability to find a suitable mate. Ed's pattern of social relationships was barren: he had never had close male friends and had only sexualized, unsatisfying, short-lived relationships with women who ultimately and invariably rejected him. His good social skills and lively sense of humor resulted in his being highly valued by other members in the early stages of the group.

As time went on and members deepened their relationships with one another, however, Ed was left behind: soon his experience in the group re-sembled closely his social life outside the group. The most obvious aspect of his behavior was his limited and offensive approach to women. His gaze was directed primarily toward their breasts or crotch; his attention was voyeuristically directed toward their sexual lives; his comments to them were typically simplistic and sexual in nature. Ed considered the men in the group unwelcome competitors; for months he did not initiate a single transaction with a man.

With so little appreciation for attachments, he, for the most part, con-sidered people interchangeable. For example, when a member described her obsessive fantasy that her boyfriend, who was often late, would be killed in an automobile accident, Ed's response was to assure her that she was young, charming, and attractive and would have little trouble finding another man of at least equal quality. To take another example, Ed was always puzzled when other members appeared troubled by the temporary absence of one of the co-therapists or, later, by the impend-ing permanent departure of a therapist. Doubtless, he suggested, there was, even among the students, a therapist of equal competence. (In fact, he had seen in the hall a bosomy psychologist whom he would particu-larly welcome as therapist.)

He put it most succinctly when he described his MDR (minimum daily requirement) for affection; in time it became clear to the group that the identity of the MDR supplier was incidental to Ed—far less relevant than its dependability.

Thus evolved the first phase of the group therapy process: the display of interpersonal pathology. Ed did not relate to others so much as he used them as equipment, as objects to supply his life needs. It was not long be-fore he had re-created in the group his habitual—and desolate—interper-sonal universe: he was cut off from everyone. Men reciprocated his total indifference; women, in general, were disinclined to service his MDR, and those women he especially craved were repulsed by his narrowly sexualized attentions. The subsequent course of Ed's group therapy was greatly informed by his displaying his interpersonal pathology inside the group, and his therapy profited enormously from focusing exhaustively on his relationships with the other group members.

THE SOCIAL MICROCOSM: A DYNAMIC INTERACTION

There is a rich and subtle dynamic interplay between the group member and the group environment. Members shape their own microcosm, which in turn pulls characteristic defensive behavior from each. The more spontaneous interaction there is, the more rapid and authentic will be the development of the social microcosm. And that in turn increases the likelihood that the central problematic issues of all the members will be evoked and addressed.

For example, Nancy, a young woman with borderline personality disorder, entered the group because of a disabling depression, a subjective state of disintegration, and a tendency to develop panic when left alone. All of Nancy's symptoms had been intensified by the threatened breakup of the small commune in which she lived. She had long been sensitized to the breakup of nuclear units; as a child she had felt it was her task to keep her volatile family together, and now as an adult she nurtured the fantasy that when she married, the various factions among her relatives would be permanently reconciled.

How were Nancy's dynamics evoked and worked through in the social microcosm of the group? Slowly! It took time for these concerns to manifest themselves. At first, sometimes for weeks on end, Nancy would work comfortably on important but minor conflict areas. But then certain events in the group would fan her major, smoldering concerns into anxious conflagration. For example, the absence of a member would unsettle her. In fact, much later, in a debriefing interview at the termination of therapy, Nancy remarked that she often felt so stunned by the absence of any member that she was unable to participate for the entire session.

Even tardiness troubled her and she would chide members who were not punctual. When a member thought about leaving the group, Nancy grew deeply concerned and could be counted on to exert maximal pressure on the member to continue, regardless of the person's best interests. When members arranged contacts outside the group meeting, Nancy became anxious at the threat to the integrity of the group. Sometimes members felt smothered by Nancy. They drew away and expressed their objections to her phoning them at home to check on their absence or lateness. Their insistence that she lighten her demands on them simply aggravated Nancy's anxiety, causing her to increase her protective efforts.

Although she longed for comfort and safety in the group, it was, in fact, the very appearance of these unsettling vicissitudes that made it possible for her major conflict areas to become exposed and to enter the stream of the therapeutic work.

Not only does the small group provide a social microcosm in which the maladaptive behavior of members is clearly displayed, but it also becomes a laboratory in which is demonstrated, often with great clarity, the meaning and the dynamics of the behavior. The therapist sees not only the behavior but also the events triggering it and sometimes, more important, the anticipated and real responses of others.

The group interaction is so rich that each member's maladaptive transaction cycle is repeated many times, and members have multiple opportunities for reflection and understanding. But if pathogenic beliefs are to be altered, the group members must receive feedback that is clear and usable. If the style of feedback delivery is too stressful or provocative, members may be unable to process what the other members offer them. Sometimes the feedback may be premature—that is, delivered before sufficient trust is present to soften its edge. At other times feedback can be experienced as devaluing, coercive, or injurious.[44] How can we avoid unhelpful or harmful feedback? Members are less likely to attack and blame one another if they can look beyond surface behavior and become sensitive to one another's internal experiences and underlying intentions.† Thus empathy is a critical element in the successful group. But empathy, particularly with provocative or aggressive clients, can be a tall order for group members and therapists alike.†

The recent contributions of the intersubjective model are relevant and helpful here.[45] This model poses members and therapists such questions as: "How am I implicated in what I construe as your provocativeness? What is my part in it?" In other words, the group members and the therapist continuously affect one another. Their relationships, their meaning, patterns, and nature, are not fixed or mandated by external influences, but jointly constructed. A traditional view of members' behavior sees the distortion with which members relate events—either in their past or within the group interaction—as solely the creation and responsibility of that member. An intersubjective perspective acknowledges the group leader's and other members' contributions to each member's here-and-now experience—as well as to the texture of their entire experience in the group.

Consider the client who repeatedly arrives late to the group meeting. This is always an irritating event, and group members will inevitably express their annoyance. But the therapist should also encourage the group to explore the meaning of that particular client's behavior. Coming late may mean "I don't really care about the group," but it may also have many other, more complex interpersonal meanings: "Nothing happens without me, so why should I rush?" or "I bet no one will even notice my absence—they don't seem to notice me while I'm there," or "These rules are meant for others, not me."

Both the underlying meaning of the individual's behavior and the impact of that behavior on others need to be revealed and processed if the members are to arrive at an empathic understanding of one another. Empathic capacity is a key component of emotional intelligence[46] and facilitates transfer of learning from the therapy group to the client's larger world. Without a sense of the internal world of others, relationships are confusing, frustrating, and repetitive as we mindlessly enlist others as players with predetermined roles in our own stories, without regard to their actual motivations and aspirations.

Leonard, for example, entered the group with a major problem of procrastination. In Leonard's view, procrastination was not only a problem but also an explanation. It explained his failures, both professionally and socially; it explained his discouragement, depression, and alcoholism. And yet it was an explanation that obscured meaningful insight and more accurate explanations.

In the group we became well acquainted and often irritated or frustrated with Leonard's procrastination. It served as his supreme mode of resistance to therapy when all other resistance had failed. When members worked hard with Leonard, and when it appeared that part of his neurotic character was about to be uprooted, he found ways to delay the group work. "I don't want to be upset by the group today," he would say, or "This new job is make or break for me"; "I'm just hanging on by my fingernails"; "Give me a break—don't rock the boat"; "I'd been sober for three months until the last meeting caused me to stop at the bar on my way home." The variations were many, but the theme was consistent.

One day Leonard announced a major development, one for which he had long labored: he had quit his job and obtained a position as a teacher. Only a single step remained: getting a teaching certificate, a matter of filling out an application requiring approximately two hours' labor.

Only two hours and yet he could not do it! He delayed until the allowed time had practically expired and, with only one day remaining, informed the group about the deadline and lamented the cruelty of his personal demon, procrastination. Everyone in the group, including the therapists, experienced a strong desire to sit Leonard down, possibly even in one's lap, place a pen between his fingers, and guide his hand along the application form. One client, the most mothering member of the group, did exactly that: she took him home, fed him, and schoolmarmed him through the application form.

As we began to review what had happened, we could now see his procrastination for what it was: a plaintive, anachronistic plea for a lost mother. Many things then fell into place, including the dynamics behind Leonard's depressions (which were also desperate pleas for love), alcoholism, and compulsive overeating.

The idea of the social microcosm is, I believe, sufficiently clear: *if the group is conducted such that the members can behave in an unguarded, unselfconscious manner, they will, most vividly, re-create and display their pathology in the group.* Thus in this living drama of the group meeting, the trained observer has a unique opportunity to understand the dynamics of each client's behavior.

RECOGNITION OF BEHAVIORAL PATTERNS IN THE SOCIAL MICROCOSM

If therapists are to turn the social microcosm to therapeutic use, they must first learn to identify the group members' recurrent maladaptive interpersonal patterns. In the incident involving Leonard, the therapist's vital clue was the emotional response of members and leaders to Leonard's behavior. These emotional responses are valid and indispensable data: they should not be overlooked or underestimated. The therapist or other group members may feel angry toward a member, or exploited, or sucked dry, or steamrollered, or intimidated, or bored, or tearful, or any of the infinite number of ways one person can feel toward another.

These feelings represent data—a bit of the truth about the other person—and should be taken seriously by the therapist. If the feelings elicited in others are highly discordant with the feelings that the client would like to engender in others, or if the feelings aroused are desired, yet inhibit growth (as in the case of Leonard), then therein lies a crucial part of the client's problem. Of course there are many complications inherent in this thesis. Some critics might say that a strong emotional response is often due to pathology not of the subject but of the respondent. If, for example, a self-confident, assertive man evokes strong feelings of fear, intense envy, or bitter resentment in another man, we can hardly conclude that the response is reflective of the former's pathology. There is a distinct advantage in the therapy group format: because the group contains multiple observers, it is easier to differentiate idiosyncratic and highly subjective responses from more objective ones.

The emotional response of any single member is not sufficient; therapists need confirmatory evidence. They look for repetitive patterns over time and for multiple responses—that is, the reactions of several other members (referred to as consensual validation) to the individual. Ultimately therapists rely on the most valuable evidence of all: their own emotional responses. Therapists must be able to attend to their own reactions to the client, an essential skill in all relational models. If, as Kiesler states, we are "hooked" by the interpersonal behavior of a member, our own reactions are our best interpersonal information about the client's impact on others.[47]

Therapeutic value follows, however, only if we are able to get "unhooked"—that is, to resist engaging in the usual behavior the client elicits from others, which only reinforces the usual interpersonal cycles. This process of retaining or regaining our objectivity provides us with meaningful feedback about the interpersonal transaction. From this perspective, the thoughts, fantasies, and actual behavior elicited in the therapist by each group member should be treated as gold. Our reactions are invaluable data, not failings. It is impossible not to get hooked by our clients, except by staying so far removed from the client's experience that we are untouched by it—an impersonal distance that reduces our therapeutic effectiveness.

A critic might ask, "How can we be certain that therapists' reactions are 'objective'?" Co-therapy provides one answer to that question. Co-therapists are exposed together to the same clinical situation. Comparing their reactions permits a clearer discrimination between their own subjective responses and objective assessments of the interactions. Furthermore, group therapists may have a calm and privileged vantage point, since, unlike individual therapists, they witness countless compelling maladaptive interpersonal dramas unfold without themselves being at the center of all these interactions.

Still, therapists do have their blind spots, their own areas of interpersonal conflict and distortion. How can we be certain these are not clouding their observations in the course of group therapy? I will address this issue fully in later chapters on training and on the therapist's tasks and techniques, but for now note only that this argument is a powerful reason for therapists to know themselves as fully as possible. Thus it is incumbent upon the neophyte group therapist to embark on a lifelong journey of self-exploration, a journey that includes both individual and group therapy.

None of this is meant to imply that therapists should not take seriously the responses and feedback of all clients, including those who are highly disturbed. Even the most exaggerated, irrational responses contain a core of reality. Furthermore, the disturbed client may be a valuable, accurate source of feedback at other times: no individual is highly conflicted in every area. And, of course, an idiosyncratic response may contain much information about the respondent.

This final point constitutes a basic axiom for the group therapist. Not infrequently, members of a group respond very differently to the same stimulus. An incident may occur in the group that each of seven or eight members perceives, observes, and interprets differently. *One common stimulus and eight different responses—how can that be?* There seems to be only one plausible explanation: there are eight different inner worlds. Splendid! After all, the aim of therapy is to help clients understand and alter their inner worlds. Thus, analysis of these differing responses is a royal road—a *via regia*—into the inner world of the group member.

For example, consider the first illustration offered in this chapter, the group containing Valerie, a flamboyant, controlling member. In accord with their inner world, each of the group members responded very differently to her, ranging from obsequious acquiescence to lust and gratitude to impotent fury or effective confrontation.

Or, again, consider certain structural aspects of the group meeting: members have markedly different responses to sharing the group's or the therapist's attention, to disclosing themselves, to asking for help or helping others. Nowhere are such differences more apparent than in the transference—the members' responses to the leader: the same therapist will be experienced by different members as warm, cold, rejecting, accepting, competent, or bumbling. This range of perspectives can be humbling and even overwhelming for therapists, particularly neophytes.

THE SOCIAL MICROCOSM—IS IT REAL?

I have often heard group members challenge the veracity of the social microcosm. Members may claim that their behavior in this particular group is atypical, not at all representative of their normal behavior. Or that this is a group of troubled individuals who have difficulty perceiving them accurately. Or even that group therapy is not real; it is an artificial, contrived experience that distorts rather than reflects one's real behavior. To the neophyte therapist, these arguments may seem formidable, even persuasive, but they are in fact truth-distorting. In one sense, the group *is* artificial: members do not choose their friends from the group; they are not central to one another; they do not live, work, or eat together; although they relate in a personal manner, their entire relationship consists of meetings in a professional's office once or twice a week; and the relationships are transient—the end of the relationship is built into the social contract at the very beginning.

When faced with these arguments, I often think of Earl and Marguerite, members in a group I led long ago. Earl had been in the group for four months when Marguerite was introduced. They both blushed to see the other, because, by chance, only a month earlier, they had gone on a Sierra Club camping trip together for a night and been "intimate." Neither wanted to be in the group with the other. To Earl, Marguerite was a foolish, empty girl, "a mindless piece of ass," as he was to put it later in the group. To Marguerite, Earl was a dull nonentity, whose penis she had made use of as a means of retaliation against her husband.

They worked together in the group once a week for about a year. During that time, they came to know each other intimately in a fuller sense of the word: they shared their deepest feelings; they weathered fierce, vicious battles; they helped each other through suicidal depressions; and, on more than one occasion, they wept for each other. Which was the real world and which the artificial?

One group member stated, "For the longest time I believed the group was a natural place for unnatural experiences. It was only later that I realized the opposite—it is an unnatural place for natural experiences."[48] One of the things that makes the therapy group real is that it eliminates social, sexual, and status games; members go through vital life experiences together, they shed reality-distorting facades and strive to be honest with one another. How many times have I heard a group member say, "This is the first time I have ever told this to anyone"? The group members are not strangers. Quite the contrary: they know one another deeply and fully. Yes, it is true that members spend only a small fraction of their lives together. But psychological reality is not equivalent to physical reality. Psychologically, group members spend infinitely more time together than the one or two meetings a week when they physically occupy the same office.

OVERVIEW

Let us now return to the primary task of this chapter: to define and describe the therapeutic factor of interpersonal learning. All the necessary premises have been posited and described in this discussion of:

1. The importance of interpersonal relationships
2. The corrective emotional experience
3. The group as a social microcosm

I have discussed these components separately. Now, if we recombine them into a logical sequence, the mechanism of interpersonal learning as a therapeutic factor becomes evident:

I. Psychological symptomatology emanates from disturbed interpersonal relationships. The task of psychotherapy is to help the client learn how to develop distortion-free, gratifying interpersonal relationships.

II. The psychotherapy group, provided its development is unhampered by severe structural restrictions, evolves into a social microcosm, a miniaturized representation of each member's social universe.

III. The group members, through feedback from others, self-reflection, and self-observation, become aware of significant aspects of their interpersonal behavior: their strengths, their limitations, their interpersonal distortions, and the maladaptive behavior that elicits unwanted responses from other people. The client, who will often have had a series of disastrous relationships and subsequently suffered rejection, has failed to learn from these experiences because others, sensing the person's general insecurity and abiding by the rules of etiquette governing normal social interaction, have not communicated the reasons for rejection. Therefore, and this is important, clients have never learned to discriminate between objectionable aspects of their behavior and a self-concept as a totally unacceptable person. The therapy group, with its encouragement of accurate feedback, makes such discrimination possible.

IV. In the therapy group, a regular interpersonal sequence occurs:
A. Pathology display: the member displays his or her behavior.
B. Through feedback and self-observation, clients
   1. become better witnesses of their own behavior;
   2. appreciate the impact of that behavior on
      a. the feelings of others;
      b. the opinions that others have of them;
      c. the opinions they have of themselves.

V. The client who has become fully aware of this sequence also becomes aware of personal responsibility for it: each individual is the author of his or her own interpersonal world.

VI. Individuals who fully accept personal responsibility for the shaping of their interpersonal world may then begin to grapple with the corollary of this discovery: if they created their social-relational world, then they have the power to change it.

VII. The depth and meaningfulness of these understandings are directly proportional to the amount of affect associated with the sequence. The more real and the more emotional an experience, the more potent is its impact; the more distant and intellectualized the experience, the less effective is the learning.

VIII. As a result of this group therapy sequence, the client gradually changes by risking new ways of being with others. The likelihood that change will occur is a function of
A. The client's motivation for change and the amount of personal discomfort and dissatisfaction with current modes of behavior;

B. The client's involvement in the group—that is, how much the client allows the group to matter;

C. The rigidity of the client's character structure and interpersonal style.

IX. Once change, even modest change, occurs, the client appreciates that some feared calamity, which had hitherto prevented such behavior, has been irrational and can be disconfirmed; the change in behavior has not resulted in such calamities as death, destruction, abandonment, derision, or engulfment.

X. The social microcosm concept is bidirectional: not only does outside behavior become manifest in the group, but behavior learned in the group is eventually carried over into the client's social environment, and alterations appear in clients' interpersonal behavior outside the group.

XI. Gradually an adaptive spiral is set in motion, at first inside and then outside the group. As a client's interpersonal distortions diminish, his or her ability to form rewarding relationships is enhanced. Social anxiety decreases; self-esteem rises; the need for self-concealment diminishes. Behavior change is an essential component of effective group therapy, as even small changes elicit positive responses from others, who show more approval and acceptance of the client, which further increases self-esteem and encourages further change.[49] Eventually the adaptive spiral achieves such autonomy and efficacy that professional therapy is no longer necessary.

Each of the steps of this sequence requires different and specific facilitation by the therapist. At various points, for example, the therapist must offer specific feedback, encourage self-observation, clarify the concept of responsibility, exhort the client into risk taking, disconfirm fantasized calamitous consequences, reinforce the transfer of learning, and so on. Each of these tasks and techniques will be fully discussed in chapters 5 and 6.

TRANSFERENCE AND INSIGHT

Before concluding the examination of interpersonal learning as a mediator of change, I wish to call attention to two concepts that deserve further discussion. Transference and insight play too central a role in most formulations of the therapeutic process to be passed over lightly. I rely heavily on both of these concepts in my therapeutic work and do not mean to slight them. What I have done in this chapter is to embed them both into the factor of interpersonal learning.

Transference is a specific form of interpersonal perceptual distortion. In individual psychotherapy, the recognition and the working through of this distortion is of paramount importance. In group therapy, working through interpersonal distortions is, as we have seen, of no less importance; however, the range and variety of distortions are considerably greater. Working through the transference—that is, the distortion in the relationship to the therapist—now becomes only one of a series of distortions to be examined in the therapy process.

For many clients, perhaps for the majority, it is the most important relationship to work through, because the therapist is the personification of parental images, of teachers, of authority, of established tradition, of incorporated values. But most clients are also conflicted in other interpersonal domains: for example, power, assertiveness, anger, competitiveness with peers, intimacy, sexuality, generosity, greed, envy.

Considerable research emphasizes the importance many group members place on working through relationships with other members rather than with the leader.[50] To take one example, a team of researchers asked members, in a twelve-month follow-up of a short-term crisis group, to indicate the source of the help each had received. Forty-two percent felt that the group members and not the therapist had been helpful, and 28 percent responded that both had been helpful. Only 5 percent said that the therapist alone was a major contributor to change.[51]

This body of research has important implications for the technique of the group therapist: rather than focusing exclusively on the client-therapist relationship, therapists must facilitate the development and working-through of interactions among members. I will have much more to say about these issues in chapters 6 and 7.

Insight defies precise description; it is not a unitary concept. I prefer to employ it in the general sense of "sighting inward"—a process encompassing clarification, explanation, and derepression. Insight occurs when one discovers something important about oneself—about one's behavior, one's motivational system, or one's unconscious.

In the group therapy process, clients may obtain insight on at least four different levels:

1. Clients may gain a more objective perspective on their interpersonal presentation. They may for the first time learn how they are seen by other people: as tense, warm, aloof, seductive, bitter, arrogant, pompous, obsequious, and so on.

2. Clients may gain some understanding into their more complex interactional patterns of behavior. Any of a vast number of patterns may become clear to them: for example, that they exploit others, court constant admiration, seduce and then reject or withdraw, compete relentlessly, plead for love, or relate only to the therapist or either the male or female members.

3. The third level may be termed motivational insight. Clients may learn why they do what they do to and with other people. A common form this type of insight assumes is learning that one behaves in certain ways because of the belief that different behavior would bring about some catastrophe: one might be humiliated, scorned, destroyed, or abandoned. Aloof, detached clients, for example, may understand that they shun closeness because of fears of being engulfed and losing themselves; competitive, vindictive, controlling clients may understand that they are frightened of their deep, insatiable cravings for nurturance; timid, obsequious individuals may dread the eruption of their repressed, destructive rage.

4. A fourth level of insight, genetic insight, attempts to help clients understand how they got to be the way they are. Through an exploration of the impact of early family and environmental experiences, the client understands the genesis of current patterns of behavior. The theoretical framework and the language in which the genetic explanation is couched are, of course, largely dependent on the therapist's school of conviction.

I have listed these four levels in the order of degree of inference. An unfortunate and long-standing conceptual error has resulted, in part, from the tendency to equate a "superficial-deep" sequence with this "degree of inference" sequence. Furthermore, "deep" has become equated with "profound" or "good," and superficial with "trivial," "obvious," or "inconsequential." Psychoanalysts have, in the past, disseminated the belief that the more profound the therapist, the deeper the interpretation (from the perspective of early life events) and thus the more complete the treatment. *There is, however, not a single shred of evidence to support this conclusion.*

Every therapist has encountered clients who have achieved considerable genetic insight based on some accepted theory of child development or psychopathology—be it that of Freud, Klein, Winnicott, Kernberg, or Kohut—and yet made no therapeutic progress. On the other hand, it is commonplace for significant clinical change to occur in the absence of genetic insight. Nor is there a demonstrated relationship between the acquisition of genetic insight and the persistence of change. In fact, there is much reason to question the validity of our most revered assumptions about the relationship between types of early experience and adult behavior and character structure.[52]

For one thing, we must take into account recent neurobiological research into the storage of memory. Memory is currently understood to consist of at least two forms, with two distinct brain pathways.[53] We are most familiar with the form of memory known as "explicit memory." This memory consists of recalled details, events, and the autobiographical recollections of one's life, and it has historically been the focus of exploration and interpretation in the psychodynamic therapies. A second form of memory, "implicit memory," houses our earliest relational experiences, many of which precede our use of language or symbols. This memory (also referred to as "procedural memory") shapes our beliefs about how to proceed in our relational world. Unlike explicit memory, implicit memory is not fully reached through the usual psychotherapeutic dialogue but, instead, through the relational and emotional component of therapy.

Psychoanalytic theory is changing as a result of this new understanding of memory. Fonagy, a prominent analytic theorist and researcher, conducted an exhaustive review of the psychoanalytic process and outcome literature. His conclusion: *"The recovery of past experience may be helpful, but the understanding of current ways of being with the other is the key to change. For this, both self and other representations may need to alter and this can only be done effectively in the here and now."*[54] In other words, the actual moment-to-moment experience of the client and therapist in the therapy relationship is the engine of change.

A fuller discussion of causality would take us too far afield from interpersonal learning, but I will return to the issue in chapters 5 and 6. For now, it is sufficient to emphasize that there is little doubt that intellectual understanding lubricates the machinery of change. It is important that insight—"sighting in"—occur, *but in its generic, not its genetic, sense.* And psychotherapists need to disengage the concept of "profound" or "significant" intellectual understanding from temporal considerations. Something that is deeply felt or has deep meaning for a client may or—as is usually the case—may not be related to the unraveling of the early genesis of behavior.

Chapter 3

GROUP COHESIVENESS

In this chapter I examine the properties of cohesiveness, the consider-able evidence for group cohesiveness as a therapeutic factor, and the various pathways through which it exerts its therapeutic influence.

What is cohesiveness and how does it influence therapeutic outcome? The short answer is that *cohesiveness is the group therapy analogue to relationship in individual therapy*. First, keep in mind that a vast body of research on individual psychotherapy demonstrates that a good therapist-client relationship is essential for a positive outcome. Is it also true that a good therapy relationship is essential in group therapy? Here again, the literature leaves little doubt that "relationship" is germane to positive outcome in group therapy. But relationship in group therapy is a far more complex concept than relationship in individual therapy. After all, there are only two people in the individual therapy transaction, whereas a number of individuals, generally six to ten, work together in group therapy. It is not enough to say that a good relationship is necessary for successful group therapy—we must specify *which* relationship: The relationship between the client and the group therapist (or therapists if there are co-leaders)? Or between the group member and other members? Or perhaps even between the individual and the "group" taken as a whole?

Over the past forty years, a vast number of controlled studies of psychotherapy outcome have demonstrated that the average person who receives psychotherapy is significantly improved and that the outcome from group therapy is virtually identical to that of individual therapy.[1] Furthermore there is evidence that certain clients may obtain greater benefit from group therapy than from other approaches, particularly clients dealing with stigma or social isolation and those seeking new coping skills.[2]

The evidence supporting the effectiveness of group psychotherapy is so compelling that it prompts us to direct our attention toward another question: What are the necessary conditions for effective psychotherapy? After all, not all psychotherapy is successful. In fact, there is evidence that treatment may be for better or for worse—although most therapists help their clients, some therapists make some clients worse.[3] Why? What makes for successful therapy? Although many factors are involved, a proper therapeutic relationship is a sine qua non for effective therapy outcome.[4] Research evidence overwhelmingly supports the conclusion that successful therapy—indeed even successful drug therapy—is mediated by a relationship between therapist and client that is characterized by trust, warmth, empathic understanding, and acceptance.[5] Although a positive therapeutic alliance is common to all effective treatments, it is not easily or routinely established. Extensive therapy research has focused on the nature of the therapeutic alliance and the specific interventions required to achieve and maintain it.[6]

Is the quality of the relationship related to the therapist's school of conviction? The evidence says, "No." Experienced and effective clinicians from different schools (Freudian, nondirective, experiential, gestalt, relational, interpersonal, cognitive-behavioral, psychodrama) resemble one another (and differ from nonexperts in their own school) in their conception of the ideal therapeutic relationship and in the relationship they themselves establish with their clients.[7]

Note that the engaged, cohesive therapeutic relationship is necessary in *all* psychotherapies, even the so-called mechanistic approaches—cognitive, behavioral, or systems-oriented forms of psychotherapy.[8] A recent secondary analysis of a large comparative psychotherapy trial, the National Institute of Mental Health's (NIMH) Treatment of Depression Collaborative Research Program, concluded that successful therapy, whether it was cognitive-behavioral therapy or interpersonal therapy, required "the presence of a positive attachment to a benevolent, supportive, and reassuring authority figure."[9] Research has shown that the client-therapist bond and the technical elements of cognitive therapy are synergistic: a strong and positive bond *in itself* disconfirms depressive beliefs and facilitates the work of modifying cognitive distortions. The absence of a positive bond renders technical interventions ineffective or even harmful.[10]

As noted, relationship plays an equally critical role in group psychotherapy. But the group therapy analogue of the client-therapist relationship in individual therapy must be a broader concept, encompassing the individual's relationship to the group therapist, to the other group members, and to the group as a whole.† At the risk of courting semantic confusion, I refer to all of these relationships in the group with the term "group cohesiveness." Cohesiveness is a widely researched basic property of groups that has been explored in several hundred research articles. Unfortunately, there is little cohesion in the literature, which suffers from the use of different definitions, scales, subjects, and rater perspectives.[11]

In general, however, there is agreement that groups differ from one another in the amount of "groupness" present. Those with a greater sense of solidarity, or "we-ness," value the group more highly and will defend it against internal and external threats. Such groups have a higher rate of attendance, participation, and mutual support and will defend the group standards much more than groups with less esprit de corps. Nonetheless it is difficult to formulate a precise definition. A recent comprehensive and thoughtful review concluded that cohesiveness "is like dignity: everyone can recognize it but apparently no one can describe it, much less measure it."[12] The problem is that cohesiveness refers to overlapping dimensions. On the one hand, there is a group phenomenon—the total esprit de corps; on the other hand, there is the individual member cohesiveness (or, more strictly, the individual's attraction to the group).[13]

In this book, cohesiveness is broadly defined as the result of all the forces acting on all the members such that they remain in the group,[14] or, more simply, the attractiveness of a group for its members.[15] Members of a cohesive group feel warmth and comfort in the group and a sense of belongingness; they value the group and feel in turn that they are valued, accepted, and supported by other members.[16]†

Esprit de corps and individual cohesiveness are interdependent, and group cohesiveness is often computed simply by summing the individual members' level of attraction to the group. Newer methods of measuring group cohesiveness from raters' evaluations of group climate make for greater quantitative precision, but they do not negate the fact that group cohesiveness remains a function and a summation of the individual members' sense of belongingness.[17] Keep in mind that group members are differentially attracted to the group and that cohesiveness is not fixed—once achieved, forever held—but instead fluctuates greatly during the course of the group.[18] Early cohesion and engagement is essential for the group to encompass the more challenging work that comes later in the group's development, as more conflict and discomfort emerges.[19] Recent research has also differentiated between the individual's sense of belonging and his or her appraisal of how well the entire group is working. It is not uncommon for an individual to feel "that this group works well, but I'm not part of it."[20] It is also possible for members (for example eating disorder clients) to value the interaction and bonding in the group yet be fundamentally opposed to the group goal.[21]

Before leaving the matter of definition, I must point out that group cohesiveness is not only a potent therapeutic force in its own right. It is a precondition for other therapeutic factors to function optimally. When, in individual therapy, we say that it is the relationship that heals, we do not mean that love or loving acceptance is enough; we mean that an ideal therapist-client relationship creates conditions in which the necessary risk taking, catharsis, and intrapersonal and interpersonal exploration may unfold. It is the same for group therapy: cohesiveness is necessary for other group therapeutic factors to operate.

THE IMPORTANCE OF GROUP COHESIVENESS

Although I have discussed the therapeutic factors separately, they are, to a great degree, interdependent. Catharsis and universality, for example, are not complete processes. It is not the sheer process of ventilation that is important; it is not only the discovery that others have problems similar to one's own and the ensuing disconfirmation of one's wretched unique-ness that are important. It is the affective sharing of one's inner world *and then the acceptance by others* that seem of paramount importance. To be accepted by others challenges the client's belief that he or she is basically repugnant, unacceptable, or unlovable. The need for belonging is innate in us all. Both affiliation within the group and attachment in the individ-ual setting address this need.[22] Therapy groups generate a positive, self-reinforcing loop: trust–self-disclosure–empathy–acceptance–trust.[23] The group will accept an individual, provided that the individual adheres to the group's procedural norms, regardless of past life experiences, trans-gressions, or social failings. Deviant lifestyles, history of prostitution, sexual perversion, heinous criminal offenses—all of these can be accepted by the therapy group, so long as norms of nonjudgmental acceptance and inclusiveness are established early in the group.

For the most part, the disturbed interpersonal skills of our clients have limited their opportunities for effective sharing and acceptance in inti-mate relationships. Furthermore, some members are convinced that their abhorrent impulses and fantasies shamefully bar them from social inter-action.† I have known many isolated clients for whom the group repre-sented their only deeply human contact. After just a few sessions, they have a stronger sense of being at home in the group than anywhere else. Later, even years afterward, when most other recollections of the group have faded from memory, they may still remember the warm sense of be-longing and acceptance.

As one successful client looking back over two and a half years of ther-apy put it, "The most important thing in it was just having a group there, people that I could always talk to, that wouldn't walk out on me. There was so much caring and hating and loving in the group, and I was a part of it. I'm better now and have my own life, but it's sad to think that the group's not there anymore."

Furthermore, group members see that they are not just passive benefi-ciaries of group cohesion, they also generate that cohesion, creating durable relationships—perhaps for the first time in their lives. One group member commented that he had always attributed his aloneness to some unidentified, intractable, repugnant character failing. It was only after he stopped missing meetings regularly because of his discouragement and sense of futility that he discovered the responsibility he exercised for his own aloneness: relationships do not inevitably wither—his had been doomed largely by his choice to neglect them.

Some individuals internalize the group: "It's as though the group is sit-ting on my shoulder, watching me. I'm forever asking, 'What would the group say about this or that?'" Often therapeutic changes persist and are consolidated because, even years later, the members are disinclined to let the group down.[24]

Membership, acceptance, and approval in various groups are of the ut-most importance in the individual's developmental sequence. The impor-tance of belonging to childhood peer groups, adolescent cliques, sororities or fraternities, or the proper social "in" group can hardly be overestimated. Nothing seems to be of greater importance for the self-esteem and well-being of the adolescent, for example, than to be included and accepted in some social group, and nothing is more devastating than exclusion.[25]

Most of our clients, however, have an impoverished group history; they have never been valuable and integral to a group. For these individuals, the sheer successful negotiation of a group experience may *in itself* be cura-tive. Belonging in the group raises self-esteem and meets members' de-pendency needs but in ways that also foster responsibility and autonomy, as each member contributes to the group's welfare and internalizes the at-mosphere of a cohesive group.[26]

Thus, in a number of ways, members of a therapy group come to mean a great deal to one another. The therapy group, at first perceived as an ar-tificial group that does not count, may in fact come to count very much. I have known groups whose members experience together severe depres-sions, psychoses, marriage, divorce, abortions, suicide, career shifts, shar-ing of innermost thoughts, and incest (sexual activity among the group members). I have seen a group physically carry one of its members to the hospital and seen many groups mourn the death of members. I have seen members of cancer support groups deliver eulogies at the funeral of a fallen group member. Relationships are often cemented by moving or haz-ardous adventures. How many relationships in life are so richly layered?

Evidence

Empirical evidence for the impact of group cohesiveness is not as extensive or as systematic as research documenting the importance of relationship in individual psychotherapy. Studying the effect of cohesiveness is more complex [27] because it involves research on variables closely related to cohesion such as group climate (the degree of engagement, avoidance, and conflict in the group)[28] and alliance (the member-therapist relationship).[29] The results of the research from all these perspectives, however, point to the same conclusion: relationship is at the heart of good therapy. This is no less important in the era of managed care and third-party oversight than it was in the past. In fact, the contemporary group therapist has an even larger responsibility to safeguard the therapeutic relationship from external intrusion and control.[30]

I now turn to a survey of the relevant research on cohesion. (Readers who are less interested in research methodology may wish to proceed directly to the summary section.)

- In an early study of former group psychotherapy clients in which members' explanations of the therapeutic factors in their therapy were transcribed and categorized, investigators found that more than half considered mutual support the primary mode of help in group therapy. Clients who perceived their group as cohesive attended more sessions, experienced more social contact with other members, and felt that the group had been therapeutic. Improved clients were significantly more likely to have felt accepted by the other members and to mention particular individuals when queried about their group experience.[31]
- In 1970, I reported a study in which successful group therapy clients were asked to look back over their experience and to rate, in order of effectiveness, the series of therapeutic factors I describe in this book.[32] Since that time, a vast number of studies using analogous designs have generated considerable data on clients' views of what aspects of group therapy have been most useful. I will examine these results in depth in the next chapter; for now, it is sufficient to note that there is a strong consensus that clients regard group cohesiveness as an extremely important determinant of successful group therapy.
- In a six-month study of two long-term therapy groups,[33] observers rated the process of each group session by scoring each member on five variables: acceptance, activity, desensitivity, abreaction, and improvement. Weekly self-ratings were also obtained from each member. Both the research raters and group members considered "acceptance" to be the variable most strongly related to improvement.
- Similar conclusions were reached in a study of forty-seven clients in twelve psychotherapy groups. Members' self-perceived personality change correlated significantly with both their feelings of involvement in the group and their assessment of total group cohesiveness.[34]

- My colleagues and I evaluated the one-year outcome of all forty clients who had started therapy in five outpatient groups.[35] Outcome was then correlated with variables measured in the first three months of therapy. Positive outcome in therapy significantly correlated with only two predictor variables: group cohesiveness[36] and general popularity—that is, clients who, early in the course of therapy, were most attracted to the group (high cohesiveness) and who were rated as more popular by the other group members at the sixth and the twelfth weeks had a better therapy outcome at the fiftieth week. The popularity finding, which in this study correlated even more positively with outcome than did cohesiveness, is, as I shall discuss shortly, relevant to group cohesiveness and sheds light on the mechanism through which group cohesiveness mediates change.
- The same findings emerge in more structured groups. A study of fifty-one clients who attended ten sessions of behavioral group therapy demonstrated that "attraction to the group" correlated significantly with improved self-esteem and inversely correlated with the group dropout rate.[37]
- The quality of intermember relationships has also been well documented as an essential ingredient in T-groups (also called sensitivity-training, process, encounter, or experiential groups; see chapter 16). A rigorously designed study found a significant relationship between the quality of intermember relationships and outcome in a T-group of eleven subjects who met twice a week for a total of sixty-four hours.[38] The members who entered into the most two-person mutually therapeutic relationships showed the most improvement during the course of the group.[39] Furthermore, the perceived relationship with the group leader was unrelated to the extent of change.
- My colleagues M. A. Lieberman, M. Miles, and I conducted a study of 210 subjects in eighteen encounter groups, encompassing ten ideological schools (gestalt, transactional analysis, T-groups, Synanon, personal growth, Esalen, psychoanalytic, marathon, psychodrama, encounter tape).[40] (See chapter 16 for a detailed discussion of this project.) Cohesiveness was assessed in several ways and correlated with outcome.[41] The results indicated that attraction to the group is indeed a powerful determinant of outcome. All methods of determining cohesiveness demonstrated a positive correlation between cohesiveness and outcome. A member who experienced little sense of belongingness or attraction to the group, even measured early in the course of the sessions, was unlikely to benefit from the group and, in fact, was likely to have a negative outcome. Furthermore, the groups with the higher overall levels of cohesiveness had a significantly better total outcome than groups with low cohesiveness.

- Another large study (N = 393) of experiential training groups yielded a strong relationship between affiliativeness (a construct that overlaps considerably with cohesion) and outcome.[42]
- MacKenzie and Tschuschke, studying twenty clients in long-term in-patient groups, differentiated members' personal "emotional relatedness to the group" from their appraisal of "group work" as a whole. The individual's personal sense of belonging correlated with future outcome, whereas the total group work scales did not.[43]
- S. Budman and his colleagues developed a scale to measure cohesiveness via observations by trained raters of videotaped group sessions. They studied fifteen therapy groups and found greater reductions in psychiatric symptoms and improvement in self-esteem in the most cohesively functioning groups. Group cohesion that was evident early—within the first thirty minutes of each session—predicted better outcome.[44]
- A number of other studies have examined the role of the relationship between the client and the group leader in group therapy. Marziali and colleagues[45] examined group cohesion and the client-group leader relationship in a thirty-session manualized interpersonal therapy group of clients with borderline personality disorder. Cohesion and member-leader relationship correlated strongly, supporting Budman's findings,[46] and both positively correlated with outcome. However, the member-group leader relationship measure was a more powerful predictor of outcome. The relationship between client and therapist may be particularly important for clients who have volatile interpersonal relationships and with whom the therapist serves an important containing function.
- In a study of a short-term structured cognitive-behavioral therapy group for social phobia[47] the relationship with the therapist deepened over the twelve weeks of treatment and correlated positively with outcome, but cohesion was static and not related to outcome. In this study the group was a setting for therapy and not an agent of therapy. Intermember bonds were not cultivated by the therapists, leading the authors to conclude that in highly structured groups, what matters most is the client-therapist collaboration around the therapy tasks.[48]
- A study of thirty-four clients with depression and social isolation treated in a twelve-session interactional problem-solving group reported that clients who described experiencing warmth and positive regard from the group leader had better therapy outcomes. The opposite also held true. Negative therapy outcomes were associated with negative client–group leader relationships. This correlative

study does not address cause and effect, however: Are clients better liked by their therapist because they do well in therapy, or does being well liked promote more well-being and effort?[49]

- Outcomes in brief intensive American Group Psychotherapy Association Institute training groups were influenced by higher levels of engagement.[50] Positive outcomes may well be mediated by group engagement that fosters more interpersonal communication and self-disclosure.[51]

Summary

I have cited evidence that group members value deeply the acceptance and support they receive from their therapy group. Self-perceived therapy outcome is positively correlated with attraction to the group. Highly cohesive groups have a better overall outcome than groups with low esprit de corps. Both emotional connectedness and the experience of group effectiveness contribute to group cohesiveness. Individuals with positive outcomes have had more mutually satisfying relationships with other members. Highly cohesive groups have greater levels of self-disclosure. For some clients and some groups (especially highly structured groups) the relationship with the leader may be the essential factor. A strong therapeutic relationship may not guarantee a positive outcome, but a poor therapeutic relationship will certainly not result in an effective treatment.

The presence of cohesion early in each session as well as in the early sessions of the group correlates with positive outcomes. It is critical that groups become cohesive and that leaders be alert to each member's personal experience of the group and address problems with cohesion quickly. Positive client outcome is also correlated with group popularity, a variable closely related to group support and acceptance. Although therapeutic change is multidimensional, these findings taken together strongly support the contention that group cohesiveness is an important determinant of positive therapeutic outcome.

In addition to this direct evidence, there is considerable indirect evidence from research with other types of groups. A plethora of studies demonstrate that in laboratory task groups, high levels of group cohesiveness produce many results that may be considered intervening therapy outcome factors. For example, group cohesiveness results in better group attendance, greater participation of members, greater influenceability of members, and many other effects. I will consider these findings in detail shortly, as I discuss the mechanism by which cohesiveness fosters therapeutic change.

MECHANISM OF ACTION

How do group acceptance, group support, and trust help troubled individuals? Surely there must be more to it than simple support or acceptance; therapists learn early in their careers that love is not enough. Although the quality of the therapist-client relationship is crucial, the therapist must do more than simply relate warmly and honestly to the client.[52] The therapeutic relationship creates favorable conditions for setting other processes in motion. What other processes? And how are they important?

Carl Rogers's deep insights into the therapeutic relationship are as relevant today as they were nearly fifty years ago. Let us start our investigation by examining his views about the mode of action of the therapeutic relationship in individual therapy. In his most systematic description of the process of therapy, Rogers states that when the conditions of an ideal therapist-client relationship exist, the following characteristic process is set into motion:

1. The client is increasingly free in expressing his feelings.
2. He begins to test reality and to become more discriminatory in his feelings and perceptions of his environment, his self, other persons, and his experiences.
3. He increasingly becomes aware of the incongruity between his experiences and his concept of self.
4. He also becomes aware of feelings that have been previously denied or distorted in awareness.
5. His concept of self, which now includes previously distorted or denied aspects, becomes more congruent with his experience.
6. He becomes increasingly able to experience, without threat, the therapist's unconditional positive regard and to feel an unconditional positive self-regard.
7. He increasingly experiences himself as the focus of evaluation of the nature and worth of an object or experience.
8. He reacts to experience less in terms of his perception of others' evaluation of him and more in terms of its effectiveness in enhancing his own development.[53]

Central to Rogers's views is his formulation of an actualizing tendency, an inherent tendency in all life to expand and to develop itself—a view stretching back to early philosophic views and clearly enunciated a century ago by Nietzsche.[54] It is the therapist's task to function as a facilitator and to create conditions favorable for self-expansion. The first task of the individual is self-exploration: the examination of feelings and experiences previously denied awareness.

This task is a ubiquitous stage in dynamic psychotherapy. Horney, for example, emphasized the individual's need for self-knowledge and self-realization, stating that the task of the therapist is to remove obstacles in the path of these autonomous processes.[55] Contemporary models recognize the same principle. Clients often pursue therapy with a plan to disconfirm pathogenic beliefs that obstruct growth and development.[56] In other words, there is a built-in inclination to growth and self-fulfillment in all individuals. The therapist does not have to inspirit clients with these qualities (as if we could!). Instead, our task is to remove the obstacles that block the process of growth. And one way we do this is by creating an ideal therapeutic atmosphere in the therapy group. A strong bond between members not only directly disconfirms one's unworthiness, it also generates greater willingness among clients to self-disclose and take interpersonal risks. These changes help deactivate old, negative beliefs about the self in relation to the world.[57]

There is experimental evidence that good rapport in individual therapy and its equivalent (cohesiveness) in group therapy encourage the client to participate in a process of reflection and personal exploration. For example, Truax,[58] studying forty-five hospitalized patients in three heterogeneous groups, demonstrated that participants in cohesive groups were significantly more inclined to engage in deep and extensive self-exploration.[59] Other research demonstrates that high cohesion is closely related to high degrees of intimacy, risk taking, empathic listening, and feedback.[60] The group members' recognition that their group is working well at the task of interpersonal learning produces greater cohesion in a positive and self-reinforcing loop.[61] Success with the group task strengthens the emotional bonds in the group.

Perhaps cohesion is vital because many of our clients have not had the benefit of ongoing solid peer acceptance in childhood. Therefore they find validation by other group members a new and vital experience. Furthermore, acceptance and understanding among members may carry greater power and meaning than acceptance by a therapist. Other group members, after all, do not have to care, or understand. They're not paid for it; it's not their "job."[62]

The intimacy developed in a group may be seen as a counterforce in a technologically driven culture that, in all ways—socially, professionally, residentially, recreationally—inexorably dehumanizes relationships.[63] In a world in which traditional boundaries that maintain relationships are increasingly permeable and transient, there is a greater need than ever for group belonging and group identity.[64] The deeply felt human experience in the group may be of great value to the individual, Rogers believes. Even if it creates no visible carryover, no external change in behavior, group members may still experience a more human, richer part of themselves and have this as an internal reference point. This last point is worth emphasizing, for it is one of those gains of therapy—especially group therapy—that enrich one's interior life and yet may not, at least for a long period of time, have external behavioral manifestations and thus may elude measurement by researchers and consideration by managed health care administrators, who determine how much and what type of therapy is indicated.

Group members' acceptance of self and acceptance of other members are interdependent; not only is self-acceptance basically dependent on acceptance by others, but acceptance of others is fully possible only after one can accept oneself. This principle is supported by both clinical wisdom and research.[65] Members of a therapy group may experience considerable self-contempt and contempt for others. A manifestation of this feeling may be seen in the client's initial refusal to join "a group of nuts" or reluctance to become closely involved with a group of pained individuals for fear of being sucked into a maelstrom of misery. A particularly evocative response to the prospect of group therapy was given by a man in his eighties when he was invited to join a group for depressed elderly men: it was useless, he said, to waste time watering a bunch of dead trees—his metaphor for the other men in his nursing home.[66]

In my experience, all individuals seeking assistance from a mental health professional have in common two paramount difficulties: (1) establishing and maintaining meaningful interpersonal relationships, and (2) maintaining a sense of personal worth (self-esteem). It is hard to discuss these two interdependent areas as separate entities, but since in the preceding chapter I dwelled more heavily on the establishment of interpersonal relationships, I shall now turn briefly to self-esteem.

Self-esteem and public esteem are highly interdependent.[67] Self-esteem refers to an individual's evaluation of what he or she is really worth, and is indissolubly linked to that person's experiences in prior social relationships. Recall Sullivan's statement: "The self may be said to be made up of reflected appraisals."[68] In other words, during early development, one's perceptions of the attitudes of others toward oneself come to determine how one regards and values oneself. The individual internalizes many of these perceptions and, if they are consistent and congruent, relies on these internalized evaluations for some stable measure of self-worth.

But, in addition to this internal reservoir of self-worth, people are, to a greater or lesser degree, always concerned and influenced by the current evaluations of others—especially the evaluation provided by the groups to which they belong. Social psychology research supports this clinical understanding: the groups and relationships in which we take part become incorporated in the self.[69] One's attachment to a group is multidimensional. It is shaped both by the member's degree of confidence in his attractiveness to the group—am I a desirable member?—and the member's relative aspiration for affiliation—do I want to belong?

The influence of public esteem—that is, the group's evaluation—on an individual depends on several factors: how important the person feels the group to be; the frequency and specificity of the group's communications to the person about that public esteem; and the salience to the person of the traits in question. (Presumably, considering the honest and intense self-disclosure in therapy groups, the salience is very great indeed, since these traits are close to a person's core identity.) In other words, the more the group matters to the person, and the more that person subscribes to the group values, the more he or she will be inclined to value and agree with the group judgment.[70] This last point has much clinical relevance. The more attracted an individual is to the group, the more he or she will respect the judgment of the group and will attend to and take seriously any discrepancy between public esteem and self-esteem. A discrepancy between the two will create a state of dissonance, which the individual will attempt to correct.

Let us suppose this discrepancy veers to the negative side—that is, the group's evaluation of the individual is less than the individual's self-evaluation. How to resolve that discrepancy? One recourse is to deny or distort the group's evaluation. In a therapy group, this is not a positive development, for a vicious circle is generated: the group, in the first place, evaluates the member poorly because he or she fails to participate in the group task (which in a therapy group consists of active exploration of one's self and one's relationships with others). Any increase in defensiveness and communicational problems will only further lower the group's esteem of that particular member. A common method used by members to resolve such a discrepancy is to devalue the group—emphasizing, for example, that the group is artificial or composed of disturbed individuals, and then comparing it unfavorably to some anchor group (for example, a social or occupational group) whose evaluation of the member is different. Members who follow this sequence (for example, the group deviants described in chapter 8) usually drop out of the group.

Toward the end of a successful course of group therapy, one group member reviewed her early recollections of the group as follows: "For the longest time I told myself you were all nuts and your feedback to me about my defensiveness and inaccessibility was ridiculous. I wanted to quit—I've done that before many times, but I felt enough of a connection here to decide to stay. Once I made that choice I started to tell myself that you cannot all be wrong about me. That was the turning point in my therapy." This is an example of the therapeutic method of resolving the discrepancy for the individual: that is, to raise one's public esteem by changing those behaviors and attitudes that have been criticized by the group. This method is more likely if the individual is highly attracted to the group and if the public esteem is not too much lower than the self-esteem.

But is the use of group pressure to change individual behavior or attitudes a form of social engineering? Is it not mechanical? Does it not neglect deeper levels of integration? Indeed, group therapy does employ behavioral principles; psychotherapy is, in all its variants, basically a form of learning. Even the most nondirective therapists use, at an unconscious level, operant conditioning techniques: they signal desirable conduct or attitudes to clients, whether explicitly or subtly.[71]

This process does not suggest that we assume an explicit behavioral, mechanistic view of the client, however. Aversive or operant conditioning of behavior and attitudes is, in my opinion, neither feasible nor effective when applied as an isolated technique. Although clients often report lasting improvement after some disabling complaint is remedied by behavioral therapy techniques, close inspection of the process invariably reveals that important interpersonal relationships have been affected. Either the therapist-client relationship in the behavioral and cognitive therapies has been more meaningful than the therapist realized (and research evidence substantiates this),[72] or some important changes, initiated by the symptomatic relief, have occurred in the client's social relationships that have served to reinforce and maintain the client's improvement. Again, as I have stressed before, all the therapeutic factors are intricately interdependent. Behavior and attitudinal change, regardless of origin, begets other changes. The group changes its evaluation of a member; the member feels more self-satisfied in the group and with the group itself; and the adaptive spiral described in the previous chapter is initiated.

A far more common occurrence in a psychotherapy group is a discrepancy in the opposite direction: the group's evaluation of a member is higher than the member's self-evaluation. Once again, the member is placed in a state of dissonance and once again will attempt to resolve the discrepancy. What can a member in that position do? Perhaps the person will lower the public esteem by revealing personal inadequacies. However, in therapy groups, this behavior has the paradoxical effect of raising public esteem—disclosure of inadequacies is a valued group norm and enhances acceptance by the group. Another possible scenario, desirable therapeutically, occurs when group members reexamine and alter their low level of self-esteem. An illustrative clinical vignette will flesh out this formulation:

• *Marietta, a thirty-four-year-old housewife with an emotionally impoverished background, sought therapy because of anxiety and guilt stemming from a series of extramarital affairs. Her self-esteem was ex-*

ceedingly low; nothing escaped her self-excoriation: her physical ap-
pearance, her intelligence, her speech, her unimaginativeness, her func-
tioning as a mother and a wife. Although she received solace from her
religious affiliation, it was a mixed blessing because she felt too un-
worthy to socialize with the church people in her community. She mar-
ried a man she considered repugnant but nonetheless a good
man—certainly good enough for her. Only in her sexual affairs, partic-
ularly when she had them with several men at once, did she seem to
come alive to feel attractive, desirable, and able to give something of
herself that seemed of value to others. However, this behavior clashed
with her religious convictions and resulted in considerable anxiety and
further self-derogation.

Viewing the group as a social microcosm, the therapist soon noted
characteristic trends in Marietta's group behavior. She spoke often of
the guilt issuing from her sexual behavior, and for many hours the
group struggled with all the titillating ramifications of her predica-
ment. At all other times in the group, however, she disengaged and of-
fered nothing. She related to the group as she did to her social
environment. She could belong to it, but she could not really relate to
the other people: the only thing of real interest she felt she could offer
was her genitals.

Over time in the group she began to respond and to question others
and to offer warmth, support, and feedback. She found other, nonsex-
ual, aspects of herself to disclose and spoke openly of a broad array of
her life concerns. Soon she found herself increasingly valued by the
other members. She gradually reexamined and eventually disconfirmed
her belief that she had little of value to offer. The discrepancy between
her public esteem and her self-esteem widened (that is, the group val-
ued her more than she regarded herself), and soon she was forced to en-
tertain a more realistic and positive view of herself. Gradually, an
adaptive spiral ensued: she began to establish meaningful nonsexual re-
lationships both in and out of the group and these, in turn, further en-
hanced her self-esteem.

The more therapy disconfirms the client's negative self-image through
new relational experience, the more effective therapy will be.[73]

Self-Esteem, Public Esteem, and Therapeutic Change: Evidence

Group therapy research has not specifically investigated the relationship
between public esteem and shifts in self-esteem. However, an interesting
finding from a study of experiential groups (see chapter 16) was that
members' self-esteem decreased when public esteem decreased.[74] (Public
esteem is measured by sociometric data, which involves asking members

to rank-order one another on several variables.) Researchers also discovered that the more a group member underestimated his or her public esteem, the more acceptable that member was to the other members. In other words, the ability to face one's deficiencies, or even to judge oneself a little harshly, increases one's public esteem. Humility, within limits, is far more adaptable than arrogance.

It is also interesting to consider data on group popularity, a variable closely related to public esteem. The group members considered most popular by other members after six and twelve weeks of therapy had significantly better therapy outcomes than the other members at the end of one year.[75] Thus, it seems that clients who have high public esteem early in the course of a group are destined to have a better therapy outcome.

What factors seem to be responsible for the attainment of popularity in therapy groups? Three variables, which did not themselves correlate with outcome, correlated significantly with popularity:

1. Previous self-disclosure.[76]
2. Interpersonal compatibility:[77] individuals who (perhaps fortuitously) have interpersonal needs that happen to blend well with those of the other group members become popular in the group.
3. Other sociometric measures; group members who were often chosen as leisure companions and worked well with colleagues became popular in the group. A clinical study of the most popular and least popular members revealed that popular members tended to be young, well-educated, intelligent, and introspective. They filled the leadership vacuum that occurs early in the group when the therapist declines to assume the traditional leader role.[78]

The most unpopular group members were rigid, moralistic, nonintrospective, and least involved in the group task. Some were blatantly deviant, attacking the group and isolating themselves. Some schizoid members were frightened of the group process and remained peripheral. A study of sixty-six group therapy members concluded that the less popular members (that is, those viewed less positively by other members) were more inclined to drop out of the group.[79]

Social psychology researchers have also investigated the attributes that confer higher social status in social groups. The personality attribute of extraversion (measured by a personality questionnaire, the NEO-PI)[80] is a very strong predictor of popularity.[81] Extraversion connotes the traits of active and energetic social engagement, that is, a person who is upbeat and emotionally robust. Depue's neurobiological research[82] suggests that such individuals invite others to approach them. The promise of the extravert's welcome response rewards and reinforces engagement.

The Lieberman, Yalom, and Miles encounter group study corroborated these conclusions.[83] Sociometric data revealed that the members with the more positive outcomes were influential and engaged in behavior in close harmony with the encounter group values of risk taking, spontaneity, openness, self-disclosure, expressivity, group facilitation, and support. Evidence has emerged from both clinical and social-psychological small-group research demonstrating that the members who adhere most closely to group norms attain positions of popularity and influence.[84] Members who help the group achieve its tasks are awarded higher status.[85]

To summarize: Members who are popular and influential in therapy groups have a higher likelihood of changing. They attain popularity and influence in the group by virtue of their active participation, self-disclosure, self-exploration, emotional expression, nondefensiveness, leadership, interest in others, and support of the group.

It is important to note that the individual who adheres to the group norms not only is rewarded by increased public esteem within the group but also uses those same social skills to deal more effectively with interpersonal problems outside the group. Thus, increased popularity in the group acts therapeutically in two ways: by augmenting self-esteem and by reinforcing adaptive social skills. The rich get richer. The challenge in group therapy is helping the poor get richer as well.

Group Cohesiveness and Group Attendance

Continuation in the group is obviously a necessary, though not a sufficient, prerequisite for successful treatment. Several studies indicate that clients who terminate early in the course of group therapy receive little benefit.[86] In one study, over fifty clients who dropped out of long-term therapy groups within the first twelve meetings reported that they did so because of some stress encountered in the group. They were not satisfied with their therapy experience and they did not improve; indeed, many of these clients felt worse.[87] Clients who remain in the group for at least several months have a high likelihood (85 percent in one study) of profiting from therapy.[88]

The greater a member's attraction to the group, the more inclined that person will be to stay in therapy groups as well as in encounter groups, laboratory groups (formed for some research purpose), and task groups (established to perform some designated task).[89] The Lieberman, Yalom, and Miles encounter group study discovered a high correlation between low cohesiveness and eventual dropping out from the group.[90] The dropouts had little sense of belongingness and left the group most often because they felt rejected, attacked, or unconnected.

The relationship between cohesiveness and maintenance of membership has implications for the total group as well. Not only do the least cohesive members terminate membership and fail to benefit from therapy, but noncohesive groups with high member turnover prove to be less therapeutic for the remaining members as well. Clients who drop out challenge the group's sense of worth and effectiveness.

Stability of membership is a necessary condition for effective short- and long-term interactional group therapy. Although most therapy groups go through an early phase of instability during which some members drop out and replacements are added, the groups thereafter settle into a long, stable phase in which much of the solid work of therapy occurs. Some groups seem to enter this phase of stability early, and other groups never achieve it. Dropouts at times beget other dropouts, as other clients may terminate soon after the departure of a key member. In a group therapy follow-up study, clients often spontaneously underscored the importance of membership stability.[91]

In chapter 15, I will discuss the issue of cohesiveness in groups led in clinical settings that preclude a stable long-term membership. For example, drop-in crisis groups or groups on an acute inpatient ward rarely have consistent membership even for two consecutive meetings. In these clinical situations, therapists must radically alter their perspectives on the life development of the group. I believe, for example, that the appropriate life span for the acute inpatient group is a single session. The therapist must strive to be efficient and to offer effective help to as many members as possible during each single session.

Brief therapy groups pay a particularly high price for poor attendance, and therapists must make special efforts to increase cohesiveness early in the life of the group. These strategies (including strong pregroup preparation, homogeneous composition, and structured interventions)[92] will be discussed in chapter 15.

Group Cohesiveness and the Expression of Hostility

It would be a mistake to equate cohesiveness with comfort. Although cohesive groups may show greater acceptance, intimacy, and understanding, there is evidence *that they also permit greater development and expression of hostility and conflict.* Cohesive groups have norms (that is, unwritten rules of behavior accepted by group members) that encourage open expression of disagreement or conflict alongside support. In fact, unless hostility can be openly expressed, persistent covert hostile attitudes may hamper the development of cohesiveness and effective interpersonal learning. Unexpressed hostility simply smolders within, only to seep out in many indirect ways, none of which facilitates the group therapeutic process. It is not easy to continue communicating honestly with someone you dislike or even hate. The temptation to avoid the other and to break off communication is very great; yet when channels of communication are closed, so are any hopes for conflict resolution and for personal growth.

This is as true on the megagroup—even the national—level as on the dyadic. The Robbers' Cave experiment, a famed research project conducted long ago, in the infancy of group dynamics research,* offers experimental evidence still relevant for contemporary clinical work.[93] A camp of well-adjusted eleven-year-old boys was divided at the outset into two groups that were placed in competition with each other in a series of contests. Soon each group developed considerable cohesiveness as well as a deep sense of hostility toward the other group. Any meaningful communication between the two groups became impossible. If, for example, they were placed in physical proximity in the dining hall, the group boundaries remained impermeable. Intergroup communication consisted of taunts, insults, and spitballs.

How to restore meaningful communication between the members of the two groups? That was the quest of the researchers. Finally they hit upon a successful strategy. Intergroup hostility was relieved only when a sense of allegiance to a single large group could be created. The researchers created some superordinate goals that disrupted the small group boundaries and forced all the boys to work together in a single large group. For example, a truck carrying food for an overnight hike stalled in a ditch and could be rescued only by the cooperative efforts of all the boys; a highly desirable movie could be rented only by the pooled contributions of the entire camp; the water supply was cut off and could be restored only by the cooperative efforts of all campers.

The drive to belong can create powerful feelings within groups. Members with a strong adherence to what is inside the group may experience strong pressure to exclude and devalue who and what is outside the bounds of the group.[94] It is not uncommon for individuals to develop prejudice against groups to which they cannot belong. It is therefore not surprising that hostility often emerges against members of ethnic or racial groups to which entry for outsiders may be impossible. The implication

---

Dynamic is a frequently used term in the vocabulary of psychotherapy and must be defined. It has a lay and a technical meaning. It derives from the Greek *dunasthi*, meaning "to have power or strength." In the lay sense, then, the word evokes energy or movement (a dynamic football player or orator), but in its technical sense it refers to the idea of "forces." In individual therapy, when we speak of a client's "psychodynamics," we are referring to the various forces in conflict within the client that result in certain configurations of experienced feelings and behavior. In common usage since the advent of Freud, the assumption is made that some of the forces in conflict with one another exist at different levels of awareness—indeed, some of them are entirely out of consciousness and, through the mechanism of repression, dwell in the dynamic unconsciousness. In group work, dynamics refers to inferred, invisible constructs or group properties (for example, cohesiveness, group pressure, scapegoating, and subgrouping) that affect the overall movements of the group.

for international conflict is apparent: intergroup hostility may dissolve in the face of some urgently felt worldwide crisis that only supranational cooperation can avert: atmospheric pollution or an international AIDS epidemic, for example. These principles also have implications for clinical work with small groups.

Intermember conflict during the course of group therapy must be contained. Above all, communication must not be ruptured, and the adversaries must continue to work together in a meaningful way, to take responsibility for their statements, and to be willing to go beyond name-calling. This is, of course, a major difference between therapy groups and social groups, in which conflicts often result in the permanent rupture of relationships. Clients' descriptions of critical incidents in therapy (see chapter 2) often involve an episode in which they expressed strong negative affect. In each instance, however, the client was able to weather the storm and to continue relating (often in a more gratifying manner) to the other member.

Underlying these events is the condition of cohesiveness. The group and the members must mean enough to each other to be willing to bear the discomfort of working through a conflict. Cohesive groups are, in a sense, like families with much internecine warfare but a powerful sense of loyalty.

Several studies demonstrate that cohesiveness is positively correlated with risk taking and intensive interaction.[95] Thus, cohesiveness is not synonymous with love or with a continuous stream of supportive, positive statements. Cohesive groups are groups that are able to embrace conflict and to derive constructive benefit from it. Obviously, in times of conflict, cohesiveness scales that emphasize warmth, comfort, and support will temporarily gyrate; thus, many researchers have reservations about viewing cohesiveness as a precise, stable, measurable, unidimensional variable and consider it instead as multidimensional.[96]

Once the group is able to deal constructively with conflict in the group, therapy is enhanced in many ways. I have already mentioned the importance of catharsis, of risk taking, of gradually exploring previously avoided or unknown parts of oneself and recognizing that the anticipated dreaded catastrophe is chimerical. Many clients are desperately afraid of anger—their own and that of others. A highly cohesive group encourages members to tolerate the pain and hurt that interpersonal learning may produce.

But keep in mind that it is the early engagement that makes such successful working-through later possible.[97] The premature expression of excess hostility before group cohesion has been established is a leading cause of group fragmentation. It is important for clients to realize that their anger is not lethal. Both they and others can and do survive an expression of their impatience, irritability, and even outright rage. For some clients, it is also important to have the experience of weathering an attack. In the process, they may become better acquainted with the reasons for their position and learn to withstand pressure from others.[98]

Conflict may also enhance self-disclosure, as each opponent tends to reveal more and more to clarify his or her position. As members are able to go beyond the mere statement of position, as they begin to understand the other's experiential world, past and present, and view the other's position from their own frame of reference, they may begin to understand that the other's point of view may be as appropriate for that person as their own is for themselves. The working through of extreme dislike or hatred of another person is an experience of great therapeutic power. A clinical illustration demonstrates many of these points (another example may be found in my novel *The Schopenhauer Cure*).[99]

• *Susan, a forty-six-year-old, very proper school principal, and Jean, a twenty-one-year-old high school dropout, became locked into a vicious struggle. Susan despised Jean because of her libertine lifestyle, and what she imagined to be her sloth and promiscuity. Jean was enraged by Susan's judgmentalism, her sanctimoniousness, her embittered spinsterhood, her closed posture to the world. Fortunately, both women were deeply committed members of the group. (Fortuitous circumstances played a part here. Jean had been a core member of the group for a year and then married and went abroad for three months. Just at that time Susan became a member and, during Jean's absence, became heavily involved in the group.)*

Both had had considerable past difficulty in tolerating and expressing anger. Over a four-month period, they interacted heavily, at times in pitched battles. For example, Susan erupted indignantly when she found out that Jean was obtaining food stamps illegally; and Jean, learning of Susan's virginity, ventured the opinion that she was a curiosity, a museum piece, a mid-Victorian relic.

Much good group work was done because Jean and Susan, despite their conflict, never broke off communication. They learned a great deal about each other and eventually realized the cruelty of their mutual judgmentalism. Finally, they could both understand how much each meant for the other on both a personal and a symbolic level. Jean desperately wanted Susan's approval; Susan deeply envied Jean for the freedom she had never permitted herself. In the working-through process, both fully experienced their rage; they encountered and then accepted previously unknown parts of themselves. Ultimately, they

*developed an empathic understanding and then an acceptance of each
other. Neither could possibly have tolerated the extreme discomfort of
the conflict were it not for the strong cohesion that, despite the pain,
bound them to the group.*

Not only are cohesive groups more able to express hostility among
members but there is evidence that they are also more able to express hostility toward the leader.[100] Regardless of the personal style or skill of
group leaders, the therapy group will nonetheless come, often within the
first dozen meetings, to experience some degree of hostility and resentment toward them. (See chapter 11 for a full discussion of this issue.)
Leaders do not fulfill members' fantasized expectations and, in the view
of many members, do not care enough, do not direct enough, and do not
offer immediate relief. If the group members suppress these feelings of
disappointment or anger, several harmful consequences may ensue. They
may attack a convenient scapegoat—another member or some institution
like "psychiatry" or "doctors." They may experience a smoldering irritation within themselves or within the group as a whole. They may, in short,
begin to establish norms discouraging open expression of feelings. The
presence of such scapegoating may be a signal that aggression is being displaced away from its more rightful source—often the therapist.[101] Leaders
who challenge rather than collude with group scapegoating not only safeguard against an unfair attack, they also demonstrate their commitment
to authenticity and responsibility in relationships.

The group that is able to express negative feelings toward the therapist
almost invariably is strengthened by the experience. It is an excellent exercise in direct communication and provides an important learning experience—namely, that one may express hostility directly without some
ensuing irreparable calamity. It is far preferable that the therapist, the true
object of the anger, be confronted than for the anger to be displaced onto
some other member in the group. Furthermore, the therapist, let us pray,
is far better able than a scapegoated member to withstand confrontation.
The entire process is self-reinforcing; a concerted attack on the leader that
is handled in a nondefensive, nonretaliatory fashion serves to increase cohesiveness still further.

One cautionary note about cohesion: misguided ideas about cohesion
may interfere with the group task.[102] Janis coined the term "groupthink"
to describe the phenomenon of "deterioration of mental efficiency, reality
testing, and moral judgment that results from group pressure."[103] Group
pressure to conform and maintain consensus may create a groupthink environment. This is not an alliance-based cohesion that facilitates the
growth of the group members; on the contrary, it is a misalliance based on

naive or regressive assumptions about belonging. Critical and analytic thought by the group members needs to be endorsed and encouraged by the group leader as an essential group norm.[104] Autocratic, closed and authoritarian leaders discourage such thought. Their groups are more prone to resist uncertainty, to be less reflective, and to close down exploration prematurely.[105]

Group Cohesiveness and Other Therapy-Relevant Variables

Research from both therapy and laboratory groups has demonstrated that group cohesiveness has a plethora of important consequences that have obvious relevance to the group therapeutic process.[106] It has been shown, for example, that the members of a cohesive group, in contrast to the members of a noncohesive group, will:

1. Try harder to influence other group members[107]
2. Be more open to influence by the other members[108]
3. Be more willing to listen to others[109] and more accepting of others[110]
4. Experience greater security and relief from tension in the group[111]
5. Participate more readily in meetings[112]
6. Self-disclose more[113]
7. Protect the group norms and exert more pressure on individuals deviating from the norms[114]
8. Be less susceptible to disruption as a group when a member terminates membership[115]
9. Experience greater ownership of the group therapy enterprise[116]

SUMMARY

By definition, cohesiveness refers to the attraction that members have for their group and for the other members. It is experienced at interpersonal, intrapersonal, and intragroup levels. The members of a cohesive group are accepting of one another, supportive, and inclined to form meaningful relationships in the group. Cohesiveness is a significant factor in successful group therapy outcome. In conditions of acceptance and understanding, members will be more inclined to express and explore themselves, to become aware of and integrate hitherto unacceptable aspects of self, and to relate more deeply to others. Self-esteem is greatly influenced by the client's role in a cohesive group. The social behavior required for members to be esteemed by the group is socially adaptive to the individual out of the group.

In addition, highly cohesive groups are more stable groups, with better attendance and less turnover. Evidence was presented to indicate that this stability is vital to successful therapy: early termination precludes benefit for the involved client and impedes the progress of the rest of the group as well. Cohesiveness favors self-disclosure, risk taking, and the constructive expression of conflict in the group—phenomenon that facilitate successful therapy.

What we have yet to consider are the determinants of cohesiveness. What are the sources of high and low cohesiveness? What does the therapist do to facilitate the development of a highly cohesive group? These important issues will be discussed in the chapters dealing with the group therapist's tasks and techniques.

Chapter 4

THE THERAPEUTIC FACTORS: AN INTEGRATION

We began our inquiry into the group therapy therapeutic factors with the rationale that the delineation of these factors would guide us to a formulation of effective tactics and strategies for the therapist. The compendium of therapeutic factors presented in chapter 1 is, I believe, comprehensive but is not yet in a form that has great clinical applicability. For the sake of clarity I have considered the factors as separate entities, whereas in fact they are intricately interdependent. In other words, I have taken the therapy process apart to examine it, and now it is time to put it back together again.

In this chapter I first consider how the therapeutic factors operate when they are viewed not separately but as part of a dynamic process. Next I address the comparative potency of the therapeutic factors. Obviously, they are not all of equal value. However, an absolute rank-ordering of therapeutic factors is not possible. Many contingencies must be considered. The importance of various therapeutic factors depends on the type of group therapy practiced. Groups differ in their clinical populations, therapeutic goals, and treatment settings—for example, eating disorders groups, panic disorder groups, substance abuse groups, medical illness groups, ongoing outpatient groups, brief therapy groups, inpatient groups, and partial hospitalization groups. They may emphasize different clusters of therapeutic factors, and some therapeutic factors are important at one stage of a group, whereas others predominate at another. Even within the same group, different clients benefit from different therapeutic factors. Like diners at a cafeteria, group members will choose their personalized menu of therapeutic factors, depending on such factors as their needs, their social skills, and their character structure.

This chapter underscores the point that some factors are not always independent mechanisms of change but instead create the conditions for change. For example, as I mentioned in chapter 1, instillation of hope may serve largely to prevent early discouragement and to keep members in the group until other, more potent forces for change come into play. Or consider cohesiveness: for some members, the sheer experience of being an accepted, valued member of a group may in itself be the major mechanism of change. Yet for other members, cohesiveness is important because it provides the conditions, the safety and support, that allow them to express emotion, request feedback, and experiment with new interpersonal behavior.

Our efforts to evaluate and integrate the therapeutic factors will always remain, to some extent, conjectural. Over the past twenty-five years there has been a groundswell of research on the therapeutic factors: recent reviews have cited hundreds of studies.[1] Yet little definitive research has been conducted on the comparative value of the therapeutic factors and their interrelation; indeed, we may never attain a high degree of certainty as to these comparative values. We have summaries at the end of sections for those readers less interested in research detail.

I do not speak from a position of investigative nihilism but instead argue that the nature of our data on therapeutic factors is so highly subjective that it largely resists the application of scientific methodology. The precision of our instrumentation and statistical analysis will always be limited by the imprecision of our primary data—the clients' assessment of what was most helpful about their group therapy experience. We may improve our data collection by asking our clients these questions at repeated intervals or by having independent raters evaluate the therapeutic factors at work,[2] but we are still left trying to quantify and categorize subjective dimensions that do not fit easily into an objective and categorical system.†[3] We must also recognize limits in our ability to infer objective therapeutic cause and effect accurately from rater observation or client reflection, both of which are inherently subjective. This point is best appreciated by those therapists and researchers who themselves have had a personal therapy experience. They need only pose themselves the task of evaluating and rating the therapeutic factors in their own therapy to realize that precise judgment can never be attained. Consider the following not atypical clinical illustration, which demonstrates the difficulty of determining which factor is most therapeutic within a treatment experience.

• *A new member, Barbara, a thirty-six-year-old chronically depressed single woman, sobbed as she told the group that she had been laid off. Although her job paid poorly and she disliked the work, she viewed the layoff as evidence that she was unacceptable and doomed to a miserable, unhappy life. Other group members offered support and reassur-*

ance but with minimal apparent impact. Another member, Gail, who was fifty years old and herself no stranger to depression, urged Barbara to avoid a negative cascade of depressive thoughts and self-derogation and added that it was only after a year of hard work in the group that she was able to attain a stable mood and to view negative events as disappointments rather than damning personal indictments.

Barbara nodded and then told the group that she had desperately needed to talk and arrived early for the meeting, saw no one else and assumed not only that the group had been canceled but also that the leader had uncaringly failed to notify her. She was angrily contemplating leaving, when the group members arrived. As she talked, she smiled knowingly, acknowledging the depressive assumptions she continually makes and her propensity to act upon them.

After a short reflection, she recalled a memory of her childhood—of her anxious mother, and her family's motto, "Disaster is always around the corner." At age eight she had a diagnostic workup for tuberculosis because of a positive skin test. Her mother had said, "Don't worry—I will visit you at the sanitarium." The diagnostic workup was negative, but her mother's echoing words still filled her with dread. Barbara then added—"I can't tell you what it's like for me today to receive this kind feedback and reassurance instead."

We can see in this illustration the presence of the several therapeutic factors—universality, instillation of hope, self-understanding, imparting information, family reenactment, interpersonal learning, and catharsis. Which therapeutic factor is primary? How can we determine that with any certainty?

Some attempts have been made to use subjectively evaluated therapeutic factors as independent variables in outcome studies. Yet enormous difficulties are encountered in such research. The methodological problems are formidable: as a general rule, the accuracy with which variables can be measured is directly proportional to their triviality. A comprehensive review of such empirical studies produced only a handful of studies that had an acceptable research design, and these studies have limited clinical relevance.[4] For example, four studies attempted to quantify and evaluate insight by comparing insight groups with other approaches, such as assertiveness training groups or interactional here-and-now groups (as though such interactional groups offered no insight).[5] The researchers measured insight by counting the number of a therapist's insight-providing comments or by observers' ratings of a leader's insight orientation. Such a design fails to take into account the crucial aspects of the experience of insight: for example, how accurate was the insight? How well timed? Was the client in a state of readiness to accept it? What was the nature of the client's relationship with the therapist? (If adversarial, the client is apt to reject any interpretation; if dependent, the client may ingest all interpretations without discrimination.) Insight is a deeply subjective experience that *cannot be rated by objective measures* (one accurate, well-timed interpretation is worth a score of interpretations that fail to hit home). Perhaps it is for these reasons that no new research on insight in group therapy and outcome has been reported in the past decade. In virtually every form of psychotherapy the therapist must appreciate the full context of the therapy to understand the nature of effective therapeutic interventions.[6]

As a result, I fear that empirical psychotherapy research will never provide the certainty we crave, and we must learn to live effectively with uncertainty. We must listen to what clients tell us and consider the best available evidence from research and intelligent clinical observation. Ultimately we must evolve a reasoned therapy that offers the great flexibility needed to cope with the infinite range of human problems.

COMPARATIVE VALUE OF THE
THERAPEUTIC FACTORS: THE CLIENT'S VIEW

How do group members evaluate the various therapeutic factors? Which factors do *they* regard as most salient to their improvement in therapy? In the first two editions of this book, it was possible to review in a leisurely fashion the small body of research bearing on this question: I discussed the two existing studies that explicitly explored the client's subjective appraisal of the therapeutic factors, and then proceeded to describe in detail the results of my first therapeutic factor research project.[7] For that undertaking, my colleagues and I administered to twenty successful group therapy participants a therapeutic factor questionnaire designed to compare the importance of the eleven therapeutic factors I identified in chapter 1.

Things have changed since then. In the past four decades, a deluge of studies have researched the client's view of the therapeutic factors (several of these studies have also obtained therapists' ratings of therapeutic factors). Recent research demonstrates that a focus on therapeutic factors is a very useful way for therapists to shape their group therapeutic strategies to match their clients' goals.[8] This burst of research provides rich data and enables us to draw conclusions with far more conviction about therapeutic factors. For one thing, it is clear that the differential value of the therapeutic factors is vastly influenced by the type of group, the stage of the therapy, and the intellectual level of the client. Thus, the overall task of reviewing and synthesizing the literature is far more difficult.

However, since most of the researchers use some modification of the therapeutic factors and the research instrument I described in my 1970 research,[9] I will describe that research in detail and then incorporate into my discussion the findings from more recent research on therapeutic factors.[10]

My colleagues and I studied the therapeutic factors in twenty successful long-term group therapy clients.[11] We asked twenty group therapists to select their most successful client. These therapists led groups of middle-class outpatients who had neurotic or characterological problems. The subjects had been in therapy eight to twenty-two months (the mean duration was sixteen months) and had recently terminated or were about to terminate group therapy.[12] All subjects completed a therapeutic factor Q-sort and were interviewed by the investigators.

Twelve categories of therapeutic factors were constructed from the sources outlined throughout this book,[13]* and five items describing each category were written, making a total of sixty items (see table 4.1). Each item was typed on a 3 × 5 card; the client was given the stack of randomly arranged cards and asked to place a specified number of cards into seven piles labeled as follows:

Most helpful to me in the group (2 cards)
Extremely helpful (6 cards)
Very helpful (12 cards)
Helpful (20 cards)
Barely helpful (12 cards)
Less helpful (6 cards)
Least helpful to me in the group (2 cards)[14]

---

*The list of sixty factor items passed through several versions and was circulated among senior group therapists for suggestions, additions, and deletions. Some of the items are nearly identical, but it was necessary methodologically to have the same number of items representing each category. The twelve categories are altruism, group cohesiveness; universality; interpersonal learning, input; interpersonal learning, output; guidance; catharsis; identification; family reenactment; self-understanding; instillation of hope; and existential factors. They are not quite identical to those described in this book; we attempted, unsuccessfully, to divide interpersonal learning into two parts: input and output. One category, self-understanding, was included to permit examination of depression and genetic insight.

The twelve factor Q-sort utilized in this research evolved into the eleven therapeutic factors identified in Chapter 1. *Imparting information* replaces *Guidance*. *The corrective recapitulation of the primary family group* replaces *Family reenactment*. *Development of socializing techniques* replaces *Interpersonal learning—output*. *Interpersonal learning* replaces *Interpersonal learning—input* and *Self-understanding*. Finally, *Imitative behavior* replaces *Identification*.

The therapeutic factor was meant to be an exploratory instrument constructed *a priori* on the basis of clinical intuition (my own and that of experienced clinicians); it was never meant to be posited as a finely calibrated research instrument. But it has been used in so much subsequent research that much discussion has arisen about construct validity and test-retest reliability. By and large, test-retest reliability has been good; factor analytic studies have yielded varied results: some studies showing only fair, others good, item-to-individual scale correlation. A comprehensive factor analytic study provided fourteen item clusters that bore considerable resemblance to my original twelve therapeutic factor categories. Sullivan and Sawilowsky have demonstrated that some differences between studies may be related to inconsistencies in brief, modified forms of the questionnaire. Stone, Lewis, and Beck have constructed a brief, modified form with considerable internal consistency.

TABLE 4.1   Therapeutic Factors: Categories and Rankings of the Sixty Individual Items

		Rank Order (The Lower the Number, the Higher the Item Is Valued by the Client)
1. Altruism	1. Helping others has given me more self-respect.	40 T*
	2. Putting others' needs ahead of mine.	52 T
	3. Forgetting myself and thinking of helping others.	37 T
	4. Giving part of myself to others.	17
	5. Helping others and being important in their lives.	33T
2. Group Cohesiveness	6. Belonging to and being accepted by a group.	16
	7 Continued close contact with other people.	20 T
	8 Revealing embarrassing things about myself and still being accepted by the group.	11 T
	9. Feeling alone no longer.	37 T
	10. Belonging to a group of people who understood and accepted me.	20 T
3. Universality	11. Learning I'm not the only one with my type of problem; "We're all in the same boat."	45 T
	12. Seeing that I was just as well off as others.	25 T
	13. Learning that others have some of the same "bad" thoughts and feelings I do.	40 T
	14. Learning that others had parents and backgrounds as unhappy or mixed up as mine.	31 T
	15. Learning that I'm not very different from other people gave me a "welcome to the human race" feeling.	33 T

* "T" denotes a tie.   *(continues)*

TABLE 4.1   (*continued*)

		Rank Order (The Lower the Number, the Higher the Item Is Valued by the Client)
4. Interpersonal Learning—Input	16. The group's teaching me about the type of impression I make on others.	5 T
	17. Learning how I come across to others.	8
	18. Other members honestly telling me what they think of me.	3
	19. Group members pointing out some of my habits or mannerisms that annoy other people.	18 T
	20. Learning that I sometimes confuse people by not saying what I really think.	13 T
5. Interpersonal Learning—Output	21. Improving my skills in getting along with people.	25 T
	22. Feeling more trustful of groups and of other people.	10
	23. Learning about the way I related to the other group members.	13 T
	24. The group's giving me an opportunity to learn to approach others.	27T
	25. Working out my difficulties with one particular member in the group.	33 T
6. Guidance	26. The doctor's suggesting or advising something for me to do.	27 T
	27. Group members suggesting or advising something for me to do.	55
	28. Group members telling me what to do.	56
	29. Someone in the group giving definite suggestions about a life problem.	48 T
	30. Group members advising me to behave differently with an important person in my life.	52 T

(*continues*)

TABLE 4.1   (*continued*)

		Rank Order (The Lower the Number, the Higher the Item Is Valued by the Client)
7. Catharsis	31. Getting things off my chest.	31 T
	32. Expressing negative and/or positive feelings toward another member.	5 T
	33. Expressing negative and/or positive feelings toward the group leader.	18 T
	34. Learning how to express my feelings.	4
	35. Being able to say what was bothering me instead of holding it in.	2
8. Identification	36. Trying to be like someone in the group who was better adjusted than I.	58
	37. Seeing that others could reveal embarrassing things and take other risks and benefit from it helped me to do the same.	8
	38. Adopting mannerisms or the style of another group member.	59
	39. Admiring and behaving like my therapist.	57
	40. Finding someone in the group I could pattern myself after.	60
9. Family Reenactment	41. Being in the group was, in a sense, like reliving and understanding my life in the family in which I grew up.	51
	42. Being in the group somehow helped me to understand old hangups that I had in the past with my parents, brothers, sisters, or other important people.	30
	43. Being in the group was, in a sense, like being in a family, only this time a more accepting and understanding family.	44

(*continues*)

TABLE 4.1   (*continued*)

			Rank Order (The Lower the Number, the Higher the Item Is Valued by the Client)
9. Family Reenactment (*continued*)		44. Being in the group somehow helped me to understand how I grew up in my family.	45 T
		45. The group was something like my family—some members or the therapists being like my parents and others being like my relatives. Through the group experience I understand my past relationships with my parents and relatives (brothers, sisters, etc.).	48 T
10. Self-Understanding		46. Learning that I have likes or dislikes for a person for reasons which may have little to do with the person and more to do with my hangups or experiences with other people in my past.	15
		47. Learning why I think and feel the way I do (that is, learning some of the causes and sources of my problems).	11 T
		48. Discovering and accepting previously unknown or unacceptable parts of myself.	1
		49. Learning that I react to some people or situations unrealistically (with feelings that somehow belong to earlier periods in my life).	20 T
		50. Learning that how I feel and behave today is related to my childhood and development (there are reasons in my early life why I am as I am).	50

(*continues*)

TABLE 4.1 *(continued)*

		Rank Order (The Lower the Number, the Higher the Item Is Valued by the Client)
11. Instillation of Hope	51. Seeing others getting better was inspiring to me.	42 T
	52. Knowing others had solved problems similar to mine.	37 T
	53. Seeing that others have solved problems similar to mine.	33 T
	54. Seeing that other group members improved encouraged me.	27 T
	55. Knowing that the group had helped others with problems like mine encouraged me.	45 T
12. Existential Factors	56. Recognizing that life is at times unfair and unjust.	54
	57. Recognizing that ultimately there is no escape from some of life's pain and from death.	42 T
	58. Recognizing that no matter how close I get to other people, I must still face life alone.	23 T
	59. Facing the basic issues of my life and death, and thus living my life more honestly and being less caught up in trivialities.	23 T
	60. Learning that I must take ultimate responsibility for the way I live my life no matter how much guidance and support I get from others.	5 T

After the Q-sort, which took thirty to forty-five minutes, each subject was interviewed for an hour by the three investigators. Their reasons for their choice of the most and least helpful items were reviewed, and a series of other areas relevant to therapeutic factors was discussed (for example, other, nonprofessional therapeutic influences in the clients' lives, critical events in therapy, goal changes, timing of improvement, therapeutic factors in their own words).

Results

A sixty-item, seven-pile Q-sort for twenty subjects makes for complex data. Perhaps the clearest way to consider the results is a simple rank-ordering of the sixty items (arrived at by ranking the sum of the twenty pile placements for each item). Turn again to table 4.1. The number after each item represents its rank order. Thus, on average, item 48 (*Discovering and accepting previously unknown or unacceptable parts of myself*) was considered the most important therapeutic factor by the subjects, item 38 (*Adopting mannerisms or the style of another group member*) the least important, and so on.

The ten items the subjects deemed most helpful were, in order of importance:

1. Discovering and accepting previously unknown or unacceptable parts of myself.
2. Being able to say what was bothering me instead of holding it in.
3. Other members honestly telling me what they think of me.
4. Learning how to express my feelings.
5. The group's teaching me about the type of impression I make on others.
6. Expressing negative and/or positive feelings toward another member.
7. Learning that I must take ultimate responsibility for the way I live my life no matter how much guidance and support I get from others.
8. Learning how I come across to others.
9. Seeing that others could reveal embarrassing things and take other risks and benefit from it helped me to do the same.
10. Feeling more trustful of groups and of other people.

Note that seven of the first eight items represent some form of catharsis or of insight. I again use *insight* in the broadest sense; the items, for the most part, reflect the first level of insight (gaining an objective perspective of one's interpersonal behavior) described in chapter 2. This remarkable finding lends considerable weight to the principle, also described in chapter 2, that therapy is a dual process consisting of emotional experience and of reflection on that experience. More, much more, about this later.

The administration and scoring of a sixty-item Q-sort is so laborious that most researchers have since used an abbreviated version—generally, one that asks a subject to rank the twelve therapeutic factor categories rather than sixty individual items. However, four studies that replicate the sixty-item Q-sort study report remarkably similar findings.[15]

If we analyze the twelve general categories,* we find the following rank order of importance:

1. Interpersonal input
2. Catharsis
3. Cohesiveness
4. Self-understanding
5. Interpersonal output
6. Existential factors
7. Universality
8. Instillation of hope
9. Altruism
10. Family reenactment
11. Guidance
12. Identification**

A number of other replicating studies describe the therapeutic factors selected by group therapy outpatients.[16] These studies are in considerable agreement: the most commonly chosen therapeutic factors are catharsis, self-understanding, and interpersonal input, closely followed by cohesiveness and universality. The same trio of most helpful therapeutic factors (interpersonal input, self-understanding, and catharsis) has been reported in studies of personal growth groups.[17] One researcher suggests that the therapeutic factors fall into three main clusters: the re-moralization factor (cluster of hope, universality, and acceptance), the self-revelation factor (self-disclosure and catharsis), and the specific psycho-

---

*The twelve categories are used only for analysis and interpretation. The clients, of course, were unaware of these categories and dealt only with the sixty randomly sorted items. The rank of each category was obtained by summing the mean rank of the five items in it. Some researchers have used brief versions of a therapeutic factor questionnaire that require clients to rank-order categories. The two approaches require different tasks of the subject, and it is difficult to assess the congruence of the two approaches.

**In considering these results, we must keep in mind that the subject's task was a forced sort, which means that the lowest ranked items are not necessarily unimportant but are simply less important than the others.

logical work factor (interpersonal learning and self-understanding).[18] This clustering resembles a factor analysis* of therapeutic factors collected from studies of American Group Psychotherapy Association Institute experiential groups suggesting that the group therapeutic factors fall into three main categories: early factors of belonging and remoralization common to all therapy groups; factors of guidance and instruction; and specific skill development factors. Despite different terminology, both of these clustering approaches suggest that the group therapeutic factors consist of universal mechanisms, mediating mechanisms, and specific change mechanisms.[19]

Which therapeutic factors are least valued? All of the studies of therapy groups and personal growth groups report the same results: family reenactment, guidance, and identification. These results all suggest that the defining core of the therapeutic process in these therapy groups is an affectively charged, self-reflective interpersonal interaction, in a supportive and trusting setting.[20] Comparisons of individual and group therapy therapeutic factors consistently underscore this finding[21] and support the importance of the basic concepts I discussed in chapter 2—the importance of the corrective emotional experience and the concept that the therapeutic here-and-now focus consists of an experiencing and a cognitive component.

In the following sections, I will incorporate these research findings in a broader discussion of the questions posed at the beginning of this chapter on the interrelationships and comparative potency of the therapeutic factors. Keep in mind throughout that these findings pertain to a specific type of therapy group: an interactionally based group with the ambitious goals of symptom relief and behavioral and characterological change. Later in this chapter I will present some evidence that other groups with different goals and shorter duration may capitalize on different clusters of therapeutic factors.

Catharsis

Catharsis has always assumed an important role in the therapeutic process, though the rationale behind its use has undergone a metamorphosis. For centuries, sufferers have been purged to be cleansed of excessive bile, evil spirits, and infectious toxins (the word itself is derived from the Greek "to clean"). Since Breuer and Freud's 1895 treatise on the treatment of hysteria,[22] many therapists have attempted to help clients rid

---

*Factor analysis is a statistical method that identifies the smallest number of hypothetical constructs needed to explain the greatest degree of consistency in a data set. It is a way to compress large quantities of data into a smaller but conceptually and practically consistent data groupings.

themselves of suppressed, choked affect. What Freud and subsequently all dynamic psychotherapists have learned is that *catharsis is not enough*. After all, we have emotional discharges, sometimes very intense ones, all our lives without their leading to change.

The data support this conclusion. Although studies of clients' appraisals of the therapeutic factors reveals the importance of catharsis, the research also suggests important qualifications. The Lieberman, Yalom, and Miles study starkly illustrates the limitations of catharsis per se.[23] The authors asked 210 members of a thirty-hour encounter group to describe the most significant incident that occurred in the course of the group. Experiencing and expressing feelings (both positive and negative) was cited frequently. *Yet this critical incident was not related to positive outcome:* incidents of catharsis were as likely to be selected by members with poor outcomes as by those with good outcomes. Catharsis was not unrelated to outcome; *it was necessary but in itself not sufficient.* Indeed, members who cited only catharsis were somewhat more likely to have had a negative experience in the group. The high learners characteristically showed a profile of catharsis *plus some form of cognitive learning.* The ability to reflect on one's emotional experience is an essential component of the change process.†

In the Q-sort therapeutic factor studies, the two items that are ranked most highly and are most characteristic of the catharsis category in factor analytic studies are items 34 *(Learning how to express my feelings)* and 35 *(Being able to say what was bothering me).* Both of these items convey something other than the sheer act of ventilation or abreaction. They connote a sense of liberation and acquiring skills for the future. The other frequently chosen catharsis item—item 32 *(Expressing negative and/or positive feelings toward another member)*—indicates the role of catharsis in the ongoing interpersonal process. Item 31, which most conveys the purest sense of sheer ventilation *(Getting things off my chest)*, was not highly ranked by group members.[24]

Interviews with the clients to investigate the reasons for their selection of items confirmed this view. Catharsis was viewed as *part of an interpersonal process;* no one ever obtains enduring benefit from ventilating feelings in an empty closet. Furthermore, as I discussed in chapter 3, catharsis is intricately related to cohesiveness. Catharsis is more helpful once supportive group bonds have formed; in other words, catharsis is more valued late rather than early in the course of the group.[25] Conversely, strong expression of emotion enhances the development of cohesiveness: members who express strong feelings toward one another and work honestly with these feelings will develop close mutual bonds. In groups of clients dealing with loss, researchers found that expression of positive affect was associated with positive outcomes. The expression of negative affect, on the other hand, was therapeutic only when it occurred in the context of genuine attempts to understand oneself or other group members.[26]

Emotional expression is directly linked with hope and a sense of personal effectiveness. Emotional disclosure is also linked to the ability to cope: articulation of one's needs permits oneself and the people in one's environment to respond productively to life's challenges. Women with early breast cancer who are emotionally expressive achieve a much better quality of life than those who avoid and suppress their distress.[27] Recently bereaved HIV-positive men who are able to express emotions, grieve, and find meaning in their losses, maintain significantly higher immune function and live longer than those who minimize their distress and avoid the mourning process.[28]

In summary, then, the open expression of affect is vital to the group therapeutic process; in its absence, a group would degenerate into a sterile academic exercise. Yet it is only part of the process and must be complemented by other factors. One last point: the intensity of emotional expression is highly relative and must be appreciated not from the leader's perspective but from that of each member's experiential world. A seemingly muted expression of emotion may, for a highly constricted individual, represent an event of considerable intensity. On many occasions I have heard students view a videotape of a group meeting and describe the session as muted and boring, whereas the members themselves experienced the session as intense and highly charged.

Self-Understanding

The therapeutic factor Q-sort also underscores the important role that the intellectual component plays in the therapeutic process. Of the twelve categories, the two pertaining to the intellectual task in therapy (interpersonal input and self-understanding) are both ranked highly. *Interpersonal input,* discussed at some length in chapter 2, refers to the individual's learning how he or she is perceived by other people. It is the crucial first step in the therapeutic sequence of the therapeutic factor of interpersonal learning.

The category of *self-understanding* is more problematic. It was constructed to permit investigation of the importance of derepression and of the intellectual understanding of the relationship between past and present (genetic insight). Refer back to table 4.1 and examine the five items of the "self-understanding" category. It is clear that the category is an inconsistent one, containing several very different elements. There is poor correlation among items, some being highly valued by group therapy members and some less so. Item 48, *Discovering and accepting previously unknown or unacceptable parts of myself,* is the *single most valued item* of all the sixty. Two items (46 and 47) that refer to understanding causes of problems and to recognizing the existence of interpersonal distortion are also highly valued. The item that most explicitly refers to genetic insight, item 50, is considered of little value by group therapy clients.

This finding has been corroborated by other researchers. One study replicated the therapeutic factor Q-sort study and, on the basis of a factor analysis, subdivided insight into two categories: self-understanding and genetic insight. The sample of seventy-two group therapy members ranked self-understanding fourth of fourteen factors and genetic insight eighth.[29] Another study concluded that genetic interpretations were significantly less effective than here-and-now feedback in producing positive group therapy outcomes. In fact, clients not only showed little benefit from genetic interpretations but in particular considered the leaders' efforts in this regard unproductive. Comembers were more effective: their efforts at linking present to past contained less jargon and were linked more directly to actual experience than were the therapists' more conceptual, less "real" explanations.[30]

When we interviewed the subjects in our study to learn more about the meaning of their choices, we found that the most popular item—48, *Discovering and accepting previously unknown or unacceptable parts of myself*—had a very specific implication to group members. More often than not, they discovered *positive* areas of themselves: the ability to care for another, to relate closely to others, to experience compassion.

There is an important lesson to be learned here. Too often psychotherapy, especially in naive, popularized, or early conceptualizations, is viewed as a detective search, as a digging or a stripping away. Rogers, Horney, Maslow, and our clients as well remind us that therapy is also horizontal and upward exploration; digging or excavation may uncover our riches and treasures as well as shameful, fearful, or primitive aspects of ourselves.[31] Our clients want to be liberated from pathogenic beliefs; they seek personal growth and control over their lives. As they gain fuller access to themselves, they become emboldened and increase their sense of ownership of their personhood. Psychotherapy has grown beyond its emphasis on eradicating the "pathological" and now aims at increasing clients' breadth of positive emotions and cognitions. A group therapy approach that encourages members to create and inhabit a powerful and caring environment is a potent approach to these contemporary goals.†[32]

Thus, one way that self-understanding promotes change is by encouraging individuals to recognize, integrate, and give free expression to previously obscured parts of themselves. When we deny or stifle parts of ourselves, we pay a heavy price: we feel a deep, amorphous sense of restriction; we are constantly on guard; we are often troubled and puzzled by internal but seemingly alien impulses that demand expression. When we are able to reclaim these disavowed parts, we experience a wholeness, and a sense of liberation.

So far, so good. But what of the other components of the intellectual task? For example, how does the highly ranked item *Learning why I think and feel the way I do* (item 47) result in therapeutic change?

First, we must recognize that there is an urgent need for intellectual understanding in the psychotherapeutic enterprise, a need that comes from both client and therapist. Our search for understanding is deeply rooted. Maslow, in a treatise on motivation, suggested that the human being has cognitive needs that are as basic as the needs for safety, love, and self-esteem.[33] Most children are exceedingly curious; in fact, we grow concerned if a child lacks curiosity about the environment. Researchers studying primates also see high levels of curiosity: monkeys in a solid enclosure will do considerable work for the privilege of being able to look through a window to see outside; they will also work hard and persistently to solve puzzles without any reward except the satisfactions inherent in the puzzle solving.

In an analogous fashion our clients automatically search for understanding, and therapists who prize the intellectual pursuit join them. Often, it all seems so natural that we lose sight of the raison d'être of therapy. After all, the object of therapy is change, not self-understanding. Or is it? Are the two synonymous? Does any and every type of self-understanding lead automatically to change? Or is the quest for self-understanding simply an interesting, appealing, reasonable exercise for clients and therapists, serving, like mortar, to keep the two joined together while something else— "relationship"—develops. Perhaps it is relationship that is the real mutative force in therapy. In fact, there is considerable evidence that a supportive psychotherapy relationship in a noninterpretive therapy can produce substantial change in interpersonal behavior.[34] It is far easier to pose these questions than to answer them. I will present some preliminary points here, and in chapter 6, after developing some material on the interpretative task and techniques of the therapist, I will attempt to present a coherent thesis.

If we examine the motives behind our curiosity and our proclivity to explore our environment, we shed some light on the process of change. These motives include *effectance* (our desire for mastery and power), *safety* (our desire to render the unexplained harmless through understanding), and *pure cognizance* (our desire for knowledge and exploration for its own sake).[35] The worried householder who explores a mysterious and frightening noise in his home; the young student who, for the first time, looks through a microscope and experiences the exhilaration of understanding the structure of an insect wing; the medieval alchemist or the New World explorer probing uncharted and proscribed regions—all receive their respective rewards: safety, a sense of personal keenness and satisfaction, and mastery in the guise of knowledge or wealth.

Of these motives, the one least relevant for the change process is pure cognizance. There is little question that knowledge for its own sake has always propelled the human being. The lure of the forbidden is an extraordinarily popular and ubiquitous motif in folk literature, from the story of Adam and Eve to the saga of Peeping Tom. It is no surprise, then, that the desire to know enters the psychotherapeutic arena. Yet there is little evidence that understanding for its own sake results in change.

But the desires for safety and for mastery play an important and obvious role in psychotherapy. They are, of course, as White has ably discussed, closely intertwined.[36] The unexplained—especially the frightening unexplained—cannot be tolerated for long. All cultures, through either a scientific or a religious explanation, attempt to make sense of chaotic and threatening situations in the physical and social environment as well as in the nature of existence itself. One of our chief methods of control is through language. Giving a name to chaotic, unruly forces provides us with a sense of mastery or control. In the psychotherapeutic situation, information decreases anxiety by removing ambiguity. There is considerable research evidence supporting this observation.[37]

The converse is, incidentally, also true: anxiety increases ambiguity by distorting perceptual acuteness. Anxious subjects show disturbed organization of visual perception; they are less capable of perceiving and organizing rapid visual cues and are distinctly slower in completing and recognizing incomplete pictures in a controlled experimental setting.[38] Unless one is able to order the world cognitively, one may experience anxiety, which, if severe, interferes with the perceptual apparatus. Thus, anxiety begets anxiety: the ensuing perplexity and overt or subliminal awareness of perceptual distortion become a potent secondary source of anxiety.[39]

In psychotherapy, clients are enormously reassured by the belief that their chaotic inner world, their suffering, and their tortuous interpersonal relationships are all explicable and thereby governable. Maslow, in fact, views the increase of knowledge as having transformative effects far beyond the realms of safety, anxiety reduction, and mastery. He views psychiatric illness as a disease caused by knowledge deficiency.[40] In this way he would support the moral philosophic contention that if we know the good, we will always act for the good. Presumably it follows that if we know what is ultimately good for us we will act in our own best interests.[41]*

---

*Recent research on the human stress response and the impact of one's exposure to potentially traumatic events demonstrates that making sense of, and finding meaning in, one's life experience reduces the psychological *and* physiological signs of stress.

Therapists, too, are less anxious if, when confronted with great suffering and voluminous, chaotic material, they can believe in a set of principles that will permit an ordered explanation. Frequently, therapists will cling tenaciously to a particular system in the face of considerable contradictory evidence—sometimes, in the case of researcher-clinicians, even evidence that has issued from their own investigations. Though such tenacity of belief may carry many disadvantages, it performs one valuable function: it enables the therapist to preserve equanimity in the face of considerable affect emerging within the transference or countertransference.

There is little in the above that is controversial. Self-knowledge permits us to integrate all parts of ourselves, decreases ambiguity, permits a sense of effectance and mastery, and allows us to act in concert with our own best interests. An explanatory scheme also permits generalization and transfer of learning from the therapy setting to new situations in the outside world.

The great controversies arise when we discuss not the process or the purpose or the effects of explanation but the *content* of explanation. As I hope to make clear in chapter 6, I think these controversies are irrelevant. When we focus on change rather than on self-understanding as our ultimate goal, we can only conclude that an explanation is correct if it leads to change. The final common result of all our intellectual efforts in therapy is change. Each clarifying, explanatory, or interpretive act of the therapist is ultimately designed to exert leverage on the client's will to change.

Imitative Behavior (Identification)

Group therapy participants rate imitative behavior among the least helpful of the twelve therapeutic factors. However, we learned from debriefing interviews that the five items in this category seem to have tapped only a limited sector of this therapeutic mode (see table 4.1). They failed to distinguish between mere mimicry, which apparently has only a restricted value for clients, and the acquisition of general styles and strategies of behavior, which may have considerable value. To clients, conscious mimicry is an especially unpopular concept as a therapeutic mode since it suggests a relinquishing of individuality—a basic fear of many group participants.

On the other hand, clients may acquire from others a general strategy that may be used across a variety of personal situations. Members of groups for medically ill patients often benefit from seeing other members manage a shared problem effectively.[42] This process also works at both overt and more subtle levels. Clients may begin to approach problems by considering, consciously or unconsciously, what some other member or the therapist would think or do in the same situation. If the therapist is tolerant and flexible, then clients may also adopt these traits. If the therapist is self-disclosing and accepts limitations without becoming insecure or defensive, then clients are more apt to learn to accept their personal shortcomings.[43] Not only do group members adopt the traits and style of the therapist, but sometimes they may even assimilate the therapist's complex value system.[44]

Initially, imitative behavior is in part an attempt to gain approval, but it does not end there. The more intact clients retain their reality testing and flexibility and soon realize that changes in their behavior result in greater acceptance by others. This increased acceptance can then act to change one's self-concept and self-esteem in the manner described in chapter 3, and an adaptive spiral is instigated. It is also possible for an individual to identify with aspects of two or more other people, resulting in an amalgam. Although parts of others are imitated, the amalgam represents a creative synthesis, a highly innovative individualistic identity.

What of spectator therapy? Is it possible that clients may learn much from observing the solutions arrived at by others who have similar problems? I have no doubt that such learning occurs in the therapy group. Every experienced group therapist has at least one story of a member who came regularly to the group for months on end, was extremely inactive, and finally terminated therapy much improved.

I clearly remember Rod, who was so shy, isolated, and socially phobic that in his adult life he had never shared a meal with another person. When I introduced him into a rather fast-paced group, I was concerned that he would be in over his head. And in a sense he was. For months he sat and listened in silent amazement as the other members interacted intensively with one another. That was a period of high learning for Rod: simply to be exposed to the possibilities of intimate interaction enriched his life. But then things changed! The group began to demand more reciprocity and placed great pressure on him to participate more personally in the meetings. Rod grew more uncomfortable and ultimately, with my encouragement, decided to leave the group. Since he worked at the same university, I had occasion to cross paths with him several times in the ensuing years, and he never failed to inform me how important and personally useful the group had been. It had shown him what was possible and how individuals could engage one another, and it offered him an internal reference point to which he could turn for reassurance as he gradually reached out to touch others in his life.

Clients learn not only from observing the substantive work of others who are like them but also from watching the process of the work. In that sense, imitative behavior is a transitional therapeutic factor that permits clients subsequently to engage more fully in other aspects of therapy. Proof of this is to be found in the fact that one of the five imitative behavior items (item 37, *Seeing that others could reveal embarrassing things and take other risks and benefit from it helped me to do the same*) was rated as the eighth (of sixty) most important therapeutic factor. A large-scale study in the Netherlands found that clients considered identification to be more important in the early stages of therapy, when novice members looked for more senior members with whom to identify.[45]

Family Reenactment

Family reenactment, or the corrective recapitulation of the primary family experience—a therapeutic factor highly valued by many therapists—is not generally considered helpful by most group members. The clinical populations that place a high value on this factor are very specific—groups for incest survivors[46] and groups for sex offenders.[47] For these members the early failure of the family to protect and care for them looms as a powerful issue.

The fact that this factor is not cited often by most group members, though, should not surprise us, since it operates at a different level of awareness from such explicit factors as catharsis or universality. Family reenactment becomes more a part of the general horizon against which the group is experienced. Few therapists will deny that the primary family of each group member is an omnipresent specter haunting the group therapy room. Clients' experience in their family of origin obviously will, to a great degree, influence the nature of their interpersonal distortions, the role they assume in the group, and their attitudes toward the group leaders.

There is little doubt in my mind that the therapy group reincarnates the primary family. It acts as a time machine, flinging the client back several decades and evoking deeply etched ancient memories and feelings. In fact, this phenomenon is one of the major sources of power of the therapy group. In my last meeting with a group before departing for a year's sabbatical, a client related the following dream: "My father was going away for a long trip. I was with a group of people. My father left us a thirty-foot boat, but rather than giving it to me to steer, he gave it to one of my friends, and I was angry about this." This is not the place to discuss this dream fully. Suffice it to say that the client's father had deserted the family when the client was young and left him to be tyrannized thereafter by an older brother. The client said that this was the first time he had thought of his father in years. The events of the group—my departure, my place being taken by a new therapist, the client's attraction to the co-therapist (a woman), his resentment toward another dominating member in the group—all acted in concert to awaken long-slumbering memories. Clients reenact early family scripts in the group and, in successful group therapy, experiment with new behavior and break free from the rigid family roles into which they had long been locked.

While I believe these are important phenomena in the therapeutic process, it is altogether a different question whether the group should focus explicitly on them. I think not, as this process is part of the internal, generally silent, homework of the group member. Major shifts in our perspective on the past occur because of the vitality of the work in the present—not through a direct summons and inquiry of the spirits of the past. There are, as I will discuss in chapter 6, many overriding reasons for the group to maintain an ahistorical focus. To focus unduly on people who are not present, on parents and siblings, on Oedipal strivings, on sibling rivalries, or patricidal desires is to avoid and deny the reality of the group and the other members as a living experience in the here-and-now.

Existential Factors

The category of existential factors was almost an afterthought. My colleagues and I first constructed the Q-sort instrument with eleven major factors. It appeared neat and precise, but something was missing. Important sentiments expressed by both clients and therapists had not been represented, so we added a factor consisting of these five items:

1. Recognizing that life is at times unfair and unjust
2. Recognizing that ultimately there is no escape from some of life's pain or from death
3. Recognizing that no matter how close I get to other people, I must still face life alone
4. Facing the basic issues of my life and death, and thus living my life more honestly and being less caught up in trivialities
5. Learning that I must take ultimate responsibility for the way I live my life no matter how much guidance and support I get from others

Several issues are represented in this cluster: responsibility, basic isolation, contingency, the capriciousness of existence, the recognition of our mortality and the ensuing consequences for the conduct of our life. What to label this category? I finally settled, with some hesitation, on *existential factors,* meaning that all these factors relate to existence—to our confrontation with the human condition—a confrontation that informs us of the harsh existential facts of life: our mortality, our freedom and responsibility for constructing our own life design, our isolation from being thrown alone into existence, and our search for life meaning despite being unfortunate enough to be thrown into a universe without intrinsic meaning.

It is clear that the existential items strike responsive chords in clients, and many cite some of the five items as having been crucially important to them. In fact, the entire category of existential factors is often ranked highly, ahead of greatly valued modes of change such as universality, altruism, recapitulation of the primary family experience, guidance, identification, and instillation of hope. Item 60, *Learning that I must take ulti-mate responsibility for the way I live my life no matter how much guid-ance and support I get from others,* was ranked fifth overall of the sixty items.

The same findings are reported by other researchers. *Every single pro-ject that includes an existential category reports that subjects rank that category at least in the upper 50 percent.* In some studies, for example, with therapy groups in prison, in day hospitals, in psychiatric hospitals, and in alcohol treatment groups, the existential category is ranked among the top three factors.[48] Existential factors are also central to many of the current group therapy interventions for the seriously medically ill.[49] A group of older women ranked existential factors first,[50] as did a sample of sixty-six patients on an alcohol unit.[51] What unites these divergent clini-cal populations is the participants' awareness of immutable limits in life—limits of time, power, or health. Even in groups led by therapists who do not conceptualize existential factors as relevant, the existential factors are highly valued by the group members.[52]

It is important to listen to our data. Obviously, the existential factors in therapy deserve far more consideration than they generally receive. It is more than happenstance that the category of existential factors was in-cluded almost as afterthought yet proved to be so important to clients. Existential factors play an important but largely unrecognized role in psy-chotherapy. There is no discrete school of existential psychotherapy, no single accepted body of existential theory and techniques. Nonetheless, a considerable proportion of American therapists (over 16 percent in a 1983 survey—as large a group as the psychoanalytic contingent) consider themselves to be existentially or "existentially-humanistically" oriented.[53] A similar proportion of senior group therapists surveyed in 1992 endorsed the existential-humanistic approach as the model that best reflects con-temporary group therapy.[54]

Even therapists who nominally adhere to other orientations are often surprised when they look deeply at their techniques and at their basic view of the human situation and find that they are existentially oriented.[55] Many psychoanalytically oriented therapists, for example, inwardly es-chew or at best ignore much of the classical analytic theory and instead consider the authentic client-therapist encounter as the mutative element of therapy.[56]

Keep in mind that classical psychoanalytic theory is based explicitly on a highly materialistic view of human nature. It is not possible to under-stand Freud fully without considering his allegiance to the Helmholtz school, an ideological school that dominated Western European medical and basic research in the latter part of the nineteenth century.[57] This doc-trine holds that we human beings are precisely the sum of our parts. It is deterministic, antivitalistic, and materialistic (that is, it attempts to explain the higher by the lower).

Freud never swerved from his adherence to this postulate and to its implications about human nature. Many of his more cumbersome formulations (for example, the dual-instinct theory, the theory of libidinal energy conservation and transformation) were the result of his unceasing attempts to fit human behavior to Helmholtzian rules. This approach constitutes a negative definition of the existential approach. If you feel restricted by its definition of yourself, if you feel that there's something missing, that we are more than a sum of parts, that the doctrine omits some of the central features that make us human—such as purpose, responsibility, sentience, will, values, courage, spirit—then to that degree you have an existentialist sensibility.

I must be careful not to slip off the surface of these pages and glide into another book. This is not the place to discuss in any depth the existential frame of reference in therapy. I refer interested readers to my book, *Existential Psychotherapy*[58] and to my other books that portray the existential clinical approach in action, *Love's Executioner*,[59] *When Nietzsche Wept*,[60] *The Gift of Therapy*,[61] *Momma and the Meaning of Life*,[62] and, *The Schopenhauer Cure*.[63] For now, it is sufficient to note that modern existential therapy represents an application of two merged philosophical traditions. The first is substantive: *Lebensphilosophie* (the philosophy of life, or philosophical anthropology); and the second is methodological: phenomenology, a more recent tradition, fathered by Edmund Husserl, which argues that the proper realm of the study of the human being is consciousness itself. From a phenomenological approach, understanding takes place from within; hence, we must bracket the natural world and attend instead to the inner experience that is the author of that world.

The existential therapeutic approach—with its emphasis on awareness of death, freedom, isolation, and life purpose—has been, until recently, far more acceptable to the European therapeutic community than to the American one. The European philosophic tradition, the geographic and ethnic confinement, and the greater familiarity with limits, war, death, and uncertain existence all favored the spread of the existential influence. The American zeitgeist of expansiveness, optimism, limitless horizons, and pragmatism embraced instead the scientific positivism proffered by a mechanistic Freudian metaphysics or a hyperrational, empirical behaviorism (strange bedfellows!).

During the past four decades, there has been a major development in American psychotherapy: the emergence of what has come to be known as the third force in American psychology (after Freudian psychoanalysis and Watsonian behaviorism). This force, often labeled "existential" or "humanistic," has had an enormous influence on modern therapeutic practice.

Note, however, that we have done more than imported the European existential tradition; we have Americanized it. Thus, although the syntax of humanistic psychology is European, the accent is unmistakably New World. The European focus is on the tragic dimensions of existence, on limits, on facing and taking into oneself the anxiety of uncertainty and nonbeing. The American humanistic psychologists, on the other hand, speak less of limits and contingency than of human potentiality, less of acceptance than of awareness, less of anxiety than of peak experiences and oceanic oneness, less of life meaning than of self-realization, less of apartness and basic isolation than of I-Thou and encounter.

Of course, when a basic doctrine has a number of postulates and the accent of each is systematically altered in a specific direction, there is a significant risk of aberration from the original doctrine. To some extent this has occurred, and some humanistic psychologists have lost touch with their existential roots and espouse a monolithic goal of self-actualization with an associated set of quick actualizing techniques. This is a most unfortunate development. It is important to keep in mind that the existential approach in therapy is not a set of technical procedures but basically an attitude, a sensibility toward the facts of life inherent in the human condition.

Existential therapy is a dynamic approach based on concerns that are rooted in existence. Earlier I mentioned that a "dynamic" approach refers to a therapy that assumes that the deep structures of personality encompass forces that are in conflict with one another, and (this point is very important) these forces exist at different levels of awareness: indeed, some exist outside of conscious awareness. But what about the *content* of the internal struggle?

The existential view of the content differs greatly from the other dynamic systems. A classical analytic approach, for example, addresses the struggle between the individual's fundamental drives (primarily sexual and aggressive) and an environment that frustrates satisfaction of those drives. Alternatively, a self psychology approach would attend to the individual's efforts to preserve a stable sense of self as vital and worthwhile in the context of resonating or disappointing self-object relationships.

The existential approach holds that the human being's paramount struggle is with the "givens" of existence, the ultimate concerns of the human condition: death, isolation, freedom, and meaninglessness. Anxiety emerges from basic conflicts in each of these realms: (1) we wish to continue to be and yet are aware of inevitable death; (2) we crave structure and yet must confront the truth that we are the authors of our own life design and our beliefs and our neural apparatus is responsible for the form of reality: underneath us there is *Nichts*, groundlessness, the abyss; (3) we desire contact, protection, to be part of a larger whole, yet experience the unbridgeable gap between self and others; and (4) we are meaning-seeking creatures thrown into a world that has no intrinsic meaning.

The items in the Q-sort that struck meaningful chords in the study subjects reflected some of these painful truths about existence. Group members realized that there were limits to the guidance and support they could receive from others and that the ultimate responsibility for the conduct of their lives was theirs alone. They learned also that though they could be close to others, there was a point beyond which they could not be accompanied: there is a basic aloneness to existence that must be faced. Many clients learned to face their limitations and their mortality with greater candor and courage. Coming to terms with their own deaths in a deeply authentic fashion permits them to cast the troublesome concerns of everyday life in a different perspective. It permits them to trivialize life's trivia.

We often ignore these existential givens, until life events increase our sensibilities. We may at first respond to illness, bereavement, and trauma with denial, but ultimately the impact of these life-altering events may break through to create a therapeutic opportunity that may catalyze constructive changes in oneself, one's relationships, and one's relationship to life in general.†[64]

After ten sessions of integrative group therapy, women with early-stage breast cancer not only experienced more optimism and reduced depression and anxiety but also concluded that their cancer had contributed positively to their lives by causing them to realign their life priorities.[65] In addition they showed a significant reduction in levels of the stress hormone cortisol.[66] Members of such support groups may benefit psychologically, emotionally, and even physically as a result of the group's support for meaningful engagement with life challenges (see chapter 15).[67]

The course of therapy of Sheila, a client who at the end of treatment selected the existential Q-sort items as having been instrumental in her improvement, illustrates many of these points.

 • *A twenty-five-year-old perennial student, Sheila complained of depression, loneliness, purposelessness, and severe gastric distress for which no organic cause could be found. In a pregroup individual session she lamented repeatedly, "I don't know what's going on!"*

 I could not discover what precisely she meant, and since this complaint was embedded in a litany of self-accusations, I soon forgot it. However, she did not understand what happened to her in the group, either: she could not understand why others were so uninterested in her, why she developed a conversion paralysis, why she entered sexually masochistic relationships, or why she so idealized the therapist.

In the group Sheila was boring and absolutely predictable. Before every utterance she scanned the sea of faces in the group searching for clues to what others wanted and expected. She was willing to be almost anything so as to avoid offending others and possibly driving them away from her. (Of course, she did drive others away, not from anger but from boredom.) Sheila was in chronic retreat from life, and the group tried endless approaches to halt the retreat, to find Sheila within the cocoon of compliance she had spun around herself.

No progress occurred until the group stopped encouraging Sheila, stopped attempting to force her to socialize, to study, to write papers, to pay bills, to buy clothes, to groom herself, but instead urged her to consider the blessings of failure. What was there in failure that was so seductive and so rewarding? Quite a bit, it turned out! Failing kept her young, kept her protected, kept her from deciding. Idealizing the therapist served the same purpose. Help was out there. He knew the answers. Her job in therapy was to enfeeble herself to the point where the therapist could not in all good conscience withhold his royal touch.

A critical event occurred when she developed an enlarged axillary lymph node. She had a biopsy performed and later that day came to the group still fearfully awaiting the results (which ultimately proved the enlarged node benign). She had never been so near to her own death before, and we helped Sheila plunge into the terrifying loneliness she experienced. There are two kinds of loneliness: the primordial, existential loneliness that Sheila confronted in that meeting, and a social loneliness, an inability to be with others.

Social loneliness is commonly and easily worked with in a group therapeutic setting. Basic loneliness is more hidden, more obscured by the distractions of everyday life, more rarely faced. Sometimes groups confuse the two and make an effort to resolve or to heal a member's basic loneliness. But, as Sheila learned that day, it cannot be taken away; it cannot be resolved; it can only be known and ultimately embraced as an integral part of existence.

Rather quickly, then, Sheila changed. She reintegrated far-strewn bits of herself. She began to make decisions and to take over the helm of her life. She commented, "I think I know what's going on" (I had long forgotten her initial complaint). More than anything else, she had been trying to avoid the specter of loneliness. I think she tried to elude it by staying young, by avoiding choice and decision, by perpetuating the myth that there would always be someone who would choose for her, would accompany her, would be there for her. Choice and freedom invariably imply loneliness, and, as Fromm pointed out long ago in Escape from Freedom, *freedom holds more terror for us than tyranny does.*[68]

Turn back again to table 4.1. Let us consider item 60, which so many clients rated so highly: *Learning that I must take ultimate responsibility for the way I live my life no matter how much guidance and support I get from others.* In a sense, this is a double-edged factor in group therapy. Group members learn a great deal about how to relate better, how to develop greater intimacy with others, how to give help and to ask for help from others. At the same time, they discover the limits of intimacy; *they learn what they cannot obtain from others.* It is a harsh lesson and leads to both despair and strength. One cannot stare at the sun very long, and Sheila on many occasions looked away and avoided her dread. But she was always able to return to it, and by the end of therapy had made major shifts within herself.

An important concept in existential therapy is that human beings may relate to the ultimate concerns of existence in one of two possible modes. On the one hand, we may suppress or ignore our situation in life and live in what Heidegger termed a state of *forgetfulness of being.*[69] In this everyday mode, we live in the world of things, in everyday diversions; we are absorbed in chatter, tranquilized, lost in the "they"; we are concerned only about the way things are. On the other hand, we may exist in a state of *mindfulness of being*, a state in which we marvel not at the way things are, but *that* they are. In this state, we are aware of being; we live authentically; we embrace our possibilities and limits; we are aware of our responsibility for our lives. (I prefer Sartre's definition of responsibility: "to be responsible is to be the "uncontested author of. . . ".)[70]

Being aware of one's self-creation in the authentic state of mindfulness of being provides one with the power to change and the hope that one's actions will bear fruit.† Thus, the therapist must pay special attention to the factors that transport a person from the *everyday* to the *authentic* mode of existing. One cannot effect such a shift merely by bearing down, by gritting one's teeth. But there are certain jolting experiences (often referred to in the philosophical literature as "boundary experiences") that effectively transport one into the mindfulness-of-being state.[71]

An extreme experience—such as Sheila's encounter with a possibly malignant tumor—is a good example of a boundary experience, an event that brings one sharply back to reality and helps one prioritize one's concerns in their proper perspective. Extreme experience, however, occurs in its natural state only rarely during the course of a therapy group, and the adept leader finds other ways to introduce these factors. The growing emphasis on brief therapy offers an excellent opportunity: the looming end of the group (or, for that matter, individual therapy) may be used by the therapist to urge clients to consider other terminations, including death, and to reconsider how to improve the quality and satisfaction of their remaining time. It is in this domain that the existential and interpersonal intersect as clients begin to ask themselves more fundamental questions:

What choices do I exercise in my relationships and in my behavior? How do I wish to be experienced by others? Am I truly present and engaged in this relationship or am I managing the relationship inauthentically to reduce my anxiety? Do I care about what this person needs from me or am I motivated by my constricted self-interest?

Other group leaders attempt to generate extreme experience by using a form of existential shock therapy. With a variety of techniques, they try to bring clients to the edge of the abyss of existence. I have seen leaders begin personal growth groups, for example, by asking clients to compose their own epitaphs. Other leaders may begin by asking members to draw their lifeline and mark their present position on it: How far from birth? How close to death? But our capacity for denial is enormous, and it is the rare group that perseveres, that does not slip back into less threatening concerns. Natural events in the course of a group—illness, death, termination, and loss—may jolt the group back, but always temporarily.

In 1974, I began to lead groups of individuals who lived continuously in the midst of extreme experience.[72] All the members had a terminal illness, generally metastatic carcinoma, and all were entirely aware of the nature and implications of their illness. I learned a great deal from these groups, especially about the fundamental but concealed issues of life that are so frequently neglected in traditional psychotherapy. (See Chapter 15 for a detailed description of this group and current applications of the supportive-expressive group approach.)

Reflecting back on that initial therapy group for cancer patients, many features stand out. For one thing, the members were deeply supportive to one another, and it was extraordinarily helpful for them to be so. Offering help so as to receive it in reciprocal fashion was only one, and not the most important, benefit of this supportiveness. Being useful to someone else drew them out of morbid self-absorption and provided them with a sense of purpose and meaning. Almost every terminally ill person I have spoken to has expressed deep fear of a helpless immobility—not only of being a burden to others and being unable to care for themselves but of being useless and without value to others. Living, then, becomes reduced to pointless survival, and the individual searches within, ever more deeply, for meaning. The group offered these women the opportunity to find meaning outside themselves: by extending help to another person, by caring for others, they found the sense of purpose that so often eludes sheer introspective reflection.*

These approaches, these avenues to self-transcendence, if well traveled, can increase one's sense of meaning and purpose as well as one's ability to

---

*The timeless and universal nature of these existential concerns is reflected in the words of the sage Hillel, 2000 years ago. Addressing his students, Hillel would say: "If I am not for myself, who will be for me? And if I am only for myself, what am I? And if not now, when?"

bear what cannot be changed. Finding meaning in the face of adversity can be transformative.[73] Long ago, Nietzsche wrote: "He who has a why to live can bear with almost any how."[74]

It was clear to me (and demonstrated by empirical research) that the members of this group who plunged most deeply into themselves, who confronted their fate most openly and resolutely, passed into a richer mode of existence.[75] Their life perspective was radically altered; the trivial, inconsequential diversions of life were seen for what they were. Their neurotic phobias diminished. They appreciated more fully the elemental features of living: the changing seasons, the previous spring, the falling leaves, the loving of others. Rather than resignation, powerlessness, and restriction, some members have experienced a great sense of liberation and autonomy.

Some even spoke of the gift of cancer. What some considered tragic, was not their death per se, but that they learned how to live life fully only after being threatened by serious illness. They wondered if it was possible to teach their loved ones this important lesson earlier in life or if it could be learned only *in extremis*? It may be that through the act of death ending life, the idea of death revitalizes life: death becomes a co-therapist pushing the work of psychotherapy ahead.

What can you as therapist do in the face of the inevitable? I think the answer lies in the verb *to be*. You do by being, by being there with the client. Presence is the hidden agent of help in all forms of therapy. Clients looking back on their therapy rarely remember a single interpretation you made, but they always remember your presence, that you were there with them. It is asking a great deal of the therapist to join this group, yet it would be hypocrisy not to join. The group does not consist of you (the therapist), and they (the dying); it is *we* who are dying, *we* who are banding together in the face of our common condition. In my book *The Gift of Therapy,* I propose that the most accurate or felicitous term for the therapeutic relationship might be "fellow traveler." Two hundred years ago, Schopenhauer suggested we should address one another as "fellow sufferers."[76]

The group well demonstrates the double meaning of the word *apartness:* we are separate, lonely, *apart from* but also a *part of.* One of my members put it elegantly when she described herself as a lonely ship in the dark. Even though no physical mooring could be made, it was nonetheless enormously comforting to see the lights of other ships sailing the same water.

COMPARATIVE VALUE OF THE THERAPEUTIC FACTORS: DIFFERENCES BETWEEN CLIENTS' AND THERAPISTS' VIEWS

Do clients and therapists agree about what helps in group psychotherapy? Research comparing therapists' and clients' assessments is instructive.

First, keep in mind that therapists' published views of the range of therapeutic factors are broadly analogous to the factors I have described.[77] But, of course, leaders from different ideological schools differ in their weighting of the therapeutic factors, even though they resemble one another in their therapeutic relationships.[78]

The research data tells us that therapists and clients differ in their valuation of the group therapeutic factors. A study of 100 acute inpatient group members and their thirty behaviorally oriented therapists showed that the therapists and clients differed significantly in their ranking of therapeutic factors. Therapists placed considerably more weight on client modeling and behavioral experimentation, whereas the group members valued other factors more: self-responsibility, self-understanding, and universality.[79] Another study showed that groups of alcoholics ranked existential factors far higher than did their therapists.[80] It should not be surprising that substance abuse clients value accountability and personal responsibility highly. These factors are cornerstones of twelve-step groups.

Fifteen HIV-positive men treated in time-limited cognitive-behavioral therapy groups for depression cited different therapeutic factors than their therapists. Members selected social support, cohesion, universality, altruism, and existential factors, whereas the therapists (in line with their ideological school) considered cognitive restructuring as the mutative agent.[81]

A large survey of prison therapy groups notes that inmates agree with their group leaders about the importance of interpersonal learning but value existential factors far more highly than their therapists do.[82] As noted earlier, incest victims in group therapy value highly the therapeutic factor of family reenactment.[83]

Therapists are wise to be alert to these divergences. Client-therapist disagreement about the goals and tasks of therapy may impair the therapeutic alliance.† This issue is not restricted to group therapy. Client-therapist discrepancies on therapeutic factors also occur in individual psychotherapy. A large study of psychoanalytically oriented therapy found that clients attributed their successful therapy to relationship factors, whereas their therapists gave precedence to technical skills and techniques.[84] In general, analytic therapists value the coming to consciousness of unconscious factors and the subsequent linkage between childhood experiences and present symptoms far more than do their clients, who deny the importance or even the existence of these elements in therapy; instead they emphasize the personal elements of the relationship and the encounter with a new, accepting type of authority figure.

A turning point in the treatment of one client starkly illustrates the differences. In the midst of treatment, the client had an acute anxiety attack and was seen by the therapist in an emergency session. Both therapist and client regarded the incident as critical, but for very different reasons. To the therapist, the emergency session unlocked the client's previously repressed memories of early incestuous sex play and facilitated a working-through of important Oedipal material. The client, on the other hand, entirely dismissed the *content* of the emergency session and instead valued the relationship implications: the caring and concern expressed by the therapist's willingness to see him in the middle of the night.

A similar discrepancy between the client's and the therapist's view of therapy is to be found in *Every Day Gets a Little Closer,* a book I coauthored with a client.[85] Throughout the treatment she and I wrote independent, impressionistic summaries of each meeting and handed them in, sealed, to my secretary. Every few months we read each other's summaries and discovered that we valued very different aspects of the therapeutic process. All my elegant interpretations? She never even heard them! What she remembered and treasured were the soft, subtle, personal exchanges, which, to her, conveyed my interest and caring for her.

Reviews of process and outcome research reveal that clients' ratings of therapist engagement and empathy are more predictive of therapeutic success than therapists' ratings of these same variables.[86] These findings compel us to pay close attention to the client's view of the most salient therapeutic factors. In research as in clinical work, we do well to heed the adage: *Listen to the client.*

To summarize: Therapists and their clients differ in their views about important therapeutic factors: clients consistently emphasize the importance of the relationship and the personal, human qualities of the therapist, whereas therapists attribute their success to their techniques. When the therapist-client discrepancy is too great, when therapists emphasize therapeutic factors that are incompatible with the needs and capacities of the group members, then the therapeutic enterprise will be derailed: clients will become bewildered and resistant, and therapists will become discouraged and exasperated. The therapist's capacity to respond to client vulnerability with warmth and tenderness is pivotal and may lie at the heart of the transformative power of therapy.†

THERAPEUTIC FACTORS: MODIFYING FORCES

It is not possible to construct an absolute hierarchy of therapeutic factors. There are many modifying forces: therapeutic factors are influenced by the type of group therapy, the stage of therapy, extragroup forces, and individual differences.

Therapeutic Factors in Different Group Therapies

Different types of group therapy favor the operation of different clusters of curative factors. Consider, for example, the therapy group on an acute inpatient ward. Members of inpatient therapy groups do not select the same constellation of three factors (interpersonal learning, catharsis, and self-understanding) as most members of outpatient groups.[87] Rather, they select a wide range of therapeutic factors that reflect, I believe, both the heterogeneous composition of inpatient therapy groups and the cafeteria theory of improvement in group therapy. Clients who differ greatly from one another in ego strength, motivation, goals, and type and severity of psychopathology meet in the same inpatient group and, accordingly, select and value different aspects of the group procedure.

Many more inpatients than outpatients select the therapeutic factors of instillation of hope and existential factors (especially the assumption of responsibility). Instillation of hope looms large in inpatient groups because so many individuals enter the hospital in a state of utter demoralization. Until the individual acquires hope and the motivation to engage in treatment, no progress will be made. Often the most effective antidote to demoralization is the presence of others who have recently been in similar straits and discovered a way out of despair. Existential factors (defined on the research instruments generally as "assumption of ultimate responsibility for my own life") are of particular importance to inpatients, because often hospitalization confronts them with the limits of other people; external resources have been exhausted; family, friends, therapists have failed; they have hit bottom and realize that, in the final analysis, they can rely only on themselves. (On one inpatient Q-sort study, the assumption of responsibility, item 60, was ranked first of the sixty items.)[88]

A vast range of homogeneously composed groups meet today. Let us review the therapeutic factors chosen by the members of several of these groups.

- Alcoholics Anonymous and Recovery, Inc. members emphasize the instillation of hope, imparting information, universality, altruism, and some aspects of group cohesiveness.
- Members of discharge planning groups in psychiatric hospitals emphasize imparting of information and development of socializing techniques.
- Participants of occupational therapy groups most valued the factors of cohesiveness, instillation of hope, and interpersonal learning.[89]
- Members of psychodrama groups in Israel, despite differences in culture and treatment format, selected factors consistent with those

selected by group therapy outpatients: interpersonal learning, catharsis, group cohesiveness, and self-understanding.[90]

- Members of self-help groups (women's consciousness raising, bereaved parents, widows, heart surgery patients, and mothers) commonly chose factors of universality, followed by guidance, altruism, and cohesiveness.[91]
- Members of an eighteen-month-long group of spouses caring for a partner with a brain tumor chose universality, altruism, instillation of hope, and the provision of information.[92]
- Psychotic clients with intrusive, controlling auditory hallucinations successfully treated in cognitive-behavioral therapy groups valued universality, hope, and catharsis. For them, finally being able to talk about their voices and feel understood by peers was of enormous value.[93]
- Spousal abusers in a psychoeducational group selected the imparting of information as a chief therapeutic factor.[94]
- Adolescents in learning disability groups cited the effectiveness of "mutual recognition"—of seeing oneself in others and feeling valued and less isolated.[95]
- Geriatric group participants who confront limits, mortality, and the passage of time select existential factors as critically important.[96]

When therapists form a new therapy group in some specialized setting or for some specialized clinical population, the first step, as I will stress in chapter 15, is to determine the appropriate goals and, after that, the therapeutic factors most likely to be helpful for that particular group. Everything else, all matters of therapeutic technique, follow from that framework. Thus, it is vitally important to keep in mind the persuasive research evidence that different types of group therapy make use of different therapeutic factors.

For example, consider a time-limited psychoeducational group for panic attacks whose members may receive considerable benefit from group leader instruction on cognitive strategies for preventing and minimizing the disruptiveness of the attacks (guidance). The experience of being in a group of people who suffer from the same problem (universality) is also likely to be very comforting. Although difficulties in relationships may indeed contribute to their symptoms, an undue focus on the therapeutic factor of interpersonal learning would not be warranted given the time frame of the group.

Understanding the client's experience of the therapeutic factors can lead to enlightened and productive group innovations. For example, an effective multimodal group approach for bulimia nervosa has been reported that integrates and sequences three independently effective treatments. This twelve-week group starts with a psychoeducation module about bulimia and nutrition; next is a cognitive-behavioral module that examines distorted cognitions about eating and body image; and the group concludes with an interpersonally oriented group segment that examines here-and-now relationship concerns and their impact on eating behaviors.[97]

Therapeutic Factors and Stages of Therapy

Intensive interactional group therapy exerts its chief therapeutic power through interpersonal learning (encompassing catharsis, self-understanding, and interpersonal input and output) and group cohesiveness, but the other therapeutic factors play an indispensable role in the intensive therapy process. To appreciate the interdependence of the therapeutic factors, we must consider the entire group process from start to finish.

Many clients expressed difficulty in rank-ordering therapeutic factors because they found different factors helpful at different stages of therapy. Factors of considerable importance early in therapy may be far less salient late in the course of treatment. Consider the early stages of development: the group's chief concerns are with survival, establishing boundaries, and maintaining membership. In this phase, factors such as the instillation of hope, guidance, and universality are especially important.†[98] A universality phase early in the group is inevitable as well, as members search out similarities and compare symptoms and problem constellations.

The first dozen meetings of a group present a high-risk period for potential dropouts, and it is often necessary to awaken hope in the members in order to keep them attending through this critical phase. Factors such as altruism and group cohesiveness operate throughout therapy, but their nature changes with the stage of the group. Early in therapy, altruism takes the form of offering suggestions or helping one another talk by asking appropriate questions and giving attention. Later it may take the form of a more profound caring and presence.

Group cohesiveness operates as a therapeutic factor at first by means of group support, acceptance, and the facilitation of attendance and later by means of the interrelation of group esteem and self-esteem and through its role in interpersonal learning. It is only after the development of group cohesiveness that members may engage deeply and constructively in the self-disclosure, confrontation, and conflict essential to the process of interpersonal learning. Therapists must appreciate this necessary developmental sequence to help prevent early group dropouts. In a study of therapeutic factors in long-term inpatient treatment in Germany, clinical improvement was related to the experience of early cohesion and belonging.

Cohesion set the stage for greater personal self-disclosure, which generated the interpersonal feedback that produced behavioral and psychological change.[99] An outpatient study demonstrated that the longer group members participated in the group, the more they valued cohesiveness, self-understanding, and interpersonal output.[100] Students in eleven-session counseling groups valued universality more in the first half of the group and interpersonal learning in the second half.[101]

In a study of twenty-six-session growth groups, universality and hope declined in importance through the course of the group, whereas catharsis increased.[102] In a study of spouse abusers, universality was the prominent factor in early stages, while the importance of group cohesion grew over time.[103] This emphasis on universality may be characteristic in the treatment of clients who feel shame or stigma. The cohesion that promotes change, however, is best built on a respect and acceptance of personal differences that takes time to mature. In another study, psychiatric inpatients valued universality, hope, and acceptance most, but later, when they participated in outpatient group psychotherapy, they valued self-understanding more.[104]

In summary, the therapeutic factors clients deem most important vary with the stage of group development. The therapist's attention to this finding is as important as the therapist's congruence with the client on therapeutic factors reviewed in the preceding section. Clients' needs and goals change during the course of therapy. In chapter 2, I described a common sequence in which group members first seek symptomatic relief and then, during the first months in therapy, formulate new goals, often interpersonal ones of relating more deeply to others, learning to love, and being honest with others. As members' needs and goals shift during therapy, so, too, must the necessary therapeutic processes. Modern enlightened psychotherapy is often termed dynamic psychotherapy because it appreciates the dynamics, the motivational aspects of behavior, many of which are not in awareness. Dynamic therapy may be thought of also as changing, evolving psychotherapy: clients change, the group goes through a developmental sequence, and the therapeutic factors shift in primacy and influence during the course of therapy.

Therapeutic Factors Outside the Group

Although I suggest that major behavioral and attitudinal shifts require a degree of interpersonal learning, occasionally group members make major changes without making what would appear to be the appropriate investment in the therapeutic process. This brings up an important principle in therapy: *The therapist or the group does not have to do the entire job.* Personality reconstruction as a therapeutic goal is as unrealistic as it is presumptuous. Our clients have many adaptive coping strengths that may have served them well in the past, and a boost from some event in therapy may be sufficient to help a client begin coping in an adaptive manner. Earlier in this text I used the term "adaptive spiral" to refer to the process in which one change in a client begets changes in his or her interpersonal environment that beget further personal change. The adaptive spiral is the reverse of the vicious circle, in which so many clients find themselves ensnared—a sequence of events in which dysphoria has interpersonal manifestations that weaken or disrupt interpersonal bonds and consequently create further dysphoria.

These points are documented when we ask clients about other therapeutic influences or events in their lives that occurred concurrently with their therapy course. In one sample of twenty clients, eighteen described a variety of extragroup therapeutic factors. Most commonly cited was a new or an improved interpersonal relationship with one or more of a variety of figures (member of the opposite sex, parent, spouse, teacher, foster family, or new set of friends).[105] Two clients claimed to have benefited by going through with a divorce that had long been pending. Many others cited success at work or school, which raised their self-esteem as they established a reservoir of real accomplishments. Others became involved in some new social venture (a YMCA group or community action group).

Perhaps these are fortuitous, independent factors that deserve credit, along with group therapy, for the successful outcome. In one sense that is true: the external event augments therapy. Yet it is also true that the potential external event had often always been there: the therapy group mobilized the members to take advantage of resources that *had long been available to them in their environment.*

Consider Bob, a lonely, shy, and insecure man, who attended a time-limited twenty-five-session group. Though he spent considerable time discussing his fear about approaching women, and though the group devoted much effort to helping him, there seemed little change in his outside behavior. But at the final meeting of the group, Bob arrived with a big smile and a going-away present for the group: a copy of a local newspaper in which he had placed an ad in the personals!

The newspapers, spouses, online sites, relatives, potential friends, social organizations, and academic or job opportunities are always out there, available, waiting for the client to seize them. The group may have given the client only the necessary slight boost to allow him or her to exploit these previously untapped resources. Frequently the group members and the therapist are unaware of the importance of these factors and view the client's improvement with skepticism or puzzlement. And frequently the group may end with no evidence of their ultimate impact on the member. Later, when I discuss combined treatment, I will emphasize the point that therapists who continue to see clients in individual therapy long after the termination of the group often learn that members make use of the internalized group months, even years, later.

A study of encounter group members who had very successful outcomes yielded corroborative results.[106] More often than not, successful members did not credit the group for their change. Instead, they described the beneficial effects of new relationships they had made, new social circles they had created, new recreational clubs they had joined, greater work satisfaction they had found. Closer inquiry indicated, of course, that the relationships, social circles, recreational clubs, and work satisfaction had not suddenly and miraculously materialized. They had long been available to the individual who was mobilized by the group experience to take advantage of these resources and exploit them for satisfaction and personal growth.

I have considered, at several places in this text, how the skills group members acquire prepare them for new social situations in the future. Not only are extrinsic skills acquired but intrinsic capacities are released. Psychotherapy removes neurotic obstructions that have stunted the development of the client's own resources. The view of therapy as *obstruction removal* lightens the burden of therapists and enables them to retain respect for the rich, never fully knowable, capacities of their clients.

Individual Differences and Therapeutic Factors

The studies cited in this chapter report average values of therapeutic factors as ranked by groups of clients. However, there is considerable individual variation in the rankings, and some researchers have attempted to determine the individual characteristics that influence the selection of therapeutic factors. Although demographic variables such as sex and education make little difference, there is evidence that level of functioning is significantly related to the ranking of therapeutic factors, for example, higher-functioning individuals value interpersonal learning (the cluster of interpersonal input and output, catharsis, and self-understanding) more than do the lower-functioning members in the same group.[107] It has also been shown that lower-functioning inpatient group members value the instillation of hope, whereas higher-functioning members in the same groups value universality, vicarious learning, and interpersonal learning.[108]

A large number of other studies demonstrate differences between individuals (high encounter group learners vs. low learners, dominant vs. nondominant clients, overly responsible vs. nonresponsible clients, high self acceptors vs. low self acceptors, highly affiliative vs. low affiliative students).[109]

Not everyone needs the same things or responds in the same way to group therapy. There are many therapeutic pathways through the group therapy experience. Consider, for example, catharsis. Some restricted individuals benefit by experiencing and expressing strong affect, whereas others who have problems of impulse control and great emotional liability may not benefit from catharsis but instead from reining in emotional expression and acquiring intellectual structure. Narcissistic individuals need to learn to share and to give, whereas passive, self-effacing individuals need to learn to express their needs and to become *more* selfish. Some clients may need to develop satisfactory, even rudimentary, social skills; others may need to work with more subtle issues—for example, a male client who needs to stop sexualizing all women and devaluing or competing with all men.

In summary, it is clear that the comparative potency of the therapeutic factors is a complex issue. Different factors are valued by different types of therapy groups, by the same group at different developmental stages, and by different clients within the same group, depending on individual needs and strengths. Overall, however, the preponderance of research evidence indicates that the power of the interactional outpatient group emanates from its interpersonal properties. Interpersonal interaction and exploration (encompassing catharsis and self-understanding) and group cohesiveness are the sine qua non of effective group therapy, and effective group therapists must direct their efforts toward maximal development of these therapeutic resources. The next chapters will consider the role and the techniques of the group therapist from the viewpoint of these therapeutic factors.

Chapter 5

THE THERAPIST:
BASIC TASKS

Now that I have considered how people change in group therapy, it is time to turn to the therapist's role in the therapeutic process. In this chapter, I consider the basic tasks of the therapist and the techniques by which they may be accomplished.

The four previous chapters contend that therapy is a complex process consisting of elemental factors that interlace in an intricate fashion. The group therapist's job is to create the machinery of therapy, to set it in motion, and to keep it operating with maximum effectiveness. Sometimes I think of the therapy group as an enormous dynamo: often the therapist is deep in the interior—working, experiencing, interacting (and being personally influenced by the energy field); at other times, the therapist dons mechanic's clothes and tinkers with the exterior, lubricating, tightening nuts and bolts, replacing parts.

Before turning to specific tasks and techniques, I wish to emphasize something to which I will return again and again in the following pages. Underlying all considerations of technique must be a consistent, positive relationship between therapist and client. The basic posture of the therapist to a client must be one of concern, acceptance, genuineness, empathy. *Nothing, no technical consideration, takes precedence over this attitude.* Of course, there will be times when the therapist challenges the client, shows frustration, even suggests that if the client is not going to work, he or she should consider leaving the group. But these efforts (which in the right circumstances may have therapeutic clout) are never effective unless they are experienced against a horizon of an accepting, concerned therapist-client relationship.

I will discuss the techniques of the therapist in respect to three fundamental tasks:

1. Creation and maintenance of the group
2. Building a group culture
3. Activation and illumination of the here-and-now

I discuss the first of these only briefly here and will pick it up in greater detail after I present the essential background material of chapters 8, 9, and 10. In this chapter, I focus primarily on the second task, *building a group culture,* and, in the next chapter turn to the third task, the *activation and illumination* of the *here-and-now.*

CREATION AND MAINTENANCE OF THE GROUP

The group leader is solely responsible for creating and convening the group. Your offer of professional help serves as the group's initial raison d'être, and you set the time and place for meetings. A considerable part of the maintenance task is performed before the first meeting, and, as I will elaborate in later chapters, the leader's expertise in the selection and the preparation of members will greatly influence the group's fate.

Once the group begins, the therapist attends to gatekeeping, especially the prevention of member attrition. Occasionally an individual will have an unsuccessful group experience resulting in premature termination of therapy, which may play some useful function in his or her overall therapy career. For example, failure in or rejection by a group may so unsettle the client as to prime him or her ideally for another therapist. Generally, however, a client who drops out early in the course of the group should be considered a therapeutic failure. Not only does the client fail to receive benefit, but the progress of the remainder of the group is adversely affected. Stability of membership is a sine qua non of successful therapy. If dropouts do occur, the therapist must, except in the case of a closed group (see chapter 10), add new members to maintain the group at its ideal size.

Initially, the clients are strangers to one another and know only the therapist, who is the group's primary unifying force. The members relate to one another at first through their common relationship with the therapist, and these therapist-client alliances set the stage for the eventual development of group cohesion.

The therapist must recognize and deter any forces that threaten group cohesiveness. Continued tardiness, absences, subgrouping, disruptive extragroup socialization, and scapegoating all threaten the functional integrity of the group and require the intervention of the therapist. Each of these issues will be discussed fully in later chapters. For now, it is necessary only to emphasize the therapist's responsibility to supra-individual needs. Your first task is to help create a physical entity, a cohesive group. There will be times when you must delay dealing with pressing needs of an individual client, and even times when you will have to remove a member from the group for the good of the other members.

A clinical vignette illustrates some of these points:

• *Once I introduced two new members, both women, into an outpatient group. This particular group, with a stable core of four male members, had difficulty keeping women members and two women had dropped out in the previous month. This meeting began inauspiciously for one of the women, whose perfume triggered a sneezing fit in one of the men, who moved his chair away from her and then, while vigorously opening the windows, informed her of his perfume allergy and of the group's "no perfume" rule.*

At this point another member, Mitch, arrived a couple of minutes late and, without even a glance at the two new members, announced, "I need some time today from the group. I was really shook up by the meeting last week. I went home from the group very disturbed by your comments about my being a time hog. I didn't like those insinuations from any of you, or from you either [addressing me]. Later that evening I had an enormous fight with my wife, who took exception to my reading a medical journal [Mitch was a physician] at the dinner table, and we haven't been speaking since."

Now this particular opening is a good beginning for most group meetings. It had many things going for it. The client stated that he wanted some time. (The more members who come to the group asking for time and eager to work, the more energized a meeting will be.) Also, he wanted to work on issues that had been raised in the previous week's meeting. (As a general rule the more group members work on themes continually from meeting to meeting, the more powerful the group becomes.) Furthermore, he began the meeting by attacking the therapist—and that was a good thing. This group had been treating me much too gently. Mitch's attack, though uncomfortable, was, I felt certain, going to produce important group work.

Thus I had many different options in the meeting, but there was one task to which I had to award highest priority: maintaining the functional integrity of the group. I had introduced two female members into a group that had had some difficulty retaining women. And how had the members of the group responded? Not well! They had virtually disenfranchised the new members. After the sneezing incident, Mitch had not even acknowledged their presence and had launched into an opening gambit—that, though personally important, systematically excluded the new women by its reference to the previous meeting.

It was important, then, for me to find a way to address this task and, if possible, also to address the issues Mitch had raised. In chapter 2, I offered the basic principle that therapy should strive to turn all issues into here-and-now issues. It would have been folly to deal explicitly with Mitch's fight with his wife. The data that Mitch would have given about his wife would have been biased and he might well have "yes, but" the group to death.

Fortunately, however, there was a way to tackle both issues at once. Mitch's treatment of the two women in the group bore many similarities to his treatment of his wife at the dinner table. He had been as insensitive to their presence and their particular needs as to his wife's. In fact, it was precisely about his insensitivity that the group had confronted him the previous meeting.

Therefore, about a half hour into the meeting, I pried Mitch's attention away from his wife and last week's session by saying, "Mitch, I wonder what hunches you have about how our two new members are feeling in the group today?"

This inquiry led Mitch into the general issue of empathy and his inability or unwillingness in many situations to enter the experiential world of the other. Fortunately, this tactic not only turned the other group members' attention to the way they all had ignored the two new women, but also helped Mitch work effectively on his core problem: his failure to recognize and appreciate the needs and wishes of others. Even if it were not possible to address some of Mitch's central issues, I still would have opted to attend to the integration of the new members. Physical survival of the group must take precedence over other tasks.

CULTURE BUILDING

Once the group is a physical reality, the therapist's energy must be directed toward shaping it into a therapeutic social system. An unwritten code of behavioral rules or *norms* must be established that will guide the interaction of the group. And what are the desirable norms for a therapeutic group? They follow logically from the discussion of the therapeutic factors.

Consider for a moment the therapeutic factors outlined in the first four chapters: acceptance and support, universality, advice, interpersonal learning, altruism, and hope—who provides these? Obviously, the other members of the group! Thus, to a large extent, *it is the group that is the agent of change.*

Herein lies a crucial difference in the basic roles of the individual therapist and the group therapist. In the individual format, the therapist functions as the solely designated direct agent of change. The group therapist functions far more indirectly. In other words, *if it is the group members who, in their interaction, set into motion the many therapeutic factors, then it is the group therapist's task to create a group culture maximally conducive to effective group interaction.*

The game of chess provides a useful analogy. Expert players do not, at the beginning of the game, strive for checkmate or outright capture of a piece, but instead aim at obtaining strategic squares on the board, thereby increasing the power of each of their pieces. In so doing, players are *indirectly* moving toward success since, as the game proceeds, this superior strategic position will favor an effective attack and ultimate material gain. So, too, the group therapist methodically builds a culture that will ultimately exert great therapeutic strength.

A jazz pianist, a member of one of my groups, once commented on the role of the leader by reflecting that very early in his musical career, he deeply admired the great instrumental virtuosos. It was only much later that he grew to understand that the truly great jazz musicians were those who knew how to augment the sound of others, how to be quiet, how to enhance the functioning of the entire ensemble.

It is obvious that the therapy group has norms that radically depart from the rules, or etiquette, of typical social intercourse. Unlike almost any other kind of group, the members must feel free to comment on the immediate feelings they experience toward the group, the other members, and the therapist. Honesty and spontaneity of expression must be encouraged in the group. If the group is to develop into a true social microcosm, members must interact freely. In schematic form, the pathways of interaction should appear like the first rather than the second diagram, in which communications are primarily to or through the therapist.

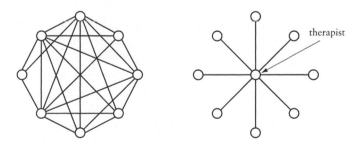

Other desirable norms include active involvement in the group, nonjudgmental acceptance of others, extensive self-disclosure, desire for self-understanding, and an eagerness to change current modes of behavior. Norms may be a *prescription for* as well as a *proscription against* certain types of behavior. Norms may be implicit as well as explicit. In fact, the members of a group cannot generally consciously elaborate the norms of the group. Thus, to learn the norms of a group, the researcher is ill advised to ask the members for a list of these unwritten rules. A far better approach is to present the members with a list of behaviors and ask them to indicate which are appropriate and which inappropriate in the group.

Norms invariably evolve in every type of group—social, professional, and therapeutic.[1] By no means is it inevitable that a therapeutic group will evolve norms that facilitate the therapeutic process. Systematic observation of therapy groups reveals that many are encumbered with crippling norms. A group may, for example, so value hostile catharsis that positive sentiments are eschewed; a group may develop a "take turns" format in which the members sequentially describe their problems to the group; or a group may have norms that do not permit members to question or challenge the therapist. Shortly I will discuss some specific norms that hamper or facilitate therapy, but first I will consider how norms come into being.

The Construction of Norms

Norms of a group are constructed both from expectations of the members for their group and from the explicit and implicit directions of the leader and more influential members. If the members' expectations are not firm, then the leader has even more opportunity to design a group culture that, in his or her view, will be optimally therapeutic. The group leader's statements to the group play a powerful, though usually implicit, role in determining the norms established in the group.† In one study, researchers observed that when the leader made a comment following closely after a particular member's actions, that member became a center of attention in the group and often assumed a major role in future meetings. Furthermore, the relative infrequency of the leader's comments augmented the strength of his or her interventions.[2] Researchers studying intensive experiential training groups for group therapists also concluded that leaders who modeled warmth and technical expertise more often had positive outcomes: members of their groups achieved greater self-confidence and greater awareness of both group dynamics and the role of the leader.[3] In general, leaders who set norms of increased engagement and decreased conflict have better clinical outcomes.[4]

By discussing the leader as norm-shaper, I am not proposing a new or contrived role for the therapist. Wittingly or unwittingly, the leader *always* shapes the norms of the group and must be aware of this function. Just as one cannot not communicate, the leader *cannot not influence norms;* virtually all of his or her early group behavior is influential. Moreover, what one does *not* do is often as important as what one does do.

Once I observed a group led by a British group analyst in which a member who had been absent the six previous meetings entered the meeting a few minutes late. The therapist in no way acknowledged the arrival of the member; after the session, he explained to the student observers that he chose not to influence the group since he preferred that they make their own rules about welcoming tardy or prodigal members. It appeared clear to me, however, that the therapist's non-welcome was an influential act and very much of a norm-setting message. His group had evolved, no doubt as a result of many similar previous actions, into a uncaring, insecure one, whose members sought methods of currying the leader's favor.

Norms are created relatively early in the life of a group and, once established, are difficult to change. Consider, for example, the small group in an industrial setting that forms norms regulating individual member output, or a delinquent gang that establishes codes of behavior, or a psychiatric ward that forms norms of expected staff and patient role behavior. To change entrenched standards is notoriously difficult and requires considerable time and often large group membership turnover.

To summarize: every group evolves a set of unwritten rules or norms that determine the procedure of the group. The ideal therapy group has norms that permit the therapeutic factors to operate with maximum effectiveness. Norms are shaped both by the expectations of the group members and by the behavior of the therapist. The therapist is enormously influential in norm setting—in fact, it is a function that the leader cannot avoid. Norms constructed early in the group have considerable perseverance. The therapist is thus well advised to go about this important function in an informed, deliberate manner.

HOW DOES THE LEADER SHAPE NORMS?

There are two basic roles the therapist may assume in a group: technical expert and model-setting participant. In each of these roles, the therapist helps to shape the norms of the group.

The Technical Expert

When assuming the role of technical expert, therapists deliberately slip into the traditional garb of expert and employ a variety of techniques to move the group in a direction they consider desirable. They explicitly attempt to shape norms during their early preparation of clients for group therapy. In this procedure, described fully in chapter 10, therapists carefully instruct clients about the rules of the group, and they reinforce the instruction in two ways: first, by backing it with the weight of authority and experience and, second, by presenting the rationale behind the suggested mode of procedure in order to enlist the clients' support.

At the beginning of a group, therapists have at their disposal a wide choice of techniques to shape the group culture. These range from explicit instructions and suggestions to subtle reinforcing techniques. For example, as I described earlier, the leader must attempt to create an interactional network in which the members freely interact rather than direct all their comments to or through the therapist. To this end, therapists may implicitly instruct members in their pregroup interviews or in the first group sessions; they may, repeatedly during the meetings, ask for all members' reactions to another member or toward a group issue; they may ask why conversation is invariably directed toward the therapist; they may refuse to answer questions when addressed; they may ask the group to engage in exercises that teach clients to interact—for example, asking each member of the group in turn to give his or her first impressions of every other member; or therapists may, in a much less obtrusive manner, shape behavior by rewarding members who address one another—therapists may nod or smile at them, address them warmly, or shift their posture into a more receptive position. Exactly the same approaches may be applied to the myriad of other norms the therapist wishes to inculcate: self-disclosure, open expression of emotions, promptness, self-exploration, and so on.

Therapists vary considerably in style. Although many prefer to shape norms explicitly, all therapists, to a degree often greater than they suppose, perform their tasks through the subtle technique of social reinforcement. Human behavior is continuously influenced by a series of environmental events (reinforcers), which may have a positive or negative valence and which exert their influence on a conscious or a subliminal level.

Advertising and political propaganda techniques are but two examples of a systematic harnessing of reinforcing agents. Psychotherapy, no less, relies on the use of subtle, often nondeliberate social reinforcers. Although few self-respecting therapists like to consider themselves social reinforcing agents, nevertheless therapists continuously exert influence in this manner, unconsciously or deliberately. They may positively reinforce behavior by numerous verbal and nonverbal acts, including nodding, smiling, leaning forward, or offering an interested "mmm" or a direct inquiry for more information. On the other hand, therapists attempt to extinguish behavior not deemed salubrious by not commenting, not nodding, ignoring the behavior, turning their attention to another client, looking skeptical, raising their eyebrows, and so on. In fact research suggests that therapists who reinforce members' pro-group behavior indirectly are often more effective than those who prompt such behavior explicitly.[5] Any obvious verbal directive from therapists then becomes especially effective because of the paucity of such interventions.

Every form of psychotherapy is a learning process, relying in part on operant conditioning. Therapy, even psychoanalysis, without some form of therapist reinforcement or manipulation is a mirage that disappears on close scrutiny.[6]

Considerable research demonstrates the efficacy of operant techniques in the shaping of group behavior.[7] Using these techniques deliberately, one can reduce silences[8] or increase personal and group comments, expressions of hostility to the leader, or intermember acceptance.[9] Though there is evidence that they owe much of their effectiveness to these learning principles, psychotherapists often eschew this evidence because of their unfounded fear that such a mechanistic view will undermine the essential human component of the therapy experience. The facts are compelling, however, and an understanding of their own behavior does not strip therapists of their spontaneity. After all, the objective of using operant techniques is to foster authentic and meaningful engagement. Therapists who recognize that they exert great influence through social reinforcement and who have formulated a central organizing principle of therapy will be more effective and consistent in making therapeutic interventions.

The Model-Setting Participant

Leaders shape group norms not only through explicit or implicit social engineering but also through the example they set in their own group behavior.[10] The therapy group culture represents a radical departure from the social rules to which clients are accustomed. Clients are asked to discard familiar social conventions, to try out new behavior, and to take many risks. How can therapists best demonstrate to their clients that new behavior will not have the anticipated adverse consequences?

One method, which has considerable research backing, is modeling: Clients are encouraged to alter their behavior by observing their therapists engaging freely and without adverse effects in the desired behavior. Bandura has demonstrated in many well-controlled studies that individuals may be influenced to engage in more adaptive behavior (for example, the overcoming of specific phobias)[11] or less adaptive behavior (for example, unrestrained aggressivity)[12] through observing and assuming other's behavior.

The leader may, by offering a model of nonjudgmental acceptance and appreciation of others' strengths as well as their problem areas, help shape a group that is health oriented. If, on the other hand, leaders conceptualize their role as that of a detective of psychopathology, the group members will follow suit. For example, one group member had actively worked on the problems of other members for months but had steadfastly declined to disclose her own problems. Finally in one meeting she confessed that one year earlier she had had a two-month stay in a state psychiatric hospital. The therapist responded reflexively, "Why haven't you told us this before?"

This comment, perceived as punitive by the client, served only to reinforce her fear and discourage further self-disclosure. Obviously, there are questions and comments that will close people down and others that will help them open up. The therapist had "opening-up" options: for example, "I think it's great that you now trust the group sufficiently to share these facts about yourself," or, "How difficult it must have been for you in the group previously, wanting to share this disclosure and yet being afraid to do so."

The leader sets a model of interpersonal honesty and spontaneity but must also keep in mind the current needs of the members and demonstrate behavior that is congruent with those needs. Do not conclude that group therapists should freely express all feelings. Total disinhibition is no more salubrious in therapy groups than in other forms of human encounter and may lead to ugly, destructive interaction. The therapist must model responsibility and appropriate restraint as well as honesty. We want to engage our clients and allow ourselves to be affected by them. In fact, "disciplined personal involvement" is an invaluable part of the group leader's armamentarium.[13] Not only is it therapeutic to our clients that we let them matter to us, we can also use our own reactions as valuable data about our clients—provided we know ourselves well enough.†

Consider the following therapeutically effective intervention:

> • *In the first session of a group of business executives meeting for a five-day human relations laboratory, a twenty-five-year-old, aggressive, swaggering member who had obviously been drinking heavily proceeded to dominate the meeting and make a fool of himself. He boasted of his accomplishments, belittled the group, monopolized the meeting, and interrupted, outshouted, and insulted every other member. All attempts to deal with the situation—feedback about how angry or hurt he had made others feel, or interpretations about the meaning and cause of his behavior—failed. Then my co-leader commented sincerely, "You know what I like about you? Your fear and lack of confidence. You're scared here, just like me. We're all scared about what will happen to us this week." That statement permitted the client to discard his facade and, eventually, to become a valuable group member. Furthermore, the leader, by modeling an empathic, nonjudgmental style, helped establish a gentle, accepting group culture.*

This effective intervention required that the co-leader first recognize the negative impact of this member's behavior and then supportively articulate the vulnerability that lay beneath the offensive behavior.[14]

Interacting as a group member requires, among other things, that group therapists accept and admit their personal fallibility. Therapists who need to appear infallible offer a perplexing and obstructing example for their clients. At times they may be so reluctant to admit error that they become withholding or devious in their relationship with the group. For example, in one group, the therapist, who needed to appear omniscient, was to be out of town for the next meeting. He suggested to the group members that they meet without him and tape-record the meeting, and he promised to listen to the tape before the next session. He forgot to listen to the tape but did not admit this to the group. Consequently, the subsequent meeting, in which the therapist bluffed by avoiding mention of the previous leaderless session, turned out to be diffuse, confusing, and discouraging.

Another example involves a neophyte therapist with similar needs. A group member accused him of making long-winded, confusing statements. Since this was the first confrontation of the therapist in this young group, the members were tense and perched on the edge of their chairs. The therapist responded by wondering whether he didn't remind the client of someone from the past. The attacking member clutched at the suggestion and volunteered his father as a candidate; the crisis passed, and the group members settled back in their chairs. However, it so happened that previously this therapist had himself been a member of a group (of psychotherapy students) and his colleagues had repeatedly focused on his tendency to make long-winded, confusing comments. In fact, then, what had transpired was that the client had seen the therapist quite correctly but was persuaded to relinquish his perceptions. If one of the goals of therapy is to help clients test reality and clarify their interpersonal relationships, then this transaction was *antitherapeutic*. This is an instance in which the therapist's needs were given precedence over the client's needs in psychotherapy.†

Another consequence of the need to be perfect occurs when therapists become overly cautious. Fearing error, they weigh their words so carefully, interacting so deliberately that they sacrifice spontaneity and mold a stilted, lifeless group. Often a therapist who maintains an omnipotent, distant role is saying, in effect, "Do what you will; you can't hurt or touch me." This pose may have the counterproductive effect of aggravating a sense of interpersonal impotence in clients that impedes the development of an autonomous group.

• *In one group a young man named Les had made little movement for months despite vigorous efforts by the leader. In virtually every meeting the leader attempted to bring Les into the discussion, but to no avail. Instead, Les became more defiant and withholding, and the therapist became more active and insistent. Finally Joan, another member, commented to the therapist that he was like a stubborn father treating Les like a stubborn son and was bound and determined to make Les change. Les, she added, was relishing the role of the rebellious son who was determined to defeat his father. Joan's comment rang true for the therapist; it clicked with his internal experience, and he acknowledged this to the group and thanked Joan for her comments.*

The therapist's behavior in this example was extremely important for the group. In effect, he said, I value you the members, this group, and this mode of learning. Furthermore, he reinforced norms of self-exploration and honest interaction with the therapist. The transaction was helpful to the therapist (unfortunate are the therapists who cannot learn more about themselves in their therapeutic work) and to Les, who proceeded to explore the payoff in his defiant stance toward the therapist.

Occasionally, less modeling is required of the therapist because of the presence of some ideal group members who fulfill this function. In fact, there have been studies in which selected model-setting members were deliberately introduced into a group.[15] In one study, researchers introduced trained confederates (not clients but psychology graduate students) into two outpatient groups.[16] The plants pretended to be clients but met regularly in group discussions with the therapists and supervisors. Their role and behavior were planned to facilitate, by their personal example, self-disclosure, free expression of affect, confrontation with the therapists, silencing of monopolists, clique busting, and so on. The two groups were studied (through participant-administered cohesiveness questionnaires and sociometrics) for twenty sessions. The results indicated that the plants, though not the most popular members, were regarded by the other participants as facilitating therapy; moreover, the authors concluded (though there were no control groups) that the plants served to increase group cohesiveness.

Although a trained plant would contribute a form of deceit incompatible with the process of group therapy, the use of such individuals has intriguing clinical implications. For example, a new therapy group could be seeded with an ideal group therapy member from another group, who then continued therapy in two groups. Or an individual who had recently completed group therapy satisfactorily might serve as a model-setting auxiliary therapist during the formative period of a new group. Perhaps an ongoing group might choose to add new members in advance of the graduation of senior members, rather than afterward, to capitalize on the modeling provided by the experienced and successful senior members.

These possibilities aside, it is the therapist who, wittingly or unwittingly, will continue to serve as the chief model-setting figure for the group members. Consequently, it is of the utmost importance that the therapist have sufficient self-confidence to fulfill this function. If therapists feel uncomfortable, they will be more likely to encounter difficulties in this aspect of their role and will often veer to one extreme or the other in their personal engagement in the group: either they will fall back into a comfortable, concealed professional role, or they will escape from the anxiety and responsibility inherent in the leader's role by abdicating and becoming simply one of the gang.†[17]

Neophyte therapists are particularly prone to these positions of exaggerated activity or inactivity in the face of the emotional demands of leading therapy groups. Either extreme has unfortunate consequences for the development of group norms. An overly concealed leader will create norms of caution and guardedness. A therapist who retreats from authority will be unable to use the wide range of methods available for the shaping of norms; furthermore, such a therapist creates a group that is unlikely to work fruitfully on important transference issues.

The issue of the transparency of the therapist has implications far beyond the task of norm setting.† When therapists are self-disclosing in the group, not only do they model behavior, but they perform an act that has considerable significance in many other ways for the therapeutic process. Many clients develop conflicted and distorted feelings toward the therapist; the transparency of the therapist facilitates members working through their transference. I shall discuss the ramifications of therapist transparency in great detail in chapter 7. Let us turn now from this general discussion of norms to the specific norms that enhance the power of group therapy.

EXAMPLES OF THERAPEUTIC GROUP NORMS

The Self-Monitoring Group

It is important that the group begin to assume responsibility for its own functioning. If this norm fails to develop, a passive group ensues, whose members are dependent on the leader to supply movement and direction. The leader of such a group, who feels fatigued and irritated by the burden of making everything work, is aware that something has gone awry in the early development of the group. When I lead groups like this, I often experience the members of the group as moviegoers. It's as though they visit the group each week to see what's playing; if it happens to interest them, they become engaged in the meeting. If not, "Too bad, Irv! Hope there'll be a better show next week!" My task in the group then is to help members understand that they *are* the movie. If they do not perform, there is no performance: the screen is blank.

From the very beginning, I attempt to transfer the responsibility of the group to the members. I keep in mind that in the beginning of a group, *I am the only one in the room who has a good definition of what constitutes a good work meeting.* It is my job to teach the members, to share that definition with them. Thus, if the group has a particularly good meeting, I like to label it so. For example, I might comment at the end, "It's time to stop. It's too bad, I hate to bring a meeting like this to an end." In future meetings, I often make a point of referring back to that meeting. In a young group, a particularly hard working meeting is often followed by a meeting in which the members step back a bit from the intensive interaction. In such a meeting, I might comment after a half hour, "I wonder how everyone feels about the meeting today? How would you compare it with last week's meeting? What did we do differently last week?"

It is also possible to help members develop a definition of a good meeting by asking them to examine and evaluate parts of a single meeting. For example, in the very early meetings of a group, I may interrupt and remark, "I see that an hour has gone by and I'd like to ask, 'How has the group gone today? Are you satisfied with it? What's been the most involving part of the meeting so far today? The least involving part?'" The general point is clear: I endeavor to shift the evaluative function from myself to the group members. I say to them, in effect, "You have the ability—and responsibility—to determine when this group is working effectively and when it is wasting its time."

If a member laments, for example, that "the only involving part of this meeting was the first ten minutes—after that we just chatted for forty-five minutes," my response is: "Then why did you let it go on? How could you have stopped it?" Or, "All of you seemed to have known this. What prevented you from acting? Why is it always my job to do what you are all able to do?" Soon there will be excellent consensus about what is productive and unproductive group work. (And it will almost invariably be the case that productive work occurs when the group maintains a here-and-now focus—to be discussed in the next chapter.)

Self-Disclosure

Group therapists may disagree about many aspects of the group therapeutic procedure, but there is great consensus about one issue: *self-disclosure is absolutely essential in the group therapeutic process.* Participants will not benefit from group therapy unless they self-disclose and do so fully. I prefer to lead a group with norms that indicate that self-disclosure must occur—but at each member's own pace. I prefer that members not experience the group as a forced confessional, where deep revelations are wrung from members one by one.[18]

During pregroup individual meetings, I make these points explicit to clients so that they enter the group fully informed that if they are to benefit from therapy, sooner or later they must share very intimate parts of themselves with the other group members.

Keep in mind that it is the subjective aspect of self-disclosure that is truly important. There may be times when therapists or group observers will mistakenly conclude that the group is not truly disclosing or that the disclosure is superficial or trivial. Often there is an enormous discrepancy between subjective and objective self-disclosure—a discrepancy that, incidentally, confounds research that measures self-disclosure on some standardized scale. Many group therapy members have had few intimate confidantes, and what appears in the group to be minor self-disclosure may be the very first time they have shared this material with anyone. The context of each individual's disclosure is essential in understanding its significance. Being aware of that context is a crucial part of developing empathy, as the following example illustrates.

• *One group member, Mark, spoke slowly and methodically about his intense social anxiety and avoidance. Marie, a young, bitter, and chronically depressed woman bristled at the long and labored elaboration of his difficulties. At one point she wondered aloud why others seemed to be so encouraging of Mark and excited about his speaking, whereas she felt so impatient with the slow pace of the group. She was concerned that she could not get to her personal agenda: to get advice about how to make herself more likable. The feedback she received surprised her: the members felt alienated from her because of her inability to empathize with others. What was happening in the meeting with Mark was a case in point, they told her. They felt that Mark's self-disclosure in the meeting was a great step forward for him. What interfered with her seeing what others saw? That was the critical question. And exploring that difficulty was the "advice" the group offered.*

What about the big secret? A member may come to therapy with an important secret about some central aspect of his or her life—for example, compulsive shoplifting, secret substance abuse, a jail sentence earlier in life, bulimia, transvestism, incest. They feel trapped. Though they wish to work in the therapy group, they are too frightened to share their secret with a large group of people.

In my pregroup individual sessions, I make it clear to such clients that sooner or later they will *have* to share the secret with the other group members. I emphasize that they may do this at their own pace, that they may choose to wait until they feel greater trust in the group, but that, ultimately, the sharing must come if therapy is to proceed. Group members who decide not to share a big secret are destined merely to re-create in the group the same duplicitous modes of relating to others that exist outside the group. To keep the secret hidden, they must guard every possible avenue that might lead to it. Vigilance and guardedness are increased, spontaneity is decreased, and those bearing the secret spin an ever-expanding web of inhibition around themselves.

Sometimes it is adaptive to delay the telling of the secret. Consider the following two group members, John and Charles. John had been a transvestite since the age of twelve and cross-dressed frequently but secretly. Charles entered the group with cancer. He stated that he had done a lot of work learning to cope with his cancer. He knew his prognosis: he would live for two or three more years. He sought group therapy in order to live his remaining life more fully. He especially wanted to relate more intimately with the important people in his life. This seemed like a legitimate goal for group therapy, and I introduced him into a regular outpatient therapy group. (I have fully described this individual's course of treatment elsewhere.[19])

Both of these clients chose not to disclose their secrets for many sessions. By that time I was getting edgy and impatient. I gave them knowing glances or subtle invitations. Eventually each became fully integrated into the group, developed a deep trust in the other members, and, after about a dozen meetings, chose to reveal himself very fully. In retrospect, their decision to delay was a wise one. The group members had grown to know each of these two members as people, as John and Charles, who were faced with major life problems, not as a transvestite and a cancer patient. John and Charles were justifiably concerned that if they revealed themselves too early, they would be stereotyped and that the stereotype would block other members from knowing them fully.

How can the group leader determine whether the client's delay in disclosure is appropriate or countertherapeutic? Context matters. Even though there has been no full disclosure, is there, nonetheless, movement, albeit slow, toward increasing openness and trust? Will the passage of time make it easier to disclose, as happened with John and Charles, or will tension and avoidance mount?

Often hanging on to the big secret for too long may be counterproductive. Consider the following example:

• *Lisa, a client in a six-month, time-limited group, who had practiced for a few years as a psychologist (after having trained with the group leader!) but fifteen years earlier had given up her practice to enter the business world, where she soon became extraordinarily successful. She entered the group because of dissatisfaction with her social life. Lisa felt lonely and alienated. She knew that she, as she put it, played her cards "too close to the vest"—she was cordial to others and a good listener but tended to remain distant. She attributed this to her enormous wealth, which she felt she must keep concealed so as not to elicit envy and resentment from others.*

By the fifth month, Lisa had yet to reveal much of herself. She retained her psychotherapeutic skills and thus proved helpful to many members, who admired her greatly for her unusual perceptiveness and sensitivity. But she had replicated her outside social relationships in the here-and-now of the group, since she felt hidden and distant from the other members. She requested an individual session with the group leader to discuss her participation in the group. During that session the therapist exhorted Lisa to reveal her concerns about her wealth and, especially, her psychotherapy training, warning her that if she waited too much longer, someone would throw a chair at her when she finally told the group she had once been a therapist. Finally, Lisa took the plunge and ultimately, in the very few remaining meetings, did more therapeutic work than in all the earlier meetings combined.

What stance should the therapist take when someone reveals the big secret? To answer that question, I must first make an important distinction. I believe that when an individual reveals the big secret, the therapist must help him or her disclose even more about the secret but in a *horizontal* rather than a *vertical mode*. By *vertical disclosure* I refer to content, to greater in-depth disclosure about the secret itself. For example, when John disclosed his transvestism to the group, the members' natural inclination was to explore the secret vertically. They asked about details of his cross-dressing: "How old were you when you started?" "Whose underclothes did you begin to wear?" "What sexual fantasies do you have when you cross-dress?" "How do you publicly pass as a woman with that mustache?" But John had already disclosed a great deal vertically about his secret, and it was more important for him now to reveal horizontally: *that is, disclosure about the disclosure (metadisclosure)—especially about the interactional aspects of disclosure.*[20]

Accordingly, when John first divulged his transvestism in the group I asked such questions as: "John, you've been coming to the group for approximately twelve meetings and not been able to share this with us. I wonder what it's been like for you to come each week and remain silent about your secret?" "How uncomfortable have you been about the prospect of sharing this with us?" "It hasn't felt safe for you to share this before now. Today you chose to do so. What's happened in the group or in your feelings toward the group today that's allowed you to do this?" "What were your fears in the past about revealing this to us? What did you think would happen? Whom did you feel would respond in which ways?"

John responded that he feared he would be ridiculed or laughed at or thought weird. In keeping with the here-and-now inquiry, I guided him deeper into the interpersonal process by inquiring, "*Who* in the group would ridicule you?" "*Who* would think you were weird?" And then, after John selected certain members, I invited him to check out those assumptions with them. By welcoming the belated disclosure, rather than criticizing the delay, the therapist supports the client and strengthens the therapeutic collaboration. As a general rule, it is always helpful to move from general statements about the "group" to more personal statements: in other words, ask members to differentiate between the members of the group.

Self-disclosure is always an interpersonal act. What is important is not that one discloses oneself but that one discloses something important in the context of a relationship to others. The act of self-disclosure takes on real importance because of its implications for the nature of ongoing relationships; even more important than the actual unburdening of oneself is the fact that disclosure results in a deeper, richer, and more complex relationship with others. (This is the reason why I do not, in contrast to other researchers,† consider self-disclosure as a separate therapeutic factor but instead subsume it under interpersonal learning.)

The disclosure of sexual abuse or incest is particularly charged in this way. Often victims of such abuse have been traumatized not only by the abuse itself but also by the way others have responded in the past to their disclosure of the abuse. Not uncommonly the initial disclosure within the victim's family is met with denial, blame, and rejection. As a result, the thought of disclosing oneself in the therapy group evokes fear of further mistreatment and even retraumatization rather than hope of working through the abuse.[21]

If undue pressure is placed on a member to disclose, I will, depending on the problems of the particular client and his or her stage of therapy, respond in one of several ways. For example, I may relieve the pressure by commenting: "There are obviously some things that John doesn't yet feel like sharing. The group seems eager, even impatient, to bring John aboard, while John doesn't yet feel safe or comfortable enough." (The word "yet" is important, since it conveys the appropriate expectational set.) I might proceed by suggesting that we examine the unsafe aspects of the group, not only from John's perspective but from other members' perspectives as well. Thus I shift the emphasis of the group from wringing out disclosures to exploring the obstacles to disclosure. What generates the fear? What are the anticipated dreaded consequences? From whom in the group do members anticipate disapprobation?

No one should ever be punished for self-disclosure. One of the most destructive events that can occur in a group is for members to use personal, sensitive material, which has been trustingly disclosed in the group, against one another in times of conflict. The therapist should intervene vigorously if this occurs; not only is it dirty fighting, but it undermines important group norms. This vigorous intervention can take many forms.

In one way or another, the therapist must call attention to the violation of trust. Often I will simply stop the action, interrupt the conflict, and point out that something very important has just happened in the group. I ask the offended member for his or her feelings about the incident, ask others for theirs, wonder whether others have had similar experiences, point out how this will make it difficult for others to reveal themselves, and so on. Any other work in the group is temporarily postponed. The important point is that the incident be underscored to reinforce the norm that self-disclosure is not only important but safe. Only after the norm has been established should we turn to examine other aspects of the incident.

Procedural Norms

The optimal procedural format in therapy is that the group be unstructured, spontaneous, and freely interacting. *But such a format never evolves naturally: much active culture shaping is required on the part of the therapist.* There are many trends the therapist must counter. The natural tendency of a new group is to devote an entire meeting to each of the members in rotation. Often the first person to speak or the one who presents the most pressing life crisis that week obtains the group floor for the meeting. Some groups have enormous difficulty changing the focus from one member to another, because a procedural norm has somehow evolved whereby a change of topic is considered bad form, rude, or rejecting. Members may lapse into silence: they feel they dare not interrupt and ask for time for themselves, yet they refuse to keep the other member supplied with questions because they hope, silently, that he or she will soon stop talking.

These patterns hamper the development of a potent group and ultimately result in group frustration and discouragement. I prefer to deal with these antitherapeutic norms by calling attention to them and indicating that since the group has constructed them, it has the power to change them.

For example, I might say, "I've been noticing that over the past few sessions the entire meeting has been devoted to only one person, often the first one who speaks that day, and also that others seem unwilling to interrupt and are, I believe, sitting silently on many important feelings. I wonder how this practice ever got started and whether or not we want to change it." A comment of this nature may be liberating to the group. The therapist has not only given voice to something that everyone knows to be true but has also raised the possibility of other procedural options.

Some groups evolve a formal "check-in" format in which each member in turn gets the floor to discuss important events of the previous week or certain moments of great distress. Sometimes, especially with groups of highly dysfunctional, anxious members, such an initial structure is necessary and facilitating but, in my experience, such a formal structure in most groups generally encourages an inefficient, taking-turns, noninteractive, "then-and-there" meeting. I prefer a format in which troubled members may simply announce at the beginning, "I want some time today," and the members and the therapist attempt, during the natural evolution of the session, to turn to each of those members.

Specialized groups, especially those with brief life spans and more deeply troubled members, often require different procedural norms. Compromises must be made for the sake of efficient time management, and the leader must build in an explicit structure. I will discuss such modifications of technique in chapter 15 but for now wish only to emphasize the general principle that the leader must attempt to structure a group in such a way as to build in the therapeutic norms I discuss in this chapter: support and confrontation, self-disclosure, self-monitoring, interaction, spontaneity, the importance of the group members as the agents of help.

The Importance of the Group to Its Members

The more important the members consider the group, the more effective it becomes. I believe that the ideal therapeutic condition is present when clients consider their therapy group meeting to be the most important event in their lives each week. The therapist is well advised to reinforce this belief in any available manner. If I am forced to miss a meeting, I inform the members well in advance and convey to them my concern about my absence. I arrive punctually for meetings. If I have been thinking about the group between sessions, I may share some of these thoughts with the members. Any self-disclosures I make are made in the service of the group. Though some therapists eschew such personal disclosure, I believe that it is important to articulate how much the group matters to you.

I reinforce members when they give testimony of the group's usefulness or when they indicate that they have been thinking about other members during the week. If a member expresses regret that the group will not meet for two weeks over the Christmas holidays, I urge them to express their feelings about their connection to the group. What does it mean to them to cherish the group? To protest its disruption? To have a place in which to describe their concerns openly rather than submerge their longings?

The more continuity between meetings, the better. A well-functioning group continues to work through issues from one meeting to the next. The therapist does well to encourage continuity. More than anyone else, the therapist is the group historian, connecting events and fitting experiences into the temporal matrix of the group. "That sounds very much like what John was working on two weeks ago," or, "Ruthellen, I've noticed that ever since you and Debbie had that run-in three weeks ago, you have become more depressed and withdrawn. What are your feelings now toward Debbie?"

I rarely start a group meeting, but when I do, it is invariably in the service of providing continuity between meetings. Thus, when it seems appropriate, I might begin a meeting: "The last meeting was very intense! I wonder what types of feelings you took home from the group and what those feelings are now?"

In chapter 14, I will describe the group summary, a technique that serves to increase the sense of continuity between meetings. I write a detailed summary of the group meeting each week (an editorialized narrative description of content and process) and mail it to the members between sessions. One of the many important functions of the summary is that it offers the client another weekly contact with the group and increases the likelihood that the themes of a particular meeting will be continued in the following one.

The group increases in importance when members come to recognize it as a rich reservoir of information and support. When members express curiosity about themselves, I, in one way or another, attempt to convey the belief that *any information members might desire about themselves is available in the group room, provided they learn how to tap it.* Thus, when Ken wonders whether he is too dominant and threatening to others, my reflex is to reply, in effect, "Ken, there are many people who know you very well in this room. Why not ask them?"

Events that strengthen bonds between members enhance the potency of the group. It bodes well when group members go out for coffee after a meeting, hold long discussions in the parking lot, or phone one another during the week in times of crisis. (Such extragroup contact is not without potential adverse effects, as I shall discuss in detail in chapter 11.)

Members as Agents of Help

The group functions best if its members appreciate the valuable help they can provide one another. If the group continues to regard the therapist as the sole source of aid, then it is most unlikely that the group will achieve an optimal level of autonomy and self-respect. To reinforce this norm, the therapist may call attention to incidents demonstrating the mutual helpfulness of members. The therapist may also teach members more effective methods of assisting one another. For example, after a client has been working with the group on some issue for a long portion of a meeting, the therapist may comment, "Reid, could you think back over the last forty-five minutes? Which comments have been the most helpful to you and which the least?" Or, "Victor, I can see you've been wanting to talk about that for a long time in the group and until today you've been unable to. Somehow Eve helped you to open up. What did she do? And what did Ben do today that seemed to close you down rather than open you up?" Behavior undermining the norm of mutual helpfulness should not be permitted to go unnoticed. If, for example, one member challenges another concerning his treatment of a third member, stating, "Fred, what right do you have to talk to Peter about that? You're a hell of a lot worse off than he is in that regard," I might intervene by commenting, "Phil, I think you've got some negative feelings about Fred today, perhaps coming from another source. Maybe we should get into them. I can't, however, agree with you when you say that because Fred is similar to Peter, he can't be helpful. In fact, quite the contrary has been true here in the group."

Support and Confrontation

As I emphasized in my discussion of cohesiveness, it is essential that the members perceive their therapy group as safe and supportive. Ultimately, in the course of therapy, many uncomfortable issues must be broached and explored. Many clients have problems with rage or are arrogant or condescending or insensitive or just plain cantankerous. The therapy group cannot offer help without such traits emerging during the members' interactions. In fact, their emergence is to be welcomed as a therapeutic opportunity. Ultimately, conflict must occur in the therapy group, and, as I will discuss in chapter 12, it is essential for the work of therapy. At the same time, however, too much conflict early in the course of a group can cripple its development. Before members feel free enough to express disagreement, they must feel safe enough and must value the group highly enough to be willing to tolerate uncomfortable meetings.

Thus, the therapist must build a group with norms that permit conflict but only after firm foundations of safety and support have been established. It is often necessary to intervene to prevent the proliferation of too much conflict too early in the group, as the following incident illustrates.

• *In a new therapy group, there were two particularly hostile members, and by the third meeting there was considerable open carping, sarcasm, and conflict. The fourth meeting was opened by Estelle (one of these two members), emphasizing how unhelpful the group had been to her thus far. Estelle had a way of turning every positive comment made to her into a negative, combative one. She complained, for example, that she could not express herself well and that there were many things she wanted to say but she was so inarticulate she couldn't get them across.*

When another member of the group disagreed and stated that she found Estelle to be extremely articulate, Estelle challenged the other member for doubting her judgment about herself. Later in the group, she complimented another member by stating, "Ilene, you're the only one here who's ever asked me an intelligent question." Obviously, Ilene was made quite uncomfortable by this hexed compliment.

At this point I felt it was imperative to challenge the norms of hostility and criticism that had developed in the group, and intervened forcefully. I asked Estelle: "What are your guesses about how your statement to Ilene makes others in the group feel?"

Estelle hemmed and hawed but finally offered that they might possibly feel insulted. I suggested that she check that out with the other members of the group. She did so and learned that her assumption was correct. Not only did every member of the group feel insulted, but Ilene also felt irritated and put off by the statement. I then inquired, "Estelle, it looks as though you're correct. You did insult the group. Also it seems that you knew that this was likely to occur. But what's puzzling is the payoff for you. What do you get out of it?"

Estelle suggested two possibilities. First she said, "I'd rather be rejected for insulting people than for being nice to them." That seemed a piece of twisted logic but nonetheless comprehensible. Her second statement was: "At least this way I get to be the center of attention." "Like now?" I asked. She nodded. "How does it feel right now?" I wondered. Estelle said, "It feels good." "How about the rest of your life?" I asked. She responded ingenuously, "It's lonely. In fact, this is it. This hour and a half is the people in my life." I ventured, "Then this group is a really important place for you?" Estelle nodded. I commented, "Estelle, you've always stated that one of the reasons you're critical of others in the group is that there's nothing more important than total honesty. If you want to be absolutely honest with us, however, I think you've got to tell us also how important we are to you and how much you like being here. That you never do, and I wonder if you can begin to investigate why it is so painful or dangerous for you to show others here how important they are to you."

By this time Estelle had become much more conciliatory and I was able to obtain more leverage by enlisting her agreement that her hostility and insults did constitute a problem for her and that it would help her if we called her on it—that is, if we instantaneously labeled any insulting behavior on her part. It is always helpful to obtain this type of contract from a member: in future meetings, the therapist can confront members with some particular aspect of their behavior that they have asked to be called to their attention. Since they experience themselves as allies in this spotting and confrontative process, they are far less likely to feel defensive about the intervention.

Many of these examples of therapist behavior may seem deliberate, pedantic, even pontifical. They are not the nonjudgmental, nondirective, mirroring, or clarifying comments typical of a therapist's behavior in other aspects of the therapeutic process. It is vital, however, that the therapist attend deliberately to the tasks of group creation and culture building. These tasks underlie and, to a great extent, precede much of the other work of the therapist.

It is time now to turn to the third basic task of the therapist: the activation and illumination of the here-and-now.

Chapter 6

THE THERAPIST: WORKING
IN THE HERE-AND-NOW

The major difference between a psychotherapy group that hopes to effect extensive and enduring behavioral and characterological change and such groups as AA, psychoeducational groups, cognitive-behavioral groups, and cancer support groups is that the psychotherapy group strongly emphasizes the importance of the here-and-now experience. Yet *all* group therapies, including highly structured groups, benefit from the group therapist's capacity to recognize and understand the here-and-now. Therapists who are aware of the nuances of the relationships between all the members of the group are more adept at working on the group task even when deeper group and interpersonal exploration or interpretation is not the therapy focus.[1]

In chapter 2, I presented some of the theoretical underpinnings of the use of the here-and-now. Now it is time to focus on the clinical application of the here-and-now in group therapy. First, keep in mind this important principle—perhaps the single most important point I make in this entire book: *the here-and-now focus, to be effective, consists of two symbiotic tiers, neither of which has therapeutic power without the other.*

The *first* tier is an experiencing one: the members live in the here-and-now; they develop strong feelings toward the other group members, the therapist, and the group. These here-and-now feelings become the major discourse of the group. The thrust is ahistorical: *the immediate events of the meeting take precedence over events both in the current outside life and in the distant past of the members.* This focus greatly facilitates the development and emergence of each member's social microcosm. It facilitates feedback, catharsis, meaningful self-disclosure, and acquisition of socializing techniques. The group becomes more vital, and *all* of the members (not only the ones directly working in that session) become intensely involved in the meeting.

But the here-and-now focus rapidly reaches the limits of its usefulness without the *second* tier, *which is the illumination of process*. If the powerful therapeutic factor of interpersonal learning is to be set in motion, the group must recognize, examine, and understand process. *It must examine itself; it must study its own transactions; it must transcend pure experience and apply itself to the integration of that experience.*

Thus, the effective use of the here-and-now requires two steps: *the group lives in the here-and-now, and it also doubles back on itself; it performs a self-reflective loop and examines the here-and-now behavior that has just occurred.*

If the group is to be effective, *both* aspects of the here-and-now are essential. If only the first—the experiencing of the here-and-now—is present, the group experience will still be intense, members will feel deeply involved, emotional expression may be high, and members will finish the group agreeing, "Wow, that was a powerful experience!" *Yet it will also prove to be an evanescent experience*: members will have no cognitive framework that will permit them to retain the group experience, to generalize from it, to identify and alter their interpersonal behavior, and to transfer their learning from the group to situations back home. This is precisely the error made by many encounter group leaders of earlier decades.

If, on the other hand, only the *second* part of the here-and-now—the examination of process—is present, then the group loses its liveliness and meaningfulness. It degenerates into a sterile intellectual exercise. This is the error made by overly formal, aloof, rigid therapists.

Accordingly, *the therapist has two discrete functions in the here-and-now: to steer the group into the here-and-now and to facilitate the self-reflective loop (or process commentary)*. Much of the here-and-now steering function can be shared by the group members, but for reasons I will discuss later, process commentary remains to a large extent the task of the therapist.

The majority of group therapists understand that their emphasis must be on the here-and-now. A large survey of seasoned group therapists underscored activation of the here-and-now as a core skill of the contemporary group therapist.[2] A smaller but careful study codified group therapists' interpretations and found that over 60 percent of interpretations focused on the here-and-now (either behavioral patterns or impact of behavior), while approximately 20 percent focused on historical causes and 20 percent on motivation.[3]

DEFINITION OF PROCESS

The term *process,* used liberally throughout this text, has a highly specialized meaning in many fields, including law, anatomy, sociology, anthropology, psychoanalysis, and descriptive psychiatry. In interactional psychotherapy, too, process has a specific technical meaning: it refers to the *nature of the relationship between interacting individuals—members and therapists.* Moreover, as we shall see, a full understanding of process must take into account a large number of factors, including the internal psychological worlds of each member, interpersonal interactions, group-as-a-whole forces, and the clinical environment of the group.†[4]

It is useful to contrast *process* with *content.* Imagine two individuals in a discussion. The *content* of that discussion consists of the explicit words spoken, the substantive issues, the arguments advanced. The *process* is an altogether different matter. When we ask about process, we ask, "What do these explicit words, the style of the participants, the nature of the discussion, *tell about the interpersonal relationship of the participants?"*

Therapists who are process-oriented are concerned not primarily with the verbal content of a client's utterance, but with the "how" and the "why" of that utterance, especially insofar as the how and the why illuminate aspects of the client's relationship to other people. Thus, therapists focus on the metacommunicational* aspects of the message and wonder why, *from the relationship aspect,* an individual makes a statement at a certain time in a certain manner to a certain person. Some of the message's impact is conveyed verbally and directly; some of the message is expressed paraverbally (by nuance, inflection, pitch, and tone); and some of the message is expressed behaviorally.† Identifying the connection between the communication's actual impact and the communicator's intent is at the heart of the therapy process.

Consider, for example, this transaction: During a lecture, a student raised her hand and asked what year did Freud die? The lecturer replied, "1938," only to have the student inquire, "But, sir, wasn't it 1939?" Since the student asked a question whose answer she already knew, her motivation was obviously not a quest for information. (A question isn't a question if you know the answer.) The process of this transaction? Most likely

---

*Metacommunication refers to the communication about a communication. Compare, for example: "Close the window!" "Wouldn't you like to close the window? You must be cold." "I'm cold, would you please close the window?" "Why is this window open?" Each of these statements contains a great deal more than a simple request or command. Each conveys a metacommunication: that is, a message about the nature of the relationship between the two interacting individuals.

that the student wished to demonstrate her knowledge or wished to humiliate or defeat the lecturer!

Frequently, the understanding of process in a group is more complex than in a two-person interaction; we must search for the process not only behind a simple statement but behind a sequence of statements made by several members. The group therapist must endeavor to understand what a particular sequence reveals about the relationship between one client and the other group members, or between clusters or cliques of members, or between the members and the leader, or, finally, between the group as a whole and its primary task.†

Some clinical vignettes may further clarify the concept.

> • *Early in the course of a group therapy meeting, Burt, a tenacious, intense, bulldog-faced graduate student, exclaimed to the group in general and to Rose (an unsophisticated, astrologically inclined cosmetologist and mother of four) in particular, "Parenthood is degrading!" This provocative statement elicited considerable response from the group members, all of whom had parents and many of whom were parents. The free-for-all that followed consumed the remainder of the group session.*

Burt's statement can be viewed strictly in terms of *content*. In fact, this is precisely what occurred in the group; the members engaged Burt in a debate over the virtues versus the dehumanizing aspects of parenthood—a discussion that was affect-laden but intellectualized and brought none of the members closer to their goals in therapy. Subsequently, the group felt discouraged about the meeting and angry with themselves and with Burt for having dissipated a meeting.

On the other hand, the therapist might have considered the *process* of Burt's statement from any one of a number of perspectives:

1. Why did Burt attack Rose? What was the interpersonal process between them? In fact, the two had had a smoldering conflict for many weeks, and in the previous meeting Rose had wondered why, if Burt was so brilliant, he was still, at the age of thirty-two, a student. Burt had viewed Rose as an inferior being who functioned primarily as a mammary gland; once when she was absent, he referred to her as a brood mare.
2. Why was Burt so judgmental and intolerant of nonintellectuals? Why did he always have to maintain his self-esteem by standing on the carcass of a vanquished or humiliated adversary?
3. Assuming that Burt's chief intent was to attack Rose, why did he proceed so indirectly? Is this characteristic of Burt's expression of

aggression? Or is it characteristic of Rose that no one dares, for some unclear reason, to attack her directly?

4. Why did Burt, through an obviously provocative and indefensible statement, set himself up for a universal attack by the group? Although the lyrics were different, this was a familiar melody for the group and for Burt, who had on many previous occasions placed himself in this position. Why? Was it possible that Burt was most comfortable when relating to others in this fashion? He once stated that he had always loved a fight; indeed, he glowed with anticipation at the appearance of a quarrel in the group. His early family environment was distinctively a fighting one. Was fighting, then, a form (perhaps the only available form) of involvement for Burt?

5. The process may be considered from the even broader perspective of the entire group. Other relevant events in the life of the group must be considered. For the past two months, the session had been dominated by Kate, a deviant, disruptive, and partially deaf member who had, two weeks earlier, dropped out of the group with the face-saving proviso that she would return when she obtained a hearing aid. Was it possible that the group needed a Kate, and that Burt was merely filling the required role of scapegoat?

Through its continual climate of conflict, through its willingness to spend an entire session discussing in nonpersonal terms a single theme, was the group avoiding something—possibly an honest discussion of members' feelings about Kate's rejection by the group or their guilt or fear of a similar fate? Or were they perhaps avoiding the anticipated perils of self-disclosure and intimacy? Was the group saying something to the therapist through Burt (and through Kate)? For example, Burt may have been bearing the brunt of an attack really aimed at the cotherapists but displaced from them. The therapists—aloof figures with a proclivity for rabbinical pronouncements—had never been attacked or confronted by the group. Their cotherapy relationship had also escaped any comment to date. Surely there were strong, avoided feelings toward the therapists, which may have been further fanned by their failure to support Kate and by their complicity through inactivity in her departure from the group.

Which one of these many process observations is correct? Which one could the therapists have employed as an effective intervention? The answer is, of course, *that any and all may be correct*. They are not mutually exclusive; each views the transaction from a slightly different vantage point. What is critical, however, is that the focus on *process* begins with the therapist's reflection on the host of factors that may underlie an interaction. By clarifying each of these in turn, the therapist could have focused the group on many different aspects of its life. *Which one, then, should the therapist have chosen?*

The therapist's choice should be based on one primary consideration: *the immediate needs of the group.* Where was the group at that particular time? The therapist had many options. If he felt there had been too much focus on Burt of late, leaving the other members feeling bored, uninvolved, and excluded, then he might have wondered aloud what the group was avoiding. The therapist might have then reminded the group of previous sessions spent in similar discussions that left them dissatisfied, or might have helped one of the members verbalize this point by inquiring about the members' inactivity or apparent uninvolvement in the discussion. If he felt that the indirectness of the group communication was a major issue he might have commented on the indirectness of Burt's attacks or asked the group to help clarify, via feedback, what was happening between Burt and Rose. If he felt that an exceptionally important group event (Kate's departure) was being strongly avoided, then he might have focused on that event and the conspiracy of silence around it.

In short, the therapist must determine what he or she thinks the group and its members need most at a particular time and help it move in that direction.

• *In another group, Saul sought therapy because of his deep sense of isolation. He was particularly interested in a group therapeutic experience because he had never before been a part of a primary group. Even in his primary family, he had felt himself an outsider. He had been a spectator all his life, pressing his nose against cold windowpanes, gazing longingly at warm, convivial groups within.*

At Saul's fourth therapy meeting, another member, Barbara, began the meeting by announcing that she had just broken up with a man who had been very important to her. Barbara's major reason for being in therapy had been her inability to sustain a relationship with a man, and she was profoundly distressed in the meeting. Barbara had an extremely poignant way of describing her pain, and the group was swept along with her feelings. Everyone in the group was very moved; I noted silently that Saul, too, had tears in his eyes.

The group members (with the exception of Saul) did everything in their power to offer Barbara support. They passed Kleenex; they reminded her of all her good qualities and assets; they reassured her that she had made a wrong choice, that the man was not good enough for her, that she was "lucky to be rid of that jerk."

Suddenly Saul interjected, "I don't like what's going on here in the group today, and I don't like the way it's being led" (a thinly veiled allusion to me, I thought). He went on to explain that the group mem-

bers had no justification for their criticism of Barbara's ex-boyfriend. They didn't really know what he was like. They could see him only through Barbara's eyes, and probably she was presenting him in a distorted way. (Saul had a personal ax to grind on this matter, having gone through a divorce a couple of years earlier. His wife had attended a women's support group, and he had been the "jerk" of that group.)

Saul's comments, of course, changed the entire tone of the meeting. The softness and support disappeared. The room felt cold; the warm bond among the members was broken. Everyone was on edge. I felt justifiably reprimanded. Saul's position was technically correct: the group was wrong to condemn Barbara's ex-boyfriend in such a sweeping and uncritical manner.

So much for the content. Now let's examine the process of this interaction. First, note that Saul's comment had the effect of putting him outside the group. The rest of the group was caught up in a warm, supportive atmosphere from which he excluded himself. Recall his chief complaint that he was never a member of a group, but always the outsider. The meeting provided an in vivo demonstration of how that came to pass. In his fourth group meeting, Saul had, kamikaze-style, attacked and voluntarily ejected himself from a group he wished to join.

A second issue had to do not with what Saul said but what he did not say. In the early part of the meeting, everyone except Saul had made warm, supportive statements to Barbara. I had no doubt that Saul felt supportive of her; the tears in his eyes indicated that. Why had he chosen to be silent? Why did he always choose to respond from his critical self and not from his warmer, more supportive self?

The examination of this aspect of the process led to some very important issues for Saul. Obviously it was difficult for him to express the softer, affectionate part of himself. He feared being vulnerable and exposing his dependent cravings. He feared losing himself and his own uniqueness by getting too close to another and by becoming a member of a group. Behind the aggressive, ever-vigilant, hard-nosed defender of honesty (but a selective honesty: honesty of expression of negative but not positive sentiments), there is often the softer, submissive child thirsting for acceptance and love.

• In a T-group (an experiential training group) of clinical psychology interns, one of the members, Robert, commented that he genuinely missed the contributions of some of the members who had been generally very silent. He turned to two of these members and asked if there was anything he or others could do that would help them participate more. The two members and the rest of the group responded by launching a withering attack on Robert. He was reminded that his own

contributions had not been substantial, that he was often silent for entire meetings himself, that he had never really expressed his emotions in the group, and so forth.

Viewed at the content level, this transaction is bewildering: Robert expressed genuine concern for the silent members and, for his solicitude, was soundly buffeted. Viewed at the process—that is, relationship—level, however, it makes perfectly good sense: the group members were much involved in a struggle for dominance, and their inner response to Robert's statement was, "Who are you to issue an invitation to speak? Are you the host or leader here? If we allow you to comment on our silence and suggest solutions, then we acknowledge your dominion over us."

• *In another group, Kevin, an overbearing business executive, opened the meeting by asking the other members—housewives, teachers, clerical workers, and shopkeepers—for help with a problem: he had received "downsizing" orders. He had to cut his staff immediately by 50 percent—to fire twenty of his staff of forty.*

The content of the problem was intriguing, and the group spent forty-five minutes discussing such aspects as justice versus mercy: that is, whether one retains the most competent workers or workers with the largest families or those who would have the greatest difficulty in finding other jobs. Despite the fact that most of the members engaged animatedly in the discussion, which involved important problems in human relations, the co-therapists regarded the session as unproductive: it was impersonal, the members remained in safe territory, and the discussion could have appropriately occurred at a dinner party or any other social gathering. Furthermore, as time passed, it became abundantly clear that Kevin had already spent considerable time thinking through all aspects of this problem, and no one was able to provide him with novel approaches or suggestions. The session was not truly a work session: instead it was a flight-from-work session.

Such a dedicated focus on content is inevitably frustrating for the group, and the therapists began to wonder about process—that is, what this content revealed about the nature of Kevin's relationship to the other members. *As the meeting progressed, Kevin, on two occasions, let slip the amount of his salary (which was more than double that of any other member). In fact, the overall interpersonal effect of Kevin's presentation was to make others aware of his affluence and power.*

The process became even more clear when the therapists recalled the previous meetings in which Kevin had attempted, in vain, to establish a special kind of relationship with one of the therapists (he had sought

some technical information on psychological testing for personnel).
Furthermore, in the preceding meeting, Kevin had been soundly at-
tacked by the group for his fundamentalist religious convictions, which
he used to criticize others' behavior but not his own propensity for ex-
tramarital affairs and compulsive lying. At that meeting, he had also
been termed "thick-skinned" because of his apparent insensitivity to
others. However, despite the criticism he had received, Kevin was a
dominant member: he was the most active and central figure in almost
every meeting.

With this information about process, let's examine the alternatives
available to consider. The therapists might have focused on Kevin's bid
for prestige, especially after the attack on him and his loss of face in the
previous meeting. Phrased in a nonaccusatory manner, a clarification of
this sequence might have helped Kevin become aware of his desperate
need for the group members to respect and admire him. At the same
time, the self-defeating aspects of his behavior could have been pointed
out. Despite his yearning for respect, the group had come to resent and
at times even to scorn him. Perhaps, too, Kevin was attempting to re-
pudiate the charge of being thick-skinned by sharing with the group in
melodramatic fashion the personal agony he experienced in deciding
how to cut his staff.

The style of the therapists' intervention would depend on Kevin's
degree of defensiveness: if he had seemed particularly brittle or prickly,
then the therapists might have underscored how hurt he must have
been at the previous meeting. If he had been more open, they might
have asked him directly what type of response he would have liked
from the others.

Other therapists might have preferred to interrupt the content dis-
cussion and simply ask the group what Kevin's question had to do with
last week's session. Still another alternative would be to call attention
to an entirely different type of process by reflecting on the group's ap-
parent willingness to permit Kevin to occupy center stage in the group
week after week. By encouraging the members to discuss their response
to his monopolization, the therapist could have helped the group initi-
ate an exploration of their relationship with Kevin.

Keep in mind that therapists need not wait until they have all the answers before asking a process question. Therapists may begin the process
inquiry by simply asking the members: "How are each of you experiencing the meeting so far?" Or they may use slightly more inference: "You
look like you are having some reaction to this." At other times, the therapist's level of inference may be raised and interventions may be more

precise and interpretive: "Kevin, I have a sense that you yearn for respect here in the group, and I wonder if the comment last week about you being 'thick-skinned' isn't in some way related to your bringing in this work dilemma."

PROCESS FOCUS: THE POWER SOURCE OF THE GROUP

The focus on process—on the here-and-now—is not just one of many possible procedural orientations; on the contrary, it is indispensable and a common denominator of all effective interactional groups. One so often hears words to this effect: "No matter what else may be said about experiential groups (therapy groups, encounter groups, and so on), one cannot deny that they are potent—that they offer a compelling experience for participants." *Why* are these groups potent? *Precisely because they encourage process exploration. The process focus is the power cell of the group.*

A process focus is the one truly unique feature of the experiential group; after all, there are many socially sanctioned activities in which one can express emotions, help others, give and receive advice, confess and discover similarities between oneself and others. But where else is it permissible, in fact encouraged, to comment, in depth, on *here-and-now behavior, on the nature of the immediately current relationship between people?* Possibly only in the parent–young child relationship, and even then the flow is unidirectional. The parent, but not the child, is permitted process comments: "Don't look away when I talk to you!" "Be quiet when someone else is speaking." "Stop saying, 'I dunno.'"

Consider the cocktail party. Imagine confronting the narcissistic self-absorbed individual who looks through or over you while talking to you, searching for someone more attractive or appealing. In place of an authentic encounter, we are most likely to comment, "Good talking with you . . ." or "I need to refill my drink . . ." The cocktail party is not the place for *process*. Responding authentically and in a process-oriented fashion would very likely thin out one's party invitations.

Process commentary among adults is taboo social behavior; it is considered rude or impertinent. Positive comments about another's immediate behavior often denote a seductive or flirtatious relationship. When an individual comments negatively about another's manners, gestures, speech, or physical appearance, we can be certain that the battle is bitter and the possibility of conciliation chancy.

Why should this be so? What are the sources of this taboo? Miles, in a thoughtful essay,[5] suggests the following reasons that process commentary is eschewed in social intercourse: socialization anxiety, social norms, fear of retaliation, and power maintenance.

Socialization Anxiety

Process commentary evokes early memories and anxieties associated with parental criticism of the child's behavior. Parents comment on the behavior of children. Although some of this process focus is positive, much more is critical and serves to control and alter the child's behavior. Adult process commentary often awakens old socialization-based anxiety and is experienced as critical and controlling.

Social Norms

If individuals felt free to comment at all times on the behavior of others, social life would become intolerably self-conscious, complex, and conflicted. Underlying adult interaction is an implicit contract that a great deal of immediate behavior will be invisible to the parties involved. Each party acts in the safety of the knowledge that one's behavior is not being noticed (or controlled) by the others; this safety provides an autonomy and a freedom that would be impossible if each continuously dwelled on the fact that others observe one's behavior and are free to comment on it.

Fear of Retaliation

We cannot monitor or stare at another person too closely, because (unless the relationship is exceedingly intimate) such intrusiveness is almost always dangerous and anxiety-provoking and evokes retribution. There exist no forums, aside from such intentional systems as therapy groups, for interacting individuals to test and to correct their observations of one another.

Power Maintenance

Process commentary undermines arbitrary authority structure. Industrial organizational development consultants have long known that an organization's open investigation of its own structure and process leads to power equalization—that is, a flattening of the hierarchical pyramid. Generally, individuals high on the pyramid not only are more technically informed but also possess organizational information that permits them to influence and manipulate: that is, they not only have skills that have allowed them to obtain a position of power but, once there, have such a central place in the flow of information that they are able to reinforce their position. The more rigid the authority structure of an organization, the more stringent are the precautions against open commentary about process (as in, for example, the military or the church). The individual who wishes to maintain a position of arbitrary authority is wise to inhibit the development of any rules permitting reciprocal process observation and commentary.

In psychotherapy, process commentary involves a great degree of therapist transparency, exposure, and even intimacy; hence many therapists resist this approach because of their own uneasiness or anxiety. Moving into process means moving into recognition that relationships are jointly created by both participants and has a mutual impact.

THE THERAPIST'S TASKS IN THE HERE-AND-NOW

In the first stage of the here-and-now focus—*the activating phase*—the therapist's task is to move the group into the here-and-now. By a variety of techniques, many of which I will discuss shortly, group leaders steer the group members *away* from outside material to focus instead on their relationship with one another. Group therapists expend more time and effort on this task early than late in the course of the group, because as the group progresses, the members begin to share much of this task, and the here-and-now focus often becomes an effortless and natural part of the group flow. In fact, many of the norms described in the last chapter, which the therapist must establish in the group, foster a here-and-now focus. For example, the leader who sets norms of interpersonal confrontation, of emotional expressivity, of self-monitoring, of valuing the group as an important source of information, is, in effect, reinforcing the importance of the here-and-now. Gradually members, too, come to value the here-and-now and will themselves focus on it and, by a variety of means, encourage their fellow members to do likewise.

It is altogether another matter with the second phase of the here-and-now orientation, *process illumination*. Forces prevent members from fully sharing that task with the therapist. Recall the T-group vignette presented earlier in which Robert commented on process and thereby set himself apart from the other members and was viewed with suspicion, as "not one of us." When a group member makes observations about what is happening in the group, the others often respond resentfully about the presumptuousness of elevating himself or herself above the others.

If a member comments, for example, that "nothing is happening today," or that "the group is stuck," or that "no one is self-revealing," or that "there seem to be strong feelings toward the therapist," then that member is courting danger. The response of the other members is predictable. They will challenge the challenging member: "*You* make something happen today," or "You reveal yourself," or "You talk about your feelings toward the therapist." Only the therapist is relatively exempt from that charge. Only the therapist has the right to suggest that others work or that others reveal themselves without having to engage personally in the act he or she suggests.

Throughout the life of the group, the members are involved in a struggle for position in the hierarchy of dominance. At times, the conflict around control and dominance is flagrant; at other times, quiescent. But it never vanishes and should be explored in therapy both because it is a rich source of material and also to prevent it from hardening into a source of continuing, fractious conflict.

Some members strive nakedly for power; others strive subtly; others desire it but are fearful of assertion; others always assume an obsequious, submissive posture. Statements by members that suggest that they place themselves above or outside the group generally evoke responses that emerge from the dominance struggle rather than from consideration of the content of the statement. Even therapists are not entirely immune from evoking this response; some clients are inordinately sensitive to being controlled or manipulated by the therapist. They find themselves in the paradoxical position of applying to the therapist for help and yet are unable to accept help because all statements by the therapist are viewed through spectacles of distrust. This is a function of the specific pathology of some clients (and it is, of course, good grist for the therapeutic mill). It is not a universal response of the entire group.

The therapist is an observer-participant in the group. The observer status affords the objectivity necessary to store information, to make observations about sequences or cyclical patterns of behavior, to connect events that have occurred over long periods of time. Therapists act as group historians. Only they are permitted to maintain a temporal perspective; only they remain immune from the charge of not being one of the group, of elevating themselves above the others. It is also only the therapists who keep in mind the original goals of the group members and the relationship between these goals and the events that gradually unfold in the group. The group therapist is the principal standard bearer of the group culture, supporting and sustaining the group and pushing it forward in its work.†⁶

• *Two group members, Tim and Marjorie, had a sexual affair that eventually came to light in the group. The other members reacted in various ways but none so condemnatory nor so vehemently as Diana, a forty-five-year-old nouveau-moralist, who criticized them both for breaking group rules: Tim, for "being too intelligent to act like such a fool," Marjorie for her "irresponsible disregard for her husband and child," and the Lucifer therapist (me) who "just sat there and let it happen." I eventually pointed out that, in her formidable moralistic broadside, some individuals had been obliterated, that the Marjorie and Tim, with all their struggles and doubts and fears, whom Diana had known for so long had suddenly been replaced by faceless one-dimensional stereotypes. Furthermore, I was the only one to recall, and to remind the group, of the reasons (expressed at the first group meeting) why Diana had sought therapy: namely, that she needed help in dealing with her rage toward a nineteen-year-old, rebellious, sexually awakening daughter who was in the midst of a search for her identity and autonomy! From there it was but a short step for the group, and then for Diana herself, to understand that her conflict with her daughter was being played out in the here-and-now of the group.*

There are many occasions when the process is obvious to all the members in the group but cannot be commented upon simply because the situation is too hot: the members are too much a part of the interaction to separate themselves from it. In fact, often, even at a distance, the therapist, too, feels the heat and is wary about naming the beast. Sometimes an inexperienced therapist may naively determine it best that some group member address an issue in the group that the leader himself feels too anxious to address. That is usually an error: the therapist has a greater ability to speak the unspeakable and to find palatable ways to say unpalatable things. Language is to the therapist what the scalpel is to the surgeon.

• *One neophyte therapist leading an experiential group of pediatric oncology nurses (a support group intended to help members decrease the stress experienced in their work) learned through collusive glances between members in the first meeting that there was considerable unspoken tension between the young, progressive nurses and the older, conservative nursing supervisors in the group. The therapist felt that the issue, reaching deep into taboo regions of authority and tradition, was too sensitive and potentially explosive to touch. His supervisor assured him that it was too important an issue to leave unexplored and that he should broach it, since it was highly unlikely that anyone else in the group could do what he dared not.*

In the next meeting, the therapist broached the issue in a manner that is almost invariably effective in minimizing defensiveness: he described his own dilemma about the issue. He told the group that he sensed a hierarchical struggle between the junior nurses and the powerful senior nurses but that he was hesitant to bring it up lest the younger nurses either deny it or attack the supervisors, who might be so wounded that they would decide to scuttle the group. His comment was enormously helpful and plunged the group into an open and constructive exploration of a vital issue.

Articulating the dilemma in a balanced, nonblaming fashion is often the most effective way to reduce the tension that obstructs the group's work. Group leaders need not have a complete answer to the dilemma—but they do need to be able to identify and speak to it.†

I do not mean that *only* the leader should make process comments. As I shall discuss later, other members are entirely capable of performing this function; in fact, there are times when their process observations will be more readily accepted than those of the therapists.

A greater ability to recognize process in interactions, perhaps a form of emotional intelligence, is an important outcome of group therapy that will serve members well in life.† (Often, students observing a mature group at work are amazed by group members' high level of psychological-mindedness.) Hence, it is a good thing for members to learn to identify and comment on process. But it is important that they not assume this function for defensive reasons—for example, to avoid the client role or in any other way to remove themselves from the group work.

Thus far in this discussion I have, for pedagogical reasons, overstated two fundamental points that I must now qualify. Those points are: (1) the here-and-now approach is an ahistorical one, and (2) there is a sharp distinction between here-and-now experience and here-and-now process illumination.

Strictly speaking, an ahistorical approach is an impossibility: every process comment refers to an act that already belongs to the past. (Sartre once said, "Introspection is retrospection.") Not only does process commentary involve behavior that has just transpired, but it frequently refers to cycles of behavior or repetitive acts that have occurred in the group over weeks or months. *Thus, the past events of the therapy group are a part of the here-and-now and an integral part of the data on which process commentary is based.*

Often it is helpful to ask clients to review their past experiences in the group. If a member feels that she is exploited every time she trusts someone or reveals herself, I often inquire about her history of experiencing that feeling in this group. Other clients, depending upon the relevant issues, may be encouraged to discuss such experiences as the times they have felt most close to others, most angry, most accepted, or most ignored.

My qualification of the ahistorical approach goes even further. As I will discuss later in a separate section, no group can maintain a total here-and-now approach. There will be frequent excursions into the "then-and-there"—that is, into personal history and into current life situations. In fact, such excursions are so inevitable that one becomes curious when they do not occur. It is not that the group doesn't deal with the past; *it is what is done with the past:* the crucial task is not to uncover, to piece together, to fully understand the past, *but to use the past for the help it offers in understanding (and changing) the individual's mode of relating to the others in the present.*

The distinction between here-and-now experience and here-and-now process commentary is not sharp: there is much overlap. For example, low-inference commentary (feedback) is both experience and commentary. When one member remarks that another refuses to look at her or that she is furious at another for continually deprecating her, she is at the same time commenting on process and involving herself in the affective here-and-now experience of the group. Process commentary, like nascent oxygen, exists for only a short time; it rapidly becomes incorporated into the experiential flow of the group and becomes part of the data from which future process comments will flow.

For example, in a experiential group of mental health trainees (a group experience that was part of their group therapy training curriculum—see chapter 17), one member, John, began the session with an account of some extreme feelings of depression and depersonalization. Instead of exploring the member's dysphoria, the group immediately began offering him practical advice about his life situation. The leader commented on the process—on the fact that the group veered away from inquiring more about John's experience. The leader's intervention seemed useful: the group members became more emotionally engaged, and several discussed their admiration of John's risk-taking and their own fear of self-revelation.

Soon afterward, however, a couple of counterdependent members objected to the leader's intervention. They felt that the leader was dissatisfied with their performance in the group, that he was criticizing them, and, in his usual subtle manner, was manipulating the group to fit in with his preconceived notions of the proper conduct of a meeting. Other members took issue with the tendency of some members to challenge every move of the therapist. Thus, the leader's process comments became part of the experiential ebb and flow of the group. Even the members' criticism of the leader (which was at first process commentary) soon also became part of the group experience and, itself, subject to process commentary.

Summary

The effective use of the here-and-now focus requires two steps: experience in here-and-now and process illumination. The combination of these two steps imbues an experiential group with compelling potency.

The therapist has different tasks in each step. First the group must be plunged into the here-and-now experience; second, the group must be helped to understand the process of the here-and-now experience: that is, what the interaction conveys about the nature of the members' relationships with one another.

The first step, here-and-now activation, becomes part of the group norm structure; ultimately the group members will assist the therapist in this task.

The second step, process illumination, *is more difficult. There are powerful injunctions against process commentary in everyday social intercourse that the therapist must overcome. The task of process commentary, to a large extent (but not exclusively), remains the responsibility of the therapist and consists, as I will discuss shortly, of a wide and complex range of behavior—from labeling single behavioral acts, to juxtaposing several acts, to combining acts over time into a pattern of behavior, to pointing out the undesirable consequences of a client's behavioral patterns, to identifying here-and-now behaviors that are analogues to the members' behavior in the world at large, to more complex inferential explanations or interpretations about the meaning and motivation of such behavior.*

TECHNIQUES OF HERE-AND-NOW ACTIVATION

In this section I wish to describe (but not prescribe) some techniques: each therapist must develop techniques consonant with his or her personal style. Indeed, therapists have a more important task than mastering a technique: they must fully comprehend the strategy and theoretical foundations upon which all effective technique must rest.

First step: I suggest that you *think* here-and-now. When you grow accustomed to thinking of the here-and-now, you automatically steer the group into the here-and-now. Sometimes I feel like a shepherd herding a flock into an ever-tightening circle. I head off errant strays—forays into personal historical material, discussions of current life situations, intellectualisms—and guide them back into the circle. Whenever an issue is raised in the group, I think, "How can I relate this to the group's primary task? How can I make it come to life in the here-and-now?" *I am relentless in this effort, and I begin it in the very first meeting of the group.*

Consider a typical first meeting of a group. After a short, awkward pause, the members generally introduce themselves and proceed, often with help from the therapist, to tell something about their life problems, why they have sought therapy, and, perhaps, the type of distress they suffer. I generally intervene at some convenient point well into the meeting and remark something like, "We've done a great deal here today so far. Each of you has shared a great deal about yourself, your pain, your reasons for seeking help. But I have a hunch that something else is also going on, and that is that you're sizing one another up, each arriving at some impressions of the others, each wondering how you'll fit in with the others. I wonder now if we could spend some time discussing what each of us has come up with thus far." Now this is no subtle, artful, shaping statement: it is a heavy-handed, explicit directive. Yet I find that most groups respond favorably to such clear guidelines and readily appreciate the therapeutic facilitation.

The therapist moves the focus from outside to inside, from the abstract to the specific, from the generic to the personal, from the personal into the interpersonal. If a member describes a hostile confrontation with a spouse or roommate, the therapist may, at some point, inquire, "If you were to be angry like that with anyone in the group, with whom would it be?" or, "With whom in the group can you foresee getting into the same type of struggle?" If a member comments that one of his problems is that he lies, or that he stereotypes people, or that he manipulates groups, the therapist may inquire, "What is the main lie you've told in the group thus far?" or, "Can you describe the way you've stereotyped some of us?" or, "To what extent have you manipulated the group thus far?"

If a client complains of mysterious flashes of anger or suicidal compulsions, the therapist may urge the client to signal to the group the very moment such feelings occur during the session, so that the group can track down and relate these experiences to events in the session.

If a member describes her problem as being too passive, too easily influenced by others, the therapist may move her directly into the issue by asking, "Who in the group could influence you the most? The least?"

If a member comments that the group is too polite and too tactful, the therapist may ask, "Who are the leaders of the peace-and-tact movement in the group?" If a member is terrified of revealing himself and fears humiliation, the therapist may bring it into the here-and-now by asking him to identify those in the group he imagines might be most likely to ridicule him. Don't be satisfied by answers of "the whole group." Press the member further. Often it helps to rephrase the question in a gentler manner, for example, "Who in the group is *least* likely to ridicule you?"

In each of these instances, the therapist can deepen interaction by encouraging further responses from the others. For example, "How do you feel about his fear or prediction that you would ridicule him? Can you imagine doing that? Do you, at times, feel judgmental in the group? Even simple techniques of asking group members to speak directly to one another, to use second-person ("you") rather than third-person pronouns, and to look at one another are very useful.

Easier said than done! Such suggestions are not always heeded. To some group members, they are threatening indeed, and the therapist must here, as always, employ good timing and attempt to experience what the client is experiencing. Search for methods that lessen the threat. *Begin by focusing on positive interaction*: "Toward whom in the group do you feel most warm?" "Who in the group is most like you?" or, "Obviously, there are some strong vibes, both positive and negative, going on between you and John. I wonder what you most envy or admire about him? And what parts of him do you find most difficult to accept?"

• A group meeting of elderly clients attending a psychiatric day hospital for treatment of depression groaned with feelings of disconnection and despair. The initial focus of the meeting was Sara—an eighty-two-year-old Holocaust survivor. Sara lamented the persistent prejudice, hatred, and racism so prominent in the news headlines. Feeling scared and helpless, she discussed her wartime memories of being dehumanized by those who hated her without knowing anything about her as a real person. Group members, including other Holocaust survivors, also shared their tortured memories.

The group leader attempted to break into the group's intense preoccupation with the past by shifting into the here-and-now. What did Sara experience talking to the group today? Did she feel that the group members were engaging her as a real person? Why had she chosen to be different today—to speak out rather than silence herself as she has done so often before? Could she take credit for that? How did others feel about Sara speaking out in this meeting?

Gradually the meeting's focus shifted from the recounting of despairing memories to lively interaction, support for Sara, and strong feelings of member connectivity.

Sometimes, it is easier for group members to work in tandem or in small subgroups. For example, if they learn that there is another member with similar fears or concerns, then a subgroup of two (or more) members can, with less threat, discuss their here-and-now concerns.[7] This may occur spontaneously or by the therapist directly creating a bridge between specific members—for example, by pointing out that the concerns just disclosed by one member have also been expressed by another.†

Using the conditional verb form provides safety and distance and often is miraculously facilitative. I use it frequently when I encounter initial resistance. If, for example, a client says, "I don't have any response or feelings at all about Mary today. I'm just feeling too numb and withdrawn," I often say something like, "If you were *not* numb or withdrawn today, what *might* you feel about Mary?" The client generally answers readily; the once-removed position affords a refuge and encourages the client to answer honestly and directly. Similarly, the therapist might inquire, "If you *were* to be angry at someone in the group, whom would it be?" or, "If you *were* to go on a date with Albert (another group member), what kind of experience might it be?"

The therapist must teach members the art of requesting and offering feedback by explicit instruction, by modeling, or by reinforcing effective feedback.[8] One important principle to teach clients is the avoidance of global questions and observations. Questions such as "Am I boring?" or

"Do you like me?" are not usually productive. A client learns a great deal more by asking, "What do I do that causes you to tune out?" "When are you most and least attentive to me?" or, "What parts of me or aspects of my behavior do you like least and most?" In the same vein, feedback such as "You're OK" or "You're a nice guy" is far less useful than "I feel closer to you when you're willing to be honest with your feelings, like in last week's meeting when you said you were attracted to Mary but feared she would scorn you. I feel most distant from you when you're impersonal and start analyzing the meaning of every word said to you, like you did early in the meeting today." *(These comments, like most of the therapist comments in this text, have equal applicability in individual therapy.)*

Resistance occurs in many forms. Often it appears in the cunning guise of total equality. Clients, especially in early meetings, often respond to the therapist's here-and-now urgings by claiming that they feel exactly the same toward all the group members: that is, they say that they feel equally warm toward all the members, or no anger toward any, or equally influenced or threatened by all. *Do not be misled. Such claims are never true.* Guided by your sense of timing, push the inquiry farther and help members differentiate one another. Eventually they will disclose that they do have slight differences of feeling toward some of the members. These slight differences are important and are often the vestibule to full interactional participation. I explore the slight differences (no one ever said they had to be enormous); sometimes I suggest that the client hold up a magnifying glass to these differences and describe what he or she then sees and feels. Often resistance is deeply ingrained and the client is heavily invested in maintaining a position that is known and familiar even though it is undermining or personally destructive.

Resistance is not usually conscious obstinacy but more often stems from sources outside of awareness. Sometimes the here-and-now task is so unfamiliar and uncomfortable to the client that it is not unlike learning a new language; one has to attend with maximal concentration in order not to slip back into one's habitual remoteness. Considerable ingenuity on the part of the therapist may be needed, as the following case study shows.

> • *Claudia resisted participation on a here-and-now level for many sessions. Typically she brought to the group some pressing current life problem, often one of such crisis proportions that the group members felt trapped. First, they felt compelled to deal immediately with the precise problem Claudia presented; second, they had to tread cautiously because she explicitly informed them that she needed all her resources to cope with the crisis and could not afford to be shaken up by interpersonal confrontation. "Don't push me right now," she might say,*

"I'm just barely hanging on." Efforts to alter this pattern were unsuccessful, and the group members felt discouraged in dealing with Claudia. They cringed when she brought in problems to the meeting.

One day she opened the group with a typical gambit. After weeks of searching she had obtained a new job but was convinced that she was going to fail and be dismissed. The group dutifully but warily investigated the situation. The investigation met with many of the familiar, treacherous obstacles that generally block the path of work on outside problems. There seemed to be no objective evidence that Claudia was failing at work. She seemed, if anything, to be trying too hard, working eighty hours a week. The evidence, Claudia insisted, simply could not be appreciated by anyone not there at work with her: the glances of her supervisor, the subtle innuendos, the air of dissatisfaction toward her, the general ambiance in the office, the failure to live up to her (self-imposed and unrealistic) sales goals. It was difficult to evaluate what she said because she was not a highly unreliable observer and typically downgraded herself and minimized her accomplishments.

The therapist moved the entire transaction into the here-and-now by asking, "Claudia, it's hard for us to determine whether you are, in fact, failing at your job. But let me ask you another question: What grade do you think you deserve for your work in the group, and what do each of the others get?"

Claudia, not unexpectedly, awarded herself a "D–" and staked her claim for at least eight more years in the group. She awarded all the other members substantially higher grades. The therapist replied by awarding Claudia a "B" for her work in the group and then went on to point out the reasons: her commitment to the group, perfect attendance, willingness to help others, great efforts to work despite anxiety and often disabling depression.

Claudia laughed it off, trying to brush off this exchange as a gag or a therapeutic ploy. But the therapist held firm and insisted that he was entirely serious. Claudia then insisted that the therapist was wrong, and pointed out her many failings in the group (one of which was the avoidance of the here-and-now). However, Claudia's disagreement with the therapist created dissonance for her, since it was incompatible with her long-held, frequently voiced, total confidence in the therapist. (Claudia had often invalidated the feedback of other members in the group by claiming that she trusted no one's judgment except the therapist's.)

The intervention was enormously useful and transferred the process of Claudia's evaluation of herself from a secret chamber lined with the distorting mirrors of her self-perception to the open, vital arena of the group. No longer was it necessary for the members to accept Claudia's perception of her boss's glares and subtle innuendoes. The boss (the therapist) was there in the group. The whole transaction was visible to the group. Finding the here-and-now *experiential* analogue of the untrustworthy "then-and-there" *reported* difficulties unlocked the therapeutic process for Claudia.

I never cease to be awed by the rich, subterranean lode of data that exists in every group and in every meeting. Beneath each sentiment expressed there are layers of invisible, unvoiced ones. But how to tap these riches? Sometimes after a long silence in a meeting, I express this very thought: "There is so much information that could be valuable to us all today if only we could excavate it. I wonder if we could, each of us, tell the group about some thoughts that occurred to us in this silence, which we thought of saying but didn't."

The exercise is more effective, incidentally, if you participate personally, even start it going. Substantial empirical evidence supports the principle that therapists who employ judicious and disciplined self-disclosure, centered in the here-and-now of the therapeutic relationship, increase their therapeutic effectiveness and facilitate clients' exploration and openness.[9] For example, you might say, "I've been feeling on edge in this silence, wanting to break it, not wanting to waste time, but on the other hand feeling irritated that it always has to be me doing this work for the group." Or, "I've been feeling uneasy about the struggle going on in the group between you and me, Mike. I'm uncomfortable with this much tension and anger, but I don't know yet how to help understand and resolve it."

When I feel there has been a particularly great deal unsaid in a meeting, I have often found the following technique useful: "It's now six o'clock and we still have half an hour left, but I wonder if you each would imagine that the meeting has ended and that you're on your way home. What disappointments would you have about the meeting today?"

Many of the inferences the therapist makes may be off-target. But objective accuracy is not the issue: *as long as you persistently direct the group from the nonrelevant, from the then-and-there, to the here-and-now, you are operationally correct.* For example, if a group spends time in an unproductive meeting discussing dull, boring parties, and the therapist wonders aloud if the members are indirectly referring to the present group session, there is no way of determining with any certainty whether that is an accurate statement. Correctness in this instance must be defined relativistically and pragmatically. By shifting the group's attention from then-and-there to here-and-now material, the therapist performs a service to the group—a service that, consistently reinforced, will ultimately result in a cohesive, interactional atmosphere maximally conducive to therapy.

Following this model, the effectiveness of an intervention should be gauged by its success in focusing the group on itself.

According to this principle, the therapist might ask a group that dwells at length on the subject of poor health or on a member's sense of guilt over remaining in bed during times of sickness, "Is the group really wondering about my [the therapist's] recent illness?" Or a group suddenly preoccupied with death and the losses each member has incurred might be asked whether they are also concerned with the group's impending four-week summer vacation. In these instances the leader attempts to make connections between the overt content and underlying unexpressed covert group-related issues.

Obviously, these interventions would be pointless if the group had already thoroughly worked through all the implications of the therapist's recent absence or the impending summer break. The technical procedure is not unlike the sifting process in any traditional psychotherapy. Presented with voluminous data in considerable disarray, the therapist selects, reinforces, and interprets those aspects he deems most helpful to the client at that particular time. Not all dreams and not all parts of a dream are attended to by the therapist; however, a dream theme that elucidates a particular issue on which the client is currently working is vigorously pursued.

Implicit here is the assumption that the therapist knows the most propitious direction for the group at a specific moment. Again, this is not a precise matter. What is most important is that the therapist has formulated broad principles of ultimately helpful directions for the group and its members—this is precisely where a grasp of the therapeutic factors is essential.

Often, when activating the group, the therapist performs two simultaneous acts: steering the group into the here-and-now and, at the same time, interrupting the content flow in the group. Not infrequently, some members will resent the interruption, and the therapist must attend to these feelings, for they, too, are part of the here-and-now. Often it is difficult for the therapist to intervene. Early in our socialization process we learn not to interrupt, not to change the subject abruptly. Furthermore, there are often times in the group when everyone seems keenly interested in the topic under discussion. Even though the therapist is certain that the group is not working, it is not easy to buck the group current. As noted in chapter 3, social-psychological small-group research demonstrates the compelling power of group pressure. To take a stand opposite to the perceived consensus of the group requires considerable courage and conviction.

My experience is that the therapist faced with this as well as many other types of dilemmas can increase the clients' receptivity by expressing both sets of feelings to the group. For example, "Lily, I feel very uncomfortable as you talk. I'm having a couple of strong feelings. One is that you're into something that is very important and painful for you, and the other is that Jason [a new member] has been trying hard to get into the group for the last few meetings and the group seems unwelcoming. This didn't happen when other new members entered the group. Why do you think it's happening now?" Or, "Lenore, I've had two reactions as you started talking. The first is that I'm delighted you feel comfortable enough now in the group to participate, but the other is that it's going to be hard for the group to respond to what you're saying because it's very abstract and far removed from you personally. I'd be much more interested in how you've been feeling about the group the last couple of meetings. Are there some incidents or interactions you've been especially tuned in to? What reactions have you had to other members here?"

There are, of course, many more such activating procedures. (In chapter 14, I describe some basic modifications in the group structure and procedure that facilitate here-and-now interaction in short-term specialty groups.) But my goal here is not to offer a compendium of techniques. Rather, I describe techniques only to illuminate the underlying principle of here-and-now activation. These group techniques, or gimmicks, are servants, not masters. To use them injudiciously, to fill voids, to jazz up the group, to acquiesce to the members' demands that the leader lead, is seductive but not constructive for the group.[10]

Overall, group leader activity correlates with outcome in a curvilinear fashion (too much or too little activity leads to unsuccessful outcomes). Too *little* leader activity results in a floundering group. Too *much* activation by a leader results in a dependent group that persists in looking to the leader to supply too much.

Remember that sheer acceleration of interaction is not the purpose of these techniques. The therapist who moves too quickly—using gimmicks to make interactions, emotional expression, and self-disclosure too easy—misses the whole point. Resistance, fear, guardedness, distrust—in short, everything that impedes the development of satisfying interpersonal relations—must be permitted expression. The goal is to create not a slick-functioning, streamlined social organization but one that functions well enough and engenders sufficient trust for the unfolding of each member's social microcosm. Working through the resistances to change is the key to the production of change.

Thus, the therapist wants to go not *around* obstacles but *through* them. Ormont puts it nicely when he points out that though we urge clients to engage deeply in the here-and-now, we expect them to fail, to default on their contract. In fact, we *want* them to default because we hope, through the nature of their failure, to identify and ultimately dispel each member's particular resistances to intimacy—including each member's resistance style (for example, detachment, fighting, diverting, self-absorption, distrust) and each member's underlying *fears of intimacy* (for example, impulsivity, abandonment, merger, vulnerability).[11]

TECHNIQUES OF PROCESS ILLUMINATION

As soon as clients have been successfully steered into a here-and-now interactional pattern, the group therapist must attend to turning this interaction to therapeutic advantage. This task is complex and consists of several stages:

- Clients must first recognize what they are doing with other people (ranging from simple acts to complex patterns unfolding over a long time).
- They must then appreciate the impact of this behavior on others and how it influences others' opinion of them and consequently its impact on their own self-regard.
- They must decide whether they are satisfied with their habitual interpersonal style.
- They must exercise the will to change.
- They must transform intent into decision and decision into action.
- Lastly, they must solidify the change and transfer it from the group setting into their larger life.

Each of these stages may be facilitated by some specific cognitive input by the therapist, and I will describe each step in turn. First, however, I must discuss several prior considerations: How does the therapist recognize process? How can the therapist help the members assume a process orientation? How can therapists increase the client receptivity of their process commentary?

Recognition of Process

Before therapists can help clients understand process, they must themselves learn to recognize it: in other words, they must be able to reflect in the midst of the group interaction and wonder, "Why is *this* unfolding in this group in this particular way and at this particular time?"† The experienced therapist does this naturally and effortlessly, observing the group proceedings from several different perspectives, including the specific individual interactions and the developmental issues in the group (see chapter 11). This difference in perspective is the major difference in role between the client and the therapist. Consider some clinical illustrations:

- *At one meeting, Alana discloses much deep personal material. The group is moved by her account and devotes much time to listening, to*

helping her elaborate more fully, and to offering support. The therapist
shares in these activities but entertains many other thoughts as well.
For example, the therapist may wonder why, of all the members, it is
invariably Alana who reveals first and most. Why does Alana so often
put herself in the role of the group member whom all the members
must nurse? Why must she always display herself as vulnerable? And
why today? And that last meeting! So much conflict! After such a meet-
ing, one might have expected Alana to be angry. Instead, she shows her
throat. Is she avoiding giving expression to her rage?

• *At the end of a session in another group, Jay, a young, rather fragile*
young man who had been inactive in the group, revealed that he was
gay—his first step out of the closet. At the next meeting the group
urged him to continue. He attempted to do so but, overcome with emo-
tion, blocked and hesitated. Just then, with indecent alacrity, Vicky
filled the gap, saying, "Well, if no one else is going to talk, I have a
problem."

Vicky, an aggressive forty-year-old cabdriver, who sought therapy
because of social loneliness and bitterness, proceeded to discuss in
endless detail a complex situation involving an unwelcome visiting
aunt. For the experienced, process-oriented therapist, the phrase "I
have a problem" is a double entendre. Far more trenchantly than her
words, Vicky's behavior declares, "I have a problem," and her problem
is manifest in her insensitivity to Jay, who, after months of silence, had
finally mustered the courage to speak.

It is not easy to tell the beginning therapist how to recognize process;
the acquisition of this perspective is one of the major tasks in your education. And it is an interminable task: throughout your career, you learn to
penetrate ever more deeply into the substratum of group discourse. This
deeper vision increases the keenness of a therapist's interest in the meeting.
Generally, beginning students who observe meetings find them far less
meaningful, complex, and interesting than do experienced therapists.

Certain guidelines, though, may facilitate the neophyte therapist's
recognition of process. Note the simple nonverbal sense data available.†
Who chooses to sit where? Which members sit together? Who chooses to
sit close to the therapist? Far away? Who sits near the door? Who comes
to the meeting on time? Who is habitually late? Who looks at whom when
speaking? Do some members, while speaking to another member, look at
the therapist? If so, then they are relating not to one another but instead
to the therapist through their speech to the others. Who looks at his
watch? Who slouches in her seat? Who yawns? Do the members pull their
chairs away from the center at the same time as they are verbally profess-

ing great interest in the group? How quickly do the group members enter the room? How do they leave it? Are coats kept on? When in a single meeting or in the sequence of meetings are they removed? A change in dress or grooming not uncommonly indicates change in a client or in the atmosphere of the entire group. An unctuous, dependent man may express his first flicker of rebellion against the leader by wearing jeans and sneakers to a group session rather than his usual formal garb.

A large variety of postural shifts may betoken discomfort; foot flexion, for example, is a particularly common sign of anxiety. Indeed, it is common knowledge that nonverbal behavior frequently expresses feelings of which a person is yet unaware. The therapist, through observing and teaching the group to observe nonverbal behavior, may hasten the process of self-exploration.

Assume that every communication has meaning and salience within the individual's interpersonal schema until proven otherwise. Make use of your own reactions to each client as a source of process data.[12] Keep attending to the reactions that group members elicit in one another. Which seem consensual reactions shared by most, and which are unique or idiosyncratic reactions?[13]

Sometimes the process is clarified by attending *not only to what is said but also to what is omitted*: the female member who offers suggestions, advice, or feedback to the male members but never to the other women in the group; the group that never confronts or questions the therapist; the topics (for example, the taboo trio: sex, money, death) that are never broached; the individual who is never attacked; the one who is never supported; the one who never supports or inquires—all these omissions are part of the transactional process of the group.

• *In one group, for example, Sonia stated that she felt others disliked her. When asked who, she selected Eric, a detached, aloof man who habitually related only to those who could be of use to him. Eric bristled, "Why me? Tell me one thing I've said to you that makes you pick me." Sonia stated, "That's exactly the point. You've never said anything to me. Not a question, not a greeting. Nothing. I just don't exist for you. You have no use for me." Eric, later, at a debriefing session after completing therapy, cited this incident as a particularly powerful and illuminating instruction.*

Physiologists commonly study the function of a hormone by removing the endocrine gland that manufactures it and observing the changes in the hormone-deficient organism. Similarly, in group therapy, we may learn a great deal about the role of a particular member by observing the here-and-now process of the group when that member is absent. For example, if the absent member is aggressive and competitive, the group may feel liberated. Other members, who had felt threatened or restricted in the missing member's presence, may suddenly blossom into activity. If, on the other hand, the group has depended on the missing member to carry the burden of self-disclosure or to coax other members into speaking, then it will feel helpless and threatened when that member is absent. Often this absence elucidates interpersonal feelings that previously were entirely out of the group members' awareness. The therapist may then encourage the group to discuss these feelings toward the absent member both at that time and later in his or her presence. A common myth that may need to be dispelled is that talking about a group member when he is not present at a meeting is politically or socially incorrect. It is not "talking behind someone's back" and it should not lead to scapegoating, provided that the group adopts the practice of sharing the discussion with that member at the following meeting.

Similarly, a rich supply of data about feelings toward the therapist often emerges in a meeting in which the therapist or a co-therapist is absent. One leader led an experiential training group of mental health professionals composed of one woman and twelve men. The woman, though she habitually took the chair closest to the door, felt reasonably comfortable in the group until a leaderless meeting was scheduled when the therapist was out of town. At that meeting the group discussed sexual feelings and experiences far more blatantly than ever before, and the woman had terrifying fantasies of the group locking the door and raping her. She realized how the therapist's presence had offered her safety against fears of unrestrained sexual behavior by the other members and against the emergence of her own sexual fantasies. (She realized, too, the meaning of her occupying the seat nearest the door!)

Search in every possible way to understand the relationship messages in any communication. Look for incongruence between verbal and nonverbal behavior. Be especially curious when there is something arrhythmic about a transaction: when, for example, the intensity of a response seems disproportionate to the stimulus statement, or when a response seems to be off target or to make no sense. At these times look for several possibilities: for example, *parataxic distortion* (the responder is experiencing the sender unrealistically), or *metacommunication* (the responder is responding, accurately, not to the manifest content but to another level of communication), or *displacement* (the responder is reacting not to the current transaction but to feelings stemming from previous transactions). A disproportionately strong emotional reaction—what one group member called "A Big Feeling"—may be the tip of an iceberg of deeper, historical concerns that get reactivated in the present.

Common Group Tensions

Remember that, to some degree, certain tensions are always present in every therapy group. Consider, for example, tensions such as the struggle for dominance, the antagonism between mutually supportive feelings and sibling rivalrous ones, between greed and selfless efforts to help the other, between the desire to immerse oneself in the comforting waters of the group and the fear of losing one's precious individuality, between the wish to get better and the wish to stay in the group, between the wish that others improve and the fear of being left behind. Sometimes these tensions are quiescent for months until some event wakens them and they erupt into plain view.

Do not forget these tensions. They are omnipresent, always fueling the hidden motors of group interaction. The knowledge of these tensions often informs the therapist's recognition of process. Consider, for example, one of the most powerful covert sources of group tension: *the struggle for dominance*. Earlier in this chapter, I described an intervention where the therapist, in an effort to steer a client into the here-and-now, gave her a grade for her work in the group. The intervention was effective for that particular person. Yet that was not the end of the story: there were later repercussions on the rest of the group. In the next meeting, two group members asked the therapist to clarify some remark he had made to them at a previous meeting. The remarks had been so supportive in nature and so straightforwardly phrased that the therapist was puzzled at the request for clarification. Deeper investigation revealed that the two members and later others, too, were requesting grades from the therapist.

• *In another experiential group of mental health professionals at several levels of training, the leader was much impressed by the group skills of Stewart, one of the youngest, most inexperienced members. The leader expressed his fantasy that Stewart was a plant, that he could not possibly be just beginning his training, since he conducted himself like a veteran with ten years' group experience. The comment evoked a flood of tensions. It was not easily forgotten by the group and, for sessions to come, was periodically revived and angrily discussed. With his comment, the therapist placed the kiss of death on Stewart's brow, since thereafter the group systematically challenged and deskilled him. It is to be expected that the therapist's positive evaluation of one member will evoke feelings of sibling rivalry among the others.*

The struggle for dominance, as I will discuss in chapter 11, fluctuates in intensity throughout the group. It is much in evidence at the beginning of the group as members jockey for position in the pecking order. Once the hierarchy is established, the issue may become quiescent, with periodic flare-ups, for example, when some member, as part of his or her therapeutic work, begins to grow in assertiveness and to challenge the established order.

When new members enter the group, especially aggressive members who do not know their place, who do not respectfully search out and honor the rules of the group, you may be certain that the struggle for dominance will rise to the surface.

> • *In one group a veteran member, Betty, was much threatened by the entrance of a new, aggressive woman, Rena. A few meetings later, when Betty discussed some important material concerning her inability to assert herself, Rena attempted to help by commenting that she, herself, used to be like that, and then she presented various methods she had used to overcome it. Rena reassured Betty that if she continued to talk about it openly in the group she, too, would gain considerable confidence. Betty's response was silent fury of such magnitude that several meetings passed before she could discuss and work through her feelings. To the uninformed observer, Betty's response would appear puzzling; but in the light of Betty's seniority in the group and Rena's vigorous challenge to that seniority, her response was entirely predictable. She responded not to Rena's manifest offer of help but instead to Rena's implicit communication: "I'm more advanced than you, more mature, more knowledgeable about the process of psychotherapy, and more powerful in this group despite your longer presence here."*

> • *In another group, Bea, an assertive, articulate woman, had for months been the most active and influential member. A new member, Bob, a psychiatric social worker (who did not reveal that fact to the group), was introduced. He was exceedingly assertive and articulate and in his first meeting, described his life situation with such candor and clarity that the other members were impressed and touched. Bea's response, however, was: "Where did you get your group therapy training?" (Not "Did you ever have therapy training?" or, "You sound like you've had some experience in examining yourself.") The wording of Bea's comment clearly revealed the struggle for dominance, for she was implicitly saying: "I've found you out. Don't think you can fool me with that jargon. You've got a long way to go to catch up with me!"*

Primary Task and Secondary Gratification

The concepts of *primary task* and *secondary gratification*, and the dynamic tension between the two, provide the therapist with a useful guide to the recognition of process (and, as I will discuss later, a guide to the factors underlying a client's resistance to process commentary).

First some definitions. The *primary task* of the client is, quite simply, to achieve his or her original goals: relief of suffering, better relationships with others, or living more productively and fully. Yet, as we examine it more closely, the task often becomes much more complicated. Generally one's view of the primary task changes considerably as one progresses in therapy. Sometimes the client and the therapist have widely different views of the primary task. I have, for example, known clients who stated that their goal is relief from pain (for example, from anxiety, depression, or insomnia) but who have a deeper and more problematic goal. One woman wished that through therapy she would become so well that she would be even more superior to her adversaries by "out mental-healthing" them; another client wished to learn how to manipulate others even more effectively; another wished to become a more effective seducer. These goals may be unconscious or, even if conscious, well hidden from others; they are not part of the initial contract the individual makes with the therapist, and yet they exert a pervasive influence in the therapeutic work. In fact, much therapy may have to occur before some clients can formulate an appropriate primary task.[14]*

Even though their goals may evolve through the course of therapy, clients initially have some clear conception of a primary task—generally, relief of some type of discomfort. By methods discussed in chapter 10, therapists, in pregroup preparations of clients and in the first group meetings, make clients aware of what they must do in the group to accomplish their primary tasks. And yet once the group begins, very peculiar things begin to happen: clients conscious wish for change there is a deeper commitment to *avoid* change—a clinging to old familiar modes of behavior. It is often through the recognition of this clinging (that is, *resistance*) that the first real opportunity for repair emerges.†

Some clinical vignettes illustrate this paradox:

• *Cal, a young man, was interested in seducing the women of the group and shaped his behavior in an effort to appear suave and charming. He concealed his feelings of awkwardness, his desperate wish to be cool,*

---

*These phenomena play havoc with outcome research strategies that focus on initial target symptoms or goals and then simply evaluate the clients' change on these measures. It is precisely for this reason that experienced therapists are dismayed at naive contemporary mental health maintenance providers who insist on evaluating therapy every few sessions on the basis of initial goals. Using more *comprehensive* global outcome questionnaires instead, such as the Outcome Questionnaire 45, can provide meaningful feedback to therapists that keeps them aligned productively with their clients.

his fear of women, and his envy of some of the men in the group. He could never discuss his compulsive masturbation and occasional voyeurism. When another male member discussed his disdain for the women in the group, Cal (purring with pleasure at the withdrawal of competition) praised him for his honesty. When another member discussed, with much anxiety, his homosexual fantasies, Cal deliberately withheld the solace he might have offered by sharing his own, similar fantasies. He never dared to discuss the issues for which he entered therapy; nothing took precedence over being cool.

Another member devoted all her energies to achieving an image of mental agility and profundity. She, often in subtle ways, continually took issue with me. She scorned any help I offered her, and took great offense at my attempts to interpret her behavior. Finally, I reflected that working with her made me feel I had nothing of value to offer. That was her finest hour! She flashed a sunny smile as she said, "Perhaps you ought to join a therapy group to work on your problem."

Another member enjoyed an enviable position in the group because of his girlfriend, a beautiful actress, whose picture he delighted in passing around in the group. She was his showpiece, living proof of his natural superiority. When one day she suddenly and peremptorily left him, he was too mortified to face the group and dropped out of therapy.

What do these examples have in common? In each, the client gave priority *not to the declared primary task but to some secondary gratification arising in the group:* a relationship with another member, an image a client wished to project, or a group role in which a client was the most sexually desirable, the most influential, the most wise, the most superior. In each instance, the client's pathology obstructed his or her pursuit of the primary goal. Clients diverted their energies from the real work of therapy to the pursuit of some gratification in the group. If this here-and-now behavior were available for study—if the members could, as it were, be pulled out of the group matrix to observe their actions in a more dispassionate manner—then the entire sequence would become part of good therapeutic work. But that did not happen! In all these instances, *the gratification took precedence over the work to be done.* Group members concealed information, misrepresented themselves, rejected the therapist's help, and refused to give help to one another.

This is a familiar phenomenon in individual therapy. Long ago, Freud spoke of the patient *whose desire to remain in therapy outweighed the desire to be cured.* The individual therapist satisfies a client's wish to be succored, to be heard, to be cradled. Yet there is a vast, quantitative difference in this respect between individual and group therapy. The individual therapy format is relatively insular; the group situation offers a far greater range of secondary gratifications, of satisfying many social needs in an individual's life. Moreover, the gratification offered is often compelling; our social needs to be dominant, to be admired, to be loved, to be revered are powerful indeed. For some, the psychotherapy group provides satisfying relationships rather than being a bridge to forming better relationships in their world at large. This presents a clinical challenge with certain populations, such as the elderly, who have reduced opportunities for human connection outside of the therapy group. In such instances, offering ongoing, less frequent booster sessions, perhaps monthly, after a shorter intensive phase may be the best way to respond to this reluctance to end therapy.[15]

Is the tension that exists between primary task and secondary gratification nothing more than a slightly different way of referring to the familiar concept of resistance and acting out? In the sense that the pursuit of secondary gratification obstructs the therapeutic work, it may generically be labeled resistance. Yet there is an important shade of difference: *Resistance* ordinarily refers to pain avoidance. Obviously, resistance in this sense is much in evidence in group therapy, on both an individual and a group level. But what I wish to emphasize is that the *therapy group offers an abundance of secondary gratifications*. Often the therapeutic work in a group is derailed not because members are too defensively anxious to work but because they find themselves unwilling to relinquish gratification.

Often, when the therapist is bewildered by the course of events in the therapy group, the distinction between primary task and secondary gratification is extremely useful. It is often clarifying for therapists to ask themselves whether the client is working on his or her primary task. And when the substitution of secondary gratification for primary task is well entrenched and resists intervention, therapists have no more powerful technique than reminding the group members of the primary task—the reasons for which they seek therapy.

The same principle applies to the *entire group*. It can be said that the entire group has a primary task that consists of the development and exploration of all aspects of the relationship of each member to each of the others, to the therapist, and to the group as an aggregate. The therapist and, later, the group members can easily enough sense when the group is working, when it is involved in its primary task, and when it is avoiding that task.

At times the therapist may be unclear about what a group is doing but knows that it is not focused on either developing or exploring relationships between members. If therapists have attended to providing the group a clear statement of its primary task, then they must conclude that the group is actively evading the task—either because of some dysphoria associated with the task itself or because of some secondary gratification that is sufficiently satisfying to supplant the therapy work.

The Therapist's Feelings

All of these guides to the therapist's recognition and understanding of process have their usefulness. But there is an even more important clue: the therapist's own feelings in the meeting, feelings that he or she has come to trust after living through many previous similar incidents in group therapy. Experienced therapists learn to trust their feelings; they are as useful to a therapist as a microscope or DNA mapping to a microbiologist. If therapists feel impatient, frustrated, bored, confused, discouraged—any of the panoply of feelings available to a human being—they should consider this valuable data and learn to put it to work.

Remember, this does not mean that therapists have to understand their feelings and arrange and deliver a neat interpretive corsage. The simple expression of feelings is often sufficient to help a client proceed further.

> • *One therapist experienced a forty-five-year-old woman in an unreal, puzzling manner because of her rapidly fluctuating method of presenting herself. He finally commented, "Sharon, I have several feelings about you that I'd like to share. As you talk, I often experience you as a competent mature woman, but sometimes I see you as a very young, almost preadolescent child, unaware of your sexuality, trying to cuddle, trying to be pleasing to everyone. I don't think I can go any farther with this now, but I wonder whether this has meaning for you." The observation struck deep chords in the client and helped her explore her conflicted sexual identity and her need to be loved by everyone.*

It is often very helpful to the group if you share feelings of being shut out by a member. Such a comment rarely evokes defensiveness, because it always implies that you wish to get closer to that person. It models important group therapy norms: risk taking, collaboration, and taking relationships seriously.

To express feelings in the therapeutic process, the therapist must have a reasonable degree of confidence in their appropriateness. The more you respond unrealistically to the client (on the basis of countertransference or possibly because of pressing personal emotional problems), the less helpful—in fact, the more antitherapeutic—will you be in presenting these feelings as if they were the client's problem rather than your own. You need to use the delicate instrument of your own feelings, and to do so frequently and spontaneously. *But it is of the utmost importance that this instrument be as reliable and accurate as possible.*

Countertransference refers broadly to the reactions therapists have to their clients. It is critically important to distinguish between your *objective* countertransference, reflecting on the client's characteristic interpersonal impact on you and others, and your *subjective* countertransference—those idiosyncratic reactions that reflect more specifically on what you, personally, carry into your relationships or interactions.[16] The former is an excellent source of interpersonal data about the client. The latter, however, says a good deal more about the therapist. To discriminate between the two requires not only experience and training but also deep self-knowledge. *It is for this reason that I believe every therapist should obtain personal psychotherapy.* (More about this in chapter 17.)

HELPING CLIENTS ASSUME A PROCESS ORIENTATION

It has long been known that observations, viewpoints, and insights arrived at through one's own efforts are valued more highly than those that are thrust upon one by another person. The mature leader resists the temptation to make brilliant virtuoso interpretations, but searches instead for methods that will permit clients to achieve self-knowledge through their own efforts. As Foulkes and Anthony put it, "There are times when the therapist must sit on his wisdom, must tolerate defective knowledge and wait for the group to arrive at solutions."[17]

The task, then, is to influence members to assume and to value the process perspective. Many of the norm-setting activities of the leader described in chapter 5 serve this end. For example, the therapist emphasizes process by periodically tugging the members out of the here-and-now and inviting them to consider more dispassionately the meaning of recent transactions. Though techniques vary depending on a therapist's style, the intention of these interventions is to switch on a self-reflective beacon. The therapist may, for example, interrupt the group at an appropriate point to comment, in effect, "We are about halfway through our time for today, and I wonder how everyone feels about the meeting thus far?" Again, by no means do you have to understand the process to ask for members' analyses. You might simply say, "I'm not sure what's happening in the meeting, but I do see some unusual things. For example, Bill has been unusually silent, Jack's moved his chair back three feet, Mary's been shooting glances at me for the past several minutes. What ideas do you all have about what's going on today?"

A process review of a highly charged meeting is often necessary. It is important for the therapist to demonstrate that intense emotional expression provides material for significant learning. Sometimes you can divide such a meeting into two parts: the experiential segment and the analysis of that experience. At other times you may analyze the process at the following meeting; you can ask about the feelings that members took home with them after the previous meeting, or simply solicit further thoughts they have since had about what occurred there.

Obviously, you teach through modeling your own process orientation. There is nothing to lose and much to gain by your sharing your perspective on the group whenever possible. Sometimes you may do this in an effort to clarify the meeting: "Here are some of the things I've seen going on today." Sometimes you may wish to use a convenient device such as summarizing the meeting to a late arrival, whether co-therapist or member. One technique I use that systematically shares my process observations with members is to write a detailed summary of the meeting afterward, including a full description of my spoken and unspoken process observations, and mail it to the members before the next meeting (see chapter 14). With this approach the therapist uses considerable personal and professional disclosure in a way that facilitates the therapy work, particularly by increasing the members' perceptivity to the process of the group.

It is useful to encourage members to describe their views on the process of group meetings. Many group therapy instructors who teach by leading an experiential group of their students often begin each meeting with a report, prepared by some designated student, of the process of the previous meeting. Some therapists learn to call upon certain members who display unusual intuitive ability to recognize process. For example, Ormont describes a marginal member in his group who had unusual sensitivity to the body language of others. The therapist made a point of harnessing that talent for the service of therapy. A question such as: "Michael, what was Pam saying to Abner with that wave of her hand?" served a double purpose: illumination of process and helping Michael gain centrality and respect.[18]

HELPING CLIENTS ACCEPT
PROCESS-ILLUMINATING COMMENTS

F. Scott Fitzgerald once wrote, "I was impelled to think. God, was it difficult! The moving about of great secret trunks." Throughout therapy, we ask our clients to think, to shift internal arrangements, to examine the consequences of their behavior. It is hard work, and it is often unpleasant, frightening work. It is not enough simply to provide clients with information or explanations; you must also facilitate the assimilation of the new information. There are strategies to help clients in this work.

Be concerned with the framing of interpretive remarks and feedback. No comments, not even the most brilliant ones, can be of value if their delivery is not accepted, if the client rejects the package unopened and uninspected. The relationship, the style of delivery, and the timing are thus as essential as the content of the message.

Clients are *always* more receptive to observations that are framed in a supportive fashion. Rarely do individuals reject an observation that they distance or shut out others, or that they are too unselfish and never ask for anything for themselves, or that they are stingy with their feelings, or that they conceal much of what they have to offer. All of these observations contain a supportive message: that the member has much to give and that the observer wishes to be closer, wishes to help, wishes to know the other more intimately.

Beware of appellations that are categorizing or limiting: they are counterproductive; they threaten; they raise defenses. Clients reject global accusations—for example, dependency, narcissism, exploitation, arrogance—and with good reason, since a person is always more than any one or any combination of labels. It is far more acceptable (and true) to speak of traits or parts of an individual—for example, "I often can sense you very much wanting to be close to others, offering help as you did last week to Debbie. But there are other times, like today, when I see you as aloof, almost scornful of the others. What do you know about this part of you?"

Often in the midst of intense group conflict, members hurl important truths at one another. Under these conditions, one cannot acknowledge the truth: it would be aiding the aggressor, committing treason against oneself. To make the conflict-spawned truths available for consumption, the therapist must appreciate and neutralize the defensiveness of the combatants.

You may, for example, appeal to a higher power (the member's desire for self-knowledge) or increase receptivity by limiting the scope of the accusation. For example, "Farrell, I see you now closed up, threatened, and fending off everything that Jamie is saying. You've been very adroit in pointing out the weaknesses of her arguments, but what happens is that you (and Jamie, too) end up getting nothing for yourself. I wonder if you could take a different tack for a while and ask yourself this (and, later: Jamie, I'd like to ask you to do the same): Is there *anything* in what Jamie is saying that is true for you? What parts seem to strike an inner chord? Could you forget for a moment the things that are not true and stay with those that *are* true?"

Sometimes group members, in an unusually open moment, make a statement that may at some future time provide the therapist with great leverage. The thrifty therapist underscores these comments in the group and stores them for later use. For example, one man who was both proud of and troubled by his ability to manipulate the group with his social charm, pleaded at one meeting, "Listen, when you see me smile like this,

I'm really hurting inside. Don't let me keep getting away with it." Another member, who tyrannized the group with her tears, announced one day, "When I cry like this, I'm angry. I'm not going to fall apart, so stop comforting me, stop treating me like a child." Store these moments of truth; they can be of great value if recalled later, in a constructive, supportive manner, when the client is closed and defensive. In the previous example, you could simply remind the member of her comment a few meetings ago and ask whether this (the smiling to cover the pain or the self protective crying) is happening now.

Often it is useful to enlist the client more actively in establishing contracts. For example, if a client has worked hard in a session on some important trait, I might say something like: "Jane, you worked hard today and were very open to our feedback about the way you mother others and the way you use that mothering to avoid facing your own needs and pain. How did it feel? Did we push you too hard?" If the client agrees that the work was helpful (as the client almost always does), then it is possible to nail down a future contract by asking, "Then is it all right for us to keep pressing you, to give you feedback whenever we note you doing this in future meetings?" This form of "contracting" consolidates the therapeutic alliance and the mutual, collaborative nature of the psychotherapy.[19]

PROCESS COMMENTARY:
A THEORETICAL OVERVIEW

It is not easy to discuss, in a systematic way, the actual practice of process illumination. How can one propose crisp, basic guidelines for a procedure of such complexity and range, such delicate timing, so many linguistic nuances? I am tempted to beg the question by claiming that herein lies the art of psychotherapy: it will come as you gain experience; you cannot, in a systematic way, come to it. To a degree, I believe this to be so. Yet I also believe that it is possible to blaze crude trails, to provide the clinician with general principles that will accelerate education without limiting the scope of artistry.

The approach I take in this section closely parallels the approach I used in the beginning of this book to clarify the basic therapeutic factors in group therapy. At that time I asked the questions: "How does group therapy help clients? In the group therapeutic process, what is core and what is front?" This approach leads to the delineation of several basic therapeutic factors and does not, I believe, constrain the therapist in any way in the choice of methods to implement them.

In this section I proceed in a similar fashion. Here the issue is not how group therapy helps but how process illumination leads to change. The issue is complex and requires considerable attention, but the length of this discussion should not suggest that the interpretive function of the therapist take precedence over other tasks.

First, let me proceed to view in a dispassionate manner the entire range of therapist interventions. I ask of each intervention the simplistic but basic question, "How does this intervention, this process-illuminating comment, help a client to change?" Underlying this approach, is a set of basic operational patterns shared by all contemporary interpersonal models of therapy.[20]

I begin by considering a series of process comments that a therapist made to a male client over several sessions of group therapy:

1. You are interrupting me.
2. Your voice is tight, and your fists are clenched.
3. Whenever you talk to me, you take issue with me.
4. When you do that, I feel threatened and sometimes frightened.
5. I wonder if you don't feel competitive with me and are trying to devalue me.
6. I've noticed that you've done the same thing with all the men in the group. Even when they try to approach you helpfully, you strike out at them. Consequently, they see you as hostile and threatening.
7. In the three meetings when there were no women present in the group, you were more approachable.
8. I think you're so concerned about your sexual attractiveness to women that you view men only as competitors and deprive yourself of the opportunity of ever getting close to a man.
9. Even though you always seem to spar with me, there seems to be another side to it. You often stay after the group to have a word with me; you frequently look at me in the group. And there's that dream you described three weeks ago about the two of us fighting and then falling to the ground in an embrace. I think you very much want to be close to me, but somehow you've got closeness and eroticism entangled and you keep pushing me away.
10. You are lonely here and feel unwanted and uncared for. That rekindles so many of your feelings of unworthiness.
11. What's happened in the group now is that you've distanced yourself, estranged yourself, from all the men here. Are you satisfied with that? (Remember that one of your major goals when you started the group was to find out why you haven't had any close men friends and to do something about that.)

Note, first of all, that the comments form a progression: they start with simple observations of single acts and proceed to a description of feelings evoked by an act, to observations about several acts over a period of time, to the juxtaposition of different acts, to speculations about the client's intentions and motivations, to comments about the unfortunate repercussions of his behavior, to the inclusion of more inferential data (dreams, subtle gestures), to calling attention to the similarity between the client's behavioral patterns in the here-and-now and in his outside social world. Inexperienced group therapists sometimes feel lost because they have not yet developed an awareness of this progressive sequence of interventions.[21]

In this progression, the comments become more inferential. They begin with sense-data observations and gradually shift to complex generalizations based on sequences of behavior, interpersonal patterns, fantasy, and dream material. As the comments become more complex and more inferential, their author becomes more removed from the other person—in short, more a therapist process-commentator. Members often make some of the earlier statements to one another but, for reasons I have already presented, rarely make the ones at the end of the sequence.

There is, incidentally, an exceptionally sharp barrier between comments 4 and 5. The first four statements issue from the experience of the commentator. They are the commentator's observations and feelings; the client can devalue or ignore them but cannot deny them, disagree with them, or take them away from the commentator. The fifth statement ("I wonder if you don't feel competitive with me and are trying to devalue me") is much more likely to evoke defensiveness and to close down constructive interactional flow. This genre of comment is intrusive; it is a guess about the other's intention and motivation and is often rejected unless an important trusting, supportive relationship has been previously established. If members in a young group make many comments of this type to one another, they are not likely to develop a constructive therapeutic climate.[22] Using the phrase "I wonder" of course softens it a bit. Where would we therapists be without the use of "I wonder?"

But back to our basic question: how does this series (or any series of process comments) help the client change? The answer is that the group therapist initiates change by escorting the client through the following sequence:

1. *Here is what your behavior is like.* Through feedback and later through self-observation, members learn to see themselves as seen by others.
2. *Here is how your behavior makes others feel.* Members learn about the impact of their behavior on the feelings of other members.
3. *Here is how your behavior influences the opinions others have of you.* Members learn that, as a result of their behavior, others value

them, dislike them, find them unpleasant, respect them, avoid them, and so on.

4. *Here is how your behavior influences your opinion of yourself.* Building on the information gathered in the first three steps, clients formulate self-evaluations; they make judgments about their self-worth and their lovability. (Recall Sullivan's aphorism that the self-concept is largely constructed from reflected self-appraisals.)

Once this sequence has been developed and is fully understood by the individual, once clients have a deep understanding that their behavior is not in their own best interests, that the texture of relationships to others and to themselves is *fashioned by their own actions*, then they have come to a crucial point in therapy: they have entered the antechamber of change.

The therapist is now in a position to pose a question that initiates the real crunch of therapy. The question, presented in a number of ways by the therapist but rarely in direct form, is: *Are you satisfied with the world you have created?* This is what you do to others, to others' opinion of you, and to your opinion of yourself—are you satisfied with your actions?*[23]

When the inevitable negative answer arrives ("No I am not satisfied with my actions") the therapist embarks on a many-layered effort to transform a sense of personal dissatisfaction into a decision to change and then into the act of change. In one way or another, the therapist's interpretive remarks are designed to encourage the act of change. Only a few psychotherapy theoreticians (for example, Otto Rank, Rollo May, Silvano Arieti, Leslie Farber, Allen Wheelis, and Irvin Yalom[24]) include the concept of will in their formulations, yet it is, I believe, implicit in most interpretive systems. I offer a detailed discussion of the role of will in psychotherapy in my text *Existential Psychotherapy.*[25] For now, broad brush strokes are sufficient.

The intrapsychic agency that initiates an act, that transforms intention and decision into action, is will. Will is the primary responsible mover within the individual. Although analytic metapsychology has chosen to emphasize the irresponsible movers of our behavior (that is, unconscious motivations and drives), it is difficult to do without the idea of will in our understanding of change.[26] We cannot bypass it under the assumption that it is too nebulous and too elusive and, consequently, consign it to the black box of the mental apparatus, to which the therapist has no access.

---

*A well-conducted multisite psychotherapy trial with over 700 clients with chronic depression clearly demonstrated the importance of therapeutic approaches that help clients develop interpersonal effectiveness and reclaim personal responsibility and accountability for their interpersonal actions. A key principle of this model of psychotherapy, cognitive behavioral analysis system psychotherapy (CBASP), is that chronic depression is directly correlated with the depressed client's loss of a sense of "cause and effect" in his or her personal world.

Knowingly or unknowingly, every therapist assumes that each client possesses the capacity to change through willful choice. Using a variety of strategies and tactics, the therapist attempts to escort the client to a crossroads where he or she can choose, willfully, in the best interests of his or her own integrity. The therapist's task is not to create will or to infuse it into the client. That, of course, you cannot do. *What you can do is to help remove encumbrances from the bound or stifled will of the client.*[27]

The concept of will provides a useful construct for understanding the procedure of process illumination. The interpretive remarks of the therapist can all be viewed in terms of how they bear on the client's will. The most common and simplistic therapeutic approach is *exhortative*: "Your behavior is, as you yourself now know, counter to your best interests. You are not satisfied. This is not what you want for yourself. Damn it, change!"

The expectation that the client will change is simply an extension of the moral philosophical belief that if one knows the good (that is, what is, in the deepest sense, in one's best interest), one will act accordingly. In the words of St. Thomas Aquinas: "Man, insofar as he acts willfully, acts according to some imagined good."[28] And, indeed, for some individuals this knowledge and this exhortation are sufficient to produce therapeutic change.

However, clients with significant and well-entrenched psychopathology will need much more than sheer exhortation. The therapist, through interpretative comments, then proceeds to exercise one of several other options that help clients disencumber their will. The therapist's goal is to guide clients to a point where they accept one, several, or all of the following basic premises:

1. Only I can change the world I have created for myself.
2. There is no danger in change.
3. To attain what I really want, I must change.
4. I can change; I am potent.

Each of these premises, if fully accepted by a client, can be a powerful stimulant to willful action. Each exerts its influence in a different way. Though I will discuss each in turn, I do not wish to imply a sequential pattern. Each, depending on the need of the client and the style of the therapist, may be effective independently of the others.

"Only I can change the world I have created for myself."

Behind the simple group therapy sequence I have described (seeing one's own behavior and appreciating its impact on others and on oneself), there is a mighty overarching concept, one whose shadow touches every part of the therapeutic process. That concept is *responsibility*. Although it is rarely discussed explicitly, it is woven into the fabric of most psychotherapeutic systems. Responsibility has many meanings—legal, religious, ethical. I use it in the sense that a person is "responsible for" by being the "basis of," the "cause of," the "author of" something.

One of the most fascinating aspects of group therapy is that *everyone is born again, born together in the group*. In other words, each member starts off on an equal footing. In the view of the others (and, if the therapist does a good job, in the view of oneself), each gradually scoops out and shapes a life space in the group. Each member, in the deepest sense of the concept, is *responsible for this space and for the sequence of events that will occur to him or her in the group*.

The client, having truly come to appreciate this responsibility, must then accept, too, that there is no hope for change *unless he or she changes*. Others cannot bring change, nor can change bring itself. One is responsible for one's past and present life in the group (as well as in the outside world) and totally responsible for one's future.

Thus, the therapist helps the client understand that the interpersonal world is arranged in a generally predictable and orderly fashion, that it is not that the client *cannot* change but that he or she *will not* change, that the client bears the responsibility for the creation of his or her world and therefore the responsibility for its transmutation. The client must regain or develop anew a sense of his or her own interpersonal agency in the world.

"There is no danger in change."

These well-intentioned efforts may not be enough. The therapist may tug and tug at the therapeutic cord and learn that individuals, even after being thus enlightened, still make no significant therapeutic movement. In this case, therapists apply additional therapeutic leverage by helping clients face the paradox of continuing to act contrary to their basic interests. In a number of ways therapists must pose the question, "How come? Why do you continue to defeat yourself?"

A common method of explaining "How come?" is to assume that there are formidable obstacles to the client's exercising willful choice, obstacles that prevent clients from seriously considering altering their behavior. The presence of the obstacle is generally inferred; the therapist makes an "as if" assumption: "You behave *as if* you feel some considerable danger would befall you if you were to change. You fear to act otherwise for fear that some calamity will befall you." The therapist helps the client clarify the nature of the imagined danger and then proceeds, in several ways, to detoxify, to disconfirm the reality of this danger.

The client's reason may be enlisted as an ally. The process of identifying and naming the fantasized danger may, in itself, enable one to understand how far removed one's fears are from reality. Another approach is to encourage the client, in carefully calibrated doses, *to commit the dreaded act in the group*. The fantasized calamity does not, of course, ensue, and the dread is gradually extinguished. This is often the pivotal piece of effective therapy. Change is probably not possible, let alone enduring, without the client's having a lived experience of direct disconfirmation of pathogenic beliefs. Insight alone is unlikely to be effective. This principle cuts powerfully across different schools of therapy.†

For example, suppose a client avoids any aggressive behavior because at a deep level he fears that he has a dammed-up reservoir of homicidal fury and must be constantly vigilant lest he unleash it and eventually face retribution from others. An appropriate therapeutic strategy is to help the client express aggression in *small doses* in the group: pique at being interrupted, irritation at members who are habitually late, anger at the therapist for charging him money, and so on. Gradually, the client is helped to relate openly to the other members and to demythologize himself as a homicidal being. Although the language and the view of human nature are different, this is precisely the same approach to change used in systematic desensitization—a major technique of behavior therapy.

"To attain what I really want, I must change."

Another explanatory approach used by many therapists to deal with a client who persists in behaving counter to his or her best interests is to consider the *payoffs* of that individual's behavior. Although the person's behavior sabotages many of his or her mature needs and goals, at the same time *it satisfies another set of needs and goals*. In other words, the client has conflicting motivations that cannot be simultaneously satisfied. For example, a male client may wish to establish mature heterosexual relationships; but at another, often unconscious, level, he may wish to be nurtured, to be cradled endlessly, to avoid the abandonment that he anticipates as the punishment for his adult strivings or, to use an existential vocabulary, to be sheltered from the terrifying freedom of adulthood. Obviously, the client cannot satisfy both sets of wishes: he cannot establish an adult heterosexual relationship with a woman if he also says (and much more loudly), "Take care of me, protect me, nurse me, let me be a part of you."

It is important to clarify this paradox for the client. We might, for example, point out: "Your behavior makes sense if we assume that you wish to satisfy the deeper, earlier, more primitive need." We try to help the client understand the nature of his conflicting desires, to choose between them, to relinquish those that cannot be fulfilled except at enormous cost to his integrity and autonomy. Once the client realizes what he really wants (as an adult) and that his behavior is designed to fulfill opposing growth-retarding needs, he gradually concludes: *To attain what I really want, I must change.*

"I can change; I am potent."

Perhaps the major therapeutic approach to the question "How come you act in ways counter to your best interests?" is to offer *explanation*. The therapist says, in effect, "You behave in certain fashions *because* . . . ," and the "because" clause generally involves motivational factors outside the client's awareness. It is true that the previous two options I have discussed also proffer explanation but—and I will clarify this shortly—the purpose of the explanation (the nature of the leverage exerted on will) is quite different in the two approaches.

What *type* of explanation does the therapist offer the client? And which explanations are correct, and which incorrect? Which "deep"? Which "superficial"? It is at this juncture that the great metapsychological controversies of the field arise, since the nature of therapists' explanations are a function of the ideological school to which they belong.

I think we can sidestep the ideological struggle by keeping a fixed gaze on the *function* of the interpretation, on the relationship between explanation and the final product: change. After all, our goal is change. Self-knowledge, derepression, analysis of transference, and self-actualization—all are worthwhile, enlightened pursuits, all are related to change, preludes to change, cousins and companions to change; and yet they are not synonymous with change.

Explanation provides a system by which we can order the events in our lives into some coherent and predictable pattern. To name something and to place it into a causal sequence is to experience it as being under our control. No longer is our behavior or our internal experience frightening, inchoate, out of control; instead, we behave (or have a particular inner experience) *because* . . . . The "because" offers us mastery (or a sense of mastery that, phenomenologically, is tantamount to mastery). It offers us freedom and self-efficacy.† As we move from a position of being motivated by unknown forces to a position of identifying and controlling those forces, we move from a passive, reactive posture to an active, acting, changing posture.

If we accept this basic premise—that a major function of explanation in psychotherapy is to provide the client with a sense of personal mastery—it follows that the value of an explanation should be measured by this criterion. To the extent that it offers a sense of potency, a causal explanation is valid, correct, or "true." Such a definition of truth is completely relativistic and pragmatic. It argues that no explanatory system has hegemony or exclusive rights, that no system is the correct, fundamental one or the "deeper" (and therefore better) one.

Therapists may offer the client any of several interpretations to clarify the same issue; each may be made from a different frame of reference, and each may be "true." Freudian, interpersonal, object relations, self psychology, attachment theory, existential, transactional analytic, Jungian, gestalt, transpersonal, cognitive, behavioral explanations—all of these may be true simultaneously. None, despite vehement claims to the contrary, have sole rights to the truth. After all, they are all based on imaginary, *as if* structures. They all say, "You are behaving (or feeling) *as if* such and such a thing were true." The superego, the id, the ego; the archetypes; the masculine protest; the internalized objects; the selfobject; the grandiose self and the omnipotent object; the parent, child, and adult ego state—*none of these really exists*. They are all fictions, all psychological constructs created for semantic convenience. *They justify their existence only by virtue of their explanatory powers*.[29]

Do we therefore abandon our attempts to make precise, thoughtful interpretations? Not at all. We only recognize the purpose and function of the interpretation. Some may be superior to others, not because they are deeper but because they have more explanatory power, are more credible, provide more mastery, and are therefore more useful. Obviously, interpretations must be tailored to the recipient. In general, therapeutic interventions are more effective if they make sense, if they are logically consistent with sound supporting arguments, if they are bolstered by empirical observation, if they "feel" right or are congruent and "click" with a client's frame of reference and internal world, and if they can be generalized and applied to many analogous situations in the client's life.

Higher-order interpretations generally offer a novel explanation to the client for some large pattern of behavior (as opposed to a single trait or act). The novelty of the therapist's explanation stems from his or her objective vantage point and unusual frame of reference, which permits an original synthesis of data. Indeed, often the data is material that the client has generally overlooked or that is outside his or her awareness.

If pushed, to what extent am I willing to defend this relativistic thesis? When I present this position to students, they respond with such questions as: Does that mean that an astrological explanation is also valid in psychotherapy? Such questions make me uneasy, but I have to respond affirmatively. If an astrological or shamanistic or magical explanation enhances a sense of mastery and leads to inner, personal change, then it is a valid explanation. There is much evidence from cross-cultural psychiatric research to support this position; the explanation must be consistent with the values and with the frame of reference of the human community in which the client dwells. In most primitive cultures, it is often *only* the magical or the religious explanation that is acceptable, and hence valid and effective.[30]

Psychoanalytic revisionists make an analogous point and argue that reconstructive attempts to capture historical "truth" are futile; it is far more important to the process of change to construct plausible, meaningful, personal narratives.[31] The past is not static: every experienced therapist knows that the process of exploration and understanding alters the recollection of the past. In fact, current neurobiological research tells us that every time we access an old memory we automatically alter it according to our current context, and the revised memory is then returned to long-term storage in place of the original memory.[32]

An interpretation, even the most elegant one, has no benefit if the client does not hear it. Therapists should take pains to review their evidence with the client and present the explanation clearly. (Be clear: if you cannot be crystal-clear, it is likely that the explanation is rickety or that you yourself do not understand it. The reason is not, as often has been claimed, that you are speaking directly to the client's unconscious.)

Do not always expect the client to accept an interpretation. Sometimes the client hears the same interpretation many times until one day it seems to "click." Why does it click that one day? Perhaps the client just came across some corroborating data from new events in the environment or from the surfacing in fantasy or dreams of some previously unconscious material. Note also that *the interpretation will not click until the client's relationship with the therapist is just right*. For example, a group member who feels threatened and competitive with the therapist is unlikely to be helped by any interpretation (except one that clarifies the transference). Even the most thoughtful interpretation will fail because the client may feel defeated or humiliated by the proof of the therapist's superior perceptivity. An interpretation becomes maximally effective only when it is delivered in a context of acceptance and trust.

Sometimes a client will accept from another member an interpretation that he or she would not accept from the therapist. (Remember, group members are entirely capable of making interpretations as useful as those of the therapists, and members will be receptive to these interpretations *provided the other member has accepted the client role and does not offer interpretations to acquire prestige, power, or a favored position with the leader.*)

A comprehensive discussion of the types of effective interpretations would require describing the vast number of explanatory schools and group therapy models—a task well beyond the scope of this book.[33]

However, three venerable concepts are so deeply associated with interpretation that they deserve coverage here:

1. The use of the past
2. Group-as-a-whole process commentary
3. Transference

I will discuss the first two in the remainder of this chapter. So many interpretative systems involve transference (indeed, traditional analytic theory decrees that *only* the transference interpretation can be effective) that I have devoted the next chapter entirely to the issue of transference and transparency.

THE USE OF THE PAST

Too often, explanation is confused with "originology" (the study of origins). Although, as I have discussed, an explanatory system may effectively postulate a "cause" of behavior from any of a large number of perspectives, many therapists continue to believe that the "real," the "deepest," causes of behavior are only to be found in the past. This position was staunchly defended by Freud, a committed psychosocial archaeologist. To the very end of his life, he relinquished neither his search for the primordial (that is, the earliest) explanation nor his tenacious insistence that successful therapy hinges on the excavation of the earliest layers of life's memories. The idea that the *present* is only a small fraction of the individual's life and that contemporary life is shaped by the overwhelmingly large contributions made by the past is powerfully embedded in the Western world's view of time.[34] This view understandably results in an emphasis on the past in traditional psychodynamic textbooks[35] of group therapy.

However, the powerful and unconscious factors that influence human behavior are *by no means* limited to the past. Current analytic theory makes a distinction between the *past unconscious* (the child within the adult) and the *present unconscious* (the currently existing unconscious thoughts, fantasies, and impulses that influence our feelings and actions).[36] Furthermore, as I shall discuss, the future, as well as the past and the present, is also a significant determinant of behavior.

The past may affect our behavior through pathways fully described by traditional psychoanalytic theorists and by learning theorists (strange bedfellows). However, the "not yet," the future, is a no less powerful determinant of behavior, and the concept of future determinism is fully defensible. We have at all times within us a sense of purpose, an idealized self, a series of goals for which we strive, a death toward which we veer.

These factors, both conscious and unconscious, all arch into the future and profoundly influence our behavior. Certainly the knowledge of our isolation, our destiny, and our ultimate death deeply influences our conduct and our inner experience. Though we generally keep them out of awareness, the terrifying contingencies of our existence play upon us without end. We either strive to dismiss them by enveloping ourselves in life's many diversions, or we attempt to vanquish death by faith in an afterlife or by striving for symbolic immortality in the form of children, material monuments, and creative expression. In addition to the explanatory potency of the past and the future, there is a third temporal concept that attempts to explain behavior: the Galilean concept of causality, which focuses on the present—on the impact of *current forces.*

In summary, explanations ensue from the exploration of the concentric rings of conscious and unconscious current motivations that envelop our clients. Take one example: clients may have a need to attack, which covers a layer of dependency wishes that they do not express for fear of rejection. Note that *we need not ask how they got to be so dependent.* In fact, the future (a person's anticipation of rejection) plays a more central role in the interpretation. Thus, as we hurtle through space, our behavioral trajectory may be thought of as triply influenced: by the past—the nature and direction of the original push; by the future—the goal that beckons us; and by the present—the current field forces operating upon it. Consider this clinical example:

• *Two clients, Ellen and Carol, expressed strong sexual feelings toward the male therapist of the group. (Both women, incidentally, had histories—indeed, chief complaints—of masochistic sexual gratification.) At one meeting, they discussed the explicit content of their sexual fantasies about the therapist. Ellen fantasized her husband being killed; herself having a psychotic breakdown; the therapist hospitalizing her and personally nurturing her, rocking her, and caring for all her bodily needs. Carol had a different set of fantasies. She wondered whether the therapist was well cared for at home. She frequently fantasized that something happened to his wife and that she would care for him by cleaning his house and cooking his meals.*

The shared sexual attraction (which, as the fantasies indicate, was not genital-sexual) had for Ellen and Carol very different explanations. The therapist pointed out to Ellen that throughout the course of the group, she had suffered frequent physical illness or severe psychological relapses. He wondered whether, at a deep level, she felt as though she could get his love and that of the other members only by a form of self-immolation. If this was the case, however, it never worked. More often than not, she discouraged and frustrated others. Even more important was the fact that as long as she behaved in ways that caused her so much shame, she could not love herself. He emphasized that it was crucial for her to change the pattern, because it defeated her in her therapy: she was afraid to get better, since she felt that to do so would entail an inevitable loss of love and nurturance.

In his comments to Carol, the therapist juxtaposed several aspects of her behavior: her self-derogation, her refusal to assume her rights, her inability to get men interested in her. Her fantasy of taking care of the therapist was illustrative of her motivations: she believed that if she could be self-sacrificing enough, if she could put the therapist deeply into her debt, then she should, in reciprocal fashion, receive the love she sought. However, Carol's search for love, like Ellen's, always failed. Her eternal ingratiation, her dread of self-assertion, her continued self-devaluation succeeded only in making her appear dull and spiritless to those whose regard she most desired. Carol, like Ellen, whirled about in a vicious circle of her own creation: the more she failed to obtain love, the more frantically she repeated the same self-destructive pattern—the only course of behavior she knew or dared to enact. It was a neatly contained, self-reinforcing, and self-defeating cycle.

So here we have two clients with a similar behavioral pattern: "sexual" infatuation with the therapist. Yet the therapist offered two different interpretations reflecting two different dynamic pathways to psychological masochism. In each, the therapist assembled several aspects of the client's behavior in the group as well as fantasy material and suggested that, if certain "as if" assumptions were made (for example, that Ellen acted as if she could obtain the therapist's love only by offering herself as severely damaged, and that Carol acted as if she could obtain his love only by so serving him and thus place him in her debt), then the rest of the behavior "made sense."

Both interpretations were potent and had a significant impact on future behavior. Yet neither broached the question *"How did you get to be that way? What happened in your earlier life to create such a pattern?"* Both dealt instead with currently existing patterns: the desire for love, the conviction that it could be obtained only in certain ways, the sacrifice of autonomy, the resulting shame, the ensuing increased need for a sign of love, and so on.

One formidable problem with explanations based on the distant past is that they contain within them the seeds of therapeutic despair. Thus the paradox: if we are fully determined by the past, whence comes the ability to change? As is evident in such later works as *Analysis Terminable and Interminable*, Freud's uncompromising deterministic view led him to, but never through, this Gordian knot.

The past, moreover, no more determines the present and the future than it is determined by them. The past exists for each of us only as we constitute it in the present against the horizon of the future. Jerome Frank remind us that clients, even in prolonged therapy, recall only a minute fraction of their past experience and may selectively recall and synthesize the past so as to achieve consistency with their present view of themselves.[37] In the same way that a client (as a result of therapy) alters her self-image, she may reconstitute the past. She may, for example, recall long-forgotten positive experiences with parents; she may humanize them and, rather than experiencing them solipsistically (as figures who existed by virtue of their service to herself), begin to understand them as harried, well-intentioned individuals struggling with the same over-whelming facts of the human condition that she faces herself. Once she reconstitutes the past, a new past can further influence her self-appraisal; however, it is the *reconstitution*, not simply the *excavation*, of the past that is crucial. Note an allied research finding: effective therapy generates further recollection of past memories, which in turn further modify the reconstitution of the past.[38]

If explanations are not to be sought from an originological perspective, and if the most potent focus of the group is the ahistorical here-and-now, does the past therefore play no role at all in the group therapeutic process? By no means! The past is an incessant visitor to the group and an even more incessant visitor to the inner world of each of the members during the course of therapy. Not infrequently, for example, a discussion of the past plays an important role in the development of group cohesiveness by increasing intermember understanding and acceptance.

The past is often invaluable in conflict resolution. Consider, for exam-ple, two members locked in a seemingly irreconcilable struggle, each of whom finds many aspects of the other repugnant. Often a full under-standing of the developmental route whereby each arrived at his or her particular viewpoint can rehumanize the struggle. A man with a regal air of hauteur and condescension may suddenly seem understandable, even winsome, when we learn of his immigrant parents and his desperate struggle to transcend the degradation of a slum childhood. Individuals benefit through being fully known by others in the group and being fully accepted; knowing another's process of becoming is a rich and often in-dispensable adjunct to knowing the person.

An ahistorical here-and-now interactional focus is never fully attain-able. Discussions of future anticipations, both feared and desired, and of past and current experiences, are an inextricable part of human discourse. What is important in group therapy is the *accent*; the past is the servant, not the master. It is important in that it explicates the current reality of the client, who is in the process of unfolding in relation to the other group members. As Rycroft states, "It makes better sense to say that the analyst makes excursions into historical research in order to understand something which is interfering with his present communication with the patient (in the same way that a translator might turn to history to elucidate an obscure text) than to say that he makes contact with the patient in order to gain access to biographical data."[39]

To employ the past in this manner involves an anamnestic technique differing from that often employed in individual therapy. Rather than a careful global historical survey, group therapists periodically attempt a sector analysis in which they explore the development of some particular interpersonal stance. Consequently, many other aspects of a client's past remain undiscussed in group therapy. It is not uncommon, for example, for group therapists to conclude a course of successful therapy with a client and yet be unfamiliar with many significant aspects of the individual's early life.

The lack of explicit discussion of the past in the ongoing therapy group does not accurately reflect the consideration of the past occurring *within* each client during therapy. The intensive focus on the here-and-now does not, of course, have as its final goal the formation of enduring relationships among group members. That is a way station, it is *a dress rehearsal* for the work that must be done with family and friends—the truly important individuals in a client's life.

At the end of therapy, clients commonly report significant attitudinal improvements in relationships that have rarely been explicitly discussed in the group. Many of these involve family members with whom one has had a relationship stretching far back into the past. Many clients, in fact, change their feelings about family members who are long dead. So the past plays a role in the working-through process, and the therapist should be aware of this silent, important homework. Yet it is an implicit role. To make repetitive use of the group meeting for explicit discussion of the past would sacrifice the therapeutic potency of the here-and-now interactional focus.

GROUP-AS-A-WHOLE PROCESS COMMENTARY

Some group leaders choose to focus heavily on group-as-a-whole phenomena. In their comments, these leaders frequently refer to the "group" or "we" or "all of us." They attempt to clarify the relationship between the group and its primary task, or between the group and the leader or one of its members, a subgroup, or some shared concern. Recall, for a moment, the "parenthood is degrading" incident described earlier in this chapter. In that incident the therapist had many process commentary options, some of which were group-as-a-whole explanations. He might, for example, have raised the issue of whether the "group" needed a scapegoat and whether, with Kate gone, Burt filled the scapegoat role; or whether the "group" was actively avoiding an important issue—that is, their guilty pleasure and fears about Kate's departure.

Throughout this text I weave in comments related to group-as-a-whole phenomena: for example, norm setting, the role of the deviant, scapegoating, emotional contagion, role suction, subgroup formation, group cohesiveness, group pressure, the regressive dependency fostered by group membership, the group's response to termination, to the addition of new members, to the absence of the leader, and so on. In addition to these common group phenomena, earlier editions of this book described some comprehensive group-as-a-whole approaches, particularly the work of Wilfred Bion, which offers an elaborate description of the psychology of groups and the unconscious forces that obstruct effective group functioning.[40] His approach, also known as the Tavistock approach, persists as a useful model for understanding group-as-a-whole dynamics. Its emphasis, however, on an inscrutable, detached, leader who serves as "conductor" of the group and limits his participation solely to group-as-a-whole interpretations has resulted in the abandonment of the Tavistock approach for group psychotherapy. Tavistock conferences, however, are still used as an educational vehicle to inform participants about the nature of group forces, leadership, and authority. (See www.yalom.com for fourth edition discussion of Bion's contributions.)

There is little question of the importance of group-as-a-whole phenomena. All group leaders would agree that inherent forces in a group significantly influence behavior; individuals behave differently in a group than they do in dyads (a factor that, as I will discuss in chapter 9, confounds the selection of group therapy members). There is wide agreement that an individual's behavior cannot be fully understood without an appreciation of his or her social and environmental context. But there remains the question of how best to apply this knowledge in the course of the therapy group. Examining the rationale of group-as-a-whole commentary provides some guidelines.

Rationale of Group-as-a-Whole Process Commentary

Group-as-a-whole phenomena influence the clinical course of the group in two significant ways: they can act in the service of the group, and they can impede effective group therapy.

Group-as-a-whole forces acting in the service of therapy. I have, throughout this text, already considered many therapeutic uses of group-as-a-whole phenomena: for example, many of the major therapeutic factors, such as cohesiveness—the esprit de corps of the entire group—obviously relate to group-as-a-whole properties, and therapists are, in fact, harnessing group-as-a-whole forces when they facilitate the development of cohesiveness. However, *it does not follow that the leader must make explicit group-as-a-whole comments.*

Group-as-a-whole forces impeding therapy. There are times when group-as-a-whole processes significantly impede therapy, and then commentary is necessary. In other words, *the purpose of a group-as-a-whole interpretation is to remove some obstacle that has arisen to obstruct the progress of the entire group.*[41] The two common types of obstacle are *anxiety-laden issues and antitherapeutic group norms.*

Anxiety-Laden Issues

Often some issue arises in the group that is so threatening that the members refuse to confront the problem and take some evasive action. This evasion takes many forms, all of which are commonly referred to as *group flight*—a regression from the group's normal functions. Here is a clinical example of flight from an anxiety-laden issue:

> • *Six members were present at the twenty-fifth group meeting; one member, John, was absent. For the first time, and without previous mention, one of the members, Mary, brought her dog to the meeting. The group members, usually animated and active, were unusually subdued and nonproductive. Their speech was barely audible, and throughout the meeting they discussed safe topics on a level of impersonality appropriate to a large social gathering or cocktail party. Much of the content centered on study habits (three of the members were graduate students), examinations, and teachers (especially their untrustworthiness and defects). Moreover, the senior member of the group discussed former members who had long since departed from the group—the "good old days" phenomenon. Mary's dog (a wretched, restless creature who spent most of the group session noisily licking its genitals) was never mentioned.*
>
> *Finally, the therapist, thinking he was speaking for all the group members, brought up the issue of Mary's having brought her dog to the meeting. Much to the therapist's surprise, Mary—a highly unpopular, narcissistic member—was unanimously defended. Everyone denied that the dog was in any way distracting, leaving the protesting therapist dangling in the wind.*

The therapist considered the entire meeting as a "flight" meeting and, accordingly, made appropriate group-as-a-whole interpretations, which I will discuss shortly. But first, what is the evidence that such a meeting is in flight? And flight from what? First, consider the age of the group. In a young group, meeting, say, for the third time—such a session may be a manifestation not of resistance but of the group members' uncertainty about their primary task and of their groping to establish procedural norms. However, this group had already met for many months and had consistently operated at a more mature level.

It becomes very evident that the group was in a flight mode when we examine the preceding group meeting. At that meeting, John, the member absent from the meeting under consideration, had been twenty minutes late and happened to walk down the corridor at the precise moment when a student opened the door of the adjoining observation room in order to enter it. For the few seconds while the door was open, John heard the voices of the other group members and saw a room full of observers viewing the group; moreover, the observers at that moment happened to be giggling at some private joke. John, like all the group members, had of course been told that the group was being observed by students. Nevertheless, this shocking and irreverent confirmation stunned him. When John, in the last moments of the meeting, was finally able to discuss it with the other members, they were equally stunned. John, as I mentioned, did not show up for the next session.

This event was a catastrophe of major proportions for the entire group—as it would be for any group. It raised serious questions in the minds of the members. Was the therapist to be trusted? Was he, like his colleagues in the observation room, inwardly giggling at them? Was anything he said genuine? Was the group, once perceived as a deeply human encounter, in fact a sterile, contrived, laboratory specimen being studied dispassionately by a therapist who probably felt closer allegiance to "them" (the others, the observers) than to the group members?

Despite—or, rather, *because* of—the magnitude of these painful group issues, the group declined to confront the matter. Instead, it engaged in flight behavior, which now begins to be understandable. Exposed to an outside threat, the group members banded tightly together for protection. They spoke softly about safe topics so as to avoid sharing anything with the outside menace (the observers and, through association, the therapist). The therapist was unsupported when he asked about the obviously distracting behavior of Mary's dog. The "good old days" was a reference to and yearning for those bygone times when the group was pure and verdant and the therapist could be trusted. The discussion of examinations and untrustworthy teachers was also a thinly veiled expression of attitudes toward the therapist.

The precise nature and timing of the intervention is largely a matter of individual style. Some therapists, myself included, tend to intervene when they sense the presence of group flight even though they do not clearly understand its source. I may, for example, comment that I feel puzzled or uneasy about the meeting and inquire, "Is there something the group is not talking about today?" or "Is the group avoiding something?" or "I have a sense there's a 'hidden agenda' today; could we talk about this?"

I may increase the power of my inquiry by citing the evidence for such a conclusion—for example, the whispering, the shift toward neutral topics and a noninteractive, impersonal mode of communication, my experience of being left out or of being deserted by the others when I mentioned the obvious distraction of the dog. Furthermore, I might add that the group is strangely avoiding all discussion both of the previous meeting and of John's absence today. In one way or another, however, the problems of the group as a whole must be addressed before any meaningful interpersonal work can resume.

In this clinical example, would we be satisfied merely with getting the group back on the track of discussing more meaningful personal material? No! More is needed: the issues being avoided were too crucial to the group's existence to be left submerged. This consideration was particularly relevant in this group, whose members had insufficiently explored their relationship to me. Therefore, I repeatedly turned the group's attention back to the main issue (their trust and confidence in me) and tried not to be misled by substitute behavior—for example, the group's offering another theme for discussion, perhaps even a somewhat charged one. My task was not simply to circumvent the resistance, to redirect the group to work areas, but to plunge the members into the source of the resistance—in other words, not *around* anxiety, but *through* it.

Another clue to the presence and strength of resistance is the group's response to therapists' resistance-piercing commentary. If therapists' comments, even when repeated, fall on deaf ears, if therapists feel ignored by the group, if they find it extraordinarily difficult to influence the meeting, then it is clear that the resistance is powerful and that the group needs to be addressed as well as the individual members. It is not an easy undertaking. It is anxiety-provoking to buck the entire group, and therapists may feel deskilled in such meetings.

The group may also avoid work by more literal flight—absence or tardiness. Whatever the form, however, the result is the same: in the language of the group dynamicist, *locomotion toward the attainment of group goals is impeded*, and the group is no longer engaged in its primary task.

Not uncommonly, the issue precipitating the resistance is discussed symbolically. I have seen groups deal with their uneasiness about observers metaphorically by long discussions about other types of confidentiality violation: for example, public posting of grades for a school course, family members opening one another's mail, and invasive credit company computers. Discomfort about the therapist's absence may prompt discussions of parental inaccessibility or death or illness. Generally, the therapist may learn something of what is being resisted by pondering the question "Why is this particular topic being discussed, and *why now?*"

An experience in a therapy group at the height of the 2003 SARS (Severe Acute Respiratory Syndrome) epidemic may be illustrative.

• *A group in a partial hospitalization program for depressed seniors was canceled for several weeks and finally reconvened, but with the proviso that all participants were required to wear uncomfortable and oppressive face masks (heeding the recommendation of infection control) that obscured nonverbal communication. The meeting was characterized by unusually hostile comments about deprivations: uncaring adult children, incompetent public health officials, unavailable, neglectful therapists. Soon the members began to attack one another and the group seemed on the brink of total disintegration.*

The therapist, also struggling with the restrictive mask, asked for a "process check"—that is, he asked the group to stop for a moment and reflect on what was happening so far in the meeting. The members all agreed that they hated what the SARS crisis had done to their group. The masks not only were physically irritating, but they also blocked them from feeling close to others in the group. They realized, too, that the generalized anger in the group was misplaced, but they did not know what to do with their strong feelings.

The therapist made a group-as-a-whole interpretation: "There's a sort of paradox here today: it's evident that you cherish this group and are angry at being deprived of it, yet, on the other hand, the anger you experience and express threatens the warm supportive group atmosphere you so value." A lot of head nodding followed the therapist's interpretation, and the anger and divisiveness soon dissipated.

Antitherapeutic Group Norms

Another type of group obstacle warranting a group-as-a-whole interpretation occurs when antitherapeutic group norms are elaborated by the group. For example, a group may establish a "take turns" format in which an entire meeting is devoted, sequentially, to each member of the group. "Taking turns" is a comfortable or convenient procedure, but it is an undesirable norm, because it discourages free interaction in the here-and-now. Furthermore, members are often forced into premature self-disclosure and, as their turn approaches, may experience extreme anxiety or even decide to terminate therapy. Or a group may establish a pattern of devoting the entire session to the first issue raised in that session, with strong invisible sanctions against changing the subject. Or there may be a "Can you top this?" format in which the members engage in a spiraling orgy of self-disclosure. Or the group may develop a tightly knit, closed pattern that excludes outlying members and does not welcome new ones.

To intervene effectively in such instances, therapists may need to make a group-as-a-whole interpretation that clearly describes the process and the deleterious effects the taking-turns format has on the members or on the group and emphasizes that there are alternatives to this mode of opening each meeting.

Frequently a group, during its development, bypasses certain important phases or never incorporates certain norms into its culture. For example, a group may develop without ever going through a period of challenging or confronting the therapist. Or a group may develop without a whisper of intermember dissension, without status bids or struggles for control. Or a group may meet at length with no hint of real intimacy or closeness arising among the members. Such avoidance is a collaborative result of the group members implicitly constructing norms dictating this avoidance.

Therapists who sense that the group is providing a one-sided or incomplete experience for the members often facilitate the progress of the group work by commenting on the missing aspect of the group's life. (Such an intervention assumes, of course, that there are regularly recurring, predictable phases of small group development with which the therapist is familiar—a topic I will discuss in chapter 11.)

The Timing of Group Interventions

For pedagogical reasons, I have discussed interpersonal phenomena and group-as-a-whole phenomena as though they were quite distinct. In practice, of course, the two often overlap, and the therapist is faced with the question of when to emphasize the interpersonal aspects of the transaction and when to emphasize the group-as-a-whole aspects. This matter of clinical judgment cannot be neatly prescribed. As in any therapeutic endeavor, judgment develops from experience (particular supervised experience) and from intuition. As Melanie Klein stated, "It is a most precious quality in an analyst to be able at any moment to pick out the point of urgency."[42]

The point of urgency is far more elusive in group therapy than in individual treatment. As a general rule, however, *an issue critical to the existence or functioning of the entire group always takes precedence over narrower interpersonal issues.* As an illustration, let me return to the group that engaged in whispering, discussion of neutral topics, and other forms of group flight during the meeting after a member had inadvertently discovered the indiscreet group observers. In that meeting, Mary, who had been absent at the previous meeting, brought her dog. Under normal circumstances, this act would clearly have become an important group issue: Mary had consulted neither with the therapist nor with other members about bringing her dog to the group; she was, because of her narcissism, an unpopular member, and her act was representative of her insensitivity to others. However, in this meeting there was a far more urgent issue—one threatening the entire group—and the dog was discussed not from the aspect of facilitating Mary's interpersonal learning but as he was used by the group in its flight. Only later, after the obstacle to the group's progress had been worked through and removed, did the members return to a meaningful consideration of their annoyance about Mary bringing the dog.

To summarize, group-as-a-whole forces are continuously at play in the therapy group. The therapist needs to be aware of them in order to harness group forces in the service of therapy and to counter them when they obstruct therapy.†

Chapter 7

THE THERAPIST:
TRANSFERENCE AND
TRANSPARENCY

Having discussed the mechanisms of therapeutic change in group therapy, the tasks of the therapist, and the techniques by which the therapist accomplishes these tasks, I turn in this chapter from *what the therapist must do* in the group to *how the therapist must be*. Do you, as therapist, play a role? To what degree are you free to be yourself? How "honest" can you be? How much transparency can you permit yourself?

Any discussion of therapist freedom should begin with transference, which can be either an effective therapeutic tool or a set of shackles that encumbers your every movement. In his first and extraordinarily prescient essay on psychotherapy (the final chapter of *Studies on Hysteria* [1895]), Freud noted several possible impediments to the formation of a good working relationship between client and therapist.[1] Most of them could be resolved easily, but one stemmed from deeper sources and resisted efforts to banish it from the therapeutic work. Freud labeled this impediment *transference*, since it consisted of attitudes toward the therapist that had been "transferred" from earlier attitudes toward important figures in the client's life. These feelings toward the therapist were "false connections"—new editions of old impulses.

Freud soon realized, however, that transference was far from being an impediment to therapy; on the contrary, if used properly, it could be the therapist's most effective tool.[2] What better way to help the clients recapture the past than to allow them to reexperience and reenact ancient feelings toward parents through the current relationship to the therapist? Furthermore, the intense and conflicted relationship that often develops

201

with the therapist, which he termed the *transference neurosis*, was amenable to reality testing; the therapist could treat it and, in so doing, simultaneously treat the infantile conflict. Although some of these terms may seem dated, many of today's psychotherapeutic approaches, including cognitive therapy, acknowledge a concept similar to transference but refer to it as the client's "schema."[3]

Although considerable evolution in theory and technique has occurred in psychoanalysis over the past half century, until recently some basic principles regarding the role of transference in psychoanalytic therapy have endured with relatively little change:[4]

1. Analysis of transference is the major therapeutic task of the therapist.
2. Because the development (and then the resolution) of transference is crucial, it is important that therapists facilitate its development by remaining opaque, so that the client can encloak them in transferred feelings and attitudes, much as one might dress a mannequin after one's own fancy. (This is the rationale behind the "blank screen" role of the analyst, a role that enjoys little currency these days even among traditional analysts.)
3. The most important type of interpretation the therapist can make is one that clarifies some aspect of transference. (In the early days of analysis the transference interpretation was referred to as the "mutative interpretation.")

In recent decades, however, many analysts have shifted their assumptions as they have recognized the importance of other factors in the therapeutic process. Judd Marmor, a prominent American analyst, anticipated this evolution in a 1973 article in which he wrote, "Psychoanalysts have begun, in general, to feel more free to enter into active communicative exchanges with patients instead of remaining bound to the incognito 'neutral mirror' model of relative silence and impassivity."[5] More recently, Stephen Mitchell, a leader in relational approaches to mainstream psychoanalysis commented:

> Many patients are now understood to be suffering not from conflictual infantile passions that can be tamed and transformed through reason and understanding but from stunted personal development. Deficiencies in caregiving in the earliest years are understood to have contributed to interfering with the emergence of a fully centered, integrated sense of self, of the patient's own subjectivity. What the patient needs is not clarification or insight so much as a sustained experience of being seen, personally engaged, and, basically valued and cared about.[6]

Mitchell and many others argue that the "curative" factor in both individual and group therapy is the *relationship*, which requires the therapist's authentic engagement and empathic attunement to the client's internal emotional and subjective experience.†[7] Note that this new emphasis on the nature of the relationship means that psychotherapy is changing its focus from a one-person psychology (emphasizing the client's pathology) to a two-person psychology (emphasizing mutual impact and shared responsibility for the relationship).†[8] In this model, the therapist's emotional experience in the therapy is a relevant and powerful source of data about the client. How to make wise use of this data will be elaborated shortly. Few would quarrel with the importance of the development, recognition, and resolution of transference in individual, dynamically oriented therapy.*

Psychoanalysts disagree about the degree of permissible therapist disclosure—ranging from extensive disclosure[9] to complete opaqueness.[10] But they do agree that transference is "inappropriate, intense, ambivalent, capricious, and tenacious"[11] and agree also about the centrality of the transference and the key role of the interpretation of transference in analytic treatment. The difference between analytic schools centers mainly on whether "transference is everything or almost everything."[12]

In group therapy the problem is not the importance of transference work; it is the *priority* of this work relative to other therapeutic factors in the treatment process. The therapist cannot focus solely on transference and at the same time perform the variety of tasks necessary to build a group that can make use of the important group therapeutic factors.

The difference between group therapists who consider the resolution of therapist-client transference as the paramount therapeutic factor[13] and those who attach equal importance to the interpersonal learning that ensues from relationships between members and from other therapeutic factors is more than theoretical: in practice, they use markedly different techniques. The following vignettes from a group led by a formal British analyst who made only transference interpretations illustrate this point:

---

*In the psychoanalytic literature, definitions of transference differ (see C. Rycroft, *Critical Dictionary of Psychoanalysis* [New York: Basic Books, 1968], and J. Sandler, G. Dave, and A. Holder, "Basic Psychoanalytic Concepts: III. Transference," *British Journal of Psychiatry* 116 [1970]: 667–72). The more rigorous definition is that transference is a state of mind of a client toward the therapist, and it is produced by displacement onto the therapist of feelings and ideas that derive from previous figures in the client's life. Other psychoanalysts extend transference to apply not only to the analysand-analyst relationship but to other interpersonal situations. In this discussion and elsewhere in this text, I use the term "transference" liberally to refer to the irrational aspects of any relationship between two people. In its clinical manifestations, the concept is synonymous with Sullivan's term "parataxic distortion." As I shall discuss, there are more sources of transference than the simple transfer or displacement of feeling from a prior to a current object.

• *At the twentieth meeting, the members discussed at great length the fact that they did not know one another's first names. They then dealt with the general problem of intimacy, discussing, for example, how difficult it was to meet and really know people today. How does one make a really close friend? Now, on two occasions during this discussion, a member had erred or forgotten the surname of another member. From this data the group leader made the transference interpretation that by forgetting the others' names, the members were expressing a wish that all the other members would vanish so that each could have the therapist's sole attention.*

• *In another session, two male members were absent, and four women members bitterly criticized the one male client present, who was gay, for his detachment and narcissism, which precluded any interest in the lives or problems of others. The therapist suggested that the women were attacking the male client because he did not desire them sexually. Moreover, he was an indirect target; the women really wanted to attack the therapist for his refusal to engage them sexually.*

In each instance, the therapist selectively attended to the data and, from the vantage point of his particular conception of the paramount therapeutic factor—that is, transference resolution—made an interpretation that was pragmatically correct, since it focused the members' attention on their relationship with the leader. However, in my view, these therapist-centered interpretations are incomplete, for they deny important intermember relationships. In fact, in the first vignette, the members, in addition to their wish for the therapist's sole attention, *were* considerably conflicted about intimacy and about their desires and fears of engaging with one another. In the second vignette, the male client *had* in fact been self-absorbed and detached from the other members of the group, and it was exceedingly important for him to recognize and understand his behavior.

Any mandate that limits group therapists' flexibility renders them less effective. I have seen some therapists hobbled by a conviction that they must at all times remain totally anonymous and neutral, others by their crusade to be at all times totally "honest" and transparent, and still others by the dictum that they must make interpretations only of transference or only of mass group phenomena, or, even more stringently, only of mass group transference.

The therapist's approach to the group can amplify or moderate the expression of members' transferences. If the therapist emphasizes his centrality, the group will become more regressive and dependent. In contrast, if the therapist values the peer interactions and peer transferences as primary expressions and not merely as displacements from the therapist, then the intensity of the transference experience in the group will be better modulated.[14]

In this chapter I make the following points about transference:

1. Transference *does* occur in therapy groups; indeed, it is omnipresent and radically influences the nature of the group discourse.
2. Without an appreciation of transference and its manifestations, the therapist will often not be able to understand fully the process of the group.
3. Therapists who ignore transference considerations may seriously misunderstand some transactions and confuse rather than guide the group members; therapists who attend *only* to the transference aspects of their relationships with members may fail to relate authentically to them.
4. There are clients whose therapy hinges on the resolution of transference distortion; there are others whose improvement will depend on interpersonal learning stemming from work not with the therapist but with another member, around such issues as competition, exploitation, or sexual and intimacy conflicts; and there are many clients who choose alternative therapeutic pathways in the group and derive their primary benefit from other therapeutic factors entirely.
5. Transference distortions between group members can be worked with as effectively, and perhaps even more effectively, than transference reactions to the therapist.[15]
6. Attitudes toward the therapist are not all transference based: many are reality based, and others are irrational but flow from other sources of irrationality inherent in the dynamics of the group. (As Freud recognized, not all group phenomena can be explained on the basis of individual psychology.)[16]
7. By maintaining flexibility, you may make good therapeutic use of these irrational attitudes toward you, without at the same time neglecting your many other functions in the group.

TRANSFERENCE IN THE THERAPY GROUP

Every client, to a greater or lesser degree, perceives the therapist incorrectly because of transference distortions, sometimes even before beginning therapy. One psychiatrist tells the story of going out to meet a new client in the waiting room and having the client dispute that the therapist was who he said he was because he was so physically different from the client's imaginings of him.[17] Few clients are entirely conflict free in their attitudes toward such issues as parental authority, dependency, God, autonomy, and rebellion—all of which are often personified in the person of the therapist. These distortions are continually at play under the surface of the group discourse. Indeed, hardly a meeting passes without some clear token of the powerful feelings evoked by the therapist.

Witness the difference in the group when the therapist enters. Often the group may have been engaged in animated conversation only to lapse into heavy silence at the sight of the therapist. (Someone once said that the group therapy meeting officially begins when suddenly nothing happens!) The therapist's arrival not only reminds the group of its task but also evokes early constellations of feelings in each member about the adult, the teacher, the evaluator. Without the therapist, the group feels free to frolic; the therapist's presence is experienced as a stern reminder of the responsibilities of adulthood.

Seating patterns often reveal some of the complex and powerful feelings toward the leader. Frequently, the members attempt to sit as far away from you as possible. As members filter into the meeting they usually occupy distant seats, leaving the seats on either side of the therapist as the penalty for late arrivals; a paranoid client often takes the seat directly opposite you, perhaps in order to watch you more closely; a dependent client generally sits close to you, often on your right. If co-therapists sit close to each other with only one vacant chair between them, you can bet it will be the last chair occupied. One member, after months of group therapy, still described a feeling of great oppression when seated between the therapists.

Over several years, for research purposes, I asked group members to fill out a questionnaire after each meeting. One of their tasks was to rank-order every member for activity (according to the total number of words each spoke). There was excellent intermember reliability in their ratings of the other group members *but exceedingly poor reliability in their ratings of the group therapist*. In the same meetings some clients rated the therapist as the *most* active member, whereas others considered him the *least* active. The powerful and unrealistic feelings of the members toward the therapist prevented an accurate appraisal, even on this relatively objective dimension.

One client, when asked to discuss his feelings toward me, stated that he disliked me greatly because I was cold and aloof. He reacted immediately to his disclosure with intense discomfort. He imagined possible repercussions: I might be too upset by his attack to be of any more help to the group; I might retaliate by kicking him out of the group; I might humiliate him by mocking him for some of the lurid sexual fantasies he had shared with the group; or I might use my psychiatric wizardry to harm him in the future.

On another occasion many years ago, a group noted that I was wearing a copper bracelet. When they learned it was for tennis elbow, their reaction was extreme. They felt angry that I should be superstitious or ascribe to any quack cures. (They had berated me for months for being too scientific and not human enough!) Some suggested that if I would spend more time with my clients and less time on the tennis court, everyone would be better off. One woman, who idealized me, said that she had seen copper bracelets advertised in a local magazine, but guessed that mine was more special—perhaps something I had bought in Switzerland.

Some members characteristically address all their remarks to the therapist, or speak to other members only to glance furtively at the therapist at the end of their statement. It is as though they speak to others in an attempt to reach the therapist, seeking the stamp of approval for all their thoughts and actions. They forget, as it were, their reasons for being in therapy: they continuously seek to gain conspiratorial eye contact; to be the last to leave the session; to be, in a multitude of ways, the therapist's favorite child.

One middle-aged woman dreamed that the group therapy room was transformed into my living room, which was bare and unfurnished. The other group members were not there; instead, the room was crowded with my family, which consisted of several sons. I introduced her to them, and she felt intense warmth and pleasure. Her association to the dream was that she was overjoyed at the thought that there was a place for her in my home. Not only could she furnish and decorate my house (she was a professional interior designer) but, since I had only sons (in her dream), there was room for a daughter.

Transference is so powerful and so ubiquitous that the dictum "the leader shall have no favorites" seems to be essential for the stability of every working group. Freud suggested that group cohesiveness, curiously, derives from the universal wish to be the favorite of the leader and the mutual identifications the group members make with the idealized leader.[18] Consider the prototypic human group: the sibling group. It is rife with intense rivalrous feelings: each child wishes to be the favorite and resents all rivals for their claims to parental love. The older child wishes to rob the younger of privileges or to eliminate the child altogether. *And yet each realizes that the rival children are equally loved by their parents* and that therefore one cannot destroy one's siblings without incurring parental wrath and thus destroying oneself.

There is only possible solution: *equality*. If one cannot be the favorite, then *there must be no favorite at all*. Everyone is granted an equal investment in the leader, and out of this demand for equality is born what we have come to know as group spirit. Freud is careful to remind us that the demand for equality applies only to the other members. They do not wish to be equal to the leader. Quite the contrary: they have a thirst for obedience—a "lust for submission," as Erich Fromm put it.[19] I shall return to this shortly. We have regrettably often witnessed the marriage of weak, devitalized, and demoralized followers to charismatic, often malignantly narcissistic group leaders.[20]

Freud was very sensitive to the powerful and irrational manner in which group members view their leader, and he systematically analyzed this phenomenon and applied it to psychotherapy.[21] Obviously, however, the psychology of member and leader has existed since the earliest human groupings, and Freud was not the first to note it.† To cite only one example, Tolstoy in the nineteenth century was keenly aware of the subtle intricacies of the member-leader relationship in the two most important groups of his day: the church and the military. His insight into the overvaluation of the leader gives *War and Peace* much of its pathos and richness. Consider Rostov's regard for the Tsar:

> He was entirely absorbed in the feeling of happiness at the Tsar's being near. His nearness alone made up to him by itself, he felt, for the loss of the whole day. He was happy, as a lover is happy when the moment of the longed-for meeting has come. Not daring to look around from the front line, by an ecstatic instance without looking around, he felt his approach. And he felt it not only from the sound of the tramping hoofs of the approaching cavalcade, he felt it because as the Tsar came nearer everything grew brighter, more joyful and significant, and more festive. Nearer and nearer moved this sun, as he seemed to Rostov, shedding around him rays of mild and majestic light, and now he felt himself enfolded in that radiance, he heard his voice—that voice caressing, calm, majestic, and yet so simple. And Rostov got up and went out to wander about among the campfires, dreaming of what happiness it would be to die—not saving the Emperor's life (of that he did not dare to dream), but simply to die before the Emperor's eyes. He really was in love with the Tsar and the glory of the Russian arms and the hope of coming victory. And he was not the only man who felt thus in those memorable days that preceded the battle of Austerlitz: nine-tenths of the men in the Russian army were at that moment in love, though less ecstatically, with their Tsar and the glory of the Russian arms.[22]

Indeed, it would seem that submersion in the love of a leader is a prerequisite for war. How ironic that more killing has probably been done under the aegis of love than of hatred!

Napoleon, that consummate leader of men, was, according to Tolstoy, not ignorant of transference, nor did he hesitate to utilize it in the service of victory. In *War and Peace*, Tolstoy had him deliver this dispatch to his troops on the eve of battle:

Soldiers! I will myself lead your battalions. I will keep out of fire, if you, with your habitual bravery, carry defeat and disorder into the ranks of the enemy. But if victory is for one moment doubtful, you will see your Emperor exposed to the enemy's hottest attack, for there can be no uncertainty of victory, especially on this day, when it is a question of the honor of the French infantry, on which rests the honor of our nation.[23]

As a result of transference, the therapy group may impute superhuman powers to the leaders. Therapists' words are given more weight and wisdom than they carry. Equally astute contributions made by other members are ignored or distorted. All progress in the group is attributed to you, the therapist. Your errors, faux pas, and absences are seen as deliberate techniques that you employ to stimulate or provoke the group for its own good. Groups, including groups of professional therapists, overestimate your power and knowledge. They believe that there are great calculated depths to each of your interventions, that you predict and control all the events of the group. Even when you confess puzzlement or ignorance, this, too, is regarded as part of your clever technique, intended to have a particular effect on the group.

Ah, to be the favorite child—of the parent, of the leader! For many group members, this longing serves as an internal horizon against which all other group events are silhouetted. However much each member cares for the other members of the group, however much each is pleased to see others work and receive help, there is a background of envy, of disappointment, that one is not basking alone in the light of the leader. The leader's inquiries into these domains—who gets the most attention? Who gets the least? Who seems most favored by the leader?—almost invariably plunge the members into a profitable examination of the group's innards.

This desire for sole possession of the leader and the ensuing envy and greed lie deeply embedded in the substructure of every group. An old colloquialism for the genital organs is "privates." However, today many therapy groups discuss sexuality with ease, even relish. The "privates" of a group are more likely to be the fee structure: money often acts as the electrodes upon which condense much of the feeling toward the leader. The fee structure is an especially charged issue in many mental health clinics, which bill members according to a sliding fee scale based on income. How much one pays is often one of the group's most tightly clutched secrets, since differing fees (and the silent, insidious corollary: different rights, different degrees of ownership) threaten the very cement of the group: equality for all members. Therapists often feel awkward talking about money: Group discussion of money and fees may open difficult issues for the therapist such as income, perceived greed, or entitlement.†

Members often expect the leader to sense their needs. One member wrote a list of major issues that troubled him and brought it to meeting after meeting, waiting for the therapist to divine its existence and ask him to read it. Obviously, the content of the list meant little—if he had really wanted to work on the problems enumerated there, he could have presented the list to the group himself. No, what was important was the belief in the therapist's prescience and presence. This member's transference was such that he had incompletely differentiated himself from the therapist. Their ego boundaries were blurred; to know or feel something was, for him, tantamount to the therapist's knowing and feeling it. Many clients carry their therapist around with them. The therapist is in them, observes their actions from over their shoulder, participates in imaginary conversations with them.

When several members of a group share this desire for an all-knowing, all-caring leader, the meetings take on a characteristic flavor. The group seems helpless and dependent. The members deskill themselves and seem unable to help themselves or others. Deskilling is particularly dramatic in a group composed of professional therapists who suddenly seem unable to ask even the simplest questions of one another. For example, in one meeting a group may talk about loss. One member mentions, for the first time, the recent death of her mother. Then silence. There is sudden group aphasia. No one is even able to say, "Tell us more about it." They are all waiting—waiting for the touch of the therapist. No one wants to encourage anyone else to talk for fear of lessening his or her chance of obtaining the leader's ministrations.

Then, at other times or in other groups, the opposite occurs. Members challenge the leader continuously. The therapist is distrusted, misunderstood, treated like an enemy. Examples of such negative transference are common. One client, just beginning the group, expended considerable energy in an effort to dominate the other members. Whenever the therapist attempted to point this out, the client regarded his intentions as malicious: the therapist was interfering with his growth; the therapist was threatened by him and was attempting to keep him subservient; or, finally, the therapist was deliberately blocking his progress lest he improve too quickly and thus diminish the therapist's income. Both of these polarized positions—slavish idealization and unrelenting devaluation, reflect destructive group norms and represent an antigroup position that demands the therapist's attention.[24]

In a group of adult female incest survivors, I, the only male in the group, was continually challenged. Unlike my female co-therapist, I could do no right. My appearance was attacked—my choice of neckties, my wearing socks that were not perfectly matched. Virtually every one of my interventions was met with criticism. My silence was labeled disinterest, and my support was viewed with suspicion. When I did not inquire deeply enough into the nature of their abuse, I was accused of lacking interest and empathy. When I did inquire, I was accused of being a "closet pervert" who got sexual kicks from listening to stories of sexual violation. Though I had known that transferential anger from a group of female abuse victims would be inevitable and useful to the therapy process, and that the attacks were against my role rather than against my person—still, the attacks were difficult to tolerate. I began to dread each meeting and felt anxious, deskilled, and incompetent. The transference was not just being felt or spoken, it was being enacted powerfully.[25] Not only was I attacked as a representative of the prototypical male in these group members' lives, but I was also being "abused" in a form of role inversion. This offered a useful window into the experience of the group members who all too often felt dread, bullied, and lacking in skill. Understanding the nature of transference and not retaliating with countertransference rage was essential in retaining a therapeutic posture.

In another group a paranoid client, who had a long history of broken leases and lawsuits brought against her by landlords, re-created her litigiousness in the group. She refused to pay her small clinic bill, claiming that there was an error in the account, but she could not find the time to come to talk to the clinic administrator. When the therapist reminded her on a number of occasions of the account, she compared him to a Jewish slumlord or a greedy capitalist who would have liked her to damage her health permanently by slaving in an environmentally toxic factory.

Another member habitually became physically ill with flu symptoms whenever she grew depressed. The therapist could find no way to work with her without her feeling he was accusing her of malingering—a replay of the accusatory process in her relationships in her family. When one therapist, on a couple of occasions, accepted a Life Saver from a female member, another member responded strongly and accused him both of mooching and of exploiting the women in the group.

Many irrational reasons exist for these attacks on the therapist, but some stem from the same feelings of helpless dependency that result in the worshipful obedience I have described. Some clients ("counterdependents") respond counterphobically to their dependency by incessantly defying the leader. Others validate their integrity or potency by attempting to triumph over the big adversary, feeling a sense of exhilaration and power from twisting the tail of the tiger and emerging unscathed.

The most common charge members level against the leader is that of being too cold, too aloof, too inhuman. This charge has some basis in reality. For both professional and personal reasons, as I shall discuss shortly, many therapists do keep themselves hidden from the group. Also, their role of process commentator requires a certain distance from the group.

But there is more to it. Although the members insist that they wish therapists to be more human, they have the simultaneous counterwish that
they be *more than human*. (See my novel *The Schopenhauer Cure* [pp.
221–253] for a fictional portrayal of this phenomenon.)

Freud often made this observation. In *The Future of an Illusion,* he
based his explanation for religious belief on the human being's thirst for
a superbeing.[26] It seemed to Freud that the integrity of the group depended on the existence of some superordinate figure who, as I discussed
earlier, fosters the illusion of loving each member equally. Solid group
bonds become chains of sand if the leader is lost. If the general perishes
in battle, it is imperative that the news be kept secret, or panic might
break out. So, too, for the leader of the church. Freud was fascinated by a
1903 novel called *When It Was Dark*, in which Christ's divinity was questioned and ultimately disproved.[27] The novel depicted catastrophic effects
on Western European civilization; previously stable social institutions de-
constituted one by one, leaving only social chaos and ideological rubble.

Hence, there is great ambivalence in the members' directive to the
leader to be "more human." They complain that you tell them nothing of
yourself, yet they rarely inquire explicitly. They demand that you be more
human yet excoriate you if you wear a copper bracelet, accept a Life Saver,
or forget to tell the group that you have conversed with a member over the
phone. They prefer not to believe you if you profess puzzlement or ignorance. The illness or infirmity of a therapist always arouses considerable
discomfort among the members, as though somehow the therapist should
be beyond biological limitation. The followers of a leader who abandons
his or her role are greatly distressed. (When Shakespeare's Richard II
laments his hollow crown and gives vent to his discouragement and need
for friends, his court bids him to be silent.)

A group of psychiatry residents I once led put the dilemma very clearly.
They often discussed the "big people" out in the world: their therapists,
group leaders, supervisors, and the adult community of senior practicing
psychiatrists. The closer these residents came to completing their training,
the more important and problematic the big people became. I wondered
aloud whether they, too, might soon become "big people." Could it be
that even I had my "big people"?

There were two opposing sets of concerns about the "big people," and
they were equally troubling: first, that the "big people" were real, that
they possessed superior wisdom and knowledge and would dispense an
honest but terrible justice to the young, presumptuous frauds who tried to
join their ranks; or, second, that the "big people" themselves were frauds,
and the members were all Dorothys facing the Oz wizard. The second
possibility had more frightening implications than the first: it brought

them face-to-face with their intrinsic loneliness and apartness. It was as if, for a brief time, life's illusions were stripped away, exposing the naked scaffolding of existence—a terrifying sight, one that we conceal from ourselves with the heaviest of curtains. The "big people" are one of our most effective curtains. As frightening as their judgment may be, it is far less terrible than that other alternative—that *there are no "big people"* and that one is finally and utterly alone.

The leader is thus seen unrealistically by members for many reasons. True transference or displacement of affect from some prior object is one reason; conflicted attitudes toward authority (dependency, distrust, rebellion, counterdependency) that become personified in the therapist is another; and still another reason is the tendency to imbue therapists with superhuman features so as to use them as a shield against existential anxiety.

An additional but entirely rational source of members' strong feelings toward the group therapist lies in the members' explicit or intuitive appreciation of the therapist's great and real power. Group leaders' presence and impartiality are, as I have already discussed, essential for group survival and stability; they have the power to expel members, add new members, and mobilize group pressure against anyone they wish.

In fact, the sources of intense, irrational feelings toward the therapist are so varied and so powerful that transference will always occur. The therapist need not make any effort—for example, striking a pose of unflinching neutrality and anonymity—to generate or facilitate the development of transference. An illustrative example of transference developing in the presence of therapist transparency occurred with a client who often attacked me for aloofness, deviousness, and hiddenness. He accused me of manipulation, of pulling strings to guide each member's behavior, of not being clear and open, of never really coming out and telling the group exactly what I was trying to do in therapy. Yet this man was a member of a group in which I had been writing very clear, honest, transparent group summaries and mailing them to the members before the next meeting (see chapter 14). A more earnest attempt to demystify the therapeutic process would be difficult to imagine. When asked by some of the members about my self-disclosure in the summaries, he acknowledged that he had not read them—they remained unopened on his desk.

As long as a group therapist assumes the responsibility of leadership, transference will occur. I have never seen a group develop without a deep, complex underpinning of transference. The problem is thus not evocation but resolution of transference. The therapist who is to make therapeutic use of transference must help clients recognize, understand, and change their distorted attitudinal set toward the leader.

How does the group resolve transference distortions? Two major approaches are seen in therapy groups: *consensual validation* and *increased therapist transparency*.

Consensual Validation

The therapist may encourage a client to validate his or her impressions of the therapist against those of the other members. If many or all of the group members concur in the client's view of and feelings toward the therapist, then it is clear that either the members' reaction stems from global group forces related to the therapist's role in the group *or* that the reaction is not unrealistic at all—the group members are perceiving the therapist accurately. If, on the other hand, there is no consensus, if one member alone has a particular view of the therapist, then this member may be helped to examine the possibility that he or she sees the therapist, and perhaps other people too, through an internal distorting prism. In this process the therapist must take care to operate with a spirit of open inquiry, lest it turn into a process of majority rule. There can be some truth even in the idiosyncratic reaction of a single member.

Increased Therapist Transparency

The other major approach relies on the therapeutic use of the self. Therapists help clients confirm or disconfirm their impressions of the therapists by gradually revealing more of themselves. The client is pressed to deal with the therapist as a real person in the here-and-now. Thus you respond to the client, you share your feelings, you acknowledge or refute motives or feelings attributed to you, you look at your own blind spots, you demonstrate respect for the feedback the members offer you. In the face of this mounting real-life data, clients are impelled to examine the nature and the basis of their powerful fictitious beliefs about the therapist.

We use our transparency and self-disclosure to maintain a therapeutic position with our clients that balances us in a position midway between the client's transference and its therapeutic disconfirmation.† Your disclosure about the client's impact on you is a particularly effective intervention because it deepens understanding for the mutual impact between therapist and group member.[28]

The group therapist undergoes a gradual metamorphosis during the life of the group. In the beginning you busy yourself with the many functions necessary in the creation of the group, with the development of a social system in which the many therapeutic factors may operate, and with the activation and illumination of the here-and-now. Gradually, as the group progresses, you begin to interact more personally with each of the members, and as you become more of a fleshed-out person, the members find it more difficult to maintain the early stereotypes they had projected onto you.

This process between you and each of the members is not qualitatively different from the interpersonal learning taking place among the members. After all, you have no monopoly on authority, dominance, sagacity, or aloofness, and many of the members work out their conflicts in these areas not with the therapist (or *not only* with the therapist) but with other members who happen to have these attributes.

This change in the degree of transparency of the therapist is by no means limited to group therapy. Someone once said that when the analyst tells the analysand a joke, you can be sure the analysis is approaching its end. However, the pace, the degree, the nature of the therapist transparency and the relationship between this activity of the therapist and the therapist's other tasks in the group are problematic and deserve careful consideration. More than any other single characteristic, the nature and the degree of therapist self-disclosure differentiate the various schools of group therapy. Judicious therapist self-disclosure is a defining characteristic of the interpersonal model of group psychotherapy.[29]

THE PSYCHOTHERAPIST AND TRANSPARENCY

Psychotherapeutic innovations appear and vanish with bewildering rapidity. Only a truly intrepid observer would attempt to differentiate evanescent from potentially important and durable trends in the diffuse, heterodox American psychotherapeutic scene. Nevertheless, there is evidence, in widely varying settings, of a shift in the therapist's basic self-presentation. Consider the following vignettes.

• *Therapists leading therapy groups that are observed through a one-way mirror reverse roles at the end of the meeting. The clients are permitted to observe while the therapist and the students discuss or rehash the meeting. Or, in inpatient groups, the observers enter the room twenty minutes before the end of the session to discuss their observations of the meeting. In the final ten minutes, the group members react to the observers' comments.[30]*

• *At a university training center, a tutorial technique has been employed in which four psychiatric residents meet regularly with an experienced clinician who conducts an interview in front of a one-way mirror. The client is often invited to observe the postinterview discussion.*

• *Tom, one of two group co-therapists, began a meeting by asking a client who had been extremely distressed at the previous meeting how he was feeling and whether that session had been helpful to him. The co-therapist then said to him, "Tom, I think you're doing just what I was doing a couple of weeks ago—pressing the clients to tell me how effective our therapy is. We both seem on a constant lookout for reassurance. I think we are reflecting some of the general discouragement in the group. I wonder whether the members may be feeling pressure that they have to improve to keep up our spirits."*

• *In several groups at an outpatient clinic, the therapists write a thorough summary (see chapter 14) after each meeting and mail it to the members before the next session. The summary contains not only a narrative account of the meeting, a running commentary on process, and each member's contribution to the session but also much therapist disclosure: the therapist's ideas about what was happening to everyone in the group that meeting; a relevant exposition of the theory of group therapy; exactly what the therapist was attempting to do in the meeting; the therapist's feelings of puzzlement or ignorance about events in the group; and the therapist's personal feelings during the session, including both those said and those unsaid at the time. These summaries are virtually indistinguishable from summaries the therapists had previously written for their own private records.*

Without discussing the merits or the disadvantages of the approaches demonstrated in these vignettes, it can be said for now that there is no evidence that these approaches corroded the therapeutic relationship or situation. On the psychiatric ward, in the tutorial, and in therapy groups, the group members did not lose faith in their all-too-human therapists but developed more faith in a process in which the therapists were willing to immerse themselves. The clients who observed their therapists in disagreement learned that although no one true way exists, the therapists are nonetheless dedicated and committed to finding ways of helping their clients.

In each of the vignettes, the therapists abandon their traditional role and share some of their many uncertainties with their clients. Gradually the therapeutic process is demystified and the therapist in a sense defrocked. The past four decades have witnessed the demise of the concept of psychotherapy as an exclusive domain of psychiatry. Formerly, therapy was indeed a closed-shop affair: psychologists were under surveillance of psychiatrists lest they be tempted to practice psychotherapy rather than counseling; social workers could do casework but not psychotherapy. Eventually these three professions—psychiatry, psychology, and social work—joined in their resistance to the emergence of new psychotherapy professions: the master's-level psychologists, the marriage and family counselors, psychiatric nurse practitioners, pastoral counselors, body workers, movement and dance therapists, art therapists. The "eggshell" era of therapy—in which the client was considered so fragile and the mysteries of technique so deep that only the individual with the ultimate diploma dared treat one—is gone forever.†

Nor is this reevaluation of the therapist's role and authority solely a modern phenomenon. There were adumbrations of such experimentation among the earliest dynamic therapists. For example, Sandor Ferenczi, a close associate of Freud who was dissatisfied with the therapeutic results of psychoanalysis, continually challenged the aloof, omniscient role of the classical psychoanalyst. Ferenczi and Freud in fact parted ways because of Ferenczi's conviction that it was the mutual, honest, and transparent relationship that therapist and client created together, not the rational interpretation, that was the mutative force of therapy.[31]

In his pioneering emphasis on the interpersonal relationship, Ferenczi influenced American psychotherapy through his impact on future leaders in the field such as William Alanson White, Harry Stack Sullivan, and Frieda Fromm-Reichman. Ferenczi also had a significant but overlooked role in the development of group therapy, underscoring the relational base of virtually all the group therapeutic factors.[32] During his last several years, he openly acknowledged his fallibility to clients and, in response to a just criticism, felt free to say, "I think you may have touched upon an area in which I am not entirely free myself. Perhaps you can help me see what's wrong with me."[33] Foulkes, a British pioneer group therapist, stated sixty years ago that the mature group therapist was truly modest—one who could sincerely say to a group, "Here we are together facing reality and the basic problems of human existence. I am one of you, not more and not less."[34]

I explore therapist transparency more fully in other literary forms: two books of stories based on my psychotherapy cases—*Love's Executioner* and *Momma and the Meaning of Life*—and in novels—*When Nietzsche Wept* (in which the client and therapist alternate roles), and *Lying on the Couch* in which the therapist protagonist reruns Ferenczi's mutual analysis experiment by revealing himself fully to a client.[35] After the publication of each of these books, I received a deluge of letters, from both clients and therapists, attesting to the widespread interest and craving for a more human relationship in the therapy venture. My most recent novel, (*The Schopenhauer Cure*)[36] is set in a therapy group in which the therapist engages in heroic transparency.

Those therapist who attempt greater transparency argue that therapy is a rational, explicable process. They espouse a humanistic attitude to therapy, in which the client is considered a full collaborator in the therapeutic venture. No mystery need surround the therapist or the therapeutic procedure; aside from the ameliorative effects stemming from expectations of help from a magical being, there is little to be lost and probably much to be gained through the demystification of therapy. A therapy based on a true alliance between therapist and enlightened client reflects a greater respect for the capacities of the client and, with it, a greater reliance on self-awareness rather than on the easier but precarious comfort of self-deception.

Greater therapist transparency is, in part, a reaction to the old authoritarian medical healer, who, for many centuries, has colluded with the distressed human being's wish for succor from a superior being. Healers have harnessed and indeed cultivated this need as a powerful agent of treatment. In countless ways, they have encouraged and fostered a belief in their omniscience: Latin prescriptions, specialized language, secret institutes with lengthy and severe apprenticeships, imposing offices, and power displays of diplomas—all have contributed to the image of the healer as a powerful, mysterious, and prescient figure.

In unlocking the shackles of this ancestral role, the overly disclosing therapist of today has at times sacrificed effectiveness on the altar of self-disclosure. However, the dangers of indiscriminate therapist transparency (which I shall consider shortly) should not deter us from exploring the judicious use of therapist self-disclosure.

The Effect of Therapist Transparency on the Therapy Group

The primary sweeping objection to therapist transparency emanates from the traditional analytic belief that the paramount therapeutic factor is the resolution of client-therapist transference. This view holds that the therapist must remain relatively anonymous or opaque to foster the development of unrealistic feelings toward him or her. It is my position, however, that other therapeutic factors are of equal or greater importance, and that the therapist who judiciously uses his or her own person increases the therapeutic power of the group by encouraging the development of these factors. In doing so, you gain considerable role flexibility and maneuverability and may, without concerning yourself about spoiling your role, directly attend to group maintenance, to the shaping of the group norms (there is considerable research evidence that therapist self-disclosure facilitates greater openness between group members[37] as well as between family members in family therapy[38]), and to here-and-now activation and process illumination. By decentralizing your position in the group, you hasten the development of group autonomy and cohesiveness. We see corroborating evidence from individual therapy: therapist self-disclosure is often experienced by clients as supportive and normalizing. It fosters deeper exploration on the client's part.† Therapist self-disclosure is particularly effective when it serves to engage the client authentically and does not serve to control or direct the therapeutic relationship.†[39]

A leader's personal disclosure may have a powerful and indelible effect. In a recent publication, a member of a group led by Hugh Mullan, a well-known group therapist, recounts a group episode that occurred forty-five years earlier. The leader was sitting with his eyes closed in a meeting, and a member addressed him: "You look very comfortable, Hugh, why's that?" Hugh responded immediately, "Because I'm sitting next to a woman." The member never forgot that odd response. It was enormously liberating and freed him to experience and express intensely personal material. As he put it, he no longer felt alone in his "weirdness."[40]

One objection to self-disclosure, a groundless objection, I believe, is the fear of escalation—the fear that once you as therapist reveal yourself, the group will insatiably demand even more. Recall that powerful forces in the group oppose this trend. The members are extraordinarily curious about you, yet at the same time wish you to remain unknown and powerful. Some of these points were apparent in a meeting many years ago when I had just begun to lead therapy groups. I had just returned from leading a weeklong residential human relations laboratory (intensive T-group; see chapter 16). Since greater leader transparency is the rule in such groups, I returned to my therapy group primed for greater self-revelation.

• *Four members, Don, Russell, Janice, and Martha, were present at the twenty-ninth meeting of the group. One member and my co-therapist were absent; one other member, Peter, had dropped out of the group at the previous meeting. The first theme that emerged was the group's response to Peter's termination. The group discussed this gingerly, from a great distance, and I commented that we had, it seemed to me, never honestly discussed our feelings about Peter when he was present, and that we were avoiding them now, even after his departure. Among the responses was Martha's comment that she was glad he had left, that she had felt they couldn't reach him, and that she didn't feel it was worth it to try. She then commented on his lack of education and noted her surprise that he had even been included in the group—an oblique swipe at the therapists.*

I felt the group had not only avoided discussing Peter but had also declined to confront Martha's judgmentalism and incessant criticism of others. I thought I might help Martha and the group explore this issue by asking her to go around the group and describe those aspects of each person she found herself unable to accept. This task proved very difficult for her, and she generally avoided it by phrasing her objections in the past tense, as in, "I once disliked some trait in you but now it's different." When she had finished with each of the members, I pointed out that she had left me out; indeed, she had never expressed her feelings toward me except through indirect attacks. She proceeded to compare me unfavorably with the co-therapist, stating that she found me too retiring and ineffectual; she then immediately attempted to undo the remarks by commenting that "Still waters run deep" and recalling examples of my sensitivity to her.

The other members suddenly volunteered to tackle the same task and, in the process, revealed many long-term group secrets: Don's effeminacy, Janice's slovenliness and desexualized grooming, and Russell's lack of empathy with the women in the group. Martha was compared to a golf ball: "tightly wound up with an enamel cover." I was attacked by Don for my deviousness and lack of interest in him.

The members then asked me to go around the group in the same manner as they had done. Being fresh from a seven-day T-group and no admirer of generals who led their army from the rear, I took a deep breath and agreed. I told Martha that her quickness to judge and condemn others made me reluctant to show myself to her, lest I, too, be judged and found wanting. I agreed with the golf ball metaphor and added that her judgmentalism made it difficult for me to approach her, save as an expert technician. I told Don that I felt his gaze on me constantly; I knew he desperately wanted something from me, and that the intensity of his need and my inability to satisfy that need often made me very uncomfortable. I told Janice that I missed a spirit of opposition in her; she tended to accept and exalt everything that I said so uncritically that it became difficult at times to relate to her as an autonomous adult.

The meeting continued at an intense, involved level, and at its end the observers expressed grave concerns about my behavior. They felt that I had irrevocably relinquished my leadership role and become a group member, that the group would never be the same, and that, furthermore, I was placing my co-therapist, who would return the following week, in an untenable position.

In fact, none of these predictions materialized. In subsequent meetings, the group plunged more deeply into work; several weeks were required to assimilate the material generated in that single meeting. In addition, the group members, following the model of the therapist, related to one another far more forthrightly than before and made no demands on me or my co-therapist for escalated self-disclosure.

There are many different types of therapist transparency, depending on the therapist's personal style and the goals in the group at a particular time. Therapists may self-disclose to facilitate transference resolution; or to model therapeutic norms; or to assist the interpersonal learning of the members who wanted to work on their relationship with the group leader; or to support and accept members by saying, in effect, "I value and respect you and demonstrate this by giving of myself"?

• *An illustrative example of therapist disclosure that facilitated therapy occurred in a meeting when all three women members discussed their strong sexual attraction to me. Much work was done on the transference aspects of the situation, on the women being attracted to a man who was obviously professionally off-limits and unattainable, older, in a position of authority, and so on. I then pointed out that there was another side to it. None of the women had expressed similar feelings toward my co-therapist (also male); furthermore, other female clients who had been in the group previously had had the same feelings. I could not deny that it gave me pleasure to hear these sentiments expressed, and I asked them to help me look at my blind spots: What was I doing unwittingly to encourage their positive response?*

My request opened up a long and fruitful discussion of the group members' feelings about both therapists. There was much agreement that the two of us were very different: I was more vain, took much more care about my physical appearance and clothes, and had an exactitude and preciseness about my statements that created about me an attractive aura of suaveness and confidence. The other therapist was sloppier in appearance and behavior: he spoke more often when he was unsure of what he was going to say; he took more risks, was willing to be wrong, and, in so doing, was more often helpful to the clients. The feedback sounded right to me. I had heard it before and told the group so. I thought about their comments during the week and, at the following meeting, thanked the group and told them that they had been helpful to me.

Making errors is commonplace: it is what is done with the error that is often critical in therapy. Therapists are not omniscient, and it is best to acknowledge that.

• *After an angry exchange between two members, Barbara and Susan, the group found it difficult to repair the damage experienced by Barbara. Although Barbara was eventually able to work through her differences with Susan, she continued to struggle with how she had been left so unprotected by the group therapist. Numerous attempts at explanation and understanding failed to break the impasse, until I stated:*

"I regret what happened very much. I have to acknowledge that Susan's criticism of you took me by surprise—it hit like a tropical storm, and I was at a loss for words. It took me some time to regroup, but by then the damage had been done. If I knew then what I know now, I would have responded differently. I am sorry for that."

Rather than feeling that I was not competent because I had missed something of great importance, Barbara felt relieved and said that was exactly what she needed to hear. Barbara did not need me to be omnipotent—she wanted me to be human, to be able to acknowledge my error, and to learn from what happened so that it would be less likely to occur in the future.

• *Another illustrative clinical example occurred in the group of women incest survivors that I mentioned earlier in this chapter. The withering anger toward me (and, to a slightly lesser degree, toward my female co-therapist) had gotten to us, and toward the end of one meeting, we both openly discussed our experience in the group. I revealed that I felt demoralized and deskilled, that everything I tried in the group had failed to be helpful, and furthermore that I felt anxious and confused in the group. My co-leader discussed similar feelings: her discomfort about the competitive way the women related to her and about the continual pressure placed on her to reveal any abuse that she may have experienced. We told them that their relentless anger and distrust of us was fully understandable in the light of their past abuse but, nonetheless, we both wanted to shriek, "These were terrible things that happened to you, but <u>we</u> didn't do them."*

This episode proved to be a turning point for the group. There was still one member (who reported having undergone savage ritual abuse as a child) who continued in the same vein ("Oh, you're uncomfortable and confused! What a shame! What a shame! But at least now you know how it feels"). But the others were deeply affected by our admission. They were astounded to learn of our discomfort and of their power over us, and gratified that we were willing to relinquish authority and to relate to them in an open, egalitarian fashion. From that point on, the group moved into a far more profitable work phase.

In addition, the "now you know how it feels" comment illuminated one of the hidden reasons for the attacks on the therapist. It was an instance of the group member both demonstrating and mastering her experience of mistreatment by being the aggressor rather than the mistreated.

It was constructive for the therapists to acknowledge and work with these feelings openly rather than simply continue experiencing them.[41]

Being so intensely devalued is unsettling to almost all therapists, especially in the public domain of the group. Yet it also creates a remarkable therapeutic opportunity if therapists can maintain their dignity and honestly address their experience in the group.†

These clinical episodes illustrate some general principles that prove useful to the therapist when receiving feedback, especially negative feedback:

1. Take it seriously. Listen to it, consider it, and respond to it. Respect the clients and let their feedback matter to you; if you don't, you merely increase their sense of impotence.
2. Obtain consensual validation: Find out how other members feel. Determine whether the feedback is primarily a transference reaction or is in fact a piece of reality about you. If it is reality, you must confirm it; otherwise, you impair rather than facilitate your clients' reality testing.
3. Check your internal experience: Does the feedback fit? Does it click with your internal experience?

With these principles as guidelines, the therapist may offer such responses as: "You're right. There are times when I feel irritated with you, but at no time do I feel I want to impede your growth, seduce you, get a voyeuristic pleasure from listening to your account of your abuse, or slow your therapy so as to earn more money from you. That simply isn't part of my experience of you." Or: "It's true that I dodge some of your questions. But often I find them unanswerable. You imbue me with too much wisdom. I feel uncomfortable by your deference to me. I always feel that you've put yourself down very low, and that you're always looking up at me." Or: "I've never heard you challenge me so directly before. Even though it's a bit scary for me, it's also very refreshing." Or: "I feel restrained, very unfree with you, because you give me so much power over you. I feel I have to check every word I say because you give so much weight to all of my statements."

Note that these therapist disclosures are *all part of the here-and-now of the group*. I am advocating that therapists relate authentically to clients in the here-and-now of the therapy hour, not that they reveal their past and present in a detailed manner—although I have never seen harm in therapists' answering such broad personal questions as whether they are married or have children, where they are going on vacation, where they were brought up, and so on. Some therapists carry it much further and may wish to describe some similar personal problems they encountered and overcame. I personally have rarely found this useful or necessary.[42]*

A study of the effects of therapist disclosure on a group over a seven-month period noted many beneficial effects from therapist transparency.[43] First, therapist disclosure was more likely to occur when therapeutic communication among members was not taking place. Second, the effect of therapist disclosure was to shift the pattern of group interaction into a more constructive, sensitive direction. Finally, therapist self-disclosure resulted in an immediate increase in cohesiveness. Yet many therapists shrink from self-disclosure without being clear about their reasons for doing so. Too often, perhaps, they rationalize by cloaking their personal inclinations in professional garb. There is little doubt, I believe, that the personal qualities of a therapist influence professional style, choice of ideological school, and preferred clinical models.†

In debriefing sessions after termination I have often discussed therapist disclosure with clients. The great majority have expressed the wish that the therapist had been more open, more personally engaged in the group. Very few would have wanted therapists to have discussed more of their private life or personal problems with them. A study of individual therapy had the same findings—clients prefer and in fact thrive on therapist engagement and prefer therapists who are "not too quiet."[44] No one expressed a preference for full therapist disclosure.

Furthermore, there is evidence that leaders are more transparent than they know. The issue is not that we reveal ourselves—that is unavoidable[45]—rather, it is what use we make of our transparency and our clinical honesty. Some self-revelation is inadvertent or unavoidable—for example, pregnancy, bereavement, and professional accomplishments.[46] In some groups, particularly homogeneous groups with a focus such as substance abuse, sexual orientation, or specific medical illness (see chapter 15), leaders will likely be asked about their personal relationship to the common group focus: Have they had personal experience with substance abuse? Are they gay? Have they personally had the medical disease that is the focus of the group? Therapists need to reveal the relevant material about themselves that helps group members realize that the therapist can understand and empathize with the clients' experiences. That does not mean, however, that the therapist must provide extensive personal historical details. Such revelations are usually unhelpful to the therapy because they blur the difference in role and function between the therapist and the group members.

---

*A small study of individual therapy demonstrated that certain non–here-and-now therapist self-disclosure could be effective in strengthening the real (nontransference) relationship between client and therapist. Personal disclosure by the therapist about common interests or activities, when it followed the client's lead, served to normalize and support clients and indirectly deepened their learning.

Though members rarely press a therapist for inappropriate disclosure, occasionally one particular personal question arises that group therapists dread. It is illustrated in a dream of a group member (the same member who likened the therapist to a Jewish slumlord): "The whole group is sitting around a long table with you (the therapist) at the head. You had in your hand a slip of paper with something written on it. I tried to snatch it away from you but you were too far away." Months later, after this woman had made some significant personal changes, she recalled the dream and added that she knew all along what I had written on the paper but hadn't wanted to say it in front of the group. It was my answer to the question, "Do you love me?" This is a threatening question for the group therapist. And there is a related and even more alarming follow-up question: "How much do you love each of us?" or, "Whom do you love best?"

These questions threaten the very essence of the psychotherapeutic contract. They challenge tenets that both parties have agreed to keep invisible. They are but a step away from a commentary on the "purchase of friendship" model: "If you really care for us, would you see us if we had no money?" They come perilously close to the ultimate, terrible secret of the psychotherapist, which is that the intense drama in the group room plays a smaller, compartmentalized role in his or her life. As in Tom Stoppard's play *Rosencrantz and Guildenstern Are Dead*, key figures in one drama rapidly become shadows in the wings as the therapist moves immediately onto the stage of another drama.

Only once have I been blasphemous enough to lay this bare before a group. A therapy group of psychiatry residents was dealing with my departure (for a year's sabbatical leave). My personal experience during that time was one of saying good-bye to a number of clients and to several groups, some of which were more emotionally involving for me than the resident group. Termination work was difficult, and the group members attributed much of the difficulty to the fact that I had been so involved in the group that I was finding it hard to say good-bye. I acknowledged my involvement in the group but presented to them the fact that they knew but refused to know: I was vastly more important to them than they were to me. After all, I had many clients; they had only one therapist. They were clearly aware of this imbalance in their psychotherapeutic work with their own clients, and yet had never applied it to themselves. There was a gasp in the group as this truth, this denial of specialness, this inherent cruelty of psychotherapy, hit home.

The issue of therapist transparency is vastly complicated by widely publicized instances of therapist-client sexual abuse. Unfortunately, the irresponsible or impulse-ridden therapists who, to satisfy their own needs, betray their professional and moral covenant have not only damaged their own clients but caused a backlash that has damaged the trust in the client-therapist relationship everywhere.

Many professional associations have taken a highly reactionary stance toward the professional relationship. Feeling threatened by legal action, they advise therapists to practice defensively and always keep potential litigation in mind. The lawyers and juries, they say, will reason that "where there is smoke, there is fire" and that since every therapist-client encounter started down the slippery slope of slight boundary crossings, human interactions between client and therapist are in themselves evidence of wrongdoing. Consequently, professional organizations warn therapists to veer away from the very humanness that is the core of the therapeutic relationship. An article with a high Victorian tone in a 1993 issue of the *American Journal of Psychiatry*,[47] for example, advocated a stifling formality and warned psychiatrists not to offer their clients coffee or tea, not to address them by their first names, not to use their own first names, never to run over the fifty-minute time period, never to see any client during the last working hour of the day (since that is when transgressions most often occur), never to touch a client—even an act such as squeezing the arm or patting the back of an AIDS patient who needs therapeutic touch should be scrutinized and documented.* Obviously, these instructions and the sentiment behind them are deeply corrosive to the therapeutic relationship. To their credit, the authors of the 1993 article recognized the antitherapeutic impact of their first article and wrote a second paper five years later aimed at correcting the overreaction generated by the first article. The second article makes a plea for common sense and for recognition of the importance of the clinical context in understanding or judging boundary issues in therapy. They encourage therapists to obtain consultation or supervision whenever they are uncertain about their therapeutic posture or interventions.[48]

But moderation in all things. There is a proper place for therapist concealment, and the most helpful therapist is by no means the one who is most fully and most consistently self-disclosing. Let us turn our attention to the perils of transparency.

Pitfalls of Therapist Transparency

Some time ago I observed a group led by two neophyte therapists who were at that time much dedicated to the ideal of therapist transparency. They formed an outpatient group and conducted themselves in an unflinchingly honest fashion, expressing openly in the first meetings their uncertainty about group therapy, their inexperience, their self-doubts,

---

*At a recent psychotherapy convention, manufacturers promoted video systems that therapists could use to record every session as a safeguard against frivolous litigation.

and their personal anxiety. One might admire their courage, but not their results. In their overzealous obeisance to transparency, they neglected their function of group maintenance, and the majority of the members dropped out of the group within the first six sessions.

Untrained leaders who undertake to lead groups with the monolithic credo "Be yourself" as a central organizing principle for all other technique and strategy generally achieve not freedom but restriction. The paradox is that freedom and spontaneity in extreme form can result in a leadership role as narrow and restrictive as the traditional blank-screen leader. Under the banner of "Anything goes if it's genuine," the leader sacrifices flexibility.[49]

Consider the issue of timing. The fully open neophyte therapists I just mentioned overlooked the fact that leadership behavior that may be appropriate at one stage of therapy may be quite inappropriate at another. If clients need initial support and structure to remain in the group, then it is the therapist's task to provide it.

The leader who strives only to create an atmosphere of egalitarianism between member and leader may in the long run provide no leadership at all. Effective leader role behavior is by no means unchanging; as the group develops and matures, different forms of leadership are required.[50] "The honest therapist" as Parloff states, "is one who attempts to provide that which the client can assimilate, verify and utilize."[51] Ferenczi years ago underscored the necessity for proper timing. The analyst, he said, must not admit his flaws and uncertainty too early.[52] First, the client must feel sufficiently secure in his own abilities before being called upon to face defects in the one on whom he leans.*

Research on group members' attitudes toward therapist self-disclosure shows that members are sensitive to the timing and the content of disclosure.[53] Therapists' disclosures that are judged as harmful in early phases of the group are considered facilitative as a group matures. Furthermore, members who have had much group therapy experience are far more desirous of therapist self-disclosure than are inexperienced group members. Content analysis demonstrates that members prefer leaders who disclose

---

*A rich example of this principle is found in *Magister Ludi,* in which Herman Hesse describes an event in the lives of two renowned ancient healers (H. Hesse, *Magister Ludi* [New York: Frederick Unger, 1949], 438–67). Joseph, one of the healers, severely afflicted with feelings of worthlessness and self-doubt, sets off on a long journey across the desert to seek help from his rival, Dion. At an oasis, Joseph describes his plight to a stranger, who miraculously turns out to be Dion, whereupon Joseph accepts Dion's invitation to go home with him in the role of patient and servant. In time, Joseph regains his former serenity and zest and ultimately becomes the friend and colleague of his master. Only after many years have passed and Dion lies on his deathbed, does he reveal that at their encounter at the oasis, he had reached a similar impasse in his life and was en route to request Joseph's assistance.

positive ambitions (for example, personal and professional goals) and personal emotions (loneliness, sadness, anger, worries, and anxieties); they disapprove of a group leader's expressing negative feelings about any individual member or about the group experience (for example, boredom or frustration).[54] Not all emotions can be expressed by the therapist. Expressing hostility is almost invariably damaging and often irreparable, contributing to premature termination and negative therapy outcomes.†

Is full disclosure even possible in the therapy group or in the outside world? Or desirable? Some degree of personal and interpersonal concealment are an integral ingredient of any functioning social order. Eugene O'Neill illustrated this in dramatic form in the play *The Iceman Cometh*.[55] A group of derelicts live, as they have for twenty years, in the back room of a bar. The group is exceedingly stable, with many well-entrenched group norms. Each man maintains himself by a set of illusions ("pipe dreams," O'Neill calls them). One of the most deeply entrenched group norms is that no members challenge another's pipe dreams. Then enters Hickey, the iceman, a traveling salesman, a totally enlightened therapist, a false prophet who believes he brings fulfillment and lasting peace to each man by forcing him to shed his self-deceptions and stare with unblinking honesty at the sun of his life. Hickey's surgery is deft. He forces Jimmy Tomorrow (whose pipe dream is to get his suit out of hock, sober up, and get a job "tomorrow") to act now. He gives him clothes and sends him, and then the other men, out of the bar to face today.

The effects on each man and on the group are calamitous. One commits suicide, others grow severely depressed, "the life goes out of the booze," the men attack one another's illusions, the group bonds disintegrate, and the group veers toward dissolution. In a sudden, last-minute convulsive act, the group labels Hickey psychotic, banishes him, and gradually reestablishes its old norms and cohesion. These "pipe dreams"—or "vital lies," as Henrik Ibsen called them in *The Wild Duck*[56]—are often essential to personal and social integrity. They should not be taken lightly or impulsively stripped away in the service of honesty.

Commenting on the social problems of the United States, Victor Frankl once suggested that the Statue of Liberty on the East Coast be counterbalanced by a Statue of Responsibility on the West Coast.[57] In the therapy group, freedom becomes possible and constructive *only* when it is coupled with responsibility. None of us is free from impulses or feelings that, if expressed, could be destructive to others. I suggest that we encourage clients and therapists to speak freely, to shed all internal censors and filters save one—the filter of responsibility to others.

I do not mean that no unpleasant sentiments are to be expressed; indeed, growth cannot occur in the absence of conflict. I do mean, however, that *responsibility*, not total disclosure, is the superordinate principle.†

The therapist has a particular type of responsibility—responsibility to clients and to the task of therapy. Group members have a human responsibility toward one another. As therapy progresses, as solipsism diminishes, as empathy increases, they come to exercise that responsibility in their interactions among themselves.

Thus, your raison d'être as group therapist is not primarily to be honest or fully disclosing. You must be clear about why you reveal yourself. Do you have a clear therapeutic intent or is countertransference influencing your approach? What impact can you anticipate from your self-disclosure? In times of confusion about your behavior, you may profit from stepping back momentarily to reconsider your primary tasks in the group. Therapist self-disclosure is an aid to the group because it sets a model for the clients and permits some members to reality-test their feelings toward you. When considering a self-disclosure, ask yourself where the group is now. Is it a concealed, overly cautious group that may profit from a leader who models personal self-disclosure? Or has it already established vigorous self-disclosure norms and is in need of other kinds of assistance? Again, you must consider whether your behavior will interfere with your group-maintenance function. You must know when to recede into the background. Unlike the individual therapist, the group therapist does not have to be the axle of therapy. In part, you are midwife to the group: you must set a therapeutic process in motion and take care not to interfere with that process by insisting on your centrality.

An overly restricted definition of the role of group therapist—whether based on transparency or any other criterion—may cause the leader to lose sight of the individuality of each client's needs. Despite your group orientation, you must retain some individual focus; not all clients need the same thing. Some, perhaps most, clients need to relax controls; they need to learn how to express their affect—anger, love, tenderness, hatred. Others, however, need the opposite: they need to gain impulse control because their lifestyles are already characterized by labile, immediately acted-upon affect.

One final consequence of more or less unlimited therapist transparency is that the cognitive aspects of therapy may be completely neglected. As I noted earlier, *mere catharsis is not in itself a corrective experience.* Cognitive learning or restructuring (much of which is provided by the therapist) seems necessary for the client to be able to generalize group experiences to outside life; without this transfer or carryover, we have succeeded only in creating better, more gracious therapy group members. Without the acquisition of some knowledge about general patterns in interpersonal relationships, the client may, in effect, have to rediscover the wheel in each subsequent interpersonal transaction.

Chapter 8

THE SELECTION
OF CLIENTS

Good group therapy begins with good client selection. Clients improperly assigned to a therapy group are unlikely to benefit from their therapy experience. Furthermore, an improperly composed group may end up stillborn, never having developed into a viable treatment mode for any of its members. It is therefore understandable that contemporary psychotherapy researchers are actively examining the effects of matching clients to psychotherapies according to specific characteristics and attributes.[1]

In this chapter I consider both the research evidence bearing on selection and the clinical method of determining whether a given individual is a suitable candidate for group therapy. In chapter 9, on group composition, I will examine a different question: once it has been decided that a client is a suitable group therapy candidate, into which specific group should he or she go? These two chapters focus particularly on a specific type of group therapy: the heterogeneous outpatient group with the ambitious goals of symptomatic relief and characterological change. However, as I shall discuss shortly, many of these general principles have relevance to other types of groups, including the shorter-term problem-oriented group. Here, as elsewhere in this book, I employ the pedagogic strategy of providing the reader with fundamental group therapy principles plus strategies for adapting these principles to a variety of clinical situations.† There is no other reasonable educative strategy. Such a vast number of problem-specific groups exist (see also chapter 15) that one cannot focus separately on selection strategy for each specific one—nor would a teacher wish to. That would result in too narrow and too rigid an education. The graduate of such a curriculum would be unable to adapt to the forms that group therapy may take in future years. Once students are grounded in the prototypical psychotherapy group they will have the base which will permit them to modify technique to fit diverse clinical populations and settings.

Effectiveness of group therapy. Let us begin with the most fundamental question in client selection: Should the client—indeed, any client—be sent to group therapy? In other words, *how effective is group therapy?* This question, often asked by individual therapists and *always* asked by third-party payers, must be addressed before considering more subtle questions of client selection. The answer is unequivocal. *Group therapy is a potent modality producing significant benefit to its participants.*[2]

A great deal of research has also attempted to determine the relative efficacy of group versus individual therapy, and the results are clear: *there is considerable evidence that group therapy is at least as efficacious as individual therapy.* An excellent, early review of the thirty-two existing well-controlled experimental studies that compared individual and group therapy* indicates that group therapy *was more effective than individual therapy in 25 percent of the studies.* In the other 75 percent, there were *no significant differences* between group and individual therapy.[3] In no study was individual therapy more effective. A more recent review using a rigorous meta-analysis** demonstrated similar findings.[4] Other reviews, some including a greater number of studies (but less rigorously controlled), have reached similar conclusions and underscore that group therapy is also more efficient than individual therapy (from the standpoint of therapist resources) by a factor of two to one and perhaps as much as four to one.[5]

Research indicates further that group therapy has specific benefits: It is for example superior to individual therapy in the provision of social learning, developing social support, and improving social networks, factors of great importance in reducing relapse for clients with substance use disorders.[6] It is more effective than individual approaches for obesity[7] (an effect achieved in part through reducing stigma), and for clients with medical illness—clients learn to enhance self-efficacy better from peers than from individual therapy.[8] Adding group therapy to the treatment of women who are survivors of childhood sexual abuse provides benefits beyond individual therapy: it results in greater empowerment and psychological well-being.[9]

---

*This review included only studies that used random assignment to treatment situations (rather than matching or nonrandom assignment), which clearly specified the independent variables employed, and which measured dependent variables by one or more standardized instruments.

**Meta-analysis is a statistical approach that examines a large number of scientific studies by pooling their data together into one large data set to determine findings that might be missed if one were only to examine smaller data sets.

The evidence for the effectiveness of group therapy is so persuasive that some experts advocate that group therapy be utilized as the primary model of contemporary psychotherapy.[10] Individual therapy, however, may be preferable for clients who require active clinical management, or when relationship issues are less important and personal insight and understanding are particularly important.[11]

So far, so good! We can be confident (and each of us should convey this confidence to sources of referral and to third-party payers) that group therapy is an effective treatment modality.

One might reasonably expect the research literature to yield useful answers to the question of which clients do best in group therapy and which are better referred to another form of therapy. After all, here's all that needs to be done: Describe and measure a panoply of clinical and demographic characteristics before clients are randomly assigned to group therapy or to other modalities and then correlate these characteristics with appropriate dependent variables, such as therapy outcome, or perhaps some intervening variable, such as attendance, mode of interaction, or cohesiveness.

But the matter turns out to be far more complex. The methodological problems are severe, not least because a true measure of psychotherapy outcome is elusive. The client variables used to predict therapy outcome are affected by a host of other group, leader, and comember variables that confound the research enterprise.†[12] Clients drop out of therapy; many obtain ancillary individual therapy; group therapists vary in competence and technique; and initial diagnostic technique is unreliable and often idiosyncratic. An enormous number of clients are needed to obtain enough therapy groups for the results to be statistically significant. Although standardized therapies are required to ensure that each of the treatment modalities is delivering proper therapy, still each person and each group is exquisitely complex and cannot simplify itself in order to be precisely measured. Hence in this chapter I draw on relevant research but also rely heavily on clinical experience—my own and that of others.

CRITERIA FOR EXCLUSION

Question: How do group clinicians select clients for group psychotherapy? Answer: The great majority of clinicians do not select for group therapy. Instead, they *deselect*. Given a pool of clients, experienced group therapists determine that certain ones cannot possibly work in a therapy group and should be excluded. *And then they proceed to accept all the other clients.*

That approach seems crude. We would all prefer the selection process to be more elegant, more finely tuned. But, in practice, it is far easier to specify exclusion than inclusion criteria; one characteristic is sufficient to exclude an individual, whereas a more complex profile must be delineated to justify inclusion.

Keep in mind that there are many group therapies, and exclusion criteria apply only for the type of group under consideration. Almost all clients (there are exceptions) will fit into *some* group. A characteristic that excludes someone from one group may be the exact feature that secures entry into another group. A secretive, non–psychologically minded client with anorexia nervosa, for example, is generally a poor candidate for a long-term interactional group, but may be ideal for a homogeneous, cognitive-behavioral eating-disorders group.†

There is considerable clinical consensus that clients are poor candidates for a heterogeneous outpatient therapy group if they are brain-damaged,[13] paranoid,[14] hypochondriacal,[15] addicted to drugs or alcohol,[16] acutely psychotic,[17] or sociopathic.† But such dry lists are of less value than identifying underlying principles. Here is the major guideline: *clients will fail in group therapy if they are unable to participate in the primary task of the group, be it for logistical, intellectual, psychological, or interpersonal reasons.* This consideration is even more compelling for brief, time-limited groups, which are particularly unforgiving of poor client selection.†

What traits must a client possess to participate in the primary task of the dynamic, interactional therapy group? They must have a capacity and willingness to examine their interpersonal behaviors, to self-disclose, and to give and receive feedback. Unsuitable clients tend to construct an interpersonal role that proves detrimental to themselves as well as to the group. In such instances the group becomes a venue for re-creating and reconfirming maladaptive patterns without the possibility of learning or change.

Consider sociopathic clients, for example, who are exceptionally poor candidates for outpatient interactional group therapy. Characteristically, these individuals are destructive in the group. Although early in therapy they may become important and active members, they will eventually manifest their basic inability to relate, often with considerable dramatic and destructive impact, as the following clinical example illustrates.

• *Felix, a highly intelligent thirty-five-year-old man with a history of alcoholism, transiency, and impoverished interpersonal relationships, was added with two other new clients to an ongoing group, which had been reduced to three by the recent graduation of members. The group had shrunk so much that it seemed in danger of collapsing, and the therapists were anxious to reestablish its size. They realized that Felix was not an ideal candidate, but they had few applicants and decided to take the risk. In addition, they were somewhat intrigued by his stated determination to change his lifestyle. (Many sociopathic individuals are forever "reaching a turning point in life.")*

By the third meeting, Felix had become the social and emotional leader of the group, seemingly able to feel more acutely and suffer more deeply than the other members. He presented the group, as he had the therapists, with a largely fabricated account of his background and current life situation. By the fourth meeting, as the therapists learned later, he had seduced one of the female members and, in the fifth meeting, he spearheaded a discussion of the group's dissatisfaction with the brevity of the meetings. He proposed that the group, with or without the permission of the therapist, meet more often, perhaps at one of the members' homes, without the therapist. By the sixth meeting, Felix had vanished, without notifying the group. The therapists learned later that he had suddenly decided to take a 2,000-mile bicycle trip, hoping to sell an article about it to a magazine.

This extreme example illustrates many of the reasons why the inclusion of a sociopathic individual in a heterogeneous ambulatory group is ill advised: his social front is deceptive; he often consumes such an inordinate amount of group energy that his departure leaves the group bereft, puzzled, and discouraged; he rarely assimilates the group therapeutic norms and instead often exploits other members and the group as a whole for his immediate gratification. *Let me emphasize that I do not mean that group therapy per se is contraindicated for sociopathic clients.* In fact, a specialized form of group therapy with a more homogeneous population and a wise use of strong group and institutional pressure may well be the treatment of choice.[18]

Most clinicians agree that clients in the midst of some acute situational crisis are not good candidates for group therapy; they are far better treated in crisis-intervention therapy in an individual, family, or social network format.[19] Deeply depressed suicidal clients are best not admitted to an interactionally focused heterogeneous therapy group either. It is difficult for the group to give them the specialized attention they require (except at enormous expense of time and energy to the other members); furthermore, the threat of suicide is too taxing, too anxiety provoking, for the other group members to manage.[20] Again, that does not mean that group therapy per se (or group therapy in combination with individual therapy) should be ruled out. A structured homogeneous group for chronic suicidality has been reported to be effective.[21]

Good attendance is so necessary for the development of a cohesive group that it is wise to exclude clients who, for any reason, may not attend regularly. Poor attendance may be due to unpredictable and hard-to-control work demands, or it may be an expression of initial resistance to therapy. I do not select individuals whose work requires extensive travel that would cause them to miss even one out of every four or five meetings. Similarly, I am hesitant to select clients who must depend on others for transportation to the group or who would have a very long commute to the group. Too often, especially early in the course of a group, a client may feel neglected or dissatisfied with a meeting, perhaps because another member may have received the bulk of the group time and attention, or the group may have been busy building its own infrastructure—work that may not offer obvious immediate gratification. Deep feelings of frustration may, if coupled with a long, strenuous commute, dampen motivation and result in sporadic attendance.

Obviously, there are many exceptions: some therapists tell of clients who faithfully fly to meetings from remote regions month after month. As a general rule, however, the therapist does well to heed this factor. For clients who live at considerable distance and have equivalent groups elsewhere, it is in everyone's interests to refer them to a group closer to home.

These clinical criteria for exclusion are broad and crude. Some therapists have attempted to arrive at more refined criteria through systematic study of clients who have failed to derive benefit from group therapy. Let me examine the research on one category of unsuccessful clients: the group therapy dropouts.

Dropouts

There is evidence that premature termination from group therapy is bad for the client and bad for the group. In a study of thirty-five clients who dropped out of long-term heterogeneous interactional outpatient groups in twelve or fewer meetings, I found that only three reported themselves as improved.[22] Moreover, those three individuals had only marginal symptomatic improvement. None of the thirty-five clients left therapy because they had satisfactorily concluded their work; they had all been dissatisfied with the therapy group experience. Their premature terminations had, in addition, an adverse effect on the remaining members of the group, who were threatened and demoralized by the early dropouts. In fact, many group leaders report a "wave effect," with dropouts begetting other dropouts. The proper development of a group requires membership stability; a rash of dropouts may delay the maturation of a group for months.

Early group termination is thus a failure for the individual and a detriment to the therapy of the remainder of the group. Unfortunately, it is common across the psychotherapies. A recent empirical analysis concluded that 47 percent of all clients leave psychotherapy (group and individual therapy as well) prematurely.[23] Even in expert hands some dropouts are unavoidable, no doubt because of the complex interplay of client, group, and therapist variables.[24] Consider the dropout rates displayed in table 8.1: group therapy attrition ranges from 17 percent to 57 percent. Although this rate is no higher than the dropout rate from individual therapy, the dropout phenomenon is of more concern to group therapists because of the deleterious effects of dropouts on the rest of the group.

A study of early dropouts may help establish sound exclusion criteria and, furthermore, may provide an important goal for the selection process. If, in the selection process, we learn merely to screen out members destined to drop out of therapy, *that in itself* would constitute a major achievement. Although the early terminators are not the only failures in group therapy, they are unequivocal failures.† We may, I think, dismiss as unlikely the possibility that early dropouts will have gained something positive that will manifest itself later. A relevant outcome study of encounter group participants noted that individuals who had a negative experience in the group did not, when studied six months later, "put it all together" and enjoy a delayed benefit from the group experience.[25] If they left the group shaken or discouraged, they were very likely to remain that way. (One exception to the rule may be individuals who enter in some urgent life crisis and terminate therapy as soon as the crisis is resolved.)

Keep in mind that the study of group dropouts tells us little about the group continuers; group continuation is a necessary but insufficient factor in successful therapy, although evidence exists that clients who continue in treatment and avoid premature or forced ending achieve the best therapy outcomes.[26]

Reasons for Premature Termination

A number of rigorous studies of group therapy in various settings (ambulatory, day hospital, Veterans Administration clinics, and private practice, including both heterogeneous groups and homogeneous groups for problems such as grief or depression, and conducted in an interactional manner or along cognitive-behavioral lines) have convergent findings.[27] These studies demonstrate that clients who drop out prematurely from group therapy are likely, at the initial screening or in the first few meetings, to have one or more of the following characteristics:

- Lower psychological-mindedness
- Reduced capacity to think about emotions without action
- Lower motivation
- More reactive than reflective
- Less positive emotion
- Greater denial
- Higher somatization
- Abuse of substances
- Greater anger and hostility
- Lower socioeconomic class and social effectiveness
- Lower intelligence
- Lack of understanding of how group therapy works

TABLE 8.1   Group Therapy Dropout Rates

Type of Group	Length of Group	Number of Sessions	Percent Dropping Out
University outpatient clinic	General, open-ended	12 or fewer	50%[a]
University outpatient clinic	Bereavement, closed	12 or fewer	28%[b]
University outpatient clinic	Short-term	8 or fewer	39%[c]
University outpatient clinic	Open-ended	3 or fewer	57%[d]
VA outpatient clinic	Open-ended	9 or fewer	51%[e]
VA outpatient clinic	Open-ended	16 or fewer	50%[f]
University outpatient clinic	Open-ended	12 or fewer	35%[g]
Private and clinic	Open-ended	3 or fewer	30%[h]
Clinic and hospital	Inpatient and outpatient	20 or fewer	25%[i]
Private practice	Long-term, analytic	12 months or less	35%[j]
Outpatient clinic	Open-ended	12 or fewer	17%[k]
Outpatient clinic	Short-term	5 or fewer	17%[l]
Private and clinic	Analytic	10 or fewer	24%[m]
Clinic	Dynamically oriented	6 months or less	17%[n]
Private practice	Dynamic/analytic	6 months or less	27% therapist A 38% therapist B[o]
Private practice	Analytic/long-term	1 year or less	55%[p]
University counseling center	Interactional/ interpersonal	12 or fewer	31% therapist A 45% therapist B[q]
Outpatient clinic	Complicated grief	8 or fewer	23%[r]
Outpatient clinic	CBT for depression	12 weeks or fewer	48%[s]

(NOTE: See endnote 28 on p. 602 for the notes for this table.)

- The experience or expectation of cultural insensitivity
- Less likable (at least according to therapists)

These conclusions suggest that, unfortunately, the rich get richer and the poor get poorer. What a paradox! The clients who have the least skills and attributes needed for working in a group—*the very ones who most need what the group has to offer*—are those most likely to fail! It is this paradox (along with economic issues) that has stimulated attempts to modify the therapy group experience sufficiently with different structures and outreach to accommodate more of these at-risk clients.†

Keep in mind that these characteristics should therefore be seen as cautions rather than absolute contraindications. The person who fails in one group or in one type of group may do well in a different one. We should aim to reduce, not eliminate dropouts. If we create groups that never experience a dropout, then it may be that we are setting our bar for entry too high, thus eliminating clients in need who we may in fact be able to help.

I will discuss one final study here in great detail, since it has considerable relevance for the selection process.[29] I studied the first six months of nine therapy groups in a university outpatient clinic and investigated all clients who terminated in twelve or fewer meetings. A total of ninety-seven clients were involved in these groups (seventy-one original members and twenty-six later additions); of these, thirty-five were early dropouts. Considerable data were generated from interviews and questionnaire studies of the dropouts and their therapists as well as from the records and observations of the group sessions and historical and demographic data from the case records.

An analysis of the data suggested nine major reasons for the clients' dropping out of therapy:

1. External factors
2. Group deviancy
3. Problems of intimacy
4. Fear of emotional contagion
5. Inability to share the therapist
6. Complications of concurrent individual and group therapy
7. Early provocateurs
8. Inadequate orientation to therapy
9. Complications arising from subgrouping

Usually more than one factor is involved in the decision to terminate. Some factors are more closely related to external circumstances or to enduring character traits that the client brings to the group, and thus are relevant to the selection process, whereas others are related to the therapist or to problems arising within the group (for example, the therapist's skill and competence, client-therapist interaction variables, and the group culture itself)† and thus are more relevant to therapist technique (I will discuss these issues in chapters 10 and 11). Most relevant to the establishment of selection criteria are the clients who dropped out because of *external factors, group deviancy, and problems of intimacy.*

External Factors. Logistical *reasons* for terminating therapy (for example, irreconcilable scheduling conflicts, moving out of the geographic area) played a negligible role in decisions to terminate. When this reason was offered by the client, closer study usually revealed group-related stress that was more pertinent to the client's departure. Nevertheless, in the initial screening session, the therapist should always inquire about any pending major life changes, such as a move. There is considerable evidence that therapy aimed at both symptom relief and making major changes in the clients' underlying character structure is not a brief form of therapy—a minimum of six months is necessary†—and that clients should not be accepted into such therapy if there is a considerable likelihood of forced termination within the next few months. Such individuals are better candidates for shorter-term, problem-oriented groups.

External stress was considered a factor in the premature dropout of several clients who were so disturbed by external events in their lives that it was difficult for them to expend the energy for involvement in the group. They could not explore their relationships with other group members while they were consumed with the threat of disruption of relationships with the most significant people in their lives. It seemed especially pointless and frustrating to them to hear other group members discuss their problems when their own problems seemed so compelling. Among the external stresses were severe marital discord with impending divorce, impending career or academic failure, disruptive relationship with family members, bereavement, and severe physical illness. In such instances referrals should be made to groups explicitly designed to deal with such situations: acute grief, for example, is generally a time-limited condition, and the acutely bereaved client is best referred to a short-term bereavement group.[30]

Note an important difference! If the goal is specifically (and nothing more than) to get rid of the pain of a break up, then a brief, problem-oriented therapy is indicated. But if the client wishes to change something in himself that causes him to thrust himself repetitively into such painful situations (for example, he continues to become involved with women who invariably leave him), then longer-term group work is indicated.

The importance of external stress as a factor in premature group termination was difficult to gauge, since often it appeared secondary to internal forces. A client's psychic turmoil may cause disruption of his or her life situation so that secondary external stress occurs; or a client may focus on an external problem, magnifying it as a means of escaping anxiety originating from the group therapy. Several clients considered external stress the chief reason for termination; but in each instance, careful study suggested that external stress was at best a contributory but not sufficient cause for the dropout. Undue focusing on external events often seemed to be one manifestation of a denial mechanism that was helping the client avoid something perceived as dangerous in the group.

In the selection process, therefore, consider an unwarranted focusing on external stress an unfavorable sign for intensive group therapy, whether it represents an extraordinary amount of stress or a manifestation of denial.

Group Deviancy. The study of clients who drop out of therapy because they are group deviants offers a rich supply of information relevant to the selection process. But first the term *deviant* must be carefully defined. Almost every group member is deviant in the sense of representing an extreme in at least one dimension—for example, the youngest member, the only unmarried member, the sickest, the only Asian-American, the only student, the angriest, the quietest.

However, one-third of the dropouts in my study deviated significantly from the rest of the group *in areas crucial to their group participation,* and this deviancy and its repercussions were considered the primary reason for their premature termination. The clients' behavior in the group varied from those who were silent to those who were loud, angry group disrupters, but all were isolates and were perceived by the therapists and by the other members as retarding the progress of the group.

The group and the therapists said of all these members that they "just didn't fit in." Indeed, often the deviants said that of themselves. This distinction is difficult to translate into objectively measurable factors. The most commonly described characteristics are lack of psychological-mindedness and lack of interpersonal sensitivity. These clients were often of lower socioeconomic status and educational level than the rest of the group. The therapists, when describing the deviants' group behavior, emphasized that they slowed the group down. They functioned on a different level of communication from that of the rest of the group. They remained at the symptom-describing, advice-giving and -seeking, or judgmental level and avoided discussion of immediate feelings and here-and-now interaction. Similar results are reported by others.[31]

An important subcategory of dropouts had chronic mental illness and were making a marginal adjustment. They had sealed over and utilized much denial and suppression and were obviously different from other group members in their dress, mannerisms, and comments. Given the negative psychological impact of high expressed emotionality on clients with chronic mental illness such as schizophrenia, an intensive interactional group therapy would be contraindicated in their treatment. Structured, supportive, and psychoeducational groups are more effective.†

Two clients in the study who did *not* drop out differed vastly from the other members in their life experience. One had a history of prostitution, the other had prior problems with drug addiction and dealing. However, these clients did not differ from the others in ways that impeded the group's progress (psychological insight, interpersonal sensitivity, and effective communication) and never became group deviants.

Group Deviancy: Empirical Research.   Considerable social-psychological data from laboratory group research[*32] helps us understand the fate of the deviant in the therapy group. Group members who are unable to participate in the group task and who impede group progress toward the completion of the task are much less attracted to the group and are motivated to terminate membership.[33] Individuals whose contributions fail to match high group standards for interaction have a high dropout rate, and the tendency to drop out is particularly marked among individuals who have a lower level of self-esteem.[34]

The task of group therapy is to engage in meaningful communication with the other group members, to reveal oneself, to give valid feedback, and to examine the hidden and unconscious aspects of one's feelings, behavior, and motivation. Individuals who fail at this task often lack the required amount of psychological-mindedness, are less introspective, less inquisitive, and more likely to use self-deceptive defense mechanisms. They also may be reluctant to accept the role of client and the accompanying implication that some personal change is necessary.

Research has shown that the individuals who are most satisfied with themselves and who are inclined to overestimate others' opinions of them tend to profit less from the group experience.[35] One study demonstrated that group members who did not highly value or desire personal changes were likely to terminate the group prematurely.[36] Questionnaire studies demonstrate that therapy group members who cannot accurately perceive how others view them are more likely to remain peripheral members.[37]

What happens to individuals who are unable to engage in the basic group task and are perceived by the group and, at some level of awareness, by themselves as impeding the group? Schachter has demonstrated that communication toward a deviant is high initially and then drops off sharply as the group rejects the deviant member.[38]

Much research has demonstrated that a member's satisfaction with the group depends on his or her position in the group communication network[39] and the degree to which that member is considered valuable by the other members of the group.[40] It also has been demonstrated that the ability of the group to influence an individual depends partly on the attractiveness of the group for that member and partly on the degree to which

---

*Laboratory group research generally involves volunteers or, more often, university students taking courses in group therapy or counseling. The participants' educational objective is to learn about group dynamics through firsthand experience in groups created for that purpose. Because these groups are well structured, time limited, and composed of members willing to answer study questionnaires, they lend themselves naturally to group research.

the member communicates with the others in the group.[41] An individual's status in a group is conferred by the group, not seized by the individual. Lower status diminishes personal well-being and has a negative impact on one's emotional experience in social groups.[42] This is an important finding, and we will return to it: Lower group status *diminishes* personal well-being; in other words, it is antitherapeutic.

It is also well known from the work of Sherif[43] and Asch[44] that an individual will often be made exceedingly uncomfortable by a deviant group role, and there is evidence that such individuals will manifest progressively more anxiety and unease if unable to speak about their position.[45] Lieberman, Yalom, and Miles demonstrated that deviant group members (members considered "out of the group" by the other members or who grossly misperceived the group norms) *had virtually no chance of benefiting from the group and an increased likelihood of suffering negative consequences.*[46]

To summarize, *experimental evidence suggests that the group deviant, compared with other group members, derives less satisfaction from the group, experiences anxiety, is less valued by the group, is less likely to be influenced by or to benefit from the group, is more likely to be harmed by the group, and is far more likely to terminate membership.*

These experimental findings coincide with the experience of deviants in the therapy groups I studied. Of the eleven deviants, one did not terminate prematurely—a middle-aged, isolated, rigidly defended man. This man managed to continue in the group because of the massive support he received in concurrent individual therapy. However, he not only remained an isolate in the group but, in the opinion of the therapists and the other members, he impeded the progress of the group. What happened in that group was remarkably similar to the phenomena in Schachter's laboratory groups described above.[47] At first, considerable group energy was expended on the deviant; eventually the group gave up, and the deviant was, to a great extent, excluded from the communicational network. But the group could never entirely forget the deviant, who slowed the pace of the work. If there is something important going on in the group that cannot be talked about, there will always be a degree of generalized communicative inhibition. With a disenfranchised member, the group is never really free; in a sense, it cannot move much faster than its slowest member.

Now, let's apply these research findings and clinical observations to the selection process. The clients who will assume a deviant role in therapy groups are not difficult to identify in screening interviews. Their denial, their de-emphasis of intrapsychic and interpersonal factors, their unwillingness to be influenced by interpersonal interaction, and their tendency to attribute dysphoria to somatic and external environmental factors will be evident in a carefully conducted interview. Some of these individuals stand out by virtue of significantly greater impairment in function. They are often referred to group therapy by their individual therapists, who feel discouraged or frustrated by the lack of progress. Occasionally, postponing entry into group therapy to provide more time for some clients to benefit from pharmacotherapy and to consolidate some stability make may group therapy possible at a later time, but in conjunction with individual treatment and management, not in place of it.

Thus, it is not difficult to identify these clients. Clinicians often err in assuming that even if certain clients will not click with the rest of the group, they will nevertheless benefit from the overall group support and the opportunity to improve their socializing techniques. In my experience, this expectation is not realized. The referral is a poor one, with neither the client nor the group profiting. Eventually the group will extrude the deviant. Therapists also tend to divest overtly and covertly from such clients, putting their therapautic energies into those clients who reward the effort.[48]

Rigid attitudes coupled with proselytizing desires may rapidly propel an individual into a deviant position. A very difficult client to work with in long-term groups is the individual who employs fundamentalist religious views in the service of denial. The defenses of this client are often impervious to ordinarily potent group pressures because they are bolstered by the norms of another anchor group—the particular religious sect. To tell the client that he or she is applying certain basic tenets with unrealistic literalness is often ineffective, and a frontal assault on these defenses merely rigidifies them.

To summarize, it is important that the therapist screen out clients who are likely to become marked deviants in the group for which they are being considered. *Clients become deviants because of their interpersonal behavior in the group sessions, not because of a deviant lifestyle or history. There is no type of past behavior too deviant for a group to accept once therapeutic group norms have been established. I have seen individuals who have been involved with prostitution, exhibitionism, incest, voyeurism, kleptomania, infanticide, robbery, and drug dealing accepted by middle-class straight groups.*

Problems of Intimacy.   Several clients dropped out of group therapy because of conflicts associated with intimacy, manifested in various ways: (1) schizoid withdrawal, (2) maladaptive self-disclosure (promiscuous self-disclosures or pervasive dread of self-disclosure), and (3) unrealistic demands for instant intimacy.*

---

*The dropout categories have substantial overlap. Many of the clients who dropped out because of problems of intimacy began to occupy a deviant role because of the behavioral manifestations of their intimacy problems. Had the stress of the intimacy conflict not forced them to terminate, it is likely that the inherent stresses of the deviant role would have created pressures leading to termination.

Several clients who were diagnosed as having schizoid personality disorder (reflecting their social withdrawal, interpersonal coldness, aloofness, introversion, and tendency toward autistic preoccupation) experienced considerable difficulty relating and communicating in the group. Each had begun the group with a resolution to express feelings and to correct previous maladaptive patterns of relating. They failed to accomplish this aim and experienced frustration and anxiety, which in turn further blocked their efforts to speak. Their therapists described their group role as "isolate," "silent member," "peripheral," and "nonrevealer."

Most of these group members terminated treatment thoroughly discouraged about the possibility of ever obtaining help from group therapy. Early in the course of a new group, I have occasionally seen such clients leave the group having benefited much from therapeutic factors such as universality, identification, altruism, and development of socializing techniques. If they remain in the group, however, the group members, in time, often grow impatient with the schizoid member's silence and weary of drawing them out ("playing twenty questions," as one group put it) and turn against them.

Another intimacy-conflicted client dropped out for different reasons: his fears of his own aggression against other group members. He originally applied for treatment because of a feeling of wanting to explode: "a fear of killing someone when I explode . . . which results in my staying far away from people." He participated intellectually in the first four meetings he attended, but was frightened by the other members' expression of emotion. When a group member monopolized the entire fifth meeting with a repetitive, tangential discourse, he was enraged with the monopolizer and with the rest of the group members for their complacency in allowing this to happen and, with no warning, abruptly terminated therapy.

Other clients experienced a constant, pervasive dread of self-disclosure, which precluded participation in the group and ultimately resulted in their dropping out. Still others engaged in premature, promiscuous self-disclosure and abruptly terminated. Some clients made such inordinate demands on their fellow group members for immediate, prefabricated intimacy that they created a nonviable group role for themselves. One early dropout unsettled the group in her first meeting by announcing to the group that she gossiped compulsively and doubted that she would be able to maintain people's confidentiality.

Clients with severe problems in the area of intimacy present a particular challenge to the group therapist both in selection and in therapeutic management (to be considered in chapter 13). The irony is that these individuals are the very ones for whom a successful group experience could be particularly rewarding. A study of experiential groups found that individuals with constricted emotionality, who are threatened by the

expression of feelings by others, and have difficulty experiencing and expressing their own emotional reactions learn more and change more than
others as a result of their group experience, even though they are significantly more uncomfortable in the group.[49] Therefore, these clients, whose
life histories are characterized by ungratifying interpersonal relationships,
stand to profit much from successfully negotiating an intimate group experience. Yet, if their interpersonal history has been too deprived, they
will find the group too threatening and will drop out of therapy more demoralized than before.[50] Clients who crave social connectedness but are
hampered by poor interpersonal skills are particularly prone to psychological distress.[51] These individuals are frustrated and distressed being in
a group bursting with opportunities for connectedness that they cannot
access for themselves.[52]

Thus, clients with problems in intimacy represent at the same time a
specific indication and contraindication for group therapy. The problem,
of course, is how to identify and screen out those who will be overwhelmed in the group. If only we could accurately quantify this critical
cutoff point! The prediction of group behavior from pretherapy screening
sessions is a complex task that I will discuss in detail in the next chapter.

Individuals with severe character and narcissistic pathology and a pervasive dread of self-disclosure may be unfavorable candidates for interactional group therapy. But if such individuals are dissatisfied with their
interpersonal styles, express a strong motivation for change, and manifest
curiosity about their inner lives, then they stand a better chance of benefiting from a therapy group. The group interaction may cause these individuals intense anxiety about losing their sense of self and autonomy.
They crave connectedness yet fear losing themselves in that very process.
Interpersonal defenses against these vulnerabilities, such as withdrawal,
devaluation, or self-aggrandizement, may push the group member into a
deviant group role.[53] Mildly or moderately schizoid clients and individuals with avoidant personality disorder, on the other hand, are excellent
candidates for group therapy and rarely fail to benefit from it.

Greater caution should be exercised when the therapist is seeking a re-
placement member for an already established, fast-moving group. Often,
combining individual and group therapy may be necessary to launch or
sustain vulnerable clients in the group. The added support and containment provided by the individual therapist may diminish the sense of risk
for the client.[54]

Fear of Emotional Contagion.   Several clients who dropped out of group
therapy reported being adversely affected by hearing the problems of the
other group members. One man stated that during his three weeks in the

group, he was very upset by the others' problems, dreamed about them every night, and relived their problems during the day. Other clients reported being upset by one particularly disturbed client in each of their groups. They were all frightened by seeing aspects of the other client in themselves and feared that they might become as mentally ill as the severely disturbed client or that continued exposure to that member would evoke a personal regression. Another client in this category who bolted from the first group meeting thirty minutes early and never returned described a severe revulsion toward the other group members. "I couldn't stand the people in the group. They were repulsive. I got upset seeing them trying to heap their problems on top of mine. I didn't want to hear their problems. I felt no sympathy for them and couldn't bear to look at them. They were all ugly, fat, and unattractive." This client had a lifelong history of being upset by other people's illnesses and avoiding sick people. Once when her mother fainted, she "stepped over her" to get away rather than trying to help. Other clinicians have noted that clients in this category have a long-term proclivity to avoid sick people, and, if they had been present at an accident were the first to leave or tended to look the other way.[55]

Such concern about contagion has many possible dynamics. Many clients with borderline personality disorder report such fears (it is a common phenomenon in inpatient group therapy), and it is often regarded as a sign of permeable ego boundaries and an inability to differentiate oneself from significant others in one's environment.

A fear of emotional contagion, unless it is extremely marked and clearly manifest in the pretherapy screening procedure, is not a particularly useful index for selection or exclusion for a group. Generally, it is difficult to predict this behavior from screening interviews. Furthermore, fear of emotional contagion is not in itself sufficient cause for failure. Therapists who are sensitive to the problem can deal with it effectively in the therapeutic process. Occasionally, clients must gradually desensitize themselves: I have known individuals who dropped out of several therapy groups but who persevered until they were finally able to remain in one. These attitudes by no means rule out group therapy. The therapist may help by clarifying for the client the crippling effects of his or her attitudes toward others' distress. How can one develop friendships if one cannot bear to hear of another's difficulties? If the discomfort can be contained, the group may well offer the ideal therapeutic format for such a client.

Other Reasons. The other reasons for group therapy dropouts—inability to share the therapist, complications of concurrent individual and group therapy, early provocateurs, problems in orientation to therapy, and complications arising from subgrouping—were generally a result less of faulty selection than of faulty therapeutic technique; they will be discussed in later chapters. None of these categories, though, belongs solely under the rubric of selection or therapy technique. For example, some clients terminated because of an inability to share the therapist. They never relinquished the notion that progress in therapy was dependent solely on the amount of goods (time, attention, and so on) they received from the group therapist.

Although it may have been true that these clients tended to be excessively dependent and authority oriented, it was also true that they had been incorrectly referred to group therapy. They had all been in individual therapy, and the group was considered a method of therapy weaning. Obviously, group therapy is not a modality to be used to facilitate the termination phase of individual therapy, and the therapist, in pretherapy screening, should be alert to inappropriate client referrals. Sometimes clients' strong reluctance to relinquish individual therapy will prevent them engaging in group therapy.†

As we saw in earlier chapters, there is compelling evidence that the strength of the therapeutic alliance predicts therapy outcome. Conversely, problems with the alliance, such as client-therapist disagreement about the goals, tasks, or therapy relationship, are associated with premature terminations and failure. A study of ten dropouts noted that several clients had been inadequately prepared for the group.[56] The therapist had been unclear about the reasons for placing them in a group. No clear set of goals had been formulated, and some clients were suspicious of the therapists' motives—questioning whether they had been placed in the group simply because the group needed a warm body. Some were wounded by being placed in a group with significantly dysfunctional members. They took this as a statement of the therapist's judgment of their condition. Some were wounded simply by being referred to a group, as though they were being reduced from a state of specialness to a state of ordinariness. Still others left the group because of a perceived imbalance in the giving-receiving process. They felt that they gave far more than they received in the group.

CRITERIA FOR INCLUSION

The most important clinical criterion for inclusion is the most obvious one: motivation.[57] The client must be highly motivated for therapy in general and for group therapy in particular. It will not do to start group therapy because one has been sent—whether by spouse, probation officer, individual therapist, or any individual or agency outside oneself. Many erroneous prejudgments of the group may be corrected in the preparation procedure (see chapter 10), but if you discern a deeply rooted unwillingness to accept responsibility for treatment or deeply entrenched unwill-ingness to enter the group, you should not accept that person as a group therapy member.

Most clinicians agree that an important criterion for inclusion is whether a client has obvious problems in the interpersonal domain: for example, loneliness, shyness and social withdrawal, inability to be inti-mate or to love, excessive competitiveness, aggressivity, abrasiveness, ar-gumentativeness, suspiciousness, problems with authority, narcissism, an inability to share, to empathize, to accept criticism, a continuous need for admiration, feelings of unlovability, fears of assertiveness, obsequious-ness, and dependency. In addition, of course, clients must be willing to take some responsibility for these problems or, at the very least, acknowl-edge them and entertain a desire for change.

Some clinicians suggest group therapy for clients who do not work well in individual therapy as a result of their limited ability to report on events in their life (because of blind spots or because of ego syntonic character pathology.)[58]

Impulsive individuals who find it difficult to control the need to act im-mediately on their feelings usually work better in groups than in individ-ual therapy.[59] The therapist working with these clients in individual therapy often finds it difficult to remain both participant and observer, whereas in the group these two roles are divided among the members: some members may, for example, rush to battle with the impulsive client, while others egg them on ("Let's you and him fight"), and others act as disinterested, reliable witnesses whose testimony the impulsive client is often far more willing to trust than the therapist's.

In cases where interpersonal problems are not paramount (or not obvi-ous to the client), group therapy may still be the treatment of choice. For example, clients who are extremely intellectualized may do better with the affective stimuli available in a group. Other clients fare poorly in individ-ual therapy because of severe problems in the transference: they may not be able to tolerate the intimacy of the dyadic situation, either so distort-ing the therapeutic relationship or becoming so deeply involved with (or oppositional to) the therapist that they need the reality testing offered by other group members to make therapy possible. Others are best treated in a group because they characteristically elicit strong negative counter-transference from an individual therapist.[60]

• *Grant, a thirty-eight-year-old man referred to group therapy by his fe-male individual therapist, struggled with anger and a near-phobic avoidance of tenderness or dependence that he believed was related to physical abuse he suffered at the hands of his brutal father. When his young son's physical playfulness became frightening to him, he sought individual therapy because of his concern that he would be an inadequate or abusive father.*

At first the individual therapy progressed well, but soon the therapist became uneasy with Grant's aggressive and crude sexual feelings toward her. She became particularly concerned when Grant suggested that he could best express his gratitude to her through sexual means. Stymied in working this through, yet reluctant to end the therapy because of Grant's gains, the therapist referred him to a therapy group, hoping that the concurrent group and individual format would dilute the intensity of the transference and countertransference. The group offered so many alternatives for both relatedness and confrontation that Grant's treatment was able to proceed effectively in both venues.

Many clients seek therapy without an explicit interpersonal complaint. They may cite the common problems that propel the contemporary client into therapy: a sense of something missing in life, feelings of meaninglessness, diffuse anxiety, anhedonia, identity confusion, mild depression, self-derogation or self-destructive behavior, compulsive workaholism, fears of success, alexithymia.[61] But if one looks closely, each of these complaints has its interpersonal underpinnings, and each generally may be treated as successfully in group therapy as in individual therapy.[62]

Research on Inclusion Criteria

Any systematic approach to defining criteria for inclusion must issue from the study of successful group therapy participants. Unfortunately, as I discussed at the beginning of this chapter, such research is extraordinarily difficult to control. I should note that prediction of outcome in individual therapy research is equally difficult, and recent reviews stress the paucity of successful, clinically relevant research.[63]

In a study of forty clients in five outpatient therapy groups through one year of group therapy, my colleagues and I attempted to identify factors that were evident before group therapy that might predict successful outcome.[64] Outcome was evaluated and correlated with many variables measured before the start of therapy. Our results indicated that none of the pretherapy factors measured were predictive of success in group therapy, including level of psychological sophistication, therapists' prediction of outcome, previous self-disclosure, and demographic data. However, two factors measured early in therapy (at the sixth and the twelfth meetings) predicted success one year later: the clients' attraction to the group and the clients' general popularity in the group.[65] The finding that popularity correlated highly with successful outcome has some implications for selection, because researchers have found that high self-disclosure, activity in the group, and the ability to introspect were some of the prerequisites for group popularity.[66] Recall that popularity and status in a group accrues to individuals who model the behaviors that advance the group's achievement of its goals.[67]

The Lieberman, Yalom, and Miles study (see chapter 16) demonstrated that, in pregroup testing, those who were to profit most from the group were those who highly valued and desired personal change; who viewed themselves as deficient both in understanding their own feelings and in their sensitivity to the feelings of others; who had high expectations for the group, anticipating that it would provide relevant opportunities for communication and help them correct their deficiencies.[68]

Melnick and Rose, in a project involving forty-five encounter group members, determined at the start of the group each member's risk-taking propensity and expectations about the quality of interpersonal behavior to be experienced in the group. They then measured each member's actual behavior in the group (including self-disclosure, feedback given, risk taking, verbal activity, depth of involvement, attraction to the group).[69] *They found that both high-risk propensity and more favorable expectations correlated with therapeutically favorable behavior in the group.*

The finding that a positive expectational set is predictive of favorable outcome has substantial research support: *the more a client expects therapy—either group or individual—to be useful, the more useful will it be.*†[70] The role of prior therapy is important in this regard: experienced clients have more positive and more realistic expectations of therapy. Agreement between therapist and client about therapy expectations strengthens the therapeutic alliance, which also predicts better therapy outcome.[71] This relationship between positive expectational set and positive outcome has important implications not only for the selection process but also for the preparation of clients for therapy. As I will discuss in chapter 10, it is possible, through proper preparation, to create a favorable expectational set.

The Client's Effect on Other Group Members

Other inclusion criteria become evident when we consider the other members of a group into which the client may be placed. Thus far, for pedagogical clarity, I have oversimplified the problem by attempting to identify only absolute criteria for inclusion or exclusion. Unlike individual therapy recruitment, where we need consider only whether the client will profit from therapy and whether he or she and a specific therapist can establish a working relationship, recruitment for group therapy cannot, in practice, ignore the other group members.

It is conceivable, for example, that a depressed suicidal client or a compulsive talker might derive some benefit from a group, but also that such a client's presence would render the group less effective for several other members. Group therapists not only commit themselves to the treatment of everyone they bring into the group, they also commit all of their other members to that individual. For example, Grant, the client described earlier in this chapter, elicited very powerful reactions from the women in the early phases of his group therapy. At one point a female member of the group responded to one of a series of Grant's angry attacks with, "I am trying to understand where Grant is coming from, but how much longer must I sacrifice myself and my progress for his therapy?"

Conversely, there may be clients who would do well in a variety of treatment modalities but are placed in a group to meet some specific group needs. For example, some groups at times seem to need an aggressive member, or a strong male, or a soft feminine member. While clients with borderline personality disorder often have a stormy course of therapy, some group therapists intentionally introduce them into a group because of their beneficial influence on the group therapy process. Generally, such individuals are more aware of their unconscious, less inhibited, and less dedicated to social formality, and they may lead the group into a more candid and intimate culture. Considerable caution must be exercised, however, in including a member whose ego strength is significantly less than that of the other members. If these clients have socially desirable behavioral traits and are valued by the other members because of their openness and deep perceptivity, they will generally do very well. If, however, their behavior alienates others, and if the group is so fast moving or threatening that they retard the group rather than lead it, then they will be driven into a deviant role and their experience is likely to be countertherapeutic.

The Therapist's Feeling Toward the Client

One final, and important, criterion for inclusion is the therapist's personal feeling toward the client. Regardless of the source, the therapist who strongly dislikes or is disinterested in a client (and cannot understand or alter that reaction) should refer that person elsewhere. This caveat is obviously relative, and you must establish for yourself which feelings would preclude effective therapy.

It is my impression that this issue is somewhat more manageable for group therapists than for individual therapists. With the consensual validation available in the group from other members and from the co-therapist, many therapists find that they are more often able to work through initial negative feelings toward clients in group therapy than in individual therapy. Nonetheless there is evidence that therapist hostility often results in premature termination in group therapy.[72] As therapists gain experience and self-knowledge, they usually develop greater generosity and tolerance and find themselves actively disliking fewer and fewer clients. Often the antipathy the therapist experiences reflects the client's characteristic impact on others and thus constitutes useful data for therapy.†

AN OVERVIEW OF THE SELECTION PROCEDURE

The material I have presented thus far about selection of clients may seem disjunctive. I can introduce some order by applying to this material a central organizing principle—a simple punishment-reward system. Clients are likely to terminate membership in a therapy group prematurely—and hence are poor candidates—*when the punishments or disadvantages of group membership outweigh the rewards or the anticipated rewards.* By "punishments" and "disadvantages," I mean the price the client must pay for group membership, including an investment of time, money, and energy as well as a variety of uncomfortable feelings arising from the group experience, including anxiety, frustration, discouragement, and rejection.

The client should play an important role in the selection process. It is preferable that one deselect oneself before entering the group rather than undergo the discomfort of dropping out of the group. However, the client can make a judicious decision only if provided with sufficient information: for example, the nature of the group experience, the anticipated duration of therapy, and what is expected of him or her in the group (see chapter 10).

The rewards of membership in a therapy group consist of the various satisfactions members obtain from the group. Let us consider those rewards, or determinants of group cohesiveness, that are relevant to the selection of clients for group therapy.[73]

Members are satisfied with their groups (attracted to their groups and likely to continue membership in them) if:

1. They view the group as meeting their personal needs—that is, their goals in therapy.
2. They derive satisfaction from their relationships with the other members.
3. They derive satisfaction from their participation in the group task.
4. They derive satisfaction from group membership vis-à-vis the outside world.

These are important factors. Each, if absent or of negative value, may outweigh the positive value of the others and result in premature termination. Let us consider each in turn.

Does the Group Satisfy Personal Needs?

The explicit personal needs of group members are at first expressed in their chief complaint, their purpose for seeking therapy. These personal needs are usually couched in terms of relief from suffering or, less frequently, in terms of self-understanding or personal growth. Several factors are important here: there must be significant personal need; the group must be viewed as an agent with the potential of meeting that need; and the group must be seen, in time, as making progress toward meeting that need.

Clients must, of course, have some discomfort in their lives to provide the required motivation for change. The relationship between discomfort and suitability for group therapy is not *linear but curvilinear*. Clients with *too little discomfort* (coupled with only a modest amount of curiosity about groups or themselves) are usually unwilling to pay the price for group membership.

Clients with *moderately high discomfort* may, on the other hand, be willing to pay a high price, provided they have faith or evidence that the group can and will help. From where does this faith arise? There are several possible sources:

- Endorsement of group therapy by the mass media, by friends who have had a successful group therapy experience, or by a previous individual therapist, referring agency, or physician
- Explicit preparation by the group therapist (see chapter 10)
- Belief in the omniscience of authority figures
- Observing or being told about improvement of other group members
- Observing changes in oneself occurring early in group therapy

Clients with *exceedingly high discomfort* stemming from extraordinary environmental stress, internal conflicts, inadequate ego strength, or some combination of these may be so overwhelmed with anxiety that many of the activities of the long-term dynamic group seem utterly irrelevant. Initially groups are unable to meet highly pressing personal needs. Dynamic, interactional group therapy is not effective or efficient in management of intense crisis and acute psychological distress.

Greatly disturbed clients may be unable to tolerate the frustration that occurs as the group gradually evolves into an effective therapeutic instrument. They may demand instant relief, which the group cannot supply—it is not designed to do so. Or they may develop anxiety-binding defenses that are so interpersonally maladaptive (for example, extreme projection or somatization) as to make the group socially nonviable for them. Again, *it is not group therapy per se that is contraindicated for clients with exceedingly high discomfort, but longer-term dynamic group therapy.* These acutely disturbed clients may be excellent candidates for a crisis group or for a specialized problem-oriented group—for example, a cognitive-behavioral group for clients with depression or panic disorder.† There too, however, they will need to participate in the group work; the difference is in the nature and focus of the work.[74]

Some clients facing an urgent major decision like divorce, abortion, or relinquishing custody of a child may not be good candidates for a dynamic group. But later, after the decision has been made, they may benefit from group therapy in dealing with the psychological and social ramifications of their choice.

Individuals variously described as non–psychologically minded, nonintrospective, high deniers, psychological illiterates, psychologically insensitive, and alexithymic may be unable to perceive the group as meeting their personal needs. In fact, they may perceive an incompatibility between their personal needs and the group goals. Psychological-mindedness is a particularly important variable, because it helps individuals engage in the "work" of therapy[75] that produces positive outcomes. Without it, clients may reason, "How can looking at my relations with the group members help me with my bad nerves?"

Satisfaction from Relationships with Other Members

Group members derive satisfaction from their relationships with other group members, and often this source of attraction to the group may dwarf the others. The importance of relationships among members both as a source of cohesiveness and as a therapeutic factor was fully discussed in chapter 3, and I need pause here only to reflect that it is rare for a client to continue membership in the prolonged absence of interpersonal satisfaction.

The development of interpersonal satisfaction may be a slow process. Psychotherapy clients are often contemptuous of themselves and are therefore likely to be initially contemptuous of their fellow group members. They have had, for the most part, few gratifying interpersonal relationships in the past and have little trust or expectation of gaining anything from close relationships with the other group members. Often they may use the therapist transitionally: by relating positively to the therapist at first, they may more easily grow closer to one another.[76]

Satisfaction from Participation in Group Activities

The satisfaction that clients derive from participation in the group task is largely inseparable from the satisfaction they derive from relationships with the other members. The group task—to achieve a group culture of intimacy, acceptance, introspection, understanding, and interpersonal honesty—is fundamentally interpersonal, and research with a wide variety of groups has demonstrated that participation in the group task is an important source of satisfaction for the group members.[77] Clients who cannot introspect, reveal themselves, care for others, or manifest their feelings will derive little gratification from participation in group activities. Such clients include many of the types discussed earlier: for example, the schizoid personality, clients with other types of overriding intimacy problems, the deniers, the somatizers, the organically impaired, and the mentally retarded. These individuals are better treated in a homogeneous, problem-specific group that has a group task consonant with their abilities.

Satisfaction from Pride in Group Membership

Members of many kinds of groups derive satisfaction from membership because the outside world regards their group as highly valued or prestigious. Not so for therapy groups because of members' share. Therapy group members will, however, usually develop some pride in their group: for example, they will defend it if it is attacked by new members. They may feel superior to outsiders—to those "in denial," to individuals who are as troubled as they but lack the good sense to join a therapy group. If clients manifest extraordinary shame at membership and are reluctant to reveal their membership to intimate friends or even to spouses, then their membership will appear to them dissonant with the values of other important anchor groups. It is not likely that such clients will become deeply attracted to the group. Occasionally, outside groups (family, military, or, more recently, industry) will exert pressure on the individual to join a therapy group.[78] Groups held together only by such coercion are tenuous at first, but the evolving group process may generate other sources of cohesiveness.

SUMMARY

Selection of clients for group therapy is, in practice, a process of deselection: group therapists exclude certain clients from consideration and accept all others. Although empirical outcome studies and clinical observation have generated *few inclusion criteria*, the study of failures in group therapy, especially of clients who drop out early in the course of the group, provides important *exclusion* criteria.

Clients should not be placed in a group if they are likely to become groups deviants. Deviants stand little chance of benefiting from the group experience and a fair chance of being harmed by it. A group deviant is one who is unable to participate in the group task. Thus, in a heterogeneous, interactional group, a deviant is one who cannot or will not examine himself and his relationship with others, especially with the other members of the group. Nor can he accept his responsibility for his life difficulties. Low psychological-mindedness is a key criterion for exclusion from a dynamic therapy group.

Clients should be excluded from long-term groups if they are in the midst of a life crisis that can be more efficiently addressed in brief, problem-specific groups or in other therapy formats.

Conflicts in the sphere of intimacy represent both indication and contraindication for group therapy. Group therapy can offer considerable help in this domain—yet if the conflicts are too extreme, the client will choose to leave (or be extruded) by the group. The therapist's task is to select those clients who are as close as possible to the border between need and impossibility. If no markers for exclusion are present, the vast majority of clients seeking therapy can be treated in group therapy.

Chapter 9

THE COMPOSITION OF THERAPY GROUPS

A chapter on group composition might at first glance seem anachronistic in the contemporary practice of group psychotherapy. Economic and managed care pressures on today's group therapist may make the idea of mindfully composing a psychotherapy group seem an impractical luxury. How can one think about the ideal method of composing therapy groups when pressures for target symptom relief, homogeneous groups, structured meetings, and brevity of therapy are the order of the day? Moreover, empirical research indicates that *the briefer and more structured the group, the less important are compositional issues.*[1] To make matters worse, research in group composition is doubtless one of the most complex and confusing areas in the group therapy literature. So what is the point of including a chapter on group composition in this text?

In this chapter my aim is to show that the principles of group composition are relevant *in all forms of therapy groups, even the most structured and seemingly homogeneous.* Group composition principles help group leaders understand the process within each group and tailor their work to meet the requirements of each client. If therapists fail to attend to issues of diversity in interpersonal, cognitive, personality, and cultural dimensions, they will fall prey to a simplistic and ineffective "one-size-fits-all" approach to group therapy. The research on group composition is voluminous and complex. Readers who are less interested in research detail may prefer in this chapter to focus on the section summaries and the final overview.

Let us begin with a thought experiment. Imagine the following situation: An ambulatory mental health clinic or counseling center with ten group therapists ready to form groups and seventy clients who, on the basis of the selection criteria outlined thus far, are suitable group therapy candidates. *Is there an ideal way to compose these ten groups?*

Or imagine this more common, analogous situation: An intake coordinator deems a client a suitable candidate for group therapy, and there are several groups operating in the clinic, each with one vacancy. Into which group should the client go? Which group would offer the best *fit?*† Both situations raise a similar question: *Is there a superior method of composing or blending a group?* Will the proper blend of individuals form an ideal group? Will the wrong blend remain inharmonious and never coalesce into a working group?

I believe that it is important to establish valid compositional principles to help us determine which clients should go into which groups. We grope in the dark if we try to build a group or fill a vacancy without any knowledge of the organization of the total system. The stakes are high: first, a number of comembers will be affected by the decision to introduce a particular client into a group, and second, the brief frame of contemporary group treatment leaves little time for correction of errors.

As in preceding chapters, I will devote particular attention to groups with ambitious goals that focus on here-and-now member interaction. But principles of composition also apply to homogeneous, problem-specific, cognitive-behavioral, or psychoeducational groups. Keep in mind that even in such groups, homogeneity in one dimension, such as diagnosis, can initially mask important heterogenity (for example, stage and severity of illness) that may powerfully interfere with the group's ability to work well together.

First, let me clarify what I mean by right and wrong "blends." Blends of what? What are the ingredients of our blend? Which of the infinite number of human characteristics are germane to the composition of an interactional therapy group? Since each member must continually communicate and interact with the other members, it is the interaction of members that will dictate the fate of a group. Therefore, if we are to deal intelligently with group composition, we must aim for a mix that will allow the members to interact in some desired manner. The entire procedure of group composition and selection of group members is thus based on the important assumption that we can, with some degree of accuracy, *predict the interpersonal or group behavior of an individual from pretherapy screening.* Are we able to make that prediction?

THE PREDICTION OF GROUP BEHAVIOR

In the previous chapter, I advised against including individuals whose group behavior would render their own therapy unproductive and impede the therapy of the rest of the group. Generally, predictions of the group behavior of individuals with extreme, fixed, maladaptive interpersonal behavior (for example, the sociopathic or the floridly manic client) are reasonably accurate: *in general, the grosser the pathology, the greater the predictive accuracy.*

In everyday clinical practice, however, the problem is far more subtle. Most clients who apply for treatment have a wider repertoire of behavior, and their ultimate group behavior is far less predictable. Let us examine the most common procedures used to predict behavior in the group.

The Standard Diagnostic Interview

The most common method of screening clients for groups is the standard individual interview. The interviewer, on the basis of data on environmental stresses, personal history, and inferences about motivation for treatment and ego strength, attempts to predict how the individual will behave in the group. These predictions, based on observations of a client's behavior in the dyadic situation, are often hazy and inaccurate. Later in the chapter I will present some strategies to increase the validity of these preliminary inferences.

One of the traditional end products of the mental health interview is a diagnosis that, in capsule form, is meant to summarize the client's condition and convey useful information from practitioner to practitioner. But does it succeed in offering practical information? Group therapists will attest it does not! Psychiatric diagnoses based on standard classificatory systems (for example, DSM-IV-TR) are, at best, of limited value as an indicator of interpersonal behavior. Diagnostic nomenclature was never meant for this purpose; it stemmed from a disease-oriented medical discipline. It is based primarily on the determination of syndromes according to aggregates of certain signs and symptoms. Personality is generally classified in a similar fashion, emphasizing discrete *categories* of interpersonal behavior rather than describing interpersonal behavior as it is actually manifested.[2]

The 2000 *Diagnostic and Statistical Manual of Mental Disorders* (DSM-IV-TR) is an improvement over earlier psychiatric diagnostic systems, and it pays far more attention to personality. It codes personality on a specific axis (Axis II) and recognizes that an individual may demonstrate clustering of personality pathology in more than one area, apart from (or in addition to) Axis I psychiatric disorders. The DSM-IV-TR provides a sharper demarcation between severe and less severe personality disorders and in general has a more empirical foundation than previous DSM systems.[3]

Nonetheless, the DSM-IV-TR, along with the most recent *International Classification of Disease* (ICD-10), has marked limitations for practitioners working with clients whose interpersonal distress and disturbance do not fit neatly into syndrome definitions. Contemporary diagnosis also emphasizes discrete and observable behavior, with little attention paid to the inner life of the individual.[4]

Overall, *the standard intake interview has been shown to have little value in predicting subsequent group behavior.*[5] For example, one study of thirty clients referred to group therapy demonstrated that the intake interviewers' ratings of five important factors—motivation for group therapy, verbal skills, chronicity of problems, history of object relations, and capacity for insight—had no predictive value for the client's subsequent group behavior (for example, verbal activity and responsivity to other members and to the leader).[6]

That a diagnostic label fails to predict much about human behavior should neither surprise nor chagrin us. No label or phrase can adequately encompass an individual's essence or entire range of behavior.[7] Any limiting categorization is not only erroneous but offensive, and stands in opposition to the basic human foundations of the therapeutic relationship. In my opinion, the less we think (during the process of psychotherapy) in terms of diagnostic labels, the better. (Albert Camus once described hell as a place where one's identity was eternally fixed and displayed on personal signs: Adulterous Humanist, Christian Landowner, Jittery Philosopher, Charming Janus, and so on.[8] To Camus, hell is where one has no way of explaining oneself, where one is fixed, classified—once and for all time.)

Standard Psychological Testing

The standard psychological diagnostic tests—among them the Rorschach test, the Minnesota Multiphasic Personality Inventory (MMPI), the Thematic Apperception Test (TAT), the Sentence Completion test, and the Draw-a-Person test—have failed to yield predictions of value to the group therapist.[9]

Specialized Diagnostic Procedures

The limited value of standard diagnostic procedures suggests that we need to develop new methods of assessing interpersonal behavior. Slowly, the field is beginning to assess personality traits and tendencies more accurately to improve our methods of matching clients to therapy.[10] Recent clinical observations and research suggest several promising directions in two general categories:

1. A formulation of an interpersonal nosological system. If the critical variable in group therapy selection is interpersonal in nature, why not develop an interpersonally based diagnostic scheme?
2. New diagnostic procedures that directly sample group-relevant behavior

An Interpersonal Nosological System. The first known attempt to classify mental illness dates back to 1700 B.C.,[11] and the intervening centuries have seen a bewildering number of systems advanced, each beset with its own internal inconsistency. The majority of systems have classified mental illness according to either symptoms or presumed etiology. The advent of the object-relations and interpersonal systems of conceptualizing psychopathology, together with the increase in the number of people seeking treatment for less severe problems in living,[12] stimulated more sophisticated attempts to classify individuals according to interpersonal styles of relating.† In previous generations psychotherapy researchers interested in the impact of personality variables on the individual's participation in groups measured such variables as externalization and resistance,[13] perceived mastery and learned resourcefulness,[14] dogmatism,[15] preference for high or low structure,[16] social avoidance,[17] locus of control,[18] interpersonal trust,[19] and social risk-taking propensity.[20]

It is of interest to note that some of the contemporary empirical schema of interpersonal relationships draw heavily from earlier clinical conceptualizations. Karen Horney's midcentury model has been particularly relevant in new formulations. Horney viewed troubled individuals as moving exaggeratedly and maladaptively *toward, against,* or *away from* other people and described interpersonal profiles of these types and various subtypes.[21]

Bowlby's work on attachment[22] has also spawned new work that categorizes individuals on the basis of four fundamental styles of relationship attachment: 1) secure; 2) anxious; 3) detached or dismissive and avoidant; and 4) fearful and avoidant.[23] Some therapists feel that these attachment styles are so important that the therapist's recognition and appropriate therapeutic responsiveness to them may make or break treatment.[24]

Contemporary interpersonal theorists† have attempted to develop a classification of diverse interpersonal styles and behavior based on data gathered through interpersonal inventories (often the Inventory of Interpersonal Problems, IIP).[25] They then place this information onto a multidimensional, interpersonal circumplex (a schematic depiction of interpersonal relations arranged around a circle in two-dimensional space; see figure 9.1).[26]

Two studies that used the interpersonal circumplex in a twelve-session training group of graduate psychology students generated the following results:

1. Group members who were avoidant and dismissive were much more likely to experience other group members as hostile.
2. Group members who were anxious about or preoccupied with relationships saw other members as friendly.
3. Strongly dominant individuals resist group engagement and may devalue or discount the group.[27]

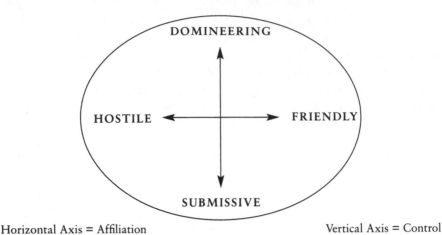

Horizontal Axis = Affiliation   Vertical Axis = Control

FIGURE 9.1   Interpersonal Circumplex

An illustrative example of this type of research may be found in a well-constructed study that tested the comparative effectiveness of two kinds of group therapy and attempted to determine the role of clients' personality traits on the results.[28] The researchers randomly assigned clients seeking treatment for loss and complicated grief (N = 107) to either a twelve-session interpretive/expressive or a supportive group therapy. Client outcome assessments included measures of depression, anxiety, self-esteem, and social adjustment. Before therapy, each client was given the NEO-Five Factor Inventory (NEO-FFI), which measures five personality variables: neuroticism, extraversion, openness, conscientiousness, and agreeableness.[29] What did the study find?

1. Both group therapies were demonstrably effective, although the interpretive group generated much greater affect and anxiety among the group members.
2. One personality factor, neuroticism, predicted poorer outcome in both types of group.
3. Three factors predicted good outcomes with both treatments: extraversion, conscientiousness, and openness.
4. The fifth factor, agreeableness predicted success in the interpretive/expressive group therapy but not in the supportive group therapy.

The authors suggest that the agreeableness factor is particularly important in sustaining relatedness in the face of the challenging work associated with this form of intensive group therapy.

Two other personality measures relevant to group therapy outcome have also been studied in depth: psychological-mindedness[30] and the

Quality of Object Relations (QOR) Scale.[31]* Both of these measures have the drawback of requiring that the client participate in a 30–60-minute semistructured interview (in contrast to the relative ease of a client self-report instrument such as the NEO-FFI).

Psychological-mindedness predicts good outcome in all forms of group therapy. Psychologically minded clients are better able to work in therapy—to explore, reflect, and understand. Furthermore, such clients are more accountable to themselves and responsible to comembers.[32] Clients with higher QOR scores, which reflect greater maturity in their relationships, are more likely to achieve positive outcomes in interpretive/expressive, emotion-activating group therapy. They are more trusting and able to express a broader range of negative and positive emotions in the group. Clients with low QOR scores are less able to tolerate this more demanding form of therapy and do better in supportive, emotion-suppressing group formats.[33]

Once we identify a key problematic interpersonal area in a client, an interesting question arises: do we employ a therapy that *avoids* or *addresses* that area of vulnerability? The large NIMH study of time-limited therapy in the treatment of depression demonstrated that clients do not necessarily do well when matched to the form of therapy that appears to target their specific problems. For example, clients with greater interpersonal difficulty did less well in the interpersonal therapy. Why would that be?

The answer is that *some* interpersonal competence is required to make use of interpersonal therapy. Clients with greater interpersonal dysfunction tend to do better in cognitive therapy, which requires less interpersonal skill. Conversely, clients with greater cognitive distortions tend to achieve better results with interpersonal therapy than with cognitive therapy. An additional finding of the NIMH study is that perfectionistic clients tend to do poorly in time-limited therapies, often becoming preoccupied with the looming end of therapy and their disappointment in what they have accomplished.[34]

Summary: Group compositional research is still a soft science. Nonetheless, some practical treatment considerations flow from the research findings. Several key principles can guide us in composing intensive interactional psychotherapy groups:

- *Clients will re-create their typical relational patterns within the microcosm of the group.*

---

*Psychological-mindedness is the ability to identify intrapsychic factors and relate them to one's difficulties. It appears to be a durable personality trait that does not change over time even with therapy. The Quality of Object Relations (QOR) Scale evaluates clients' characteristic manner of relating along a continuum ranging from mature to primitive.

- *Personality and attachment variables are more important predictors of in-group behavior than diagnosis alone.*
- *Clients require a certain amount of interpersonal competence to make the best use of interactional group therapy.*
- *Clients who are rigidly domineering or dismissive will impair the work of the therapy group.*
- *Members eager for engagement and willing to take social risks will advance the group's work.*
- *Psychologically minded clients are essential for an effective, interactional therapy group; with too few such clients, a group will be slow and ineffective.*
- *Clients who are less trusting, less altruistic, or less cooperative will likely struggle with interpersonal exploration and feedback and may require more supportive groups.*
- *Clients with high neuroticism or perfectionism will likely require a longer course of therapy to effect meaningful change in symptoms and functioning.*

Direct Sampling of Group-Relevant Behavior. The most powerful method of predicting group behavior is to observe the behavior of an individual who is engaged in a task closely related to the group therapy situation.[35] In other words, *the closer we can approximate the therapy group in observing individuals, the more accurately we can predict their in-group behavior.* Substantial research evidence supports this thesis. An individual's behavior will show a certain consistency over time, even though the people with whom the person interacts change—as has been demonstrated with therapist-client interaction and small group interaction.[36] For example, it has been demonstrated that a client seen by several individual therapists in rotation will be consistent in behavior (and, surprisingly, will change the behavior of each of the therapists!).[37]

Since we often cannot accurately predict group behavior from an individual interview, *we should consider obtaining data on behavior in a group setting.* Indeed, business and government have long found practical applications for this principle. For example, in screening applicants for positions that require group-related skills, organizations observe applicants' behavior in related group situations. A group interview test has been used to select Air Force officers, public health officers, and many types of public and business executives and industry managers. Universities have also made effective use of group assessment to hire academic faculty.[38]

This general principle can be refined further: group dynamic research also demonstrates that behavior in one group is consistent with behavior in previous groups, especially if the groups are similar in composition,[39] in group task,[40] in group norms,[41] in expected role behavior,[42] or in global group characteristics (such as climate or cohesiveness).[43] In other words, even though one's behavior is broadly consistent from one group to the next, the individual's specific behavior in a new group is influenced by the task and the structural properties of the group and by the specific interpersonal styles of the other group members.

The further implication, then, is that we can obtain the most relevant data for prediction of group behavior by observing an individual behave in a group that is *as similar as possible to the one for which he or she is being considered*. How can we best apply this principle? The most literal application would be to arrange for the applicant to meet with the therapy group under consideration and to observe his or her behavior in this setting. In fact, some clinicians have attempted just that: they invite prospective members to visit the group on a trial basis and then ask the group members to participate in the selection process.[44] Although there are several advantages to this procedure (to be discussed in chapter 11), I find it clinically unwieldy: it tends to disrupt the group; the members are disinclined to reject a prospective member unless there is some glaring incompatibility; furthermore, prospective members may not act naturally when they are on trial.

An interesting research technique with strong clinical implications is the waiting-list group—a temporary group constituted from a clinic waiting list. Clinicians observe the behavior of a prospective group therapy member in this group and, on the basis of the data they obtain there, refer the individual to a specific therapy or research group. In an exploratory study, researchers formed four groups of fifteen members each from a group therapy waiting list; the groups met once a week for four to eight weeks.[45] Waiting-list group behavior of the clients not only predicted their behavior in their subsequent long-term therapy group but also enhanced the clients' engagement in their subsequent therapy group. They concluded, as have other researchers using a group diagnostic procedure for clients applying for treatment, that clients did not react adversely to the waiting-list group.[46] It is challenging to lead waiting list groups. It requires an experienced leader who has the skill to sustain a viable group in an understaffed setting dealing with vulnerable and often demoralized clients.[47]

In one well-designed project, thirty clients on a group therapy waiting list were placed into four one-hour training sessions. The sessions were all conducted according to a single protocol, which included an introduction to here-and-now interaction.[48] The researchers found that each client's verbal participation and interpersonal responsivity in the training sessions correlated with their subsequent behavior during their first sixteen group therapy sessions. These findings were subsequently replicated in another, larger project.[49]

Summary: A number of studies attest to the predictive power of observed pretherapy group behavior. Furthermore, there is a great deal of corroborating evidence from human relations and social-psychological group research that subsequent group behavior may be satisfactorily predicted from pretherapy waiting or training groups.†

The Interpersonal Intake Interview.   For practitioners or clinics facing time or resource pressures, the use of trial groups may be an intriguing but highly impractical idea. A less accurate but more pragmatic method of obtaining similar data is an interpersonally oriented interview in which the therapist tests the prospective group client's ability to deal with the interpersonal here-and-now reality. Is the client able to comment on the process of the intake interview or to understand or accept the therapist's process commentary? For example, is the client obviously tense but denies it when the therapist asks? Is the client able and willing to identify the most uncomfortable or pleasant parts of the interview? Or comment on how he or she wishes to be thought of by the therapist?

Detailed inquiry should be made into the client's interpersonal and group relationships, relationships with early chums, closest prolonged friendships, and degree of intimacy with members of both sexes. Many of Harry Stack Sullivan's interview techniques are of great value in this task.[50] It is informative, for example, when inquiring about friendships to ask for the names of best friends and what has become of them. It is valuable to obtain a detailed history of formal and informal groups, childhood and adult cliques, fraternities, club memberships, gangs, teams, elected offices, and informal roles and status positions. I find it valuable to ask the client to give a detailed description of a typical twenty-four hours and to take particular note of the way the client's life is peopled.

The predictive power of this type of interview has yet to be determined empirically, but it seems to me far more relevant to subsequent group behavior than does the traditional intake clinical interview. This interview approach has become a standard assessment component in interpersonal therapy (IPT) and cognitive behavioral analysis system psychotherapy (CBASP).[51]

Fifty years ago, Powdermaker and Frank described an interpersonal relations interview that correctly predicted several patterns of subsequent group therapy behavior, such as "will dominate the group by a flood of speech and advice"; "will have considerable difficulty in showing feelings but will have compulsion to please the therapist and other members"; "will be bland and socially skillful, tending to seek the leader's attention while ignoring the other members"; "will have a wait-and-see attitude"; or "will have a sarcastic, superior 'show-me' attitude and be reluctant to discuss his problems."[52] Contemporary psychotherapists have made an important addition to this approach: they emphasize the client's beliefs and expectations about relationships, which give form to the client's interpersonal behavior. This behavior in turn pulls characteristic responses from others.[53]

Such a sequence is illustrated in the following vignette, which also illustrates the necessity of the therapist attending to his own emotional and behavioral reactions and responses to the client.

> • *Connie, a woman in her forties, was referred by her family physician for group therapy because of her social anxiety, dysthymia, and interpersonal isolation. Immediately on entering the office she told me she had a "bone to pick" with me. "How could you leave a message on my answering machine calling me Connie and yourself Doctor So-and-so? Don't you understand the power imbalance that perpetuates? Haven't you heard of feminism and empowerment? Do you treat all the women you know like this, or only your clients?"*
>
> *I was at first stunned, and then felt threatened and angry. After a few moments' reflection I considered that she indeed had a point, and I acknowledged my carelessness.*
>
> *Later in the session I asked whether we might explore the extent of her anger, and we soon began discussing her expectation that she would be silenced and devalued in this process, as she had been so many times in the past. I told her that she had, in a sense, presented a powerful test to me —hoping, perhaps, that I would not take the bait, that I would not confirm her expectations about how her world always treats her, a pattern that often resulted in her feeling rebuked, attacked, and shut down. I suggested that she no doubt came to these beliefs honestly and that they reflected her experiences in life. She may well initially relate to the group members in the same way that she did with me, but she did have a choice. She could make the group experience yet another in a series of angry rejections, or she could begin a process of learning and understanding that could interrupt this self-fulfilling prophecy.*

Summary

Group behavior can be predicted from a pretherapy encounter. Of all the prediction methods, the traditional intake individual interview oriented toward establishing a diagnosis appears the least accurate, and yet it is the most commonly used. An individual's group behavior will vary depending on internal psychological needs, the manner of expressing them, the interpersonal composition and the norms of the group. A general principle, however, is that the more similar the intake procedure is to the actual group situation, the more accurate will be the prediction of a client's behavior. *The most promising single clinical method may be observation of*

a client's behavior in an intake, role-play, or waiting-list group. If circum-
stances and logistics do not permit this method, I recommend that group
therapists modify their intake interview to focus primarily on a client's in-
terpersonal functioning.

PRINCIPLES OF GROUP COMPOSITION

To return now to the central question: Given ideal circumstances—a large
number of client applicants, plenty of time, and a wealth of information by
which we can predict behavior—how then to compose the therapy group?

Perhaps the reason for the scarcity of interest in the prediction of group
behavior is that the information available about the next step—group
composition—is even more rudimentary. Why bother refining tools to
predict group behavior if we do not know how to use this information?
Although all experienced clinicians sense that the composition of a group
profoundly influences its character, the actual mechanism of influence has
eluded clarification.[54] I have had the opportunity to study closely the conception, birth, and development of more than 250 therapy groups—my
own and my students'—and have been struck repeatedly by the fact that
some groups seem to jell immediately, some more slowly, and other
groups founder painfully and either fail entirely or spin off members and
emerge as working groups only after several cycles of attrition and addition of members. It has been my impression that whether a group jells is
only partly related to the competence or efforts of the therapist or to the
number of "good" members in the group. To a degree, the critical variable
is some as yet unclear blending of the members.

A clinical experience many years ago vividly brought this principle
home to me. I was scheduled to lead a six-month experiential group of
clinical psychology interns, all at the same level of training and approximately the same age. At the first meeting, over twenty participants appeared—too many for one group—and I decided to break them into two
groups, and asked the participants simply to move in random fashion
around the room for five minutes and at the end of that time position
themselves at one or the other end of the room. Thereafter, each group
met for an hour and a half, one group immediately following the other.

Although superficially it might appear that the groups had similar compositions, the subtle blending of personalities resulted in each having a
radically different character. The difference was apparent in the first meeting and persisted throughout the life of the groups. One group assumed an
extraordinarily dependent posture. In the first meeting, I arrived on
crutches with my leg in a cast because I had injured my knee playing football a couple of days earlier. Yet the group made no inquiry about my condition. Nor did they themselves arrange the chairs in a circle. (Remember

that all were professional therapists, and most had led therapy groups!) They asked my permission for such acts as opening the window and closing the door. Most of the group life was spent analyzing their fear of me, the distance between me and the members, my aloofness and coldness.

In the other group, I wasn't halfway through the door before several members asked, "Hey, what happened to your leg?" The group moved immediately into hard work, and each of the members used his or her professional skills in a constructive manner. In this group I often felt unnecessary to the work and occasionally inquired about the members' disregard of me.

This "tale of two groups" underscores the fact that the composition of the groups dramatically influenced the character of their subsequent work. If the groups had been ongoing rather than time limited, the different environments they created might eventually have made little difference in the beneficial effect each group had on its members. In the short run, however, the members of the first group felt more tense, more deskilled, and more restricted. Had it been a therapy group, some members might have felt so dissatisfied that they would have dropped out of the group. The group was dominated by what Nitsun describes as "antigroup" forces (elements present in each group that serve to undermine the group's work).[55] Because of their narrower range of experience in the group, they learned less about themselves than the members of the other group did.

A similar example may be drawn from two groups in the Lieberman, Yalom, and Miles group study.[56] These two short-term groups were randomly composed but had an identical leader—a tape recording that provided instructions about how to proceed at each meeting (the Encountertape Program). Within a few meetings, two very different cultures emerged. One group was dependably obedient to the taped instructions and faithfully followed all the prescribed exercises. The other group developed a disrespectful tone to the tape, soon referring to it as "George." It was common for these members to mock the tape. For example, when the tape gave an instruction to the group, one member commented derisively, "That's a great idea, George!" Not only was the culture different for these groups, but so was the outcome. At the end of the thirty-hour group experience—ten meetings—the irreverent group had an appreciably better outcome.

Thus, we can be certain that composition affects the character and process of the group. Still, we are a long way from concluding that a given method X composes a group more effectively than method Y does. Group therapy outcome studies are complex, and rigorous research has not yet defined the relationship between group composition and the ultimate criterion: therapy outcome. Despite some promising work using the personality variables reviewed earlier in this chapter, we still must rely largely on nonsystematic clinical observations and studies stemming from nonther-apy settings.

Clinical Observations

The impressions of individual clinicians on the effects of group composi-tion must be evaluated with caution. The lack of a common language for describing behavior, the problems of outcome evaluation, the theoretical biases of the therapist, and the limited number of groups that any one clinician may treat all limit the validity of clinical impressions in this area.

There appears to be a general clinical sentiment that heterogeneous groups have advantages over homogeneous groups for *long-term intensive interactional group therapy*.†[57] Homogeneous groups, on the other hand, have many advantages if the therapist wishes to offer support for a shared problem or help clients develop skills to obtain symptomatic relief over a brief period.[58] Even with these groups, however, composition is not irrel-evant. A homogeneous group for men with HIV or women with breast cancer will be strongly affected by the stage of illness of the members. An individual with advanced disease may represent the other members' great-est fears and lead to members' disengagement or withdrawal.[59]

Even in highly specialized, homogeneous, manual-guided group thera-pies, such as groups for individuals dealing with a genetic predisposition to developing breast or colorectal cancer, the therapist can expect compo-sition to play a substantial role.[60] Like the group of psychology interns de-scribed earlier, some therapy groups quickly come together, whereas others stumble along slowly, even with the same leader.

In general, though, *homogeneous groups jell more quickly, become more cohesive, offer more immediate support to group members, are bet-ter attended, have less conflict, and provide more rapid relief of symp-toms*. However, many clinicians believe that they do not lend themselves to long-term psychotherapeutic work with ambitious goals of personality change. The homogeneous group, in contrast to the heterogeneous group, has a tendency to remain at superficial levels and is a less effective medium for the altering of character structure.

The issue becomes clouded when we ask, "Homogeneous for what?" "Heterogeneous for what?" "For age?" "Sex?" "Symptom complex?" "Marital status?" "Education?" "Socioeconomic status?" "Verbal skills?" "Psychosexual development?" "Psychiatric diagnostic categories?" "Inter-personal needs?" Which of these are the critical variables? Is a group com-posed of women with bulimia or seniors with depression *homogeneous* because of the shared symptom, or *heterogeneous* because of the wide range of personality traits of the members?

A number of authors seek to clarify the issue by suggesting that the group therapist strive for *maximum heterogeneity in the clients' conflict areas and patterns of coping, and at the same time strive for homogeneity of the clients' degree of vulnerability and capacity to tolerate anxiety.* For example, a homogeneous group of individuals who all have major conflicts about hostility that they dealt with through denial could hardly offer therapeutic benefit to its members. However, a group with a very wide range of vulnerability (loosely defined as ego strength) will, for different reasons, also be retarded: the most vulnerable member will place limits on the group, which will become highly restrictive to the less vulnerable ones. Foulkes and Anthony suggest blending diagnoses and disturbances to form a therapeutically effective group. The greater the span between the polar types, the higher the therapeutic potential.[61] But the head and tail of the group both must stay connected to the body of the group for therapeutic benefit to emerge.

Unfolding from these clinical observations is the rule that a degree of incompatibility must exist between the client and the interpersonal culture of the group if change is to occur. This principle—*that change is preceded by a state of dissonance or incongruity*—is backed by considerable clinical and social-psychological research; I will return to it later in this chapter. In the absence of adequate ego strength, however, group members cannot profit from the dissonance.

Therefore, for the long-term intensive therapy group, the rule that will serve clinicians in good stead is: *heterogeneity for conflict areas and homogeneity for ego strength.* We seek *heterogeneity* of individuals with regard to gender, level of activity or passivity, thinking and feeling, and interpersonal difficulties, but *homogeneity* with regard to intelligence, capacity to tolerate anxiety, and ability to give and receive feedback and to engage in the therapeutic process.

But heterogeneity must not be maintained at the price of creating a group isolate. Consider the age variable: If there is one sixty-year-old member in a group of young adults, that individual may choose (or be forced) to personify the older generation. Thus, this member is stereotyped (as are the younger members), and the required interpersonal honesty and intimacy will fail to materialize. A similar process may occur in an adult group with a lone late adolescent who assumes the unruly teenager role. Yet there are advantages to having a wide age spread in a group. Most of my ambulatory groups have members ranging in age from twenty-five to sixty-five. Through working out their relationships with other members, they come to understand their past, present, and future relationships with a wider range of significant people: parents, peers, and children.

Sexual orientation, cultural, and ethno-racial factors similarly need to be considered. Group members from minority backgrounds will need to trust that other group members are willing to consider each individual's specific context and not to view that individual as a stereotype of his culture.†

Some therapists employ another concept—*role heterogeneity*—in their approach to group composition. Their primary consideration when adding a new member is what role in the group is open. Theoretically, such an orientation seems desirable. Practically, however, it suffers from lack of clarity. An extraordinary range of therapy group roles have been suggested: task leader, social-emotional leader, provocateur, doctor's helper, help-rejecting complainer, self-righteous moralist, star, fight/flight leader, dependency leader, pairing leader, group hysteric, technical executive leader, social secretary, group stud, group critic, group romantic, guardian of democracy, timekeeper, aggressive male, vigilante of honesty, the sociable role, the structural role, the divergent role, the cautionary role, the scrutinizer, the innocent, the scapegoat, the intellectualizer, the child, the puritan, the reintegrater, and so on. Can we expand the list arbitrarily and indefinitely by including all behavior trait constellations? Or is there a fixed set of roles, constant from group to group, that members are forced to fill? Until we have some satisfactory frame of reference to deal with these questions, asking "What role is open in the group?" will contribute little toward an effective approach to group composition.

Clinical experience demonstrates that groups do better if some members can be exemplars and advocates of constructive group norms. Placing one or two "veterans" of group therapy into a new group may pay large dividends. Conversely, we can sometimes predict that clients will fit poorly with a particular group because of the likelihood that they will assume an unhealthy role in it. Consider this clinical illustration:

• *Eve, a twenty-nine-year-old woman with prominent narcissistic personality difficulties, was evaluated for group therapy. She was professionally successful but interpersonally isolated, and she experienced chronic dysthymia that was only partially ameliorated with antidepressants. When she came to my office for a pregroup consultation, within minutes I experienced her as brittle, explosive, highly demanding, and devaluing of others. In many ways, Eve's difficulties echoed those of another woman, Lisa, who had just quit this group (thereby creating the opening for which Eve was being evaluated). Lisa's intense, domineering need to be at the center of the group, coupled with an exquisite vulnerability to feedback, had paralyzed the group members, and her departure had been met with clear relief by all. At another time, this group and Eve could have been a constructive fit. So soon after Lisa's departure, however, it was very likely that Eve's characteristic style of relating would trigger strong feelings in the group of "here we go again," shifting the group members back into feelings that they had just painfully processed. An alternative group for Eve was recommended.*

One final clinical observation. As a supervisor and researcher, I had an opportunity to study closely the entire thirty-month course of an ambulatory group led by two competent psychiatric residents. The group consisted of seven members, all in their twenties, six of whom could be classified as having schizoid personality disorder. The most striking feature of this homogeneous group was its extraordinary dullness. Everything associated with the group meetings, tape recordings, written summaries, and supervisory sessions seemed low-keyed and plodding. Often nothing seemed to be happening: there was no discernible movement individually among the members or in the group as a whole. And yet attendance was near perfect, and the group cohesiveness extraordinarily high.

At that time many ambulatory groups in the Stanford outpatient clinic were part of a study involving the measurement of group cohesiveness. This homogeneous schizoid group scored higher on cohesiveness (measured by self-administered questionnaires) than any other group. Since all the group participants in the Stanford clinic during this period were subjects in outcome research,[62] thorough evaluations of clinical progress were available at the end of one year and again at thirty months. The members of this group, both the original members and the replacements, did extraordinarily well and underwent substantial characterological changes as well as complete symptomatic remission. In fact, few other groups I've studied have had comparably good results. My views about group composition were influenced by this group, and I have come to attach great importance to group stability, attendance, and cohesiveness.

Although in theory I agree with the concept of composing a group of individuals with varied interpersonal stresses and needs, I feel that in practice it may be a spurious issue. Given the limited predictive value of our traditional screening interview, it is probable that our expectations exceed our abilities if we think we can achieve the type of subtle balance and personality interlocking necessary to make a real difference in group functioning. For example, although six of the seven members in the group I just discussed were diagnosed as schizoid personalities, they differed far more than they resembled one another. This apparently homogeneous group, contrary to the clinical dictum, did not remain at a superficial level and effected significant personality changes in its members. Although the interaction seemed plodding to the therapists and researchers, it did not to the participants. None of them had ever had intimate relationships, and many of their disclosures, though objectively unremarkable, were subjectively exciting first-time disclosures.

Many so-called homogeneous groups remain superficial, *not because of homogeneity but because of the psychological set of the group leaders and the restricted group culture they fashion*. Therapists who organize a group of individuals around a common symptom or life situation must be careful not to convey powerful implicit messages that generate group norms of restriction, a search for similarities, submergence of individuality, and discouragement of self-disclosure and interpersonal honesty. Norms, as I elaborated in chapter 5, once set into motion, may become self-perpetuating and difficult to change. We should aim to reduce negative outcomes by forming groups with members who offer care, support, mutual engagement, regular attendance, and openness, but *composition itself is not always destiny.*†

What about gender and group composition? Some authors, arguing from theory or clinical experience, advocate single-gender groups, but the limited empirical research does not support this.[63] Men in all-male groups are less intimate and more competitive, whereas men in mixed-gender groups are more self-disclosing and less aggressive. Unfortunately, the benefit of gender heterogeneity does not accrue to the women in these groups: women in mixed-gender groups may become less active and deferential to the male participants. Men may do poorly in mixed-gender groups composed of only one or two men and several women; men in this instance may feel peripheral, marginalized, and isolated.[64]

OVERVIEW

It would be most gratifying at this point to integrate these clinical and experimental findings, to point out hitherto unseen lines of cleavage and coalescence, and to emerge with a crisp theory of group composition that has firm experimental foundations as well as immediate practicality. Unfortunately, the data do not permit such a definitive synthesis. But there is value in highlighting major research findings that pertain to group composition.

The culture and functioning of every group—its ethos, values, and modus vivendi—will be influenced by the composition of its members. Our approach to composition must be informed by our understanding of the group's tasks. The group must be able to respond to members' needs for emotional support *and* for constructive challenge. In psychotherapy groups we should aim for a composition that balances similarity and divergence in interpersonal engagement and behavior; relationship to authority; emotional bonding; and task focus. Moreover, it is essential that members agree with the values that guide the therapeutic enterprise.

The research also points to certain unequivocal findings. *The composition of a group does make a difference and influences many aspects of group function.*† A group's composition influences certain predictable short-term characteristics—for example, high cohesion and engagement, high conflict, high flight, high dependency. Furthermore, we can, if we choose to use available procedures, predict to some degree the group behavior of the individual.

What we are uncertain of, however, is the relationship between any of these group characteristics and the ultimate therapy outcome of the group members. Furthermore, we do not know how much the group leader may alter these characteristics of the group or how long an ongoing group will manifest them. We do know, however, that cohesive groups with higher engagement generally produce better clinical outcomes.†

In practice there are two major theoretical approaches to group composition: the homogeneous and the heterogeneous approach. Let us examine briefly the theoretical underpinnings of these two approaches. Underlying the *heterogeneous* approach to composition are two theoretical rationales that may be labeled the social microcosm theory and the dissonance theory. Underlying the *homogeneous* group composition approach is the group cohesiveness theory.

The Heterogeneous Mode of Composition

The social microcosm theory postulates that because the group is regarded as a miniature social universe in which members are urged to develop new methods of interpersonal interaction, the group should be heterogeneous in order to maximize learning opportunities. It should resemble the real social universe by being composed of individuals of different sexes, professions, ages, and socioeconomic and educational levels. In other words, it should be a demographic assortment.

The dissonance theory as applied to group therapy also suggests a heterogeneous compositional approach, but for a different reason. Learning or change is likely to occur when the individual, in a state of dissonance, acts to reduce that dissonance. Dissonance creates a state of psychological discomfort and propels the individual to attempt to achieve a more consonant state. Individuals who find themselves in a group in which membership has many desirable features (for example, hopes of alleviation of suffering, attraction to the leader and other members) but which, at the same time, makes tension-producing demands (for example, self-disclosure or interpersonal confrontation) will experience a state of dissonance or imbalance.[65]

Similarly, a state of discomfort occurs when, in a valued group, one finds that one's interpersonal needs are unfulfilled or when one's customary style of interpersonal behavior produces discord. The individual in these circumstances will search for ways to reduce discomfort—for example, by leaving the group or, preferably, by beginning to experiment with new forms of behavior. To facilitate the development of adaptive discomfort, the heterogeneous argument suggests that clients be exposed to other individuals in the group who will not reinforce neurotic positions by fulfilling interpersonal needs but instead will be frustrating and challenging, making clients aware of different conflict areas and also demonstrating alternative interpersonal modes.

Therefore, it is argued, *a group should include members with varying interpersonal styles and conflicts.* It is a delicate balance, because if frustration and challenge are too great, and the staying forces (the attraction to the group) too small, no real asymmetry or dissonance occurs; the individual does not change but instead physically or psychologically leaves the group. If, on the other hand, the challenge is too small, no learning occurs; members will collude, and exploration will be inhibited. The dissonance theory thus argues for a broad personality assortment.

The Homogeneous Mode of Composition

The cohesiveness theory, underlying the homogeneous approach to group composition, postulates, quite simply, that *attraction to the group is the intervening variable critical to outcome and that the paramount aim should be to assemble a cohesive, compatible group.*

Summary

How can we reconcile or decide between these two approaches? First, note that no group therapy research supports the dissonance model. There is great clinical consensus (my own included) that group therapy clients should be exposed to a variety of conflict areas, coping methods, and conflicting interpersonal styles, and that conflict in general is essential to the therapeutic process. However, there is no empirical evidence that deliberately composed heterogeneous groups *facilitate therapy, and I have just cited modest evidence to the contrary.*

On the other hand, a large body of small-group research supports the cohesiveness concept. Interpersonally compatible therapy groups will develop greater cohesiveness. Members of cohesive groups have better attendance, are more able to express and tolerate hostility, are more apt to attempt to influence others, and are themselves more readily influenced. Members with greater attraction to their group have better therapeutic outcome; members who are less compatible with the other members tend to drop out of the group. Members with the greatest interpersonal compatibility become the most popular group members, and group popularity is highly correlated with successful outcome.

The fear that a homogeneous group will be unproductive, constricted, or conflict free or that it will deal with a only narrow range of interpersonal concerns is unfounded, for several reasons. First, there are few individuals whose pathology is indeed monolithic—that is, who, despite their chief conflict area, do not also encounter conflicts in intimacy or authority, for example. Second, the group developmental process may demand that clients deal with certain conflict areas. For example, the laws of group development (see chapter 11) demand that the group ultimately deal with issues of control, authority, and the hierarchy of dominance. In a group with several control-

conflicted individuals, this phase may appear early or very sharply. In a group lacking such individuals, other members who are less conflicted or whose conflicts are less overt in the area of dependency and authority may be forced nonetheless to deal with it as the group inevitably moves into this stage of development. If certain developmentally required roles are not filled in the group, most leaders, consciously or unconsciously, alter their behavior to fill the void.[66] Furthermore—and this is an important point—no therapy group with proper leadership can be too comfortable or fail to provide dissonance for its members, because the members must invariably clash with the group task. To develop trust, to disclose oneself, to develop intimacy, to examine oneself, to confront others—are all discordant tasks to individuals who have significant problems in interpersonal relationships.

Many problem-specific brief groups can easily be transformed into a productive interactional group with proper guidance from the leader. For example, two rigorous studies compared homogeneous groups of clients with bulimia who were randomly assigned to behavioral group therapy, cognitive-behavioral group therapy, or interactional group therapy (therapy that did not explicitly address eating behavior but instead focused entirely on interpersonal interaction). Not only did these homogeneous interactional groups function effectively, but their outcome was in every way equal to the cognitive-behavioral groups, including their positive effect on the eating disorder.[67]

On the basis of our current knowledge, therefore, I propose that cohesiveness be the primary guideline in the composition of therapy groups. *The hoped-for dissonance will unfold in the group, provided the therapist functions effectively in the pretherapy orientation of clients and during the early group meetings. Group integrity should be given highest priority, and group therapists must select clients with the lowest likelihood of premature termination. Individuals with a high likelihood of being irreconcilably incompatible with the prevailing group ethos and culture, or with at least one other member, should not be included in the group. It bears repeating that* group cohesiveness is not synonymous with group comfort or ease. *Quite the contrary: it is only in a cohesive group that conflict can be tolerated and transformed into productive work.*

A FINAL CAVEAT

Admittedly, the idea of crafting an ideal group is seductive. It is a siren's wail that has lured many researchers and generated a large body of research, little of which, alas, has proved substantial, replicable, or clinically relevant. Not only that, but, in many ways, the topic of group composition is out of touch with the current everyday realities of clinical practice. As noted earlier, contemporary pressures on the practice of group therapy discourage the therapist's attention to group composition as a relevant concern.

Many contemporary group clinicians in private practice and in public clinics are more concerned with group integrity and survival. Generally, these clinicians have difficulty accumulating enough clients to form and maintain groups. (And I have no doubt that this difficulty will grow with each passing year because of the rapid increase in numbers of practicing psychotherapists from ever more professional disciplines.) The more therapists available, the more professional competition for clients, the harder it is to begin and maintain therapy groups in private practice. Therapists prefer to fill their individual hours and are reluctant to risk losing a client through referral to a therapy group. If clinicians attempt to put some group candidates on hold while awaiting the perfect blend of group participants—assuming that we know the formula of the blend (which we do not)—they will never form a group. Referrals accumulate so slowly that the first prospective members interviewed may tire of waiting and find suitable therapy elsewhere.

Thus contemporary clinicians, myself included, generally form groups by accepting, within limits, the first suitable seven or eight candidates screened and deemed to be good group therapy candidates. Only the crudest principles of group composition are employed, such as having an equal number of men and women or a wide range of age, activity, or interactional style. For example, if two males already selected for the group are particularly passive, it is desirable to create balance by adding more active men.

Other excellent options exist in practice, however. First, the clinician may compose a group from clients in his individual practice. As I shall discuss in chapter 15, concurrent therapy is a highly effective format. Second, clinicians who are in a collaborative practice, often sharing a suite of offices, may coordinate referrals and fill one group at a time. In many communities, group therapists have successfully created a specialty practice by marketing themselves through speaking engagements and advertising.

The therapist's paramount task is to create a group that coheres. Time and energy spent on delicately casting and balancing a group cannot be justified, given the current state of our knowledge and clinical practice. I believe that therapists do better to invest their time and energy in careful selection of clients for group therapy and in pretherapy preparation (to be discussed in the next chapter). There is no question that composition radically affects the group's character, but if the group holds together and if you appreciate the therapeutic factors and are flexible in your role, you can make therapeutic use of any conditions (other than lack of motivation) that arise in the group.

Chapter 10

CREATION OF THE GROUP: PLACE, TIME, SIZE, PREPARATION

PRELIMINARY CONSIDERATIONS

Before convening a group, therapists must secure an appropriate meeting place and make a number of practical decisions about the structure of the therapy: namely, the size and the life span of the group, the admission of new members, the frequency of meetings, and the duration of each session. In addition, the contemporary practitioner often must negotiate a relationship with a third-party payer, HMO, or managed care organization.[1] The tension between therapeutic priorities and the economic priorities of managed care regarding the scope and duration of treatment must also be addressed.[2] Dissonance between therapists and third-party administrators may have a deleterious impact on the client-therapist relationship.† The entire practice of therapy, including therapists' morale, will benefit from greater partnership and less polarization.

Today clinicians have an ethical responsibility to advocate for effective therapy. They must educate the public, destigmatize group therapy, build strong clinical practice organizations with well-trained and properly credentialed clinicians, and urge third-party payers to attend to the robust empirical research supporting group therapy's effectiveness.†

The Physical Setting
Group meetings may be held in any room that affords privacy and freedom from distractions. In institutional settings, the therapist must negotiate with the administration to establish inviolate time and space for therapy groups. The first step of a meeting is to form a circle so that members can

281

all see one another. For that reason, a seating arrangement around a long, rectangular table or the use of sofas that seat three or four people is unsatisfactory. If members are absent, most therapists prefer to remove the empty chairs and form a tighter circle.

If the group session is to be videotaped or observed through a one-way mirror by trainees, the group members' permission must be obtained in advance and ample opportunity provided for discussion of the procedure. Written consent is essential if any audiovisual recording is planned. A group that is observed usually seems to forget about the viewing window after a few weeks, but often when working through authority issues with the leader, members again become concerned about it. If only one or two students are regular observers, it is best to seat them in the room but outside of the group circle. This avoids the intrusion of the mirror and allows the students to sample more of the group affect, which inexplicably is often filtered out by the mirror. Observers should be cautioned to remain silent and to resist any attempts of the group members to engage them in the discussion. (See chapter 17 for further discussion about group observation.)

Open and Closed Groups

At its inception, a group is designated by its leader as open or closed. A closed group, once begun, shuts its gates, accepts no new members except within the first 2 or 3 sessions and meets for a predetermined length of time. An open group, by contrast, maintains a consistent size by replacing members as they leave the group. An open group may have a predetermined life span—for example, groups in a university student health service may plan to meet only for the nine-month academic year. Many open groups continue indefinitely even though every couple of years there may be a complete turnover of group membership and even of leadership. I have known of therapy groups in psychotherapy training centers that have endured for twenty years, being bequeathed every year or two by a graduating therapist to an incoming student. Open groups tolerate changes in membership better if there is some consistency in leadership. One way to achieve this in the training setting is for the group to have two co-therapists; when the senior co-therapist leaves, the other one continues as senior group leader, and a new co-therapist joins.[3]

Most closed groups are brief therapy groups that meet weekly for six months or less. A longer closed group may have difficulty maintaining stability of membership. Invariably, members drop out, move away, or face some unexpected scheduling incompatibility. Groups do not function well if they become too small, and new members must be added lest the group perish from attrition. A long-term closed-group format is feasible in a setting that assures considerable stability, such as a prison, a military base, a long-term psychiatric hospital, and occasionally an ambulatory group in which all members are concurrently in individual psychotherapy with the group leader. Some therapists lead a closed group for six months, at which time members evaluate their progress and decide whether to commit themselves to another six months.

Some intensive partial hospitalization programs begin with an intensive phase with closed group therapy, which is followed by an extended, less intensive open group therapy aftercare maintenance phase. The closed phase emphasizes common concerns and fundamental skills that are best acquired if the whole group can move in concert. The open phase, which aims to reduce relapse, reinforces the gains made during the intensive phase and helps clients apply their gains more broadly in their own social environments. This model has worked well in the treatment of substance abuse, trauma, and depression.[4]

DURATION AND FREQUENCY OF MEETINGS

Until the mid-1960s, the length of a psychotherapy session seemed fixed: the fifty-minute individual hour and the eighty- to ninety-minute group therapy session were part of the entrenched wisdom of the field. Most group therapists agree that, even in well-established groups, at least sixty minutes is required for the warm-up interval and for the unfolding and working through of the major themes of the session. There is also some consensus among therapists that after about two hours, the session reaches a point of diminishing returns: the group becomes weary, repetitious, and inefficient. Many therapists appear to function best in segments of eighty to ninety minutes; with longer sessions therapists often become fatigued, which renders them less effective in subsequent therapy sessions on the same day.

Although the frequency of meetings varies from one to five times a week, the overwhelming majority of groups meet once weekly. It is often logistically difficult to schedule multiple weekly ambulatory group meetings, and most therapists have never led an outpatient group that meets more than once a week. But if I had my choice, I would meet with groups twice weekly: such groups have a greater intensity, the members continue to work through issues raised in the previous session, and the entire process takes on the character of a continuous meeting. Some therapists meet twice weekly for two or three weeks at the start of a time-limited group to turbocharge the intensity and launch the group more effectively.[5]

Avoid meeting too infrequently. Groups that meet less than once weekly generally have considerable difficulty maintaining an interactional focus. If a great deal has occurred between meetings in the lives of the members, such groups have a tendency to focus on life events and on crisis resolution.

The Time-Extended Group.   In efforts to achieve "time-efficient ther-apy,"[6] group leaders have experimented with many aspects of the frame of therapy, but none more than the duration of the meeting. Today's economically driven climate pressures therapists to abbreviate therapy, but the opposite was true in the 1960s and 1970s, the heyday of the en-counter groups (see chapter 16), when group therapists experimented boldly with the length of meetings. Therapists held weekly meetings that lasted four, six, even eight hours. Some therapists chose to meet less frequently but for longer periods—for example, a six-hour meeting every other week. Individual therapists often referred their clients to a weekend time-extended group. Some group therapists referred their en-tire group for a weekend with another therapist or, more commonly, conducted a marathon meeting with their own group sometime during the course of therapy.

The "marathon group" was widely publicized during that time in U.S. magazines, newspapers, and fictionalized accounts.† It met for a pro-longed session, perhaps lasting twenty-four or even forty-eight hours, with little or no time permitted for sleep. Participants were required to re-main together for the entire designated time. Meals were served in the therapy room, and sleep, if needed, was snatched during quick naps in the session or in short scheduled sleep breaks. The emphasis of the group was on total self-disclosure, intensive interpersonal confrontation, and affec-tive involvement and participation. Later the time-extended format was adapted by such commercial enterprises as est and Lifespring; today, these large group awareness training programs have virtually disappeared.[7]

Proponents of the time-extended group claimed that it accelerated group development, intensified the emotional experience, and efficiently condensed a lengthy course of therapy into a day or a weekend.† The emotional intensity and fatigue resulting from lack of sleep was also thought to accelerate the abandonment of social facades. The results of marathon group therapy reported in the mass media and in scientific jour-nals at the time were mind-boggling, exceeding even today's claims of the personality-transforming effects of new miracle drugs: "Eighty percent of the participants undergo significant change as the result of a single meet-ing";[8] "ninety percent of 400 marathon group members considered the meeting as one of the most significant and meaningful experiences of their lives";[9] "marathon group therapy represents a breakthrough in psy-chotherapeutic practice";[10] "the marathon group has become a singular agent of change which allows rapidity of learning and adaptation to new patterns of behavior not likely to occur under traditional arrange-ments";[11] "if all adults had been in a marathon, there would be no more war; if all teenagers had been in a marathon, there would be no more ju-venile delinquency";[12] and so on.

Yet despite these claims, the marathon movement has come and gone. The therapists who still regularly or periodically hold time-extended group meetings represent a small minority of practitioners. Though there have been occasional recent reports of intensive, and effective, retreat weekends for various conditions ranging from substance abuse to bulimia,[13] these enterprises consist of a comprehensive program that includes group therapy, psychoeducation, and clear theory rather than a reliance on the intensive confrontation and fatigue characteristic of the marathon approach. This approach is also used today to augment weekly group therapy for clients with cancer, in the form of an intensive weekend retreat for skill building, reflection, and meditation.[14]

Nonetheless, it is important to inform ourselves about the marathon movement—not because it has much current usage, nor to pay homage to it as a chapter in the history of psychotherapy, but because of what it reveals about how therapists make decisions about clinical practice. Over the past several decades, psychotherapy in general and group therapy in particular have been taken by storm by a series of ideological and stylistic fads. Reliance on the fundamentals and on well-constructed research is the best bulwark against will-o'-the-wisp modes of therapy dominated by the fashion of the day.

Many therapeutic fads come and go so quickly that research rarely addresses the issues they raise. Not so for the time-extended meeting, which has spawned a considerable research literature. Why? For one thing, the format lends itself to experimentation: it is far easier to do outcome research on a group that lasts, say, one day than on one that lasts for six months: there are fewer dropouts, fewer life crises, no opportunities for subjects to obtain ancillary therapy. Another reason is that time-extended groups arose in an organization (the National Training Laboratories—see chapter 16) that had a long tradition of coupling innovation and research.

The highly extravagant claims I quoted above were based entirely on anecdotal reports of various participants or on questionnaires distributed shortly after the end of a meeting—an exceedingly unreliable approach to evaluation. In fact, any outcome study based solely on interviews, testimonials, or client self-administered questionnaires obtained at the end of the group is of questionable value. At no other time is the client more loyal, more grateful, and less objective about a group than at termination, when there is a powerful tendency to recall and to express only positive, tender feelings. Experiencing and expressing negative feelings about the group at this point would be unlikely for at least two reasons: (1) there is strong group pressure at termination to participate in positive testimonials—few group participants, as Asch[15] has shown, can maintain their objectivity in the face of apparent group unanimity; and (2) members reject critical feelings toward the group at this time to avoid a state of cognitive dissonance: in other words, once an individual invests considerable emotion and time in a group and develops strong positive feelings toward other members, it becomes difficult to question the value or activities of the group. To do so thrusts the individual into a state of uncomfortable dissonance.

Research on marathon groups is plagued with a multitude of design defects.[16] Some studies failed to employ proper controls (for example, a non–time-extended comparison group). Others failed to sort out the effects of artifact and other confounding variables. For example, in a residential community of drug addicts, an annual marathon group was offered to rape survivors. Because the group was offered only once a year, the participants imbued it with value even before it took place.[17]

The rigorous controlled studies comparing differences in outcome between time-extended and non–time-extended groups conclude that there is no evidence for the efficacy of the time-extended format. The positive results reported in a few studies were unsystematic and evaporated quickly.[18]

Is it possible, as is sometimes claimed, that a time-extended meeting accelerates the maturation of a therapy group, that it increases openness, intimacy, and cohesiveness and thus facilitates insight and therapeutic breakthroughs? My colleagues and I studied the effect of a six-hour meeting on the development of cohesiveness and of a here-and-now, interactive communicational mode.[19] We followed six newly formed groups in an ambulatory mental health program for the first sixteen sessions. Three of the groups held a six-hour first session, whereas the other three held a six-hour eleventh session.[20]

We found that *the marathon session did not favorably influence the communication patterns in subsequent meetings.*[21] In fact, there was a trend in the opposite direction: after the six-hour meetings, the groups appeared to engage in *less* here-and-now interaction. The influence of the six-hour meeting on cohesiveness was quite interesting. In the three groups that held a six-hour *initial* meeting, there was a trend toward *decreased* cohesiveness in subsequent meetings. In the three groups that held a six-hour *eleventh* meeting, however, there was a significant *increase* in cohesiveness in subsequent meetings. Thus, timing is a consideration: it is entirely possible that, at a particular juncture in the course of a group, a time-extended session may help increase member involvement in the group. Hence, the results showed that cohesiveness can be accelerated but not brought into being by time-extended meetings.

During the 1960s and 1970s, many therapists referred individual therapy patients to weekend marathon groups; in the 1980s, many sent patients to intensive large-group awareness training weekends (for example, est and Lifespring). *Is it possible that an intensive, affect-laden time-extended group may open up a client who is stuck in therapy?* My colleagues and I studied thirty-three such clients referred by individual therapists for a weekend encounter group. We assigned them to one of three groups: two affect-evoking gestalt marathons and a control group (a weekend of meditation, silence, and tai chi).[22] Six weeks later, the experimental subjects showed slight but significant improvement in their individual therapy compared to the control subjects. By twelve weeks, however, all differences had disappeared, and *there were no remaining measurable effects on the process of individual therapy.*

The marathon group phenomenon makes us mindful of the issue of transfer of learning. There is no question that the time-extended group can evoke powerful affect and can encourage members to experiment with new behavior. But does a change in one's behavior in the group invariably beget a change in one's outside life? Clinicians have long known that change in the therapy session is not tantamount to therapeutic success, that change, if it is to be consolidated, must be carried over into important outside interpersonal relationships and endeavors and tested again and again in these natural settings. Of course therapists wish to accelerate the process of change, but the evidence suggests that the duration of treatment is more influential than the number of treatments. *The transfer of learning is laborious and demands a certain irreducible amount of time.*[23]

Consider, for example, a male client who, because of his early experience with an authoritarian, distant, and harsh father, tends to see all other males, especially those in a position of authority, as having similar qualities. In the group he may have an entirely different emotional experience with a male therapist and perhaps with some of the male members. What has he learned? Well, for one thing he has learned that not all men are frightening bastards—at least there are one or two who are not. Of what lasting value is this experience to him? Probably very little unless he can generalize the experience to future situations. As a result of the group, the individual learns that at least *some* men in positions of authority can be trusted. But which ones? He must learn how to differentiate among people so as not to perceive all men in a predetermined manner. A new repertoire of perceptual skills is needed. Once he is able to make the necessary discriminations, he must learn how to go about forming relationships on an egalitarian, distortion-free basis. For the individual whose interpersonal relationships have been impoverished and maladaptive, these are formidable and lengthy tasks that often require the continual testing and reinforcement available in the long-term therapeutic relationship.

BRIEF GROUP THERAPY

Brief group therapy is rapidly becoming an important and widely used therapy format. To a great extent, the search for briefer forms of group therapy is fueled by economic pressures. Managed care plans and HMOs strive relentlessly for briefer, less expensive, and more efficient forms of therapy.* A survey of managed care administrators responsible for the health care of over 73 million participants[24] noted that they were interested in the use of more groups but favored brief, problem-homogeneous, and structured groups. In the same survey, a range of therapists favored process, interpersonal, and psychodynamic group therapy without arbitrary time restrictions. Other factors also favor brief therapy: for example, many geographic locations have high service demands and low availability of mental health professionals; here, brevity translates into greater access to services.

How long is "brief"? The range is wide: some clinicians say that fewer than twenty to twenty-five visits is brief,[25] others sixteen to twenty sessions,[26] and still others fifty or sixty meetings.[27] Inpatient groups may be thought of as having a life span of a single session (see chapter 15). Perhaps it is best to offer a functional rather than a temporal definition: a brief group is the shortest group life span that can achieve some specified goal—hence the felicitous term "time-efficient group therapy".[28] A group dealing with an acute life crisis, such as a job loss, might last four to eight sessions, whereas a group addressing major relationship loss, such as divorce or bereavement, might last twelve to twenty sessions. A group for dealing with a specific symptom complex, such as eating disorders or the impact of sexual abuse, might last eighteen to twenty-four sessions. A "brief" group with the goal of changing enduring characterological problems might last sixty to seventy sessions.[29]

These time frames are somewhat arbitrary, but recent explorations into the "dose-effect" of individual psychotherapy shed some light on the question of duration of therapy.[30] This research attempts to apply the drug dose-response curve model to individual psychotherapy by studying large numbers of clients seeking psychotherapy in ambulatory settings. Typically the form of therapy provided is eclectic, integrating supportive, exploratory, and cognitive therapy approaches without the use of therapy manuals. Although no comparable dose-effect research in group therapy has been reported, it seems reasonable to assume that there are similar patterns of response to group therapy.

Researchers note that clients with less disturbance generally require fewer therapy hours to achieve a significant improvement. Remoralization can occur quickly, and eight sessions or fewer are sufficient to return many clients to their precrisis level. The vast majority of clients with more

---

*One is reminded of the farmer who attempted to train his horse to do with smaller and smaller amounts of food, but eventually lamented, "Just as I had taught it to manage with no food at all, the darn critter went and died on me."

chronic difficulties require about fifty to sixty sessions to improve, and those with significant personality disturbances require even more. The greater the impairment in trust or emotional deprivation and the earlier in development the individual has suffered loss or trauma, the greater the likelihood that a brief therapy will be insufficient. Failure of prior brief therapies is also often a sign of the need for a longer therapy.[31]

Whatever the precise length of therapy, all brief psychotherapy groups (excluding psychoeducational groups) share many common features. They all strive for efficiency; they contract for a discrete set of goals and attempt to stay focused on goal attainment; they tend to stay in the present (with either a here-and-now focus or a "there-and-now" recent-problem-oriented focus); they attend throughout to the temporal restrictions and the approaching ending of therapy; they emphasize the transfer of skills and learning from the group to the real world; their composition is often homogeneous for some problem, symptomatic syndrome, or life experience; they focus more on *interpersonal than on intrapersonal concerns.*[32]

A course of brief group therapy need not be viewed as the definitive treatment. Instead it could be considered an installment of treatment—an opportunity to do a piece of important, meaningful work, which may or may not require another installment in the future.[33]

When leading a brief therapy group, a group therapist must heed some general principles:

- The brief group is not a truncated long-term group;[34] group leaders must have a different mental set: they must clarify goals, focus the group, manage time, and be active and efficient. Since groups tend to deny their limits, leaders of brief groups must act as group time-keeper, periodically reminding the group how much time has passed and how much remains. The leader should regularly make comments such as: "This is our twelfth meeting. We're two-thirds done, but we still have six more sessions. It might be wise to spend a few minutes today reviewing what we've done, what goals remain, and how we should invest our remaining time."
- Leaders must also attend to the transfer of learning, encouraging clients to apply what they have learned in the group to their situations outside the group. They must emphasize that treatment is intended to set change in motion, but not necessarily to complete the process within the confines of the scheduled treatment. The work of therapy will continue to unfold long after the sessions stop.
- Leaders should attempt to turn the disadvantages of time limitations into an advantage. Since the time-limited therapy efforts of Carl Rogers, we have known that imposed time limits may increase efficiency and energize the therapy.[35] Also, the fixed, imminent ending

may be used to heighten awareness of existential dimensions of life: time is not eternal; everything ends; there will be no magic problem solver; the immediate encounter matters; the ultimate responsibility rests within, not without.[36]

- Keep in mind that the official name of the group *does not determine the work of therapy*. In other words, just because the group is made up of recently divorced individuals or survivors of sex abuse does not mean that the focus of the group is "divorce" or "sexual abuse." It is far more effective for the group's focus to be interactional, directed toward those aspects of divorce or abuse that have ramifications in the here-and-now of the group. For example, clients who have been abused can work on their shame, their rage, their reluctance to ask for help, their distrust of authority (that is, the leaders), and their difficulty in establishing intimate relationships. Groups of recently divorced members will work most profitably not by a prolonged historical focus on what went wrong in the marriage but by examining each member's problematic interpersonal issues as they manifest in the here-and-now of the group. Members must be helped to understand and change these patterns so that they do not impair future relationships.

- The effective group therapist should be flexible and use all means available to increase efficacy. Techniques from cognitive or behavioral therapy may be incorporated into the interactional group to alleviate symptomatic distress. For example, the leader of a group for binge eating may recommend that members explore the relationship between their mood and their eating in a written journal, or log their food consumption, or meditate to reduce emotional distress. But this is by no means essential. Brief group work that focuses on the interpersonal concerns that reside beneath the food-related symptoms *is as effective as brief group work that targets the disordered eating directly*.[37] In other words, therapists can think of symptoms as issuing from disturbances in interpersonal functioning and alleviate the symptom by repairing the interpersonal disturbances.†

- Time is limited, but leaders must not make the mistake of trying to save time by abbreviating the pregroup individual session. On the contrary, leaders must exercise particularly great care in preparation and selection. The most important single error made by busy clinics and HMOs is to screen new clients by phone and immediately introduce them into a group without an individual screening or preparatory session. Brief groups are less forgiving of errors than long-term groups. When the life of the group is only, say, twelve sessions, and two or three of those sessions are consumed by attending to an unsuitable member who then drops out (or must be asked to leave), the cost is very high: the development of the group is retarded, levels of trust and cohesion are slower to develop, and a significant proportion of the group's precious time and effectiveness is sacrificed.

- Use the pregroup individual meeting not only for standard group preparation but also to help clients reframe their problems and sharpen their goals so as to make them suitable for brief therapy.[38] Some group therapists will use the first group meeting to ask each client to present his/her interpersonal issues and treatment goals.[39]

Some clinicians have sought ways to bridge the gap between brief and longer-term treatment. One approach is to follow the brief group with booster group sessions scheduled at greater intervals, perhaps monthly, for another six months.[40] Another approach offers clients a brief group but provides them with the option of signing on for another series of meetings. One program primarily for clients with chronic illness consists of a series of twelve-week segments with a two-week break between segments.[41] Members may enter a segment at any time until the sixth week, at which time the group becomes a closed group. A client may attend one segment and then choose at some later point to enroll for another segment. The program has the advantage of keeping all clients, even the long-term members, goal-focused, as they reformulate their goals each segment.

Are brief groups effective? Outcome research on brief group therapy has increased substantially over the past ten years. An analysis of forty-eight reports of brief therapy groups (both cognitive-behavioral and dynamic/interpersonal) for the treatment of depression demonstrated that groups that meet, on average, for twelve sessions produced significant clinical improvement: group members were almost three times more likely to improve than clients waiting for treatment.[42] Furthermore, therapy groups add substantially to the effect of pharmacotherapy in the treatment of depression.[43] Brief groups for clients with loss and grief have also been proven effective and are significantly more effective than no treatment.[44] Both expressive-interpretive groups and supportive groups have demonstrated significant effects with this clinical population.[45]

A study of brief interpersonal group therapy for clients with borderline personality disorder reported improvement in clients' mood and behavior at the end of twenty-five sessions.[46] Brief group therapy is also effective in the psychological treatment of the medically ill:[47] it improves coping and stress management, reduces mood and anxiety symptoms, and improves self-care.

Some less salubrious findings have also been reported. In a comparison study of short-term group, long-term group, brief individual, and long-term individual therapies, the short-term group was the least effective of the four modalities.[48] In a study in which subjects were randomly assigned to short-term group treatment and short-term individual treatment, the investigators found significant improvement in both groups and no significant differences between them—except that *subjectively* the members preferred brief individual to brief group treatment.[49]

In sum, research demonstrates the effectiveness of brief group therapy. However, there is no evidence that brief therapy is superior to longer-term therapy.[50] In other words, if brief groups are necessary, we can lead them with confidence: we know there is much we can offer clients in the brief format. But don't be swept away by the powerful contemporary press for efficiency. Don't make the mistake of believing that a brief, streamlined therapy approach offers clients more than longer-term therapy. One of the architects of the NIMH Collaborative Treatment of Depression Study, one of the largest psychotherapy trial conducted, has stated that the field has likely oversold the power of brief psychotherapy.[51]

Size of the Group

My own experience and a consensus of the clinical literature suggest that the ideal size of an interactional therapy group is seven or eight members, with an acceptable range of five to ten members. The lower limit of the group is determined by the fact that a critical mass is required for an aggregation of individuals to become an interacting group. When a group is reduced to four or three members, it often ceases to operate as a group; member interaction diminishes, and therapists often find themselves engaged in individual therapy within the group. The groups lack cohesiveness, and although attendance may be good, it is often due to a sense of obligation rather than a true alliance. Many of the advantages of a group, especially the opportunity to interact and analyze one's interaction with a large variety of individuals, are compromised as the group's size diminishes. Furthermore, smaller groups become passive, suffer from stunted development, and frequently develop a negative group image.[52] Obviously the group therapist must replace members quickly, but appropriately. If new members are unavailable, therapists do better to meld two small groups rather than to continue limping along with insufficient membership in both.

The upper limit of therapy groups is determined by sheer economic principles. As the group increases in size, less and less time is available for the working through of any individual's problems. Since it is likely that one or possibly two clients will drop out of the group in the course of the initial meetings, it is advisable to start with a group slightly larger than the preferred size; thus, to obtain a group of seven or eight members, many therapists start a new group with eight or nine. Starting with a group size much larger than ten in anticipation of dropouts may become a self-fulfilling prophecy. Some members will quit because the group is simply too large for them to participate productively. Larger groups of twelve to sixteen members may meet productively in day hospital settings, because each member is likely to have many other therapeutic opportunities over the course of each week and because not all members will necessarily participate in each group session.

To some extent, the optimal group size is a function of the duration of the meeting: the longer the meeting, the larger the number of participants who can profitably engage in the group. Thus, many of the marathon therapy groups of past years had as many sixteen members. Groups such as Alcoholics Anonymous and Recovery, Inc. that do not focus on interaction may range from twenty to eighty. Psychoeducational groups for conditions such as generalized anxiety may meet effectively with twenty to thirty participants. These groups actively discourage individual disclosure and interaction, relying instead on the didactic imparting of information about anxiety and stress reduction.[53] Similar findings have been reported in the treatment of panic disorder and agoraphobia.[54]

The large-group format has also been used with cancer patients, often with training in stress reduction and self-management of illness symptoms and medical treatment side effects. These groups may contain forty to eighty participants meeting weekly for two hours over a course of six weeks.[55] If you think of the health care system as a pyramid, large groups of this type are part of the broad base of accessible, inexpensive treatment at the system's entry level. For many, this provision of knowledge and skills is sufficient. Clients who require more assistance may move up the pyramid to more focused or intensive interventions.[56]

A range of therapeutic factors may operate in these groups. Large homogeneous groups normalize, destigmatize, activate feelings of universality, and offer skills and knowledge that enhance self-efficacy. AA groups use inspiration, guidance, and suppression; the large therapeutic community relies on group pressure and interdependence to encourage reality testing, to combat regression, and to instill a sense of individual responsibility toward the social community.

Group size is inversely proportional to interaction. One study investigated the relationship between group size and the number of different verbal interactions initiated between members in fifty-five inpatient therapy groups. The groups ranged in size from five to twenty participants. A marked reduction in interactions between members was evident when group size reached nine members, and another when it reached seventeen members. The implication of the research is that, in inpatient settings, groups of five to eight offer the greatest opportunity for total client participation.[57]

Several studies of non-therapy groups suggest that as the size of a group increases, there is a corresponding tendency for members to feel disenfranchised and to form cliques and disruptive subgroups.[58] Further-more, only the more forceful and aggressive members are able to express their ideas or abilities.[59] A comparison of twelve-member and five-member problem-solving groups indicates that the larger groups experience more dissatisfaction and less consensus.[60]

PREPARATION FOR GROUP THERAPY

There is great variation in clinical practice regarding individual sessions with clients prior to group therapy. Some therapists, after seeing prospective clients once or twice in selection interviews, do not meet with them individually again, whereas others continue individual sessions until the client starts in the group. If several weeks are required to accumulate sufficient members, the therapist is well advised to continue to meet with each member periodically to prevent significant attrition. Even in settings with plenty of appropriate group therapy referrals it is important to maintain client momentum and interest. One way to do this is to set a firm start date for the group and then focus energetically on recruitment and assessment. A group leader may need to invest twenty to twenty-five hours to assemble one group.

Some therapists prefer to see the client several times in individual sessions in order to build a relationship that will keep members in the group during early periods of discouragement and disenchantment. It is my clinical impression that the more often clients are seen before entering the group, the less likely they are to terminate prematurely from the group. Often the first step in the development of bonds among members is their mutual identification with a shared person: the therapist. Keep in mind that the purpose of the individual pregroup sessions is to build a therapeutic alliance. To use the sessions primarily for anamnestic purposes is not a good use of clinical time; it suggests to the client that anamnesis is central to the therapy process.

One other overriding task must be accomplished in the pregroup interview or interviews: *the preparation of the client for group therapy*. If I had to choose the one area where research has the greatest relevance for practice, it would be in the preparation of clients for group therapy. *There is highly persuasive evidence that pregroup preparation expedites the course of group therapy.* Group leaders must achieve several specific goals in the preparatory procedure:

- Clarify misconceptions, unrealistic fears, and expectations
- Anticipate and diminish the emergence of problems in the group's development

- Provide clients with a cognitive structure that facilitates effective group participation
- Generate realistic and positive expectations about the group therapy

Misconceptions About Group Therapy

Certain misconceptions and fears about group therapy are so common that if the client does not mention them, the therapist should point them out as potential problems. Despite powerful research evidence on the efficacy of group therapy, many people still believe that group therapy is second-rate. Clients may think of group therapy as cheap therapy—an alternative for people who cannot afford individual therapy or a way for managed health care systems to increase profits. Others regard it as diluted therapy because each member has only twelve to fifteen minutes of the therapist's time each week. Still others believe that the raison d'être of group therapy is to accommodate a number of clients that greatly exceeds the number of staff therapists.

Let us examine some surveys of public beliefs about group therapy. A study of 206 college students consisting of students seeking counseling and a comparable number of psychology students identified three common misconceptions:

1. Group therapy is unpredictable or involves a loss of personal control—for example, groups may coerce members into self-disclosure.
2. Group therapy is not as effective as individual therapy because effectiveness is proportional to the attention received from the therapist.
3. Being in a group with many individuals with significant emotional disturbance is in itself detrimental.[61]

A British National Health Service study of sixty-nine moderately distressed clients seeking therapy reported that more than 50 percent declared that they would not enter group therapy even if no other treatment were available. Concerns cited included the fear of ridicule and shame, the lack of confidentiality, and the fear of being made worse through some form of contagion. What are some of the sources of this strong anti-group bias? For many clients seeking therapy, difficulties with their peer and social group or family is *the* problem. Hence, groups in general are distrusted, and the individual therapy setting is considered the protected, safe, and familiar zone. This is particularly the case for those with no prior experience in therapy.[62]

In general, the media and fictional portrayals of group therapy are vastly inaccurate and often portray therapy groups in a mocking, ridiculing fashion.* Reality television shows may also play a role. They speak to our unconscious fears of being exposed and extruded from our group because we are found to be defective, deficient, stimulate envy or are deemed to be the "weakest link."[63] Whatever their sources, such misconceptions and apprehensions must be countered; otherwise these strong negative expectations may make successful group therapy outcome unlikely.†

Nor are these unfavorable expectations limited to the general public or to clients. A survey of psychiatric residents found similar negative attitudes toward the efficacy of group therapy.[64] Lack of exposure in one's training is part of the problem, but the strength of resistances to remedying these training shortfalls suggest that antigroup attitudes may be deeply rooted and even unconscious. Thus, it should not surprise us to find such attitudes within institutional and administrative leadership.

In addition to evaluative misconceptions, clients usually harbor procedural misconceptions and unrealistic interpersonal fears. Many of these are evident in the following dream, which a client reported at her second pregroup individual session shortly before she was to attend her first group meeting:

> • I dreamed that each member of the group was required to bring cookies to the meeting. I went with my mother to buy the cookies that I was to take to the meeting. We had great difficulty deciding which cookies would be appropriate. In the meantime, I was aware that I was going to be very late to the meeting, and I was becoming more and more anxious about getting there on time. We finally decided on the cookies and proceeded to go to the group. I asked directions to the room where the group was to meet, and was told that it was meeting in room 129A. I wandered up and down a long hall in which the rooms were not numbered consecutively and in which I couldn't find a room with an "A." I finally discovered that 129A was located behind another room and went into the group. When I had been looking for the room, I had encountered many people from my past, many people whom I had gone to school with and many people whom I had known for a number of years. The group was very large, and about forty or fifty people were milling around the room. The members of the group included members of my family—most specifically, two of my brothers. Each member of the group was required to stand in front of a large audience and say what they thought was their difficulty and why they were there and what their problems were. The whole dream was

---

*It is for this very reason that I decided to write a group therapy novel, *The Schopenhauer Cure* (New York: HarperCollins, 2005), in which I attempt to offer an honest portrayal of the effective therapy group in action.

very anxiety-provoking, and the business of being late and the business of having a large number of people was very distracting.

Several themes are abundantly clear in this dream. The client anticipated the first group meeting with considerable dread. Her concern about being late reflected a fear of being excluded or rejected by the group. Furthermore, since she was starting in a group that had already been meeting for several weeks, she feared that the others had progressed too far, that she would be left behind and could never catch up. (She could not find a room with an "A" marked on it.) She dreamed that the group would number forty or fifty. Concerns about the size of the group are common; members fear that their unique individuality will be lost as they become one of the mass. Moreover, clients erroneously apply the model of the economic distribution of goods to the group therapeutic experience, assuming that the size of the crowd is inversely proportional to the goods received by each individual.

The dream image of each member confessing problems to the group audience reflects one of the most basic and pervasive fears of individuals entering a therapy group: the horror of having to reveal oneself and to confess shameful transgressions and fantasies to an alien audience. What's more, members imagine a critical, scornful, ridiculing, or humiliating response from the other members. The experience is fantasized as an apocalyptic trial before a stern, uncompassionate tribunal. The dream also suggests that pregroup anticipation resulted in a recrudescence of anxiety linked to early group experiences, including those of school, family, and play groups. It is as if her entire social network—all the significant people and groups she had encountered in her life— would be present in this group. (In a metaphorical sense, this is true: to the degree that she had been shaped by other groups and other individuals, to the degree that she internalized them, she would carry them into the group with her since they are part of her character structure; furthermore, she would, transferentially, re-create in the therapy group her early significant relationships.)

It is clear from the reference to room 129 (an early schoolroom in her life) that the client was associating her impending group experience with a time in her life when few things were more crucial than the acceptance and approval of a peer group. Furthermore, she anticipated that the therapist would be like her early teachers: an aloof, unloving evaluator.

Closely related to the dread of forced confession is the concern about confidentiality. The client anticipated that there would be no group boundaries, that every intimacy she disclosed would be known by every significant person in her life. Other common concerns of individuals entering group therapy, not evident in this dream, include a fear of mental contagion, of being made sicker through association with ill comembers. Often, but not exclusively, this is a preoccupation of clients with fragile ego boundaries who lack a solid, stable sense of self.

The anxiety about regression in an unstructured group and being helpless to resist the pull to merge and mesh with others can be overwhelming. In part, this concern is also a reflection of the self-contempt of individuals who project onto others their feelings of worthlessness. Such dynamics underlie the common query, "How can the blind lead the blind?" Convinced that they themselves have nothing of value to offer, some clients find it inconceivable that they might profit from others like themselves. Others fear their own hostility. If they ever unleash their rage, they think, it will engulf them as well as others. The notion of a group where anger is freely expressed is terrifying, as they think silently, "If others only knew what I really thought about them."

All of these unrealistic expectations that, unchecked, lead to a rejection or a blighting of group therapy can be allayed by adequate preparation of the client. Before outlining a preparation procedure, I will consider four problems commonly encountered early in the course of the group that may be ameliorated by preparation before therapy begins.

Common Group Problems

1. One important source of perplexity and discouragement for clients early in therapy is *perceived goal incompatibility*. They may be unable to discern the congruence between group goals (such as group integrity, construction of an atmosphere of trust, and an interactional focus) and their individual goals (relief of suffering). What bearing, members may wonder, does a discussion of their personal reactions to other members have on their symptoms of anxiety, depression, phobias, impotence, or insomnia?

2. A *high turnover* in the early stages of a group is, as I have discussed, a major impediment to the development of an effective group. The therapist, from the very first contact with a client, should discourage irregular attendance and premature termination. The issue is more pressing than in individual therapy, where absences and tardiness can be profitably investigated and worked through. In the initial stages of the group, irregular attendance results in a discouraged and disconnected group.

3. Group therapy, unlike individual therapy, often *does not offer immediate comfort*. Clients may be frustrated by not getting enough "airtime" in the first few meetings, they may feel deprived of their specialness,† or they may feel anxious about the task of direct interpersonal interaction. The therapist should anticipate and address this frustration and anxiety in the preparatory procedure. This is a

particular challenge for clients who have found individual therapy to be narcissistically gratifying.

4. *Subgrouping and extragroup socializing*, which has been referred to as the Achilles' heel of group therapy, may be encountered at any stage of the group. This complex problem will be considered in detail in chapter 12. Here it is sufficient to point out that the therapist may begin to shape the group norms regarding subgrouping in the very first contact with the clients.

A System of Preparation

There are many approaches to preparing clients for group therapy. The simplest and most practical in the harried world of everyday clinical practice is to offer the client the necessary information in the pregroup interview(s). I am careful to set aside sufficient time for this presentation. I attempt to see clients at least twice before introducing them into the group. But even if I see someone only once, I reserve at least half the time to address each of the foregoing misconceptions and initial problems of group therapy.

Misconceptions should be explored in detail and each one corrected by an accurate and complete discussion. I share with the client my predictions about the early problems in therapy and present a conceptual framework and clear guidelines for effective group behavior. Each client's preparation must be individualized according to the presenting complaints, questions and concerns raised in the interview, and level of sophistication regarding the therapy process. Two situations require particular attention from the therapist: the therapy neophyte and the client who presents with cross-cultural issues. The client who has never been in any form of therapy may find group therapy particularly challenging and may require additional pregroup individual preparation.† Clients from other cultures may be particularly threatened by the intimate personal exposure in the group. The pregroup preparation sessions provide the therapist the opportunity to explore the impact of the client's culture on his or her attitudes, beliefs, and identity and to demonstrate the therapist's genuine willingness to enter the client's world.[65]

I have found a preparatory interview with the following objectives to be of considerable value:

1. Enlist clients as informed allies. Give them a conceptual framework of the interpersonal basis of pathology and how therapy works.
2. Describe how the therapy group addresses and corrects interpersonal problems.
3. Offer guidelines about how best to participate in the group, how to maximize the usefulness of group therapy.

4. Anticipate the frustrations and disappointments of group therapy, especially of the early meetings.
5. Offer guidelines about duration of therapy. Make a contract about attendance in group.
6. Instill faith in group therapy; raise expectations about efficacy.
7. Set ground rules about confidentiality and subgrouping.

Now, to flesh out each of these points in turn.

1. First, I present clients with a brief explanation of the interpersonal theory of psychiatry, beginning with the statement that although each person manifests his or her problems differently, *all who seek help from psychotherapy have in common the basic difficulty of establishing and maintaining close and gratifying relationships with others.* I remind them of the many times in their lives that they have undoubtedly wished to clarify a relationship, to be really honest about their positive and negative feelings with someone and get reciprocally honest feedback. The general structure of society, however, does not often permit such open communication. Feelings are hurt, relationships are ruptured, misunderstandings arise, and, eventually, communication ceases.

2. I describe the therapy group, in simple, clear language, as a social laboratory in which such honest interpersonal exploration is not only permitted but encouraged. If people are conflicted in their methods of relating to others, then a social situation encouraging honest interaction provides a precious opportunity to learn many valuable things about themselves. I emphasize that working on their relationships directly with other group members will not be easy; in fact, it may even be stressful. But it is crucial *because if they can completely understand and work out their relationships with the other group members, there will be an enormous carryover into their outside world:* they will discover pathways to more rewarding relationships with significant people in their life now and with people they have yet to meet.

3. I advise members that the way to use therapy best is to be honest and direct with their feelings in the group at that moment, especially their feelings toward the other group members and the therapists. I emphasize this point many times and refer to it as the core of group therapy. I say that clients may, as they develop trust in the group, reveal intimate aspects of themselves, but that the group is not a forced confessional and that people have different rates of developing trust and revealing themselves. The group is a forum for risk taking, I emphasize, and I urge members to try new types of behavior in the group setting.

4. I predict certain stumbling blocks and warn clients that they may feel puzzled and discouraged in the early meetings. It will, at times, not be apparent how working on group problems and intermember relationships

can be of value in solving the problems that brought them to therapy. This puzzlement, I stress, is to be expected in the typical therapy process. I tell them that many people at first find it painfully difficult to reveal themselves or to express directly positive or negative feelings, and I discuss the tendency to withdraw emotionally, to hide feelings, to let others express one's feelings, to form concealing alliances with others. I also predict that they are likely to develop feelings of frustration or annoyance with the therapist and that they will expect answers that the therapist cannot supply. Help will often be forthcoming from other group members, however difficult it may be for them to accept this fact.

5. For clients entering an open-ended psychotherapy group I emphasize that the therapeutic goals of group therapy are ambitious because we desire to change behavior and attitudes many years in the making. Treatment is therefore gradual and may be long, often with no important change occurring for months. I strongly urge clients to stay with the group and to ignore any inclination to leave the group before giving it a real chance. It is almost impossible to predict the eventual effectiveness of the group during the first dozen meetings. Thus, I urge them to suspend judgment and to make a good-faith commitment of at least twelve meetings before even attempting to evaluate the ultimate usefulness of the group. For clients who are entering a briefer group therapy, I say that the group offers an outstanding opportunity to do a piece of important work that they can build upon in the future. Each session is precious, and it is in their interest and the interest of the other group members to attend each one of the limited number scheduled.

6. It is vitally important for the therapist to raise expectations, to instill faith in group therapy, and to dispel the false notion that group therapy is second-class therapy. Research tells us that clients who enter therapy expecting it to be successful will exert much greater effort in the therapy, will develop a stronger therapeutic alliance, and are significantly more likely to succeed.[66] This effect of client pretherapy expectancies is even greater for less structured therapies that may generate more client anxiety and uncertainty.[67] In my preparation, therefore, I provide a brief description of the history and development of group therapy—how group therapy passed from a stage during World War II when it was valued for its economic advantages (that is, it allowed psychotherapists to reach a large number of people in need), to its current position in the field, where it clearly has something unique to offer and is often the treatment of choice. I inform clients that psychotherapy outcome studies demonstrate that group therapy is as efficacious as any mode of individual therapy.

7. There are a few ground rules. Nothing is more important than honestly sharing perceptions and feelings about oneself and other members in the group. *Confidentiality*, I state, is as essential in group therapy as it is

in any therapist-client relationship. For members to speak freely, they must have confidence that their statements will remain within the group. In my group therapy experience, I can scarcely recall a single significant breach of confidence and can therefore reassure group members on this matter.*[68]

It is important not to corrode client trust regarding confidentiality. However, at the same time, in the spirit of obtaining informed consent for treatment, I also inform the client of my mandatory professional duties to report certain offenses.[69] In virtually all jurisdictions the therapist must report situations in which the actions of the client are, or will imminently be, harmful to self or others. Occasionally, members may inquire whether they can relate aspects of the group therapy discussion with a spouse or a confidant. I urge them to discuss only their own experience: the other members' experiences and certainly their names should be kept in strictest confidence.

In addition to the ground rules of honesty and confidentiality, I make a point of discussing the issue of contacts outside the group between members which, in one form or another, will occur in every psychotherapy group. Two particularly important points must be stressed:

1. The group provides an opportunity for learning about one's problems in social relationships; *it is not an assembly for meeting and making social friends*. On the contrary, if the group is used as a source of friends it loses its therapeutic effectiveness. In other words, the therapy group teaches one *how to* develop intimate, long-term relationships, but it does not *provide* these relationships. It is a bridge, not the destination. It is not life but a dress rehearsal for life.

2. If by chance or design, however, members *do* meet outside the group, it is their responsibility to discuss the salient aspects of that meeting inside the group. It is particularly useless for therapists to prohibit extragroup socializing or, for that matter, to declare any injunctions about client behavior. Almost invariably during the therapy, group members will engage in some outside socializing and in the face of the therapist's prohibition may be reluctant to disclose it in the group. As I shall elaborate in the next chapter, extragroup relationships are not harmful per se (in fact, they may be extremely important in the therapeutic process); *what impedes therapy is the conspiracy of silence that often surrounds such meetings*.

An approach of injunction and prohibition merely draws group members into the issue of rule setting and rule breaking. It is far more effective

---

*The limits of confidentiality in group therapy is an area that has not been broadly explored in the professional literature, but rare reports do surface of comembers being called to testify in criminal or civil proceedings. One questionnaire survey of 100 experienced group therapists noted that over half of the respondents experienced some minor confidentiality breach.

to explain at length why certain actions may interfere with therapy. With subgrouping, for example, I explain that friendships among group members often prevent them from speaking openly to one another in the group. Members may develop a sense of loyalty to a dyadic relationship and may thus hesitate to betray the other by reporting their conversations back to the group. Yet such secrecy will conflict with the openness and candor so essential to the therapy process. *The primary task of therapy group members is, I remind them, to learn as much as possible about the way each individual relates to each other person in the group.* All events that block that process ultimately obstruct therapy. Occasionally group members may wish to make a secret disclosure to the group leader. Almost always it is best that the disclosure be shared with the group. Group leaders must never, in advance, agree to secrecy but instead promise to use discretion and their best clinical judgment.

This strategy of providing full information to the members about the effects of extragroup socializing provides the therapist with far greater leverage than the strategy of the *ex cathedra* "thou shall not." If group members engage in secretive subgrouping, you do not have to resort to the ineffectual, misdirected "Why did you break my rules?" but instead can plunge into the heart of resistance by inquiring, "How come you're sabotaging your own therapy?"

In summary, this cognitive approach to group therapy preparation has several goals: to provide a rational explanation of the therapy process; to describe what types of behavior are expected of group members; to establish a contract about attendance; to raise expectations about the effects of the group; to predict (and thus to ameliorate) problems and discomfort in early meetings. Underlying these words is the process of demystification. *Therapists convey the message that they respect the client's judgment and intelligence, that therapy is a collaborative venture, that leaders are experts who operate on a rational basis and are willing to share their knowledge with the client. One final point is that comprehensive preparation also enables the client to make an informed decision about whether to enter a therapy group.*

Though this discussion is geared toward a longer-term interactional group, its basic features may be adapted to any other type of group therapy. In brief therapy groups relying on different therapeutic factors—for example, cognitive-behavioral groups—the relevant details of the presentation would have to be altered, but every therapy group profits from preparation of its members.† *If clinical exigencies preclude a thorough preparation, then a short preparation is better than none at all. In chapter 15, I describe a three-minute preparation I provide at the start of an acute inpatient group.*

Other Approaches to Preparation

Straightforward cognitive preparation presented a single time to a client may not be sufficiently powerful. Clients are anxious during their pre-group interviews and often recall astonishingly little of the content of the therapist's message or grossly misunderstand key points. For example, some group participants whom I asked to remain in the group for twelve sessions before evaluating its usefulness understood me to say that the group's entire life span would be twelve sessions.

Consequently, it is necessary to repeat and to emphasize deliberately many key points of the preparation both during the pregroup sessions and during the first few sessions of the group. For my ambulatory groups that meet once a week, I prepare a weekly written summary that I mail out to all the group members after each session (see chapter 14). These summaries provide an excellent forum to repeat in writing essential parts of the preparation procedure. When a new member joins an ongoing group, I provide additional preparation by requesting that he or she read the group summaries of the previous six meetings.

Many therapists have described other methods to increase the potency of the preparatory procedure. Some have used another group member to sponsor and to prepare a new member.[70] Others have used a written document for the new client to study before entering a group. The appendix to this book contains an example of a written handout to be used as a supplement for preparing clients entering a group. It stresses focusing on the here-and-now, assuming personal responsibility, avoiding blaming others, avoiding giving suggestions and fostering dependency, learning to listen to others, becoming aware both of feelings and of thoughts, and attempting to experiment with intimacy and with new behavior. We emphasize feedback and offer prospective members specific instructions about how to give and receive feedback: for example, be specific, give it as soon as possible, be direct, share the positive and the negative, tell how the other makes you feel, don't deal with *why* but with *what* you see and feel, acknowledge the feedback, don't make excuses, seek clarification, think about it, and beware of becoming defensive.[71]

Other preparation techniques include observation of an audiotape or videotape of meetings.† For reasons of confidentiality, this must be a professionally marketed tape in the public domain or a tape of a simulated group meeting with staff members or professional actors playing the roles of members. The scripts may be deliberately designed to demonstrate the major points to be stressed in the preparatory phase.

An even more powerful mode of preparing clients is to provide them with personal training in desired group behavior.†[72] Several experiential formats have been described. One brief group therapy team, for example, employs a two-part preparation. First, each group member has an individual meeting to establish a focus and goals for therapy. Afterward, prospective group members participate in an experiential single-session workshop at which eighteen to twenty clients perform a series of carefully selected structured interactional exercises, some involving dyads, some triads, and some the entire group.[73]

Another study used four preparatory sessions, each of which focused on a single concept of pregroup training: (1) using the here-and-now, (2) learning how to express feelings, (3) learning to become more self-disclosing, and (4) becoming aware of the impact one has and wishes to have on others. The researchers handed out cognitive material in advance and designed structured group exercises to provide experiential learning about each concept.[74] Other projects use role playing to simulate group therapy interaction.[75]

In general, the more emotionally alive and relevant the preparation is, the greater its impact will be. Some research suggests that it is the active, experiential rather than the cognitive or passive, observing component of the pretraining that may have the greatest impact.[76]

Much current preparation research centers on the client's motivation and change readiness.*[77] The focus on motivation as a target for intervention (rather than a prerequisite for treatment) originated in the treatment of addiction and has subsequently been applied effectively for clients with eating disorders and perpetrators of sexual abuse—clinical populations well recognized for denial and resistance to change.[78]

In the future, we can expect interactive computer technology to generate even more effective preparatory programs. However, the existing approaches, used singly or in combination, can be highly effective. Much research evidence, to which I now turn, attests to the general effectiveness of these techniques.

Research Evidence

In a controlled experiment, my colleagues and I tested the effectiveness of a brief cognitive preparatory session.[79] Of a sample of sixty clients awaiting group therapy, half were seen in a thirty-minute preparatory session, and the other half were seen for an equal period in a conventional interview dedicated primarily to history-taking. Six therapy groups (three of prepared clients, three of unprepared clients) were organized and led by group therapists unaware that there had been an experimental manipulation.

---

*The transtheoretical model of change postulates that individuals advance through five phases in the change process. Therapy will be more effective if it is congruent with the client's particular state of change readiness. The stages are precontemplation, contemplation, preparation, action, and maintenance.

(The therapists believed only that all clients had been seen in a standard intake session.) A study of the first twelve meetings demonstrated that the prepared groups had more faith in therapy (which, in turn, positively influences outcome) and engaged in significantly more group and interpersonal interaction than did the unprepared groups, and that this difference was as marked in the twelfth meeting as in the second.[80] The research design required that identical preparation be given to each participant. Had the preparation been more thorough and more individualized for each client, its effectiveness might have been greater.

The basic design and results of this project—a pregroup preparation sample, which is then studied during its first several group therapy meetings and shown to have a superior course of therapy compared with a sample that was not properly prepared—has been replicated many times. The clinical populations have varied, and particular modes of preparation and process and outcome variables have grown more sophisticated. But the amount of corroborative evidence supporting the efficacy *on both group processes and client outcomes* of pregroup preparation is impressive.[81] Furthermore, few studies fail to find positive effects of preparation on clients' work in group therapy.[82]

Pregroup preparation improves attendance[83] and increases self-disclosure, self-exploration, and group cohesion,[84] although the evidence for lower dropout rates is less consistent.[85] Prepared group members express more emotion;[86] assume more personal responsibility in a group;[87] disclose more of themselves;[88] show increased verbal, work-oriented participation;[89] are better liked by the other members;[90] report less anxiety;[91] are more motivated to change;[92] show a significant decrease in depression;[93] improve in marital adjustment and ability to communicate;[94] are more likely to attain their primary goals in therapy;[95] and have fewer erroneous conceptions about the group procedure.[96] Research shows that cognitive preparation of clients in lower socioeconomic classes results in greater involvement, group activity, and self-exploration.[97] Even notoriously hard to engage populations, such as domestic abusers, respond very positively to measures aimed at enhancing attendance and participation.[98]

In summary, a strong research consensus endorses the value of pregroup client preparation. Most of the findings demonstrate the beneficial impact of preparation on intervening variables; a direct effect on global client outcome is more difficult to demonstrate because the contributions of other important therapy variables obscure the effect of preparation.[99]

The Rationale Behind Preparation

Let us consider briefly the rationale behind preparation for group therapy. The first meetings of a therapy group are both precarious and vitally important: many members grow unnecessarily discouraged and terminate therapy, and the group is in a highly fluid state and maximally responsive to the influence of the therapist—who has the opportunity to help the group elaborate therapeutic norms. The early meetings are a time of considerable client anxiety, both *intrinsic*, unavoidable anxiety and *extrinsic*, unnecessary anxiety.

The *intrinsic* anxiety issues from the very nature of the group. Individuals who have encountered lifelong disabling difficulties in interpersonal relationships will invariably be stressed by a therapy group that demands not only that they attempt to relate deeply to other members but also that they discuss these relationships with great candor. In fact, as I noted in chapter 9, clinical consensus and empirical research both indicate that anxiety seems to be an essential condition for the initiation of change.[100] In group therapy, anxiety arises not only from interpersonal conflict but from dissonance, which springs from one's desire to remain in the group while at the same time feeling highly threatened by the group task. An imposing body of evidence, however, demonstrates that there are limits to the adaptive value of anxiety in therapy.[101] An optimal degree of anxiety enhances motivation and increases vigilance, but excessive anxiety will obstruct one's ability to cope with stress. White notes, in his masterful review of the evidence supporting the concept of an exploratory drive, that excessive anxiety and fear are the enemies of environmental exploration; they retard learning and decrease exploratory behavior in proportion to the intensity of the fear.[102] In group therapy, crippling amounts of anxiety may prevent the introspection, interpersonal exploration, and testing of new behavior essential to the process of change.

Much of the anxiety experienced by clients early in the group is not intrinsic to the group task but is *extrinsic,* unnecessary, and sometimes iatrogenic. This anxiety is a natural consequence of being in a group situation in which one's expected behavior, the group goals, and their relevance to one's personal goals are exceedingly unclear. Research with laboratory groups demonstrates that if the group's goals, the methods of goal attainment, and expected role behavior are ambiguous, the group will be less cohesive and less productive and its members more defensive, anxious, frustrated, and likely to terminate membership.[103]

Effective preparation for the group will reduce the *extrinsic* anxiety that stems from uncertainty. By clarifying the group goals, by explaining how group and personal goals are confluent, by presenting unambiguous guidelines for effective behavior, by providing the client with an accurate formulation of the group process, the therapist reduces uncertainty and the accompanying extrinsic anxiety.

A systematic preparation for group therapy by no means implies a rigid structuring of the group experience. I do not propose a didactic, directive approach to group therapy but, on the contrary, suggest a technique that will enhance the formation of a freely interacting, autonomous group. By averting lengthy ritualistic behavior in the initial sessions and by diminishing initial anxiety stemming from ambiguity, the group is enabled to plunge quickly into group work.

Although some group therapists eschew systematic preparation for the group, all group therapists attempt to clarify the therapeutic process and the behavior expected of clients: Differences between therapists or between therapeutic schools are largely in the timing and style of preparation. By subtle or even subliminal verbal and nonverbal reinforcement, even the most nondirective therapist attempts to persuade a group to accept his or her values about what is or is not important in the group process.[104]

Bureaucratic considerations add another component to preparation: informed consent. Contemporary therapists are under increasing pressure to provide (and to document in the record that it has been provided) sufficient information about treatment benefits, side effects, costs, and alternatives to make an informed choice about their therapy.[105] Furthermore, informed consent cannot be dispensed with in a single discussion but must be revisited on a timely basis. Obtaining informed consent is rapidly evolving into a standard of practice enshrined in the Ethics Guidelines of the American Psychological Association[106] and the American Psychiatric Association.[107] Though this procedure may seem onerous, it is here to stay, and adaptive therapists must find a way to transform it into something useful: periodic frank discussions about the course of therapy convey respect for the client and strengthen the therapeutic alliance.

One final practical observation about preparation is in order. Group therapists often find themselves pressed to find group members. A sudden loss of members may provoke therapists into hasty activity to rebuild the group, often resulting in the selection of unsuitable, inadequately prepared members. The therapist then has to assume the position of selling the group to the prospective member—a position that is generally obvious to the client. The therapist does better to continue the group with reduced membership, to select new members carefully, and then to present the group in such a way as to maximize a client's desire to join it. In fact, research indicates that the more difficult it is to enter a group and the more one wants to join, the more the individual will subsequently value the group.[108] This is the general principle underlying initiation rites to fraternities and arduous selection and admission criteria for many organizations. An applicant cannot but reason that a group so difficult to join must be very valuable indeed.

Chapter 11

IN THE BEGINNING

The work of the group therapist begins long before the first group meeting. As I have already emphasized, successful group outcome depends largely on the therapist's effective performance of the pretherapy tasks. In previous chapters, I discussed the crucial importance of proper group selection, composition, setting, and preparation. In this chapter I consider the birth and development of the group: first, the stages of development of the therapy group, and then problems of attendance, punctuality, membership turnover, and addition of new members—important issues in the life of the developing group.

FORMATIVE STAGES OF THE GROUP

Every therapy group, with its unique cast of characters and complex interaction, undergoes a singular development. All the members begin to manifest themselves interpersonally, each creating his or her own social microcosm. In time, if therapists do their job effectively, members will begin to understand their interpersonal style and eventually to experiment with new behavior. Given the richness of human interaction, compounded by the grouping of several individuals with maladaptive styles, it is obvious that the course of a group over many months or years will be complex and, to a great degree, unpredictable. Nevertheless, group dynamic forces operate in all groups to influence their development, and it is possible to describe an imperfect but nonetheless useful schema of developmental phases.

One well-known group developmental theory postulates five stages: forming, storming, norming, performing, and adjourning.[1] This simple, rhythmic phrase captures well the range of group development models articulated by diverse researchers and applies to both time-limited and open-ended groups.†[2]

In general, groups are first preoccupied with the tasks of initial member engagement and affiliation. This phase is followed by one with a focus on control, power, status, competition, and individual differentiation. Next comes a long, productive working phase marked by intimacy, engagement, and genuine cohesion. The final stage is termination of the group experience. These models also share a premise that development is *epigenetic*—that is, each stage builds on the success of preceding ones. Hence, early developmental failures will express themselves throughout the group's life. Another premise of development is that groups are likely to regress under conditions threatening group integrity.†

As group development unfolds, we see shifts in group member behavior and communication. As the group matures, increased empathic, positive communication will be evident. Members describe their experience in more personal, affective and less intellectual ways. Group members focus more on the here-and-now, are less avoidant of productive conflict, offer constructive feedback, are more disclosing, and are more collaborative. Advice is replaced with exploration, and the group is more interactional, self-directed and less leader centered.[3] This developmental shift to more meaningful work has also been demonstrated repeatedly in reliable studies of task and work groups and correlates significantly with enhanced productivity and achievement.[4]

There are compelling reasons for you as the therapist to familiarize yourself with the developmental sequence of groups. If you are to perform your task of assisting the group to form therapeutic norms and to prevent the establishment of norms that hinder therapy, then you must have a clear conception of the optimal development of a therapy group. If you are to diagnose group blockage and to intervene strategically to encourage healthy development, you must have a sense of favorable and of flawed development. Furthermore, knowledge of a broad developmental sequence will provide you with a sense of mastery and direction in the group; a confused and anxious leader engenders similar feelings in the group members.

The First Meeting

The first group therapy session is invariably a success. Clients (as well as neophyte therapists) generally anticipate it with such dread that they are always relieved by the actual event. Any actions therapists take to reduce clients' anxiety and unease are generally useful. It is often helpful to call members a few days before the first meeting to reestablish contact and remind them of the group's beginning. Greeting group members outside the group room before the first meeting or posting signs on the hallway directing clients to the group room for the first meeting are easy and reassuring steps to take.

Some therapists begin the meeting with a brief introductory statement about the purpose and method of the group (especially if they have not thoroughly prepared the clients beforehand); others may simply mention one or two basic ground rules—for example, honesty and confidentiality. The therapist may suggest that the members introduce themselves; if the therapist instead remains silent, invariably some member will suggest that the members introduce themselves. In North American groups the use of first names is usually established within minutes. Then a very loud silence ensues, which, like most psychotherapy silences, seems eternal but lasts only a few seconds.

Generally, the silence is broken by the individual destined to dominate the early stages of the group, who will say, "I guess I'll get the ball rolling," or words to that effect. Usually that person then recounts his or her reasons for seeking therapy, which often elicits similar descriptions from other members. An alternative course of events occurs when a member (perhaps spurred by the tension of the group during the initial silence) comments on his or her social discomfort or fear of groups. This remark may stimulate related comments from others who have similar feelings.

As I stressed in chapter 5, the therapist wittingly or unwittingly begins to shape the norms of the group at its inception. This task can be more efficiently performed while the group is still young. The first meeting is therefore no time for the therapist to be passive and inactive;[5] in chapter 5 I described a number of techniques to shape norms in a beginning group.

The Initial Stage: Orientation, Hesitant Participation, Search for Meaning, Dependency

Two tasks confront members of any newly formed group. First, they must understand how to achieve their primary task—the purpose for which they joined the group. Second, they must attend to their social relationships in the group so as to create a niche for themselves that will provide not only the comfort necessary to achieve their primary task but also gratification from the sheer pleasure of group membership. In many groups, such as athletic teams, college classrooms, and work settings, the primary task and the social task are well differentiated.[6] In therapy groups, although this fact is not often appreciated at first by members, the tasks are confluent—a fact vastly complicating the group experience of socially ineffective individuals.

Several simultaneous concerns are present in the initial meetings. Members, especially if not well prepared by the therapist, search for the rationale of therapy; they may be confused about the relevance of the group's activities to their personal goals in therapy. The initial meetings are often peppered with questions reflecting this confusion. Even months later, members may wonder aloud, "How is this going to help? What does all this have to do with solving my problems?"

At the same time, the members are attending to their social relationships: they size up one another and the group. They search for viable roles for themselves and wonder whether they will be liked and respected or ignored and rejected. Although clients ostensibly come to a therapy group for treatment, social forces impel them to invest most of their energy in a search for approval, acceptance, respect, or domination. To some, acceptance and approval appear so unlikely that they defensively reject or depreciate the group by mentally derogating the other members and by reminding themselves that the group is unreal and artificial, or that they are too special to care about a group that requires sacrificing even one particle of their prized individuality. Many members are particularly vulnerable at this time.†[7]

In the beginning, the therapist is well advised to keep one eye on the group as a whole, and the other eye on each individual's subjective experience in this new group. Members wonder what membership entails. What are the admission requirements? How much must one reveal or give of oneself? What type of commitment must one make? At a conscious or near-conscious level, they seek the answers to questions such as these and maintain a vigilant search for the types of behavior that the group expects and approves. Most clients crave both a deep, intimate one-to-one connection and a connection to the whole group.†[8] Occasionally, however, a member with a very tenuous sense of self may fear losing his identity through submersion in the group. If this fear is particularly pronounced it may impede engagement in the group. For such individuals, differentiation trumps belonging.[9]

If the early group is puzzled, testing, and hesitant, then it is also dependent. Overtly and covertly, members look to the leader for structure and answers as well as for approval and acceptance. Many comments and reward-seeking glances are cast at you as members seek to gain approval from authority. Your early comments are carefully scrutinized for directives about desirable and undesirable behavior. Clients appear to behave as if salvation emanates solely or primarily from you, if only they can discover what it is you want them to do. There is considerable realistic evidence for this belief: you have a professional identity as a healer, you host the group by providing a room, you prepare members, and you charge a fee for your services. All of this reinforces their expectation that you will take care of them. Some therapists unwittingly compound this belief by absorbing the client projections of special powers and unconsciously offering unfulfillable promise of succor.[10]

The existence of initial dependency thus stems from many sources: the therapeutic setting, the therapist's behavior, a morbid dependency state on the part of the client and, as I discussed in chapter 7, the many irrational sources of the members' powerful feelings toward the therapist.

Among the strongest of these is the human need for an omnipotent, omniscient, all-caring parent or rescuer—a need that colludes with the infinite human capacity for self-deception to create a yearning for and a belief in a superbeing.†

In young groups, the members' fantasies play in concert to result in what Freud referred to as the group's "need to be governed by unrestricted force, its extreme passion for authority, its thirst for obedience."[11] (Yet, who is God's god? I have often thought that the higher suicide rate among psychiatrists relative to other specialists is one tragic commentary on this dilemma.[12] Psychotherapists who are deeply depressed and who know that they must be their own superbeing, their own ultimate rescuer, are more likely than many of their clients to plunge into final despair.)

The content and communicational style of the initial phase tends to be relatively stereotyped and restricted, resembling the interaction occurring at a cocktail party or similar transient social encounters. Problems are approached rationally; the client suppresses irrational aspects of his concerns in the service of support, etiquette, and group tranquillity. Thus, at first, groups may endlessly discuss topics of apparently little substantive interest to any of the participants; these cocktail party issues, however, serve as a vehicle for the first interpersonal exploratory forays. Hence, the content of the discussion is less important than the unspoken process: members size up one another, they attend to such things as who responds favorably to them, who sees things the way they do, whom to fear, whom to respect.

In the beginning, therapy groups often spend time on symptom description, previous therapy experience, medications, and the like. The members often search for similarities. Members are fascinated by the notion that they are not unique in their misery, and most groups invest considerable energy in demonstrating how the members are similar. This process often offers considerable relief to members (see the discussion of universality in chapter 1) and provides part of the foundation for group cohesiveness. These first steps set the stage for the later deeper engagement that is a prerequisite for effective therapy.[13]

Giving and seeking advice is another characteristic of the early group: clients seek advice for problems with spouses, children, employers, and so on, and the group attempts to provide some practical solution. As discussed in chapter 1, this guidance is rarely of functional value but serves as a vehicle through which members can express mutual interest and caring. It is also a familiar mode of communication that can be employed before members understand how to work fully in the here-and-now.

In the beginning the group needs direction and structure. A silent leader will amplify anxiety and foster regression.† This phenomenon occurs even in groups of psychologically sophisticated members. For example, a training group of psychiatry residents led by a silent, nondirective leader grew anxious at their first meeting and expressed fears of what could happen in the group and who might become a casualty of the experience. One member spoke of a recent news report of a group of seemingly "normal" high school students who beat a homeless man to death. Their anxiety lessened when the leader commented that they were all concerned about the harmful forces that could be unleashed as a result of joining this group of seemingly "normal" residents.

The Second Stage: Conflict, Dominance, Rebellion

If the first core concern of a group is with "in or out," then the next is with "top or bottom."[14] In this second, "storming" stage, the group shifts from preoccupation with acceptance, approval, commitment to the group, definitions of accepted behavior, and the search for orientation, structure, and meaning, to a preoccupation with dominance, control, and power. The conflict characteristic of this phase is among members or between members and leader. Each member attempts to establish his or her preferred amount of initiative and power. Gradually, a control hierarchy, a social pecking order, emerges.

Negative comments and intermember criticism are more frequent; members often appear to feel entitled to a one-way analysis and judgment of others. As in the first stage, advice is given but in the context of a different social code: social conventions are abandoned, and members feel free to make personal criticism about a complainer's behavior or attitudes. Judgments are made of past and present life experiences and styles. It is a time of "oughts" and "shoulds" in the group, a time when the "peer-court"[15] is in session. Members make suggestions or give advice, not as a manifestation of deep acceptance and understanding—sentiments yet to emerge in the group—but in the service of jockeying for position.

The struggle for control is part of the infrastructure of every group. It is always present, sometimes quiescent, sometimes smoldering, sometimes in full conflagration. If there are members with strong needs to dominate, control may be the major theme of the early meetings. A dormant struggle for control often becomes more overt when new members are added to the group, especially new members who do not "know their place" and, instead of making obeisance to the older members in accordance with their seniority, make strong early bids for dominance.

The emergence of hostility toward the therapist is inevitable in the development of a group. Many observers have emphasized an early stage of ambivalence to the therapist coupled with resistance to self-examination and self-disclosure. Hostility toward the leader has its source in the unrealistic, indeed magical, attributes with which clients secretly imbue the therapist. Their expectations are so limitless that they are bound to be disappointed by any therapist, however competent. Gradually, as they recognize the therapist's limitations, reality sets in and hostility to the leader dissipates.

This is by no means a clearly conscious process. The members may intellectually advocate a democratic group that draws on its own resources but nevertheless may, on a deeper level, crave dependency and attempt first to create and then destroy an authority figure. Group therapists refuse to fill the traditional authority role: they do not lead in the ordinary manner; they do not provide answers and solutions; they urge the group to explore and to employ its own resources. The members' wish lingers, however, and it is usually only after several sessions that the group members come to realize that the therapist will frustrate their yearning for the ideal leader.

Yet another source of resentment toward the leader lies in the gradual recognition by each member that he or she will not become the leader's favorite child. During the pretherapy session, each member comes to harbor the fantasy that the therapist is his or her very own therapist, intensely interested in the minute details of that client's past, present, and fantasy world. In the early meetings of the group, however, each member begins to realize that the therapist is no more interested in him or her than in the others; seeds are sown for the emergence of rivalrous, hostile feelings toward the other members. Each member feels, in some unclear manner, betrayed by the therapist. Echoes of prior issues with siblings may emerge and members begin to appreciate the importance of peer interactions in the work of the group.†

These unrealistic expectations of the leader and consequent disenchantment are by no means a function of childlike mentality or psychological naivete. The same phenomena occur, for example, in groups of professional psychotherapists. In fact, there is no better way for the trainee to appreciate the group's proclivity both to elevate and to attack the leader than to be a member of a training or therapy group and to experience these powerful feelings firsthand. Some theorists[16] take Freud's *Totem and Taboo*†[17] literally and regard the group's pattern of relationship with the leader as a recapitulation of the primal horde patricide. Freud does indeed suggest at one point that modern group phenomena have their prehistoric analogues in the mist of ancient, primal horde events: "Thus the group appears to us as a revival of the primal horde. Just as primitive man survives potentially in every individual, so the primal horde may arise once more out of any random collection; insofar as men are habitually under the sway of group formation, we recognize in it the survival of the primal horde."[18] The primal horde is able to free itself from restrictive, growth-inhibiting bonds and progress to a more satisfying existence only after the awesome leader has been removed.

The members are never unanimous in their attack on the therapist. Invariably, some champions of the therapist will emerge from the group. The lineup of attackers and defenders may serve as a valuable guide for the understanding of characterological trends useful for future work in the group. Generally, the leaders of this phase, those members who are earliest and most vociferous in their attack, are heavily conflicted in the area of dependency and have dealt with intolerable dependency yearnings by reaction formation. These individuals, sometimes labeled counterdependents,[19] are inclined to reject prima facie all statements by the therapist and to entertain the fantasy of unseating and replacing the leader.

For example, approximately three-fourths of the way through the first meeting of a group for clients with bulimia, I asked for the members' reflections on the meeting: How had it gone for them? Disappointments? Surprises? One member, who was to control the direction of the group for the next several weeks, commented that it had gone precisely as she had expected; in fact, it had been almost disappointingly predictable. The strongest feeling that she had had thus far, she added, was anger toward me because I had asked one of the members a question that evoked a brief period of weeping. She had felt then, "They'll never break me down like that!" Her first impressions were very predictive of her behavior for some time to come. She remained on guard and strove to be self-possessed and in control at all times. She regarded me not as an ally but as an adversary and was sufficiently forceful to lead the group into a major emphasis on control issues for the first several sessions.

If therapy is to be successful, counterdependent members must at some point experience their flip side and recognize and work through deep dependency cravings. The challenge in their therapy is first to understand that their counterdependent behavior often evokes rebuke and rejection from others before their wish to be nourished and protected can be experienced or expressed.

Other members invariably side with the therapist. They must be helped to investigate their need to defend the therapist at all costs, regardless of the issue involved. Occasionally, clients defend you because they have encountered a series of unreliable objects and misperceive you as extraordinarily frail; others need to preserve you because they fantasize an eventual alliance with you against other powerful members of the group. Beware that you do not unknowingly transmit covert signals of personal distress to which the rescuers appropriately respond.

Many of these conflicted feelings crystallize around the issue of the leader's name. Are you to be referred to by professional title (Dr. Jones or, even more impersonally, the doctor or the counselor) or by first name? Some members will immediately use the therapist's first name or even a diminutive of the name, before inquiring about the therapist's preference.

Others, even after the therapist has wholeheartedly agreed to proceeding on a first-name basis, still cannot bring themselves to mouth such irreverence and continue to bundle the therapist up in a professional title. One client, a successful businessman who had been consistently shamed and humiliated by a domineering father insisted on addressing the therapist as "Doctor" because he claimed this was a way to ensure that he was getting his money's worth.

Although I have posited disenchantment and anger with the leader as a ubiquitous feature of small groups, by no means is the process constant across groups in form or degree. The therapist's behavior may potentiate or mitigate both the experience and the expression of rebellion. Thus, one prominent sociologist, who has for many years led sensitivity-training groups of college students, reports that inevitably there is a powerful insurrection against the leader, culminating in the members removing him or her bodily from the group room.[20] I, on the other hand, led similar groups for more than a decade and never encountered a rebellion so extreme that members physically ejected me from the room. Such a difference can be due only to differences in leader styles and behavior. What kind of leader evokes the most negative responses? Generally it is those who are ambiguous or deliberately enigmatic; those who are authoritative yet offer no structure or guidelines; or those who covertly make unrealistic promises to the group early in therapy.[21]

This stage is often difficult and personally unpleasant for group therapists. Let me remind neophyte therapists that you are essential to the survival of the group. The members cannot afford to liquidate you: you will always be defended. For your own comfort, however, you must learn to discriminate between an attack on your person and an attack on your role in the group. The group's response to you is similar to transference distortion in individual therapy in that it is not directly related to your behavior, but its source in the group must be understood from both an individual psychodynamic and a group dynamic viewpoint.

Therapists who are particularly threatened by a group attack protect themselves in a variety of ways.†[22] Once I was asked to act as a consultant for two therapy groups, each approximately twenty-five sessions old, that had developed similar problems: both groups seemed to have reached a plateau, no new ground appeared to have been broken for several weeks, and the members seemed to have withdrawn their interest in the groups. A study of current meetings and past protocols revealed that neither group had yet directly dealt with any negative feelings toward the therapists. However, the reasons for this inhibition were quite different in the two groups. In the first group, the two co-therapists (first-time leaders) had clearly exposed their throats, as it were, to the group and, through their obvious anxiety, uncertainty, and avoidance of hostility-laden issues, pleaded frailty. In addition, they both desired to be loved by all the members and had been at all times so benevolent and so solicitous that an attack by the group members would have appeared unseemly and ungrateful.

The therapists of the second group had forestalled an attack in a different fashion: they remained aloof, Olympian figures whose infrequent, ostensibly profound interventions were delivered in an authoritarian manner. At the end of each meeting, they summarized, often in unnecessarily complex language, the predominant themes and each member's contributions. To attack these therapists would have been both impious and perilous.

Therapist countertransference in these two instances obstructed the group's work. Placing one's own emotional needs ahead of the group's needs is a recipe for failure.[23] Either of these two leadership styles tends to inhibit a group; suppression of important ambivalent feelings about the therapist results in a counterproductive taboo that opposes the desired norm of interpersonal honesty and emotional expression. Furthermore, an important model-setting opportunity is lost. The therapist who withstands an attack without being either destroyed or vindictive but instead responds by attempting to understand and work through the sources and effects of the attack demonstrates to the group that aggression need not be lethal and that it can be expressed and understood in the group.

One of the consequences of suppression of therapist-directed anger for the two groups in question, and for most groups, is the emergence of displaced, off-target aggression. For example, one group persisted for several weeks in attacking doctors. Previous unfortunate experiences with doctors, hospitals, and individual therapists were described in detail, often with considerable group consensus on the injustices and inhumanity of the medical profession. In one group, a member attacked the field of psychotherapy by bringing in a *Psychology Today* article that purported to prove that psychotherapy is ineffective. At other times, police, teachers, and other representatives of authority are awarded similar treatment.

Scapegoating of other members is another off-target manifestation. It is highly improbable for scapegoating to persist in a group in the absence of the therapist's collusion. The leader who cannot be criticized openly generally is the source of scapegoating. Peer attack is a safer way of expressing aggression and rivalry or of elevating one's status in the group. Added to this dynamic is the group members' unconscious need to project unacceptable aspects of self onto a group member in an attempt to reduce the risk of personal rejection by the group. At its worst, this scapegoated member can be sacrificed by the group under the covert and misguided belief that if only it were not for this one member, the group would become a utopia.[24]

Yet another source of group conflict originates in the intrinsic process of change. Rigidly entrenched attitudes and behavioral patterns are challenged by other members, and each individual is faced with the discomfort of letting go of old patterns. A useful paradigm of change in group work consists of the sequence of unfreezing, change, and refreezing.[25] The stage of "unfreezing" naturally entails a degree of challenge and conflict. Individuals adhere to their beliefs about relationships and cling to what is familiar to them. At first many clients lack the ability to examine themselves and to accept feedback. Gradually clients acquire the capacity to participate, feel emotion, and then reflect on that experience. Once that is possible, harmful, habitual patterns of behavior can be altered.[26]

The Third Stage: Development of Cohesiveness

A third commonly recognized formative phase of a group is the development of mature group cohesiveness. After the previous period of conflict, the group gradually develops into a cohesive unit. Many varied phrases with similar connotations have been used to describe this phase: in-group consciousness;[27] common goal and group spirit;[28] consensual group action, cooperation, and mutual support;[29] group integration and mutuality;[30] we-consciousness unity;[31] support and freedom of communication;[32] and establishment of intimacy and trust between peers.

In this phase the interpersonal world of the group is one of balance, resonance, safety, increased morale, trust, and self-disclosure.[33] Some members reveal the real reason they have come for treatment: sexual secrets and long-buried transgressions are shared. Postgroup coffee meetings may be arranged. Attendance improves, and clients evince considerable concern about missing members.

The chief concern of the group is with intimacy and closeness. If we characterize clients' concerns in the first phase as "in or out" and the second as "top or bottom," then we can think of the third phase as "near or far." The members' primary anxieties have to do with not being liked, not being close enough to others, or being too close to others.[34]

Although there may be greater freedom of self-disclosure in this phase, there may also be communicational restrictions of another sort: often the group suppresses all expression of negative affect in the service of cohesion. Compared with the previous stage of group conflict, all is sweetness and light, and the group basks in the glow of its newly discovered unity.[35] Eventually, however, the glow will pale and the group embrace will seem ritualistic unless differentiation and conflict in the group are permitted to emerge. Only when all affects can be expressed and constructively worked through in a cohesive group does the group become a mature work group—a state lasting for the remainder of the group's life, with periodic short-lived recrudescences of each of the earlier phases. Thus one may think of the stage of growing cohesiveness as consisting of two phases: an early stage of great mutual support (group against external world) and a more advanced stage of group work or true teamwork in which tension emerges not out of the struggle for dominance but out of each member's struggle with his or her own resistances.

Overview

Now that I have outlined the early stages of group development, let me qualify my statements lest the novice take the proposed developmental sequence too literally. The developmental phases are in essence constructs— entities that exist for the group leaders' semantic and conceptual convenience. Although the research shows persuasively, using different measures, client populations, and formal change theories, that group development occurs, the evidence is less clear on whether there is a precise, inviolate sequence of development. At times the development appears linear; at other times it is cyclical with a reiterative nature.[36] It is also apparent that *the boundaries between phases are not clearly demarcated and that a group does not permanently graduate from one phase.*

Another approach to group development research is to track the course of particular variables such as cohesion,[37] emotionality,[38] or intimacy[39] through the course of the group. No linear course exists. In considering group development, think of replacing an automobile wheel: one tightens the bolts one after another just enough so that the wheel is in place; then the process is repeated, each bolt being tightened in turn, until the wheel is entirely secure. In the same way, phases of a group emerge, become dominant, and then recede, only to have the group return to the same issues with greater thoroughness later. Thus, it is more accurate to speak of developmental tasks rather than developmental phases or a predictable developmental sequence. We may, for example, see a sequence of high engagement and low conflict, followed by lower engagement and higher conflict, followed by a return to higher engagement.[40] Hamburg suggests the term *cyclotherapy* to refer to this process of returning to the same issues but from a different perspective and each time in greater depth.[41] Often a therapy group will spend considerable time dealing with dominance, trust, intimacy, fears, the relationship between the co-therapists, and then, months later, return to the same topic from an entirely different perspective.

The group leader is well advised to consider not only the forces that promote the group's development, but also those that have been identified as antigroup.[42] These common forces encompass individual and societal resistance to joining—the fear of merging; the fear of loss of one's sense of independence; the loss of one's fantasy of specialness; the fear of seeking but being turned away.

THE IMPACT OF CLIENTS ON GROUP DEVELOPMENT

The developmental sequence I have described perhaps accurately portrays the unfolding of events in a theoretical, unpeopled therapy group and is much like the major theme of an ultramodern symphony that is unintelligible to the untrained ear. In the group, obfuscation derives from the richness and unpredictability of human interaction, which complicates the course of treatment and yet contributes to its excitement and challenge.

My experience is that the development of therapy groups is heavily and invariably influenced by chance—by the particular and unique composition of the group. Often the course of the group is set by a single member, generally the one with the loudest interpersonal pathology. By *loudest* I refer not to severity of pathology but to pathology that is most immediately manifest in the group. For example, in the first meeting of a group of incest victims, a member made a number of comments to the effect that she was disappointed that so many members were present whose healing was at such an earlier state than hers. Naturally, this evoked considerable anger from the others, who attacked her for her condescending remarks. Before long this group developed into the angriest, and least caring, group I'd ever encountered. We cannot claim that this one member put anger into the group. It would be more accurate to say that she acted as a lightning rod to release anger that was already present in each of the participants. But had she not been in the group, it is likely that the anger may have unfolded more slowly, perhaps in a context of more safety, trust, and cohesiveness. Groups that do not start well face a far more difficult challenge than ones that follow the kind of developmental sequence described in this chapter.

Many of the very individuals who seek group therapy struggle with relating and engaging. That is often why they seek therapy. Many say of themselves, "I am not a group person."[43] A group composed of several such individuals will doubtless struggle with the group tasks more than a group containing several members who have had constructive and effective experience with groups.[44]

Other individuals who may alter typical group developmental trends include those with monopolistic proclivities, exhibitionism, promiscuous self-disclosure, or an unbridled inclination to exert control. Not infrequently, such individuals receive covert encouragement from the therapist and other group members. Therapists value these clients because they provide a focus of irritation in the group, stimulate the expression of affect, and enhance the interest and excitement of a meeting. The other members often initially welcome the opportunity to hide behind the protagonist as they themselves hesitantly examine the terrain.

In a study of the dropouts of nine therapy groups, I found that in five of them, a client with a characteristic pattern of behavior fled the therapy

group within the first dozen meetings.[45] These clients ("early provocateurs") differed from one another dynamically but assumed a similar role
in the group: They stormed in, furiously activated the group, and then
vanished. The therapists described their role in the group in such terms as
"catalysts," "targets," "hostile interpreters," or "the only honest one."
Some of these early provocateurs were active counterdependents and challenged the therapist early in the group. One, for example, challenged the
leader in the third meeting in several ways: he suggested that the members
hold longer meetings and regular leaderless meetings, and, only half jok-
ingly, tried to launch an investigation into the leader's personal problems.
Other provocateurs prided themselves on their honesty and bluntness,
mincing no words in giving the other members candid feedback. Still others, heavily conflicted in intimacy, both seeking it and fearing it, engaged
in considerable self-disclosure and exhorted the group to reciprocate,
often at a reckless pace. Although the early provocateurs usually claimed
that they were impervious to the opinions and evaluations of others, in
fact they cared very much and, in each instance, deeply regretted the nonviable role they had created for themselves in the group.[46]

Therapists must recognize this phenomenon early in the group and,
through clarification and interpretation of their role, help prevent these
individuals from committing social suicide. Perhaps even more important,
therapists must recognize and discontinue their own covert encouragement of the early provocateur's behavior. It is not uncommon for therapists to be stunned when the early provocateur drops out. They may so
welcome the behavior of these clients that they fail to appreciate the
client's distress as well as their own dependence on these individuals for
keeping the group energized.

It is useful for therapists to take note of their reactions to the absence
of the various members of the group. If some members are never absent,
you may fantasize their absences and your reaction to it. Consider what
thoughts, feelings, fantasies and actions these individuals generate in you,
and what they do to generate that impact.[47] If you dread the absence of
certain members, feeling that there would be no life in the group that day,
then it is likely that there is too much burden on those individuals and so
much secondary gratification that they will not be able to deal with their
primary task in therapy. Given the responsibility projected onto them,
they may well be considered a form of scapegoat, although a positively
viewed one, at least at first.*

---

*In a classic paper on scapegoating, Scheidlinger recalls the Biblical origins of the scapegoat. One
goat is the bearer of all the people's sins and is banished from the community. A second goat is the
bearer of all the positive features of the people and is sacrificed on the altar. To be a scapegoat of
either sort bodes poorly for one's survival (S. Scheidlinger, "Presidential Address: On Scapegoating in Group Psychotherapy," *International Journal of Group Psychotherapy* 32 (1982): 131–43).

I believe much of the confusion about group development is that each group is, at the same time, *like all groups, like some groups, and like no other group! Of course,* all therapy groups go through some change as they proceed. *Of course* there is some early awkwardness, as the group deals with its raison d'être and its boundaries. *Of course* this is followed by some tension and by repeated attempts to develop intimacy. And *of course* all groups must face termination—the final phase. And from time to time, but only from time to time, one encounters a group that runs "on schedule."

Some time ago at an A. K. Rice two-week group workshop, I took part in an intergroup exercise in which the sixty participants were asked to form four groups in any manner they wished and then to study the ongoing relationships among the groups. The sixty participants, in near panic, stampeded from the large room toward the four rooms designated for the four small groups. The panic, an inevitable part of this exercise, probably stemmed from primitive fears of exclusion from a group.[48] In the group in which I participated, the first words spoken after approximately sixteen members had entered the room were, "Close the door. Don't let anyone else in!" The first act of the group was to appoint an official doorkeeper. Once the group's boundaries were defined and its identity vis-à-vis the outside world established, the group turned its attention to regulating the distribution of power by speedily electing a chairman, before multiple bids for leadership could immobilize the group. Only later did the group experience and discuss feelings of trust and intimacy and then, much later, feelings of sadness as the group approached termination.

In summary, there are some advantages to group therapists' possessing some broad schema of a group developmental sequence: It enables them to maintain objectivity and to chart the voyage of a group despite considerable yawing, and to recognize if a group never progresses past a certain stage or omits some. At times, therapists may demand something for which the group is not yet ready: mutual caring and concern develop late in the group; in the beginning, caring may be more pro forma as members view one another as interlopers or rivals for the healing touch of the therapist. The therapist who is aware of normative group development is able to remain more finely tuned to the group.

But there is a downside to the clinical application of group developmental ideas. The inexperienced therapist may take them too seriously and use them as a template for clinical practice. I have seen beginning therapists exert energy on forcing a group, in procrustean fashion, to progress in lockstep through set phases. Such formulaic therapy—and it grows more common in these days of standardized therapy via treatment manual—lessens the possibility of real therapist-client engagement. The sacrifice of realness, of authenticity, in the therapeutic relationship is no minor loss: It is the loss of the very heart of psychotherapy.

Certainly, the first generations of psychotherapy manuals diminished the authenticity of therapy by their slavish attention to adherence to the model. More contemporary therapy manuals do less micromanaging of treatment and provide more scope for therapist flexibility and naturalness.[49]

Psychotherapy, whether with a group or with an individual client, should be a shared journey of discovery. There is danger in every system of "stages"—in the therapist having fixed, preconceived ideas and procedural protocols in any kind of growth-oriented therapy. It is precisely for this reason that some trends forced on the field by managed care are so toxic.

In the mid-1970s, I began the first group for cancer patients with Katy Weers, a remarkable woman with advanced breast cancer. She often railed about the harm brought to the field by Elisabeth Kübler-Ross's "stages" of dying, and dreamed of writing a book to refute this concept. To experience the client against a template of stages interferes with the very thing so deeply desired by clients: "therapeutic presence." Katy and I both suspected that therapists cloaked themselves in the mythology of "stages" to muffle their own death anxiety.

MEMBERSHIP PROBLEMS

The early developmental sequence of a therapy group is powerfully influenced by membership problems. Turnover in membership, tardiness, and absence are facts of life in the developing group and often threaten its stability and integrity. Considerable absenteeism may redirect the group's attention and energy away from its developmental tasks toward the problem of maintaining membership. It is the therapist's task to discourage irregular attendance and, when necessary, to replace dropouts appropriately by adding new members.

Turnover

In the normal course of events, a substantial number of members drop out of interactionally based groups in the first twelve meetings (see table 8.1). If two or more members drop out, new members are usually added—but often a similar percentage of these additions drop out in their first dozen or so meetings. Only after this does the group solidify and begin to engage in matters other than those concerning group stability. Generally, by the time clients have remained in the group for approximately twenty meetings, they have made the necessary long-term commitment. In an attendance study of five groups, there was considerable turnover in membership within the first twelve meetings, a settling in between the twelfth and twentieth, and near-perfect attendance, with excellent punctuality and no dropouts, between the twentieth and forty-fifth meetings (the end of the study).[50] Most studies demonstrate the same findings.[51] It is unusual for the number of later dropouts to exceed that of earlier phases.[52] In one study in which attrition in later phases was higher, the authors attributed the large numbers of later dropouts to mounting discomfort arising from the greater intimacy of the group. Some groups had a wave of dropouts; one dropout seemed to seed others. As noted in chapter 8, prior or concurrent individual therapy substantially reduces the risk of premature termination.[53]

In general, short-term groups report lower dropout rates.[54] In closed, time-limited groups, it is useful to start with a large enough number of clients that the group can withstand some attrition and yet be sufficiently robust for the duration of the group's course. Too large a starting size invites dropouts from individuals who will feel detached and peripheral to the group. Starting with nine or ten members is probably ideal in this situation.

Attendance and Punctuality

Despite the therapist's initial encouragement of regular attendance and punctuality, difficulties usually arise in the early stages of a group. At times the therapist, buffeted by excuses from clients—baby-sitting problems, vacations, transportation difficulties, work emergencies, out-of-town guests—becomes resigned to the impossibility of synchronizing the schedules of eight busy people. Resist that course! Tardiness and irregular attendance usually signify resistance to therapy and should be regarded as they are in individual therapy. When several members are often late or absent, search for the source of the group resistance; for some reason, cohesiveness is limited and the group is foundering. If a group solidifies into a hard-working cohesive group, then—*mirabile dictu*—the baby-sitting and scheduling problems vanish and there may be perfect attendance and punctuality for many months.

At other times, the resistance is individual rather than group based. I am continually amazed by the transformation in some individuals, who for long periods have been tardy because of "absolutely unavoidable" contingencies—for example, periodic business conferences, classroom rescheduling, child care emergencies—and then, after recognizing and working through the resistance, become the most punctual members for months on end. One periodically late member hesitated to involve himself in the group because of his shame about his impotence and homosexual fantasies. After he disclosed these concerns and worked through his feelings of shame, he found that the crucial business commitments responsible for his lateness—commitments that, he later revealed, consisted of perusing his mail—suddenly evaporated.

Whatever the basis for resistance, it is behavior that must, for several reasons, be modified before it can be understood and worked through. For one thing, irregular attendance is destructive to the group. It is contagious and leads to group demoralization. Obviously, it is impossible to work on an issue in the absence of the relevant members. Few exercises are more futile than addressing the wrong audience by deploring irregular attendance with the group members who are present—the regular, punctual participants. Groups are generally supportive of individuals who are genuinely trying to attend regularly but fall short, in contrast to their intolerance of those who lack real commitment to the group.

Various methods of influencing attendance have been adopted by therapists. During pretherapy interviews, many therapists stress the importance of regular attendance. Clients who appear likely to have scheduling or transportation problems are best referred for individual therapy, as are those who must be out of town once a month or who, a few weeks after the group begins, plan an extended out-of-town vacation. Charging full fees for missed sessions is standard practice. Many private practitioners set a fixed monthly fee, which is not reduced for missed meetings for any reason.

There are few more resistant group clients than men who have physically abused their partners. At the same time, there is robust evidence that group interventions are effective with this population, if the men continue in treatment. However, dropout rates of 40–60 percent within three months are not uncommon. Clinicians working with this population have tackled the problem of poor motivation directly with intensive pregroup training, including psychoeducational videos to increase empathy for the victims and inform abusers about the physiology and psychology of violence.[55] An even simpler intervention has proven powerfully effective. In a study of 189 men, group leaders who reached out actively via phone calls, expressions of concern, and personalized alliance-building measures produced dramatic results. These simple, low-tech interventions significantly increased both attendance and tenure in both interpersonal and cognitive-behavioral group therapies and significantly reduced the incidence of domestic violence.[56]

It is critical that the therapist be utterly convinced of the importance of the therapy group and of regular attendance. The therapist who acts on this conviction will transmit it to the group members. Thus, therapists should arrive punctually, award the group high priority in their own schedule, and, if they must miss a meeting, inform the group of their absence weeks in advance. It is not uncommon to find that therapist absence or group cancellation may be followed by poor attendance.

• *Upon arriving at a psychotherapy group for elderly men, I discovered that half the group of eight was absent. Illness, family visits, and conflicting appointments all conspired to diminish turnout. As I surveyed the room strewn with empty chairs, one man spoke up and suggested with some resignation that we cancel the group since so many members were away. My first reaction was one of quiet relief at the prospect of unexpected free time in my day. My next thought was that canceling the meeting was a terrible message to those present. In fact, the message would echo the diminishment, isolation, and unwantedness that the men felt in their lives. Therefore I suggested that it might be even more important than ever to meet today. The men actively embraced my comment as well as my suggestion that we remove the unnecessary chairs and tighten the circle so that we could hear one another better.*

A member who has a poor attendance record (whatever the reason) is unlikely to benefit from the group. In a study of ninety-eight group participants, Stone and his colleagues found that poor attendance early in the group was linearly related to late dropout (at six to twelve months).[57] Thus, inconsistent attendance demands decisive intervention.

• *In a new group, one member, Dan, was consistently late or absent. Whenever the co-therapists discussed his attendance, it was clear that Dan had valid excuses: his life and his business were in such crisis that unexpected circumstances repeatedly arose to make attendance impossible. The group as a whole had not jelled; despite the therapists' efforts, other members were often late or absent, and there was considerable flight during the sessions. At the twelfth meeting, the therapists decided that decisive action was necessary. They advised Dan to leave the group, explaining that his schedule was such that the group could be of little value to him. They offered to help Dan arrange individual therapy, which would provide greater scheduling flexibility. Although the therapists' motives were not punitive and although they were thorough in their explanation, Dan was deeply offended and walked out in anger midway through the meeting. The other members, extremely threatened, supported Dan to the point of questioning the therapists' authority to ask a member to leave.*

Despite the initial, raucous reaction of the group, it was soon clear that the therapists had made the proper intervention. One of the co-therapists phoned Dan and saw him individually for two sessions, then referred him to an appropriate therapist for individual therapy. Dan soon appreciated that the therapists were acting not punitively but in his best interests: irregularly attending a therapy group would not have been effective therapy for him. The group was immediately affected: attendance abruptly improved and remained near perfect over the next several months. The members, once they had recovered from their fear of similar banishment, gradually disclosed their approval of

the therapists' act and their great resentment toward Dan and, to a
lesser extent, toward some of the other members for having treated the
group in such a cavalier fashion.

Some therapists attempt to improve attendance by harnessing group
pressure—for example, by refusing to hold a meeting until a predetermined number of members (usually three or four) are present. Even without formalization of this sort, the pressure exerted by the rest of the
group is an effective lever to bring to bear on errant members. The group
is often frustrated and angered by the repetitions and false starts necessitated by irregular attendance. The therapist should encourage the members to express their reactions to late or absent members. Be mindful,
though, that the therapist's concern about attendance is not always shared
by the members: a young or immature group often welcomes the small
meeting, regarding it as an opportunity for more individual attention
from the leader. Similarly, be cautious not to punish the regular participants by withholding treatment in the process of applying group pressure
on the absent members.

Like any event in the group, absenteeism or tardiness is a form of behavior that reflects an individual's characteristic patterns of relating to
others. Be sure to examine the personal meaning of the client's action. If
Mary arrives late, does she apologize? Does Joe enter in a thoughtless, exhibitionistic manner? Does Sally arrive late because she experiences herself as nonentity who makes no contribution to the group's life in any
event? Does Ralph come as he chooses because he believes nothing of substance happens without him anyway? Does Peg ask for a recap of the
events of the meeting? Is her relation with the group such that the members provide her with a recap? If Stan is absent, does he phone in advance
to let the group know? Does he offer complex, overelaborate excuses, as
though convinced he will not be believed? Not infrequently, a client's psychopathology is responsible for poor attendance. For example, one man
who sought therapy because of a crippling fear of authority figures and
a pervasive inability to assert himself in interpersonal situations was
frequently late because he was unable to muster the courage to interrupt
a conversation or a conference with a business associate. An obsessive-
compulsive client was late because he felt compelled to clean his desk over
and over before leaving his office.

Thus, absenteeism and lateness are part of the individual's social microcosm and, if handled properly, may be harnessed in the service of self-
understanding. For both the group's and the individual's sake, however,
they must be corrected before being analyzed. No interpretation can be
heard by an absent group member. In fact, the therapist must attend to
the timing of his comments to the returning member. Clients who have

been absent or are late often enter the meeting with some defensive guilt or shame and are not in an optimal state of receptiveness for observations about their behavior. The therapist does well to attend first to group maintenance and norm-setting tasks and then, later, when the timing seems right and defensiveness diminished, attempt to help the individual explore the meaning of his or her behavior. The timing of feedback is particularly important for members who have greater psychological vulnerability and less mature relationships.[58]

Group members who must miss a meeting or arrive late should, as they were advised in pregroup preparation, phone the therapist in advance in order to spare the group from wasting time expressing curiosity or concern about their absence. Often, in advanced groups, the fantasies of group members about why someone is absent provide valuable material for the therapeutic process; in early groups, however, such speculations tend to be superficial and unfruitful.

An important adage of interactional group therapy, which I emphasize many times throughout this book, is that any event in the group can serve as grist for the interpersonal mill. Even the absence of a member can generate important, previously unexplored material.

> • *A group composed of four women and three men held its eighth meeting in the absence of two of the men. Albert, the only male present, had previously been withdrawn and submissive in the group, but in this meeting a dramatic transformation occurred. He erupted into activity, talked about himself, questioned the other members, spoke loudly and forcefully, and, on a couple of occasions, challenged the therapist. His nonverbal behavior was saturated with quasi-courtship bids directed at the women members: for example, frequent adjustment of his shirt collar and preening of the hair at his temples. Later in the meeting, the group focused on Albert's change, and he realized and expressed his fear and envy of the two missing males, both of whom were aggressive and assertive. He had long experienced a pervasive sense of social and sexual impotence, which had been reinforced by his feeling that he had never made a significant impact on any group of people and especially any group of women. In subsequent weeks, Albert did much valuable work on these issues—issues that might not have become accessible for many months without the adventitious absence of the two other members.*

My clinical preference is to encourage attendance but never, regardless of how small the group is, to cancel a session. There is considerable therapeutic value in the client's knowing that the group is always there, stable and reliable: its constancy will in time beget constancy of attendance. I have led many small group sessions, with as few as two members, that have proved to be critical for those attending. The technical problem with such meetings is that without the presence of interaction, the therapist may revert to focusing on intrapsychic processes in a manner characteristic of individual therapy and forgo group and interpersonal issues. It is far more therapeutically consistent to focus in depth on group and interpersonal processes even in the smallest of sessions. Consider the following clinical example from a ten-month-old group:

• *For various reasons—vacations, illnesses, resistance—only two members attended: Wanda, a thirty-eight-year-old depressed woman with borderline personality disorder who had twice required hospitalization, and Martin, a twenty-three-year-old man with schizoid personality disorder who was psychosexually immature and suffered from moderately severe ulcerative colitis.*

Wanda spent much of the early part of the meeting describing the depth of her despair, which during the past week had reached such proportions that she had been preoccupied with suicide and, since the group therapist was out of town, had visited the emergency room at the hospital. While there, she had surreptitiously read her medical chart and seen a consultation note written a year earlier by the group therapist in which he had diagnosed her as borderline. She said that she had been anticipating this diagnosis and now wanted the therapist to hospitalize her.

Martin then recalled a fragment of a dream he had several weeks before but had not discussed: the therapist was sitting at a large desk interviewing Martin, who stood up and looked at the paper on which the therapist is writing. There he saw in huge letters one word covering the entire page: IMPOTENT. The therapist helped both Wanda and Martin discuss their feelings of awe, helpless dependence, and resentment toward him as well as their inclination to shift responsibility and project onto him their bad feelings about themselves.

Wanda proceeded to underscore her helplessness by describing her inability to cook for herself and her delinquency in paying her bills, which was so extreme that she now feared police action against her. The therapist and Martin both discussed her persistent reluctance to comment on her positive accomplishments—for example, her continued excellence as a teacher. The therapist wondered whether her presentation of herself as helpless was not designed to elicit responses of caring and concern from the other members and the therapist—responses that she felt would be forthcoming in no other way.

Martin then mentioned that he had gone to the medical library the previous day to read some of the therapist's professional articles. In response to the therapist's question about what he really wanted to find out, Martin answered that he guessed he really wanted to know how the therapist felt about him and proceeded to describe, for the first time, his longing for the therapist's sole attention and love.

Later, the therapist expressed his concern at Wanda's reading his note in her medical record. Since there is a realistic component to a client's anxiety on learning that her therapist has diagnosed her as borderline, the therapist candidly discussed both his own discomfort at having to use diagnostic labels for hospital records and the confusion surrounding psychiatric nosological terminology; he recalled as best he could his reasons for using that particular label and its implications.

Wanda then commented on the absent members and wondered whether she had driven them from the group (a common reaction). She dwelled on her unworthiness and, at the therapist's suggestion, made an inventory of her baleful characteristics, citing her slovenliness, selfishness, greed, envy, and hostile feelings toward all those in her social environment. Martin both supported Wanda and identified with her, since he recognized many of these feelings in himself. He discussed how difficult it was for him to reveal himself in the group (Martin had disclosed very little of himself previously in the group). Later, he discussed his fear of getting drunk or losing control in other ways: for one thing, he might become indiscreet sexually. He then discussed, for the first time, his fear of sex, his impotence, his inability to maintain an erection, and his last-minute refusals to take advantage of sexual opportunities. Wanda empathized deeply with Martin and, although she had for some time regarded sex as abhorrent, expressed the strong wish (a wish, not an intention) to help him by offering herself to him sexually. Martin then described his strong sexual attraction to her, and later both he and Wanda discussed their sexual feelings toward the other members of the group. The therapist made the observation, one that proved subsequently to be of great therapeutic importance to Wanda, that her interest in Martin and her desire to offer herself to him sexually belied many of the items in her inventory: her selfishness, greed, and ubiquitous hostility to others.

Although only two members were present at this meeting, they met as a group and not as two individual clients. The other members were discussed in absentia, and previously undisclosed interpersonal feelings between the two clients and toward the therapist were expressed and analyzed. It was a valuable session, deeply meaningful to both participants. It is worth noting here that talking about group members in their absence is not "talking behind people's backs." A member's absence cannot dictate what gets addressed by those in attendance, although it is essential that absent members be brought back into the loop upon their return. Mailing out a group summary (see chapter 14) is a good way to accomplish this.

Dropouts

There is no more threatening problem for the neophyte group therapist (and for many experienced therapists as well) than the dropout from group therapy. Dropouts concerned me greatly when I first started to lead groups, and my first group therapy research was a study of all the group participants who had dropped out of the therapy groups in a large psychiatric clinic.[59] It is no minor problem. As I discussed earlier, the group therapy demographic research demonstrates that a substantial number of clients will leave a group prematurely regardless of what the therapist does. In fact, some clinicians suggest that dropouts are not only inevitable but necessary in the sifting process involved in achieving a cohesive group.[60]

Consider, too, that the existence of an escape hatch may be essential to allow some members to make their first tentative commitments to the group. The group must have some decompression mechanism: mistakes in the selection process are inevitable, unexpected events occur in the lives of new members, and group incompatibilities develop. Some intensive weeklong human relations laboratories or encounter groups that meet at a geographically isolated place lack a way of escape; on several occasions, I have seen psychotic reactions in participants forced to continue in an incompatible group.

There are various reasons for premature termination (see chapter 8). It is often productive to think about the dropout phenomenon from the perspective of the interaction of three factors: the client, the group, and the therapist.[61] In general, client contributions stem from problems caused by deviancy, conflicts in intimacy and disclosure, the role of the early provocateur, external stress, complications of concurrent individual and group therapy, inability to share the leader, and fear of emotional contagion. Underlying all these reasons is the potential stress early in the group. Individuals who have maladaptive interpersonal patterns are exposed to unaccustomed demands for candor and intimacy; they are often confused about procedure; they suspect that the group activities bear little relevance to their problem; and, finally, they feel too little support in the early meetings to sustain their hope.

Group factors include the consequences of subgrouping, poor compositional match of clients, scapegoating, member-member impasses, or unresolved conflict. The therapists also play a role: they may select members too hurriedly, they may not prepare members adequately, they may not attend to building group cohesion, or they may be influenced by unresolved countertransference reactions.

Preventing Dropouts. As I discussed earlier, the two most important methods of decreasing the dropout rate are proper selection and comprehensive pretherapy preparation. It is especially important that in the preparation procedure, the therapist make it clear that periods of discouragement are to be expected in the therapy process. Clients are less likely to lose confidence in a therapist who appears to have the foreknowledge that stems from experience. In fact, the more specific the prediction, the greater its power. For example, it may be reassuring to a socially anxious and phobic individual to anticipate that there will be times in the group when he will wish to flee, or that he will dread coming to the next meeting. The therapist can emphasize that the group is a social laboratory and suggest that the client has the choice of making the group yet another instance of failure and avoidance or, for the first time, staying in the group and experimenting, in a low-risk situation, with new behaviors. Some groups contain experienced group members who assume some of this predictive function, as in the following case:

• *One group graduated several members and was reconstituted by adding five new members to the remaining three veteran members. In the first two meetings, the old members briefed the new ones and told them, among other things, that by the sixth or seventh meeting some member would decide to drop out and then the group would have to drop everything for a couple of meetings to persuade him to stay. The old members went on to predict which of the new members would be the first to decide to terminate. This form of prediction is a most effective manner of ensuring that it is not fulfilled.*

Despite painstaking preparation, however, many clients will consider dropping out. When a member informs a therapist that he or she wishes to leave the group, a common approach is to urge the client to attend the next meeting to discuss it with the other group members. Underlying this practice is the assumption that the group will help the client work through resistance and thereby dissuade him or her from terminating. This approach, however, is rarely successful. In one study of thirty-five dropouts from nine therapy groups (with a total original membership of ninety-seven clients), I found that *every one of the dropouts had been urged to return for another meeting, but not once did this final session avert premature termination.*[62] Furthermore, there were no group continuers who had threatened to drop out and were salvaged by this technique, despite considerable group time spent in the effort. In short, asking the client who has decided to drop out to return for a final meeting is usually an ineffective use of group time.

Generally, the therapist is well advised to see a potential dropout for a short series of individual interviews to discuss the sources of group stress. Occasionally an accurate, penetrating interpretation will keep a client in therapy.

> • *Joseph, an alienated client with schizoid personality disorder, announced in the eighth meeting that he felt he was getting nowhere in the group and was contemplating termination. In an individual session, he told the therapist something he had never been able to say in the group—namely, that he had many positive feelings toward a couple of the group members. Nevertheless, he insisted that the therapy was ineffective and that he desired a more accelerated and precise form of therapy. The therapist correctly interpreted Joseph's intellectual criticism of the group therapy format as a rationalization: he was, in fact, fleeing from the closeness he had felt in the group. The therapist again explained the social microcosm phenomenon and clarified for Joseph that in the group he was repeating his lifelong style of relating to others. He had always avoided or fled intimacy and no doubt would always do so in the future unless he stopped running and allowed himself the opportunity to explore his interpersonal problems in vivo. Joseph continued in the group and eventually made considerable gains in therapy.*

In general the therapist can decrease premature termination by attending assiduously to early phase problems. I will have much to say later in this text about self-disclosure, but for now keep in mind that outliers—excessively active members and excessively quiet members—are both dropout risks. Try to balance self-disclosure. It may be necessary to slow the pace of a client who too quickly reveals deeply personal details before establishing engagement. On the other hand, members who remain silent session after session may become demoralized and increasingly frightened of self-disclosure.

Negative feelings, misgivings, and apprehensions about the group or the therapeutic alliance must be addressed and not pushed underground. Moreover, the expression of positive affects should also be encouraged and, whenever possible, modeled by the therapist.[63]

Inexperienced therapists are particularly threatened by the client who expresses a wish to drop out. They begin to fear that, one by one, their group members will leave and that they will one day come to the group and find themselves alone in the room. (And what, then, do they tell their group supervisor?) Therapists for whom this fantasy truly takes hold cease to be therapeutic to the group. The balance of power shifts. They feel blackmailed. They begin to be seductive, cajoling—anything to entice the clients back to future meetings. Once this happens, of course, any therapeutic leverage is lost entirely.

After struggling in my own clinical work with the problem of group dropouts over many years, I have finally achieved some resolution of the issue. By shifting my personal attitude, I no longer have group therapy dropouts. But I do have group therapy throwouts! I do not mean that I frequently ask members to leave a therapy group, but I am perfectly prepared to do so if it is clear that the member is not working in the group. I am persuaded (from my clinical experience and from empirical research findings) that group therapy is a highly effective mode of psychotherapy. If an individual is not going to be able to profit from it, then I want to get that person out of the group and *into a more appropriate mode of therapy*, and bring someone else into the group who will be able to use what the group has to offer.

This method of reducing dropouts is more than a specious form of bookkeeping; it reflects a posture of the therapist that increases the commitment to work. Once you have achieved this particular mental set, you communicate it to your clients in direct and indirect ways. You convey your confidence in the therapeutic modality and your expectation that each client will use the group for effective work.

Removing a Client from a Group. Taking a client out of a therapy group is an act of tremendous significance for both that individual and the group. Hence it must be approached thoughtfully. Once a therapist determines that a client is not working effectively, the next step is to identify and remove all possible obstacles to the client's productive engagement in the group. If the therapist has done everything possible yet is still unable to alter the situation, there is every reason to expect one of the following outcomes: (1) the client will ultimately drop out of the group without benefit (or without further benefit); (2) the client may be harmed by further group participation (because of negative interaction or the adverse consequences of the deviant role—see chapter 8); or (3) the client will substantially obstruct the group work for the remaining group members. Hence, it is folly to adopt a laissez-faire posture: *the time has come to remove the client from the group.*

How? There is no adroit, subtle way to remove a member from a group. Often the task is better handled in an individual meeting with the client than in the group. The situation is so anxiety-provoking for the other members that generally the therapist can expect little constructive group discussion; moreover, an individual meeting reduces the member's public humiliation. It is not helpful to invite the client back for a final meeting to work things through with the group: if the individual were able to work things through in an open, nondefensive manner, there would have been no need to ask him or her to leave the group in the first place. In my experience, such final working-through meetings are invariably closed, nonproductive, and frustrating.

Whenever you remove a client from the group, you should expect a powerful reaction from the rest of the group. The ejection of a group member stirs up deep levels of anxiety associated with rejection or abandonment by the primal group. You may get little support from the group, even if there is unanimous agreement among the members that the client should have been asked to leave. Even if, for example, the client had developed a manic reaction and was disrupting the entire group, the members will still feel threatened by your decision.

There are two possible interpretations the members may give to your act of removing the member. One interpretation is rejection and abandonment: that is, that you do not like the client, you resent him, you're angry, and you want him out of the group and out of your sight. Who might be next?

The other interpretation (the correct one, let us hope) is that you are a responsible mental health professional acting in the best interests of that client and of the remaining group members. Every individual's treatment regimen is different, and you made a responsible decision about the fact that this form of therapy was not suited to a particular client at this moment. Furthermore, you acted in a professionally responsible manner by ensuring that the client will receive another form of therapy more likely to be helpful.

The remaining group members generally embrace the first, or rejection, interpretation. Your task is to help them arrive at the second interpretation. You may facilitate the process by making clear the reasons for your actions and sharing your decisions about future therapy for the extruded client, such as individual therapy with you or a referral to a colleague. Occasionally, the group may receive the decision to remove a member with relief and appreciation. A sexually abused woman described the extrusion of a sadistic, destructive male group member as the first time in her life that the "people in charge" were not helpless or blind to her suffering.

The Departing Member: Therapeutic Considerations.   When a client is asked to leave or chooses to leave a group, the therapist must endeavor to make the experience as constructive as possible. Such clients ordinarily are considerably demoralized and tend to view the group experience as one more failure. Even if the client denies this feeling, the therapist should still assume that it is present and, in a private discussion, provide alternative methods of viewing the experience. For example, the therapist may present the notion of readiness or group fit. Some clients are able to profit from group therapy only after a period of individual therapy; others, for reasons unclear to us, are never able to work effectively in therapy groups. It is also entirely possible that the client may achieve a better fit and a successful course of therapy in another group, and this possibility should be explored. In any case, you should help the removed member understand that this outcome is not a failure on the client's part but that, for several possible reasons, a form of therapy has proved unsuccessful.

It may be useful for the therapist to use the final interview to review in detail the client's experience in the group. Occasionally, a therapist is uncertain about the usefulness or the advisability of confronting someone who is terminating therapy. Should you, for example, confront the denial of an individual who attributes his dropping out of the group to his hearing difficulties when, in fact, he had been an extreme deviant and was clearly rejected by the group? As a general principle, it is useful to consider the client's entire career in therapy. If the client is very likely to reenter therapy, a constructive gentle confrontation will, in the long run, make any subsequent therapy more effective. If, on the other hand, there is little likelihood that the client will pursue a dynamically oriented therapy, there is little point in presenting a final interpretation that he or she will never be able to use or extend. Test the denial. If it is deep, leave it be: there is no point in undermining defenses, even self-deceptive ones, if you cannot provide a satisfactory substitute. Avoid adding insight to injury.[64]

The Addition of New Members

Whenever the group census falls too low (generally five or fewer members), the therapist should introduce new members. This may occur at any time during the course of the group, but in the long-term group there are major junctures when new members are usually added: during the first twelve meetings (to replace early dropouts) and after twelve to eighteen months (to replace improved, graduating members). With closed, time-limited groups, there is a narrow window of the first 3–4 weeks in which it is possible to add new members, and yet provide them with an adequate duration of therapy.

Timing.   The success of introducing new members depends in part on proper timing: there are favorable and unfavorable times to add members. Generally, a group that is in crisis, is actively engaged in an internecine struggle, or has suddenly entered into a new phase of development does not favor the addition of new members; it will often reject the newcomers or else evade confrontation with the pressing group issue and instead redirect its energy toward them.

Examples include a group that is dealing for the first time with hostile feelings toward a controlling, monopolistic member or a group that has recently developed such cohesiveness and trust that a member has, for the first time, shared an extremely important secret. Some therapists postpone the addition of new members if the group is working well, even when the census is down to four or five. I prefer not to delay, and promptly begin to screen candidates. Small groups, even highly cohesive ones, will eventually grow even smaller through absence or termination and soon will lack the interaction necessary for effective work. The most auspicious period for adding new members is during a phase of stagnation in the group. Many groups, especially older ones, sensing the need for new stimulation, actively encourage the therapist to add members.

In groups for women with metastatic breast cancer,[65] the members were very clear about the timing of new members joining. If the group was dealing with a very ill, dying, or recently deceased member, the members preferred not to have new additions because they needed all of their energy and time to address their loss and grief.

Response of the Group.   A cartoon cited by a British group therapist portrays a harassed woman and her child trying to push their way into a crowded train compartment. The child looks up at his mother and says, "Don't worry, Mother, at the next stop it will be our turn to hate!"[66] The parallel to new members entering the group is trenchant. Hostility to the newcomer is evident even in the group that has beseeched the therapist to add new members, and it may reach potent levels. The extent of the antipathy has even been labeled "infanticide."[67]

I have observed many times that when new members are slated to enter a meeting, the old members arrive late and may even remain for a few minutes talking together animatedly in the waiting room while the therapists and the new clients wait in the therapy room. A content analysis of the session in which a new member or members are introduced reveals several themes that are hardly consonant with benevolent hospitality. The group suddenly spends far more time than in previous meetings discussing the good old days. Long-departed group members and events of bygone meetings are avidly recalled, as new members are guilelessly reminded, lest they have forgotten, of their novitiate status. Old battles are reengaged to make the group as unpalatable as possible.

Similarly, members may remark on resemblances they perceive between the new member and some past member. The newcomer may get grilled. In a meeting I once observed in which two members were introduced, the group noted a similarity between one of them and a past member who (the newcomer shortly learned) had committed suicide a year before; the other client was compared to someone who had dropped out, discouraged and unimproved, after three months of therapy. These members, unaware of the invidiousness of their greetings, consciously felt that they were extending a welcome, whereas in fact they projected much unpleasant emotion onto the newcomers.

A group may also express its ambivalence by discussing, in a newcomer's first meeting, threatening and confidence-shaking issues. For example, in its seventeenth session, in which two new members entered, one group discussed for the first time the therapists' competence. The members noted that the therapists were listed in the hospital catalogue as resident-students and that they might be leading their first group. This issue—an important one that should be discussed—was nonetheless highly threatening to new members. It is of interest that this information was already known to several group members but had never until that meeting been broached in the group.

There can, of course, be strong feelings of welcome and support if the group has been searching for new members. The members may exercise great gentleness and patience in dealing with new members' initial fear or defensiveness. The group, in fact, may collude in many ways to increase its attractiveness to the newcomer. Often members gratuitously offer testimonials and describe the various ways in which they have improved. In one such group, a newcomer asked a disgruntled, resistive woman member about her progress, and before she could reply, two other members, sensing that she would devalue the group, interrupted and described their own progress. Although groups may unconsciously wish to discourage newcomers, members are generally not willing to do so by devaluing their own group.

There are several reasons for a group's ambivalent response to new members. Some members who highly prize the solidarity and cohesiveness of the group may be threatened by any proposed change to the status quo. Will the new members undermine the group? Powerful sibling rivalry issues may be evoked at the entrance of a new drain on the group's supplies: members may envision newcomers as potential rivals for the therapist's and the group's attention and perceive their own fantasized role as favored child to be in jeopardy.[68]

Still other members, particularly those conflicted in the area of control and dominance, may regard the new member as a threat to their position in the hierarchy of power. In one group where a new attractive female client was being introduced, the two incumbent female members, desperately protecting their stake, employed many prestige-enhancing devices, including the recitation of poetry. When John Donne is quoted in a therapy group as part of the incoming ritual, it is hardly for an aesthetic end.

A common concern of a group is that, even though new members are needed, they will nonetheless slow the group down. The group fears that familiar material will have to be repeated for the newcomers and that the group must recycle and relive the tedious stages of gradual social introduction and ritualistic etiquette. This expectation fortunately proves to be unfounded: new clients introduced into an ongoing group generally move quickly into the prevailing level of group communication and bypass the early testing phases characteristic of members in a newly formed group. Another, less frequent, source of ambivalence issues from the threat posed to group members who have improved and who fear seeing themselves in the newcomer, as they were at the beginning of their own therapy. In order to avoid reexposure to painful past periods of life, they will frequently shun new clients who appear as reincarnations of their earlier selves.

Commonly, the new members of the group have a unique and constructive perspective on the group members. They see the older members as they are currently, reinforcing the reality of the changes achieved, often admiring the veteran members' perceptiveness, social comfort, and interpersonal skills. This form of feedback can serve as a powerful reminder of the value of the therapeutic work done to date. The morale of both the new and the old members can be enhanced simultaneously.

Therapeutic Guidelines.   Clients entering an ongoing group require not only the standard preparation to group therapy I discussed in chapter 10 but also preparation to help them deal with the unique stresses accompanying entry into an established group. Entry into any established culture—a new living situation, job, school, hospital, and so on—produces anxiety and, as extensive research indicates, demands orientation and support.†[69] A review of the new member's prior experiences of joining can be instructive and identify potential challenges that may emerge.

I tell clients that they can expect feelings of exclusion and bewilderment on entering an unusual culture, and I reassure them that they will be allowed to enter and participate at their own rate. New clients entering established groups may be daunted by the sophistication, openness, interpersonal facility, and daring of more experienced members; they may also be frightened or fear contagion, since they are immediately confronted with members revealing more of their pathology than is revealed in the first meetings of a new group. These contingencies should be discussed with the client. It is generally helpful to describe to the incoming participant the major events of the past few meetings. If the group has been going through some particularly intense, tumultuous events, it is wise to provide an even more thorough briefing. If the group is being videotaped or the therapist uses a written summary technique (see chapter 14), then the new member, with the group's permission, may be asked to view the tapes or read the summaries of the past few meetings.

I make an effort to engage the new client in the first meeting or two. Often it is sufficient merely to inquire about his or her experience of the meeting—something to the effect of: "Sara, this has been your first session. What has the meeting felt like for you? Does it seem like it will be difficult to get into the group? What concerns about your participation are you aware of so far?" It's often useful to help new clients assume some control over their participation. For example, the therapist might say, "I note that several questions were asked of you earlier. How did that feel? Too much pressure? Or did you welcome them?" Or, "Sara, I'm aware that you were silent today. The group was deeply engaged in business left over from meetings when you were not present. How did that make you feel? Relieved? Or would you have welcomed questions directed at you?" Note that all of these questions are here-and-now centered.

Many therapists prefer to introduce two new members at a time, a practice that may have advantages for both the group and the new members. Occasionally, if one client is integrated into the group much more easily than the other, it may backfire and create even greater discomfort for a newcomer, who may feel that he is already lagging behind his cohort. Nevertheless, introduction in pairs has much to recommend it: the group conserves energy and time by assimilating two members at once; the new members may ally with each other and thereby feel less alien.

The number of new members introduced into the group distinctly influences the pace of absorption. A group of six or seven can generally absorb a new member with scarcely a ripple; the group continues work with only the briefest of pauses and rapidly pulls the new member along. On the other hand, a group of four confronted with three new members often comes to a screeching halt as all ongoing work ceases and the group devotes all its energy to the task of incorporating the new members. The old members will wonder how much they can trust the new ones. Dare they continue with the same degree of self-disclosure and risk taking? To what extent will their familiar, comfortable group be changed forever? The new members will be searching for guidelines to behavior. What is acceptable in this group? What is forbidden? If their reception by the established members is not gracious, they may seek the comfort inherent in an alliance of newcomers. The therapist who notes frequent use of "we" and "they," or "old members" and "new members," should heed these signs of schism. Until incorporation is complete, little further therapeutic work can be done.

A similar situation often arises when the therapist attempts to amalgamate two groups that have been reduced in number. This procedure is not easy. A clash of cultures and cliques formed along the lines of the previous groups can persist for a remarkably long time, and the therapist must actively prepare clients for the merger. It is best in this situation to end both groups and then resume as a totally new entity.

The introduction of new members may, if properly considered, enhance the therapeutic process of the old members, who may respond to a newcomer in highly idiosyncratic styles. An important principle of group therapy, which I have discussed, is that every major stimulus presented to the group elicits a variety of responses by the group members. The investigation of the reasons behind these different responses is generally rewarding and clarifies aspects of character structure. For members to observe others respond to a situation in ways remarkably different from the way they do is an arresting experience that can provide them with considerable insight into their behavior. Such an opportunity is unavailable in individual therapy but constitutes one of the chief strengths of the group therapeutic format. An illustrative clinical example may clarify this point.

• *A new member, Alice—forty years old, attractive, divorced—was introduced at a group's eighteenth meeting. The three men in the group greeted her in strikingly different fashions.*

Peter arrived fifteen minutes late and missed the introduction. For the next hour, he was active in the group, discussing issues left over from the previous meeting as well as events occurring in his life during the past week. He totally ignored Alice, avoiding even glancing at her—a formidable feat in a group of six people in close physical proximity. Later in the meeting, as others attempted to help Alice participate, Peter, still without introducing himself, fired questions at her like a harsh prosecuting attorney. A twenty-eight-year-old devout Catholic father of four, Peter had sought therapy because he "loved women too much," as he phrased it, and had had a series of extramarital affairs. In subsequent meetings, the group used the events of Alice's first meeting to help Peter investigate the nature of his "love" for women. Gradually, he came to recognize how he used women, including his wife, as sex objects, valuing them for their genitals only and remaining insensitive to their feelings and experiential world.

The two other men in the group, Arthur and Brian, on the other hand, were preoccupied with Alice during her first meeting. Arthur, a twenty-four-year-old who sought therapy because of his massive sexual inhibition, reacted strongly to Alice and found that he could not look at her without experiencing an acute sense of embarrassment. His discomfort and blushing were apparent to the other members, who helped him explore far more deeply than he had previously his relationship with the women in the group. Arthur had desexualized the other two women in the group by establishing in his fantasy a brother-sister relationship with them. Alice, who was attractive and available and at the same time old enough to evoke in him affect-laden feelings about his mother, presented a special problem for

Arthur, who had previously been settling into too comfortable a niche in the group.

Brian, on the other hand, transfixed Alice with his gaze and delivered an unwavering broad smile to her throughout the meeting. An extraordinarily dependent twenty-three-year-old, Brian had sought therapy for depression after the breakup of a love affair. Having lost his mother in infancy, he had been raised by a succession of nannies and had had only occasional contact with an aloof, powerful father of whom he was terrified. His romantic affairs, always with considerably older women, had invariably collapsed because of the insatiable demands he made on the relationship. The other women in the group in the past few meetings had similarly withdrawn from him and, with progressive candor, had confronted him with, as they termed it, his puppy-dog presentation of himself. Brian thus welcomed Alice, hoping to find in her a new source of succor. In subsequent meetings, Alice proved helpful to Brian as she revealed her feeling, during her first meeting, of extreme discomfort at his beseeching smile and her persistent sense that he was asking for something important from her. She said that although she was unsure of what he wanted, she knew it was more than she had to give.

Freud once compared psychotherapy to chess in that far more is known and written about the opening and the end games than about the middle game. Accordingly, the opening stages of therapy and termination may be discussed with some degree of precision, but the vast bulk of therapy cannot be systematically described. Thus, the subsequent chapters follow no systematic group chronology but deal in a general way with the major issues and problems of later stages of therapy and with some specialized therapist techniques.

Chapter 12

THE ADVANCED GROUP

O nce a group achieves a degree of maturity and stability, it no longer exhibits easily described, familiar stages of development. The rich and complex working-through process begins, and the major therapeutic factors I described earlier operate with increasing force and effectiveness. Members gradually engage more deeply in the group and use the group interaction to address the concerns that brought them to therapy. The advanced group is characterized by members' growing capacity for reflection, authenticity, self-disclosure, and feedback.[1] Hence, it is impossible to formulate specific procedural guidelines for all contingencies. In general, the therapist must strive to encourage development and operation of the therapeutic factors. The application of the basic principles of the therapist's role and technique to specific group events and to each client's therapy (as discussed in chapters 5, 6, and 7) constitutes the art of psychotherapy, and for this there is no substitute for clinical experience, reading, supervision, and intuition.

Certain issues and problems, however, occur with sufficient regularity to warrant discussion. In this chapter, I consider subgrouping, conflict, self-disclosure, and termination of therapy. In the next chapter, I discuss certain recurrent behavioral configurations in individuals that present a challenge to the therapist and to the group.

SUBGROUPING

Fractionalization—the splitting off of smaller units—occurs in every social organization. The process may be transient or enduring, helpful or harmful, for the parent organization. Therapy groups are no exception. Subgroup formation is an inevitable and often disruptive event in the life of the group, yet there too the process, if understood and harnessed properly, may further the therapeutic work.† How do we account for the phenomenon of subgrouping? We need to consider both individual and group factors.

Individual Factors

Members' concerns about personal connection and status often motivate the creation of the subgroup.† A subgroup in the therapy group arises from the belief of two or more members that they can derive more gratification from a relationship with one another than from the entire group. Members who violate group norms by secret liaisons are opting for need gratification rather than for pursuit of personal change—their primary reason for being in therapy (see the discussion of primary task and secondary gratification in chapter 6). Need frustration occurs early in therapy: for example, members with strong needs for intimacy, dependency, sexual conquests, or dominance may soon sense the impossibility of gratifying these needs in the group and often attempt to gratify them outside the formal group.

In one sense, these members are "acting out": they engage in behavior *outside* the therapy setting that relieves inner tensions and avoids direct expression or exploration of feeling or emotion. Sometimes it is only possible in retrospect to discriminate "acting out" from acting or participating in the therapy group. Let me clarify.

Keep in mind that the course of the therapy group is a continual cycle of action and analysis of this action. The social microcosm of the group depends on members' engaging in their habitual patterns of behavior, which are then examined by the individual and the group. Acting out becomes resistance only *when one refuses to examine one's behavior.* Extragroup behavior that is not examined in the group becomes a particularly potent form of resistance, whereas *extragroup behavior that is subsequently brought back into the group and worked through may prove to be of considerable therapeutic import.*[2]

Group Factors

Subgrouping may be a manifestation of a considerable degree of undischarged hostility in the group, especially toward the leader. Research on styles of leadership demonstrates that a group is more likely to develop disruptive in-group and out-group factions under an authoritarian, restrictive style of leadership.[3] Group members, unable to express their anger and frustration directly to the leader, release these feelings obliquely by binding together and mobbing or scapegoating one or more of the other members.

At other times, subgrouping is a sign of problems in group development. A lack of group cohesion will encourage members to retreat from large and complex group relationships into simpler, smaller, more workable subgroups.

Clinical Appearance of Subgrouping

Extragroup socializing is often the first stage of subgrouping. A clique of three or four members may begin to have telephone conversations, to meet over coffee or dinner, to visit each other's homes, or even to engage in business ventures together. Occasionally, two members will become sexually involved. A subgroup may also occur completely within the confines of the group therapy room, as members who perceive themselves to be similar form coalitions.

There may be any number of common bonds: comparable educational level, similar values, ethno-cultural background, similar age, marital status, or group status (for example, the old-timer original members). Social organizations characteristically develop opposing factions—two or more conflicting subgroups. But such is not often the case in therapy groups: one clique forms but the excluded members lack effective social skills and do not usually coalesce into a second subgroup.

The members of a subgroup may be identified by a general code of behavior: they may agree with one another regardless of the issue and avoid confrontations among their own membership; they may exchange knowing glances when a member not in the clique speaks; they may arrive at and depart from the meeting together; their wish for friendship overrides their commitment to examination of their behavior.[4]

The Effects of Subgrouping

Subgrouping can have an extraordinarily disruptive effect on the course of the therapy group. In a study of thirty-five clients who prematurely dropped out from group therapy, I found that eleven (31 percent) did so largely because of problems arising from subgrouping.[5] Complications arise whether the client is included in or excluded from a subgroup.

Inclusion.   Those included in a twosome or a larger subgroup often find that group life is vastly more complicated and, ultimately, less rewarding. As a group member transfers allegiance from the group goals to the subgroup goals, loyalty becomes a major and problematic issue. For example, should one abide by the group procedural rules of free and honest discussion of feelings if that means breaking a confidence established secretly with another member?

> • *Christine and Jerry often met after the therapy session to have long, intense conversations. Jerry had remained withdrawn in the group and had sought out Christine because, as he informed her, he felt that she alone could understand him. After obtaining her promise of confidentiality,*

he soon was able to reveal to her his pedophilic obsessions and his deep distrust of the group leader. Back in the group, Christine felt restrained by her promise and avoided interaction with Jerry, who eventually dropped out unimproved. Ironically, Christine was an exceptionally sensitive member of the group and might have been particularly useful to Jerry by encouraging him to participate in the group had she not felt restrained by the antitherapeutic subgroup norm (that is, her promise of confidentiality).

Sharing with the rest of the members what one has learned in extra-group contacts is tricky. The leader addressing such an issue must take care to avoid situations where members feel humiliated or betrayed.

• An older, paternal man often gave two other group members a ride. On one occasion he invited them to watch television at his house. The visitors witnessed an argument between the man and his wife and at a subsequent group session told him that they felt he was mistreating his wife. The older group member felt so betrayed by the two members, whom he had considered his friends, that he began concealing more from the group and ultimately dropped out of treatment.

Severe clinical problems occur when group members engage in sexual relations: they often hesitate to "besmirch" (as one client phrased it) an intimate relationship by giving it a public airing. Freud never practiced clinical group therapy, but in 1921 he wrote a prescient essay on group psychology in which he underscored the incompatibility between a sexual love relationship and group cohesiveness.[6] Though we may disagree with the cornerstone of his argument (that inhibited sexual instincts contribute to the cohesive energy of the group), his conclusions are compelling: that is, no group tie—be it race, nationality, social class, or religious belief—can remain unthreatened by the overriding importance that two people in love can have for each other.

Obviously, the ties of the therapy group are no exception. Members of a therapy group who become involved in a love/sexual relationship *will almost inevitably come to award their dyadic relationship higher priority than their relationship to the group.* In doing so, they sacrifice their value for each other as helpmates in the group; they refuse to betray confidences; rather than being honest in the group, they engage in courtship behavior—they attempt to be charming to each other, they assume poses in the group, they perform for each other, blotting out the therapists, other members of the group, and, most important, their primary goals in therapy. Often the other group members are dimly aware that something important is being actively avoided in the group discussion, a state of affairs that usually results in global group inhibition. An unusual chance incident provided evidence substantiating these comments.[7]

> • *A research team happened to be closely studying a therapy group in which two members developed a clandestine sexual relationship. Since the study began months before the liaison occurred, good baseline data are available. Several observers (as well as the clients themselves, in post-group questionnaires) had for months rated each meeting along a seven-point scale for amount of affect expressed, amount of self-disclosure, and general value of the session. In addition, the communication-flow system was recorded with the number and direction of each member's statements charted on a who-to-whom matrix.*
>
>   *During the observation period, Bruce and Geraldine developed a sexual relationship and kept it secret from the therapist and the rest of the group for three weeks. During these three weeks, the data (when studied in retrospect) showed a steep downward gradient in the scoring of the quality of the meetings, and reduced verbal activity, expression of affect, and self-disclosure. Moreover, scarcely any verbal exchanges between Geraldine and Bruce were recorded!*

This last finding is the quintessential reason that subgrouping impedes therapy. The primary goal of group therapy is to facilitate each member's exploration of his or her interpersonal relationships. Here were two people who knew each other well, had the potential of being deeply helpful to each other, and yet barely spoke to each other in the group.

The couple resolved the problem by deciding that one of them would drop out of the group (not an uncommon resolution). Geraldine dropped out, and in the following meeting, Bruce discussed the entire incident with relief and great candor. (The ratings by both the group members and the observers indicated this meeting to be valuable, with active interaction, strong affect expression, and much disclosure from others as well as Bruce.)

The positive, affiliative effects of subgrouping *within* the therapy group may be turned to therapeutic advantage.[8] From the perspective of a general systems approach, the therapy group is a large and dynamic group made up of several smaller subgroups. Subgrouping occurs (and may be encouraged by the therapist) as a necessary component of elucidating, containing, and ultimately integrating areas of conflict or distress within the group. Clients who have difficulty acknowledging their feelings or disclosing themselves may do better if they sense they are not alone. Hence, the therapist may actively point out functional, but shifting, subgroups of members who share some basic intra- or interpersonal concern and urge that the subgroup work together in the group and share the risks of disclosure as well as the relief of universality.

Exclusion. Exclusion from the subgroup also complicates group life. Anxiety associated with earlier peer exclusion experiences is evoked, and if it is not discharged by working-through, it may become disabling. Often it is exceptionally difficult for members to comment on their feelings of exclusion: they may not want to reveal their envy of the special relationship, or they may fear angering the involved members by "outing" the subgroup in the session.

Nor are therapists immune to this problem. I recall, a group therapist, one of my supervisees, observed two of his group members (both married) walking arm in arm along the street. The therapist found himself unable to bring his observation back into the group. Why? He offered several reasons:

- He did not want to assume the position of spy or disapproving parent in the eyes of the group.
- He works in the here-and-now and is not free to bring up nongroup material.
- The involved members would, when psychologically ready, discuss the problem.

These are rationalizations, however. There is no more important issue than the interrelationship of the group members. Anything that happens between group members is part of the here-and-now of the group. The therapist who is unwilling to bring in all material bearing on member relationships can hardly expect members to do so. If you feel yourself trapped in a dilemma—on the one hand, knowing that you must bring in such observations and, on the other, not wanting to seem a spy—then generally the best approach is to *share your dilemma with the group*, both your observations *and* your personal uneasiness and reluctance to discuss them.†

Therapeutic Considerations

By no means is subgrouping, with or without extragroup socializing, invariably disruptive. If the goals of the subgroup are consonant with those of the parent group, subgrouping may ultimately enhance group cohesiveness. For example, a coffee group or a bowling league may operate successfully and increase the morale of a larger social organization. In therapy groups, some of the most significant incidents occur as a result of some extragroup member contacts that are then fully worked through in therapy.

- *Two women members who went to a dance together after a meeting discussed, in the following meeting, their observations of each other in that purely social setting. One of them had been far more flirtatious, even openly seductive, than she had been in the group; furthermore, much of this was "blind spot" behavior—out of her awareness.*

• *Another group scheduled a beer party for one member who was terminating. Unfortunately, he had to leave town unexpectedly, and the party was canceled. The member acting as social secretary notified the others of the cancellation but by error neglected to contact one member, Jim. On the night of the party Jim waited, in vain, at the appointed place for two hours, experiencing many familiar feelings of rejection, exclusion, and bitter loneliness. The discussion of these reactions and of Jim's lack of any annoyance or anger and his feeling that his being excluded was natural, expected, the way it should be, led to much fruitful therapeutic work for him. When the party was finally held, considerable data was generated about the group. Members displayed different aspects of themselves. For example, the member who was least influential in the group because of his emotional isolation and his inability or unwillingness to disclose himself assumed a very different role because of his wit, store of good jokes, and easy social mannerisms. A sophisticated and experienced member reencountered his dread of social situations and inability to make small talk, and took refuge behind the role of host, devoting his time busily to refilling empty glasses.*

• *In another group, a dramatic example of effective subgrouping occurred when the members became concerned about one member who was in such despair that she considered suicide. Several group members maintained a weeklong telephone vigil, which proved to be beneficial both to that client and to the cohesiveness of the entire group.*

• *The vignette of the man who liked Robin Hood, described in chapter 2, is another example of subgrouping that enhanced therapeutic work. The client attempted to form an extragroup alliance with every member of the group and ultimately, as a result of his extragroup activity, arrived at important insights about his manipulative modes of relating to peers and about his adversarial stance toward authority figures.*

The principle is clear: any contact outside a group may prove to be of value *provided that the goals of the parent group are not relinquished.* If such meetings are viewed as part of the group rhythm of action and subsequent analysis of this action, much valuable information can be made available to the group. To achieve this end, the involved members must inform the group of all important extragroup events. If they do not, the disruptive effects on cohesiveness I have described will occur. The cardinal principle is: *it is not the subgrouping per se that is destructive to the group, but the conspiracy of silence that generally surrounds it.*

In practice, groups that meet only once a week often experience more of the disruptive than the beneficial effects of subgrouping. Much extragroup socializing never comes directly to the group's attention, and the behavior of the involved members is never made available for analysis in the group. For example, the extragroup relationship I described between Christine and Jerry, in which Jerry revealed in confidence his pedophilic obsessions, was never made known to the group. Christine disclosed the incident more than a year later to a researcher who interviewed her in a psychotherapy outcome study.

The therapist should encourage open discussion and analysis of all extragroup contacts and all in-group coalitions and continue to emphasize the members' responsibility to bring extragroup contacts into the group. The therapist who surmises from glances between two members in the group, or from their appearance together outside the group, that a special relationship exists between them should not hesitate to present this thought to the group. No criticism or accusation is implied, since the investigation and understanding of an affectionate relationship between two members may be as therapeutically rewarding as the exploration of a hostile impasse. The therapist must attempt to disconfirm the misconception that psychotherapy is reductionistic in its ethos, that all experience will be reduced to some fundamental (and base) motive. Furthermore, other members must be encouraged to discuss their reaction to the relationship, whether it be envy, jealousy, rejection, or vicarious satisfaction.[9]

One practical caveat: clients engaged in some extragroup relationship that they are not prepared to discuss in the therapy group may ask the therapist for an individual session and request that the material discussed not be divulged to the rest of the group. If you make such a promise, you may soon find yourself in an untenable collusion from which extrication is difficult. I would suggest that you refrain from offering a promise of confidentiality but instead assure the clients that you will be guided by your professional judgment and act sensitively, in their therapeutic behalf. Though this may not offer sufficient reassurance to all members, it will protect you from entering into awkward, antitherapeutic pacts.

Therapy group members may establish sexual relationships with one another, but not with great frequency. The therapy group is not prurient; clients often have sexual conflicts resulting in such problems as impotence, nonarousal, social alienation, and sexual guilt. I feel certain that far less sexual involvement occurs in a therapy group than in any equally long-lasting social or professional group.

The therapist cannot, by edict, prevent the formation of sexual relations or any other form of subgrouping. Sexual acting out and compulsivity are often symptoms of relationship difficulties that led to therapy in the first place. The emergence of sexual acting out in the group may well present a unique therapeutic opportunity to examine the behavior.

Consider the clinical example of the Grand Dame described in chapter 2. Recall that Valerie seduced Charles and Louis as part of her struggle for power with the group therapist. The episode was, in one sense, disruptive for the group: Valerie's husband learned of the incident and threatened Charles and Louis, who, along with other members, grew so distrustful of Valerie that dissolution of the group appeared imminent. How was the crisis resolved? The group expelled Valerie, who then, somewhat sobered and wiser, continued therapy in another group. Despite these potentially catastrophic complications, some considerable benefits occurred. The episode was thoroughly explored within the group, and the participants obtained substantial help with their sexual issues. For example, Charles, who had a history of a Don Juan style of relationships with women, at first washed his hands of the incident by pointing out that Valerie had approached him and, as he phrased it, "I don't turn down a piece of candy when it's offered." Louis also tended to disclaim responsibility for his relationships with women, whom he customarily regarded as a "piece of ass." Both Charles and Louis were presented with powerful evidence of the implications of their act—the effects on Valerie's marriage and on their own group—and so came to appreciate their personal responsibility for their acts. Valerie, for the first time, realized the sadistic nature of her sexuality; not only did she employ sex as a weapon against the therapist but, as I have already described, as a means of depreciating and humiliating Charles and Louis.

Though extragroup subgrouping cannot be forbidden, neither should it be encouraged. I have found it most helpful to make my position on this problem explicit to members in the preparatory or initial sessions. I tell them that extragroup activity often impedes therapy, and I clearly describe the complications caused by subgrouping. I emphasize that if extragroup meetings occur, fortuitously or by design, then it is the subgroupers' responsibility to the other members and to the group to keep the others fully informed. As I noted in chapter 10, the therapist must help the members understand that the group therapy experience is a dress rehearsal for life; it is the bridge, not the destination. It will teach the skills necessary to establish durable relationships but will not provide the relationships. If group members do not transfer their learning, they derive their social gratification exclusively from the therapy group and therapy becomes interminable.

It is my experience that it is unwise to include two members in a group who already have a long-term special relationship: husband and wife, roommates, business associates, and so on. Occasionally, the situation may arise in which two members naively arrive for a first meeting and discover that they know one another from a prior or preexisting personal or employment relationship. It is not the most auspicious start to a group, but the therapist must not avoid examining the situation openly and thoroughly. Is the relationship ongoing? Will the two members be less likely to be fully open in the group? Are there concerns about confidentiality? How will it affect other group members? Is there a better or more workable option? A quick and a shared decision must be reached about how to proceed.

It is possible for group therapy to focus on current long-term relationships, but that entails a different kind of therapy group than that described in this book—for example, a marital couples' group, conjoint family therapy, and multiple-family therapy.†

In inpatient psychotherapy groups and day hospital programs, the problem of extragroup relationships is even more complex, since the group members spend their entire day in close association with one another. The following case is illustrative.

> • *In a group in a psychiatric hospital for criminal offenders, a subgrouping problem had created great divisiveness. Two male members—by far the most intelligent, articulate, and educated of the group—had formed a close friendship and spent much of every day together. The group sessions were characterized by an inordinate amount of tension and hostile bickering, much of it directed at these two men, who by this time had lost their separate identities and were primarily regarded, and regarded themselves, as a dyad. Much of the attacking was off target, and the therapeutic work of the group had become overshadowed by the attempt to destroy the dyad.*
>
> *As the situation progressed, the therapist, with good effect, helped the group explore several themes. First, the group had to consider that the two members could scarcely be punished for their subgrouping, since everyone had had an equal opportunity to form such a relationship. The issue of envy was thus introduced, and gradually the members discussed their own longing and inability to establish friendships. Furthermore, they discussed their feelings of intellectual inferiority to the dyad as well as their sense of exclusion and rejection by them. The two members had, however, augmented these responses by their actions. Both had, for years, maintained their self-esteem by demonstrating their intellectual superiority whenever possible. When addressing other members, they deliberately used polysyllabic words and maintained a conspiratorial attitude, which accentuated the others' feelings of inferiority and rejection. Both members profited from the group's description of the subtle rebuffs and taunts they had meted out and came to realize that others had suffered painful effects from their behavior.*

Nota bene that my comments on the potential dangers of subgrouping apply to groups that rely heavily on the therapeutic factor of interpersonal learning. In other types of groups, such as cognitive-behavioral groups for eating disorders, extragroup socializing has been shown to be beneficial in altering eating patterns.[10] Twelve-step groups, self-help groups, and support groups also make good use of extragroup contact. In support groups of, for example, cancer patients extragroup contact becomes an essential part of the process, and participants may be actively encouraged to contact one another between sessions as an aid in coping with the illness and its medical treatment.[11] On many occasions, I have seen the group rally around members in deep despair and provide extraordinary support through telephone contact.

Clinical Example

I end this section with a lengthy clinical illustration—the longest in the book. I include it because it shows in depth not only many of the issues involved in subgrouping but also other aspects of group therapy discussed in other chapters, including the differentiation between primary task and secondary gratification and the assumption of personal responsibility in therapy.

The group met twice weekly. The participants were young, ranging in age from twenty-five to thirty-five. At the time we join the group, two women had recently graduated, leaving only four male clients. Bill, the male lead in the drama to unfold, was a tall, handsome thirty-two-year-old divorced dentist and had been in the group for about eight months without making significant progress. He originally sought therapy because of chronic anxiety and episodic depressions. He was socially self-conscious to the degree that simple acts—for example, saying good night at a party—caused him much torment. If he could have been granted one wish by some benevolent therapeutic muse, it would have been to be "cool." He was dissatisfied with work, he had no male friends, and he highly sexualized his relationships with women. Though he had been living with a woman for a few months, he felt neither love nor commitment toward her.

The group, waiting for new members, met for several sessions with only the four men and established a virile, Saturday-night, male-bonding subculture. Issues that had rarely surfaced while women were in the group frequently occupied center stage: masturbatory practices and fantasies, fear of bullies and feelings of cowardice about fighting, concerns about physique, lustful feelings about the large breasts of a woman who had been in the group, and fantasies of a "gang bang" with her.

Two women were then introduced into the group, and never has a well-established culture disintegrated so quickly. The Saturday-night camaraderie was swept away by a flood of male dominance behavior. Bill boldly and brazenly competed for not one but both women. The other men in the group reacted to the first meeting with the two women members in accordance with their dynamic patterns.

Rob, a twenty-five-year-old graduate student, arrived at the meeting in lederhosen, the only time in eighteen months of therapy he thus bedecked himself, and during the meeting was quick to discuss, in detail, his fears of (and his attraction to) other men. Another member made an appeal to the maternal instincts of the new female additions by presenting himself as a fledgling with a broken wing. The remaining member removed himself from the race by remarking, after the first forty minutes, that he wasn't going to join the others in the foolish game of competing for the women's favors; besides, he had been observing the new members and concluded that they had nothing of value to offer him.

One of the women, Jan, was an attractive twenty-eight-year-old, divorced woman with two children. She was a language professor who sought therapy for many reasons: depression, promiscuity, and loneliness. She complained that she could not say no to an attractive man. Men used her sexually: they would drop by her home for an hour or two in the evening for sex but would not be willing to be seen with her in daylight. There was an active willingness on her part, too, as she boasted of having had sexual relations with most of the heads of the departments at the college where she taught. Because of poor judgment, she was in deep financial trouble. She had written several bad checks and was beginning to flirt with the idea of prostitution: If men were exploiting her sexually, then why not charge them for her favors?

In the pregroup screening interviews and preparatory sessions, I realized that her promiscuity made her a likely candidate for self-destructive sexual acting-out in the group. Therefore, I had taken much greater pains than usual to emphasize that outside social involvement with other group members would not be in her or the group's best interests.

After the entrance of the two women, Bill's group behavior altered radically: he disclosed himself less; he preened; he crowed; he played a charming, seductive role; he became far more deliberate and self-conscious in his actions. In short, in pursuit of secondary sexual gratification, he appeared to lose all sense of why he was in a therapy group. Rather than welcoming my comments to him, he resented them: he felt they made him look bad in front of the women. He rapidly jettisoned his relationship with the men in the group and thenceforth related to them dishonestly. For example, in the first meeting, when one of the male members told the women he felt they had nothing of value to offer him, Bill rushed in to praise him for his honesty, even though Bill's real feeling at that moment was exhilaration that the other had folded his tent and left him in sole possession of the field of women. At this stage, Bill resisted any intervention. I tried many times during these weeks to illuminate his behavior for him, but I might as well have tried to strike a match in a monsoon.

After approximately three months, Jan made an overt sexual proposition to Bill, which I learned of in a curious way. Bill and Jan happened to arrive early in the group room, and in their conversation, Jan invited Bill to her apartment to view some pornographic movies. Observers viewing the group through a one-way mirror had also arrived early, overheard the proposition, and related it to me after the meeting. I felt uneasy about how the information had been obtained; nonetheless, I brought up the incident in the next meeting, only to have Jan and Bill deny that a sexual invitation had been made. The discussion ended with Jan angrily stomping out midway through the meeting.

In succeeding weeks, after each meeting she and Bill met in the parking lot for long talks and embraces. Jan brought these incidents back into the meeting but, in so doing, incurred Bill's anger for betraying him. Eventually, Bill made an overt sexual proposition to Jan, who, on the basis of much work done in the group, decided it would be against her best interests to accept. For the first time, she said no to an attractive, interested, attentive man and received much group support for her stance.

(I am reminded of an episode Victor Frankl once told me of a man who had consulted him on the eve of his marriage. He had had a sexual invitation from a strikingly beautiful woman, a friend of his fiancée, and felt he could not pass it up. When would such an opportunity come his way again? It was, he insisted, a unique, once-in-a-lifetime opportunity! Dr. Frankl—quite elegantly, I think—pointed out that he did indeed have a unique opportunity and, indeed, it was one that would never come again. It was the opportunity to say "no" in the service of his responsibility to himself and his chosen mate!)

Bill, meanwhile, was finding life in the group increasingly complex. He was pursuing not only Jan but also Gina, who had entered the group with Jan. At the end of each meeting, Bill struggled with such conundrums as how to walk out of the group alone with each woman at the same time. Jan and Gina were at first very close, almost huddling together for comfort as they entered an all-male group. It was to Bill's advantage to separate them, and in a number of ways he contrived to do so. Not only did Bill have a "divide and seduce" strategy, but he also found something intrinsically pleasurable in the process of splitting. He had had a long history of splitting and seducing roommates and, before that, of interposing himself between his mother and his sister.

Gina had, with the help of much prior therapy, emerged from a period of promiscuity similar to Jan's. Compared with Jan, though, she was more desperate for help, more committed to therapy, and committed to a relationship with her boyfriend. Consequently, she was not eager to consummate a sexual relationship with Bill. However, as the group progressed she developed a strong attraction to him and an even stronger determination that, if she could not have him, neither would Jan. One day in the group, Gina unexpectedly announced that she was getting married in three weeks and invited the group to the wedding. She described her husband-to-be as a rather passive, clinging, ne'er-do-well. It was only many months later that the group learned he was a highly gifted mathematician who was considering faculty offers from several leading universities.

Thus, Gina, too, pursued secondary gratification rather than her primary task. In her efforts to keep Bill interested in her and to compete with Jan, she misrepresented her relationship with another man, underplaying the seriousness of her involvement until her marriage forced her hand. Even then, she presented her husband in a fraudulently unfavorable light so as to nourish Bill's hopes that he still had an opportunity for a liaison with her. In so doing, Gina sacrificed the opportunity to work in the group on her relationship with her fiancé—one of the urgent tasks for which she had sought therapy!

After several months in the group, Jan and Bill decided to have an affair and announced to the group their planned assignation two weeks later. The members reacted strongly. The other two women (another had entered the group by this time) were angry. Gina felt secretly hurt at Bill's rejection of her, but expressed anger only at how his and Jan's liaison would threaten the integrity of the group. The new member, who had a relationship with a man similar to Bill, identified with Bill's girlfriend. Some of the men participated vicariously, perceiving Jan as a sexual object and rooting for Bill to "score." Another said (and as time went by this sentiment was heard more often) that he wished Bill would "hurry up and screw her" so that they could talk about something else in the group. He was an anxious, timid man who had had no heterosexual experience whatsoever. The sexual goings-on in the group were, as he phrased it, so far "out of his league" that he could not participate in any way.

Rob, the man in the group who had had worn lederhosen at Jan and Gina's first meeting, silently wished that the heterosexual preoccupation of the group were different. He had been having increasing concern about his homosexual obsessions but had delayed discussing them in the group for many weeks because of his sense that the group would be unreceptive to his needs and that he would lose the respect of the members, who placed such extraordinary value on heterosexual prowess.

Eventually, however, he did discuss these issues, with some relief. It is important to note that Bill, aside from advice and solicitude, offered Rob very little. Some ten months later, after Rob left the group and after the

Bill-Jan pairing had been worked through, Bill disclosed his own homo-sexual concerns and fantasies. Had Bill, whom Rob admired very much, shared these at the appropriate time, it might have been of considerable help to Rob. Bill would not at that time, however, disclose anything that might encumber his campaign to seduce Jan—another instance of how the pursuit of secondary gratification rendered the group less effective.

Once their sexual liaison began, Jan and Bill became even more inac-cessible for group scrutiny and for therapeutic work. They began speak-ing of themselves as "we" and resisted all exhortations from me and the other members to learn about themselves by analyzing their behavior. At first it was difficult to know what was operating between the two aside from powerful lust. I knew that Jan's sense of personal worth was cen-tered outside herself. To keep others interested in her she needed, she felt, to give gifts—especially sexual ones.

Furthermore, there was a vindictive aspect: she had previously tri-umphed over important men (department chairmen and several employ-ers) by sexual seduction. It seemed likely that Jan felt powerless in her dealings with me. Her chief coinage with men—sex—afforded her no sig-nificant influence over me, but it did permit an indirect victory through the medium of Bill. I learned much later how she and Bill would gleefully romp in bed, relishing the thought of how they had put something over on me. In the group, Bill not only recapitulated his sexualization of relation-ships and his repetitive efforts to prove his potency by yet another seduc-tion, but he also found particularly compelling the opportunity for Oedipal mastery—taking women away from the leader.

Thus, Bill and Jan, in a rich behavioral tapestry, displayed their dy-namics and re-created their social environment in the microcosm of the group. Bill's narcissism and inauthentic mode of relating to women were clearly portrayed. He often made innuendoes to the effect that his rela-tionship with the woman he lived with was deteriorating, thus planting a seed of matrimonial hope in Jan's imagination. Bill's innuendoes colluded with Jan's enormous capacity for self-deception: She alone of any of the group members considered marriage to Bill a serious possibility. When the other members tried to help her hear Bill's primary message—that she was not important to him, that she was merely another sexual conquest—she reacted defensively and angrily.

Gradually, the dissonance between Bill's private statements and the group's interpretations of his intentions created so much discomfort that Jan considered leaving the group. I reminded her, as forcibly as possible, that this was precisely what I had warned her about before she entered the group. If she dropped out of therapy, all the important things that had happened in the group would come to naught. She had had many brief and unrewarding relationships in the past. The group offered her the unique opportunity to stay with a relationship and, for once, play the drama through to its end. In the end Jan decided to stay.

Jan and Bill's relationship was exclusive: neither related in any significant way to anyone else in the group, except that Bill attempted to keep erotic channels open to Gina (to keep his "account open at the bank," as he put it). Gina and Jan persisted in a state of unrelenting enmity so extreme that each had homicidal fantasies about the other. (When Gina married, she invited to the wedding everyone in the group except Jan. Only when a boycott was threatened by the others was a frosty invitation proffered her.) Bill's relationship to me had been very important to him before Jan's entry. During the first months of his liaison with Jan, he seemed to forget my presence, but gradually his concern about me returned. One day, for example, he related a dream in which I escorted all the members but him into an advanced postgraduate group, while he was pulled by the hand to a more elementary, "losers" group.

Jan and Bill's relationship consumed enormous amounts of group energy and time. Relatively few unrelated themes were worked on in the group, but all of the members worked on personal issues relating to the pairing: sex, jealousy, envy, fears of competition, concerns about physical attractiveness. There was a sustained high level of emotion in the group. Attendance was astoundingly high: over a thirty-meeting stretch there was not a single absence.

Gradually, Jan and Bill's relationship began to sour. She had always maintained that all she wanted from him was his sheer physical presence. One night every two weeks with him was what she required. Now she was forced to realize that she wanted much more. She felt pressured in life: she had lost her job and was beset by financial concerns; she had given up her promiscuity but felt sexual pressures and now began to say to herself, "Where is Bill when I really need him?" She grew depressed, but rather than work on the depression in the group, she minimized it. Once again, secondary considerations were given priority over primary, therapeutic ones, for she was reluctant to give Gina and the other members the satisfaction of seeing her depressed: They had warned her months ago that a relationship with Bill would ultimately be self-destructive.

And where, indeed, was Bill? That question plunged us into the core issue of Bill's therapy: responsibility. As Jan grew more deeply depressed (a depression punctuated by accident proneness, including a car crash and a painful burn from a kitchen mishap), the group confronted Bill with the question: *Had he known in advance the outcome of the adventure, would he have done anything different?*

Bill said, "No! I would have done nothing different! If I don't look after my own pleasure, who will?" The other members of the group and now Jan, too, attacked him for his self-indulgence and his lack of responsibility to others. Bill pondered over this confrontation, only to advance a series of rationalizations at the subsequent meeting.

"Irresponsible? No, I am not irresponsible! I am high-spirited, impish, like Peer Gynt. Life contains little enough pleasure," he said. "Why am I not entitled to take what I can? Who sets those rules?" He insisted that the group members and the therapist, guilefully dressed in the robes of responsibility, were, in fact, trying to rob him of his life force and freedom.

For many sessions, the group plunged into the issues of love, freedom, and responsibility. Jan, with increasing directness, confronted Bill. She jolted him by asking exactly how much he cared for her. He squirmed and alluded both to his love for her and to his unwillingness to establish an enduring relationship with any woman. In fact, he found himself "turned off" by any woman who wanted a long-term relationship.

I was reminded of a comparable attitude toward love in the novel *The Fall*, where Camus expresses Bill's paradox with shattering clarity:

> It is not true, after all, that I never loved. I conceived at least one great love in my life, of which I was always the object . . . sensuality alone dominated my love life. . . . In any case, my sensuality (to limit myself to it) was so real that even for a ten-minute adventure I'd have disowned father and mother, even were I to regret it bitterly. Indeed—especially for a ten-minute adventure and even more so if I were sure it was to have no sequel.[12]

The group therapist, if he were to help Bill, had to make certain that there was to be a sequel.

Bill did not want to be burdened with Jan's depression. There were women all around the country who loved him (and whose love made him feel alive), yet for him these women did not have an independent existence. He preferred to think that his women came to life only when he appeared to them. Once again, Camus spoke for him:

> I could live happily only on condition that all the individuals on earth, or the greatest possible number, were turned toward me, eternally in suspense, devoid of independent life and ready to answer my call at any moment, doomed in short to sterility until the day I should deign to favor them. In short, for me to live happily it was essential for the creatures I chose not to live at all. They must receive their life, sporadically, only at my bidding.[13]

Jan pressed Bill relentlessly. She told him that there was another man who was seriously interested in her, and she pleaded with Bill to level with her, to be honest about his feelings to her, to set her free. By now Bill was quite certain that he no longer desired Jan. (In fact, as we were to learn later, he had been gradually increasing his commitment to the woman with whom he lived.) Yet he could not allow the words to pass his lips—a strange type of freedom, then, as Bill himself gradually grew to understand: the freedom to take but not to relinquish. (Camus, again: "Believe me, for certain men at least, not taking what one doesn't desire is the hardest thing in the world!")[14] He insisted that he be granted the freedom to choose his pleasures, yet, as he came to see, he did not have the freedom to choose for himself. His choice almost invariably resulted in his thinking less well of himself. And the greater his self-hatred, the more compulsive, the less free, was his mindless pursuit of sexual conquests that afforded him only an evanescent balm.

Jan's pathology was equally patent. She ceded her freedom to Bill (a logical paradox); only he had the power to set her free. I confronted her with her pervasive refusal to accept her freedom: Why couldn't she say no to a man? How could men use her sexually unless she allowed it? It was evident, too, that she punished Bill in an inefficient, self-destructive manner: she attempted to induce guilt through accidents, depression, and lamentations that she had trusted a man who had betrayed her and that now she would be ruined for life.

Bill and Jan circled these issues for months. From time to time they would reenter their old relationship but always with slightly more sobriety and slightly less self-deception. During a period of nonwork, I sensed that the timing was right and confronted them in a forcible manner. Jan arrived late at the meeting complaining about the disarray of her financial affairs. She and Bill giggled as he commented that her irresponsibility about money made her all the more adorable. I stunned the group by observing that Jan and Bill were doing so little therapeutic work that I wondered whether it made sense for them to continue in the group.

Jan and Bill accused me of hypermoralism. Jan said that for weeks she came to the group only to see Bill and to talk to him after the group; if he left, she did not think she would continue. I reminded her that the group was not a dating bureau: surely there were far more important tasks for her to pursue. Bill, I continued, would play no role in the long scheme of her life and would shortly fade from her memory. Bill had no commitment to her, and if he were at all honest he would tell her so. Jan rejoined that Bill was the only one in the group who truly cared for her. I disagreed and said that Bill's caring for her was clearly not in her best interests.

Bill left the meeting furious at me (especially at my comment that he would soon fade from Jan's mind). For a day, he fantasized marrying her to prove me wrong, but he returned to the group to plunge into serious work. As his honesty with himself deepened, as he faced a core feeling of emptiness that a woman's love had always temporarily filled, he worked his way through painful feelings of depression that his acting out had kept at bay. Jan was deeply despondent for two days after the meeting, and then suddenly made far-reaching decisions about her work, money, men, and therapy.

The group then entered a phase of productive work, which was further deepened when I introduced a much older woman into the group who brought with her many neglected themes in the group: aging, death, physical deterioration. Jan and Bill fell out of love. They began to examine their relationships with others in the group, including the therapists. Bill stopped lying, first to Jan, then to Gina, then to the other members, and finally to himself. Jan continued in the group for six more months, and Bill for another year.

The outcome for both Jan and Bill was—judged by any outcome criteria—stunning. In interviews nine months after their termination, both showed impressive changes. Jan was no longer depressed, self-destructive, or promiscuous. She was involved in the most stable and satisfying relationship with a man she had ever had, and she had gone into a different and more rewarding career. Bill, once he understood that he had made his relationship with his girlfriend tenuous to allow him to seek what he really didn't want, allowed himself to feel more deeply and married shortly before leaving the group. His anxious depressions, his tortured self-consciousness, his pervasive sense of emptiness had all been replaced by their respective, vital counterparts.

I am not able in these few pages to sum up all that was important in the therapy of Jan and Bill. There was much more to it, including many important interactions with other members and with me. *The development and working through of their extragroup relationship was, I believe, not a complication but an indispensable part of their therapy.* It is unlikely that Jan would have had the motivation to remain in therapy had Bill not been present in the group. It is unlikely that without Jan's presence, Bill's central problems would have surfaced clearly and become accessible for therapy.

The price paid by the group, however, was enormous. Vast amounts of group time and energy were consumed by Jan and Bill. Other members were neglected, and many important issues went untouched. Most often, such extragroup subgrouping would create a destructive therapy impasse.† It is most unlikely that a new group, or a group that met less frequently than twice a week, could have afforded the price. It is also unlikely that Jan and Bill would have been willing to persevere in their therapeutic work and to remain in the group had they not already been committed to the group before their love affair began.

CONFLICT IN THE THERAPY GROUP

Conflict cannot be eliminated from human groups, whether dyads, small groups, macrogroups, or such megagroups as nations and blocs of nations. If overt conflict is denied or suppressed, invariably it will manifest itself in oblique, corrosive, and often ugly ways. Although our immediate association with conflict is negative—destruction, bitterness, war, violence—a moment of reflection brings to mind positive associations: drama, excitement, change, and development. Therapy groups are no exception. Some groups become "too nice" and diligently avoid conflict and confrontation, often mirroring the therapist's avoidance of aggression. Yet conflict is so inevitable in the course of a group's development that its absence suggests some impairment of the developmental sequence. Furthermore, conflict can be exceeding valuable to the course of therapy, provided that its intensity does not exceed the members' tolerance and that proper group norms have been established. Learning how to deal effectively with conflict is an important therapeutic step that contributes to individual maturation and emotional resilience.[15] In this section, I consider conflict in the therapy group—its sources, its meaning, and its contribution to therapy.

Sources of Hostility

There are many sources of hostility in the therapy group and an equal number of relevant explanatory models and perspectives, ranging from ego psychology to object relations to self psychology.[16] The group leader's capacity to identify the individual, interpersonal, and group dynamic contributions to the hostility in the group is essential.[17]

Some antagonisms are projections of the client's self-contempt. Indeed, often many sessions pass before some individuals really begin to hear and respect the opinions of other members. They have so little self-regard that it is at first inconceivable that others similar to themselves have something valuable to offer. Devaluation begets devaluation, and a destructive interpersonal loop can be readily launched.

Transference or parataxic distortions often generate hostility in the therapy group. One may respond to others not on the basis of reality but on the basis of an image of the other distorted by one's own past relationships and current interpersonal needs and fears. Should the distortion be negatively charged, then a mutual antagonism may be easily initiated. The group may function as a "hall of mirrors,"†[18] which may aggravate hostile and rejecting feelings and behaviors. Individuals may have long suppressed some traits or desires of which they are much ashamed; when they encounter another person who embodies these very traits, they generally shun the other or experience a strong but inexplicable antagonism toward the person. The process may be close to consciousness and recognized easily with guidance by others, or it may be deeply buried and understood only after many months of investigation.

• *One patient, Vincent, a second-generation Italian-American who had grown up in the Boston slums and obtained a good education with great difficulty, had long since dissociated himself from his roots. Having invested his intellect with considerable pride, he spoke with great care in order to avoid betraying any nuance of his accent or background. In fact, he abhorred the thought of his lowly past and feared that he would be found out, that others would see through his front to his core, which he regarded as ugly, dirty, and repugnant. In the group, Vincent experienced extreme antagonism for another member, also of Italian descent, who had, in his values and in his facial and hand gestures, retained his identification with his ethnic group. Through his investigation of his antagonism toward this man, Vincent arrived at many important insights about himself.*

• *In a group of psychiatric residents, Pat agonized over whether to transfer to a more academically oriented residency. The group, with one member, Clem, as spokesman, resented the group time Pat took for this problem, rebuking him for his weakness and indecisiveness and insisting that he "crap or get off the pot." When the therapist guided the group members into an exploration of the sources of their anger toward Pat, many dynamics became evident (several of which I will discuss in chapter 17). One of the strongest sources was uncovered by Clem, who discussed his own paralyzing indecisiveness. He had, a year earlier, faced the same decision as Pat and, unable to act decisively, had resolved the dilemma passively by suppressing it. Pat's behavior reawakened that painful scenario for Clem, who resented the other man not only for disturbing his uneasy slumber but also for struggling with the issue more honestly and more courageously than he had.*

J. Frank described a reverberating double-mirror reaction:

• *In one group, a prolonged feud developed between two Jews, one of whom flaunted his Jewishness while the other tried to conceal it. Each finally realized that he was combating in the other an attitude he repressed in himself. The militant Jew finally understood that he was disturbed by the many disadvantages of being Jewish, and the man who hid his background confessed that he secretly nurtured a certain pride in it.*[19]

Another source of conflict in groups arises from *projective identification,* an unconscious process which consists of projecting some of one's own (but disavowed) internal attributes into another, toward whom one subsequently feels an uncanny attraction-repulsion. A stark literary example of projective identification occurs in Dostoevsky's nightmarish tale "The Double," in which the protagonist encounters a man who is his physical double and yet a personification of all the dimly perceived, hated aspects of himself.[20] The tale depicts with astonishing vividness both the powerful attraction and the horror and hatred that develop between the protagonist and his double.

Projective identification has intrapsychic and interpersonal components.[21] It is both a defense (primitive in nature because it polarizes, distorts, and fragments reality), and a form of interpersonal relationship.†[22] Elements of one's disowned self are put not only *onto* another and shunned, as in simple projection, but *into* another. The behavior of the other actually changes within the ongoing relationship because the overt and covert communication of the projector influences the recipient's psychological experience and behavior. Projective identification resembles two distorting mirrors facing each other producing increasing distortions as the reflected images bounce back and forth.[23]

There are many other sources of anger in group therapy. Individuals with a fragile sense of self can respond with rage to experiences of shame, dismissal, empathic failure, or rejection and seek to bolster their personal stature by retaliation or interpersonal coercion. At times anger can be a desperate reaction to one's sense of fragmentation in the face of interpersonal rejection and may represent the client's best effort at avoiding total emotional collapse.[24]

Rivalry and envy may also fuel conflict. Group members may compete with one another in the group for the largest share of the therapist's attention or for some particular role: for example, the most powerful, respected, sensitive, disturbed, or needy person in the group. Members (fueled perhaps by unconscious remnants of sibling rivalry) search for signs that the therapist may favor one or another of the members. In one group, for example, one member asked the therapist where he was going on vacation and he answered with uncharacteristic candor. This elicited a bitter response from another member, who recalled how her sister had always received things from her parents that she had been denied.†[25]

The addition of new members often ignites rivalrous feelings:

• *In the fiftieth meeting of one group, a new member, Ginny,* was added. In many aspects she was similar to Douglas, one of the original members: they were both artists, mystical in their approach to life, often steeped in fantasy, and all too familiar with their unconscious. It*

---

*This is the same Ginny with whom I coauthored a book about our psychotherapy: *Every Day Gets a Little Closer: A Twice-Told Therapy* (New York: Basic Books, 1975; reissued 1992).

was not affinity, however, but antagonism that soon developed between the two. Ginny immediately established her characteristic role by behaving in a spiritlike, irrational, and disorganized fashion in the group. Douglas, who saw his role as the sickest and most disorganized member being usurped, reacted to her with intolerance and irritation. Only after active interpretation of the role conflict and Douglas's assumption of a new role ("most improved member") was an entente between the two members achieved.

As the group progresses, the members may grow increasingly impatient and angry with those who have not adopted the group's norms of behavior. If someone, for example, continues to hide behind a facade, the group may coax her and attempt to persuade her to participate. After some time patience gives out and the members may angrily demand that she be more honest with herself and the others.

Certain members, because of their character structure, will invariably be involved in conflict and will engender conflict in any group. Consider a man with a paranoid personality disorder whose assumptive world is that there is danger in the environment. He is eternally suspicious and vigilant. He examines all experience with an extraordinary bias as he searches for clues and signs of danger. He is tight, ready for an emergency. He is never playful and looks suspiciously upon such behavior in others, anticipating their efforts to exploit him. Obviously, these traits will not endear that individual to the other group members. Sooner or later, anger will erupt all around him; and the more severe and rigid his character structure, the more extreme will be the conflict. Eventually, if therapy is to succeed, the client must access and explore the feelings of vulnerability that reside beneath the hostile mistrust.

In chapter 11, I discussed yet another source of hostility in the group: members become disenchanted and disappointed with the therapist for frustrating their (unrealistic) expectations.† If the group is unable to confront the therapist directly, it may create a scapegoat—a highly unsatisfactory solution for both victim and group. In fact, scapegoating is a method by which the group can discharge anger arising from threats to the group's integrity and function, and it is a common phenomenon in any therapy group. The choice of a scapegoat generally is not arbitrary. Some people repeatedly find themselves in a scapegoat role, in a variety of social situations. It is useful for therapists to view scapegoating as created jointly by the group members and the scapegoat.[26]

Hostility in the group can also be understood from the perspective of stages of group development. In the early phase, the group fosters regression and the emergence of irrational, uncivilized parts of individuals. The young group is also beset with anxiety (from fear of exposure, shame, stranger anxiety, powerlessness) that may be expressed as hostility. Prejudice (which is a way of reducing anxiety through a false belief that one knows the other) may make an early appearance in the group and, of course, elicits reciprocal anger from others. Throughout the course of the group, narcissistic injury (wounds to self-esteem from feedback or being overlooked, unappreciated, excluded, or misunderstood) is often suffered and is often expressed by angry retaliation. Still later in the course of the group, anger may stem from other sources: projective tendencies, sibling rivalry, transference, or the premature termination of some members.†

Management of Hostility

Regardless of its source, the discord, once begun, follows a predictable sequence. The antagonists develop the belief that they are right and the others are wrong, that they are good and the others bad. Moreover, although it is not recognized at the time, these beliefs are characteristically held with equal conviction and certitude by each of the two opposing parties. Where such a situation of opposing beliefs exists, we have all the ingredients for a deep and continuing tension, even to the point of impasse.

Generally, a breakdown in communication ensues. The two parties cease to listen to each other with any understanding. If they were in a social situation, the two opponents would most likely completely rupture their relationship at this point and never be able to correct their misunderstandings.

Not only do the opponents stop listening, but they may also unwittingly distort their perceptions of one another. Perceptions are filtered through a screen of stereotype. The opponent's words and behavior are distorted to fit a preconceived view. Contrary evidence is ignored; conciliatory gestures may be perceived as deceitful tricks. (The analogy to international relations is all too obvious.) In short, there is a greater investment in verification of one's beliefs than in understanding the other.[27]

Distrust is the basis for this sequence. Opponents view their own actions as honorable and reasonable, and the behavior of others as scheming and evil. If this sequence, so common in human events, were permitted to unfold in therapy groups, the group members would have little opportunity for change or learning. A group climate and group norms that preclude such a sequence must be established early in the life of the group.

Cohesiveness is the primary prerequisite for the successful management of conflict. Members must develop a feeling of mutual trust and respect and come to value the group as an important means of meeting their personal needs. They must understand the importance of maintaining communication if the group is to survive; all parties must continue to deal directly with one another, no matter how angry they become. Furthermore, everyone is to be taken seriously. When a group treats one member as a "mascot," someone whose opinions and anger are lightly regarded, the hope of effective treatment for that individual has all but officially been abandoned. Covert exchanges between members, sometimes bordering on the "rolling of one's eyes" in reaction to the mascotted member's participation is an ominous sign. Mascotting jeopardizes group cohesiveness: no one is safe, particularly the next most peripheral member, who will have reason to fear similar treatment.

The cohesive group in which everyone is taken seriously soon elaborates norms that obligate members to go beyond name calling. Members must pursue and explore derogatory labels and be willing to search more deeply within themselves to understand their antagonism and to make explicit those aspects of others that anger them. Norms must be established that make it clear that group members are there to understand themselves, not to defeat or ridicule others. It is particularly useful if members try to reach within themselves to identify similar trends and impulses. Terence (a second-century B.C. Roman dramatist) gave us a valuable perspective when he said, "I am human and nothing human is alien to me."[28]

A member who realizes that others accept and are trying to understand finds it less necessary to hold rigidly to beliefs and may be more willing to explore previously denied aspects of self. Gradually, such members may recognize that not all of their motives are as they have proclaimed, and that some of their attitudes and behavior are not so fully justified as they have been proclaiming. When this breakthrough step has been achieved, individuals reappraise the situation and realize that the problem can be viewed in more than one way.

Empathy is an important element in conflict resolution and facilitates humanization of the struggle. Often, understanding the past plays an important role in the development of empathy: Once an individual appreciates how aspects of an opponent's earlier life have contributed to the current stance, then the opponent's position not only makes sense but may even appear right. *Tout comprendre, c'est tout pardonner.*

Conflict resolution is often impossible in the presence of off-target or oblique hostility:

> • *Maria began a group session by requesting and obtaining the therapist's permission to read a letter she was writing in conjunction with a court hearing on her impending divorce, which involved complex issues of property settlement and child custody. The letter reading consumed considerable time and was often interrupted by the other members, who disputed the contents of the letter. The sniping by the group and defensive counterattacks by the protagonist continued until the group atmosphere crackled with irritability. The group made no constructive headway until the therapist explored with the members*

the process of the meeting. The therapist was annoyed with himself for having permitted the letter to be read and with Maria for having put him in that position. The group members were angry at the therapist for having given permission and at Maria both for consuming so much time and for relating to them in the frustrating, impersonal manner of letter reading. Once the anger had been directed away from the oblique target of the letter's contents onto the appropriate targets—the therapist and Maria—steps toward conflict resolution could begin.

Permanent conflict abolition, let me note, is *not* the final goal of the therapy group. Conflict will continually recur in the group despite successful resolution of past conflicts and despite the presence of considerable mutual respect and warmth. However, unrestrained expression of rage is not a goal of the therapy group either.

Although some people relish conflict, the vast majority of group members (and therapists) are highly uncomfortable when expressing or receiving anger. The therapist's task is to harness conflict and use it in the service of growth. One important principle is to find the right level: too much or too little conflict is counterproductive. The leader is always fine-tuning the dial of conflict. When there is persistent conflict, when the group cannot agree on anything, the leader searches for resolution and wonders why the group denies any commonality; on the other hand, when the group consistently agrees on everything, the leader searches for diversity and differentiation. Thus, you need to titrate conflict carefully. Generally, it is unnecessary to evoke conflict deliberately; if the group members are interacting with one another openly and honestly, conflict will emerge. More often, the therapist must intervene to keep conflict within constructive bounds.†

Keep in mind that the therapeutic use of conflict, like all other behavior in the here-and-now, is a two-step process: experience (affect expression) and reflection upon that experience. You may control conflict by switching the group from the first to the second stage. Often a simple, direct appeal is effective: for example, "We've been expressing some intense negative feelings here today as well as last week. To protect us from overload, it might be valuable to stop what we're doing and try together to understand what's been happening and where all these powerful feelings come from." Group members will have different capacities to tolerate conflict. One client responded to the therapist's "freezing the frame" (shifting the group to a reflective position) by criticizing the therapist for cooling things off just when things were getting interesting. A comember immediately commented that she could barely tolerate more tension and was grateful for a chance to regroup. It may be useful to think of the shift to process as creating a space for reflection—a space in which members may explore their *mutual* contributions to the conflict. The creation of this space for thoughtful reflection may be of great import—indeed, it may make the difference between therapeutic impasse and therapeutic growth.[29]

Receiving negative feedback is painful and yet, if accurate and sensitively delivered, helpful. The therapist can render it more palatable by making the benefits of feedback clear to the recipient and enlisting that client as an ally in the process. Often you can facilitate that sequence by remembering the original presenting interpersonal problems that brought the individual to therapy or by obtaining verbal contracts from group members early in therapy, which you can refer back to when the member obtains feedback.

For example, if at the onset of therapy a client comments that her fiancé accuses her of trying to tear him down, and that she wishes to work on that problem in the group, you may nail down a contract by a statement such as: "Carolyn, it sounds as though it would be helpful to you if we could identify similar trends in your relationships to others in the group. How would you feel if, from now on, we point this out to you as soon as we see it happen?" Once this contract has been agreed upon, store it in your mind and, when the occasion arises (for example when the client receives relevant similar feedback from men in the group), remind the client that, despite the discomfort, this precise feedback may be exceptionally useful in understanding her relationship with her fiancé.

Almost invariably, two group members who feel considerable mutual antagonism have the potential to be of great value to each other (see my novel *The Schopenhauer Cure* for a dramatic example of this phenomenon).† Each obviously cares about how he is viewed by the other. Generally, there is much envy or much mutual projection, which offers the opportunity to uncover hidden parts of themselves. In their anger, each will point out to the other important (though unpalatable) truths. The self-esteem of the antagonists may be increased by the conflict. When people become angry at one another, this in itself may be taken as an indication that they are important to one another and take one another seriously. Some have aptly referred to such angry relationships as "tough love" (a term originating in the Synanon groups for addicts). Individuals who truly care nothing for each other ignore each other. Individuals may learn another important lesson: that others may respond negatively to some trait, mannerism, or attitude but still value them.

For clients who have been unable to express anger, the group may serve as a testing ground for taking risks and learning that such behavior is neither dangerous nor necessarily destructive. In chapter 2, I described incidents cited by group members as turning points in their therapy. A majority of these critical incidents involved the expression, for the first time, of strong negative affect. It is also important for clients to learn that they can withstand attacks and pressure from others. Emotional resilience and healthy insulation can be products of work involving conflict.†

Overly aggressive individuals may learn some of the interpersonal consequences of blind outspokenness. Through feedback, they come to appreciate the impact they have on others and gradually come to terms with the self-defeating pattern of their behavior. For many, angry confrontations may provide valuable learning opportunities, since group members learn to remain in mutually useful contact despite their anger.

Clients may be helped to express anger more directly and more fairly. Even in all-out conflict, there are tacit rules of war, which, if violated, make satisfactory resolution all but impossible. For example, in therapy groups combatants will occasionally take information disclosed by the other in a previous spirit of trust and use it to scorn or humiliate that person. Or they may refuse to examine the conflict because they claim to have so little regard for the other that they do not wish to waste any further time. These postures require vigorous intervention by the therapist. When therapists belatedly realize that an earlier or different intervention would have been helpful, they should acknowledge that—as Winnicott once said—the difference between good parents and bad parents was not the number of mistakes made but what they did with them.[30]

Sometimes in unusually sustained and destructive situations the leader must forcefully assume control and set limits. The leader cannot leave such situations to the group alone if doing so gives license to an individual's destructive behavior. Consider this description of limit-setting by Ormont:[31]

> Gabriel crackled with ill will toward everybody. He would not let anyone talk without shouting them down. When the members demanded I get rid of him, I cut in on him sharply: "Look, Gabriel, I understand how you feel. I might say the same things, but with a lighter touch. The difference is that you're out of control. You have a fertile imagination. But you're not moving things along in the group—you're simply finding fault and hurting feelings.
>
> He seemed to be listening, so I ventured an interpretation. "You're telling us Miriam is no good. I get the impression you're saying you are no good—a no-good guy. Either you're going to cooperate or you're going to get out!" His reaction astonished us. Without saying a word to me he turned to Miriam and apologized to her. Later he told us how he felt my ability to set limits reassured him. Somebody was in control.

One of the most common indirect and self-defeating modes of fighting is the one used by Jan in the clinical illustration of subgrouping I described earlier in this chapter. This strategy calls for the client, in one form or another, to injure himself or herself in the hope of inducing guilt in the other—the "see what you've done to me" strategy. Usually, much therapeutic work is required to change this pattern. It is generally deeply ingrained, with roots stretching back to earliest childhood (as in the common childhood fantasy of watching at your own funeral as parents and other grief-stricken tormentors pound their breasts in guilt).

Group leaders must endeavor to turn the process of disagreeing into something positive—a learning situation that encourages members to evaluate the sources of their position and to relinquish those that are irrationally based. Clients must also be helped to understand that regardless of the source of their anger, their method of expressing it may be self-defeating. Feedback is instrumental in this process. For example, members may learn that, unbeknownst to themselves, they characteristically display scorn, irritation, or disapproval. Human sensitivity to facial gestures and nuances of expression far exceeds proprioceptive sensitivity.[32] Only through feedback do we learn that we communicate something that is not intended or, for that matter, even consciously experienced. Focusing attention on the divergence between a client's intent and actual impact can significantly enhance self-awareness.†[33]

The therapist should also attempt to help the conflicting members learn more about their opponent's position. Therapists who feel comfortable using structured exercises may find that role-switching may be a useful intervention. Members are asked to take the part of their opponent for a few minutes in order to apprehend the other's reasons and feelings. Focused anger-management groups have been applied effectively in a range of settings and clinical populations, stretching from burdened caregivers of family members with dementia to war veterans suffering posttraumatic stress disorder. These groups usually combine psychoeducation (focusing on the connections between thoughts, emotions, and behavior) and skill building.†

Many group members have the opposite problem of suppressing and avoiding angry feelings. In groups they learn that others in their situation would feel angry; they learn to read their own body language ("My fists are clenched so I must be angry"); they learn to magnify rather than suppress the first flickerings of anger; they learn that it is safe, permissible, and in their best interests to be direct and to feel and express anger. Most important, their fear of such behavior is extinguished: their fantasized catastrophe does not occur, their comments do not result in destruction, guilt, rejection, or escalation of anger.

Strong shared affect may enhance the importance of the relationship. In chapter 3, I described how group cohesiveness is increased when members of a group go through intense emotional experiences together, regardless of the nature of the emotion. In this manner, members of a successful therapy group are like members of a closely knit family, who may battle each other yet derive much support from their family allegiance. A dyadic relationship, too, that has weathered much stress is likely to be especially rewarding. A situation in which two individuals in group therapy experience an intense mutual hatred and then, through some of the mechanisms I have described, resolve the hatred and arrive at mutual understanding and respect is always of great therapeutic value.

SELF-DISCLOSURE

Self-disclosure, both feared and valued by participants, plays an integral part in all group therapies. Without exception, group therapists agree that it is important for clients to reveal personal material in the group—material that the client would rarely disclose to others. The self-disclosure may involve past or current events in one's life, fantasy or dream material, hopes or aspirations, and current feelings toward other individuals. In group therapy, feelings toward other members often assume such major importance that the therapist must devote energy and time to creating the preconditions for disclosure: trust and cohesiveness.†

Risk

Every self-disclosure involves some risk on the part of the discloser—how much risk depends in part on the nature of what is disclosed. Disclosing material that has previously been kept secret or that is highly personal and emotionally charged obviously carries greater risk. First-time disclosure, that is, the first time one has shared certain information with anyone else, is felt to be particularly risky.

The amount of risk also depends on the audience. Disclosing members, wishing to avoid shame, humiliation, and rejection, feel safer if they know that the audience is sensitive and has also previously disclosed highly personal material.†[34]

Sequence of Self-Disclosure

Self-disclosure has a predictable sequence. If the receiver of the disclosure is involved in a meaningful relationship with the discloser (and not merely a casual acquaintance at a cocktail party) the receiver is likely to feel obligated to reciprocate with some personal disclosure. Now the receiver as well as the original discloser is vulnerable, and the relationship usually deepens, with the participants continuing to make slightly more open and intimate disclosures in turn until some optimal level of intimacy is reached. Thus, in the cohesive group self-disclosure draws more disclosure, ultimately generating a constructive loop of trust, self-disclosure, feedback, and interpersonal learning.[35]

Here is an illustrative example:

• *Halfway through a thirty-session course of group therapy, Cam, a thirty-year-old avoidant, socially isolated, engineer, opened a session by announcing that he wanted to share a secret with the group: for the past several years, he had frequented strip clubs, befriending the strippers. He had a fantasy that he would rescue a stripper, who would then, in gratitude, fall in love with him. Cam went on to describe how he had spent thousands of dollars on his "rescue missions." The group members welcomed his disclosure, especially since it was the first substantially personal disclosure he had made in the group. Cam responded that time was running out and he wanted to relate to the others in a real way before the group ended. This encouraged Marie, a recovering alcoholic, to reciprocate with a major disclosure: many years ago she had worked as an exotic dancer and prostitute, and she assured Cam that he could expect nothing but disappointment and exploitation in that environment. She had never disclosed her past for fear of the group's judgment, but felt compelled to respond to Cam: She hated to see such a decent man engaging in self-destructive relationships. The mutual disclosure, support, and caring accelerated the work in the subsequent meeting for all the members.*

Adaptive Functions of Self-Disclosure

As disclosures proceed in a group, the entire membership gradually increases its involvement and responsibility to one another. If the timing is right, nothing will commit an individual to a group more than receiving or revealing some intimate secret material. There is nothing more exhilarating than for a member to disclose for the first time material that has been burdensome for years and to be genuinely understood and fully accepted.† Interpersonalists such as Sullivan and Rogers maintained that self-acceptance must be preceded by acceptance by others; in other words, to accept oneself, one must gradually permit others to know one as one really is.

Research evidence validates the importance of self-disclosure in group therapy.[36] In chapter 3, I described the relationship between self-disclosure and popularity in the group. Popularity (as determined from sociometrics) correlates with therapy outcome.[37] Group members who disclose extensively in the early meetings are often very popular in their groups.[38] People reveal more to individuals they like; conversely, those who reveal themselves are more likely to be liked by others.[39] Several research inquiries have demonstrated that high disclosure (either naturally occurring or experimentally induced) increases group cohesiveness.[40] But the relationship between liking and self-disclosure is not linear. One who discloses too much arouses anxiety in others rather than affection.[41] In other words, both the content and process of self-disclosure need to be considered. Self-disclosure should be viewed as a means and not an end in itself.[42]

Much research supports the crucial role of self-disclosure in successful therapy outcome.[43] Successfully treated participants in group therapy made almost twice as many self-disclosing personal statements during the course of therapy as did unsuccessfully treated clients.[44] Lieberman, Yalom, and Miles found that in encounter groups, individuals who had negative outcomes revealed less of themselves than did the other participants.[45]

The concept of transfer of learning is vital here: *not only are clients rewarded by the other group members for self-disclosure, but the behavior, thus reinforced, is integrated into their relationships outside the group, where it is similarly rewarded.* Often the first step toward revealing something to a spouse or a potential close friend is the first-time disclosure in the therapy group.

Hence, to a significant degree, the impact of self-disclosure is shaped by the relationship context in which the disclosure occurs. What is truly validating to the client is to reveal oneself and *then* to be accepted and supported. Once that happens, the client experiences a genuine sense of connection and of understanding.[46] Keep in mind also that here-and-now disclosure in particular has a far greater effect on cohesion than then-and-there disclosure.[47]

Often clients manifest great resistance to self-disclosure. Frequently a client's dread of rejection or ridicule from other members coexists with the hope of acceptance and understanding.[48] Group members often entertain some calamitous fantasy about self-disclosure; *to disclose and to have that calamitous fantasy disconfirmed is highly therapeutic.*

In a bold undergraduate teaching experiment, students confidentially shared a deep secret with the class. Great care was taken to ensure anonymity. Secrets were written on uniform paper, read by the instructor in a darkened classroom so as to conceal blushing or other facial expressions of discomfort, and immediately destroyed. The secrets included various sexual preferences, illegal or immoral acts (including sexual abuse, cheating, stealing, drug sales), psychological disturbances, abuse suffered in alcoholic families, and so on. Immediately after the reading of the secrets, there was a powerful response in the classroom: "a heavy silence . . . the atmosphere is palpable . . . the air warm, heavy, and electric . . . you could cut the tension with a knife." Students reported a sense of relief at hearing their secrets read—as though a weight had been lifted from them.

But there was even greater relief in the subsequent class discussion, in which students shared their responses to hearing various secrets, exchanged similar experiences, and not uncommonly chose to identify which secret they wrote. The peer support was invariably positive and powerfully reassuring.[49]

Maladaptive Self-Disclosure

Self-disclosure is related to optimal psychological and social adjustment in a curvilinear fashion: too much or too little self-disclosure signifies maladaptive interpersonal behavior.

Too little self-disclosure usually results in severely limited opportunity for reality testing. Those who fail to disclose themselves in a relationship generally forfeit the opportunity to obtain valid feedback. Furthermore, they prevent the relationship from developing further; without reciprocation, the other party will either desist from further self-disclosure or else rupture the relationship entirely.

Group members who do not disclose themselves have little chance of genuine acceptance by the other members and therefore little chance of experiencing a rise in self-esteem.[50] If a member is accepted on the basis of a false image, no enduring boost in self-esteem occurs; moreover, that person will then be even less likely to engage in valid self-disclosure because of the added risk of losing the acceptance gained through the false presentation of self.[51]

Some individuals dread self-disclosure, not primarily because of shame or fear of nonacceptance but because they are heavily conflicted in the area of control. To them, self-disclosure is dangerous because it makes them vulnerable to the control of others. It is only when several other group members have made themselves vulnerable through self-disclosure that such a person is willing to reciprocate.

Self-disclosure blockages will impede individual members as well as entire groups. Members who have an important secret that they dare not reveal to the group may find participation on any but a superficial level very difficult, because they will have to conceal not only the secret *but all possible avenues to it*. In chapter 5, I discussed in detail how, in the early stages of therapy, the therapist might best approach the individual who has a big secret. To summarize, it is advisable for the therapist to counsel the client to share the secret with the group in order to benefit from therapy. The pace and timing are up to the client, but the therapist may offer to make the act easier in any way the client wishes. When the long-held secret is finally shared, it is often illuminating to learn what made it possible to come forward at this point in time. I will often make such statements as "You've been coming to this group for many weeks wanting to tell us about this secret. What has changed in you or in the group to make it possible to share it today? What has happened to allow you to trust us more today?"† See *The Schopenhauer Cure* for a graphic example.

Therapists sometimes unwittingly discourage self-disclosure. The most terrifying secret I have known a client to possess was in a newly formed group that I supervised, which was led by a neophyte therapist. One year earlier, this woman had murdered her two-year-old child and then attempted suicide. (The court ruled her insane and released her on the provision that she undergo therapy.) After fourteen weeks of therapy, not only had she told nothing of herself but by her militant promulgation of denial and suppressive strategies (such as invoking astrological tables and ancient mystical sects) had impeded the entire group. Despite his best efforts and much of my supervisory time, the therapist could find no method to help the client (or the group) move into therapy. I then observed several sessions of the group through the two-way mirror and noted, to my surprise, that the client provided the therapist with many opportunities to help her discuss the secret. A productive supervisory session was devoted to the therapist's countertransference. His feelings about his own two-year-old child and his horror (despite himself) at the client's act colluded with her guilt to silence her in the group. In the following meeting, the gentlest question by the therapist was sufficient to free the client's tongue and to change the entire character of the group.

In some groups, self-disclosure is discouraged by a general climate of judgmentalism. Members are reluctant to disclose shameful aspects of themselves for fear that others will lose respect for them. In training or therapy groups of mental health professionals, this issue is even more pressing. Since our chief professional instrument is our own person, at risk is professional as well as personal loss of respect. In a group of psychiatric residents, for example, one member, Joe, discussed his lack of confidence as a physician and his panic whenever he was placed in a life-or-death clinical situation. Ted, an outspoken, burly member, acknowledged that Joe's fear of revealing this material was well founded, since Ted did lose respect for him and doubted whether he would, in the future, refer patients to Joe. The other members supported Joe and condemned Ted for his judgmentalism and suggested that they would be reluctant to refer patients to *him*. An infinite regress of judgmentalism can easily ensue, and it is incumbent on the therapist at these times to make a vigorous process intervention.

The therapist must differentiate, too, between a healthy need for privacy and neurotic compulsive secrecy.† Some people, who seldom find their way into groups, are private in an adaptive way: they share intimacies with only a few close friends and shudder at the thought of self-disclosure in a group. Moreover, they enjoy private self-contemplative activities. This is a very different thing from privacy based on fear, shame, or crippling social inhibitions. Men appear to have more difficulty in self-disclosure than women: they tend to view relationships from the perspective of competition and dominance rather from tenderness and connectedness.[52]

Too much self-disclosure can be as maladaptive as too little. Indiscriminate self-disclosure is neither a goal of mental health nor a pathway to it. Some individuals make the grievous error of reasoning that if self-disclosure is desirable, then total and continuous self-disclosure must be a very good thing indeed. Urban life would become unbearably sticky if every contact between two people entailed sharing personal concerns and secrets. Obviously, the relationship that exists between discloser and receiver should be the major factor in determining the pattern of self-disclosure. Several studies have demonstrated this truth experimentally: individuals disclose different types and amounts of material depending on whether the receiver is a mother, father, best same-sex friend, opposite-sex friend, work associate, or spouse.[53]

However, some maladaptive disclosers disregard, and thus jeopardize, their relationship with the receiver. The self-disclosing individual who fails to discriminate between intimate friends and distant acquaintances perplexes associates. We have all, I am certain, experienced confusion or betrayal on learning that supposedly intimate material confided to us has been shared with many others. Furthermore, a great deal of self-disclosure may frighten off an unprepared recipient. In a rhythmic, flowing relationship, one party leads the other in self-disclosures, but never by too great a gap.

In group therapy, members who reveal early and promiscuously will often drop out soon in the course of therapy. Group members should be encouraged to take risks in the group; but if they reveal *too much too early*, they may feel so much shame that any interpersonal rewards are offset; furthermore, their overabundant self-disclosure may threaten others who would be willing to support them but are not yet prepared to reciprocate.[54] High disclosers are then placed in a position of such great vulnerability in the group that they often choose to flee.

All of these observations suggest that self-disclosure is a complex social act that is situation and role bound. One does not self-disclose in solitude: time, place, and person must always be considered. Appropriate self-disclosure in a therapy group, for example, may be disastrously inappropriate in other situations, and appropriate self-disclosure for one stage of a therapy group may be inappropriate for another stage.

These points are particularly evident in the case of self-disclosure of feelings toward other members, or feedback. It is my belief that the therapist should help the members be guided as much by responsibility to others as by freedom of expression. I have seen vicious, destructive events occur in groups under the aegis of honesty and self-revelation: "You told us that we should be honest about expressing our feelings, didn't you?" *But, in fact, we always selectively reveal our feelings.* There are always layers of reactions toward others that we rarely share—feelings about unchangeable attributes, physical characteristics, deformity, professional or intellectual mediocrity, social class, lack of charm, and so on.

For some individuals, disclosure of overt hostile feelings is "easy-honest." But they find it more difficult to reveal underlying meta-hostile feelings— feelings of fear, envy, guilt, sadistic pleasure in vindictive triumph. And how many individuals find it easy to disclose negative feelings but avoid expressing positive feelings—feelings of admiration, concern, empathy, physical attraction, love?

A group member who has just disclosed a great deal faces a moment of vulnerability and requires support from the members and/or the therapist. Regardless of the circumstances, no client should be attacked for important self-disclosure. A clinical vignette illustrates this point.

• *Five members were present at a meeting of a year-old group. (Two members were out of town, and one was ill.) Joe, the protagonist of this episode, began the meeting with a long, rambling statement about feeling uncomfortable in a smaller group. Since Joe had started the group, his style of speaking had turned members off. Everyone found it hard to listen to him and longed for him to stop. But no one had really dealt honestly with these vague, unpleasant feelings about Joe until this meeting, when, after several minutes, Betsy interrupted him: "I'm going to scream—or burst! I can't contain myself any longer! Joe, I wish you'd stop talking. I can't bear to listen to you. I don't know who you're talking to—maybe the ceiling, maybe the floor, but I know you're not talking to me. I care about everyone else in this group. I think about them. They mean a lot to me. I hate to say this, but for some reason, Joe, you don't matter to me."*

Stunned, Joe attempted to understand the reason behind Betsy's feelings. Other members agreed with Betsy and suggested that Joe never said anything personal. It was all filler, all cotton candy—he never revealed anything important about himself; he never related personally to any of the members of the group. Spurred, and stung, Joe took it upon himself to go around the group and describe his personal feelings toward each of the members.

I thought that, even though Joe revealed more than he had before, he still remained in comfortable, safe territory. I asked, "Joe, if you were to think about revealing yourself on a ten-point scale, with "one" representing cocktail-party stuff and "ten" representing the most you could ever imagine revealing about yourself to another person, how would you rank what you did in the group over the last ten minutes?" He thought about it for a moment and said he guessed he would give himself "three" or "four." I asked, "Joe, what would happen if you were to move it up a rung or two?"

He deliberated for a moment and then said, "If I were to move it up a couple of rungs, I would tell the group that I was an alcoholic."

This was a staggering bit of self-disclosure. Joe had been in the group for a year, and no one in the group—not even me and my co-therapist—had known of this. Furthermore, it was vital information. For weeks, for example, Joe had bemoaned the fact that his wife was pregnant and had decided to have an abortion rather than have a child by him. The group was baffled by her behavior and over the weeks became highly critical of his wife—some members even questioned why Joe stayed in the marriage. The new information that Joe was an alcoholic provided a crucial missing link. Now his wife's behavior made sense!

My initial response was one of anger. I recalled all those futile hours Joe had led the group on a wild-goose chase. I was tempted to exclaim, "Damn it, Joe, all those wasted meetings talking about your wife! Why didn't you tell us this before?" But that is just the time to bite your tongue. The important thing is not that Joe did not give us this information earlier but that he did tell us today. Rather than being punished for his previous concealment, he should be reinforced for having made a breakthrough and been willing to take an enormous risk in the group. The proper technique consisted of supporting Joe and facilitating further "horizontal" disclosure, that is, about the experience of disclosure (see chapter 5).†

It is not uncommon for members to withhold information, as Joe did, with the result that the group spends time inefficiently. Obviously, this has a number of unfortunate implications, not the least of which is the toll on the self-esteem of the withholding member who knows he or she is being duplicitous—acting in bad faith toward the other members. Often group leaders do not know the extent to which a member is withholding, but (as I discuss in chapter 14) as soon as they begin doing combined therapy (that is, treating the same individual both in individual and group therapy), they are amazed at how much new information the client reveals.

In chapter 7, I discussed aspects of group leader self-disclosure. The therapist's transparency, particularly within the here-and-now, can be an effective way to encourage member self-disclosure.† But leader transparency must always be placed in the context of what is useful to the functioning of a particular group at a particular time. The general who, after making an important tactical decision, goes around wringing his hands and expressing his uncertainty will undercut the morale of his entire command.[55] Similarly, the therapy group leader should obviously not disclose feelings that would undermine the effectiveness of the group, such as impatience with the group, a preoccupation with a client or a group seen earlier in the day, or any of a host of other personal concerns.[56]

TERMINATION

The concluding phase of group therapy is termination, a critically important but frequently neglected part of treatment.[57] Group therapy termination is particularly complex: members may leave because they have achieved their goals, they may drop out prematurely, the entire group may end, and the therapist may leave. Furthermore, feelings about termination must be explored from different perspectives: the individual member, the therapist, the group as a whole.

Even the word termination has unfavorable connotations; it is often used in such negative contexts as an unwanted pregnancy or a poorly performing employee.[58] In contrast, a mutual, planned ending to therapy is a positive, integral part of the therapeutic work that includes review, mourning, and celebration of the commencement of the next phase of life. The ending should be clear and focused—not a petering out. Confronting the ending of therapy is a boundary experience, a confrontation with limits.[59] It reminds us of the precious nature of our relationships and the requirement to conclude with as few regrets as possible about work undone, emotions unexpressed, or feelings unstated.

Termination of the Client

If properly understood and managed, termination can be an important force in the process of change. Throughout, I have emphasized that group therapy is a highly individual process. Each client will enter, participate in, use, and experience the group in a uniquely personal manner. The end of therapy is no exception.

Only general assumptions about the length and overall goals of therapy may be made. Managed health care decrees that most therapy groups be brief and problem oriented—and, indeed, as reviewed in chapter 10, there is evidence that brief group approaches may effectively offer symptomatic relief. There is also evidence, however, that therapy is most effective when the ending of treatment is collaboratively determined and not arbitrarily imposed by a third party.[60] Managed care is most interested in what will be most useful for the majority of a large pool of clients. Psychotherapists are less interested in statistics and aggregates of clients than in the individual distressed client in their office.

How much therapy is enough? That is not an easy question to answer. Although remoralization and recovery from acute distress often occur quickly, substantial change in character structure generally requires twelve to twenty-four months, or more, of therapy.†[61]

The goals of therapy have never been stated more succinctly than by Freud: "to be able to love and to work."[62] Freud believed that therapy should end when there is no prospect for further gains and the individual's pathology has lost its hold. Some people would add other goals: the ability to love oneself, to allow oneself to be loved, to be more flexible, to learn to play, to discover and trust one's own values, and to achieve greater self-awareness, greater interpersonal competence, and more mature defenses.[63]

Some group members may achieve a great deal in a few months, whereas others require years of group therapy. Some individuals have far more ambitious goals than others; it would not be an exaggeration to state that some individuals, satisfied with their therapy, terminate in approximately the same state in which others begin therapy. Some clients may have highly specific goals in therapy and, because much of their psychopathology is ego-syntonic, choose to limit the amount of change they are willing to undertake. Others may be hampered by important external circumstances in their lives. All therapists have had the experience of helping a client improve to a point at which further change would be countertherapeutic. For example, a client might, with further change, outgrow, as it were, his or her spouse; continued therapy would result in the rupture of an irreplaceable relationship unless concomitant changes occur in the spouse. If that contingency is not available (if, for example, the spouse adamantly refuses to engage in the change process), the therapist may be well advised to settle for the positive changes that have occurred, even though the personal potential for greater growth is clear.

Termination of professional treatment is but a stage in the individual's career of growth. Clients continue to change, and one important effect of successful therapy is to enable individuals to use their psychotherapeutic resources constructively in their personal environment. Moreover, treatment effects may be time delayed: I have seen many successful clients in long-term follow-up interviews who have not only continued to change after termination but who, after they have left the group, recall an observation or interpretation made by another member or the therapist that only then—months, even years, later—became meaningful to them.

Setbacks, too, occur after termination: many successfully treated clients will, from time to time, encounter severe stress and need short-term help. In addition, almost all members experience anxiety and depression after leaving a group. A period of mourning is an inevitable part of the termination process. Present loss may evoke memories of earlier losses, which may be so painful that the client truncates the termination work. Indeed, some cannot tolerate the process and will withdraw prematurely with a series of excuses. This must be challenged: the client needs to internalize the positive group experience and the members and leader; without proper separation, that process will be compromised and the client's future growth constricted.[64]

Some therapists find that termination from group therapy is less problematic than termination from long-term individual therapy, in which clients often become extremely dependent on the therapeutic situation. Group therapy participants are usually more aware that therapy is not a way of life but a process with a beginning, a middle, and an end. In the open therapy group, there are many living reminders of the therapeutic sequence. Members see new members enter and improved members graduate; they observe the therapist beginning the process over and over again to help the beginners through difficult phases of therapy. Thus, they realize the bittersweet fact that, although the therapist is a person with whom they have had a real and meaningful relationship, he or she is also a professional whose attention must shift to others and who will not remain as a permanent and endless source of gratification for them.

Not infrequently, a group places subtle pressure on a member not to terminate because the remaining members will miss that person's presence and contributions. There is no doubt that members who have worked in a therapy group for many months or years acquire interpersonal and group skills that make them particularly valuable to the other members. (This is an important qualitative difference between group therapy and individual therapy outcome: Group therapy members routinely increase in emotional intelligence and become expert process diagnosticians and facilitators.)†

• *One graduating member pointed out in his final meeting that Al usually started the meeting, but recently that role had switched over to Donna, who was more entertaining. After that, he noted that Al, aside from occasional sniping, often slumped into silence for the rest of the meeting. He also remarked that two other members never communicated directly to each other; they always used an intermediary. Another graduating member remarked that she had noted the first signs of the breakdown of a long-term collusion between two members in which they had, in effect, agreed never to say anything challenging or unpleasant to the other. In the same meeting, she chided the members of the group who were asking for clarification about the groups ground rules about subgrouping: "Answer it for yourselves. It's your therapy. You know what you want to get out of the group. What would it mean to you? Will it get in your way or not?" All of these comments are so-*

*phisticated and interpersonally astute—worthy of any experienced
group therapist.*

Therapists may so highly value such a member's contributions that
they also are slow in encouraging him or her to terminate—of course,
there is no justification for such a posture, and therapists should explore
this openly as soon as they become aware of it. I have, incidentally, noted
that a "role suction" operates at such times: once the senior member
leaves, another member begins to exercise skills acquired in the group.
Therapists, like other members, will feel the loss of departing members
and by expressing their feelings openly do some valuable modeling for the
group and demonstrate that this therapy and these relationships matter,
not just to the clients but to them as well.

Some socially isolated clients may postpone termination because they
have been using the therapy group for social reasons rather than as a
means for developing the skills to create a social life for themselves in
their home environment. The therapist must help these members focus on
transfer of learning and encourage risk taking outside the group. Others
unduly prolong their stay in the group because they hope for some guarantee that they are indeed safe from future difficulties. They may suggest
that they remain in the group for a few more months, until they start a
new job, or get married, or graduate from college. If the improvement
base seems secure, however, these delays are generally unnecessary. Members must be helped to come to terms with the fact that one can never be
certain; one is always vulnerable.

Not infrequently, clients experience a brief recrudescence of their original symptomatology shortly before termination. Rather than prolong
their stay in the group, the therapist should help the clients understand
this event for what it is: protest against termination. There are times,
however, when this pretermination regression can serve as a last opportunity to revisit the concerns that led to treatment initially and allow some
relapse prevention work. Ending does not undo good work, but it can
profitably revisit the beginnings of the work.

• *One man, three meetings before termination, re-experienced much of
the depression and sense of meaninglessness that had brought him into
therapy. The symptoms rapidly dissipated with the therapist's interpretation that he was searching for reasons not to leave the group. That
evening, the client dreamed that the therapist offered him a place in another group in which he would receive training as a therapist: "I felt
that I had duped you into thinking I was better." The dream represents
an ingenious stratagem to defeat termination and offers two alternatives: the client goes into another of the therapist's groups, in which he*

receives training as a therapist; or he has duped the therapist and has not really improved (and thus should continue in the group). Either way, he does not have to terminate.

Some members improve gradually, subtly, and consistently during their stay in the group. Others improve in dramatic bursts. I have known many members who, though hard working and committed to the group, made no apparent progress whatsoever for six, twelve, even eighteen months and then, suddenly, in a short period of time, seemed to transform themselves. (What do we tell our students? That change is often slow, that they should not look for immediate gratification from their clients. If they build solid, deep therapeutic foundations, change is sure to follow. So often we think of this as just a platitude designed to bolster neophyte therapists' morale—we forget that it is true.)

The same staccato pattern of improvement is often true for the group as a whole. Sometimes groups struggle and lumber on for months with no visible change in any member, and then suddenly enter a phase in which everyone seems to get well together. Rutan uses the apt metaphor of building a bridge during a battle.[65] The leader labors mightily to construct the bridge and may, in the early phases, suffer casualties (dropouts). But once the bridge is in place, it escorts many individuals to a better place.

There are certain clients for whom even a consideration of termination is problematic. These clients are particularly sensitized to abandonment; their self-regard is so low that they consider their illness to be their only currency in their traffic with the therapist and the group. In their minds growth is associated with dread, since improvement would result in the therapist's leaving them. Therefore they must minimize or conceal progress. Of course, it is not until much later that they discover the key to this absurd paradox: Once they truly improve, they will no longer need the therapist!†

One useful sign suggesting readiness for termination is that the group becomes less important to the client. One terminating member commented that Mondays (the day of the group meetings) were now like any other day of the week. When she began in the group, she lived for Mondays, with the rest of the days inconsequential wadding between meetings.

I make a practice of recording the first individual interview with a client. Not infrequently, these tapes are useful in arriving at the termination decision. By listening many months later to their initial session, clients can obtain a clearer perspective of what they have accomplished and what remains to be done.

The group members are an invaluable resource in helping one another decide about termination, and a unilateral decision made by a member without consulting the other members is often premature. Generally, a well-timed termination decision will be discussed for a few weeks in the group, during which time the client works through feelings about leaving. There are times when clients make an abrupt decision to terminate membership in the group immediately. I have often found that such individuals find it difficult to express gratitude and positive feeling; hence they attempt to abbreviate the separation process as much as possible. These clients must be helped to understand and correct their jarring, unsatisfying method of ending relationships. In fact, for some, the dread of ending dictates their whole pattern of avoiding connections and avoiding intimacy. To ignore this phase is to neglect an important area of human relations. Ending is, after all, a part of almost every relationship, and throughout one's life one must say good-bye to important people.

Many terminating members attempt to lessen the shock of departure by creating bridges to the group that they can use in the future. They seek assurances that they may return, they collect telephone numbers of the other members, or they arrange social meetings to keep themselves informed of important events of the group. These efforts are only to be expected, and yet the therapist must not collude in the denial of termination. On the contrary, you must help the members explore it to its fullest extent. Clients who complete individual therapy may return, but clients who leave the group can never return. They are truly leaving: the group will be irreversibly altered; replacements will enter the group; the present cannot be frozen; time flows on cruelly and inexorably. These facts are evident to the remaining members as well—there is no better stimulus than a departing member to encourage the group to deal with issues about the rush of time, loss, separation, death, aging, and the contingencies of existence. Termination is thus more than an extraneous event in the group. It is the microcosmic representation of some of life's most crucial and painful issues.

The group members may need some sessions to work on their loss and to deal with many of these issues. The loss of a member provides an unusual work opportunity for individuals sensitized to loss and abandonment. Since they have compatriots sharing their loss, they mourn in a communal setting and witness others encompass the loss and continue to grow and thrive.[66]

After a member leaves the group, it is generally wise not to bring in new members without a hiatus of one or more meetings. A member's departure is often an appropriate time for others to take inventory of their own progress in therapy. Members who entered the group at the same time as the terminating member may feel some pressure to move more quickly.

Some members may misperceive the member's leaving as a forced departure and may feel a need to reaffirm a secure place in the group—by regressive means if necessary. More competitive members may rush toward termination prematurely. Senior members may feel envy or react with shame, experiencing the success of the comember as a reminder of their own self-deficiency and failing.† In extreme cases, the shame- or envy-ridden client may seek to devalue and spoil the achievement of the graduating member. Newer members may feel inspired or awed and left doubting whether they will ever be able to achieve what they have just witnessed.

Should the group engage in some form of ritual to mark the termination of a member? Sometimes a member or several members may present a gift to the graduating member or bring coffee and cake to the meeting—which may be appropriate and meaningful, as long as, like any event in the group, it can be examined and processed. For example, the group may examine the meaning of the ritual; who suggests and plans it? Is it intended to avoid necessary and appropriate sadness?[67]

We therapists must also look to our own feelings during the termination process, because occasionally we unaccountably and unnecessarily delay a client's termination. Some perfectionist therapists may unrealistically expect too much change and refuse to accept anything less than total resolution. Moreover, they lack faith in a client's ability to continue growth after the termination of formal therapy.[68] Other clients bring out Pygmalion pride in us: we find it difficult to part with someone who is, in part, our own creation; saying good-bye to some clients is saying good-bye to a part of ourselves. Furthermore, it is a permanent good-bye. If we have done our job properly, the client no longer needs us and breaks all contact.

Termination of the Therapist

In training programs, it is common practice for trainees to lead a group for six months to a year and then pass it on to a new student as their own training takes them elsewhere. This is generally a difficult period for the group members, and often they respond with repeated absences and threatened termination. It is a time for the departing therapist to attend to any unfinished business he or she has with any of the members. Some members feel that this is their last chance and share hitherto concealed material. Others have a recrudescence of symptoms, as though to say, "See what your departure has done to me!"[69] Therapists must not avoid any of these concerns: the more complete their ending with the group, the greater the potential for an effective transfer of leadership. It is an excellent opportunity for helping members appreciate their own resources.

The same principles apply in situations in which a more established leader needs to end his leadership due to a move, illness, or professional change. If the group members decide to continue, it is the leader's responsibility to secure new leadership. The transition process takes considerable time and planning, and the new leader must set about as quickly as possible to take over group leadership. One reported approach is to meet with all the group members individually in a pregroup format as described in chapter 9, while the old leader is still meeting with the group. After the first leader concludes, the new one begins to meet with the group at the set group time or at a mutually agreed-upon new time.[70]

Termination of the Group

Groups terminate for various reasons. Brief therapy groups, of course, have a preset termination date. Often external circumstances dictate the end of a group: for example, groups in a university mental health clinic usually run for eight to nine months and disband at the beginning of the summer vacation. Open groups often end only when the therapist retires or leaves the area (although this is not inevitable; if there is a co-therapist, he or she may continue the group). Occasionally, a therapist may decide to end a group because the great majority of its members are ready to terminate at approximately the same time.

Often a group avoids the difficult and unpleasant work of termination by denying or ignoring termination, and the therapist must keep the task in focus for them. In fact, as I discussed in chapter 10, it is essential for the leader of the brief therapy group to remind the group regularly of the approaching termination and to keep members focused on the attainment of goals. Groups hate to die, and members generally try to avoid the ending. They may, for example, pretend that the group will continue in some other setting—for example, reunions or regularly scheduled social meetings. But the therapist is well advised to confront the group with reality: the end of a group is a real loss. It never really can be reconvened, and even if relationships are continued in pairs or small fragments of the group, the entire group as the members then know it—in this room, in its present form, with the group leaders—will be gone forever.

The therapist must call attention to maladaptive modes of dealing with the impending termination. Some individuals have always dealt with the pain of separating from those they care about by becoming angry or devaluing the others. Some choose to deny and avoid the issue entirely. If anger or avoidance is extreme—manifested, for example, by tardiness or increased absence—the therapist must confront the group with this behavior. Usually with a mature group, the best approach is direct: the members can be reminded that it is their group, and they must decide how they want to end it. Members who devalue others or attend irregularly must be helped to understand their behavior. Do they feel their behavior or their absence makes no difference to the others, or do they so dread expressing positive feelings toward the group, or perhaps negative feelings toward the therapist for ending it, that they avoid confrontation?

Pain over the loss of the group is dealt with in part by a sharing of past experiences: exciting and meaningful past group events are remembered; members remind one another of the way they were then; personal testimonials are invariably heard in the final meetings. It is important that the therapist not bury the group too early, or the group will limp through ineffective lame-duck sessions. You must find a way to hold the issue of termination before the group and yet help the members keep working until the very last minute.

Some leaders of effective time-limited groups have sought to continue the benefits of the group by helping the group move into an ongoing leaderless format. The leader may help the transition by attending the meetings as a consultant at regular but decreasing intervals, for example biweekly or monthly. In my experience, it is particularly desirable to make such arrangements when the group is primarily a support group and constitutes an important part of the members' social life—for example, groups of the elderly who, through the death of friends and acquaintances, are isolated. Others have reported to me the successful launching of ongoing leaderless groups for men, for women, for AIDS sufferers, Alzheimer's caregivers, and the bereaved.

Keep in mind that the therapist, too, experiences the discomfort of termination. Throughout the final group stage, we must join the discussion. We will facilitate the group work by disclosing our own feelings. Therapists, as well as members, will miss the group. We are not impervious to feelings of loss and bereavement. We have grown close to the members and we will miss them as they miss us. To us as well as to the client, termination is a jolting reminder of the built-in cruelty of the psychotherapeutic process. Such openness on the part of the therapist invariably makes it easier for the group members to make their good-bye more complete. For us, too, the group has been a place of anguish, conflict, fear, and also great beauty: some of life's truest and most poignant moments occur in the small and yet limitless microcosm of the therapy group.

Chapter 13

PROBLEM GROUP MEMBERS

I have yet to encounter the unproblematic client, the one who coasts through the course of therapy like a newly christened ship gliding smoothly down the ramps into the water. Each group member *must* be a problem: the success of therapy depends on each individual's encountering and then mastering basic life problems in the here-and-now of the group. Each problem is complex, overdetermined, and unique. The intent of this book is not to provide a compendium of solutions to problems but to describe a strategy and set of techniques that will enable a therapist to adapt to any problem arising in the group.

The term "problem client" is itself problematic. Keep in mind that the problem client rarely exists in a vacuum but is, instead, an amalgam consisting of several components: the client's own psychodynamics, the group's dynamics, and the client's interactions with comembers and the therapist. We generally overestimate the role of the client's character while underestimating the role of the interpersonal and social context.[1]

Certain illustrative behavioral constellations merit particular attention because of their common occurrence. A questionnaire sent by the American Group Psychotherapy Association to practicing group therapists inquired about the critical issues necessary for group therapists to master. Over fifty percent responded, "Working with difficult patients."[2] Accordingly, in this chapter, we shall turn our attention to difficult clients and specifically discuss eight problematic clinical types: the monopolist, the silent client, the boring client, the help-rejecting complainer, the psychotic or bipolar client, the schizoid client, the borderline client, and the narcissistic client.

THE MONOPOLIST

The bête noire of many group therapists is the habitual monopolist, a person who seems compelled to chatter on incessantly. These individuals are anxious if they are silent; if others get the floor, they reinsert themselves with a variety of techniques: rushing in to fill the briefest silence, responding to every statement in the group, continually addressing the problems of the speaker with a chorus of "I'm like that, too."

The monopolist may persist in describing, in endless detail, conversations with others (often taking several parts in the conversation) or in presenting accounts of newspaper or magazine stories that may be only slightly relevant to the group issue. Some monopolists hold the floor by assuming the role of interrogator. One member barraged the group with so many questions and "observations" that it occluded any opportunity for members to interact or reflect. Finally, when angrily confronted by comembers about her disruptive effect, she explained that she dreaded silence because it reminded her of the "quiet before the storm" in her family—the silence preceding her father's explosive, violent rages. Others capture the members' attention by enticing them with bizarre, puzzling, or sexually piquant material.

Labile clients who have a dramatic flair may monopolize the group by means of the crisis method: They regularly present the group with major life upheavals, which always seem to demand urgent and lengthy attention. Other members are cowed into silence, their problems seeming trivial in comparison. ("It's not easy to interrupt *Gone with the Wind*," as one group member put it.)

Effects on the Group

Although a group may, in the initial meeting, welcome and perhaps encourage the monopolist, the mood soon turns to one of frustration and anger. Other group members are often disinclined to silence a member for fear that they will thus incur an obligation to fill the silence. They anticipate the obvious rejoinder of, "All right, I'll be quiet. You talk." And, of course, it is not possible to talk easily in a tense, guarded climate. Members who are not particularly assertive may not deal directly with the monopolist for some time; instead, they may smolder quietly or make indirect hostile forays. Generally, oblique attacks on the monopolist will only aggravate the problem and fuel a vicious circle. The monopolist's compulsive speech is an attempt to deal with anxiety; as the client senses the growing group tension and resentment, his or her anxiety rises, and the tendency to speak compulsively correspondingly increases. Some monopolists are consciously aware, at these times, of assembling a smoke screen of words in order to divert the group from making a direct attack.

Eventually, this source of unresolved tension will have a detrimental effect on cohesiveness—an effect manifested by such signs of group disruption as indirect, off-target fighting, absenteeism, dropouts, and subgrouping. When the group does confront the monopolist, it is often in an explosive, brutal style; the spokesperson for the group usually receives unanimous support—I have even witnessed a round of applause. The monopolist may then sulk, be completely silent for a meeting or two ("See what they do without me"), or leave the group. In any event, little that is therapeutic has been accomplished for anyone.

Therapeutic Considerations

How can the therapist interrupt the monopolist in a therapeutically effective fashion? Despite the strongest provocation and temptation to shout the client down or to silence the client by edict, such an assault has little value (except as a temporary catharsis for the therapist). The client is not helped: no learning has accrued; the anxiety underlying the monopolist's compulsive speech persists and will, without doubt, erupt again in further monopolistic volleys or, if no outlet is available, will force the client to drop out of the group. Neither is the group helped. Regardless of the circumstances, the others are threatened by the therapist's silencing, in a heavy-handed manner, one of the members. A seed of caution and fear is implanted in the mind of all the members; they begin to wonder if a similar fate might befall them.

Nevertheless, the monopolistic behavior must be checked, and generally it is the therapist's task to do so. Although often the therapist does well to wait for the group to handle a group problem, the monopolistic member is one problem that the group, and especially a young group, often *cannot* handle. The monopolistic client poses a threat to its procedural underpinnings: group members are encouraged to speak in a group, yet this particular member must be silenced. The therapist must prevent the elaboration of therapy-obstructing norms and at the same time prevent the monopolistic client from committing social suicide. A two-pronged approach is most effective: consider both the monopolizer *and* the group that has allowed itself to be monopolized. This approach reduces the hazard of scapegoating and illuminates the role played by the group in each member's behavior.

From the standpoint of the group, bear in mind the principle that individual and group psychology are inextricably interwoven. No monopolistic client exists in a vacuum: The client always abides in a dynamic equilibrium with a group that permits or encourages such behavior.[3] Hence, the therapist may inquire why the group permits or encourages one member *to carry the burden of the entire meeting*. Such an inquiry may startle the members, who have perceived themselves only as passive victims of the monopolist. After the initial protestations are worked through, the group members may then, with profit, examine their exploitation of the monopolist; for example, they may have been relieved by not having to participate verbally in the group. They may have permitted the monopolist to do all the self-disclosure, or to appear foolish, or to act as a lightning rod for the group members' anger, while they themselves assumed little responsibility for the group's therapeutic tasks. Once the members disclose and discuss their reasons for inactivity, their personal commitment to the therapeutic process is augmented. They may, for example, discuss their fears of assertiveness, or of harming the monopolist, or of a retaliatory attack by some specific member or by the therapist; they may wish to avoid seeking the group's attention lest their greed be exposed; they may secretly revel in the monopolist's plight and enjoy being a member of the victimized and disapproving majority. A disclosure of any of these issues by a hitherto uninvolved client signifies progress and greater engagement in therapy.

In one group, for example, a submissive, chronically depressed woman, Sue, exploded in an uncharacteristic expletive-filled rage at the monopolistic behavior of another member. As she explored her outburst, Sue quickly recognized that her rage was really inwardly directed, stemming from her own stifling of her self, her own passivity, her avoidance of her own emotions. "My outburst was twenty years in the making," Sue said as she apologized and thanked her startled "antagonist" for crystallizing this awareness.

The group approach to this problem must be complemented by work with the monopolistic individual. The basic principle is a simple one: you do not want to silence the monopolist; you do not want to hear less from the client—*you want to hear more.* The seeming contradiction is resolved when we consider that the monopolist uses compulsive speech for self-concealment. The issues the monopolist presents to the group do not accurately reflect deeply felt personal concerns but are selected for other reasons: to entertain, to gain attention, to justify a position, to present grievances, and so on. Thus, the monopolist sacrifices the opportunity for therapy to an insatiable need for attention and control. Although each therapist will fashion interventions according to personal style, the essential message to monopolists must be that, through such compulsive speech, they hold the group at arm's length and prevent others from relating meaningfully to them. Thus you do not reject but instead issue an invitation to engage more fully in the group. If you harbor only the singular goal of silencing the client, then you have, in effect, abandoned the therapeutic goal and might as well remove the member from the group.

At times, despite considerable therapist care, the client will continue to hear only the message, "So you want me to shut up!" Such clients will ultimately leave the group, often in embarrassment or anger. Although this is an unsettling event, the consequences of therapist inactivity are far worse. Though the remaining members may express some regret at the departure of the member, it is not uncommon for them to acknowledge that they were on the verge of leaving themselves had the therapist not intervened.

In addition to grossly deviant behavior, the social sensory system of monopolists has a major impairment. They seem peculiarly unaware both of their interpersonal impact and of the response of others to them. Moreover, they lack the capacity or inclination to empathize with others.

Data from an exploratory study support this conclusion.[4] Clients and student observers were asked to fill out questionnaires at the end of each group meeting. One of the areas explored was activity. The participants were asked to rank the group members, including themselves, for the total number of words uttered during a meeting. There was excellent reliability in the activity ratings among group members and observers, with two exceptions: (1) the ratings of the therapist's activity by the clients showed large discrepancies (a function of transference; see chapter 7); and (2) monopolistic clients placed themselves far lower on the activity rankings than did the other members, who were often unanimous in ranking a monopolist as the most active member in the meeting.

The therapist must, then, help the monopolist be self-observant by encouraging the group to provide him or her with continual, empathic feedback about his impact on the others.[5] Without this sort of guidance from the leader, the group may provide the feedback in a disjunctive, explosive manner, which only makes the monopolist defensive. Such a sequence has little therapeutic value and merely recapitulates a drama and a role that the client has performed far too often.

• *In the initial interview, Matthew, a monopolist, complained about his relationship with his wife, who, he claimed, often abruptly resorted to such sledgehammer tactics as publicly humiliating him or accusing him of infidelity in front of his children. The sledgehammer approach accomplished nothing durable for this man; once his bruises had healed, he and his wife began the cycle anew. Within the first few meetings of the group, a similar sequence unfolded in the social microcosm of the group: because of his monopolistic behavior, judgmentalism, and inability to hear the members' response to him, the group pounded harder and harder until finally, when he was forced to listen, the message sounded cruel and destructive.*

Often the therapist must help increase a client's receptivity to feedback. You may have to be forceful and directive, saying, for example, "Charlotte, I think it would be best now for you to stop speaking because I sense there are some important feelings about you in the group that I think would be very helpful for you to know." You should also help the members disclose their responses to Charlotte rather than their interpretations of her motives. As described earlier in the sections on feedback and interpersonal learning, it is far more useful and acceptable to offer a statement such as "When you speak in this fashion I feel . . ." rather than "You are behaving in this fashion because. . . . " The client may often perceive motivational interpretations as accusatory but finds it more difficult to reject the validity of others' subjective responses.†

Too often we confuse or interchange the concepts of interpersonal manifestation, response, and cause. The *cause* of monopolistic behavior may vary considerably from client to client: some individuals speak in order to control others; many so fear being influenced or penetrated by others that they compulsively defend each of their statements; others so overvalue their own ideas and observations that they cannot delay and all thoughts must be immediately expressed. Generally the cause or actual intent of the monopolist's behavior is not well understood until much later in therapy, and interpretation of the cause may offer little help in the early management of disruptive behavior patterns. It is far more effective to concentrate on the client's *manifestation* of self in the group and on the other members' *response* to his or her behavior. Gently but repeatedly, members must be confronted with the paradox that however much they may wish to be accepted and respected by others, they persist in behavior that generates only irritation, rejection, and frustration.

A clinical illustration of many of these issues occurred in a therapy group in a psychiatric hospital/prison in which sexual offenders were incarcerated:

• *Walt, who had been in the group for seven weeks, launched into a familiar, lengthy tribute to the remarkable improvement he had undergone. He described in exquisite detail how his chief problem had been that he had not understood the damaging effects his behavior had on others, and how now, having achieved such understanding, he was ready to leave the hospital.*

The therapist observed that some of the members were restless. One softly pounded his fist into his palm, while others slumped back in a posture of indifference and resignation. He stopped the monopolist by asking the group members how many times they had heard Walt relate this account. All agreed they had heard it at every meeting—in fact, they had heard Walt speak this way in the very first meeting. Furthermore, they had never heard him talk about anything else and knew him only as a story. The members discussed their irritation with Walt, their reluctance to attack him for fear of seriously injuring him, of losing control of themselves, or of painful retaliation. Some spoke of their hopelessness about ever reaching Walt, and of the fact that he related to them only as stick figures without flesh or depth. Still others spoke of their terror of speaking and revealing themselves in the group; therefore, they welcomed Walt's monopolization. A few members expressed their total lack of interest or faith in therapy and therefore failed to intercept Walt because of apathy.

Thus the process was overdetermined: A host of interlocking factors resulted in a dynamic equilibrium called monopolization. By halting the runaway process, uncovering and working through the underlying factors, the therapist obtained maximum therapeutic benefit from a potentially crippling group phenomenon. Each member moved closer to group involvement. Walt was no longer permitted or encouraged to participate in a fashion that could not possibly be helpful to him or the group.

It is essential to guide the monopolistic client into the self-reflective process of therapy. I urge such clients to reflect on the type of response they were originally hoping to receive from the group and then to compare that with what eventually occurred. How do they explain that discrepancy? What role did they play in it?

Often monopolistic clients may devalue the importance of the group's reaction to them. They may suggest that the group consists of disturbed people or protest, "This is the first time something like this has ever happened to me." If the therapist has prevented scapegoating, then this statement is always untrue: the client is in a particularly familiar place. What is different in the group is the presence of norms that permit the others to comment openly on her behavior.

The therapist increases therapeutic leverage by encouraging these clients to examine and discuss interpersonal difficulties in their life: loneliness, lack of close friends, not being listened to by others, being shunned without reason—all the reasons for which therapy was first sought. Once these are made explicit, the therapist can, more convincingly, demonstrate to monopolistic clients the importance and relevance of examining their in-group behavior. Good timing is necessary. There is no point in attempting to do this work with a closed, defensive individual in the midst of a firestorm. Repeated, gentle, properly timed interventions are required.

THE SILENT CLIENT

The silent member is a less disruptive but often equally challenging problem for the therapist. Is the silent member always a problem? Perhaps the client profits silently. A story, probably apocryphal, that has circulated among group therapists for decades tells of an individual who attended a group for a year without uttering a word. At the end of the fiftieth meeting, he announced to the group that he would not return; his problems had been resolved, he was due to get married the following day, and he wished to express his gratitude to the group for the help they had given him.

Some reticent members may profit from vicariously engaging in treatment through identifying with active members with similar problems. It is possible that changes in behavior and in risk taking can gradually occur in such a client's relationships outside the group, although the person remains silent and seemingly unchanged in the group. The encounter group study of Lieberman, Yalom, and Miles indicated that some of the participants who changed the most seemed to have a particular ability to maximize their learning opportunities in a short-term group (thirty hours) *by engaging vicariously in the group experience of other members.*[6]

In general, though, the evidence indicates that the more active and influential a member is in the group matrix, the more likely he or she is to benefit. Research in experiential groups demonstrates that regardless of what the participants said, *the more words they spoke, the greater the positive change in their picture of themselves.*[7] Other research demonstrates that vicarious experience, as contrasted with direct participation, was ineffective in producing either significant change, emotional engagement, or attraction to the group process.[8]

Moreover, there is much clinical consensus that in long-term therapy, silent members do not profit from the group. Group members who self-disclose very slowly may never catch up to the rest of the group and at best achieve only minimal gains.[9] The greater the verbal participation, the greater the sense of involvement and the more clients are valued by others and ultimately by themselves. Self-disclosure is not only essential to the development of group cohesion, it is directly correlated to positive therapeutic outcome, as is the client's "work" in therapy. I would suggest, then, that we not be lulled by the legendary story of the silent member who got well. *A silent client is a problem client and rarely benefits significantly from the group.*†

Clients may be silent for many reasons. Some may experience a pervasive dread of self-disclosure: every utterance, they feel, may commit them to progressively more disclosure. Others may feel so conflicted about aggression that they cannot undertake the self-assertion inherent in speaking. Some are waiting to be activated and brought to life by an idealized caregiver, not yet having abandoned the childhood wish for magical rescue. Others who demand nothing short of perfection in themselves never speak for fear of falling shamefully short, whereas others attempt to maintain distance or control through a lofty, superior silence. Some clients are especially threatened by a particular member in the group and habitually speak only in the absence of that member. Others participate only in smaller meetings or in alternate (leaderless) meetings. Some are silent for fear of being regarded as weak, insipid, or mawkish. Others may silently sulk to punish others or to force the group to attend to them.[10]

Here too, group dynamics may play a role. Group anxiety about potential aggression or about the availability of emotional supplies in the group may push a vulnerable member into silence to reduce the tension or competition for attention. Distinguishing between a transient "state" of silence or a more enduring "trait" of silence is therefore quite useful.

The important point, though, is that *silence is never silent*; it is behavior and, like all other behavior in the group, has meaning in the here-and-now as a representative sample of the client's way of relating to his or her interpersonal world. The therapeutic task, therefore, is not only to change the behavior (that is essential if the client is to remain in the group) but to explore the meaning of the behavior.

Proper management depends in part on the therapist's understanding of the dynamics of the silence. A middle course must be steered between placing undue pressure on the client and allowing the client to slide into an extreme isolate role. The therapist may periodically include the silent client by commenting on nonverbal behavior: that is, when, by gesture or demeanor, the client is evincing interest, tension, sadness, boredom, or amusement. Not infrequently a silent member introduced into an ongoing group will feel awed by the clarity, directness, and insight of more experienced members. It is often helpful for the therapist to point out that many of these admired veteran group members also struggled with silence and self-doubt when they began. Often the therapist may hasten the member's participation by encouraging other members to reflect on their own proclivities for silence.[11] Even if repeated prodding or cajoling is necessary, the therapist should encourage client autonomy and responsibility by repeated process checks. "Is this a meeting when you want to be prodded?" "How did it feel when Mike put you on the spot?" "Did he go too far?" "Can you let us know when we make you uncomfortable?" "What's the ideal question we could ask you today to help you come into the group?" The therapist should seize every opportunity to reinforce the client's activity and underscore the value of pushing against his fears (pointing out, for example, the feelings of relief and accomplishment that follow his risk-taking.)[12]

If a client resists all these efforts and maintains a very limited participation even after three months of meetings, my experience has been that the prognosis is poor. The group will grow frustrated and tire of coaxing and encouraging the silent, blocked member. In the face of the group's disapprobation, the client becomes more marginalized and less likely than ever to participate. Concurrent individual sessions may be useful in helping the client at this time. If this fails, the therapist may need to consider withdrawing the client from the group. Occasionally, entering a second therapy group later may prove profitable, since the client is now well-informed of the hazards of silence.

THE BORING CLIENT

Rarely does anyone seek therapy because of being boring. Yet, in a different garb, thinly disguised, the complaint is not uncommon. Clients complain that they never have anything to say to others; that they are left standing alone at parties; that no one ever invites them out more than once; that others use them only for sex; that they are inhibited, shy, socially awkward, empty, or bland. Like silence, monopolization, or selfishness, boredom is to be taken seriously. It is an extremely important problem, whether the client explicitly identifies it as such or not.

In the social microcosm of the therapy group, boring members re-create these problems and bore the members of the group—and the therapist. The therapist dreads a small meeting in which only two or three boring members are present. If they were to terminate, they would simply glide out of the group, leaving nary a ripple in the pond.

Boredom is a highly individual experience. Not everyone is bored by the same situation, and it is not easy to make generalizations. In general, though, the boring client in the therapy group is one who is massively inhibited, who lacks spontaneity, who never takes risks. Boring patients' utterances are always "safe" (and, alas, always predictable). Obsequious and carefully avoiding any sign of aggressivity, they are often masochistic (rushing into self-flagellation before anyone else can pummel them—or, to use another metaphor, catching any spears hurled at them in midair and then stabbing themselves with them). They say what they believe the social press requires—that is, before speaking, they scan the faces of the other members to determine what is expected of them to say and squelch any contrary sentiment coming from within. The particular social style of the individual varies considerably: one may be silent; another stilted and hyperrational; another timid and self-effacing; still another dependent, demanding, or pleading.

Some boring clients are alexithymic—an expressive difficulty stemming not only from neurotic inhibition but from cognitive deficits in the ability to identify and communicate feelings. The alexithymic client is concrete, lacks imaginative capacity, and focuses on operational details, not emotional experience.[13] Individual therapy with such clients can be excruciatingly slow and arid, similar to work with clients with schizoid personality disorder. Group therapy alone, or concurrent with individual therapy, may be particularly helpful in promoting emotional expressiveness through modeling, support, and the opportunity to experiment with feelings and expressiveness.[14]

The inability to read their own emotional cues also may make these individuals vulnerable to medical and psychosomatic illness.[15] Group therapy, because of its ability to increase emotional awareness and expression, can reduce alexithymia and has been shown to improve medical outcomes, for example in heart disease.[16]

Group leaders and members often work hard to encourage spontaneity in boring clients. They ask such clients to share fantasies about members, to scream, to curse—anything to pry something unpredictable from them.

• *One of my clients, Nora, drove the group to despair with her constant clichés and self-deprecatory remarks. After many months in the group, her outside life began to change for the better, but each report of success was accompanied by the inevitable self-derogatory neutralizer. She was accepted by an honorary professional society ("That is good," she said, "because it is one club that can't kick me out"); she received her graduate degree ("but I should have finished earlier"); she had gotten all A's ("but I'm a child for bragging about it"); she looked better physically ("shows you what a good sunlamp can do"); she had been asked out by several new men in her life ("must be slim pickings in the market"); she obtained a good job ("it fell into my lap"); she had had her first vaginal orgasm ("give the credit to marijuana").*

The group tried to tune Nora in to her self-effacement. An engineer in the group suggested bringing an electric buzzer to ring each time she knocked herself. Another member, trying to shake Nora into a more spontaneous state, commented on her bra, which he felt could be improved. (This was Ed, discussed in chapter 2, who generally related only to the sexual parts of women.) He said he would bring her a present, a new bra, next session. Sure enough, the following session he arrived with a huge box, which Nora said she would prefer to open at home. So there it sat, looming in the group and, of course, inhibiting any other topic. Nora was asked at least to guess what it contained, and she ventured, "A pair of falsies."

She was finally prevailed upon to open the gift and did so laboriously and with enormous embarrassment. The box contained nothing but Styrofoam stuffing. Ed explained that this was his idea for Nora's new bra: that she should wear no bra at all. Nora promptly apologized to Ed (for guessing he had given her falsies) and thanked him for the trouble he had taken. The incident launched much work for both members. (I shall not here discuss the sequel for Ed.) The group told Nora that, though Ed had humiliated and embarrassed her, she had responded by apologizing to him. She had politely thanked someone who had just given her a gift of precisely nothing! The incident created the first robust spark of self-observation in Nora. She began the next meeting with: "I've just set the world ingratiation record. Last night I received an obscene phone call and I apologized to the man!" (She had said, "I'm sorry, you must have the wrong number.")

The underlying dynamics of the boring patient vary enormously from individual to individual. Many have a core dependent position and so dread rejection and abandonment that they are compulsively compliant, eschewing any aggressive remark that might initiate retaliation. They mistakenly confuse healthy self-assertion with aggression and by refusing to acknowledge their own vitality, desires, spontaneity, interests, and opinions, they bring to pass (by boring others) the very rejection and abandonment they had hoped to forestall.†[17]

If you, as the therapist, are bored with a client, that boredom is important data. (The therapy of all difficult clients necessitates thoughtful attention to your countertransference).[18]* Always assume that if you are bored by the member, so are others. You must counter your boredom with curiosity. Ask yourself: "What makes the person boring? When am I most and least bored? How can I find the person—the real, the lively, spontaneous, creative, person—within this boring shell?" No urgent "breakthrough" technique is indicated. Since the boring individual is tolerated by the group much better than the abrasive, narcissistic, or monopolistic client, you have much time.

Lastly, keep in mind that the therapist must take a Socratic posture with these clients. Our task is not to put something *into* the individual but quite the opposite, to let something out that was there all the time. Thus we do not attempt to *inspirit* boring clients, or inject color, spontaneity, or richness *into* them, but instead to identify their squelched creative, vital, childlike parts and to help remove the obstacles to their free expression.

THE HELP-REJECTING COMPLAINER

The help-rejecting complainer, a variant of the monopolist, was first identified and named by J. Frank in 1952.[19] Since then the behavior pattern has

---

*Therapist countertransference is always a source of valuable data about the client, never more so than with provocative clients whose behavior challenges our therapeutic effectiveness. Group leaders should determine their role in the joint construction of the problem client's difficulties. Any therapist reaction or behavior that deviates from one's baseline signals that interpersonal pulls are being generated. Therapists must take care to examine their feelings before responding. Together, these perspectives inform and balance the therapist's use of empathic processing, confrontation and feedback.

been recognized by many group clinicians, and the term appears frequently in the psychiatric literature, particularly in the psychotherapy and psychosomatic areas.[20] In this section, I discuss the rare fully developed help-rejecting complainer; however, this pattern of behavior is not a distinct, all-or-nothing clinical syndrome. Individuals may arrive at this style of interaction through various psychological pathways. Some may persistently manifest this behavior in an extreme degree with no external provocation, whereas others may demonstrate only a trace of this pattern. Still others may become help-rejecting complainers only at times of particular stress. Closely associated with help-rejecting complaining is the expression of emotional distress through somatic complaints. Clients with medically unexplainable symptoms constitute a large and frustrating primary care burden.[21]

Description

Help-rejecting complainers (or HRCs) show a distinctive behavioral pattern in the group: they implicitly or explicitly *request* help from the group by presenting problems or complaints and then *reject* any help offered. HRCs continually present problems in a manner that makes them to appear insurmountable. In fact, HRCs seems to take pride in the insolubility of their problems. Often HRCs focus wholly on the therapist in a tireless campaign to elicit intervention or advice and appear oblivious to the group's reaction to them. They seem willing to appear ludicrous so long as they are allowed to persist in the search for help. They base their relationship to the other members along the singular dimension of being more in need of aid. HRCs rarely show competitiveness in any area except when another member makes a bid for the therapist's or group's attention by presenting a problem. Then HRCs often attempt to belittle that person's complaints by comparing them unfavorably with their own. They often tend to exaggerate their problems and to blame others, often authority figures on whom they depend in some fashion. HRCs seem entirely self-centered, speaking only of themselves and their problems.

When the group and the therapist do respond to the HRC's plea, the entire bewildering, configuration takes form as the client rejects the help offered. The rejection is unmistakable, though it may assume many varied and subtle forms: sometimes the advice is rejected overtly, sometimes indirectly; sometimes while accepted verbally, it is never acted upon; if it is acted upon, it inevitably fails to improve the member's plight.

Effects on the Group

The effects on the group are obvious: the other members become irritated, frustrated, and confused. The HRC seems a greedy whirlpool, sucking the group's energy. Worse yet, no deceleration of the HRC's demands is evident. Faith in the group process suffers, as members experience a sense of impotence and despair of making their own needs appreciated by the group. Cohesiveness is undermined as absenteeism occurs or as clients subgroup in an effort to exclude the HRC.

Dynamics

The behavioral pattern of the HRC appears to be an attempt to resolve highly conflicted feelings about dependency. On the one hand, the HRC feels helpless, insignificant, and totally dependent on others, especially the therapist, for a sense of personal worth. Any notice and attention from the therapist temporarily enhance the HRC's self-esteem. On the other hand, the HRC's dependent position is vastly confounded by a pervasive distrust and enmity toward authority figures. Consumed with need, the HRC turns for help to a figure he or she anticipates will be unwilling or unable to help. The anticipation of refusal so colors the style of requesting help that the prophecy is fulfilled, and further evidence is accumulated for the belief in the malfeasance of the potential caregiver.[22] A vicious circle results, one that has been spinning for much of the client's life.

Guidelines for Management

A severe HRC is an exceedingly difficult clinical challenge, and many such clients have won a Pyrrhic victory over therapist and group by failing in therapy. It would thus be presumptuous and misleading to attempt to prescribe a careful therapeutic plan; however, certain generalizations may be posited. Surely it is a blunder for the therapist to confuse the help requested for the help required.†[23] The HRC solicits advice not for its potential value but in order to spurn it. Ultimately, the therapist's advice, guidance, and treatment will be rejected or, if used, will prove ineffective or, if effective, will be kept secret. It is also a blunder for the therapist to express any frustration and resentment. Retaliation merely completes the vicious circle: the clients' anticipation of ill treatment and abandonment is once again realized: They feel justified in their hostile mistrust and are able to affirm once again that no one can ever really understand them.

What course, then, is available to the therapist? One clinician suggests, perhaps in desperation, that the therapist interrupt the vicious circle by indicating that he or she "not only understands but shares the patient's feelings of hopelessness about the situation," thus refusing to perpetuate his or her part in a futile relationship. Two brave co-therapists who led a group composed only of help-rejecting complainers warn us against investing in a sympathetic, nurturing relationship with the client. They suggest that therapists sidestep any expression of optimism, encouragement, or advice and adopt instead a pose of irony in which they agree with the content of the client's pessimism while maintaining a detached affect. Eric Berne, who considers the HRC pattern to be the most common of all social and psychotherapy group games, labeled it "Why don't you—yes but." The use of such easily accessible descriptive labels often makes the process more transparent to the group members, but great caution must be exercised when using any bantering approach: there is a fine line separating therapeutic playful caring from mockery and humiliation.[24]

In general, the therapist should attempt to mobilize the major therapeutic factors in the service of the client. When a cohesive group has been formed and the client—through universality, identification, and catharsis—has come to value membership in the group, then the therapist can encourage interpersonal learning by continually focusing on feedback and process in much the same manner as I have described in discussing the monopolistic client. HRCs are generally not aware of their lack of empathy to others. Helping them see their interpersonal impact on the other members is a key step in their coming to examine their characteristic pattern of relationships.

THE PSYCHOTIC OR BIPOLAR CLIENT

Many groups are designed specifically to work with clients with significant Axis I disturbance. In fact, when one considers groups on psychiatric wards, partial hospitalization units, veterans' hospitals, and aftercare programs, the total number of therapy groups for severely impaired clients likely outnumbers those for higher-functioning clients. I will discuss groups composed for hospitalized clients in chapter 15 (for more on this topic, see my text *Inpatient Group Psychotherapy*, Basic Books, 1983) but for now consider the issue of what happens to the course of an interactive therapy group of higher-functioning individuals when one member develops a psychotic illness during treatment.

The fate of the psychotic client, the response of the other members, and the effective options available to the therapist all depend in part on *timing*, that is, *when in the course of the group the psychotic illness occurs*. In general, in a mature group in which the psychotic client has long occupied a central, valued role, the group members are more likely to be tolerant and effective during the crisis.

The Early Phases of a Group
In chapter 8, I emphasized that in the initial screening, the grossly psychotic client should be excluded from ambulatory interactional group therapy. However, it is common practice to refer clients with apparently stable bipolar disease to group therapy to address the interpersonal consequences of their illness.

At times, despite cautious screening, an individual decompensates in the early stages of therapy, perhaps because of unanticipated stress from life circumstances, or from the group, or perhaps because of poor adherence to a medication regimen. This is a major event for the group and always creates substantial problems for the newly formed group (and, of course, for the client, who is likely to slide into a deviant role in the group and eventually terminate treatment, often much the worse for the experience).

In this book I have repeatedly stressed that the early stages of the group are a time of great flux and great importance. The young group is easily influenced, and norms that are established early are often exceedingly durable. An intense sequence of events unfolds as, in a few weeks, an aggregate of frightened, distrustful strangers evolves into an intimate, mutually helpful group. Any event that consumes an inordinate amount of time early on and diverts energy from the tasks of the developmental sequence is potentially destructive to the group. Some of the relevant problems are illustrated by the following clinical example.

• *Sandy was a thirty-seven-year-old housewife who had once, many years before, suffered a major and recalcitrant depression requiring hospitalization and electroconvulsive therapy. She sought group therapy at the insistence of her individual therapist, who thought that an understanding of her interpersonal relationships would help her to improve her relationship with her husband. In the early meetings of the group, she was an active member who tended to reveal far more intimate details of her history than did the other members. Occasionally, Sandy expressed anger toward another member and then engaged in excessively profuse apologies coupled with self-deprecatory remarks. By the sixth meeting, her behavior became still more inappropriate. She discoursed at great length on her son's urinary problems, for example, describing in intricate detail the surgery that had been performed to relieve his urethral stricture. At the following meeting, she noted that the family cat had also developed a blockage of the urinary tract; she then urged the other members to describe their pets.*

In the eighth meeting, Sandy became increasingly manic. She behaved in a bizarre, irrational manner, insulted members of the group, openly flirted with the male members to the point of stroking their bodies, and finally lapsed into punning, clang associations, inappropriate laughter, and tears. One of the therapists finally escorted her from the room, phoned her husband, and arranged for immediate psychiatric hospitalization. Sandy remained in the hospital in a manic, psychotic state for a month and then gradually recovered.

The members were obviously extremely uncomfortable during the meeting, their feelings ranging from bafflement and fright to annoyance. After Sandy left, some expressed their guilt for having, in some unknown manner, triggered her behavior. Others spoke of their fear, and one recalled someone he knew who had acted in a similar fashion but had also brandished a gun.

During the subsequent meeting, the members discussed many feelings related to the incident. One member expressed his conviction that no one could be trusted: even though he had known Sandy for seven weeks, her behavior proved to be totally unpredictable. Others expressed their relief that they were, in comparison, psychologically healthy; others, in response to their fears of similarly losing control, employed considerable denial and veered away from discussing these problems. Some expressed a fear of Sandy's returning and making a shambles of the group. Others expressed their diminished faith in group therapy; one member asked for hypnosis, and another brought to the meeting an article from a scientific journal claiming that psychotherapy was ineffective. A loss of faith in the therapists and their competence was expressed in the dream of one member, in which the therapist was in the hospital and was rescued by the client.

In the next few meetings, all these themes went underground. The meetings became listless, shallow, and intellectualized. Attendance dwindled, and the group seemed resigned to its own impotence. At the fourteenth meeting, the therapists announced that Sandy was improved and would return the following week. A vigorous, heated discussion ensued. The members feared that:

1. They would upset her. An intense meeting would make her ill again and, to avoid that, the group would be forced to move slowly and superficially.
2. Sandy would be unpredictable. At any point she might lose control and display dangerous, frightening behavior.
3. Sandy would, because of her lack of control, be untrustworthy. Nothing in the group would remain confidential.

At the same time, the members expressed considerable anxiety and guilt for wishing to exclude Sandy from the group, and soon tension and a heavy silence prevailed. The extreme reaction of the group persuaded the therapist to delay reintroducing Sandy (who was, incidentally, in concurrent individual therapy) for a few weeks.

When she finally reentered the group, she was treated as a fragile object, and the entire group interaction was guarded and defensive. By the *twentieth meeting, five of the seven members had dropped out of the group, leaving only Sandy and one other member.*

The therapists reconstituted the group by adding five new members. It is of interest that, despite the fact that only two of the old members and the therapists continued in the reconstituted group, the old group culture persisted—a powerful example of the staying power of norms even in the presence of a limited number of culture bearers.[25] The group dynamics had locked the group and Sandy into severely restricted roles and functions. Sandy was treated so delicately and obliquely by the new members that the group moved slowly, floundering in its own politeness and social conventionality. Only when the therapists openly confronted this issue and discussed in the group their own fears of upsetting Sandy and thrusting her into another psychological decompensation were the members able to deal with their feelings and fears about her. At that point, the group moved ahead more quickly. Sandy remained in the new group for a year and made decided improvements in her ability to relate with others and in her self-concept.

Later in the Course of a Group

An entirely different situation may arise when an individual who has been an involved, active group member for many months decompensates into a psychotic state. Other members are then primarily concerned for that member rather than for themselves or for the group. Since they have previously known and understood the now-psychotic member as a person, they often react with great concern and interest; the client is less likely to be viewed as a strange and frightening object to be avoided.[26]*

Although perceiving similar trends in themselves may enhance the other members' ability to continue relating to a distressed group member, it also creates a personal upheaval in some, who begin to fear that they, too, can lose control and slide into a similar abyss. Hence, the therapist does well to anticipate and express this fear to the others in the group.

When faced with a psychotic client in a group, many therapists revert to a medical model and symbolically dismiss the group by intervening forcefully in a one-to-one fashion. In effect, they say to the group, "This is too serious a problem for you to handle." Such a maneuver, however, is often antitherapeutic: the client is frightened and the group infantilized.

---

*Moos and I demonstrated, for example, that medical students assigned for the first time to a psychiatric ward regarded the psychotic patients as extremely dangerous, frightening, unpredictable, and dissimilar to themselves. At the end of the five-week assignment, their attitudes had undergone considerable change: the students were less frightened of their patients and realized that psychotic individuals were just confused, deeply anguished human beings, more like themselves than they had previously thought.

It has been my experience that a mature group is perfectly able to deal with the psychiatric emergency and, although there may be false starts, to consider every contingency and take every action that the therapist might have considered. Consider the following clinical example.

• *In the forty-fifth meeting, Rhoda, a forty-three-year-old divorced woman, arrived a few minutes late in a disheveled, obviously disturbed state. Over the previous few weeks, she had gradually been sliding into a depression, but now the process had suddenly accelerated. She was tearful, despondent, and exhibited psychomotor retardation. During the early part of the meeting, she wept continuously and expressed feelings of great loneliness and hopelessness as well as an inability to love, hate, or, for that matter, have any deeply felt emotion. She described her feeling of great detachment from everyone, including the group, and, when prompted, discussed suicidal ruminations.*

The group members responded to Rhoda with great empathy and concern. They inquired about events during the past week and helped her discuss two important occurrences that seemed related to the depressive crisis: (1) for months she had been saving money for a summer trip to Europe; during the past week, her seventeen-year-old son had decided to decline a summer camp job and refused to search for other jobs—a turn of events that, in Rhoda's eyes, jeopardized her trip; (2) she had, after months of hesitation, decided to attend a dance for divorced middle-aged people, which proved to be a disaster: no one had asked her to dance, and she had ended the evening consumed with feelings of total worthlessness.

The group helped her explore her relationship with her son, and for the first time, she expressed rage at him for his lack of concern for her. With the group's assistance, she attempted to explore and express the limits of her responsibility toward him. It was difficult for Rhoda to discuss the dance because of the amount of shame and humiliation she felt. Two other women in the group, one single and one divorced, empathized deeply with her and shared their experiences and reactions to the scarcity of suitable males. Rhoda was also reminded by the group of the many times she had, during sessions, interpreted every minor slight as a total rejection and condemnation of herself. Finally, after much attention, care, and warmth had been offered her, one of the members pointed out to Rhoda that the experience of the dance was being disconfirmed right in the group: several people who knew her well were deeply concerned and involved with her. Rhoda rejected this idea by claiming that the group, unlike the dance, was an artificial situation in which people followed unnatural rules of conduct. The members quickly pointed out that quite the contrary was true: the dance—the contrived congregation of

*strangers, the attractions based on split-second, skin-deep impressions—
was the artificial situation and the group was the real one. It was in the
group that she was more completely known.*

*Rhoda, suffused with feelings of worthlessness, then berated herself
for her inability to feel reciprocal warmth and involvement with the
group members. One of the members quickly intercepted this maneuver by pointing out that Rhoda had a familiar and repetitive pattern of
experiencing feelings toward the other members, evidenced by her facial expression and body posture, but then letting her "shoulds" take
over and torture her by insisting that she should feel more warmth and
more love than anyone else. The net effect was that the real feeling she
did have was rapidly extinguished by the winds of her impossible self-
demands.*

*In essence, what then transpired was Rhoda's gradual recognition of
the discrepancy between her public and private esteem (described in
chapter 3). At the end of the meeting, Rhoda responded by bursting
into tears and crying for several minutes. The group was reluctant to
leave but did so when the members had all convinced themselves that
suicide was no longer a serious consideration. Throughout the next
week, the members maintained an informal vigil, each phoning Rhoda
at least once.*

A number of important and far-reaching principles emerge from this illustration. Rather early in the session, the therapist realized the important
dynamics operating in Rhoda's depression and, had he chosen, might
have made the appropriate interpretations to allow the client and the
group to arrive much more quickly at a cognitive understanding of the
problem—but that would have detracted considerably from the meaningfulness and value of the meeting to both the protagonist and the other
members. For one thing, the group would have been deprived of an opportunity to experience its own potency; every success adds to the group's
cohesiveness and enhances the self-regard of each of the members. It is
difficult for some therapists to refrain from interpretation, and yet it is essential to learn to sit on your wisdom. There are times when it is foolish
to be wise and wise to be silent.

At times, as in this clinical episode, the group chooses and performs the
appropriate action; at other times, the group may decide that the therapist
must act. But there is a vast difference between a group's hasty decision
stemming from infantile dependence and unrealistic appraisal of the therapist's powers and a decision based on the members' thorough investigation of the situation and mature appraisal of the therapist's expertise.

These points lead me to an important principle of group dynamics,
one substantiated by considerable research. *A group that reaches an au-*

tonomous *decision based on a thorough exploration of the pertinent problems will employ all of its resources in support of its decision; a group that has a decision thrust upon it is likely to resist that decision and be even less effective in making valid decisions in the future.*

Let me take a slight but relevant tangent here and tell you a story about a well-known study in group dynamics. The focus of this illustration is a pajama-producing factory in which periodic changes in jobs and routine were necessitated by advances in technology. For many years, the employees resisted these changes; with each change, there was an increase in absenteeism, turnover, and aggression toward the management as well as decreased efficiency and output.

Researchers designed an experiment to test various methods of overcoming the employees' resistance to change. The critical variable to be studied was the degree of participation of the group members (the employees) in planning the change. The employees were divided into three groups, and three variations were tested. The first variation involved no participation by the employees in planning the changes, although they were given an explanation. The second variation involved participation through elected representation of the workers in designing the changes to be made in the job. The third variation consisted of total participation by all the members of the group in designing the changes. The results showed conclusively that, *on all measures studied (aggression toward management, absenteeism, efficiency, number of employees resigning from the job), the success of the change was directly proportional to the degree of participation of the group members.*[27]

The implications for group therapy are apparent: members who personally participate in planning a course of action will be more committed to the enactment of the plan. They will, for example, invest themselves more fully in the care of a disturbed member if they recognize that it is their problem and not the therapist's alone.

At times, as in the previous clinical example, the entire experience is beneficial to the development of group cohesiveness. Sharing intense emotional experiences usually strengthens ties among members. The danger to the group occurs when the psychotic client consumes a massive amount of energy for a prolonged period. Then other members may drop out, and the group may deal with the disturbed individual in a cautious, concealed manner or attempt to ignore him or her. These methods never fail to aggravate the problem. In such critical situations, one important option always available to the therapist is to see the disturbed client in individual sessions for the duration of the crisis (this option will be dealt with more fully in the discussion of combined therapy). Here too, however, the group should thoroughly explore the implications and share in the decision.

One of the worst calamities that can befall a therapy group is the presence of a manic member. A client in the midst of a severe hypomanic episode is perhaps the single most disruptive problem for a group. (In contrast, a full-blown manic episode presents little problem, since the immediate course of action is clear: hospitalization.)

The client with acute, poorly contained bipolar affective disorder is best managed pharmacologically and is not a good candidate for interactionally oriented treatment. It is obviously unwise to allow the group to invest much energy and time in treatment that has such little likelihood of success. There is mounting evidence, however, for the use of specific, homogeneous group interventions for clients with bipolar illness. These groups offer psychoeducation about the illness and stress the importance of pharmacotherapy adherence and maintenance of healthy lifestyle and self-regulation routines. These groups are best employed in conjunction with pharmacotherapy in the maintenance phase of this chronic illness, after any acute disturbances have settled. Substantial benefits from therapy have been demonstrated, including improved pharmacotherapy adherence; reduced mood disturbance; fewer illness relapses; less substance abuse; and improved psychosocial functioning.[28]

THE CHARACTEROLOGICALLY DIFFICULT CLIENT

The final three types of problem clients in group therapy I shall discuss are the schizoid client, the borderline client, and the narcissistic client. These clients are often discussed together in the clinical literature under the rubric of characterologically difficult or Axis II clients.[29] Traditional DSM diagnostic criteria do not do justice to the complexity of these clients and fail to capture adequately their inner psychological experience.[30]

Most characterologically difficult clients have in common problems in regulation of affect, in interpersonal engagement, and in sense of self. Their pathology is thought to be based on serious problems in the first few years of life. They lack internal soothing or comforting parental representations, and instead their internal world is peopled by abandoning, withholding, and disappointing parental representations. They often lack the ability to integrate ambivalent feelings and interpersonal reactions, splitting the world into black and white, good and bad, loving and hating, idealizing and devaluing. At any moment they have little recall of feelings other than the powerful ones felt at that moment. Prominent difficulties include rage, vulnerability to abandonment and to narcissistic injury, and a tendency toward projective identification. Such clients also often lack a sense of their role in their difficulties or of their impact on others.[31]

Because these difficulties generally manifest in troubled and troubling interpersonal relationships, group therapy has a prominent role in both ambulatory and partial hospitalization settings. Group therapy is promising but challenging with these clients, but the psychological and health care cost-benefit ratios are very encouraging, particularly when adequate time in treatment is provided.[32]

Often the characterologically difficult client has experienced traumatic abuse early in life as well, which further amplifies the challenge in treatment. In some samples the comorbidity of posttraumatic stress disorder (PTSD) and borderline personality disorder exceeds 50 percent. When the traumatic experiences and consequent symptoms—chiefly intrusive reexperiencing of the trauma, avoidance of any reminder of the trauma, and general hyperarousal—have a profound combined impact on the individual, the term "complex PTSD" is often applied. This term captures the way in which the traumatic events and psychological reactions to these events shape the individual's personality.[33]

Characterologically difficult clients are prevalent in most clinical settings. They are often referred to groups by an individual therapist when (1) the transference has grown too intense for dyadic therapy; (2) the client has become so defensively isolated that group interaction is required to engage the client; (3) therapy has proceeded well but a plateau has been reached and interactive experience is necessary to produce further gains.

The Schizoid Client

Many years ago, in a previous edition of this book, I began this section with the following sentence: "The schizoid condition, the malady of our times, perhaps accounts for more patients entering therapy than does any other psychopathological configuration." This no longer rings true. The fashions of mental illness change: Today, clients more commonly enter treatment because of substance abuse, eating disorders, and sequelae of sexual and physical abuse. Even though the schizoid condition is no longer the malady of our times, schizoid individuals are still common visitors to therapy groups. They are emotionally blocked, isolated, and distant and often seek group therapy out of a vague sense that something is missing: they cannot feel, cannot love, cannot play, cannot cry. They are spectators of themselves; they do not inhabit their own bodies; they do not experience their own experience. Superficially, the schizoid client and the avoidant client resemble each other. There are, however, clear differences. The avoidant individual is anxiously inhibited, self-aware, and able to engage when sufficiently reassured that rejection will not ensue. In contrast, the schizoid client suffers a deficit in key emotional and reflective capacities.[34]

No one has described the experiential world of the schizoid individual more vividly than Sartre in *The Age of Reason*:

He closed the paper and began to read the special correspondent's dispatch on the front page. Fifty dead and three hundred wounded had already been counted, but that was not the total, there were certainly corpses under the debris. There were thousands of men in France who had not been able to read their paper that morning without feeling a clot of anger rise in their throat, thousands of men who had clenched their fists and muttered: "Swine!" Mathieu clenched his fists and muttered: "Swine!" and felt himself still more guilty. If at least he had been able to discover in himself a trifling emotion that was veritably if modestly alive, conscious of its limits. But no: he was empty, he was confronted by a vast anger, a desperate anger, he saw it and could almost have touched it. But it was inert—if it were to live and find expression and suffer, he must lend it his own body. It was other people's anger. Swine! He clenched his fists, he strode along, but nothing came, the anger remained external to himself. Something was on the threshold of existence, a timorous dawn of anger. At last! But it dwindled and collapsed, he was left in solitude, walking with the measured and decorous gait of a man in a funeral procession in Paris. He wiped his forehead with his handkerchief and he thought: One can't force one's deeper feelings. Yonder was a terrible and tragic state of affairs that ought to arouse one's deepest emotions. It's no use, the moment will not come.[35]

Schizoid individuals are often in a similar predicament in the therapy group. In virtually every group meeting, they have confirmatory evidence that the nature and intensity of their emotional experience differs considerably from that of the other members. Puzzled at this discrepancy, they may conclude that the other members are melodramatic, excessively labile, phony, overly concerned with trivia, or simply of a different temperament. Eventually, however, schizoid clients, like Sartre's protagonist, Mathieu, begin to wonder about themselves, and begin to suspect that somewhere inside themselves is a vast frozen lake of feeling.

In one way or another, by what they say or do not say, schizoid clients convey this emotional isolation to the other members. In chapter 2, I described a male client who could not understand the members' concern about the therapist's leaving the group or a member's obsessive fears about her boyfriend being killed. He saw people as interchangeable. He had his need for a minimum daily requirement of affection (without, it seemed, proper concern about the source of the affection). He was "bugged" by the departure of the therapist only because it would slow down his therapy, but he did not share the feeling expressed by the others: grief at the loss of the person who is the therapist. In his defense, he maintained, "There's not much sense in having any strong feelings about the therapist leaving, since there's nothing I can do about it."

Another member, chided by the group because of his lack of empathy toward two highly distressed members, responded, "So, they're hurting. There are millions of people hurting all over the world at this instant. If I let myself feel bad for everyone who is hurting, it would be a full-time occupation." Most of us get a rush of feelings and then we sometimes try to comprehend the meaning of the feelings. In schizoid clients, feelings come later—they are awarded priority according to the dictates of rationality. Feeling must be justified pragmatically: if they serve no purpose, why have them?

The group is often keenly aware of discrepancies among a member's words, experience, and emotional response. One member, who had been criticized for withholding information from the group about his relationship with a girlfriend, frostily asked, "Would you like to bring your camera and climb into bed with us?" When questioned, however, he denied feeling any anger and could not account for the tone of sarcasm.

At other times, the group reads the schizoid member's emotions from postural or behavioral cues. Indeed, such individuals may relate to themselves in a similar way and join in the investigation, commenting, for example, "My heart is beating fast, so I must be frightened," or "My fist is clenched, so I must be mad." In this regard they share a common difficulty with the alexithymic clients described earlier.

The response of the other members is predictable; it proceeds from curiosity and puzzlement through disbelief, solicitude, irritation, and frustration. They will repeatedly inquire, "What do you feel about . . . ?" and only much later come to realize that they were demanding that this member quickly learn to speak a foreign language. At first, members become very active in helping to resolve what appears to be a minor affliction, telling schizoid clients what to feel and what *they* would feel if they were in that situation. Eventually, the group members grow weary; frustration sets in; and then they redouble their efforts—almost always with no noticeable results. They try harder yet, in an attempt to force an affective response by increasing the intensity of the stimulus. Ultimately, they resort to a sledgehammer approach.

The therapist must avoid joining in the quest for a breakthrough. I have never seen a schizoid client significantly change by virtue of a dramatic incident; change is a prosaic process of grinding labor, repetitive small steps, and almost imperceptible progress. It is tempting and often useful to employ some activating, nonverbal, or gestalt techniques to hasten a client's movement. These approaches may speed up the client's recognition and expression of nascent or repressed feelings, but keep in mind that if you do excessive, one-to-one directive work, the group may become less potent, less autonomous, and more dependent and leader centered. (I will discuss these issues at length in chapter 14.) Furthermore, schizoid clients not only need new skills but, more important, they need a new internalized experience of the world of relationships—and that takes time, patience, and perseverance.

In chapter 6, I described several here-and-now activating techniques that are useful in work with the schizoid client. Work energetically in the here-and-now. Encourage the client to differentiate among members; despite protestations, the client does not feel *precisely* the same way toward everyone in the group. Help such members move into feelings they pass off as inconsequential. When the client admits, "Well, I may feel slightly irritated or slightly hurt," suggest staying with these feelings; no one ever said it was necessary to discuss only big feelings. "Hold up a magnifying glass to the hurt," you might suggest; "describe exactly what it is like." Invite the client to imagine what others in the group are feeling. Try to cut off the client's customary methods of dismissal: "Somehow, you've gotten away from something that seemed important. Can we go back to where we were five minutes ago? When you were talking to Julie, I thought you looked near tears. Something was going on inside."†

Encourage the client to observe his or her body. Often the client may not experience affect but will be aware of the affective autonomic equivalents: tightness in the stomach, sweating, throat constriction, flushing, and so on. Gradually the group may help the client translate those feelings into their psychological meaning. The members may, for example, note the timing of the client's reactions in conjunction with some event in the group.

Therapists must beware of assessing events solely according to their own experiential world. As I have discussed previously, clients may experience the same event in totally different ways: An event that is seemingly trivial to the therapist or to one member may be an exceedingly important experience to another member. A slight show of irritation by a restricted schizoid individual may be a major breakthrough for that person. It may be the first time in adulthood that he or she has expressed anger and may enable further testing out of new behavior, both in and out of the group.

In the group, these individuals are high risk and high reward. Those who can manage to persevere, to continue in the group and not be discouraged by the inability to change their relationship style quickly, are almost certain to profit considerably from the group therapy experience.

The Borderline Client

For decades, psychotherapists have known about a large cluster of individuals who are unusually difficult to treat and who fall between the major diagnostic criteria of severity of impairment: more disorganized than neurotic clients but more integrated than psychotic clients. A thin veneer of integration conceals a primitive personality structure. Under stress, these borderline clients are highly unstable; some develop psychoses that may resemble schizophrenic psychosis but are circumscribed, short-lived, and episodic.

DSM-IV-TR states that borderline personality disorder is a pervasive pattern of instability of interpersonal relationships, self-image, affects, and control over impulses requiring at least five of these nine features: frantic efforts to avoid real or imagined abandonment; unstable and intense interpersonal relationships characterized by alternation between extremes of idealization and devaluation; identity disturbance—persistent and markedly disturbed, distorted, or unstable self-image or sense of self; impulsiveness in two self-damaging areas, such as substance abuse, spending, sex, binge eating, and reckless driving; recurrent suicidal threats or behavior, or self-mutilation; affective instability due to a marked reactivity of mood; chronic feelings of emptiness; inappropriate intense anger or lack of control of anger; transient, stress-related paranoid ideation or severe dissociative symptoms.[36]

In recent years, a great deal more clarity about clients with borderline personality disorder has emerged, thanks especially to the work of Otto Kernberg, who emphasized the overriding instability of the borderline client—instability of mood, thought, and interpersonal involvement.[37] Yet the category still lacks precision, has unsatisfactory reliability,[38] and often serves as a catchall for a personality disorder that clinicians cannot otherwise diagnose. It will, in all likelihood, undergo further transformation in future classificatory systems.

Although there is considerable debate about the psychodynamics and the developmental origins of the borderline personality disturbance,[39] this debate is tangential to group therapy practice and need not be discussed here. What is important for the group therapist, as I have stressed throughout this book, is not the elusive and unanswerable question—how one *got to be the way one is*—but rather the nature of the current forces, both conscious and unconscious, that influence the way the characterologically difficult client relates to others.

Not only has there been a recent explosion of interest in the diagnosis, the psychodynamics, and the individual therapy of the borderline client, but also much group therapy literature has focused on the borderline personality disturbance. Group therapists have developed an interest in these clients for two major reasons. First, because borderline personality disorder is difficult to diagnose in a single screening session, many clinicians unintentionally introduce borderline clients into therapy groups consisting of clients functioning at a higher level of integration. Second, there is growing evidence that group therapy is an effective form of treatment. Some of the most impressive research results emerge from homogeneous and intensive partial hospitalization programs in which therapy groups offer the borderline individual containment, emotional support, and interpersonal learning while demanding personal accountability in an environment that counters regression and unhealthy intensification of transference reactions. Significant and enduring improvements in mood, psychosocial stability, and self-harm behavior have been reported.[40]

The majority of borderline clients, however, are likely to be treated in heterogeneous ambulatory groups. There is mounting consensus that combined or concurrent individual and group treatment may be the treatment of choice for the borderline client. Some experts have arrived at the conclusion that the preferred treatment is combined treatment with two group meetings and one individual meeting weekly. Furthermore, research evidence indicates that borderline clients highly value their group therapy experience—often more than their individual therapy experience.[41]

Keep in mind that the client's pathology places great demands on the treating therapist, who may at times be frustrated by the inability to make secure gains in therapy and may at other times experience strong wishes to rescue these clients, even to modify the traditional procedures and boundaries of the therapeutic situation. Keep in mind also that many therapists suggest group therapy for borderline clients *not because these clients work well or easily in therapy groups but because they are extraordinarily difficult to treat in individual therapy.*

Often, individual therapists find that the borderline client cannot easily tolerate the intensity and intimacy of the one-to-one treatment setting. Crippling transference and countertransference problems regularly emerge in therapy. Therapists often find it difficult to deal with the demands and the primitive anger of the borderline client, particularly since the client so often acts them out (for example, through absence, lateness, drug abuse, or self-mutilation). Massive regression often occurs, and many clients are so threatened by the emergence of painful, primitive affects that they flee therapeutic engagement or cause the therapist to reject them. Though the evidence suggests that group therapy may be quite effective for these clients, their primitive affects and highly distorted perceptual tendencies vastly influence the course of group therapy and severely tax the resources of the group. The duration of therapy is long: There is considerable clinical consensus that borderline clients require many years of therapy and will generally stay in a group longer than any of the other members.

Separation anxiety and the fear of abandonment play a crucial role in the dynamics of the borderline client. A threatened separation (the therapist's vacation, for example—and sometimes even the end of a session) characteristically evokes severe anxiety and triggers the characteristic defenses of this syndrome: splitting, projective identification, devaluation, and flight.

The therapy group may assuage separation anxiety in two ways. First, one or (preferably) two group therapists are introduced into the client's life, thus shielding the client from the great dysphoria occurring when the individual therapist is unavailable. Second, the group itself becomes a stable entity in the client's life, one that exists even when some of its members are absent. Repeated loss (that is, the termination of members) within the secure continued existence of the group helps clients come to terms with their extreme sensitivity to loss. The therapy group offers a singular opportunity to mourn the loss of an important relationship in the comforting presence of others who are simultaneously dealing with the same loss. Real relationships can offset the intense hunger the borderline client feels, but in a more mutual, less intense fashion.[42] Once the borderline client develops trust in the group, he or she may serve as a major stabilizing influence. Because borderline clients' separation anxiety is so great and they are so anxious to preserve the continued presence of important figures in their environment, they help keep the group together, often becoming the most faithful attendees and chiding other members for being absent or tardy.

One of the major advantages a therapy group may have for the treatment of a borderline client is the powerful reality testing provided by the ongoing stream of feedback and observations from the members. Thus, regression is far less pronounced. The client may distort, act out, or express primitive, chaotic needs and fears, but the continuous reminders of reality in the therapy group keep these feelings muted.

• *Marge, forty-two, was referred to the group by her individual therapist, who had been unable to make headway with her. Marge's feelings toward her therapist alternated between great rage at him and hunger for him. The intensity of these feelings was so great that no work could be done on them and the therapist was on the verge of discontinuing therapy. Placing her in a therapy group was his last resort.*

Upon entry into the group, Marge refused to talk for several meetings because she wanted to determine how the group ran. After four meetings in silence, she suddenly unleashed a ferocious attack on one of the group co-leaders, labeling him as cold, powerful, and rejecting. She offered no reasons or data for her comments aside from her gut feeling about him. Furthermore, she expressed contempt for those members of the group who felt affection for this co-therapist.

Her feelings for the other leader were quite the opposite: she experienced him as soft, warm, and caring. Other members were startled by her black-and-white view of the co-therapists and urged her, unsuccessfully, to work on her great propensity for judgment and anger. Her positive attachment to the one leader contained her sufficiently to permit her to continue in the group and allowed her to tolerate the intense hostile feeling toward the other leader and to work on other issues in the group— though she continued to snipe intermittently at the hated leader.

A notable change occurred with the "bad" therapist's vacation. When Marge expressed a fantasy of wanting to kill him, or at least to see him suffer, members expressed astonishment at the degree of her rage. Perhaps, one member suggested, she hated him so much because she badly wanted to be closer to him and was convinced it would never happen. This feedback had a dramatic impact on Marge. It touched not only on her feelings about the therapist but also on deep, conflicted feelings about her mother. Gradually, her anger softened, and she described her longing for a different kind of relationship with the therapist. She expressed sadness also at her isolation in the group and described her wish for more closeness with other members. Some weeks after the return of the "bad" therapist, her anger had diminished sufficiently to work with him in a softer, more productive manner.

This example illustrates how, in a number of ways, the group therapy situation can reduce intense and crippling transference distortions. First, other members offered different views of the therapist, which ultimately helped Marge correct her distorted views. Second, borderline clients who develop powerful negative transference reactions are able to continue working in the group because they so often develop opposite, balancing feelings toward the co-therapist or toward other members of the group— which is why many clinicians strongly advise a co-therapy format in the group treatment of borderline clients.[43] It is also possible for a client to rest temporarily, to withdraw, or to participate in a less intensified fashion in the therapy group. Such respites from intensity are rarely possible in the one-to-one format.

The work ethic of psychotherapy is often more readily apparent in a group. Individual therapy with borderline clients may be marked by the absence of a therapeutic alliance.[44] Some clients lose sight of the goal of personal change and instead expend their energy in therapy seeking revenge for inflicted pain or demanding gratification from therapist. Witnessing other members working on therapy goals in the group often supplies an important corrective to derailed therapy.

Since the borderline individuals' core problems lie in the sphere of intimacy, the therapeutic factor of cohesiveness is often of decisive import. If these clients are able to accept the reality testing offered by the group, and if their behavior is not so disruptive as to cast them in a deviant or scapegoat role, then the group may become a holding environment—an enormously important, supportive refuge from the stresses borderline clients experience in everyday life. The borderline clients' sense of belongingness is augmented by the fact that they are often a great asset to the therapy group. These individuals have great access to affect, unconscious needs, fantasies, and fears, and they may loosen up a group and facilitate the therapeutic work, especially the therapy of schizoid, inhibited, constricted individuals. Of course, this can be a double-edged sword. Some group members may be negatively affected by the borderline client's intense rages and negativity, which can undermine the work of comembers who are victims of abuse or trauma.[45]

The borderline client's vulnerability and tendency to distort are so extreme that concurrent or combined individual therapy is required. Many therapists suggest that the most common reason for treatment failure of borderline clients in therapy groups is the omission of adjunctive individual therapy.[46] If conjoint therapy is used, it is particularly important for the group and the individual therapists to be in ongoing communication. The dangers of splitting are real, and it is important that the client experience the therapists as a solid, coherent team.

Despite the heroic efforts of DSM-IV-TR, the borderline personality disorder does not represent a homogeneous diagnostic category. One borderline client may be markedly dissimilar clinically to another. The frequently hospitalized chaotic individual is grossly different (and has a very different course of therapy) from the less severely disabled individual with an unanchored self.[47] Thus, the decision to include a borderline client in a group depends on the characteristics of the particular individual being screened rather than on the broad diagnostic category. The therapist has to assess not only a client's ability to tolerate the intensity of the therapy group but also the group's ability to tolerate the demands of that particular client at that point. Most heterogeneous ambulatory groups can, at best, tolerate only one or possibly two borderline individuals. The major considerations influencing the selection process are the same as those described in chapter 8. It is particularly important to assess the possibility of the client's becoming a deviant in the group. Rigidity of behavioral patterns, especially patterns that antagonize other people, should be carefully scrutinized. Clients who are markedly grandiose, contemptuous, and disdainful are unlikely to have a bright future in a group. It is necessary for a client to have the capacity to tolerate minimal amounts of frustration or criticism without serious acting out. A client with an erratic work record, a history of transitory relationships, or a history of quickly moving on to a new situation when slightly frustrated in an old one is likely to respond in the same way in the therapy group.

The Narcissistic Client

The term *narcissistic* may be used in different ways. It is useful to think about narcissistic clients representing a range and dimension of concerns rather than a narrow diagnostic category.[48] Although there is a formal diagnosis of narcissistic personality disorder, there are many more individuals with narcissistic traits who create characteristic interpersonal problems in the course of group therapy.

The nature of the narcissistic individual's difficulties is captured comprehensively in the DSM-IV-TR diagnostic criteria for the personality disorder. A diagnosis of the personality disorder requires that at least five of nine criteria be met: grandiose sense of self-importance; preoccupation with fantasies of unlimited success, power, love, or brilliance; a belief that he or she is special and can be understood only by other special, high-status people; a need for excessive admiration; a sense of entitlement; interpersonally exploitative behavior; lack of empathy; often envious of others; arrogant, haughty behaviors or attitudes.[49]

More commonly, many individuals with narcissistic difficulties present with features of grandiosity, a need for admiration from others, and a lack of empathy. These individuals also tend to have a shallow emotional life, derive little enjoyment from life other than tributes received from others, and tend to depreciate those from whom they expect few narcissistic supplies.[50] Their self-esteem is brittle and easily diminished, often generating outrage at the source of insult.

Appropriate narcissism, a healthy love of oneself, is essential to the development of self-respect and self-confidence. *Excessive* narcissism takes the form of loving oneself to the exclusion of others, of losing sight of the fact that others are sentient beings, that others, too, are constituting egos, each constructing and experiencing a unique world. In extreme form, narcissists are solipsists who experience the world and other individuals as existing solely for them.

General Problems.   The narcissistic client often has a stormier but more productive course in group than in individual therapy. In fact, the individual format provides so much gratification that the core problem emerges much more slowly: the client's every word is listened to; every feeling, fantasy, and dream are examined; much is given to and little demanded from the client.

In the group, however, the client is expected to share time, to understand, to empathize with and to help others, to form relationships, to be concerned with the feelings of others, to receive constructive but sometimes critical feedback. Often narcissistic individuals feel alive when onstage: they judge the group's usefulness to them on the basis of how many minutes of the group's and the therapist's time they have obtained at a meeting. They guard their specialness fiercely and often object when anyone points out similarities between themselves and other members. For the same reason, they also object to being included with the other members in group-as-a-whole interpretations.

They may have a negative response to some crucial therapeutic factors—for example, cohesiveness and universality. To belong to a group, to be like others, may be experienced as a homogenizing and cheapening experience. Hence the group experience readily brings to light the narcissistic client's difficulties in relationships. Other members may feel unsympathetic to the narcissistic member because they rarely see the vulnerability and fragility that resides beneath the grandiose and exhibitionistic behavior, a vulnerable core that the narcissistic client often keeps well hidden.[51]

• *One group member, Vicky, was highly critical of the group format and frequently restated her preference for the one-to-one therapy format. She often supported her position by citing psychoanalytic literature critical of the group therapy approach. She felt bitter at having to share time in the group. For example, three-fourths of the way through a meeting, the therapist remarked that he perceived Vicky and John to be under much pressure. They both admitted that they needed and wanted time in the meeting that day. After a moment's awkwardness, John gave way, saying he thought his problem could wait until the next session. Vicky consumed the rest of the meeting and, at the following session, continued where she left off. When it appeared that she had every intention of using the entire meeting again, one of the members commented that John had been left hanging in the last session. But there was no easy transition, since, as the therapist pointed out, only Vicky could entirely release the group, and she gave no sign of doing so graciously (she had lapsed into a sulking silence).*

Nonetheless, the group turned to John, who was in the midst of a major life crisis. John presented his situation, but no good work was done. At the very end of the meeting, Vicky began weeping silently. The group members, thinking that she wept for John, turned to her. But she wept, she said, for all the time that was wasted on John—time that she could have used so much better. What Vicky could not appreciate for at least a year in the group was that this type of incident did not indicate that she would be better off in individual therapy. Quite the contrary: the fact that such difficulties arose in the group was precisely the reason that the group format was especially indicated for her.

Though narcissistic clients are frustrated by their bids for attention being so often thwarted in the group as well in their outside life, that very enlivening frustration constitutes a major advantage for the group therapeutic mode. Furthermore, the group is catalyzed as well: some members profit from having to take assertive stands against the narcissist's greediness, and members who are too nonassertive may use aspects of the narcissistic client's behavior as modeling.

Another narcissistic patient, Ruth, who sought therapy for her inability to maintain deep relationships, participated in the group in a highly stylized fashion: she insisted on filling the members in every week on the minute details of her life and especially on her relationships with men, her most pressing problem. Many of these details were extraneous, but she was insistent on a thorough recitation (much like the "watch me" phase of early childhood). Aside from watching her, there seemed no way the group could relate to Ruth without making her feel deeply rejected. She insisted that friendship consisted of sharing intimate details of one's life, yet we learned through a follow-up interview with a member who terminated the group that Ruth frequently called her for social evenings—but she could no longer bear to be with Ruth because of her propensity to use friends in the same way one might use an analyst: as an ever-patient, ever-solicitous, ever-available ear.

Some narcissistic individuals who have a deep sense of specialness and entitlement feel not only that they deserve maximum group attention but also that it should be forthcoming without any effort on their part. They expect the group to care for them, to reach out for them despite the fact that they reach out for no one. They expect gifts, surprises, compliments, concern, though they give none. They expect to be able to express anger and scorn but to remain immune from retaliation. They expect to be loved and admired for simply being there. I have seen this posture especially pronounced in beautiful women who have been praised all their lives simply by virtue of their appearance and their presence.

The lack of awareness of, or empathy for, others is obvious in the group. After several meetings, members begin to note that although the client does personal work in the group, he or she never questions, supports, or assists others. The narcissistic client may describe life experiences with great enthusiasm, but is a poor listener and grows bored when others speak. One narcissistic man often fell asleep in the meeting if the issues discussed were not immediately relevant to him. When confronted about his sleeping, he would ask for the group's forbearance because of his long, hard day (even though he was frequently unemployed, a phenomenon he attributed to employers' failure to recognize his unique skills). There are times when it is useful to point out that there is only one relationship in life where one individual can constantly receive without reciprocating to the other—the mother and her young infant.

In chapter 12, in the account of Bill and Jan's relationship, I described many of Bill's narcissistic modes of relating to other people. Much of his failure or inability to view the world from the position of the other was summed up in a statement he made to the other woman in the group, Gina, after sixteen months of meetings. He wistfully said that he regretted that nothing had happened between them. Gina sharply corrected him: "You mean nothing sexual, but a great deal has happened for me. You tried to seduce me. For once I refused. I didn't fall in love with you, and I didn't go to bed with you. I didn't betray myself or my husband. I learned to know you and to care for you very deeply with all your faults and with all your assets. Is that nothing happening?"

Several months after the end of therapy, I asked Bill in a follow-up interview to recall some of the most significant events or turning points in therapy. He described a session late in therapy when the group watched a videotape of the previous session. Bill was stunned to learn that he had completely forgotten most of the session, remembering only those few points in which he was centrally involved. His egocentricity was powerfully brought home to him and affirmed what the group had been trying to tell him for months.

Many therapists distinguish between the *overgratified* narcissistic individual, like Bill, and the *undergratified* narcissistic individual, who tends to be more deprived and enraged, even explosive. The group behavior of the latter is misunderstood by the other members, who interpret the anger as an attack on the group rather than as a last-ditch attempt to defend the otherwise unprotected self. Consequently, these members are given little nurturance for their unspoken wounds and deficits and are at risk of bolting from the group. It is essential that therapists maintain an empathic connection to these clients and focus on their subjective world, particularly when they feel diminished or hurt. At times, the group leader may even need to serve as an advocate for the understanding of the emotional experience of these provocative group members.[52]

A clinical illustration:

• *Val, a narcissistic woman, was insulting, unempathic, and highly sensitive to even the mildest criticism. In one meeting, she lamented at length that she never received support or compliments from anyone in the group, least of all from the therapists. In fact, she could remember only three positive comments to her in the seventy group meetings she had attended. One member responded immediately and straightforwardly: "Oh, come on, Val, get off it. Last week both of the therapists supported you a whole lot. In fact, you get more stroking in this group than anyone else." Every other member of the group agreed and offered several examples of positive comments that had been given to Val over the last few meetings.*

Later in the same meeting, Val responded to two incidents in a highly maladaptive fashion. Two members were locked in a painful battle over control. Both were shaken and extremely threatened by the degree of anger expressed, both their own and their antagonist's. Many of the other group members offered observations and support. Val's response was that she didn't know what all the commotion was about, and that the two were "jerks" for getting themselves so upset about nothing at all.

A few minutes later, Farrell, a member who had been very concealed and silent, was pressed to reveal more about herself. With considerable resolve, she disclosed, for the first time, intimate details about a relationship she had recently entered into with a man. She talked about her fear that the relationship would collapse because she desperately wanted children and, once again, had started a relationship with a man who had made it clear that he did not want children. Many members of the group responded empathically and supportively to her disclosure. Val was silent, and when called upon, she stated that she could see Farrell was having a hard time talking about this, but couldn't understand why. "It didn't seem like a big-deal revelation." Farrell responded, "Thanks, Val, that makes me feel great—it makes me want to have nothing to do with you. I'd like to put as much distance as possible between the two of us."

The group's response to Val in both of these incidents was immediate and direct. The two people she had accused of acting like jerks let her know that they felt demeaned by her remarks. One commented, "If people talk about some problem that you don't have, then you dismiss it as being unimportant or jerky. Look, I don't have the problems that you have about not getting enough compliments from the therapists or other members of the group. It simply is not an issue for me. How would you feel if I called you a jerk every time you complained about that?"

This meeting illustrates several features of group work with a characterologically difficult client. Val was inordinately adversarial and had developed an intense and disabling negative transference in several previous attempts in individual therapy. In this session, she expressed distorted perceptions of the therapists (that they had given her only three compliments in seventy sessions when, in fact, they had been strongly supportive of her). In individual therapy, Val's distortion might have led to a major impasse because her transferential distortions were so marked that she did not trust the therapists to provide an accurate view of reality. Therapy groups have a great advantage in the treatment of such clients because, as illustrated in this vignette, group therapists do not have to serve as champions of reality: the other group members assume that role and commonly provide powerful and accurate reality testing to the client.

Val, like many narcissistic patients, was overly sensitive to criticism. (Such individuals are like the hemophiliac patient, who bleeds at the slightest injury and lacks the resources to staunch the flow of blood.)[53] The group members were aware that Val was highly vulnerable and tolerated criticism poorly. Yet they did not hesitate to confront her directly and consistently. Although Val was wounded in this meeting, as in so many others, she also heard the larger message: the group members took her seriously and respected her ability to take responsibility for her actions and to change her behavior. I believe that it is crucially important that a group assume this stance toward the vulnerable client. It may be experienced as a powerful affirmation. Once a group begins to ignore, patronize, or mascot a narcissistic individual, then therapy for that client fails. The group no longer provides reality testing, and the client assumes the noxious deviant role.

The major task for the group therapist working with all of these problematic clients is neither precise diagnosis nor a formulation of early causative dynamics. Whether the diagnosis is schizoid, borderline, or narcissistic personality disorder, the primary issue is the same: the therapeutic management of the highly vulnerable individual in the therapy group.

Chapter 14

THE THERAPIST: SPECIALIZED FORMATS AND PROCEDURAL AIDS

The standard group therapy format in which one therapist meets with six to eight members is often complicated by other factors: the client may concurrently be in individual therapy; there may be a co-therapist in the group; the client may be involved in a twelve-step group; occasionally the group may meet without the therapist. I shall discuss these variations in this chapter and describe, in addition, some specialized techniques and approaches that, although not essential, may at times facilitate the course of therapy.

CONCURRENT INDIVIDUAL AND GROUP THERAPY

First, some definitions. *Conjoint therapy* refers to a treatment format in which the client is seen by one therapist in individual therapy and a different therapist (or two, if co-therapists) in group therapy. In *combined therapy*, the client is treated by the *same* therapist simultaneously in individual and group therapy. No systematic data exists about the comparative effectiveness of these variations. Consequently, guidelines and principles must be formulated from clinical judgment and from reasoning based on the posited therapeutic factors.

Whenever we integrate two treatment modalities, we must first consider their compatibility. More is not always better! Are the different treatments working at cross-purposes, or do they enhance one another? If compatible, are they complementary, working together by addressing different aspects of the client's therapy needs, or are they facilitative, each supporting and enhancing the work of the other?[1]

The relative frequencies of the two types of concurrent therapy are un-known, although it is likely that in private practice *combined* therapy is more commonly employed than *conjoint* therapy.[2] The opposite appears to be true in institutional and mental health treatment settings.[3] By no means should one consider conjoint and combined therapy equivalent. They have exceedingly different features and clinical indications, and I shall discuss them separately.

Conjoint Therapy

I believe that, with some exceptions, conjoint individual therapy is not *essential* to the practice of group therapy. If members are selected with a mod-erate degree of care, a therapy group meeting once or (preferably) twice a week is ample therapy and should benefit the great majority of clients. But there are exceptions. The characterologically difficult client, as I discussed in chapter 13, frequently needs to be in concurrent therapy—either combined or conjoint. In fact, the earliest models of concurrent group and individual therapy developed in response to the needs of these challenging clients.[4] Clients with a history of childhood sexual abuse or for whom issues around shame are significant also often require concurrent therapy.[5]

Not infrequently, group members may go through a severe life crisis (for example, bereavement or a divorce) that requires temporary individ-ual therapy support. Some clients are so fragile or blocked by anxiety or fearful of aggression that individual therapy is required to enable them to participate in the group. From time to time, individual therapy is required to prevent a client from dropping out of the group or to monitor more closely a suicidal or impulsive client.

• *Joan, a young woman with borderline personality disorder partici-pating in her first group, was considerably threatened by the first few meetings. She had felt increasingly alienated because her bizarre fan-tasy and dream world seemed so far from the experience of the other members. In the fourth meeting, she verbally attacked one of the mem-bers and was, in turn, attacked. For several nights thereafter, she had terrifying nightmares. In one, her mouth turned to blood, which ap-peared related to her fear of being verbally aggressive because of her world-destructive fantasies. In another, she was walking along the beach when a huge wave engulfed her—this related to her fear of los-ing her boundaries and identity in the group. In a third dream, Joan was held down by several men who guided the therapist's hands as he performed an operation on her brain—obviously related to her fears of therapy and of the therapist being overpowered by the male members.*

Her hold on reality grew more tenuous, and it seemed unlikely that she could continue in the group without added support. Concurrent individual therapy with another therapist was arranged; it helped her to contain her anxiety and enabled her to remain in the group.

• Jim was referred to a group by his psychoanalyst, who had treated him for six years and was now terminating analysis.[6] Despite considerable improvement, Jim still had not mastered the symptom for which he had originally sought treatment: fear of women. He found it difficult even to dictate to his secretary. In one of his first group meetings, he was made extremely uncomfortable by a woman in the group who complimented him. He stared at the floor for the rest of the session, and afterward called his analyst to say that he wanted to drop out of the group and reenter analysis. His analyst discussed the situation with the group therapist and agreed to resume individual treatment on the condition the client return to the group as well. For the next few months, they had an individual hour after each group session. The two therapists had frequent consultations, and the group therapist was able to modulate the noxious stimuli in the group sufficiently to allow the client to continue in therapy. Within a few months, he was able to reach out emotionally to women for the first time, and he gradually grew more at ease with women in the real world.

Thus far, we have considered how individual therapy may facilitate the client's course in group therapy. The reverse is also true: group therapy may be used to augment or facilitate the course of individual therapy.†[7] In fact, the majority of clients in conjoint therapy enter the group through referral by their individual therapist. The individual therapist might find a client exceptionally restricted and arid and unable to produce the material necessary for productive work. Often the rich, affective interpersonal interaction of the group is marvelously evocative and generates ample data for both individual and group work. At other times, clients have major blind spots that prevent them from reporting accurately or objectively what actually transpires in their life.

One older man was referred to group therapy by his individual therapist because the individual therapy was at an impasse due to an intense paternal transference. The male therapist could say nothing to this client without its being challenged and obsessively picked apart for its inaccuracy or incompleteness. Although both client and therapist were aware of the reenactment in the therapy of the relationship between oppressed son and bullying father, no real progress was made until the client entered the more democratic, leveled group environment and was able to hear feedback that was disentangled from paternal authority.

Other clients are referred to a therapy group because they have improved in the safe setting of the one-to-one therapy hour, yet are unable to transfer the learning to outside life. The group setting may serve as a valuable way station for the next stage of therapy: experimentation with behavior in a low-risk environment, which may effectively disconfirm the client's fantasies of the calamitous consequences of new behavior.

Sometimes in the individual therapy of characterologically difficult clients, severe, irreconcilable problems in the transference arise, and the therapy group may be particularly helpful in diluting transference and facilitating reality testing (see chapter 13). The individual therapist may also benefit from a deintensification of the countertransference. The group and the individual therapist may function effectively as peer consultants and supports in the treatment of particularly taxing clients who use splitting and projective identification in ways that may be quite overwhelming to the therapist. In essence, conjoint therapy capitalizes on the presence in treatment of multiple settings, multiple transferences, multiple observers, multiple interpreters, and multiple maturational agents.[8]

Complications.   Along with these advantages of conjoint therapy come a number of complications. When there is a marked difference in the basic approach of the individual therapist and the group therapist, the two therapies may work at cross-purposes.

If, for example, the individual approach is oriented toward understanding genetic causality and delves deeply into past experiences while the group focuses primarily on here-and-now material, the client is likely to become confused and to judge one approach on the basis of the other. An overarching sense of a synthesis of the group and individual work is necessary for success.

Not infrequently, clients beginning group therapy are discouraged and frustrated by the initial group meetings that offer less support and attention than their individual therapy hours. Sometimes such clients, when attacked or stressed by the group, may defend themselves by unfavorably comparing their group to their individual therapy experience. Such an attack on the group invariably results in further deterioration of the situation. It is not uncommon, however, for clients later in therapy to appreciate the unique offerings of the group and to reverse their comparative evaluations of the two modes.

Another complication of conjoint therapy arises when clients use individual therapy to drain off affect from the group. The client may interact like a sponge in the group, taking in feedback and carrying it away to gnaw on like a bone in the safe respite of the individual therapy hour. Clients may resist working in the group through the pseudo-altruistic rationalization, "I will allow the others to have the group time since I have my own hour." Another form of resistance is to deal with important material in the opposite venue— to use the group to address the transference to the individual therapist and to use the individual therapy to address reactions to group members. When these patterns are particularly pronounced and resist all other interventions, the group therapist, in collaboration with the individual therapist, may insist that either the group or the individual therapy be terminated. I have known several clients whose involvement in the group dramatically accelerated when their concurrent individual therapy was stopped.

In my experience, the individual and the group therapeutic approaches complement each other particularly well if two conditions are met. First, there must be a good working collaboration between the individual and group therapists. They must have the client's permission to share all information with each other. It is important that both therapists be equally committed to the idea of conjoint therapy and in agreement about the rationale for the referral to group therapy. A referral to a group for conjoint treatment should not be a cover for the sloughing of clinical responsibility because the individual therapist is paving the way to terminate the treatment.[9] Furthermore, it is essential that the therapists are mutually respectful—both of the competence and therapeutic approach of the other.

A solid relationship between the individual and group therapists may prove essential in addressing the inevitable tensions as clients compare their group and individual therapists, at times idealizing one and devaluing the other. This is a particularly uncomfortable issue for less experienced group therapists working conjointly with more senior individual therapists whose invisible glowering presence in the group may inhibit the group therapist and undermine confidence, stimulating the group therapist's concern about how they are being portrayed by the client to the individual therapist.[10] These considerations are especially evident in the treatment of more difficult clients who employ defenses of splitting. It is exceedingly tough to be the vilified therapist in a conjoint treatment. The position of the idealized therapist may be easier to bear, but it is only somewhat less precarious and no less ineffective.

Thus, the first condition for an effective conjoint therapy experience is that the individual and group therapists have an open, solid, mutually respectful working relationship. The second condition is that the individual therapy must complement the group approach—it must be here-and-now oriented and must devote time to an exploration of the client's feelings toward the group members and toward incidents and themes of current meetings. Such an exploration can serve as rehearsal for deeper involvement in the life of the group.

Individual therapists who are experienced in group methods may significantly help their client (and the rest of the group) by coaching the client on how to work in the group. I recently referred a young man I was seeing in individual therapy to a therapy group. He was characteristically suffused with rage, which he usually expressed in explosions toward his wife or as road rage (which had gotten him into several dangerous situations).

After a few weeks of group therapy, he reported in his individual hours that he had varying degrees of anger toward many of the group members. When I raised the question of his expressing this in the group, he paled: "No one ever confronts anyone directly in this group—that's not the way this group works . . . I would feel awful . . . I'd devastate the others . . . I couldn't face them again . . . I'd be drummed out of the group." We rehearsed how he might confront his anger in the group. Sometimes I role-played how I might talk about it in the group if I were him. I gave him examples of how to give feedback that would be unlikely to evoke retaliation. For example, "I've a problem I haven't been able to discuss here before. I got a lot of anger. I blow up to my wife and kids and have serious road rage. I'd like help with it here and I'm not sure how to work on it, I wonder if I could start to tackle it by talking about some flashes of anger I feel sometimes in the group meeting." At this point, any group therapist I have ever known would purr with pleasure and encourage him to try.

He might then continue, I suggested, by saying, "For example, you, John (one of the other members): I have tremendous admiration toward you in so many ways, your intelligence, your devotion to the right causes, but nonetheless last week I noted a wave of irritation when you were speaking toward the end of the meeting about your attitude toward the women you date—was that all me or did others feel that way?" My client took notes during our session and followed my lead, and within a few weeks one of the group therapists told me that not only was this client doing good work, but he had turned the whole group around and that meetings had become more lively and interactional for everyone in the group.

The individual therapist also can with great profit focus on transfer of learning, on helping the client apply what he or she has learned in the group to new situations—for example, to the relationship with the individual therapist and to other important figures in the client's social world.

Although it is more common for group therapy to be added to an ongoing individual therapy, the opposite may also occur. It may be that the group work catalyzes changes or evokes memories that evoke great distress warranting time and attention that the group may not be able to provide.[11] In general, it is best to launch one treatment first and then add the second if required, rather than start both at once, to avoid confusing or overwhelming the client.

Combined Therapy

Earlier I said that concurrent therapy is not *essential* to group therapy. I feel the same way about combined therapy. Yet I also agree with the many clinicians who find that combined therapy is an exceptionally productive and powerful therapeutic format. I continue to be impressed by the results of placing my individual clients into a group: almost invariably, therapy is accelerated and enriched.

Generally, in clinical practice, combined therapy begins with individual therapy. After several weeks or months of individual therapy, therapists place a client into one of their therapy groups—one generally composed entirely of clients who are also in individual therapy with the leader. Homogeneity in this regard is helpful—that is, that all the members of the group also be in individual therapy with the group leader—but it is not essential. The pressures of everyday practice sometimes result in some clients being in individual therapy with the group leader while one or two are not. Not infrequently issues of envy may arise in members who do not meet with the group leader individually.

Typically, the client attends one group session and one individual session weekly. Other, more cost-effective variants have been described, for example, a format in which each group member meets for one individual session every few weeks.[12] Although such a format has much to offer, it has a different rationale from combined therapy, in that the occasional meeting is an adjunct to the group: it is designed to facilitate norm formation and to optimize the members' use of the group.

In combined therapy, the group is usually open-ended, with clients remaining in both therapies for months, even years. But combined therapy may also involve a time-limited group format. I have, on many occasions, formed a six-month group of my long-term individual clients. After the group terminates, the clients continue individual therapy, which has been richly fertilized by group-spawned data.

Advantages.   There is no doubt that combined therapy (as well as conjoint therapy) decreases dropouts.†[13] My own informal survey of combined therapy groups—my own and those of supervisees and colleagues—over a period of several years reveals that early dropouts are exceedingly rare. In fact, of clients who were already established in individual therapy before entering a group led by their individual therapist, *not a single one* dropped out in the first twelve sessions. This, of course, contrasts starkly with the high dropout rates for group therapy without concurrent individual therapy (see table 8.1). The reasons are obvious. First, therapists know their individual therapy clients very well and can be more accurate in the selection process. Second, the therapists in their individual therapy sessions are able to prevent impending dropouts by addressing and resolving issues that preclude the client's work in the group.

• *After seven meetings, David, a somewhat prissy, fifty-year-old confirmed bachelor, was on the verge of dropping out. The group had given him considerable feedback about several annoying characteristics: his frequent use of euphemisms, his concealment behind long, boring repetitious anecdotes, and his persistence in asking distracting cocktail-party questions. Because David seemed uninfluenced by the feedback, the group ultimately backed away and began to mascot him (to tolerate him in a good-natured fashion, but not to take him seriously).*

In an individual session, he lamented about being "out of the loop" in the group and questioned whether he should continue. He also mentioned that he had not been wearing his hearing aid to the group (which I had not noticed) because of his fear of being ridiculed or stereotyped. Under ordinary circumstances, David would have dropped out of the group, but, in his individual therapy, I could capitalize on the group events and explore the meaning of his being "out of the loop." It turned out to be a core issue for David. Throughout his childhood and adolescence, he had felt socially shunned and ultimately resigned himself to it. He became a loner and entered a profession (freelance computer consultation) that permitted a "lone-eagle" lifestyle.

At my urging, he reconnected his hearing aid in the group and expressed his feelings of being out of the loop. His self-disclosure and, even more important, his examination of his role in putting himself out of the loop were sufficient to reverse the process and bring him into the group. He remained in combined therapy with much profit for a year.

This example highlights another advantage of concurrent treatment: the rich and unpredictable interaction in the group commonly opens up areas in therapy that might otherwise never have surfaced in the more insular individual format. David never felt "out of the loop" in his individual therapy—after all, I listened to his every word and strove to be present with him continually.

• *Another example involves Steven, a man who, for years, had many extramarital encounters but refused to take safer-sex precautions. In individual therapy I discussed this with him for months from every possible vantage point: his grandiosity and sense of immunity from biological law, his selfishness, his concerns about impotence with a condom. I communicated my concern for him, for his wife, and for his sex partners. I experienced and expressed paternal feelings: outrage at his selfish behavior, sadness at his self-destructiveness. All to no avail. When I placed Steven in a therapy group, he did not discuss his sexual risk-taking behavior, but some relevant experiences occurred.*

On a number of occasions, he gave feedback to women members in a cruel, unfeeling manner. Gradually, the group confronted him on this and reflected on his uncaring, even vindictive, attitudes to women. Most of his group work centered on his lack of empathy. Gradually, he learned to enter the experiential world of others. The group was time limited (six months), and many months later in individual therapy, when we again focused in depth on Steven's sexual behavior, he recalled, with considerable impact, the group members' accusing him of being uncaring. Only then was he able to consider his choices in the light of his lack of loving, and only then did his behavioral pattern yield.

• A third example involves Roger, a young man who for a year in individual therapy had been continually critical of me. Roger acknowledged that he had made good gains—but, after all, that was precisely what he had hired me for, and, he never forgot to add, he was paying me big bucks for my services. Where were his positive, tender feelings? They never surfaced in individual therapy. When he entered my six-month combined therapy group, the pattern continued, and the members perceived him as cold, unfeeling, and often hostile—they called him the "grenade launcher." Much to everyone's surprise, it was Roger who expressed the strongest regret at the ending of the group. When pressed, he said that he would miss the group and miss his contact with some of the members. "Which of us in particular?" the group inquired. Before he could respond, I intervened and asked if the group could guess. No one had the vaguest idea. When Roger singled out two members, they were astonished, having had no hint that Roger cared for them.

The two therapies worked together. My experience with Roger in individual therapy cued me to pursue Roger's affective block but it was the group members' reaction—their inability to read him or to know of his feelings for them—that had a far more powerful impact on Roger. After all, their feelings could not be rationalized away—it was not part of their job.

• Sam, a man who entered therapy because of his inhibitions and lack of joie de vivre, encountered his lack of openness and his rigidity far more powerfully in the therapy group than in the individual format. He kept from the group three particularly important secrets: that he had been trained as a therapist and practiced for a few years; that he had retired after inheriting a large fortune; and that he felt superior and held others in contempt. He rationalized keeping secrets in the group (as he *did in his social life) by believing that self-revelation would result in greater distance from others: he would be stereotyped in one way or another, "used," envied, revered, or hated.*

After three months of participation in a newly formed group, he became painfully aware of how he had re-created in the group the same peripheral onlooker role that he assumed in his real life. All the members had started together, all the others had revealed themselves and participated in a personal, uninhibited manner—he alone had chosen to stay outside.

In our individual work, I urged Sam to reveal himself in the group. Individual session after session, I felt like a second in a boxing ring exhorting him to take a chance. In fact, as the group meetings went by, I told him that delay was making things much worse. If he waited much longer to tell the group he had been a therapist, he would get a lot of flak when he did. (Sam had been receiving a steady stream of compliments about his perceptivity and sensitivity.)

Finally, Sam took the plunge and revealed his three secrets. Immediately he and the other members began to relate in a more genuine fashion. He enabled other members to work on related issues. A member who was a student therapist discussed her fear of being judged for superficial comments; another wealthy member revealed his concerns about others' envy; another revealed that she was a closet snob. Still others discussed strong, previously hidden feelings about money—including their anger at the therapist's fees. After the group ended, Sam continued to discuss these interactions in individual therapy and to take new risks with the therapist. The members' acceptance of him after his disclosures was a powerfully affirming experience. Previously, they had accepted him for his helpful insights, but that acceptance meant little, because it was rooted in bad faith: his false presentation of himself and his concealment of his training, wealth, and personal traits.

Sam's case points out some of the inherent pitfalls in combined therapy. For one thing, the role of the therapist changes significantly and increases in complexity. There is something refreshingly simple in leading a group when the leader knows the same thing about each member as everyone else does. But the combined therapist knows so much that life gets complicated. A member once referred to my role as that of the Magus: I knew everything: what members felt toward one another, what they chose to say, and, above all, what they chose to withhold.

Group therapists who see none of their group clients in individual therapy can be more freewheeling: they can ask for information, take blind guesses, ask broad, general questions, call on members to describe their feelings about another member or some group incident. But the combined therapist knows too much! It becomes awkward to ask questions of members when you know the answer. Consequently, many therapists find that they are less active in groups of their own individual clients than when leading other groups.

Input of group members often opens up rich areas for exploration, areas into which the individual therapist may enter. For example, Irene, a middle-aged woman, had left her husband months earlier and was, in a state of great indecision, living in a small rented apartment. Other group members asked how she had furnished the place, and gradually it came out that she had done virtually nothing to make her surroundings comfortable or attractive. An investigation into her need to deprive herself, to wear a hair shirt, proved enormously valuable to her.

The combined therapist often struggles with the issue of boundaries. (This is also true in conjoint therapy at times when the group therapist has learned from the individual therapist about important feelings or events that their mutual client has not yet addressed in the group.) Is the content of the client's individual therapy the property of the group? As a general rule, it is almost always important to urge clients to bring up group-relevant material in the group. If, for example, in the individual therapy hour, the client brings up angry feelings toward another member, the therapist must urge the client to bring these feelings back to the group.

Suppose the client resists? Again, most therapists will pursue the least intrusive options: first, repeated urging of the client and investigation of the resistance; then focusing on in-group conflict between the two members, even if the conflict is mild; then sending knowing glances to the client; and, the final step, asking the client for permission to introduce the material into the group. Good judgment, of course, must be exercised. No technical rationale justifies humiliating a client. As noted earlier, a promise of absolute therapist confidentiality can rarely be provided without negatively constraining the therapy. Therapists can only promise that they will use their discretion and best professional judgment. Meanwhile, they must work toward helping the client accept the responsibility of bringing forward relevant material from one venue to the other.

Combined group and individual therapy may present special problems for neophyte group therapists. Some find it difficult to see the same client in two formats because they customarily assume a different role in the two types of therapy: in group, therapists tend to be more informal, open, and actively engaged with the client; in individual therapy, the therapist tends to remain somewhat impersonal and distant. Often therapists in training prefer that clients have a pure treatment experience—that is, solely group therapy without any concurrent individual therapy with themselves or other therapists—in order to discover for themselves what to expect from each type of therapy.

COMBINING GROUP THERAPY
AND TWELVE-STEP GROUPS

An increasingly common form of concurrent therapy is the treatment in group psychotherapy of clients who are also participating in twelve-step groups. Historically, a certain antipathy has existed between the proponents of these two modalities, with subtle and at times overt denigration of one another.[14] Recently there has been a growing recognition that substance use disorders are an appropriate focus for the mental health field. The vast economic costs and psychosocial scope of addiction disorders, the high comorbidity rates with other psychological problems, and the social and relational context of addiction make group therapy particularly relevant.†[15]

Individuals who abuse substances also typically experience substantial interpersonal disturbance at every stage of their illness: first, they have predisposing interpersonal difficulties resulting in emotional pain that the individual attempts to abate by substance use; second, they have relational difficulties resulting from the substance abuse; third, they have interpersonal difficulties that complicate the maintenance of sobriety. There is good evidence that group therapy can play an important role in recovery by alcoholics helping them develop coping skills that sustain sobriety and enhance resilience to relapse.[16]

There is also strong evidence that twelve-step groups are both effective and valued by clients.[17] (Alcoholics Anonymous is the most prevalent of the twelve-step groups, but there are over 100 variations, for such conditions as cocaine and other narcotics addiction, gambling, sexual addiction, and overeating.) It is inevitable that some of the many million of members of AA attending the thousands of weekly group meetings in the United States alone will also participate in group psychotherapy. Furthermore, there is emerging evidence that twelve-step groups and mainstream therapies can be effectively integrated.†[18]

Group therapy and AA can complement one another if certain obstacles are removed. First, group leaders must become informed about the mechanism of twelve-step group work and learn to appreciate the inherent wisdom in the twelve-step program as well as the enormous support it offers to those struggling with addiction. Second, there are several common misconceptions that must be cleared up—misconceptions held by group therapists and/or by members of AA. These include:[19]

1. Twelve-step groups are opposed to psychotherapy or medication.
2. Twelve-step groups encourage the abdication of personal responsibility.
3. Twelve-step groups discourage the expression of strong affects.

4. Mainstream group therapy neglects spirituality.
5. Mainstream group therapy is powerful enough to be effective without twelve-step groups.
6. Mainstream group therapy views the AA relationships and the relationship between sponsor and sponsee as regressive.

Keep in mind that it is difficult to make blanket statements about AA meetings, because AA meetings are not all the same: there is much variability from group to group. In general, however, there are two major differences between the AA approach and the group therapy approach.

AA relies heavily on the members' relationship to a higher power, submission to that power, and understanding of the self in relation to that higher power.

Group therapy encourages member-to-member interaction, especially in the here-and-now: it is the lifeblood of the group. AA, by contrast, specifically prohibits "crosstalk"—that is, direct interaction between members during a meeting. "Crosstalk" could be any direct inquiry, suggestion, advice, feedback, or criticism. (This, too, is a generalization, however: if one searches, one can find AA groups that engage in considerable interaction.) The prohibition of "crosstalk" by no means leads to an impersonal meeting, however. AA members have pointed out to me that the knowledge that there will be no judgment or criticism is freeing to members and encourages them to self-disclose at deep levels. Since there is no designated trained group leader to modulate and process here-and-now interaction, it seems to me that AA's decision to avoid intensive interpersonal interaction is a wise and instrumental one.

Therapy group leaders introducing an AA member into their therapy group must keep in mind that group feedback will be an unfamiliar concept and should take extra time and care in pregroup preparation sessions to explain the difference between the AA model and the therapy group model regarding the use of the here-and-now.

I recommend that group leaders attend some AA meetings and thoroughly familiarize themselves with the twelve steps. Demonstrate your respect for the steps and attempt to convey to the client that most of the twelve steps have meaning in the context of the therapy group and, if followed, will enhance the work of therapeutic change.

Table 14.1 lists the twelve steps and suggests related group therapy themes. I do not suggest a reinterpretation of the twelve steps but a loose translation of ideas in the steps into related interpersonal group concepts. With this framework, group leaders can readily employ a common language that covers both approaches and reinforces the idea that therapy and the recovery process are mutually facilitative.

TABLE 14.1   The Convergence of Twelve-Step and Interpersonal Group
Therapy Approaches

The Twelve Steps	Interpersonal Group Psychotherapy
1. We admitted that we were powerless over alcohol and that our lives had become unmanageable	Relinquish grandiosity and counterdependence. Begin the process of trusting the process and the power of the group.
2. Came to believe that a Power greater than ourselves could restore us to sanity	Self-repair through relationships and human connection. Reframe "Higher Power" into a source of soothing, nurturance, and hope that may replace the reliance on substances.
3. Made a decision to turn our will and our lives over to the care of God as we understood Him	Make a leap of trust in the therapy procedure and the good will of fellow group members.
4. Made a searching and fearless moral inventory of ourselves	Self-discovery. Search within. Learn as much about yourself as possible.
5. Admitted to God, to ourselves, and to another human being the exact nature of our wrongs	Self-disclosure. Share your inner world with others—the experiences that fill you with shame and guilt as well as your dreams and hopes.
6. Were entirely ready to have God remove all these defects of character	Explore and illuminate, in the here-and-now of the treatment, all destructive interpersonal actions that invite relapses. The task of the group is to help members find the resources within themselves to prepare to take action.
7. Humbly asked Him to remove our shortcomings	Acknowledge interpersonal feelings and behaviors that hinder satisfying relationships. Modify these by experimenting with new behaviors. Request and accept feedback in order to broaden your interpersonal repertoire. Though the group offers the opportunity to work on issues, it is your responsibility to do the work.
8. Made a list of all persons we had harmed, and became willing to make amends to them all	Identify interpersonal injuries you have been responsible for; develop empathy for others' feelings. Try to appreciate the impact of your actions on others and develop the willingness to repair injury.

(continues)

TABLE 14.1 *(continued)*

The Twelve Steps	Interpersonal Group Psychotherapy
9. Made direct amends to such people wherever possible, except when to do so would injure them or others	Use the group as a testing ground for the sequence of recognition and repair. Start the ninth step work by making amends to other group members whom you have in any manner impeded or offended.
10. Continued to take personal inventory and when we were wrong promptly admit it	Internalize the process of self-reflection, assumption of responsibility, and self-revelation. Make these attributes part of your way of being in the therapy group and in your outside life.
11. Sought through prayer and meditation to improve our conscious contact with God as we understand Him, praying only for knowledge of His will for us and the power to carry that out	No direct psychotherapeutic focus, but the therapy group may support mind-calming meditation and spiritual exploration.
12. Having had a spiritual awakening as the result of these steps, we tried to carry this message to other addicts, and to practice these principles in all our affairs	Become actively concerned for others, beginning with your fellow group members. Embracing an altruistic way of being in the world will raise your love and respect for yourself.

Adapted from Matano and Yalom.[20]

CO-THERAPISTS

Some group therapists choose to meet alone with a group, but the great majority prefer to work with a co-therapist.[21] Limited research has been conducted to determine the relative efficacy of the two methods, although a study of co-therapy in family and marital therapy demonstrates that that in those modalities co-therapy is at least as effective as single therapist treatment and in some ways superior.[22] Clinicians differ in their opinions.[23] My own clinical experience has taught me that co-therapy presents both special advantages and potential hazards.

First, consider the advantages, both for the therapists and the clients. Co-therapists complement and support each other. Together, they have greater cognitive and observational range, and with their dual points of view they may generate more hunches and more strategies. When one therapist, for example, is intensively involved with one member, the co-therapist may be far more aware of the remaining members' responses to the interchange and hence may be in a better position to broaden the range of the interaction and exploration.

Co-therapists also catalyze transferential reactions and make the nature of distortions more evident, because clients will differ so much among themselves in their reactions to each of the co-therapists and to the co-therapists' relationship. In groups in which strong therapist countertransference reactions are likely (for example, groups for clients with HIV or cancer or in trauma groups), the supportive function of co-therapy becomes particularly important for both clients and therapists.†[24]

Most co-therapy teams deliberately or, more often, unwittingly split roles: one therapist assumes a provocative role—much like a Socratic gadfly—while the other is more nurturing and serves as a harmonizer in the group.† When the co-therapists are male and female, the roles are usually (but not invariably) assumed accordingly. In well-functioning co-therapy teams these roles are fluid, not rigid. Each leader should have access to the full range of therapeutic postures and interventions.

Many clinicians agree that a male-female co-therapist team may have unique advantages: the image of the group as the primary family may be more strongly evoked; many fantasies and misconceptions about the relationship between the two therapists arise and may profitably be explored. Many clients benefit from the model setting of a male-female pair working together with mutual respect and inclusiveness, without the destructive competition, mutual derogation, exploitation, or pervasive sexuality they may associate with male-female pairings. For victims of early trauma and sexual abuse, a male-female co-therapy team increases the scope of the therapy by providing an opportunity to address issues of mistrust, abuse of power, and helplessness that are rooted in early paradigms of male-female relationships. Clients from cultures in which men are dominant and women are subservient may experience a co-therapy team of a strong, competent woman and a tender, competent man as uniquely facilitative.[25]

From my observations of over eighty therapy groups led by neophyte therapists, I consider the co-therapy format to have special advantages for the beginning therapist. Many students, in retrospect, consider the co-leader experience one of their most effective learning experiences. Where else in the training curriculum do two therapists have the opportunity to participate simultaneously in the same therapy experience and supervision?[26] For one thing, the presence of a co-therapist lessens initial therapist anxiety and permits therapists to be more objective in their efforts to understand the meeting. In the post-meeting rehash, the co-therapists can provide valuable feedback about each other's behavior. Until therapists obtain sufficient experience to be reasonably clear of their own self-presentation in the group, such feedback is vital in enabling them to differentiate what is real and what is transference distortion in clients' perceptions. Similarly, co-therapists may aid each other in the identification and working-through of countertransference reactions toward various members.

It is especially difficult for beginning therapists to maintain objectivity in the face of massive group pressure. One of the more unpleasant and difficult chores for neophyte therapists is to weather a group attack on them and to help the group make constructive use of it. When you are under the gun, you may be too threatened either to clarify the attack or to encourage further attack without appearing defensive or condescending. There is nothing more squelching than an individual under fire saying, "It's really great that you're attacking me. Keep it going!" A co-therapist may prove invaluable here in helping the members continue to express their anger at the other therapist and ultimately to examine the source and meaning of that anger.

Whether co-therapists should openly express disagreement during a group session is an issue of some controversy. I have generally found co-therapist disagreement unhelpful to the group in the first few meetings. The group is not yet stable or cohesive enough to tolerate such divisiveness in leadership. Later, however, therapist disagreement may contribute greatly to therapy. In one study, I asked twenty clients who had concluded long-term group therapy about the effects of therapist disagreement on the course of the group and on their own therapy.[27] They were unanimous in their judgment that it was beneficial. For many it was a model-setting experience: They observed individuals whom they respected disagree openly and resolve their differences with dignity and tact.

Consider a clinical example:

• *During a group meeting my co-leader, a resident, asked me why I seemed so quick to jump in with support whenever one of the men, Rob, received feedback. The question caught me off guard. I commented first that I had not noticed that until she drew it to my attention. I then invited feedback from others in the group, who agreed with her observation. It soon became clear to me that I was overly protective of Rob, and I commented that although he had made substantial gains in controlling his anger and explosiveness, I still regarded him as fragile and felt I needed to protect him from overreacting and undoing his success. Rob thanked me and my co-leader for our openness and added that although he may have needed extra care in the past, he no longer did at this point. He was correct!*

In this way, group members experience therapists as human beings who, despite their imperfections, are genuinely attempting to help the members. Such a humanization process is inimical to irrational stereotyping, and clients learn to differentiate others according to their individual attributes rather than their roles. Unfortunately, co-therapists take far too little advantage of this wonderful modeling opportunity. Research into communicational patterns in therapy groups shows exceedingly few therapist-to-therapist remarks.[28]

Although some clients are made uncomfortable by co-therapists' disagreement, which may feel like witnessing parental conflict, for the most part it strengthens the honesty and the potency of the group. I have observed many stagnant groups spring to life when the two therapists differentiated themselves as individuals.

The disadvantages of the co-therapy format flow from problems in the relationship between the two co-therapists. How the co-therapy goes, so will the group. That is one of the main criticisms of the use of co-therapy outside of training environments.[29] Why add another relationship (and one that drains professional resources) to the already interpersonally complex group environment?[30]

Hence, it is important that the co-therapists feel comfortable and open with each other. They must learn to capitalize on each other's strengths: one leader may be more able to nurture and support and the other more able to confront and to tolerate anger. If the co-therapists are competitive, however, and pursue their own star interpretations rather than support a line of inquiry the other has begun, the group will be distracted and unsettled.

It is also important that co-therapists speak the same professional language. A survey of forty-two co-therapy teams revealed that the most common source of co-therapy dissatisfaction was differing theoretical orientation.[31]

In some training programs a junior therapist is paired with a senior therapist, a co-therapy format that which offers much but is fraught with problems. Senior co-therapists must teach by modeling and encouragement, while junior therapists must learn to individuate while avoiding both nonassertiveness and destructive competition. Most important, they must be willing, as equals, to examine their relationship—not only for themselves but as a model for the members.† The choice of co-therapist is not to be taken lightly. I have seen many classes of psychotherapists choose co-therapists and have had the opportunity to follow the progress of these groups, and I am convinced that the ultimate success or failure of a group depends largely on the correctness of that choice. If the two therapists are uncomfortable with each other or are closed, rivalrous, or in wide disagreement about style and strategy (and if these differences are not resolvable through supervision), there is little likelihood that their group will develop into an effective work group.[32]

Differences in temperament and natural rhythm are inevitable. What is not inevitable, however, is that these differences get locked into place in ways that limit each co-therapist's role and function. Sometimes the group's feedback can be illuminating and lead to important work, as occurred in a group for male spousal abusers who questioned why the male co-therapist collected the group fee and the female co-therapist did the "straightening up."

When consultants or supervisors are called in to assist with a group that is not progressing satisfactorily, they can often offer the greatest service by directing their attention to the relationship between the co-therapists. (This will be fully discussed in chapter 17.) One study of neophyte group leaders noted that the factor common to all trainees who reported a disappointing clinical experience was unaddressed and unresolved co-therapy tensions.[33] One frustrated and demoralized co-therapist reported a transparent dream in supervision, just after her arrogant but incompetent co-therapist withdrew from the training program. In the dream she was a hockey goalie defending her team's net, and one of her own players (guess who?) kept firing the puck at her.

Co-therapist choice should not be made blindly: do not agree to colead a group with someone you do not know well or do not like. Do not make the choice because of work pressures or an inability to say no to an invitation: it is far too important and too binding a relationship.*

You are far better off leading a solo group with good supervision than being locked into an incompatible co-therapy relationship. If, as part of your training, you become a member of an experiential group, you have an ideal opportunity to gather data about the group behavior of other students. I always suggest to my students that they delay decisions about co-therapists until after meeting in such a group. You do well to select a co-therapist toward whom you feel close but who in personal characteristics is dissimilar to you: such complementarity enriches the experience of the group.

There are, as I discussed, advantages in a male-female team, but you will also be better off leading a group with someone compatible of the same sex than with a colleague of the opposite sex with whom you do not work well. Husbands and wives frequently co-lead marital couples groups (generally short term and focused on improvement of dyadic relationships); co-leadership of a long-term traditional group, however, requires an unusually mature and stable marital relationship. I advise therapists who are involved in a newly formed romantic relationship with each other not to lead a group together; it is advisable to wait until the relationship has developed stability and permanence. Two former lovers, now estranged, do not make a good co-therapy team.

---

*In Evelyn Waugh's *Brideshead Revisited* (Boston: Little, Brown, 1945), the protagonist is counseled that if he is not circumspect, he will have to devote a considerable part of his second year at college to get rid of undesirable friends he has made during his first year.

Characterologically difficult clients (see chapter 13) who are unable to integrate loving and hateful feelings may project feelings on the therapists that end up "splitting" the co-therapy team. One co-therapist may become the focus of the positive part of the split and is idealized while the other becomes the focus of hateful feelings and is attacked or shunned. Often client's overwhelming fears of abandonment or of engulfment trigger this kind of splitting.

Some groups become split into two factions, each co-therapist having a "team" of clients with whom he or she has a special relationship. Sometimes this split has its genesis in the relationship the therapist established with those clients before the group began, in prior individual therapy or in consultation. (For this reason, it is advisable that *both* therapists interview all clients, preferably simultaneously, in the pregroup screening. I have seen clients continue to feel a special bond throughout their entire group therapy course with the member of the co-therapy team who first interviewed them.) Other clients align themselves with one therapist because of his or her personal characteristics, or because they feel a particular therapist is more intelligent, more senior, or more sexually attractive than the other or more ethnically or personally similar to themselves. Whatever the reasons for the subgrouping, *the process should be noted and openly discussed.*

One essential ingredient of a good co-therapy team is discussion time. The co-therapy relationship takes time to develop and mature. Co-therapists must *set aside time to talk and tend to their relationship.*[34] At the very least, they need a few minutes before each meeting (to talk about the last session and to examine possible agendas for that day's meeting) and fifteen to twenty minutes at the end to debrief and to share their reflections about each other's behavior. If the group is supervised, it is imperative that *both* therapists attend the supervisory session. Many busy HMO clinics, in the name of efficiency and economy, make the serious mistake not setting aside time for co-therapist discussion.

THE LEADERLESS MEETING

Beginning in the 1950s, some clinicians experimented with leaderless meetings. Groups would meet without the leader when he was on vacation, or the group might meet more than once weekly and schedule regular leaderless meetings. Over the past two decades, however, interest in leaderless meetings has waned. Almost no articles on the subject have appeared, and my own informal surveys indicate that few contemporary clinicians use regularly scheduled leaderless meetings in their practice.[35]

In contemporary practice, therapists occasionally arrange for a leaderless meeting on the infrequent occasions when they are out of town. This is one option for dealing with the absence of the therapist. Other options include, of course, canceling the meeting, rescheduling it, extending the time of the next group, and providing a substitute leader.[36]

Members generally do not initially welcome the suggestion of the leaderless meeting. It evokes many unrealistic fears and consequences of the therapist's absence. In one study, I asked a series of clients who had been in group therapy for at least eight months what would have happened in the group if the group therapists were absent.[37] (This is another way of asking what function the group therapists perform in the group.) The replies were varied. Although a few members stated that they would have welcomed leaderless meetings, most of the others expressed, in order of frequency, these general concerns:

1. The group would stray from the primary task. A cocktail-hour atmosphere would prevail; members would avoid discussing problems, there would be long silences, and the discussions would become increasingly irrelevant: "We would end up in left field without the doctor to keep us on the track"; "I could never express my antagonisms without the therapist's encouragement"; "We need him there to keep things stirred up"; "Who else would bring in the silent members?"; "Who would make the rules? We'd spend the entire meeting simply trying to make rules."

2. The group would lose control of its emotions. Anger would be unrestrained, with no one there either to rescue the damaged members or to help the aggressive ones maintain control.

3. The group would be unable to integrate its experiences and to make constructive use of them: "The therapist is the one who keeps track of loose ends and makes connections for us. She helps clear the air by pointing out where the group is at a certain time." The members viewed the therapist as the time binder—the group historian who sees patterns of behavior longitudinally and points out that what a member did today, last week, and last month fits into a coherent pattern. The members were saying, in effect, that however great the action and involvement without the therapist, they would be unable to make use of it.

Many of the members' concerns are clearly unrealistic and reflect a helpless, dependent posture. It is for this very reason that a leaderless meeting may play an important role in the therapy process. The alternate meeting helps members experience themselves as autonomous, responsible, resourceful adults who, though they may profit from the therapist's expertise, are nevertheless able to control their emotions, to pursue the primary task of the group, and to integrate their experience.

The way a group chooses to communicate to the therapist the events of the alternate meeting is often of great interest. Do the members attempt to conceal or distort information, or do they compulsively brief the therapist on all details? Sometimes the ability of a group to withhold information from the therapist is in itself an encouraging sign of group maturation, although therapists are usually uncomfortable with being excluded. In the group, as in the family, members must strive for autonomy, and the leaders must facilitate that striving. Often the leaderless session and subsequent events allow the therapist to experience and understand his or her own desires for control and feelings of being threatened as clients become less dependent.

DREAMS

The number and types of dreams that group members bring to therapy are largely a function of the therapist's attentiveness to dreams. The therapist's response to the first dreams presented by clients will influence the choice of dreams subsequently presented. The intensive, detailed, personalized investigation of dreams practiced in analytically oriented individual therapy is hardly feasible in group therapy. For groups that meet once weekly, such a practice would require that a disproportionate amount of time be spent on one client; the process is, furthermore, minimally useful to the remaining members, who become mere bystanders.

What useful role, then, can dreams play in group therapy? In individual analysis or analytically oriented treatment, therapists are usually presented with many dreams and dream fragments. They never strive for complete analysis of all dreams (Freud held that a total dream analysis should be a research, not a therapeutic, endeavor) but, instead, elect to work on dreams or aspects of dreams that seem *pertinent to the current phase of therapy*. Therapists may ignore some dreams and ask for extensive associations to others.† For example, if a bereaved client brings in a dream full of anger toward her deceased husband as well as heavily disguised symbols relating to confusion about sexual identity, the therapist will generally select the former theme for work and ignore or postpone the second. Moreover, the process is self-reinforcing. It is well known that clients who are deeply involved in therapy dream or remember dreams compliantly: that is, they produce dreams that corroborate the current thrust of therapy and reinforce the theoretical framework of the therapist ("tag-along" dreams, Freud termed them).

Substitute "group work" for "individual work," and the group therapist may use dreams in precisely the same fashion. The investigation of certain dreams accelerates group therapeutic work. Most valuable are group dreams—dreams that involve the group as an entity—or dreams that reflect the dreamer's feelings toward one or more members of the group. Either of these types may elucidate not only the dreamer's but other members' concerns that until then have not become fully conscious. Some dreams may introduce, in disguised form, material that is conscious but that members have been reluctant to discuss in the group. Hence, inviting the group members to comment on the dream and associate to it or its impact on them is often productive. It is important also to explore the context of the disclosure of the dream: why dream or disclose this dream at this particular time?[38]

• *In a meeting just preceding the entry of two new members to the group, one self-absorbed man, Jeff, reported his first dream to the group after several months of participation. "I am polishing my new BMW roadster to a high sheen. Then, just after I clean the car interior to perfection, seven people dressed as clowns arrive, get into my car carrying all sorts of food and mess it up. I just stand there watching and fuming."*

Both he and the group members presented associations to the dream around an old theme for Jeff—his frustrating pursuit of perfection and need to present a perfect image to the world. The leader's inquiry about "why this dream now?" led to more significant insight. Jeff said that over the last few months he had begun to let the group into his less-than-perfect "interior" world. Perhaps, he said, the dream reflected his fear that the new members coming the next week would not take proper care of his interior. He was not alone in this anxiety: Other members also worried that the new members might spoil the group.

Some illustrative examples of members' dreams in group therapy may clarify these points.

At the twentieth meeting, a woman related this dream:

• *I am walking with my younger sister. As we walk, she grows smaller and smaller. Finally I have to carry her. We arrive at the group room, where the members are sitting around sipping tea. I have to show the group my sister. By this time she is so small she is in a package. I unwrap the package but all that is left of her is a tiny bronze head.*

The investigation of this dream clarified several previously unconscious concerns of the client. The dreamer had been extraordinarily lonely and had immediately become deeply involved in the group—in fact, it was her only important social contact. At the same time, however, she feared her intense dependence on the group; it had become *too* important to her. She modified herself rapidly to meet group expectations and, in so doing, lost sight of her own needs and identity. The rapidly shrinking sister symbolized herself becoming more infantile, more undifferentiated, and finally inanimate, as she immolated herself in a frantic quest for the group's approval. Perhaps there was anger in the image of the group "sipping tea." Did they really care about her? The lifeless, diminutive bronzed head—was that what they wanted? Dreams may reflect the state of the dreamer's sense of self. The dream needs to be treated with great care and respect as an expression of self and not as a secret message whose code must be aggressively cracked.[39]

Some of the manifest content of this dream becomes clearer through a consideration of the content of the meeting preceding the dream: the group had spent considerable time discussing her body (she was moderately obese). Finally, another woman had offered her a diet she had recently seen in a magazine. Thus, her concerns about losing her personal identity took the dream form of shrinking in size.

The following dream illustrates how the therapist may selectively focus on those aspects that further the group work:

• *My husband locks me out of our grocery store. I am very concerned about the perishables spoiling. He gets a job in another store, where he is busy taking out the garbage. He is smiling and enjoying this, though it is clear he is being a fool. There is a young, attractive male clerk there who winks at me, and we go out dancing together.*

This member was the middle-aged woman who was introduced into a group of younger members, two of whom, Jan and Bill, were involved in a sexual relationship (discussed in chapter 13). From the standpoint of her personal dynamics, the dream was highly meaningful. Her husband, distant and work-oriented, locked her out of his life. She had a strong feeling of her life slipping by unused (the perishables spoiling). Previously in the group, she had referred to her sexual fantasies as "garbage." She felt considerable anger toward her husband, to which she could not give vent (in the dream, she made an absurd figure of him).

These were tempting dream morsels, yet the therapist instead chose to focus on the *group-relevant* themes. The client had many concerns about being excluded from the group: she felt older, less attractive, and very isolated from the other members. Accordingly, the therapist focused on the theme of being locked out and on her desire for more attention from others in the group, especially the men (one of whom resembled the winking clerk in the dream).

Dreams often reveal unexpressed group concerns or shed light on group blockages and impasses.[40] The following dream illustrates how conscious but avoided group material may, through dreams, be brought into the group for examination.

• *There are two rooms side by side with a mirror in my house. I feel there is a burglar in the next room. I think I can pull the curtain back and see a person in a black mask stealing my possessions.*

This dream was brought in at the twentieth meeting of a therapy group that was observed through a one-way mirror by the therapist's students. Aside from a few comments in the first meeting, the group members had never expressed their feelings about the observers. A discussion of the dream led the group into a valuable and much-needed conversation about the therapist's relationship to the group and to his students. Were the observers "stealing" something from the group? Was the therapist's primary allegiance toward his students, and were the group members merely a means of presenting a good show or demonstration for them?

AUDIOVISUAL TECHNOLOGY

The advent of audiovisual technology has elicited enormous interest among group therapists. Videotaping seems to offer enormous benefits for the practice, teaching, and understanding of group therapy. After all, do we not wish clients to obtain an accurate view of their behavior? Do we not search for methods to encourage self-observation and to make the self-reflective aspect of the here-and-now as salient as the experiencing aspect? Do we not wish to illuminate the blind spots of clients (and therapists, as well)?[41] Audiovisual technology seemed a great boon to the practicing group clinician, and the professional group therapy literature of the late 1960s and 1970s reflected an initial wave of tremendous enthusiasm,[42] but succeeding years have seen a steep decline in articles and books about the clinical use of audiovisual technology—and of those that have been published, the majority focused on populations that are particularly concerned by self-image issues: for example, adolescents and clients with eating disorders or speech disorders. The use of audiovisual techniques in teaching and in research, on the other hand, has been more enduring.

It is hard to explain the diminishing interest in the clinical application of audiovisual technology. Perhaps it is related to the ethos of efficiency and expediency: the clinical use of audiovisual equipment is often awkward and time-consuming. Nonetheless I feel that this technology still has much potential and, at the very least, merits a brief survey of how it has been used in group therapy.

Some clinicians taped each meeting and used immediate playback ("focused feedback") during the session. Obviously, certain portions must be selected by the group members or by leaders for viewing.[43] Some therapists used an auxiliary therapist whose chief task was to operate the camera and associated gadgetry and to select suitable portions for playback. Other therapists taped the meeting and devoted the following session to playback of certain key sections asking the member to react to it.[44]

Some therapists scheduled an extra playback meeting in which most of the previous tape is observed; others taped the first half of the meeting and observed the tape during the second half. Still other therapists used a serial-viewing technique: they videotaped every session and retained short representative segments of each, which they later played back to the group.[45] Other therapists simply made the tapes available to clients who wished to come in between meetings to review some segment of the meeting. The tapes were also made available for absent members to view the meeting they missed.

Client response depends on the timing of the procedure. Clients will respond differently to the first playback session than to later sessions. In the first playback, clients attend primarily to their own image and are less attentive to their styles of interacting with others or to the process of the group. My own experience, and that of others, is that group members may have a keen interest in videotape viewing early in therapy but, once the group becomes cohesive and highly interactive, rapidly lose interest in the viewing and resent time taken away from the live group meeting.[46] Thus, any viewing time may have to be scheduled outside of the regular group meeting.

Often a member's long-cherished self-image is radically challenged by a first videotape playback and they may recall, and be more receptive to, previous feedback offered by other members. Self observation is powerful; nothing is as convincing as information one discovers for oneself.

Many initial playback reactions are concerned with physical attractiveness and mannerisms, whereas in subsequent playback sessions, clients note their interactions with others, withdrawal, self-preoccupation, hostility, or aloofness. They are much more able to be self-observant and objective than when actually involved in the group interaction.

I have on occasion found video recording to be of great value in crisis situations. For example, a man in a group for alcoholics arrived at a meeting intoxicated and proceeded to be monopolistic, insulting, and crude. Heavily intoxicated individuals obviously do not profit from meetings because they are not capable of retaining and integrating the events of the session. This meeting was videotaped, however, and a subsequent viewing was enormously helpful to the client. He had been told but never really apprehended how destructive his alcohol use was to himself and others.

On another occasion in an alcoholic group, a client arrived heavily intoxicated and soon lost consciousness and lay stretched out on the sofa while the group, encircling him, discussed various courses of action. Some time later, the client viewed the tape and was profoundly affected. People had often told him that he was he was killing himself with alcohol, but the sight of himself on videotape, laid out as if on a bier, brought to mind his twin brother, who died of alcoholism.

In another case, a periodically manic client who had never accepted that her behavior was unusual had an opportunity to view herself in a particularly frenetic, disorganized state.[47] In each of these instances, the videotape provided a powerful self-observatory experience—a necessary first step in the therapeutic process.

Videotaping has also been used to prepare long-term patients for a transition out of the hospital. One team reports a structured twelve-session group in which the members engage in a series of nonthreatening exercises and view videotapes in order to improve their communicational and social skills.[48]

Many therapists are reluctant to inflict a video camera on a group. They feel that it will inhibit the group's spontaneity and that the group members will resent the intrusion—though not necessarily overtly. In my experience, the person who often experiences the most discomfort is the therapist. The fear of being exposed and shamed, particularly in supervision, is a leading cause of therapist resistance and must be addressed in supervision (see chapter 17).[49]

Clients who are to view the playback are usually receptive to the suggestion of videotaping. Of course, they are concerned about confidentiality and need reassurance on this issue. If the tape is to be viewed by anyone other than the group members (for example, students, researchers, or supervisors), the therapist must be explicit about the purpose of the viewing and the identity of the viewers and must also obtain written permission from each member with regard to each intended use: clinical, educational, and research. Clients should be full participants in the decision about the secure storage or erasure of the videotapes.

Videotaping in Teaching

Video recording has proven its value in the teaching of all forms of psychotherapy. Students and supervisors are able to view a session with a minimum of distortion. Important nonverbal aspects of behavior by both students and clients, which may be completely missed in the traditional supervisory format, become available for study. The student-therapist has a rich opportunity to observe his or her own presentation of self and body language. Frequently what gets missed in traditional supervision is not the students' "mistakes," but the very effective interventions that they employ intuitively without conscious awareness. Confusing aspects of the meeting may be viewed several times until some order appears. Valuable teaching sessions that clearly illustrate basic principles of therapy may be stored and a teaching videotape library created. This has become a mainstay of training psychotherapists for both clinical practice and for leading manual-based groups in clinical trials.†[50]

Videotaping in Research

The use of videotaping has also advanced the field significantly by allowing researchers to ensure that the psychotherapy being tested in clinical trials is delivered competently and adheres to the intent of the study.[51] It is no less important in a psychotherapy trial than it is in a drug therapy trial to monitor the treatment delivery and demonstrate that clients received the right kind and right amount of treatment. In pharmacotherapy research, blood level assays are used for this purpose. In psychotherapy research, video recordings are an excellent monitoring tool for the same purpose.

WRITTEN SUMMARIES

For the past thirty years, I have regularly used the ancillary technique of written summaries in my group therapy. At the end of each session, I dictate a detailed summary of the group session.[52] The summary is an editorialized narrative that describes the flow of the session, each member's contribution, my contributions (not only what I said but what I wished I had said and what I did say but regretted), and any hunches or questions that occur to me after the session. This dictation is transcribed either by a typist or via voice recognition program and mailed to the members the following day. Dictation of the summaries (two to three single-spaced pages) requires approximately twenty to thirty minutes of a therapist's time and is best done immediately after the session. To date, my students and colleagues and I have written and mailed thousands of group summaries to group members. It is my strong belief that the procedure greatly facilitates therapy.

But in these days of economically pressured psychotherapy, who can accommodate a task that requires yet another thirty minutes of therapist time and an hour or two of secretarial time? For that matter, look back through this chapter: Who has time for setting up cameras and selecting portions of the videotape to replay to the group? Who has time for even brief meetings with a co-therapist before and after meetings? Or for conferring with group members' individual therapists? The answer, of course, is that harried therapists must make choices and often, alas, must sacrifice some potentially powerful but time-consuming adjuncts to therapy in order to meet the demands of the marketplace. Every therapist is dismayed by the draining off of time and effort in completing mountains of paperwork.

Managed health care administrators believe that time can be saved by streamlining therapy—making it slicker, briefer, more uniform. But in psychotherapy, uniformity is not synonymous with efficiency, let alone with effectiveness. Therapists sacrifice the very core of therapy if they sacrifice their ingenuity and their ability to respond to unusual clinical situations with creative measures. Hence, even though the practice is not in wide clinical use at present, I devote space in this text to such techniques as the written summary. I believe it is a potent facilitating technique. My experience has been that all group therapists willing to try it have found that it enhances the course of group therapy.†[53] Moreover, a description of the summary technique raises many issues of great importance in the education of the young therapist.†[54]

The written summary may even do double service as a mechanism for documenting the course of therapy and meeting the requirements of third-party payers, turning the usually unrewarding and dry process of record keeping into a functional intervention.[55] We are wise to remember that the client's record belongs to the client and can be accessed by the client at any point. In all instances, it is appropriate to write notes expecting that they may be read by the client. Notes should therefore provide a transparent, therapeutic, depathologizing, considered, and empathic account of the treatment (and not include group members' last names).

My first experience with the written summary was in individual therapy. A young woman, Ginny, had attended a therapy group for six months but had to terminate because she moved out of town and could not arrange transportation to get to the group on time. Moreover, her inordinate shyness and inhibition had made it difficult for her to participate in the group. Ginny was inhibited in her work as well: a gifted writer, she was crippled by severe writer's block.

I agreed to treat her in individual therapy but with one unusual proviso: after each therapy hour, she had to write an impressionistic, freewheeling summary of the underground of the session, that is, what she was really thinking and feeling but had not verbally expressed. My hope was that the assignment would help penetrate the writing block and encourage greater spontaneity. I agreed to write an equally candid summary. Ginny had a pronounced positive transference. She idealized me in every way, and my hope was that a written summary conveying my honest feelings—pleasure, discouragement, puzzlement, fatigue—would permit her to relate more genuinely to me.

For a year and a half, Ginny and I wrote weekly summaries. We handed them, sealed, to my secretary, and every few months we read each other's summaries. The experiment turned out to be highly successful: Ginny did well in therapy, and the summaries contributed greatly to that success.* I developed sufficient courage from the venture (and courage is needed: it is difficult at first for a therapist to be so self-revealing) to think about adapting the technique to a therapy group. The opportunity soon arose in two groups of alcoholic clients.[56]

My co-therapists and I had attempted to lead these groups in an interactional mode. The groups had gone well in that the members were interacting openly and productively. However, here-and-now interaction always entails anxiety, and alcoholic clients are notoriously poor anxiety binders. By the eighth meeting, members who had been dry for months were drinking again (or threatening to drink again if they "ever had another meeting like the one last week!"). We hastily sought methods of modulating anxiety: increased structure, a suggested (written) agenda for each meeting, video playback, and written summaries distributed after each meeting. The group members considered the written summary to be the most efficacious method by far, and soon it replaced the others.

I believe that the summaries are most valuable if they are honest and straightforward about the process of therapy. They are virtually identical to summaries I make for my own files (which provide most of the clinical material for this book) and are based on the assumption that the client is a full collaborator in the therapeutic process—that *psychotherapy is strengthened, not weakened, by demystification.*

The summary serves several functions: it provides understanding of the events of the session, takes note of good (or resistive) sessions; comments on client gains; predicts (and, by doing so, generally prevents) undesirable developments; brings in silent members; increases cohesiveness (by underscoring similarities and caring in the group, and so on); invites new behavior and interactions; provides interpretations (either repetition of interpretations made in the group or new interpretations occurring to the therapist later); and provides hope to the group members (helping them realize that the group is an orderly process and that the therapists have some coherent sense of the group's long-term development). In fact, the summary may be used to augment every one of the group leader's tasks in a group. In the following discussion of the functions of the summary, I

---

*I learned a great deal about psychotherapy from this experiment. For one thing, it brought home to me the *Rashomon* nature of the therapeutic venture (see chapter 4). The client and I had extraordinarily different perspectives of the hours we shared. All my marvelous interpretations? She had never even heard them! Instead, Ginny heard, and valued, very different parts of the therapy hour: the deeply human exchanges; the fleeting supportive, accepting glances; the brief moments of real intimacy. The exchange of summaries also provided interesting instruction about psychotherapy, and I used the summaries in my teaching. Years later the client and I decided to write a prologue and an afterword and publish the summaries as a book. (*Every Day Gets a Little Closer.* New York: Basic Books, 1974.)

shall cite excerpts from summaries and end the section with an entire summary.

Revivification and Continuity

The summary becomes another group contact during the week. The meeting is revivified for the members, and the group is more likely to assume continuity. In chapter 5 I stated that groups assume more power if the work is continuous, if themes begun one week are not dropped but explored, more deeply, in succeeding meetings. The summary augments this process. Not infrequently, group members begin a meeting by referring to the previous summary—either a theme they wish to explore or a statement with which they disagree.

Understanding Process

The summary helps clients reexperience and understand important events of a meeting. In chapter 6, I described the here-and-now as consisting of two phases: *experience* and *the understanding of that experience. The summary facilitates the second stage*, the understanding and integration of the affective experience. Sometimes group sessions may be so threatening or unsettling that members close down and move into a defensive, survival position. Only later (often with the help of the summary) can they review significant events and convert them into constructive learning experiences. The therapist's interpretations (especially complex ones) delivered in the midst of a melee tend to fall on deaf ears. Interpretations repeated in the summary are often effective because the client is able to consider them at length, far from the intensity of engagement.

Shaping Group Norms

The summaries may be used to reinforce norms both implicitly and explicitly. For example, the following excerpt reinforces the here-and-now norm:

> • *Phil's relationship with his boss is very important and difficult for him at this time, and as such is certainly material for the group. However, the members do not know the boss, what he is like, what he is thinking and feeling and thus are limited in offering help. However, they are beginning to know one another and can be more certain of their own reactions to one another in the group. They can give more accurate feedback about feelings that occur between them rather than trying to guess what the boss may be thinking.*

Or consider the following excerpt, which encourages the group members to comment on process and to approach the therapist in an egalitarian manner:

> • *Jed did something very different in the group today, which was to make an observation about the bind that Irv [the therapist] was in. He noted, quite correctly, that Irv was in a bind of not wishing to change the topic from Dinah because of Irv's reluctance to stir up any of Dinah's bad feelings about being rejected or abandoned in the group, but on the other hand Irv wanted very much to find out what was happening to Pete, who was obviously hurting today.*

Therapeutic Leverage

The therapist may, in the summary, reinforce risk taking and focus clients on their primary task, their original purpose in coming to therapy. For example:

> • *Irene felt hurt at Jim's calling her an observer of life and fell silent for the next forty-five minutes. Later she said she felt clamped up and thought about leaving the group. It is important that Irene keep in mind that her main reason for being in therapy was that she felt estranged from others and unable to create closer, sustained relationships, especially with men. In that context, it is important for her to recognize, understand, and eventually overcome her impulse to clamp up and withdraw as a response to feedback.*

Or the therapist may take care to repeat statements by clients that will offer leverage in the future. For example:

> • *Nancy began weeping at this point, but when Ed tried to console her, she snapped, "Stop being so kind. I don't cry because I'm miserable, I cry when I'm pissed off. When you console me or let me off the hook because of my tears, you always stop me from looking at my anger."*

New Thoughts

Often the therapist understands an event after the fact. On other occasions, the timing is not right for a clarifying remark during a session (there are times when too much cognition might squelch the emotional experience), or there has simply been no time available in the meeting, or a member has been so defensive that he or she would reject any efforts at clarification. The summaries provide the therapist with a second chance to convey important thoughts. This excerpt communicates a message that emerged in the cotherapist's postmeeting discussion. The summary describes and attempts to counteract undesirable developments in the session—the shaping of countertherapeutic norms and scapegoating:

• *Ellen and Len were particularly vehement today in pointing out several times that Cynthia had been confrontative and insensitive to Ted and, as Len put it, was very, very hard on people. Is it possible that what was going on in the group today might be viewed from another perspective: the perspective of what types of message the group was giving to the new members about how they would like them to be in the group? Is it possible that the group was suggesting to Rick and Carla [new members] that they take pains not to be critical and that open criticism is something that simply is not done here in this group? It may also be true that, to some degree, Cynthia was "set up," that she was made the "fall person" for this transaction: that is, is it possible that, at some unconscious level, the group concluded that she was tough enough to take this and they could get a message to the new members through Cynthia, through a criticism of her behavior?*

Transmission of the Therapist's Temporal Perspective

Far more than any member of the group, the therapist maintains a long-range temporal perspective and is cognizant of changes occurring over many weeks or months, both in the group and in each of the members. There are many times when the sharing of these observations offers hope, support, and meaning for the members. For example:

• *Seymour spoke quite openly in the group today about how hurt he was by Jack and Burt switching the topic off him. We [the co-therapists] were struck by the ease and forthrightness with which he was able to discuss these feelings. We can clearly remember his hurt, passive, silence in similar situations in the past, and are impressed with how markedly he has changed his ability to express his feelings openly.*

The summaries provide temporal perspective in yet another way. Since the clients almost invariably save and file the reports, they have a comprehensive account of their progression through the group, an account to which they may, with great profit, refer in the future.

Therapist Self-Disclosure

Therapists, in the service of the clients' therapy, may use the summary as a vehicle to disclose personal here-and-now feelings (of puzzlement, of discouragement, of irritation, of pleasure) and their views about the theory and rationale underlying their own behavior in the group. Consider the therapist self-disclosure in these illustrative excerpts:

• *Irv and Louise [the co-therapists] both felt considerable strain in the meeting. We felt caught between our feelings of wanting to continue more with Dinah, but also being very much aware of Al's obvious hurting in the meeting. Therefore, even at the risk of Dinah's feeling that we were deserting her, we felt strongly about bringing in Al before the end of the meeting.*

* *We felt very much in a bind with Seymour. He was silent during the meeting. We felt very much that we wanted to bring him into the group and help him talk, especially since we knew that the reason he had dropped out of his previous group was because of his feeling that people were uninterested in what he had to say. On the other hand, today we decided to resist the desire to bring him in because we knew that by continually bringing Seymour into the group, we are infantilizing him, and it will be much better if, sooner or later, he is able to do it by himself.*

* *Irv had a definite feeling of dissatisfaction with his own behavior in the meeting today. He felt he dominated things too much, that he was too active, too directive. No doubt this is due in large part to his feeling of guilt at having missed the previous two meetings and wanting to make up for it today by giving as much as possible.*

Filling Gaps

An obvious and important function of the summary is to fill in gaps for members who miss meetings because of illness, vacation, or any other reason. The summaries keep them abreast of events and enable them to move more quickly back into the group.

New Group Members

The entrance of a new member may also be facilitated by providing summaries of the previous few meetings. I routinely ask new members to read such summaries before attending the first meeting.

General Impressions

I believe that the written summary facilitates therapy. Clients have been unanimous in their positive evaluation: most read and consider the summaries very seriously; many reread them several times; almost all file them for future use. The client's therapeutic perspective and commitment is deepened; the therapeutic relationship is strengthened; and no serious transference complications occur. The dialogue and disagreement about summaries is always helpful and makes this a collaborative process. The intent of the summary should never be to convey a sense of the "last word" on something.

I have noted no adverse consequences. Many therapists have asked about confidentiality, but I have encountered no problems in this area. Clients are asked to regard the summary with the same degree of confidentiality as any event in the group. As an extra precaution, I use only first names, avoid explicit identification of any particularly delicate issue (for example, an extramarital affair), and mail it out in a plain envelope with no return address. E-mail may be another, even more time-efficient vehicle if security can be assured.

The only serious objection to written summaries I have encountered occurred in a six-month pilot research group of adult survivors of incest. In that group there was one member with a history of extreme abuse who slipped in and out of paranoid thinking. She was convinced that her abusers were still after her and that the summary would somehow constitute a paper trail leading them to her. She did not want any summaries mailed to her. Soon two other members expressed discomfort with any written record because of the extent of their shame around the incest. Consequently, my co-therapist and I announced that we would discontinue the written summary. However, the other members expressed so much grumbling disappointment that we ultimately agreed on a compromise: for the last ten minutes of each session, my co-therapist and I summarized our impressions and experiences of the meeting. Although the oral summary could not provide everything a written one did, it nonetheless proved a satisfactory compromise.

Like any event in the group, the summaries generate differential responses. For example, clients with severe dependency yearnings will cherish every word; those with a severe counterdependent posture will challenge every word or, occasionally, be unable to spare the time to read them at all; obsessive clients obsess over the precise meaning of the words; and paranoid individuals search for hidden meanings. Thus, although the summaries provide a clarifying force, they do not thwart the formation of the distortions whose corrections are intrinsic to therapy.

A Summary of a Group's Twentieth Meeting

The complete summary below is unedited aside from minor stylistic improvements and change of names. I dictated it on a microcassette recorder in approximately twenty minutes (driving home after the session). A few weeks are required to learn to dictate meetings comfortably and quickly, but it is not a difficult feat. My co-therapists, generally psychiatry residents, do the dictating on alternate weeks, and after only a few weeks the clients cannot differentiate whether I or my co-leader did the summary. *It is essential that the summary be dictated immediately after a session* and, if co-leading, after the postgroup debriefing with your co-therapist. This is very important! The sequence of events in the group fades quickly. Do not let even a phone call intervene between the meeting and your dictation.

I suggest this dictating plan: first try to construct the skeleton of the meeting by recalling the two to four major issues of the meeting. When that is in place, next try to recall the transitions between issues. Then go back to each issue and try to describe each member's contribution to the discussion of each issue. Pay special attention to your own role, including what you said (or didn't say) and what was directed toward you.

Do not be perfectionistic: One cannot recall or remember everything. Do not try to refresh your memory by listening to a tape of a meeting—that would make the task far too time-consuming. I mail it out without proof-reading it; clients overlook errors and omissions. Voice-activated computer technology makes the task even simpler and less time-consuming.

This is a sample summary of a meeting of a long-term open ambulatory group. It is better written (polished for this text) and more lucid than the great majority of my summaries. Do not be dissuaded from trying the summary technique after reading this. Don't be dismayed, either, by the length of this summary. Because I want to take advantage of this opportunity to describe a meeting in great detail, I have selected a summary that is about 25 percent longer than most.

> • *Terri was absent because of illness. Laura opened the meeting by raising an important question for her left over from last week. During her interchange with Edith, she thought that she had seen Paul give Kathy a knowing glance. Paul assured Laura that that was, indeed, not the case. He had looked at Kathy—but it was for a different reason entirely: it had been because of his deep concern about Kathy's depression last week, hoping to find a way to involve Kathy more in the group. The matter was dropped there, but it seemed a particularly useful way for Laura to have used the group. It is not an uncommon experience for individuals to feel that others exchange glances when they are talking, and it seemed as though Laura had a certain sense of being excluded or perhaps of Paul dismissing her or possibly Paul being uninterested in what she and Edith were up to.*
>
> *The next issue that emerged consumed a considerable portion of the meeting and, in some ways, was tedious for many of the members but, at the same time, was an exceptionally valuable piece of work. Paul took the floor and began talking about certain types of insight he had had during the couple of weeks. He took a very long time to describe what he had been feeling, and did so in a highly intelligent but intellectualized and vague fashion. People in the group, at this point, were either straining to stay with Paul and understand what he was coming to or, as in the case of Bill and Ted, had begun to tune Paul out. Eventually what transpired was that Paul communicated to the group that he had some real doubts about whether or not he, indeed, really wanted to go back to law school, and was wrestling with those doubts.*

During Paul's entire presentation he seemed, at some level, aware that he was being unclear and that he was communicating what he had to say in a highly oblique fashion. He asked, on several occasions, whether the group was following him and whether he was clear. At the end of his presentation, he puzzled individuals in the group by commenting that he felt very good about what had happened in the group and felt that he was in exactly the place he wanted to be in. Kathy questioned this. She, like others in the group, felt a little puzzled about what on earth it was that Paul had gotten from the whole sequence.

But apparently what had happened was that Paul had been able to convey to the group the struggle he was having about this decision and, at the same time, covertly to make it clear to the group that he did not want any active help with the content of the decision. When we wondered why Paul couldn't just come out and say what it took him a very long time to say in just a sentence or two—that is, "I'm struggling with the decision to enter law school and I'm not certain if I want to go"— he said he would have felt extremely frightened had he said that. It seemed, as we analyzed it, that what he was frightened of was that somehow the group, as his family had, would take the decision away from him, would rob him of his autonomy, would leap in and make the decision for him in some fashion.

Then we suggested another approach for Paul. Would it have been possible for him to have started the meeting by being explicit about the whole process: that is, "I'm struggling with an important decision. I don't know if I really want to go to law school. I want you all to know this and be able to share this with you, but I don't want anyone in the group to help me actually make the decision." Paul reflected upon this and commented that sounded very possible—something, indeed, he could have done. We'll need to keep that in mind for the future: when Paul becomes intellectualized and vague, we should help him find ways to communicate his thoughts and needs succinctly and directly. That is, if he wants to get something from others and, at the same time, not puzzle or discourage them.

At the very end of this, the group seemed to have some difficulty letting Paul go, and more questions kept being asked of him. Al, in particular, asked Paul several questions about the content of his decision, until Edith finally commented that she'd like to change the topic, and it was clear that Paul was more than glad to do so.

We did not discuss in the group today Al's questioning of Paul, which is not dissimilar from some other meetings in the past where Al became intensely interested in the content of the enterprise. One speculation we have (which will undoubtedly be rejected outright!) is that

Al may be filling the time of the group as a way to keep the group away from asking him some questions about the pain in his life.

There was a very brief interchange between Edith and Laura. After their confrontation last week, Edith said that Laura had come up to her after the meeting and made it clear to her that Edith should not be upset about what was, at least in part, Laura's problem. Edith felt grateful at that and let Laura know that. At the same time, however, Laura could comment to Edith that when Edith first started to talk to her in the meeting today, she felt this rush of fear again.

We did not pursue that any further, but we wonder if that's not an important event: that is, that it might be important not only to Laura but to Edith as well to know that Laura has this fear of her—a fear that Paul commented he also shared at times. The reason this might be important is that Edith stated that she wants to do some work on the attitude of attack that she often assumes.

The man she is dating has made similar comments to her. Is it possible that the aspect of Laura's fear that may be important to Edith is that Laura has been attacked by Edith on several occasions in the past and that Laura remembers these and is (understandably) cautious? Edith, on the other hand, has a sense that, because she has forgotten or dismissed the previous attack, Laura should therefore, of course, do so also—and that's where the discrepancy begins to come in. Indeed, in the previous meeting, Edith seemed rather astonished that Laura would still continue to feel that fear. This may be an important theme that should be examined in future meetings. People forget different things at different rates.

Irv attempted to bring Ted into the meeting because everyone has been aware that Ted has been withdrawn and silent in the meetings, and his participation has been much missed. Ted talked, once again, about feeling that the group was unsafe and feeling fearful of talking because he keeps being attacked for almost anything he says. But not so, the group said! We then talked about the fact that, as Laura pointed out, when he talked about issues that were personal and close to himself—like his loneliness or his difficulties making friends—then, indeed, there was no attack at all.

The group began to try to help differentiate that there are things that Ted may do that evoke attack, but there are plenty of other ways he could interact in the group that would, indeed, not culminate in any type of attack. What ways? Ted asked.

Well, Irv pointed out that Ted might make positive comments about people or focus on some of the things he liked about people in the group, and it was suggested that he do this. Edith asked him for some

positive feedback, and for a few moments Ted was blocked and then fi-
nally commented that Edith had "a pleasant personality . . . usually."

The phrasing of this sentence soon resulted in some antagonistic ex-
changes, and soon Ted was back in a very familiar and very unsafe sit-
uation in the group. Laura and others pointed out that he had phrased
that compliment in such a way as to undo it and make it seem less like
a compliment and almost more like something negative. Al and others
pointed out how the adding of the word "usually" made it seem ironi-
cal rather than a genuine compliment. Ted defended himself by saying
that he had to be honest and had to be accurate. He also pointed out
that, if he were simply to say that Edith was intelligent or sensitive, she
would immediately conclude that he meant that she was the most in-
telligent person in the room.

Edith pointed out that, indeed, that was not the case, and she would
have been pleased to hear him give that kind, any kind, of compliment.
Ted might have been in a little less of a bind, as Bill pointed out, had
he made a more limited type of compliment: that is, rather than talk
about something as global as personality, make it somewhat more nar-
row. For example, Ted might have commented on some aspect of Edith
that he liked, some single act, something she said, even her dress or her
hair or some particular mannerism.

When we questioned Ted about how he had gotten back into this sit-
uation in the group and whether he bore any responsibility for it, Ted
was very quick to point out that, indeed, he had and that he did share
a good part of the burden of responsibility for the position of being at-
tacked that he was in. We attempted to point out to Ted that feeling the
group as unsafe is an extremely important issue for him to work on be-
cause this is very much the way he experiences the world outside, and
the more he can explore ways to live in the group so that it appears less
dangerous, the more he will be able to generalize to his life outside.

In the last few minutes of the group, the focus turned to Bill. Edith
and others commented that they had been missing his participation.
Bill stated he'd been aware of his inactivity and been disappointed that
he'd shared so little of himself. His silence has been somewhat different
from Ted's silence in that he does not experience the group as unsafe
but instead has a sense of letting things pass by. If he has some ques-
tions or opinions, he's perfectly willing to let them go by without ex-
pressing them. This posture of letting the life in the group go by may be
extremely important for Bill because it reflects how he lives in the
world at large—where he lets much of life go by and often experiences
himself more as an observer than as a participant. Changing that pos-
ture in the group would be the first step to changing that posture in life.

Kathy was rather quiet in the group today, but the comments she did make earlier in the meeting reflected that she, at least visibly, appears less depressed and distressed than she was during the previous meeting.

This summary illustrates several of the functions I described earlier. It clarifies process. A good deal of the meeting was consumed by Paul's obsessive, confusing monologue (which was rendered more confusing yet by his comment that he had gotten a great deal from his recitation). The summary explained the process of that transaction. It also reinforced norms (by, for example, supporting Laura for checking out surreptitious glances passing between two members). It increased therapeutic leverage by linking in-group behavior with out-group problems (two instances of this: Edith's relationship with her boyfriend and Bill's observer posture in life).

It added some afterthoughts (the comment to Al about filling time with questions about content to keep the group from questioning him). It attempted to identify behavioral and dynamic patterns (for example, Edith's narcissistic sense of entitlement—that is, that she should be able to attack when she was angry and that the others should forget about it when she felt better). Lastly, it left no one out, reminding each that they were being seen and cared for.

GROUP THERAPY RECORD KEEPING

Documentation of therapy must protect confidentiality and meet a number of objectives: to demonstrate that an appropriate standard of care has been provided; to describe the process and effectiveness of the treatment; to facilitate continuity of care by another therapist at a later time; to verify that a billable service has been provided at a certain time and date.

For these purposes many recommend that the group therapist keep a combined record: a group record and a separate file for each individual member.[57] If written group summaries are used, they should be included in the group record. For students the group record may also serve as the group *process notes* that will be reviewed in supervision. The group record should note attendance, scheduling issues, prominent group themes, the state of group cohesion, prominent interactions, transference and countertransference, what was engaged and what was avoided, and anticipations of what will need to be addressed in the next session. The group therapist should *always* review this record immediately before the following meeting.

In addition, a personal chart or record must be kept for each individual client. This record serves as the client's personal *progress notes*, noting initial goals, symptoms; safety concerns if any; engagement with the psychotherapy process; and achievement of therapy goals. Whereas the group record should be made after each group meeting, the individual progress notes can be made at less frequent but regular intervals, with more frequent entries as the clinical situation warrants.

STRUCTURED EXERCISES

I use the term *structured exercise* to denote an activity in which a group follows some specific set of directions. It is an experiment carried out in the group, generally suggested by the leader but occasionally by some experienced member. The precise rationale of the structured exercises varies, but in general they are considered accelerating devices. Unlike some of the more time-consuming techniques described in this chapter, these exercises may be regarded as efficiency oriented and hence may be of special interest to managed health care therapists and policymakers.

Structured exercises attempt to speed up the group with warm-up procedures that bypass the hesitant, uneasy first steps of the group; they speed up interaction by assigning to interacting individuals tasks that circumvent ritualized, introductory social behavior; and they speed up each individual member's work by techniques designed to help members move quickly to get in touch with suppressed emotions, with unknown parts of themselves, and with their physical selves.† In some settings and with some clinical populations, the structured exercise may be the central focus of the meeting. Some common models include action- and activity-oriented groups for the elderly (such as art, dance, and movement groups) that aim to reconnect clients to a sense of effectiveness, competence, and social interaction; structured activity groups for hospitalized psychotic patients; and body awareness for victims of trauma.[58]

Mindfulness-based stress reduction (MBSR) groups that teach meditation, deep breathing, and relaxation and focus awareness on members' moment-to-moment state of being are also prominent and have been used to remarkably good effect in the treatment of medical illnesses and anxiety disorders and in the prevention of relapse in depression.[59] These techniques can also be incorporated as smaller components of broader-based group interventions.

The structured exercise in interactional groups may require only a few minutes, or it may consume an entire meeting. It may be predominantly verbal or nonverbal. Almost all nonverbal procedures, however, include a verbal component; generally, the successful structured exercise will generate data that is subsequently discussed. Such exercises, common in the encounter groups but far less used in the therapy group, may involve the *entire group as a group* (the group may be asked, for example, to build something or to plan an outing); *one member vis-à-vis the group* (the "trust fall," for example, in which one member stands, eyes closed, in the center and falls, allowing the group to catch, support, and then cradle and rock the person); *the entire group as individuals* (members may be asked in turn to give their initial impressions of everyone else in the group); *the entire group as dyads* (the "blind walk," for example, in which the group is broken into dyads and each pair takes a walk with one member blindfolded and led by the other); *one designated dyad* (two members locked in a struggle may be asked to take turns pushing the other to the ground and then lifting him or her up again); or *one designated member* ("switching chairs"—a member may be asked to give voice to two or more conflicting inner roles, moving from one chair to another as he or she assumes one or the other role). Any prescribed exercise that involves physical contact needs to be carefully considered. If the usual boundaries of therapy are to be crossed, even in the best of faith and with clear therapeutic intent, it is essential to obtain informed consent from the group members.

Structured exercises were widely used in the T-group and later in the encounter group (see chapter 16), and their popularity received a boost from gestalt therapy in the 1960s and 1970s. For a time, such exercises were used to excess by many leaders and training programs. Some group leader training programs relied heavily on texts of structured exercises and trained technique-oriented leaders who reach into a grab bag of gimmicks whenever the proceedings flag. During the 1980s, the general public came to identify group therapy with structured exercises through large group awareness courses (for example, est and Lifespring). Such courses consisted entirely of a two-to-four-day potpourri of structured exercises and didactic and inspirational instruction.[60]

This injudicious use of structured exercises was a miscarriage of the intent of the approaches that spawned these techniques. The T-group field formulated exercises that were designed to demonstrate principles of group dynamics (both between and within groups) and to accelerate group development. Since the typical T-group met for a sharply limited period of time, the leaders sought methods to speed the group past the initial reserve and social ritualized behavior. Their aim was for members to experience as much as possible of the developmental sequence of the small group.

Gestalt therapy, another major source of structured exercises, is based on existential roots. Fritz Perls (the founder of gestalt therapy) left many recorded sessions with clients as well as theoretical essays that demonstrate that he was basically concerned with problems of existence, self-awareness, responsibility, contingency, and wholeness both within an individual and within the individual's social and physical universe.[61] Although Perls's technical approach was novel, his conception of the human being's basic dilemma is one he shares with a long line of philosophers of life, stretching back to the beginning of recorded thought.

Paradoxically, gestalt therapy has come to be considered by some clinicians as a speedy, gimmick-oriented therapy, whereas, in fact, it is an ambitious and thoughtful venture. It attempts to penetrate denial systems and to bring clients to a new perspective on their position in the world. Although it decries a technical, packaged approach, some gestalt therapy trainees do not progress past technique, do not grasp the theoretical assumptions on which all technique must rest.

How has it come about that the substance has so often been mistaken for the essence of the gestalt approach? The cornerstone for the error was unwittingly laid by Perls himself, whose creative, technical virtuosity acted in such consort with his flair for showmanship as to lead many people to mistake the medium for the message. Perls had to do battle with the hyperintellectualized emphasis of the early analytic movement and often overreacted and overstated his opposition to theory. "Lose your mind and come to your senses," Perls proclaimed. Consequently, he did not write a great deal but taught by illustration, trusting that his students would discover their own truths through experience rather than through the intellectual process. Descriptions of the contemporary practice of gestalt therapy emphasize a more balanced approach, which employs structured exercises (or "therapist-induced experiments") in a judicious fashion.[62]

How useful are structured exercises? What does research tell us about the effects of these procedures on the process and outcome of the group? Lieberman, Yalom, and Miles's encounter group project (see chapter 16) closely studied the impact of the structured exercise and came to the following conclusions.[63] Leaders who used many exercises were popular with their groups. Immediately at the end of a group, the members regarded them as *more competent, more effective, and more perceptive* than leaders who used these techniques sparingly. *Yet the members of groups that used the most exercises had significantly less favorable outcomes than did the members of groups with the fewest exercises.* (The groups with the most exercises had fewer high changers, fewer total positive changers, and more negative changers. Moreover, the high changers of the encounter groups with the most exercises were *less* likely to maintain change over time.)

In short, the moral of this study is that *if your goal is to have your group members think you're competent and that you know what you're doing, then use an abundance of structured interventions*; in doing so, in leading by providing explicit directions, in assuming total executive function, you fulfill the group's fantasies of what a leader should do. However, your group members will *not be improved; in fact, excessive reliance on these techniques renders a group less effective.*

The study explored other differences between the groups with the most and the least exercises. The amount of self-disclosure and the emotional climate of the groups was the same. But there were differences in the themes emphasized: *The groups with more exercises focused on the expression of positive and negative feelings; those with fewer exercises had a greater range of thematic concerns: the setting of goals; the selection of procedural methods; closeness versus distance; trust versus mistrust; genuineness versus phoniness; affection; and isolation.*

It would seem, then, that groups using many structured exercises never deal with several important group themes. There is no doubt that the structured exercises appear to plunge the members quickly into a great degree of expressivity, *but the group pays a price for its speed*; it circumvents many group developmental tasks and does not develop a sense of autonomy and potency.

It is not easy for group clinicians to evaluate their own use of structured techniques. In the encounter group project almost all leaders used some structured exercises. Some of the more effective leaders attributed their success in large measure to these techniques. To take one example, many leaders used the "hot seat" technique (a format popularized by Perls in which one member sits in the central chair, and the leader in particular as well as the other members focus on that member exclusively and exhaustively for a long period of time).

However, the approach was as highly valued by the most ineffective leaders as by the effective ones. Obviously, other aspects of leader behavior accounted for the effective leaders' success, but if they erroneously credit their effectiveness to the structured exercise, then it is given a value it does not deserve (and is unfortunately passed on to students as the central feature of the process of change).

The Lieberman, Yalom, and Miles encounter group project also demonstrated that it was not just the leaders' interactions with a member that mediated change. Of even greater importance were many psychosocial forces in the change process: Change was heavily influenced by an individual's role in the group (centrality, level of influence, value congruence, and activity) and by characteristics of the group (cohesiveness, climate of high intensity and harmoniousness, and norm structure). In other words, the data failed to support the importance of the leaders' direct therapeutic interaction with each member.

Though these findings issue from short-term encounter groups, they have much relevance for the therapy group. First, consider speed: structured exercises do indeed bypass early, slow stages of group interaction and do indeed plunge members quickly into an expression of positive and negative feelings. But whether or not they accelerate the process of therapy is another question entirely.

In short-term groups—T-groups or very brief therapy groups—it is often legitimate to employ techniques to bypass certain difficult stages, to help the group move on when it is mired in an impasse. In long-term therapy groups, the process of bypassing is less germane; the leader more often wishes to guide the group *through* anxiety, *through* the impasse or difficult stages, rather than *around* them. Resistance, as I have emphasized throughout this text, is not an impediment to therapy but is the stuff of therapy. The early psychoanalysts conceived of the analytic procedure in two stages: the analysis of resistance and then the true analysis (which consists of strip-mining the infantile unconscious roots of behavior). Later they realized that the analysis of resistance, if pursued thoroughly, is sufficient unto itself.

Interactional group therapy functions similarly: There is more to be gained by experiencing and exploring great timidity or suspiciousness or any of a vast number of dynamics underlying a member's initial guardedness than by providing the member with a vehicle that plunges him or her willy-nilly into deep disclosure or expressivity. Acceleration that results in material being wrenched in an untimely way from individuals may be counterproductive if the proper context of the material has not been constructed.

Yet another reason for urging caution in the use of multiple structured exercises in therapy groups is that leaders who do so run the risk of infantilizing the group. Members of a highly structured, leader-centered group begin to feel that help (all help) emanates from the leader; they await their turn to work with the leader; they deskill themselves; they cease to avail themselves of the help and resources available in the group. They divest themselves of responsibility.

I do not wish to overstate the case against the use of structured exercises. Surely there is a middle ground between allowing the group, on the one hand, to flounder pointlessly in some unproductive sequence and, on the other, assuming a frenetically active, overly structured leadership role. Indeed, that is the conclusion the Lieberman, Yalom, and Miles study reached.[64] The study demonstrated that an active, executive, managerial leadership style function relates to outcome in a curvilinear fashion: that is, *too much structure and too little structure were negatively correlated with good outcome.* Too much structure created the types of problem discussed above (leader-centered, dependent groups), and too little (a laissez-faire approach) resulted in plodding, unenergetic, high-attrition groups.

We do not need to look toward any unusual types of groups to find structured exercises—many of the techniques I described in chapter 5, which the leader employs in norm setting, in here-and-now activation, and in process-illumination functions, have a prescriptive quality. ("Who in the group do you feel closest to?" "Can you look at Mary as you talk to her?" "If you were going to be graded for your work in the group, what grade would you receive?" And so on.) Therapists also may use a guided-fantasy structured exercise during a meeting. For example, they might ask members to close their eyes and then describe to them some relaxing scene (like a barefoot walk on the beach with warm, gentle waves rippling in), then ask them to imagine meeting one or more of the group members or leaders and to complete the fantasy. Later, members would be asked to share and explore their fantasies in the group.

Every experienced group leader employs some structured exercises. For example, if a group is tense and experiences a silence of a minute or two (a minute's silence feels very long in a group), I often ask for a go-around in which each member says, quickly, what he or she has been feeling or has thought of saying, but did not, during that silence. This simple exercise usually generates much valuable data.†

What is important in the use of structured exercises are the degree, accent, and purpose associated with them. If structured interventions are suggested to help mold an autonomously functioning group, or to steer the group into the here-and-now, or to explicate process, they may be of value. In a brief group therapy format, they may be invaluable tools for focusing the group on its task and plunging the group more quickly into its task. If used, they should be properly timed; nothing is as disconcerting as the right idea in the wrong place at the wrong time. It is a mistake to use exercises as emotional space filler—that is, as something interesting to do when the group seems at loose ends.

Nor should a structured exercise be used to generate affect in the group. A properly led therapy group should not need energizing from outside. If there seems insufficient energy in the group, if meetings seem listless, if time and time again the therapist feels it necessary to inject voltage into the group, there is most likely a significant developmental problem that a reliance on accelerating devices will only compound. What is needed instead is to explore the obstructions, the norm structure, the members' passive posture toward the leader, the relationship of each member to his or her primary task, and so forth. My experience is that if the therapist prepares clients adequately and actively shapes expressive, interactional, self-disclosing norms in the manner described in chapter 5, there will be no paucity of activity and energy in the group.

Structured exercises often play a more important role in brief, specialized therapy groups than in the long-term general ambulatory group. In the next chapter, I shall describe uses of structured exercises in a number of specialty therapy groups.

Chapter 15

SPECIALIZED
THERAPY GROUPS

Group therapy methods have proved to be so useful in so many different clinical settings that it is no longer correct to speak of group therapy. Instead, we must refer to the group *therapies*. Indeed, as a cursory survey of professional journals would show, the number and scope of the group therapies are mind-boggling.

There are groups for incest survivors, for people with HIV/AIDS, for clients with eating disorders or with panic disorder, for the suicidal, the aged, for parents of sexually abused children, for parents of murdered children, for compulsive gamblers and for sex addicts, for people with herpes, for women with postpartum depression, for sexually dysfunctional men, and for sexually dysfunctional gay men. There are groups for people with hypercholesteremia, for survivors of divorce, for children of people with Alzheimer's, for spouses of people with Alzheimer's, for alcoholics, for children of alcoholics, for male batterers, for mothers of drug addicts, for families of the mentally ill, for fathers of delinquent daughters, for depressed older women, for angry adolescent boys, for survivors of terrorist attacks, for children of Holocaust survivors, for women with breast cancer, for dialysis patients, for people with multiple sclerosis, leukemia, asthma, sickle-cell anemia, deafness, agoraphobia, mental retardation. And for transsexuals and people with borderline personality disorder, gastric dyspepsia, or irritable bowel, for amputees, paraplegics, insomniacs, kleptomaniacs, asthmatics, nonorgasmic women, college dropouts, people who have had a myocardial infarction or a stroke, adopting parents, blind diabetics, clients in crisis, bereaved spouses, bereaved parents, the dying, and many, many others.†[1]

Obviously no single text could address each of these specialized groups. Even if that were possible, it would not constitute an intelligent approach to education. Does any sensible teacher of zoology, to take one example, undertake to teach vertebrate anatomy by having the students memorize the structures of each subspecies separately? Of course not. Instead, the teacher teaches basic and general principles of form, structure, and function and then proceeds to teach the anatomy of a *prototypic* primal specimen that serves as a template for all other vertebrates. Commonly teachers use a representative amphibian. Remember those frog dissection laboratories?

The extension of this analogy to group therapy is obvious. The student must first master fundamental group therapy theory and then obtain a deep understanding of a prototypic therapy group. But which group therapy represents the most archaic common ancestor? There has been such a luxuriant growth of group therapies that it requires some perspicacity to find, amid the thicket, the primal trunk of group therapy.

If there is an ancestral group therapy, it is the *open, long-term outpatient group therapy* described in this book. It was the first group therapy, and it has been deeply studied, since its members are sufficiently motivated, cooperative, and stable to have allowed systematic research. Furthermore, it has stimulated, over the past fifty years, an imposing body of professional literature containing the observations and conclusions of thoughtful clinicians.

Now that you have come this far in this text, now that you are familiar with the fundamental principles and techniques of the prototypical therapy group, you are ready for the next step: *the adaptation of basic group therapy principles to any specialized clinical situation.* That step is the goal of this chapter. First I describe the basic principles that allow the group therapy fundamentals to be adapted to different clinical situations, and then I present two distinct clinical illustrations—the adaptation of group therapy for the acute psychiatric inpatient ward, and the widespread use of groups for clients coping with medical illness. The chapter ends with a discussion of important developments in group therapy: the structured group therapies, self-help groups, and online groups.

MODIFICATION OF TRADITIONAL GROUP THERAPY FOR SPECIALIZED CLINICAL SITUATIONS: BASIC STEPS

To design a specialized therapy group, I suggest the following three steps: (1) assess the clinical situation; (2) formulate appropriate clinical goals; and (3) modify traditional technique to be responsive to these two steps—the new clinical situation and the new set of clinical goals.

Assessment of the Clinical Situation

It is important to examine carefully all the clinical facts of life that will bear on the therapy group. Take care to differentiate the *intrinsic* limiting factors from the *extrinsic* factors. The *intrinsic* factors (for example, mandatory attendance for clients on legal probation, prescribed duration of group treatment in an HMO clinic, or frequent absences because of medical hospitalizations in an ambulatory cancer support group) are built into the clinical situation and cannot be changed.

Then there are *extrinsic* limiting factors (factors that have become tradition or policy), which are arbitrary and within the power of the therapist to change—for example, an inpatient ward that has a policy of rotating the group leadership so that each group meeting has a different leader, or an incest group that traditionally opens with a long "check-in" (which may consume most of the meeting) in which each member recounts the important events of the week.

In a sense, the AA serenity prayer is pertinent here: therapists must accept that which they cannot change (intrinsic factors), change that which can be changed (extrinsic factors) and be wise enough to know the difference. Keep in mind, though, that as therapists gain experience, they often find that more and more of the intrinsic factors are actually extrinsic and hence mutable. For example, by educating the program's or institution's decision makers about the rationale and effectiveness of group therapy, it is possible to create a more favorable atmosphere for the therapy group.[2]

Formulation of Goals

When you have a clear view of the clinical facts of life—number of clients, length of therapy, duration and frequency of group meetings, type and severity of pathology, availability of co-leadership—your next step is to construct a reasonable set of clinical goals.

You may not like the clinical situation, you may feel hampered by the many intrinsic restraints that prevent you from leading the ideal group, but do not wear yourself out by protesting an immutable situation. (Better to light a candle than to curse the darkness.) With proper modification of goals and technique, you will always be able to offer some form of help.

I cannot overemphasize the importance of setting clear and appropriate goals: it may be the most important step you take in your therapeutic work. Nothing will so inevitably ensure failure as inappropriate goals. The goals of the long-term outpatient group I describe in this book are ambitious: to offer symptomatic relief and to change character structure. If you attempt to apply these same goals to, say, an aftercare group of clients with chronic schizophrenia you will rapidly become a therapeutic nihilist and stamp yourself and group therapy as hopelessly ineffective.

It is imperative that you shape a set of goals that is *appropriate to the clinical situation and achievable in the available time frame.* The goals must be clear not only to the therapists but to participants as well. In my discussion of group preparation in chapter 10, I emphasized the importance of enlisting the client as a full collaborator in treatment. You facilitate collaboration by making the goals and the group task explicit and by linking the two: that is, by clarifying for the members how the procedure of the therapy group will help them attain those goals.

In time-limited specialized groups, the goals must be focused, achievable, and tailored to the capacity and potential of the group members. It is important that the group be a success experience: clients enter therapy often feeling defeated and demoralized; the last thing they need is another failure. In the discussion of the inpatient group in this chapter, I shall give a detailed example of this process of goal setting.

Modification of Technique

When you are clear about the clinical conditions and have formulated appropriate, realizable goals, you must next consider the implication these conditions and goals have for your therapeutic technique. In this step, it is important to consider the therapeutic factors and to determine which will play the greatest role in the achievement of the goals. It is a phase of disciplined experimentation in which you alter technique, style, and, if necessary, the basic form of the group to adapt to the clinical situation and to the new goals of therapy.

To provide a brief hypothetical example, suppose you are asked to lead a group for which there is relatively little precedent—say a suicide-prevention center asks you to lead a twenty-session group of older, hemiparetic, suicidal clients. Your primary and overriding goal, of course, is to prevent suicide, and all technical modifications must first address that goal. A suicide during the life of the group would not only be an individual tragedy, it would also be catastrophic for the successful development of the group.

During your screening interviews, you develop some additional goals: you may discover that many clients are negligent about taking medication and that all the clients suffer from severe social isolation, from a pervasive sense of hopelessness and meaninglessness. So, given the additional goals of working on these issues as well, how do you modify standard group techniques to achieve them most efficiently?

First, it is clear that the risk is so high that you must assiduously monitor the intensity of and fluctuations in suicidality. You might, for example, require conjoint individual therapy and/or ask members to fill in a brief depression scale each week. Or you could begin each meeting with a *brief* check-in focused on suicidal feelings. Because of the high risk of suicide and the extent of social isolation, you may wish to *encourage* rather than discourage extragroup contact among the members, perhaps even mandating a certain number of phone calls or e-mail messages from clients to therapists and between clients each week. You may decide to encourage an additional coffee hour after the meeting or between meetings. Or you may address both the isolation and the sense of uselessness by tapping the therapeutic factor of altruism—for example, by experimenting with a "buddy system" in which new members are assigned to one of the experienced members. The experienced member would check in with the new member during the week to make sure the client is taking his or her medication and to "sponsor" that individual in the meeting—that is, to make sure the new member gets sufficient time and attention during the meeting.

There is no better antidote to isolation than deep therapeutic engagement in the group, and thus you must strive to create positive here-and-now interactions in each meeting. Since instillation of hope is so important, you may decide to include some recovered clients in the group—clients who are no longer suicidal and have discovered ways to adapt to their hemiparesis. Shame about physical disability is also an isolating force. The therapist might wish to counteract shame through physical contact—for example, asking group members to touch or hold each others' paralyzed hands and arms, or asking members to join hands at the end of meetings for a brief guided meditation. In an ideal situation, you may launch a support group that will evolve, after the group therapy ends, into a freestanding self-help group for which you act as consultant.

It is clear from this example that therapists must know a good deal about the special problems of the clients who will be in their group. And that is true for each clinical population—there is no all-purpose formula. Therapists must do their homework in order to understand the unique problems and dynamics likely to develop during the course of the group.

Thus, therapists leading long-term *groups of alcoholics* must expect to deal with issues surrounding sobriety, AA attendance, sneak drinking, conning, orality, dependency, deficiencies in the ability to bind anxiety, and a proneness to act out.

Bereavement groups must often focus on guilt (for not having done more, loved more, been a better spouse), on loneliness, on major life decisions, on life regrets, on adapting to a new, unpalatable life role, on feeling like a "fifth wheel" with old friends, on the pain and the need to "let go" of the dead spouse. Many widows and widowers feel that building a new life would signify insufficient love and constitute a betrayal of their dead spouse. Groups must also focus on dating (and the ensuing guilt) and the formation of new relationships, and, if the therapist is skillful, on personal growth.

Retirement groups must address such themes as recurrent losses, increased dependency, loss of social role, need for new sources to validate sense of self-worth, diminished income and expectancies, relinquishment of a sense of continued ascendancy, and shifts in spousal relationship as a result of more time shared together.[3]

Groups for *burdened family caregivers* of people with Alzheimer's disease often focus on the experience of loss, on the horrific experience of caring for spouses or parents who are but a shell of their former self, unable to acknowledge the caregiver's effort or even to identify the caregiver by name. They focus also on isolation, on understanding the causes of dementia and elaborating strategies for coping with the consuming burden, on guilt about wishing for or achieving some emancipation from the burden.[4]

Groups of *incest survivors* are likely to display considerable shame, fear, rage toward male authorities (and male therapists), and concerns about being believed.

Groups for psychological trauma would likely address a range of concerns, perhaps in a sequence of different group interventions. Safety, trust, and security would be important at first. Being together with others who have experienced a similar trauma and receiving psychoeducation about the impact of trauma on the mind and body can serve to reduce feelings of isolation and confusion. Later these groups might use structured behavioral interventions to treat specific trauma symptoms. Next the groups might address how trauma has altered members' basic beliefs and assumptions about the world. These groups would ideally be homogeneous for the earlier work and later a heterogeneous, mixed-gender group may be necessary to complete the process of the client's reentry into the post-trauma world.[5]

In summary, to develop a specialized therapy group I recommend the following steps:

1. *Assessment of the clinical setting.* Determine the immutable clinical restraints.
2. *Formulation of goals.* Develop goals that are appropriate and achievable within the existing clinical restraints.
3. *Modification of traditional technique.* Retain the basic principles and therapeutic factors of group therapy but alter techniques to achieve the specified goals: therapists must adapt to the clinical situation and the dynamics of the special clinical population.

Be mindful that all groups, even the most structured ones, also have a *group process* that may impact the group. You may determine that it is outside of the scope of the group to explore directly that process in depth, but you must be able to recognize its presence and how best to utilize, manage, or contain it.†

These steps are clear but too aseptic to be of immediate clinical usefulness. I shall now proceed to illustrate the entire sequence in detail by describing in depth the development of a therapy group for the acute psychiatric inpatient ward.

I have chosen the acute inpatient therapy group for two reasons. First, it offers a particularly clear opportunity to demonstrate many principles of strategic and technical adaptation. The clinical challenge is severe: as I shall discuss, *the acute inpatient setting is so inhospitable to group therapy that radical modifications of technique are required*. Second, this particular example may have intrinsic value to many readers since the inpatient group is the *most common specialized group*: therapy groups are led on most acute psychiatric wards in the country and, as a comprehensive survey documents, over 50 percent of clients admitted to acute psychiatric units nationwide participate in group psychotherapy.[6] For many, it is their first group exposure, hence it behooves us to make it a constructive experience.

THE ACUTE INPATIENT THERAPY GROUP

The Clinical Setting

The outpatient group that I describe throughout this book is freestanding: all important negotiations occur between the group therapist(s) and the seven or eight group members. Not so for the inpatient group! When you lead an inpatient group, the first clinical fact of life you must face is that your group is never an independent, freestanding entity. It always has a complex relationship to the larger group: the inpatient ward in which it is ensconced.†[7] What unfolds between members in the *small* therapy group reverberates unavoidably with what transpires within the *large* group of the institution.

The inpatient group's effectiveness, often its very existence, is heavily dependent upon administrative backing. If the ward medical director and the clinical nursing coordinator are not convinced that the group therapy approach is effective, they are unlikely to support the group program and will undermine the prestige of the therapy groups in many ways: they will not assign staff members to group leader positions on a regular schedule, they will not provide supervision, nor even schedule group sessions at a convenient, consistent time. Therapy groups on such wards are rendered ineffective. The group leaders are untrained and rapidly grow demoralized. Meetings are scheduled irregularly and are often disrupted by members being yanked out for individual therapy or for a variety of other hospital appointments.†

Is this state of affairs an *intrinsic, immutable* problem? Absolutely not! Rather, it is an *extrinsic, attitudinal* problem and stems from a number of sources, especially the professional education of the ward administrators. Many psychiatric training programs and nursing schools do not offer a comprehensive curriculum in group therapy (and virtually no programs offer sound instruction in inpatient group psychotherapy). Hence, it is completely understandable that ward directors will not invest ward resources and energy in a treatment program about which they have little knowledge or faith. Without a potent psychosocial therapeutic intervention, inpatient wards rely only on medication and the work of the staff is reduced to custodial care. But I believe that these attitudes can change: it is difficult to ignore the research that demonstrates the effectiveness of inpatient group therapy.[8] The ramifications of a foundering group program are great. A well-functioning group program can permeate and benefit the milieu as a whole, and the small group should be seen as a resource to the system as a whole.[9]

Sometimes the debate about the role of group therapy on the inpatient unit has nothing to do with the effectiveness of the therapy but in actuality is a squabble over professional territory. For many years, the inpatient therapy group has been organized and led by the psychiatric nursing profession. But what happens if the ward has a medical director who does not believe that psychiatric nurses (or occupational therapists, activity therapists, or recreational therapists) should be practicing psychotherapy? In this instance, the group therapy program is scuttled, not because it is ineffective but to safeguard professional territory.

The professional interdisciplinary struggles about psychotherapy—now involving a number of nonmedical disciplines: psychology, nursing, and master's-level counselors and psychologists—need to be resolved in policy committees or staff meetings. The small therapy group must not be used as a battleground on which professional interests are contested.

In addition to these extrinsic, programmatic problems, the acute inpatient ward poses several major *intrinsic* problems for the group therapist. There are two particularly staggering problems that must be faced by every inpatient group therapist: *the rapid turnover of patients on inpatient wards and the heterogeneity of psychopathology.*

Rapid Client Turnover.   The duration of psychiatric hospitalization has inexorably shortened. On most wards, hospital stays range from a few days to a week or two. This means, of course, that the composition of the small therapy group will be highly unstable. I led a daily group on an inpatient unit for five years and rarely had the identical group for two consecutive meetings—almost never for three.

This appears to be an immutable situation. The group therapist has little influence on ward admission and discharge policy. In fact, more and more commonly, discharge decisions are based on fiscal rather than clinical concerns. Nor is there any reason to suspect that this situation will change in the foreseeable future. The revolving-door inpatient unit is here to stay, and even as the door whirls ever faster, clinicians must keep their primary focus on the client's treatment, doing as much as they can within the imposed constraints.[10]

Heterogeneity of Pathology. The typical contemporary psychiatric inpatient unit (often in a community general hospital) admits patients with a wide spectrum of pathology: acute schizophrenic psychosis, decompensated borderline or neurotic conditions, substance abuse, major affective disorders, eating disorders, post-traumatic stress disorders, and situational reactions.

Not only is there a wide diagnostic spread, but there are also broad differences in attitudes toward, and capacity for, psychotherapy: many patients may be unmotivated; they may be psychologically unsophisticated; they may be in the hospital involuntarily or may not agree that they need help; they often are not paying for therapy; they may have neither introspective propensity nor inner-directed curiosity about themselves. They seek relief, not growth.

The presence of these two factors alone—*the brief duration of treatment and the range of psychopathology*—makes it evident that a radical modification of technique is required for the inpatient therapy group.

Consider how these two intrinsic clinical conditions violate some of the necessary conditions of group therapy I described earlier in this text. In chapter 3, I stressed the crucial importance of stability of membership. Gradually, over weeks and months, the sense of cohesiveness—a major therapeutic factor—develops, and participants often derive enormous benefit from the experience of being a valued member of an ongoing, stable group. How, then, to lead a whirligig group in which new members come and go virtually every session?

Similarly, in chapter 9, I stressed the importance of composing a group carefully and of paying special attention to avoiding deviants and to selecting members with roughly the same amount of ego strength. How, then, to lead a group in which one has almost no control over the membership, a group in which there may be floridly psychotic individuals sitting side by side with better-functioning, integrated members?

In addition to the major confounding factors of rapid patient turnover and the range of psychopathology, several other intrinsic clinical factors exert significant influence on the functioning of an inpatient psychotherapy group.

Time. The therapist's time is very limited. Generally, there is no time to see a patient in a pregroup interview to establish a relationship and to prepare the person for the group. There is little time to integrate new members into the group, to work on termination (someone terminates the group almost every meeting), to work through issues that arise in the group, or to focus on transfer of learning.

Group Boundaries.   The group boundaries are often blurred. Members are generally in other groups on the ward with some or many of the same members. Extragroup socializing is, of course, the rule rather than the exception: patients spend their entire day together. The boundaries of confidentiality are similarly blurred. There can be no true confidentiality in the small inpatient group: patients often share important small group events with others on the ward, and staff members freely share information with one another during rounds, nursing reports, and staff meetings. In fact it is imperative that the small inpatient group boundary of confidentiality be elastic and encompass the entire ward rather than being confined to any one group within that ward. Otherwise the small group becomes disconnected from the unit.†

The Role of the Group Leader.   The role of inpatient group leaders is complex since they may be involved with clients throughout the day in other roles. Their attendance may often be often erratic. Group leaders are frequently psychiatric nurses who, because of the necessity of weekend, evening, and night coverage, are on a rotating schedule and often cannot be present at the group for several consecutive meetings.

Therapist autonomy is limited in other ways as well. For example, therapists have, as I shall discuss shortly, only limited control over group composition. They often have no choice about co-therapists, who are usually assigned on the basis of the rotation schedule. Each client has several therapists at the same time. Inpatient group therapists usually feel more exposed than their outpatient colleagues. Difficulties in the group will be readily known by all. Lastly, the pace of the acute inpatient ward is so harried that there is little opportunity for supervision or even for post-meeting discussion between therapists.

Formulation of Goals

Once you have grasped these clinical facts of life of the inpatient therapy group and differentiated intrinsic from extrinsic factors, it is time to ask this question: *Given the many confounding intrinsic factors that influence (and hobble) the course of the inpatient group, what can the group accomplish?* What are reasonable goals of therapy—goals that are attainable by the inpatient clinical population in the available time?

Let us start by noting that the goals of the acute inpatient group are *not identical to those of acute inpatient hospitalization.* The goal of the group is not to resolve a psychotic depression, not to decrease psychotic panic, not to slow down a patient with mania, not to diminish hallucinations or delusions. Groups can do none of these things. That's the job of other aspects of the ward treatment program—primarily of the psychopharmacological regimen. To set these goals for a therapy group is not only unrealistic but it sentences the group to failure.

So much for what the inpatient group cannot do. What *can* it offer? I will describe six achievable goals:

1. Engaging the patient in the therapeutic process
2. Demonstrating that talking helps
3. Problem spotting
4. Decreasing isolation
5. Being helpful to others
6. Alleviating hospital-related anxiety

1. Engaging the patient in the therapeutic process

The contemporary pattern of acute psychiatric hospitalization—brief but repeated admissions to psychiatric wards in general hospitals—can be more effective than longer hospitalization only if hospitalization is followed with adequate aftercare treatment.[11] Furthermore, there is persuasive evidence that group therapy aftercare is a particularly efficacious mode of aftercare treatment—more so than individual aftercare therapy.[12]

A primary goal of inpatient group therapy emerges from these findings—namely, to engage the patient in a process that he or she perceives as constructive and supportive and will wish to continue after discharge from the hospital. Keep in mind that for many patients, the inpatient psychotherapy experience is their first introduction to therapy. If the group therapy experience is sufficiently positive and supportive to encourage them to attend an aftercare group, then—all other factors aside—the inpatient therapy group will have served a very important function.

2. Demonstrating that talking helps

The inpatient therapy group helps patients learn that talking about their problems is helpful. They learn that there is relief to be gained in sharing pain and in being heard, understood, and accepted by others. From listening to others, members also learn that others suffer from the same type of disabling distress as they do—one is not unique in one's suffering. In other words, the inpatient group introduces members to the therapeutic factors of cohesiveness and universality.

3. Problem spotting

The duration of therapy in the inpatient therapy group is far too brief to allow clients to work through problems. But the group can efficiently help clients spot problems that they may, with profit, work on in ongoing individual therapy, both during their hospital stay and in their post-discharge therapy. By providing a discrete focus for therapy, which clients value highly,[13] inpatient groups increase the efficiency of other therapies.

It is important that the groups identify problems with some therapeutic handle—problems that the client perceives as circumscribed and malleable (not problems such as chronic unhappiness, depression, or suicidal inclinations that are too generalized to offer a discrete handhold for therapy). The group is most adept at helping members identify problems in their mode of relating to other people. It is the ideal therapy arena in *which to learn about maladaptive interpersonal behavior*. Emily's story is a good illustration of this point.

> • *Emily was an extremely isolated young woman who was admitted to the inpatient unit for depression. She complained that she was always in the position of calling others for a social engagement. She never received invitations; she had no close girlfriends who sought her out. Her dates with men always turned into one-night stands. She attempted to please them by going to bed with them, but they never called for a second date. People seemed to forget her as soon as they met her. During the three group meetings she attended, the group gave her consistent feedback about the fact that she was always pleasant and always wore a gracious smile and always seemed to say what she thought would be pleasing to others. In this process, however, people soon lost track of who Emily was. What were her own opinions? What were her own desires and feelings? Her need to be eternally pleasing had a serious negative consequence: people found her boring and predictable.*
>
> *A dramatic example occurred in her second meeting, when I forgot her name and apologized to her. Her response was, "That's all right, I don't mind." I suggested that the fact that she didn't mind was probably one of the reasons I had forgotten her name. In other words, had she been the type of person who would have minded or made her needs more overt, then most likely I would not have forgotten her name. In her three group meetings, Emily identified a major problem that had far-reaching consequences for her social relationships outside: her tendency to submerge herself in a desperate but self-defeating attempt to capture the affection of others.*

4. Decreasing isolation

The inpatient group can help break down the isolation that exists between members. The group is a laboratory exercise intended to sharpen communication skills: the better the communication, the less the isolation. It helps individuals share with one another and permits them to obtain feedback about how others perceive them and to discover their blind spots.

Decreasing isolation between inpatient group members has *two distinct payoffs*. First, improved communication skills will help patients in their relationships with others outside the hospital. Virtually everyone who is admitted in crisis to an inpatient ward suffers from a breakdown or an absence of important supportive relationships with others. If the patient is able to transfer communication skills from the group to his or her outside life, then the group will have fulfilled a very important goal.

A second payoff is evident in the patient's behavior on the ward: as isolation decreases, the patient becomes increasingly able to use the therapeutic resources available, including relationships with other patients.[14]

5. Being helpful to others

This goal, the therapeutic factor of altruism, is closely related to the previous one. Clients are not just helped by their peers, they are also helped by the knowledge that they themselves have been useful to others. Clients generally enter psychiatric hospitals in a state of profound demoralization. They feel that not only have they no way of helping themselves but they have nothing to offer others. The experience of being valuable to other ward members is enormously affirming to one's sense of self-worth.

6. Alleviating hospital-related anxiety

The process of psychiatric hospitalization can be intensely anxiety provoking. Many patients experience great shame; they may be concerned about stigmatization and the effects of hospitalization on their job and friendships. Many patients are distressed by events on the ward—not only the bizarre and frightening behavior of other patients, but also the staff tensions.

Many of these secondary sources of tension compound the patient's primary dysphoria and must be addressed in therapy. The small therapy groups (as well as the therapeutic community group) provide a forum in which patients can air these issues and often achieve reassurance simply from learning that these concerns are shared by other members. They can learn, for example, that their roommate is not hostile and intentionally rejecting of them, but rather is preoccupied and fearful.

Modification of Technique

We have now accomplished the first two steps of designing a group for the contemporary inpatient ward: (1) assessing the clinical setting, including identifying the intrinsic clinical facts of life, and (2) formulating an appropriate and realistic set of goals. Now we are ready to turn to the third step: designing (on the basis of intrinsic restraints and goals) a clinical strategy and technique.[15]

The Therapist's Time Frame.   In the outpatient therapy group I have described in this text, the therapist's time frame is many weeks or months, sometimes years. Therapists must be patient, must build cohesiveness over many sessions, must work through issues repetitively from meeting to meeting (they recognize that psychotherapy is often cyclotherapy, because they must return again and again to the same issues in the therapeutic work). *The inpatient group therapist faces an entirely different situation*: the group composition changes almost every day; the duration of therapy for members is often very brief—indeed, many attend the group for only a single session.

It is clear that the inpatient group therapist must adopt a radically shortened time frame: I believe that *the inpatient group therapist must consider the life of the group to be only a single session*. Perhaps there will be continuity from one meeting to the next; perhaps there will be culture bearers who will be present in several consecutive meetings, but do not count on it. The most constructive attitude to assume is that your group will last for only a single session and that you must strive to offer something useful for as many participants as possible during that session.

Efficiency and Activity.   The single-session time frame demands *efficiency*. You have no time to allow issues to build, to let things develop in the group and slowly work them through. You have no time to waste; you have only a single opportunity to engage a patient, and you must not squander it.

Efficiency demands activity on the part of the therapist. There is no place in inpatient group psychotherapy for the passive, reflective group therapist. A far higher level of activity is demanded in inpatient than in outpatient groups. You must activate the group and call on, actively support, and interact personally with members. This increased level of activity requires a major shift in technique for the therapist who has been trained in long-term group therapy, but it is an absolutely essential modification of technique.

Support.   Keep in mind that one of the major goals of the inpatient therapy group is to engage clients in a therapeutic process *they will wish to continue after leaving the hospital*. Thus, it is imperative that the therapist create in the group an atmosphere that members experience as supportive, positive, and constructive. Members must feel safe; they must learn to trust the group and to experience it as a place where they will be understood and accepted.

The inpatient therapy group is not the place for confrontation, for criticism, for the expression and examination of intense anger. There will often be patients in the group who are conning or manipulative and who may need powerful confrontation, but it is far better to let them pass unchallenged than to run the risk of making the group feel unsafe to the vast majority of patients. Group leaders need to recognize and incorporate both the needs of the group and the needs of the individual into their intervention. Consider, for example, Joe, an angry man with bipolar disorder who arrived at the small group the day after being forcibly restrained and secluded by unit staff after threatening to harm a nurse who refused his request for a pass off the ward. Joe pointedly sat silently outside of the circle with his back to the group members. Addressing Joe's behavior was essential—it was too threatening to ignore—but it was also potentially inflammatory to engage Joe against his manifest wish. The group leader chose to acknowledge Joe's presence, noting that it likely was hard for Joe to come to the group after the tensions of the night before. He was welcome to participate more fully if he chose, but if not, just coming would be viewed as a step toward his reentry. Joe maintained his silent posture, but the group was liberated and able to proceed.

In the long-term outpatient group, therapists provide support both directly and indirectly: *direct* support by personal engagement, by empathic listening, by understanding, by accepting glances, nods, and gestures; *indirect* support by building a cohesive group that then becomes a powerful agent of support.

Inpatient group therapists must learn to offer support more quickly and directly. Support is not something that therapists reflexively provide. In fact, many training programs in psychotherapy unwittingly extinguish a therapist's natural propensity to support patients. Therapists are trained to become sniffers of pathology, experts in the detection of weaknesses. They are often so sensitized to transferential and countertransferential issues that they hold themselves back from engaging in basically human, supportive behavior with their clients.

Support may be offered in a myriad of ways.† The most direct, the most valued by clients, and the most often overlooked by well-trained professional therapists is to acknowledge openly the members' efforts, intentions, strengths, positive contributions, and risks.[16] If, to take an obvious example, one member states that he finds another member in the group very attractive, it is important that this member be supported for the risk he has taken. You may wonder whether he has previously been able to express his admiration of another so openly and note, if appropriate, that this is reflective of real progress for him in the group. Or, suppose you note that several members have been more self-disclosing after one particular member took a risk and revealed delicate and important material—then openly comment on it! Do not assume that members automatically realize that their disclosures have helped others take risks. Identify and reinforce the adaptive parts of the client's presentation.[17]

Try to emphasize the positive rather than the negative aspects of a defensive posture. Consider, for example, members who persist in playing assistant therapist. Do not confront them by challenging their refusal to work on personal issues, but offer instead positive comments about how helpful they have been to others and then gently comment on their unselfishness and reluctance to ask for something personal from the group. It is the rare individual who resists the therapist's suggestion that he or she needs to learn to be more selfish and to ask for more from others.

The therapist also supports by helping members obtain support from the group. Some clients, for example, obtain very little support because they characteristically present themselves in a highly objectionable fashion. A self-centered member who incessantly ruminates about a somatic condition will rapidly exhaust the patience of any group. When you identify such behavior, it is important to intervene quickly before animosity and rejection have time to well up. You may try any number of tactics— for example, directly instructing the client about other modes of behaving in the group or assigning the client the task of introducing new members into the group, giving feedback to other members, or attempting to guess and express what each person's evaluation of the group is that day.

Consider a woman who talked incessantly about her many surgical procedures.[18] It became clear from listening to this woman's description of her life situation that she felt she had given everything to her children and had received nothing in return. She also described a deep sense of unworthiness and of being inferior to the other members of the group. I suggested that when she talked about her surgical procedures she was really saying, "I have some needs, too, but I have trouble asking for them. My preoccupation with my surgery is a way of asking, 'Pay some attention to me.'" Eventually, she agreed with my formulation and to my request for her permission, whenever she talked about her surgery, to translate that into the real message, "Pay more attention to me." This client's explicit request for help was effective, and the members responded to her positively—which they never had when she recited her irritating litany of somatic complaints.

Another approach to support is to make certain the group is safe by anticipating and avoiding conflict whenever possible. If clients are irritable or want to learn to be more assertive or to challenge others, it is best to channel that work onto yourself: you are, let us hope, in a far better position to handle criticism than are any of the group members.

If two members are locked in conflict, it is best to intervene quickly and to search for positive aspects of the conflict. For example, keep in mind that sparks often fly between two individuals because of the group phenomenon of *mirroring*: one sees aspects of oneself (especially negative aspects) in another whom one dislikes because of what one dislikes in oneself. Thus, you can deflect conflict by asking individuals to discuss the various ways in which they resemble their adversary.

There are many other conflict-avoiding strategies. *Envy* is often an integral part of interpersonal conflict (see chapter 10); it is often constructive to ask adversaries to talk about those aspects of each other that they admire or envy. Role switching is sometimes a useful technique: ask adversaries to switch places and present the other's point of view. Often it is helpful to remind the group that opponents generally prove to be very helpful to each other, whereas those who are indifferent rarely help each other grow. Sometimes an adversarial position is a method of showing that one cares.†

One reason some members experience the group as unsafe is that they fear that things will go too far, that the group may coerce them to lose control—to say, think, or feel things that will result in interpersonal catastrophe. You can help these members feel safe in the group by allowing them to exercise control over their own participation. Check in with members repeatedly with such questions as: "Do you feel we're pushing you too hard?" "Is this too uncomfortable for you?" "Do you think you've revealed too much of yourself today?" "Have I been too intrusive by asking you such direct questions today?"

When you lead groups of severely disturbed, regressed patients, you must provide even more direct support. Examine the behavior of the severely regressed patients and find in it some positive aspect. Support the mute patient for staying the whole session; compliment the patient who leaves early for having stayed twenty minutes; support the member who arrives late for having shown up; support inactive members for having paid attention throughout the meeting. If members try to give advice, even inappropriate advice, reward them for their intention to help. If statements are unintelligible or bizarre, nonetheless label them as attempts to communicate. One group member, Jake, hospitalized because of a psychotic decompensation, angrily blurted out in the group that he intended to get Satan to rain "Hellfire and Brimstone upon this God-forsaken hospital." Group members withdrew into silence. The therapist wondered aloud what provoked this angry explosion. Another member commented that Jake had been agitated since his discharge planning meeting. Jake then added that he did not want to go to the hostel that was recommended. He wanted to go back to his boarding house, because it was safer from theft and assault. That was something all in the group could understand and support. Finding the underlying and understandable human concern brought Jake and the group members back together—a far better situation than Jake being isolated because of his bizarre behavior.

Focus of the Inpatient Group: The Here-And-Now. Throughout this text, I have repeatedly emphasized the importance of here-and-now interaction in the group therapeutic process. I have stressed that work in the here-and-now is the heart of the group therapeutic process, the power cell that energizes the therapy group. Yet, whenever I have visited inpatient wards throughout the country, I have found that groups there rarely focus on here-and-now interaction. Such avoidance of the here-and-now is, in my opinion, precisely the reason so many inpatient groups are ineffective.

If the inpatient group does not focus on the here-and-now, what other options are there? Most inpatient groups adopt a then-and-there focus in which members, following the therapist's cues, take turns presenting their "back-home problems"—those that brought them into the hospital—while the rest of the group attempts to address those problems with exhortation and advice. *This approach to inpatient group therapy is the least effective way to lead a therapy group and almost invariably sentences the group to failure.*

The problems that brought a patient into the hospital are complex and overwhelming. They have generally foiled the best efforts of skilled mental health professionals and will, without question, stump the therapy group members. For one thing, distressed patients are generally unreliable self-reporters: the information they present to the group will invariably be biased and, given the time constraints, limited. The then-and-there focus has many other disadvantages as well. For one thing, it results in highly inequitable time sharing. If much or all of a meeting is devoted to one member, many of the remaining members will feel cheated or bored. Unlike outpatient group members, they cannot even bank on the idea that they have credit in the group—that is, that the group owes them time and attention. Since they will most likely soon be discharged or find themselves in a group composed of completely different members, patients are left clutching worthless IOUs.

Some inpatient groups focus on *ward problems*—ward tensions, staff-patient conflict, housekeeping disputes, and so on. Generally, this is an unsatisfactory mode of using the small group. The average inpatient ward has approximately twenty patients. In any small group meeting, only half the members and one or two staff members will be present; invariably, the patients or staff members discussed will be in the other group. A much better arena for dealing with ward problems is the therapeutic community meeting, in which all patients and staff are present.

Other inpatient groups focus on *common themes*—for example, suicidal ideation, hallucinations, or drug side effects. Such meetings may be of value to some but rarely all members. Often such meetings serve primarily to dispense information that could easily be provided to patients in other formats. It is not the most effective way of using the inherent power of the small group modality.

The clinical circumstances of the inpatient group do not make the here-and-now focus any less important or less advisable. In fact, *the here-and-now focus is as effective in inpatient as in outpatient therapy.* However, the clinical conditions of inpatient work (especially the brief duration of treatment and the group members' severity of illness) demand modifications in technique. As I mentioned earlier, there is no time for working through interpersonal issues. Instead, you must help patients spot interpersonal problems and reinforce interpersonal strengths, while encouraging them to attend aftercare therapy, where they can pursue and work through the interpersonal issues identified in the group.

The most important point to be made about the use of the here-and-now in inpatient groups is already implicit in the foregoing discussion of support. I cannot emphasize too heavily that the here-and-now is *not synonymous with conflict, confrontation, and critical feedback.* I am certain that it is because of this erroneous assumption that so few inpatient group therapists capitalize on the value of here-and-now interaction.

Conflict is only one, and by no means the most important, facet of here-and-now interaction. The here-and-now focus helps patients learn many invaluable interpersonal skills: to communicate more clearly, to get closer to others, to express positive feelings, to become aware of personal mannerisms that push people away, to listen, to offer support, to reveal oneself, to form friendships.

The inpatient group therapist must pay special attention to the issue of the relevance of the here-and-now. The members of an inpatient group are in crisis. They are preoccupied with their life problems and immobilized by dysphoria or confusion. Unlike many outpatient group members who are interested in self-exploration, in personal growth, and in improving their ability to cope with crisis, inpatients are closed, in a survival mode, and unlikely to apprehend the relevance of the here-and-now focus for their problems.

Therefore, you must provide explicit instruction about its relevance. I begin each group meeting with a brief orientation in which I emphasize that, though individuals may enter the hospital for different reasons, everyone can benefit from examining how he or she relates to other people. Everyone can be helped by learning how to get more out of relationships with others. I stress that I focus on relationships in group therapy because *that is what group therapy does best.*† In the group, there are other members and two mental health experts who are willing to provide feedback about how they see each person in the group relating to others. I also acknowledge that members have important and painful problems, other than interpersonal ones, but that these problems need to be addressed in other therapeutic modalities: in individual therapy, in social service interviews, in couples or marital therapy, or with medication.

Modes of Structure

Just as there is no place in acute inpatient group work for the inactive therapist, there is no place for the nondirective group therapist. The great majority of patients on an inpatient ward are confused, frightened, and disorganized; they crave and require some external structure and stability. Consider the experience of patients newly admitted to the psychiatric unit: they are surrounded by other troubled, irrationally behaving patients; their mental acuity may be obtunded by medication; they are introduced to many staff members who, because they are on a complex rotating schedule, may not appear to have consistent patterns of attendance; they are exposed, sometimes for the first time, to a wide array of therapies and therapists.

Often the first step to acquiring internal structure is exposure to a clearly perceived, externally imposed structure. Anxiety is relieved when one is provided with clear, firm expectations for behavior in a new situation.

In a study of debriefing interviews with newly discharged patients, the overwhelming majority expressed a preference for *group leaders who provided an active structure for the group.*[19] They appreciated a therapist who started the group meeting and who provided crystal-clear direction for the procedure of the group. They preferred leaders who actively invited members to participate, who focused the group's attention on work, who assured equal distribution of time, who reminded the group of its basic group task and direction. The research literature demonstrates that such leaders obtain superior clinical results.[20]

Group leaders can provide structure for the group in many ways: by orienting members at the start of each group; by providing a written description of the group in advance of the meeting, by setting clear spatial and temporal boundaries; by using a lucid, confident personal style; by following a consistent and coherent group procedure.

Spatial and Temporal Boundaries.   The ideal physical arrangement for an inpatient therapy group, as for any type of group, is *a circle of members meeting in an appropriately sized room with a closed door.* Sounds simple, yet the physical plan of many wards makes these basic requirements difficult to meet. Some units, for example, have only one group room and yet must schedule two groups to meet at the same time. In this case, one group may have to meet in a very large, busy general activity room or in an open hallway without clear spatial demarcation. I believe that the lack of clear spatial boundaries vitiates intimacy and cohesiveness and compromises the work of the group; it is far preferable to find some closed space, even if it means meeting off the ward.

Structure is also provided by *temporal stability*. The ideal meeting begins with all members present and punctual, and runs with no interruptions until its conclusion. It is difficult to approximate these conditions in an inpatient setting for several reasons: disorganized patients arrive late because they forget the time and place of the meeting; members are called out for some medical or therapy appointment; members with a limited attention span may ask to leave early; heavily medicated members fall asleep during a session and interrupt the group flow; agitated or panicked patients may bolt from the group.

Therapists must intervene in every way possible to provide maximum stability. They should urge the unit administration to declare the group time inviolable so that group members cannot be called out of the group for *any* reason (not because the group is the most important therapy on the unit, but because these disruptions undermine it, and group therapy, by its nature, has little logistical flexibility). They may ask the staff members to remind disorganized patients about the group meeting and escort them into the room. It should be the ward staff's responsibility, not the group leaders' alone, to ensure that patients attend. And, of course, the group therapists should always model promptness.

The problem of bolters—members who run out of a group meeting—can be approached in several ways. First, patients are made more anxious if they perceive that they will not be permitted to leave the room. Therefore, it is best simply to express the hope that they can stay the whole meeting. If they cannot, suggest that they return the next day, when they feel more settled. A patient who attempts to leave the room in midsession cannot, of course, be physically blocked, but there are other options. You may reframe the situation in a way that provides a rationale for putting up with the discomfort of staying: for example, in the case of a person who has stated that he or she often flees from uncomfortable situations and is resolved to change that pattern, you might remind him or her of that resolution. You may comment: "Eleanor, it's clear that you're feeling very uncomfortable now. I know you want to leave the room, but I remember your saying just the other day that you've always isolated yourself when you felt bad and that you want to try to find ways to reach out to others. I wonder if this might not be a good time to work on that by simply trying extra hard to stay in the meeting today?" You may decrease her anxiety by suggesting that she simply be an observer for the rest of the session, or you may suggest that she change her seat to a place that feels more comfortable to her—perhaps next to you.

Groups led for higher-level patients may be made more stable by a policy that prohibits latecomers from entering the group session. This policy, of course, is only effective with an optional group. It may present problems for therapists who feel uncomfortable with being strict gate-keepers; it runs against the grain of traditional clinical training to refuse admission to clients who want therapy. Of course, this policy creates resentment in clients who arrive at a meeting only a few minutes late, but it also conveys to them that you value the group time and work and that you want to get the maximum amount of uninterrupted work each session. The group may employ a five-minute window for late arrivals with the door open, but once the door is closed, the meeting should not be interrupted. Debriefing interviews with recently discharged patients invariably reveal that they resent interruptions and approve of all the therapists' efforts to ensure stability.[21] Latecomers who are denied entrance to the group may sulk for an hour or two but generally will be punctual the following day.

Therapist Style.   The therapist also greatly contributes to the sense of structure through personal style and presence.† Confused or frightened patients are reassured by therapists who are firm, explicit, and decisive, yet who, at the same time, share with patients the reasons for their actions. Many long-term outpatient group therapists allow events to run their course and then encourage the examination and integration of the event. Inpatient groups, however, are disrupted repeatedly by major events. Members are often too stressed and vulnerable to deal effectively with such events and are reassured if therapists act decisively and firmly. If, for example, a manic patient veers out of control and monopolizes the group's time, it is best to intervene and prevent the patient from obstructing the group work in that session. You may, for example, tell the patient that it is time to be quiet and to work on listening to others, or, if the patient is unable to exercise any control, you may escort him or her from the room. Generally, it is excellent modeling for therapists to talk about their ambivalent feelings in such a situation. They may, for example, share both their conviction that they have made the proper move for the welfare of the entire group and their great discomfort at assuming an authoritarian pose.

At other times, the group may engage in long discussions that the inpatient therapist realizes are not effective and do not constitute effective work. Again, the therapist has options, including waiting and then analyzing the resistance. However, in inpatient groups it is far more efficient to be direct—for example, to interrupt the group with some explicit message such as, "I have a sense that this topic is of much interest to several of the people in the room, but it seems to me that you could easily have this discussion outside the group. I want to suggest that there might be a more valuable way to use the group time. Groups are much more helpful if we help members learn more about how they relate and communicate with others, and I think it would be better if we could get back to . . . "—here you would supply some clear alternative.

Group Session Protocol.   One of the most potent ways of providing structure is to build into each session a *consistent, explicit sequence.* This is a radical departure from traditional outpatient group therapy technique, but in specialized groups it makes for the most efficient use of a limited number of sessions, as we shall see later when we examine cognitive-behavioral therapy groups. In the inpatient group, a structured protocol for each session has the advantage not only of efficiency but also of ameliorating anxiety and confusion in severely ill patients. I recommend that rapid-turnover inpatient groups take the following form.

1. *The first few minutes.* This is when the therapist provides explicit structure for the group and prepares the group members for therapy. (Shortly, I will describe a model group in which I give a verbatim example of a preparatory statement.)
2. *Definition of the task.* The therapist attempts in this phase to determine the most profitable direction for the group to take in a particular session. Do not make the error of plunging in great depth into the first issue raised by a member, for, in so doing, you may miss other potentially productive agendas. You may determine the task in a number of ways. You may, for example, simply listen to get a feel of the urgent issues present that day, or you may provide some structured exercise that will permit you to ascertain the most valuable direction for the group to take that day (I will give a description of this technique later).†
3. *Filling the task.* Once you have a broad view of the potentially fertile issues for a session, you attempt, in the main body of the meeting, to address these issues, involving as many members as possible in the group session.
4. *The final few minutes.* The last few minutes is the summing-up period. You indicate that the work phase is over, and you devote the remaining time to review and analysis of the meeting. This is the self-reflective loop of the here-and-now, in which you attempt to clarify, in the most lucid possible language, the interaction that occurred in the session. You may also wish to do some final mopping up: you may inquire about any jagged edges or ruffled feelings that members may take out of the session or ask the members, both the active and the silent ones, about their experience and evaluation of the meeting.

Disadvantages of Structure.   Several times in this text, I have remonstrated against excessive structure. For example, in discussing norm setting, I urged that the therapist strive to make the group as autonomous as possible and noted that an effective group takes maximum responsibility for its own functioning. I have also suggested that an excessively active therapist who structures the group tightly will create a dependent group; surely if the leader does everything for the members, they will do too little for themselves. As noted in chapter 14, empirical research demonstrates that leaders who provide excessive structure may be positively evaluated by their members, but their groups fail to have positive outcomes. Again, *leader behavior that is structuring in nature* (total verbal activity and amount of managerial behavior) *is related in curvilinear fashion to positive outcome* (both at the end of the group and at the six-month follow-up).[22] In other words, the rule of the golden mean prevails: *too much or too little leader structuring is detrimental to growth*.

Thus, we face a dilemma. In many brief, specialized groups, we must provide structure; but if we provide too much, our group members will not learn to use their own resources. This is a major problem for the inpatient group therapist who must, for all the reasons I have described, structure the group and yet avoid infantilizing its members.

There is a way out of this dilemma—a way so important that it constitutes a fundamental principle of therapy technique in many specialized groups. *The leader must structure the group so as to encourage each member's autonomous functioning.* If this principle seems paradoxical wait! The following model of an inpatient group will clarify it.

The Higher-Level Group: A Working Model

In this section I describe in some detail a format for the higher-level functioning inpatient group. Keep in mind that my intention here, as throughout this chapter, is not to provide a blueprint but to illustrate an approach to the modification of group therapy technique. My hope, thus, is not that you will attempt to apply this model faithfully to your clinical situation but that it will serve *to illustrate the general strategy of modification and will assist you in designing an effective model for the specific clinical situations you face.*[23]

I suggest that an optional group be held for higher-level clients,* meeting three to five times a week for approximately seventy-five minutes. I have experimented with a variety of models over the years; the model I de-

---

*Higher-level clients are the more verbal clients who are motivated to work in therapy and whose attention span permits them to attend an entire meeting. Elsewhere I describe a group design for lower-functioning, more regressed clients (Yalom, *Inpatient Group Psychotherapy,* 313–35).

scribe here is the most effective one I have found, and I have used it for several hundred inpatient group therapy sessions. This is the basic protocol of the meeting:

1. Orientation and Preparation   . . . 3 to 5 minutes
2. Personal Agenda Setting   . . . 20 to 30 minutes
3. Agenda Filling   . . . 20 to 35 minutes
4. Review   . . . 10 to 20 minutes

Orientation and Preparation.   The preparation of patients for the therapy group is no less important in inpatient than in outpatient group therapy. The time frame, of course, is radically different. Instead of spending twenty to thirty minutes preparing an individual for group therapy during an individual session, the inpatient group therapist must accomplish such preparation in the first few minutes of the inpatient group session. I suggest that the leader begin every meeting with a simple and brief introductory statement that includes a description of the ground rules (time and duration of meeting, rules about punctuality), a clear exposition of the purpose of the group, and an outline of the basic procedure of the group, including the sequence of the meeting. The following is a typical preparatory statement:

> I'm Irv Yalom and this is Mary Clark. We'll co-lead this afternoon therapy group, which meets daily for one hour and fifteen minutes beginning at two o'clock. The purpose of this group is to help members learn more about the way they communicate and relate to others. People come into the hospital with many different kinds of important problems, but one thing that most individuals have in common here is some unhappiness about the way some of their important relationships are going.
>
> There are, of course, many other urgent problems that people have, but those are best worked on in some of your other forms of therapy. What this kind of group does best of all is to help people understand more about their relationships with others. One of the ways we can work best is to focus on the relationships that exist between the people in this room. The better you learn to communicate with each of the people here, the better it will become with people in your outside life. Other groups on our unit may emphasize other approaches.
>
> It's important to know that observers are present almost every day to watch the group through this one-way mirror. [Here, point toward the mirror and also toward the microphone if appropriate, in an attempt to orient the patient as clearly as possible to the spatial surroundings.] The observers are professional mental health workers, often medical or nursing students, or other members of the ward staff.

We begin our meetings by going around the group and checking with each person and asking each to say something about the kinds of problems they're having in their lives that they'd like to try to work on in the group. That should take fifteen to thirty minutes. It is very hard to come up with an agenda during your first meetings. But don't sweat it. We will help you with it. That's our job. After that, we then try to work on as many of these problems as possible. In the last fifteen minutes of the group, the observers will come into the room and share their observations with us. Then, in the last few minutes, we check in with everyone here about how they size up the meeting and about the leftover feelings that should be looked at before the group ends. We don't always get to each agenda fully each meeting, but we will do our best. Hopefully we can pick it up at the next meeting and you may find also that you can work on it between sessions.

Note the basic components of this preparation: (1) a description of the ground rules; (2) a statement of the purpose and goals of the group; (3) a description of the procedure of the group (including the precise structure of the meeting). Some inpatient therapists suggest that this preparation can be partly communicated to patients outside of the group and should be even more detailed and explicit by, for example, including a discussion of blind spots, supportive and constructive feedback (providing illustrative examples), and the concept of the social microcosm.[24]

Personal Agenda Setting.   The second phase of the group is the elaboration of the task. The overriding task of the group (from which the various goals of the group emanate) is to help each member explore and improve his or her interpersonal relationships. An efficient method of task definition is a structured exercise that asks each member to formulate a brief personal agenda for the meeting. The agenda must be realistic and doable in the group that day. It must focus on interpersonal issues and, if possible, on issues that in some way relate to one or more members in the group.

Formulating an appropriate agenda is a complex task. Patients need considerable assistance from the therapist, especially in their first couple of meetings. Neophyte therapists may also find this challenging at first. Each patient is, in effect, asked to make a personal statement that involves three components: (1) an acknowledgment of the wish to change (2) in some interpersonal domain (3) that has some here-and-now manifestation. Think about this as an evolution from the general to the specific, the impersonal to the personal, and the personal to the interpersonal. "I feel unhappy" evolves into "I feel unhappy because I am isolated," which evolves into "I want to be better connected," which evolves into ". . . with another member of the group." Notwithstanding the many ways patients can begin their exposition, there are no more than eight to ten basic agendas that express the vast majority of patient concerns: wanting to be less isolated, more assertive, a better communicator, less bottled up, closer with others, more effective in dealing with anger, less mistrustful, or better known to others, or wanting to receive specific feedback about a characteristic or aspect of behavior. Having these examples in mind may make it easier for therapists to help patients create a workable focus.

Patients have relatively little difficulty with the first two aspects of the agenda but require considerable help from the therapist in the third—that is, framing the agenda in the here-and-now. The third part, however, is less complex than it seems, and the therapist may move any agenda into the here-and-now by mastering only a few basic guidelines.

Consider the following common agenda: "I want to learn to communicate better with others." The patient has already accomplished the first two components of the agenda: (1) he or she has expressed a desire for change (2) in an interpersonal area. All that remains is to move the agenda into the here-and-now, a step that the therapist can easily facilitate with a comment such as: "Please look around the room. With whom in the group do you communicate well? With whom would you like to improve your communication?"

Another common agenda is the statement, "I'd like to learn to get closer to people." The therapist's procedure is the same: thrust it into the here-and-now by asking, "Who in the group do you feel close to? With whom would you like to feel closer?" Another common agenda is: "I want to be able to express my needs and get them met. I keep my needs and pain hidden inside and keep trying to please everybody." The therapist can shift that into the here-and-now by asking: "Would you be willing to try to let us know today what you need?" or "What kind of pain do you have? What would you like from us?"

Nota bene, the agenda is generally *not* the reason the patient is in the hospital. But, often unbeknownst to the patient, the agenda may be an underlying or contributory reason. The patient may have been hospitalized because of substance abuse, depression, or a suicide attempt. Underlying such behaviors or events, however, there are almost invariably important tensions or disruptions in interpersonal relationships.

Note also that the therapist strives for agendas that are gentle, positive, and nonconfrontational. In the examples just cited of agendas dealing with communication or closeness, I made sure of inquiring first about the positive end of the scale.

Many patients offer an agenda that directly addresses anger: for example, "I want to be able to express my rage. The doctors say I turn my anger inward and that causes me to be depressed." This agenda must be handled with care. You do *not* want patients to express anger at one another, and you must reshape that agenda into a more constructive form.

I have found it helpful to approach the patient in the following manner: "I believe that anger is often a serious problem because people let it build up to high levels and then are unable to express it. The release of so much anger would feel like a volcano exploding. It's frightening both to you and to others. It's much more useful in the group to work with *young anger*, before it turns into red anger. I'd like to suggest to you that today you focus on young anger—for example, impatience, frustration, or very minor feelings of annoyance. Would you be willing to express in the group any minor flickerings of impatience or annoyance when they first occur—for example, irritation at the way I lead the group today?"

The agenda exercise has many advantages. For one thing, it is a solution to the paradox that *structure is necessary but, at the same time, growth inhibiting*. The agenda exercise provides structure for the group, but it simultaneously encourages autonomous behavior on the part of the patient. Members are required to take responsibility for the therapy and to say, in effect, "Here is what I want to change about myself. Here's what I choose to work on in the group today." Thus, the agenda encourages members to assume a more active role in their own therapy and to make better use of the group. They learn that straightforward, explicit agendas involving another member of the group will guarantee that they do productive work in the session: for example, "I tried to approach Mary earlier today to talk to her, and I have the feeling that she rejected me, wanted nothing to do with me, and I'd like to find out why."

Some patients have great difficulty stating their needs directly and explicitly. In fact, many enter the hospital because of self-destructive attempts that are *indirect methods of signifying that they need help*. The agenda task teaches them to state their needs clearly and directly and to ask explicitly for help from others. In fact, for many, *the agenda exercise, rather than any subsequent work in the group meeting, is itself the therapy*. If these patients can simply be taught to ask for help verbally rather than through some nonverbal, self-destructive mode, then the hospitalization will have been very useful.

The agenda exercise also provides a wide-angle view of the group work that may be done that day. The group leader is quickly able to make an appraisal of what each patient is willing to do and which patients' goals may interdigitate with other those of others in the group.

The agenda exercise is valuable but cannot immediately be installed in a group. Often a therapy group needs several meetings to catch on to the task and to recognize its usefulness. Personal agenda setting is *not* an exercise that the group members can accomplish on their own: the therapist must be extremely facilitative, persistent, inventive, and often directive to make it work. If members are extremely resistant, sometimes a suitable agenda is for them to examine why it is so hard to formulate an agenda.

Profound resistance or demoralization may be expressed by comments such as "What difference will it make?" "I don't want to be here at all!" If it is quickly evident that you have no real therapeutic leverage, you may choose to ally with the resistance rather than occupy the group's time in a futile struggle with the resistant member. You may simply say that it is not uncommon to feel this way on admission to the hospital, and perhaps the next meeting will feel different. You might add that the patient may choose to participate at some point in the session. If anything catches his interest, he should speak about it.

Sometimes if a patient cannot articulate an agenda, one can be prescribed that involves listening and then providing feedback to a member the patient selects. At other times it is useful to ask other members to suggest a suitable agenda for a given individual.

For example, a nineteen-year-old male offered an unworkable agenda: "My dad treats me like a kid." He could not comprehend the agenda concept in his first meeting, and I asked for suggestions from the other members. There were several excellent ones: "I want to examine why I'm so scared in here," or, "I want to be less silent in the group." Ultimately, one member suggested a perfect agenda: "I want to learn what I do that makes my dad treat me like a kid. You guys tell me: do I act like a kid in this group?"

Take note of why this was the perfect agenda. It addressed his stated concern about his father treating him like a kid, it addressed his behavior in the group that had made it difficult for him to use the group, and it focused on the here-and-now in a manner that would undoubtedly result in the group's being useful to him.

Agenda Filling. Once the personal agenda setting has been completed, the next phase of the group begins. In many ways, this segment of the group resembles any interactionally based group therapy meeting in which members explore and attempt to change maladaptive interpersonal behavior. *But there is one major difference*: therapists have at their disposal agendas for each member of the group, which allows them to focus the work in a more customized and efficient manner. The presumed life span of the inpatient group is only a single session, and the therapist *must* be efficient in order to provide the greatest good for the greatest number of patients.

If the group is large—say, twelve members—and if there are new members who require a good bit of time to formulate an agenda, then there may be only thirty minutes in which to fill the twelve agendas. Obviously, work cannot be done on each agenda in the session, and it is important that patients be aware of this possibility. You may tell members explicitly that the personal agenda setting does not constitute a promise that each agenda will be focused on in the group. You may also convey this possibility through conditional language in the agenda formation phase: "If time permits, what would you like to work on today?"

Nonetheless, the efficient and active therapist should be able to work on the majority of agendas in each session. The single most valuable guideline I can offer is try to fit agendas together so that you work on several at once. If, for example, John's agenda is that he is very isolated and would like some feedback from the members about why it's hard to approach him, then you can fill several agendas simultaneously by calling for feedback for John from members with agendas such as: "I want to learn to express my feelings," "I want to learn how to communicate better to others," or, "I want to learn how to state my opinions clearly."

Similarly, if there's a member in the group who is weeping and highly distressed, why should you, the therapist, but the only one to comfort that individual when you have, sitting in the group, members with the agenda of: "I want to learn to express my feelings," or, "I want to learn how to be closer to other people"? By calling on these members, you stitch several agendas together.

Generally, during the personal agenda setting, the therapist collects several letters of credit—commitments from patients about certain work they want to do during the meeting. If, for example, one member states that she thinks it important to learn to take risks in the group, it is wise to store this and, at some appropriate time, call on her to take a risk by, for example, giving feedback or evaluating the meeting. If a member expresses the wish to open up and share his pain with others, it is facilitative to elicit some discrete contract—you may even make a contract for only two or three minutes of sharing—and then make sure that individual gets the time in the group and the opportunity to stop at the allotted time. It is possible, with such contracts, to increase responsibility assumption by asking the patient to nominate one or two members to monitor him to ensure he has fulfilled the contract by a certain time in the session. This kind of "maestro-like conducting" may feel heavy-handed to the beginning therapist, but it leads to a more effective inpatient group.

The End-of-Meeting Review.   The final phase of the group meeting signals a formal end to the body of the meeting and consists of review and evaluation. I have often led an inpatient group on a teaching unit and generally had two to four students observing the session through a one-way mirror. I prefer to divide the final phase of the group into two equal segments: a discussion of the meeting by the therapists and observers, and the group members' response to this discussion.

In the first segment, therapists and observers form a small circle in the room and conduct an open analysis of a meeting, just as though there were no patients in the room listening and watching. (If there are no observers in the meeting that day, the co-therapists hold a discussion between themselves or invite the group members to contribute to a discussion in which everyone attempts to review and analyze the meeting.) In this discussion, leaders and observers review the meeting and focus on the group leadership and the experience of each of the members. The leaders question what they missed, what else they might have done in the group, whether they left out certain members. The discussants take pains to make some comment about each member: the type of agenda formulated, the work done on that agenda, guesses about a patient's satisfaction with the group.

Although this group wrap-up format is unorthodox, it is, in my experience, effective. For one thing, it makes constructive use of observers. In the traditional teaching format, student-observers stay invisible and meet with the therapist in a postgroup discussion to which the members, of course, do not have access. Members generally resent this observation format and sometimes develop paranoid feelings about being watched. To bring the observers into the group transforms them from a negative to a positive force. In fact, group members often express disappointment when no observers are present.

This format requires therapist transparency and is an excellent opportunity to do invaluable modeling. Co-therapists may discuss their dilemmas or concerns or puzzlement. They may ask the observers for feedback about their behavior. Did, for example, the observers think they were too intrusive or that they put too much pressure on a particular individual? What did the observers think about the relationship between the two leaders?

In the final segment of the review phase, the discussion is thrown open to the members. Generally this is a time of great animation, since the therapist-observer discussion generates considerable data. There are two directions that the final few minutes can take. First, the members may respond to the therapist-observer discussion: for example, they may comment on the openness, or lack thereof, of the therapists and observers. They may react to hearing the therapist express doubt or fallibility. They may agree with or challenge the observations that have been made about their experience in the group.

The other direction is for the group members to process and evaluate their own meeting. The therapist may guide a discussion, making such inquiries as: "How did you feel about the meeting today?" "Did you get what you wanted out of it?" "What were your major disappointments with this session?" "If we had another half hour to go, how would you use the time?" The final few minutes are also a time for the therapist to make contact with the silent members and inquire about their experience: "Were there times when you wanted to speak in the group?" "What stopped you?" "Had you wanted to be called on, or were you grateful not to have participated?" "If you *had* said something, what would it have been?" (This last question is often remarkably facilitative.)

The final phase of the meeting thus has many functions: review, evaluation, pointing to future directions. But it is also a time for reflection and tying together loose ends before the members leave the group session.

In a study that specifically inquired into patients' reactions to this format, there was strong consensus among the group members that the final phase of the group was an integral part of the group session.[25] When members were asked what percentage of the value of the group stemmed from this final segment, they gave it a value that far exceeded the actual time involved. Some respondents, for example, ascribed to the final twenty minutes of the meeting a value of 75 percent of the total group value.

GROUPS FOR THE MEDICALLY ILL

Group psychosocial interventions play an increasingly important role in comprehensive medical care and are likely to proliferate in the future, given their effectiveness and potential for reducing health care costs.[26] Reports of their use and efficacy in a wide range of ailments abound in the literature. Group therapy interventions have been employed for all the major medical illnesses, including cardiac disease, obesity, lupus, infertility, irritable bowel syndrome, inflammatory bowel disease, pregnancy, postpartum depression, transplantation, arthritis, chronic obstructive lung disease, brain injury, Parkinson's, multiple sclerosis, diabetes, HIV/AIDS, and cancer.[27]

There are many reasons that psychological treatment is important in medical illness. First, there is the obvious, well-known linkage between psychological distress and medical illness—namely, that depression, anxiety, and stress reactions are common consequences of serious medical illness and not only impair quality of life but also amplify the negative impact of the medical illness.[28] We know, for example, that depression after a heart attack occurs in up to 50 percent of men and significantly elevates the risk of another heart attack.[29] Furthermore, the anxiety and depression accompanying serious medical illness tend to increase health-compromising behaviors, such as alcohol use and smoking, and disrupt compliance with recovery regimens of diet, exercise, medication, and stress reduction.[30]

Paradoxically, a new source of psychological stress stems from recent advances in medical technology and treatment. Consider, for example, the many formerly fatal illnesses that have been transformed into chronic illnesses: for example, fully 4 percent of Americans are cancer survivors—a state of being that carries with it its own inherent stress.[31] Or consider recent breakthroughs in prevention. Genetic testing now plays an important role in medical practice: physicians can compute the risk of an individual's developing such illnesses as Huntington's disease or breast, ovarian, and colon cancer.[32] That, of course, is undeniably a good thing. Yet this technology comes with a price. Large numbers of individuals are tormented by momentous, anxiety-laden decisions. When one learns, for example, of a genetic predisposition to a serious illness, one is forced to face such questions as: Should I have a prophylactic mastectomy? (or other preventive surgery?) Is it fair for me to get married? To have children? Do I share this information with siblings who prefer not to know?

And do not forget the psychological stigma attached to many medical illnesses, for example, HIV/AIDS, irritable bowel syndrome, and Parkinson's. At a time when individuals are in great need of social support, the shame and stigma of illness can cause social withdrawal and stress-inducing isolation.

Additionally, seriously ill individuals and their families fear uttering anything that might amplify worry or fear in loved ones. The press for "thinking positive" invites shallowness in communication, which further increases a sense of isolation.[33]

More than ever before, we are aware of the psychological importance of patient-doctor communication in chronic medical disease. Collaborative, trusting communication between patient and doctor is generally associated with greater well-being and better decision making.[34] Yet many patients, dissatisfied with their relationship with their physician, feel powerless to improve it.

Medical illness confronts us with our fundamental vulnerability and limits. Illusions that have sustained us and offered comfort are challenged. We lose, for example, the sense that life is under our control, that we are special, immune to natural law, that we have unlimited time, energy, and choice. Serious illness evokes fundamental questions about the meaning of life, death, transiency, responsibility, and our place in the universe.[35]

And, of course, the strain of medical illness extends far beyond the person with the illness. Family members and caregivers may suffer significant stress and dysphoria.[36] Groups often play an important role in their support:

for example, consider the enormous growth in groups for caretakers of patients with Alzheimer's disease.[37]

General Characteristics

Typically, groups for the medically ill are homogeneous for the illness and time-limited, meeting four to sixteen times. Groups that help patients with coping and adaptation[38]* may be offered at every step of the individual's illness and medical treatment.

As I discussed in chapter 10, brief groups require clear structure and high levels of focused therapist activity. But even in brief, highly structured, manual-guided group interventions, the group leader must attend to group dynamics and group process, not necessarily to explore them, but to manage them effectively so that the group does not get derailed and become counterproductive.[39]

Although homogeneous groups tend to jell quickly, the leader must be careful to bring in outliers who resist group involvement. Certain behaviors may need to be tactfully and empathically reframed into a more workable fashion. Consider, for example, the bombastic, hostile man in a post–myocardial infarction ten-session group who angrily complains about the lack of concern and affection he feels from his sons. Since deep interpersonal work is not part of the group contract, the therapist needs to have constructive methods of addressing the patient's concerns without violating the groups norms. In general, therapists would seek to contain, rather than amplify the client's distress, or have it generate a charged negative emotional climate in the group. They might, for example, take a psychoeducational stance and discuss how anger and hostility are noxious to one's cardiac health, or they might address the latent hurt, fear or sadness that the anger masks, and invite a more direct expression of those primary emotions.

Although these groups do not emphasize interpersonal learning (in fact, the leader generally avoids here-and-now focus), many of the other therapeutic factors are particularly potent in group therapy with the medically ill. *Universality* is highly evident and serves to diminish stigmatization and isolation. *Cohesiveness* provides social support directly. Extragroup contact is often encouraged and viewed as a successful outcome, not as resistance to the work of the group. Seeing others cope effectively with a

---

*We can think of coping as *the means* and adaptation as *the end*. Maximizing adaptation generally improves quality of life. One may categorize the medical groups according to their basic coping emphasis:

1. Emotion-based coping—social support, emotional ventilation
2. Problem-based coping—active cognitive and behavioral strategies, psychoeducation, stress reduction techniques
3. Meaning-based coping—increasing existential awareness, realigning life priorities

shared illness *instills hope,* which can take many forms: hope for a cure, for courage, for dignity, for comfort, for companionship, or for peace of mind. Generally, members learn coping skills more effectively from the *modeling* of peers than from experts.[40] *Imparting of information* (psychoeducation— in particular about one's illness and in general about health-related matters) plays a major role in these groups and comes not only from the leaders but from the exchange of information and advice between members. *Altruism* is strongly evident and contributes to well-being through one's sense of usefulness to others. *Existential factors* are also prominent, as the group supports its members in confronting the fundamental anxieties of life that we conceal from ourselves until we are forcibly confronted with their presence.†

Clinical Illustration

In this section I describe the formation, the structure, and the usefulness of a specific therapy group for the medically ill: a group for women with breast cancer.

The Clinical Situation.   At the time of the first experimental therapy groups for breast cancer patients, in the mid-1970s, women with breast cancer were in serious peril. Surgery was severely deforming and chemotherapy poorly developed. Women whose disease had metastasized had little hope for survival, were often in great pain, and felt abandoned and isolated. They were reluctant to discuss their despair with their family and friends lest they bring them down into despair as well. Moreover, friends and family avoided them, not knowing how best to speak to them. All this resulted in a bidirectional and ever-increasing isolation.

Breast cancer patients felt hopeless and powerless: they often felt uncared for and unheard by their physicians but unable to complain or to seek help elsewhere. Often they felt guilty: the pop psychology of the day promulgated the belief that they were in some manner responsible for their own disease.

Finally, there was considerable resistance in the medical field to forming a group because of the widespread belief that talking openly about cancer and hearing several women share their pain and fears would only make things worse.*

Goals for the Therapy Group.   The primary goal was reduction of isolation. My colleagues and I hoped that if we could bring together several individuals facing the same illness and encourage them to share their

---

*For a full description of the first group led for cancer patients, see my story "Travels with Paula" in *Momma and the Meaning of Life* (New York: HarperCollins, 1999, 15–53).

experiences and feelings, we could create a supportive social network, destigmatize the illness, and help the members share resources and coping strategies. Many of the patients' closest friends had dropped away, and we committed ourselves to continued presence: to stay with them—to the death if necessary.

Modification of Group Therapy Technique. After some experimentation with groups of patients with different types and stages of cancer, we concluded that a homogeneous group offered the most support: we formed a group of women with metastatic breast cancer that met weekly for ninety minutes. It was an open group with new women joining the group, cognizant that others before them had died from the illness.

Support was the most important guiding principle. We wanted each member to experience "presence"—to know others facing the same situation. As one member put it, "I know I'm all alone in my little boat, but when I look and see the lights on in all the other boats in the harbor, I don't feel so alone."

In order to increase the members' sense of personal control, the therapists turned over as much as possible of the direction of the group to the members. They invited members to speak, to share their experiences, to express the many dark feelings they could not discuss elsewhere. They modeled empathy, attempted to clarify confused feelings, and sought to mobilize the resources available in the membership. For example, if members described their fear of their physicians and their inability to ask their oncologist questions, the leaders encouraged other members to share the ways they had dealt with their physicians. At times the leaders suggested that a member role-play a meeting with her oncologist. Not infrequently a member invited another group member to accompany her to her medical appointment. One of the most powerful interventions the women learned was to respond to a rushed appointment with a doctor with the compellingly simple and effective statement, "I know that you are rushed, but if you can give me five more minutes of your time today, it may give me a month's peace of mind."

The leaders found that expression of affect, whatever it might be, was a positive experience—the members had too few opportunities elsewhere to express their feelings. They talked about everything: all their macabre thoughts, their fear of death and oblivion, the sense of meaninglessness, the dilemma of what to tell their children, how to plan their funeral. Such discussions served to detoxify some of these fearsome issues.

The therapists were always supportive, never confrontational. The here-and-now, if used at all, always focused on positive feelings between members. Members differed greatly in their coping styles. Some members, for example, wanted to know everything about their illness, others preferred not to inquire too deeply. Leaders never challenged behavior that offered comfort, mindful never to tamper with a group member's coping style unless they had something far superior to offer. Some groups formed cohesion-building rituals such as a few minutes of hand-holding meditation at the end of meetings.

The members were encouraged to have extragroup contacts: phone calls, luncheons, and the like, and even occasional suicide phone vigils, were part of the ongoing process. Some members delivered eulogies at the funerals of members, fulfilling their pledge never to abandon one another.

Many members had overcome panic and despair and found something positive emanating from the confrontation with death. Some spoke of entering a golden period in which they prized and valued life more vividly. Some reprioritized their life activities and stopped doing the things they did not wish to do. Instead they turned their attention to the things that mattered most: loving exchanges with family, the beauty of the passing seasons, discovering creative parts of themselves. One patient noted wisely, "Cancer cures psychoneurosis." The petty things that used to agonize her no longer mattered. More than one patient said she had become wiser but that it was a pity she had to wait until her body was riddled with cancer before learning how to live. How much she wished her children could learn these lessons while they were healthy. These attitudes resulted in their welcoming rather than resenting student observers. Having learned something valuable from their encounter with death, they could imbue the final part of life with meaning by passing their wisdom on to others, to students and to children.

Leading such a group is emotionally moving and highly demanding. Co-therapy and supervision are highly recommended. Leaders cannot remain distant and objective: the issues addressed touched leaders as well as members. When it comes to the human condition, there is no "us and them." We are all fellow travelers or fellow sufferers facing the same existential threats.[41]

This particular group approach, which is now identified as supportive-expressive group therapy (SEGT), has been described in a series of publications[42] and been taught to a range of psycho-oncology professionals.[43] SEGT has also been used for related conditions: for women with primary breast cancer, a disease that carries a good prognosis for the vast majority of women, as well as for women with a strong genetic or familial predisposition to develop breast cancer. Reports describe effective homogeneous groups that meet for a course of twelve weekly sessions. The last four meetings may be used as boosters, meeting once monthly for four months, which extends exposure to the intervention for six months. In these groups, one's own death may not be a primary focus, but coping with life's uncertainty, prophylactic mastectomy, and shattered illusions of invulnerability are central concerns. Grief and loss issues related to mothers and family members who may have died of breast cancer are also prominent.[44]

Effectiveness.   Outcome research over the past fifteen years has demonstrated the effectiveness of these groups. SEGT for women at risk of breast cancer, women with primary breast cancer, and women with metastatic disease has been shown to reduce pain, and improve psychological coping. The medical profession's apprehension that talking about death and dying would make women feel worse or cause them to withdraw from the group has also been disconfirmed.[45] Can groups for cancer patients increase survival time?[46] The first controlled study of groups for women with metastatic breast cancer reported longer survival, but several other studies, have failed to replicate those findings. All of the studies, however, show significant positive psychological results: although the group intervention most likely is not life prolonging, there is little doubt that it can be life altering.[47]

ADAPTATION OF CBT AND IPT TO GROUP THERAPY

It can be valuable indeed to use a pluralistic approach to psychotherapy—that is, to integrate into one's approach helpful aspects of other approaches to therapy. In this section I explore two widely used current models of group therapy in order to identify methods that all therapists can effectively incorporate into their work (a far more constructive stance than to assume a competitive approach that narrows our therapeutic vision).

Cognitive-behavioral therapy (CBT) and interpersonal therapy (IPT) were originally constructed, described, and empirically tested in individual therapy,[48] but both now are used as brief group therapy interventions. Readers will no doubt find many concepts in these next pages familiar, although with different terminology attached.†

It is important not to be misled by labels. A recent review of the current literature on group therapy for women with breast cancer noted that many of the groups identified as CBT were in fact integrative models that synthesized contributions from multiple models.[49] This important finding is by no means the exception: it is often the case that effective, well-conducted therapy of purportedly different ideological models shares more in common than good and bad therapy conducted within the same model. One of the major conclusions of the encounter group study reported in chapter sixteen was exactly that: *the behavior of the effective therapists resembled one another far more than they resembled the other (less effective) practitioners of their own ideological school.*[50]

Cognitive-Behavioral Group Therapy

Group CBT (also referred to as CBT-G) arose from the search for greater clinical efficiency. Cognitive-behavioral therapists used the group venue to deliver individual CBT to a large number of clients simultaneously. Note this important and fundamental difference. *CBT therapists were using groups to increase the efficiency of delivering CBT to individual clients, not to tap the unique benefits inherent in the group arena I have emphasized throughout this text.* At first, cognitive-behavioral therapists had a narrow focus: they wanted to provide psychoeducation and cognitive and behavioral skill training. What about peer support, universality, imitative behavior, altruism destigmatization, social skills training, interpersonal learning? They were considered merely backdrop benefits. What about the presence of group process, cohesion, or phases of group development? They represented noise in the system, often interfering with the work of delivering CBT: in fact, some therapists raised concern that the group format diluted the power of CBT.[51]

We have passed now into a second generation of more sophisticated CBT group applications, in which the essential elements of group life are being acknowledged and productively utilized by CBT group therapists.[52] Today the task of the group and the relationships of the members within the group are not considered antagonistic.

The CBT approach postulates that psychological distress is the result of impaired information-processing and disruption in patterns of social behavioral reinforcement.[53] Although thoughts, feelings, and behaviors were known to be interrelated, the CBT approach considered one's thoughts in particular to be central to the process. Often automatic and flying beneath the radar of one's awareness, one's thoughts initiate alterations in mood and behavior. CBT therapists attempt to access and illuminate these thoughts through probing, Socratic questioning, and the encouragement of self-examination and self-monitoring.

Once automatic thoughts that shape behavior, mood, and sense of self are identified, the therapist initiates an exploration of the client's conditional beliefs—"if this happens, then that will follow." These conditional beliefs are then translated into hypotheses that the client systematically tests by acquiring actual evidence that refutes or confirms the beliefs. This testing leads to further identification of the client's core beliefs, those that reside at the center of the individual's view of self.

What type of core beliefs are uncovered? Core beliefs fall into two main categories—relationships and competence. "Am I worth loving?" and "Can I achieve what I need to confirm my worth?" Interpersonally oriented therapists have noted that both core beliefs are strongly interpersonal at their center.[54] Once these dysfunctional core beliefs (for example,

"I am entirely unlovable") are identified, the next objective of treatment is to restructure them into more adaptive and self-affirming beliefs.

Group CBT has been applied effectively to an array of clinical conditions: acute depression,[55] chronic depression,[56] chronic dysthymia,[57] depression relapse prevention,[58] post-traumatic stress disorder (PTSD),[59] eating disorders,[60] insomnia,[61] somatization and hypochondriasis,[62] spousal abuse,[63] panic disorder,[64] obsessive compulsive disorder,[65] generalized anxiety disorder,[66] social phobia,[67] anger management,[68] schizophrenia (both for negative symptoms such as apathy and withdrawal, and, positive symptoms such as hallucinations),[69] and other conditions, including medical illnesses.

Substantial and durable benefits have been reported in all these applications. Group CBT has been found to be no less effective than individual CBT, and it does not have a higher rate of premature termination of therapy. Exposure-based group treatment for PTSD, however, does have a greater frequency of dropouts. Group members are often so overwhelmed by exposure to traumatic memories that a brief format is not feasible, and desensitization must be conducted over a considerable period of time.[70]

The application of CBT in groups varies according to the particular needs of the clients in each type of specialty group, but all share certain well-identified features.[71] Group CBT is homogeneous, time limited, and relatively brief, generally with a course of eight to twelve meetings that last two to three hours.[72] Group CBT emphasizes structure, focus, and acquisition of cognitive and behavioral skills. Therapists make it clear that group members are each accountable for advancing their therapy, and they assign homework between sessions. The type of homework is tailored to the concerns of the individual client. It might involve keeping a log of one's automatic thoughts and how these thoughts relate to mood, or it might involve a behavioral task that challenges avoidance.

The review of the homework is a key component of each group meeting and represents a key difference between group CBT and interactional group therapy, in that it substitutes "cold processing" of the client's at-home functioning for the "hot processing" that typifies interactional group therapy.[73] In other words, the group focuses on clients' descriptions of their back-home functioning rather than on their real-time functioning in the here-and-now interaction.

Measurement of clients' distress and progress through self-report questionnaires is ongoing, providing regular feedback that either supports the therapy or signals the need to realign therapy.

The group CBT therapist makes use of a set of strategies and techniques, in various combinations, that clients employ and then discuss together in the group.[74] These interventions deconstruct the clients' difficulties into workable segments and combat their tendency to generalize, magnify, and distort. For example, clients are asked to:

- *Record automatic thoughts.* Make overt what is covert; link thoughts to mood and behavior. For example, "I will never be able to meet anyone who will find me attractive."
- *Challenge automatic thoughts.* Challenge negative beliefs; identify distortions in thinking; explore the deeper personal assumptions underlying the automatic thoughts. For example, "How can I actually meet people if I keep refusing invitations to go out for drinks after work?"
- *Monitor mood.* Explore the relationship between mood and thoughts and behaviors; for example, "I think I started to feel lousy when no one invited me for lunch today."
- *Create an arousal hierarchy.* Rank anxiety-generating situations that are to be gradually confronted, building from easiest to hardest. For example, a client with agoraphobia would rank the venues that create anxiety from the easiest to the most challenging. Going to church on Sunday morning with a spouse might be at the low end of arousal. Going shopping alone at a new mall at night might be at the high end of arousal. Ultimately, gradual exposure desensitizes the client and extinguishes the anxious and avoidant response.
- *Monitor activity.* Track how time and energy are spent. For example, monitoring how much time is actually lost to rumination about work competence and how that in turn interferes with completing required tasks.
- *Problem-solve.* Find solutions to everyday problems. Therapists challenge clients' belief in their incompetence by breaking a problem down into instrumental and workable components.
- *Learn relaxation training.* Reduce emotional tension by progressive muscle relaxation, guided imagery, breathing exercises and meditation. Generally a meeting or two is devoted to training in these techniques.
- *Perform a risk appraisal.* Identify the source of clients' sense of threat and the resources they have to meet these threats. This might include, for example, examining the client's belief that his panic attack is actually a heart attack and reminding him that he can use deep breathing to settle himself effectively.
- *Acquire knowledge through psychoeducation.* This might include, for example, education about the physiology of anxiety.

The group CBT treatment of social phobia is representative.[75] Each group consists of five to seven members and meets for twelve sessions of two and a half hours each. An individual pregroup or postgroup meeting may be used in some instances. Each meeting has a beginning agenda and check-in, a middle working phase, and an end-of-session review.

The first two sessions address the clients' automatic thoughts regarding situations that evoke anxiety, such as "If I speak up, I will certainly make a fool of myself and be ridiculed." Skills are taught to challenge these automatic thoughts and errors in logic. For example: "You assume the worst outcome possible and yet when you voice your concerns here, you have been repeatedly told by others in the group that you are clear and articulate." Alternative ways of making sense of the situation are encouraged.

The middle sessions address each individual's target goals, using homework, in-group role simulations, and behavioral exposure to the source of anxiety. The last few sessions consolidate gains and identify future situations that could trigger a relapse. Thus the entire sequence consists of identifying dysfunctional thinking, challenging these thoughts, restructuring thoughts, and modifying behavior.

Group Interpersonal Therapy

Individual interpersonal therapy (IPT), first described by Klerman and colleagues,[76] has recently been adapted for group use. In the same way that CBT views psychological dysfunction as a problem of information processing and behavioral reinforcement, IPT views psychological dysfunction as a problem based in one's interpersonal relationships. As the client's social functioning and interpersonal competence improve, the client's disorder—for example, depression or binge eating—also improves. This occurs with little specific attention to the actual disorder other than psychoeducation about its nature, course, and impact.†

Group IPT (sometimes referred to as IPT-G) emphasizes the acquisition of interpersonal skills and strategies for dealing with social and interpersonal problems.[77] Group applications of IPT emerge not only from the drive toward greater efficiency but also from the recognition of the therapeutic opportunities group members can provide one another in addressing interpersonal dysfunction. The first group IPT application was developed for clients with binge eating disorder, but recent applications have addressed depression, social phobia, and trauma.[78] It has been used effectively as a stand-alone treatment and conjointly with pharmacotherapy, either concurrently or sequentially.[79] Its applicability has also been demonstrated in another culture (in Uganda), and it has the potential to be taught effectively to trainees who have little psy-chotherapeutic background.[80]

Group IPT closely follows the individual IPT model. A positive, sup-portive, transparent and collaborative client-therapist relationship is strongly encouraged. Each client's interpersonal difficulties are ascer-tained beforehand in an intensive evaluation of relationship patterns and categorized into one or two of four main areas: grief, role disputes, role transitions, or interpersonal deficits. Self-report questionnaires may be used to refine the client's focus and to measure progress. The most com-monly used self-report measurements address the client's chief areas of distress—mood, eating behaviors, or interpersonal patterns.† One to three goals are identified for each client to help focus the work and to jump-start the group therapy.

A typical course of therapy consists of one or two preliminary individ-ual meetings and eight to twenty group meetings of ninety minutes each, with an individual follow-up session three or four months later; some practitioners use a midgroup individual evaluation meeting. Group meet-ings may also be scheduled as booster sessions at regular intervals in the months following the intensive phase of therapy.

The group therapy consists of an initial introduction and orientation phase, a middle working phase, and a final consolidation and review seg-ment.[81] Written group summaries (see chapter 14) may be sent to each group member before the next session.

The first phase of the group, in which members present personal goals, helps to catalyze cohesion and universality. Psychoeducation, interper-sonal problem solving, advice, and feedback are provided to each client by the group members and the therapist. The ideal posture for the therapist is one of active concern, support, and encouragement. Transference issues are managed rather than explored. Clients are encouraged to analyze and clarify their patterns of communication with figures in their environment but not to work through member-to-member tensions.

What are the differences between group IPT and the interactional, in-terpersonal model described in this text? In the service of briefer therapy and more limited goals, group IPT generally deemphasizes both the here-and-now and the group's function as a social microcosm. These modifi-cations reduce interpersonal tensions and the potential for disruptive disagreements. (Such conflicts may be instrumental for far-reaching change but may impede the course of brief therapy.) The group nonethe-less becomes an important social network, through its supportive and modeling functions. In some carefully selected instances, group here-and-now interaction may be employed and linked to the client's focus and goals.

SELF-HELP GROUPS AND
INTERNET SUPPORT GROUPS

A contemporary focus on specialized groups would be incomplete without considering self-help groups and their youngest offspring—Internet support groups.

Self-Help Groups

The number of participants in self-help groups is staggering. A 1997 study that antedates Internet support groups reported that 10 million Americans had participated in a self-help group in the preceding year, and a total of 25 million Americans had participated in a self-help group sometime in the past. That study focused exclusively on self-help groups that had no professional leadership. In fact, more than 50 percent of self-help groups have professional leadership of some sort, which means that a truer measure of participation in self-help groups is 20 million individuals in the previous year and 50 million overall—figures that far exceed the number of people receiving professional mental health care.[82]

Although it is difficult to evaluate the effectiveness of freestanding self-help groups, given that membership is often anonymous, follow-up is difficult, and no records are kept, some systematic studies attest to the efficacy of these groups. Members value the groups, report improved coping and well-being, greater knowledge of their condition, and reduced use of other health care facilities.[83]*

These findings have led some researchers to call for a much more active collaboration between professional health care providers and the self-help movement. Is there a way that self-help groups can effectively address the widening gap between societal need and professional resources?[84] One important advance is the number of active self-help clearinghouses accessible online or by phone that have emerged to guide consumers to the nearly 500 diverse types of self-help groups in operation. Examples include the American Self-Help Clearinghouse and the National Mental Health Consumers Self-Help Clearinghouse.

Self-help groups have such high visibility that it is barely necessary to list their various forms. One can scarcely conceive of a type of distress, behavioral aberration, or environmental misfortune for which there is not some corresponding group. The roster, far larger than the psychopathologies described in DSM-IV-TR, includes widespread groups such as AA,

---

*The authors of a large meta-analysis concluded that although problems with addictions respond well to self-help groups, clients with medical problems in such groups do not demonstrate objective benefits commensurate with how highly the participants value the groups.

Recovery, Inc., Compassionate Friends (for bereaved parents), Mended Hearts (for clients with heart disease), Smoke Enders, Weight Watchers, Overeaters Anonymous, and highly specialized groups such as Spouses of Head Injury Survivors, Gay Alcoholics, Late-Deafened Adults, Adolescent Deaf Children of Alcoholics, Moms in Recovery, Senior Crime Victims, Circle of Friends (friends of someone who has committed suicide), Parents of Murdered Children, Go-Go Stroke Club (victims of stroke), Together Expecting a Miracle (adoption support). Some self-help groups transform into social action and advocacy groups as well, such as MADD (Mothers Against Drunk Driving).

Although the self-help groups resemble that of the therapy group, there are some significant differences. The self-help group makes extensive use of almost all the therapeutic factors—especially altruism, cohesiveness, universality, imitative behavior, instillation of hope, and catharsis. But there is one important exception: the therapeutic factor of interpersonal learning plays a far less important role in the self-help group than in the therapy group.[85] It is rare for a group to be able to focus significantly and constructively on the here-and-now without the participation of a well-trained leader. In general, self-help groups differ from therapy groups in that they have far fewer personality interpretations, less confrontation, and far more positive, supportive statements.[86]

Most self-help groups employ a consistent, sensible cognitive framework that the group veterans who serve as the group's unofficial leaders can easily describe to incoming members. Although members benefit from universality and instillation of hope, those who actively participate and experience stronger cohesiveness are likely to benefit the most.[87]

What accounts for the widespread use and apparent efficacy of self-help groups? They are open and accessible, and they offer psychological support to anyone who shares the group's defining characteristics. They emphasize *internal* rather than *external* expertise—in other words, the resources available in the group rather than those available from external experts. The members' shared experience make them both peers and credible experts. Constructive comparisons, even inspiration, can be drawn from one's peers in a way that does not happen with external experts. Members are simultaneously providers *and* consumers of support, and they profit from both roles—their self-worth is raised through altruism, and hope is instilled by their contact with others who have surmounted problems similar to theirs. Pathology is deemphasized and dependency reduced. It is well known that passive and avoidant coping diminish functional outcomes. Active strategies, such as those seen in self-help groups, enhance functional outcome.[88]

Ailments that are not recognized or addressed by the professional health care system are very likely to generate self-help groups. Because these groups effectively help members accept and normalize their malady, they are particularly helpful to victims of stigmatizing ailments.[89]

Groups for substance use disorders are doubtless the most widely found self-help groups. More than 100,000 AA groups exist around the world in over 150 countries.[90] The twelve-step model is not only used in AA, but variants of it are used by many other professional providers and by many other self-help groups, such as Narcotics Anonymous, Overeaters Anonymous, Sex Addicts Anonymous, and Gamblers Anonymous. Although some members have misgivings about AA's spiritual focus, research shows that a lack of a personal commitment to spirituality does not interfere with treatment effectiveness.[91]

Although twelve-step groups do not use professional leadership, many other self-help groups (perhaps more than half) have a professional leader who is active in the meeting or serves in an advisory or consultant capacity. Occasionally a mental health professional will help launch a self-help group and then withdraw, turning over the running of the group to its members.[92] Any mental health professional serving as a consultant must be aware of the potential dangers in too strenuous a demonstration of professional expertise: the self-help group does better if the expertise resides with the members.

A final note: group therapists should not look at the self-help group movement as a rival but as a resource. As I have discussed in chapter 14, many clients will benefit from participation in both types of group experience.

Internet Support Groups

Just a few years ago, the idea of Internet virtual group therapy seemed the stuff of fantasy and satire. Today, it is the real-life experience of millions of people around the world. Consider the following data: 165,640,000 Americans are Internet users; 63,000,000 have sought health information online; 14,907,000 have participated in an online symposium at some time, *and in a recent polling a remarkable 1,656,400 participated in an Internet support group the preceding day!*[93]

Internet support groups take the form of *synchronous*, real-time groups (not unlike a chat line) or *asynchronous* groups, in which members post messages and comments, like a bulletin board. Groups may be time limited or of indeterminate duration. In many ways they are in a state of great flux: it is too early in their evolution for clear structures or procedures to have been established. Internet support groups may be actively led, moderated, or run without any peer or professional executive input. If moderators are used, their responsibility is to coordinate, edit, and post participants' messages in ways that maximize therapeutic opportunity and group functioning.[94]

How can we account for this explosive growth? Internet support group participants and providers have described many advantages. Many individuals, for example, wish to participate in a self-help group but are not able to attend face-to-face meetings because of geographic distance, physical disability, or infirmity. Clients with stigmatizing ailments or social anxiety may prefer the relative anonymity of an Internet support group. For many people in search of help, it is the equivalent of putting a toe in the water, in preparation for full immersion in some therapy endeavor. After all, what other support system is available 24/7 and allows its members time to rehearse, craft, and fine-tune their stories so as to create an ideal, perhaps larger-than-life narrative?[95]

A recent experience as a faculty member in a month-long American Group Psychotherapy Association online training symposium was eye-opening. The program was an asynchronous (that is, bulletin board model) moderated virtual group for mental health professionals on the treatment of trauma. More than 2,000 people around the world signed up, although only a small fraction posted messages. The experience was vital and meaningful, and the faculty, like many of the participants, thought much about the postings during the day and eagerly checked each night to read the latest informative or evocative posting. Although we never met face to face, we indeed became a group that engaged, worked, and terminated.

Internet support groups have several intrinsic problems. The current technology is still awkward and lacks reliability and privacy safeguards. Members may, intentionally or through oversight, post inaccurate messages. Identities and stories may be fictionalized. Communication of emotional states may be limited or distorted by the absence of nonverbal cues. Some experts worry that the Internet contact may deflect members from much-needed professional care or squeeze out actual support in the lives of some participants.[96] Keep in mind, too, that a group is a group and Internet groups do have a process. They are not immune to destructive norms, antigroup behavior, unhealthy group pressures, client overstimulation, and scapegoating.[97]

There are ethical concerns about professional involvement in Internet support groups.* Professionals who serve as facilitators need to clarify the nature of their contract, how they will be paid for their services, and the limits of their responsiveness online to any emergencies. They must

---

*The American Counseling Association has issued specific ethics guidelines for online therapists (American Counseling Association, "Ethical Standards for Internet Online Counseling" [1999]; available at www.counseling.org). Other organizations, such as the American Psychological Association, have not yet distinguished online from face-to-face care. It is certain that the future will see new statements from licensing bodies and professional organizations addressing this area.

obtain informed consent, acknowledge that there are limits to confidentiality, and provide a platform for secure communication. In addition they must identify each participant accurately and be certain of how to contact each person, and they must indicate clearly how they themselves can be reached in an emergency. Keep in mind geographic limits with regard to licensure and malpractice insurance. A therapist licensed in one state may not be legally able to treat a client residing in another state.[98]

Many questions about Internet support groups clamor for attention. Are they effective? If so, is it the result of a particular intervention approach or of more general social support and interaction? Can face-to-face group models translate to an online format? What are the implications for health care costs? What kind of special training do online therapists require? Can therapists communicate empathy in prose as readily as in face-to-face interaction?

Although Internet support groups are at an early stage of development, some notable preliminary findings have emerged. In many ways, such groups lend themselves well to research. The absence of nonverbal interaction may be a disadvantage clinically, but it is a boon for the researcher, since everything (100 percent of the interaction) that goes on in the group is in written form and hence available for analysis.

One team of researchers adapted a loneliness-reducing face-to-face cognitive-behavioral group intervention[99] to a synchronous, therapist-led support group that met for twelve two-hour sessions. Significant reductions of loneliness in the nineteen subjects were achieved and sustained at four-month follow-up. The small sample size limits the validity of the conclusions, but the researchers demonstrated the feasibility of applying a specific intervention designed for a face-to-face group to an online format.

"Student Bodies" is an Internet support group that is part of a large public health intervention and research enterprise. It is essentially an asynchronous moderated Internet support group intended to prevent eating disorders in adolescent and young women.[100] On a secure Web site, it offers participants psychoeducation about eating disorders and encourages them to journal online about their body, eating, and their responses to the psychoeducation. They may also post messages through the moderator about personal challenges and successes in the modification of disordered thinking about eating. This intervention resulted in improvements in weight, body image concerns, and eating attitudes and behaviors.[101]

In a study of sixty college students, researchers added to the "Student Bodies" program an eight-session, moderated, *synchronous* (that is, meeting in real time) Internet support group component. They found that the synchronous online group format expanded client gains.[102]

A study of 103 participants in an asynchronous, open-ended peer Internet support group for depression found that many of the members of the group valued it highly, spending at least five hours online over the preceding two weeks. More than 80 percent continued to receive face-to-face care, viewing the online group as a supportive adjunct, not a substitute for traditional care.[103] One participant's account of her experience describes many of the unique benefits of the Internet support group:

> I find online message boards to be a very supportive community in the absence of a "real" community support group. I am more likely to interact with the online community than I am with people face to face. This allows me to be honest and open about what is really going on with me. There are lots of shame and self-esteem issues involved in depression, and the anonymity of the online message board is very effective in relieving some of the anxiety associated with "group therapy" or even individual therapy. I am not stating that it is a replacement for professional assistance, but it has been very supportive and helped motivate me to be more active in my own recovery program.[104]

CHESS (Comprehensive Health Enhancement Support System), a sophisticated Internet group program developed at the University of Wisconsin, has provided support for people with AIDS, cancer, and for caregivers of Alzheimer's patients. The group program consists of three elements. First, it provides relevant information and resources through online access to experts and question-and-answer sessions. Second, a facilitator-mediated discussion group offers an opportunity for members to obtain social support by sharing their personal story and reacting to the stories of the other members. Third, it helps clients formulate and then implement an action plan for constructive change, such as scheduling time away from caregiving for self-care. Over many years, thousands of participants with a range of medical concerns have completed questionnaires about the impact of these interventions. Reported benefits include briefer hospitalizations, improved communication with health care providers, and an increased sense of personal empowerment.†[105]

The results of two different Internet support group approaches for women with breast cancer have been reported. One program evaluated seventy-two women with primary breast cancer in a twelve-week, moderated, Web-based asynchronous group, structured according to the supportive-expressive group therapy model described earlier in this chapter and run in partnership with Bosom Buddies, a peer support network for women with cancer. The groups reduced depression and cancer-related stress scores. Women typically logged on three times a week and used this group experience to launch an informal support network that has continued long after the twelve-week treatment ended.[106]

The second program, a synchronous, sixteen-session group led by trained facilitators from the Wellness Community (an international, not-for-profit organization supporting the medically ill) for thirty-two women with primary breast cancer, also reduced depression and reactions to pain.[107]

All Internet support groups develop their own specific set of norms and dynamics. An analysis of text postings in groups for women with breast cancer demonstrated that groups with a trained moderator were more likely to express distressing emotions, which has the effect of reducing depression.[108] The moderator's skill in activating, containing, and exploring strong emotion appears to be as important in online support groups as in face-to-face groups.[109]

We are just at the beginning of the use of electronic technology in the provision of mental health care. If it does turn out to help us connect meaningfully, it would be a pleasant and welcome surprise—an all-too-rare instance of technology increasing rather than decreasing human engagement.

Chapter 16

GROUP THERAPY:
ANCESTORS AND COUSINS

During the 1960s and 1970s, the encounter group phenomenon, a heady, robust social movement, swept through the nation. Huge numbers of individuals participated in small groups sometimes described as "therapy group for normals." Today whenever I mention encounter groups to students I am greeted by quizzical looks that ask, "What's that?" Although encounter groups are largely a thing of the past, their influence on group therapy practice continues today.

There are several reasons the contemporary group therapist should have, at the very least, some passing knowledge of them.

1. First, as I discuss in chapter seventeen, the proper training of the group therapist must include some personal group experience. Few training programs offer a traditional therapy group for trainees; instead they provide some variant of an encounter group, today often labeled a "process group." (For the moment, I refer to all experiential groups as encounter groups, but shortly I will define terms more precisely.) Thus, many group therapists enter the field through the portals of the encounter group.
2. Secondly, the form of contemporary group therapy has been vastly influenced by the encounter group. No historical account of the development and evolution of group therapy is complete without a description of the cross-fertilization between the therapy and the encounter traditions.
3. Lastly, and this may seem surprising, the encounter group, or at least the tradition from which it emerged, has been responsible for developing the best, and the most sophisticated, small group research technology. In comparison, the early group therapy research was

crude and unimaginative; much of the empirical research I have cited throughout this text has its roots in the encounter group tradition.

In this chapter I provide a lean overview of the encounter group and then expand on these three points. Readers who would like more information about the rise, efflorescence, and decline of this curious social movement may read a more detailed account (the chapter on encounter groups from the previous edition of this text) on my Web site, www.yalom.com.

WHAT IS AN ENCOUNTER GROUP?

"Encounter group" is a rough, inexact generic term that encompasses a great variety of forms and has many aliases: human relations groups, training groups, T-groups, sensitivity groups, personal growth groups, marathon groups, human potential groups, sensory awareness groups, basic encounter groups, and experiential groups.

Although the nominal plumage is dazzling and diverse, all these experiential groups have several common elements. They range in size from eight to twenty members—large enough to encourage face-to-face interaction, yet small enough to permit all members to interact. The groups are time limited and are often compressed into hours or days. They are referred to as "experiential groups" because they focus to a large extent on their own experience, that is, the here-and-now. They transcend etiquette and encourage the doffing of traditional social facades; they value interpersonal honesty, exploration, confrontation, heightened emotional expressiveness, and self-disclosure. The group goals are often vague: occasionally they stress merely the provision of an experience—joy, entertainment, being turned on—but more often they implicitly or explicitly strive for some *change*—in behavior, in attitudes, in values, in lifestyle, in self-actualization, in one's relationship to others, to the environment, to one's own body. The participants are considered "seekers" and "normals," not "patients" or "clients"; the experience is considered not therapy but "growth."

ANTECEDENTS AND EVOLUTION OF THE ENCOUNTER GROUP

The term "encounter group" became popular in the mid-1960s, but the experiential group had already existed for twenty years and was most commonly referred to as a "T-group"—"T" for training (in human relations).

The first T-group, the ancestral experiential group, was held in 1946. Here is the story of its birth.[1] The State of Connecticut had passed the

Fair Employment Practices Act and asked Kurt Lewin, a prominent social psychologist, to train leaders who could deal effectively with tensions among ethnic groups and thus help to change the racial attitudes of the public. Kurt Lewin organized a workshop that consisted of groups of ten members each. These groups were led in the traditional manner of the day; they were basically discussion groups and analyzed "back-home" problems presented by the group members.

Lewin, a strong believer in the dictum *"No research without action; no action without research,"* assigned research observers to record and code the behavioral interactions of each of the small groups. During evening meetings, the group leaders and the research observers met and pooled their observations of leaders, members, and group process. Soon some participants learned of these evening meetings and asked permission to attend. This was a radical request; the staff hesitated: not only were they reluctant to reveal their own inadequacies, but they were uncertain about how participants would be affected by hearing their behavior discussed openly.

Finally they decided to permit members to observe the evening meetings on a trial basis. Observers who have written about this experience report that the effect on both participants and staff was "electric."[2] There was something galvanizing about witnessing an in-depth discussion of one's own behavior. The format of the evening meetings was widened to permit the participants to respond to the observations and soon all parties were involved in the analysis and interpretation of their interaction. Before long, all the participants were attending the evening meetings, which often ran as long as three hours. There was widespread agreement that the meetings offered participants a new and rich understanding of their own behavior.

The staff immediately realized that they had, somewhat serendipitously, discovered a powerful technique of human relations education—*experiential learning.* Group members learn most effectively by studying the interaction of the network in which they themselves are enmeshed. (By now the reader will have recognized the roots of the "here-and-now" in contemporary group therapy.) The staff discovered that members profit enormously by being confronted, in an objective manner, with on-the-spot observations of their own behavior and its effects on others. These observations instruct members about their interpersonal styles, the responses of others to them, and about group behavior in general.

From this beginning, research was woven into the fabric of the T-group—not only the formal research conducted but also *a research attitude* on the part of the leader, who collaborates with the group members in a research inquiry designed to enable participants to experience, understand, and change their behavior. This research attitude, together with the concept of the T-group as a technique of education, gradually changed during the 1950s and 1960s, as Rogerian and Freudian clinicians began participating in human relations laboratory training and chose to focus ever more heavily on interpersonal interaction and personal change.

These clinically oriented leaders heavily emphasized the here-and-now and discouraged discussion of any outside material, including theory, sociological and educational reflections, or any "there-and-then" material, including "back-home" current problems or past personal history. I attended and led encounter groups in the 1960s in which leaders customarily began the group with only one request, "Let's try to keep all our comments in the here-and-now." It sounds impossible, and yet it worked well. Sometimes there was a long initial silence, and then members might begin describing their different feelings about the silence. Or often there were differential responses to the leader's request—anxiety, puzzlement, impatience, or irritation. These different responses to either the silence or the leader's instructions were all that was needed to launch the group, and in a short time it would be up and running.

In addition to the here-and-now focus, the T-group made many other major technical innovations destined to exert much influence on the psychotherapy group. Let's examine four particularly important contributions: feedback, observant participation, unfreezing, and cognitive aids.

Feedback

Feedback, a term borrowed from electrical engineering, was first applied to the behavioral sciences by Lewin (who was teaching at MIT at the time).[3] The early group leaders considered that an important flaw in society was that too little opportunity existed for individuals to obtain accurate feedback from their "back-home" associates—bosses, coworkers, husbands, wives, teachers. Feedback, which became an essential ingredient of all T-groups (and later, of course, all interactional therapy groups) was found to be most effective when it stemmed from here-and-now observations, when it followed the generating event as closely as possible, and when the recipient checked it out with other group members to establish its validity and reduce perceptual distortion.

Observant Participation

The early T-group leaders considered *observant participation* the optimal method of group participation. Members must not only engage emotionally in the group, but they must simultaneously and objectively observe themselves and the group. Often this is a difficult task to master, and members chafe at the trainer's attempts to subject the group to objective analysis. Yet the dual task is essential to learning; alone, either action or intellectual scrutiny yields little learning. Camus once wrote, "My greatest wish: to remain lucid in ecstasy." So, too, the T-group (and the therapy group, as well) is most effective when its members can couple clarity of vision with emotional experience.

Unfreezing

Unfreezing, also adopted from Lewin's change theory,[4] refers to the process of disconfirming an individual's former belief system. Motivation for change must be generated before change can occur. One must be helped to reexamine many cherished assumptions about oneself and one's relations to others. The familiar must be made strange; thus, many common props, social conventions, status symbols, and ordinary procedural rules were eliminated from the T-group, and one's values and beliefs about oneself were challenged. This was a most uncomfortable state for group participants, a state tolerable only under certain conditions: Members must experience the group as a safe refuge within which it is possible to entertain new beliefs and experiment with new behavior without fear of reprisal. Though "unfreezing" is not a familiar term to clinicians, the general concept of examining and challenging familiar assumptions is a core part of the psychotherapeutic process.

Cognitive Aids

Cognitive guides around which T-group participants could organize their experience were often presented in brief lecturettes by T-group leaders. This practice foreshadowed and influenced the current widespread use of cognitive aids in contemporary psychoeducational and cognitive-behavioral group therapy approaches. One example used in early T-group work (I choose this particular one because it remains useful in the contemporary therapy group) is the Johari window[5] a four-cell personality paradigm that clarifies the function of feedback and self-disclosure.

	Known to Self	Unknown to Self
Known to Others	A	B
Unknown to Others	C	D

Cell A, "Known to self and Known to others," is the public area of the self; cell B, "Unknown to self and Known to others," is the blind area; cell C, "Known to self and Unknown to others," is the secret area; cell D, "Unknown to self and Unknown to others," is the unconscious self. The goals of the T-group, the leader suggests, are to increase the size of cell A by decreasing cell B (blind spots) through feedback and cell C (secret area) through self-disclosure. In traditional T-groups, cell D (the unconscious) was considered out of bounds.

GROUP THERAPY FOR NORMALS

In the 1960s, the clinically oriented encounter group leaders from the West Coast began endorsing a model of a T-group as "group therapy for normals." They emphasized personal growth,[6] and though they still considered the experiential group an instrument of education, not of therapy, they offered a broader, more humanistically based definition of education. Education is not, they argued, the process of acquiring interpersonal and leadership skills, not the understanding of organizational and group functioning; education is nothing less than comprehensive self-discovery, the development of one's full potential.

These group leaders worked with normal healthy members of society, indeed with individuals who, by most objective standards, had achieved considerable success yet still experienced considerable tension, insecurity, and value conflict. They noted that many of their group members were consumed by the building of an external facade, a public image, which they then strove to protect at all costs. Their members swallowed their doubts about personal adequacy and maintained constant vigilance lest any uncertainty or discomfort slip into visibility.

This process curtailed communication not only with others but with themselves. The leaders maintained that in order to eliminate a perpetual state of self-recrimination, the successful individual gradually comes to believe in the reality of his or her facade and attempts, through unconscious means, to ward off internal and external attacks on that self-image. Thus, a state of equilibrium is reached, but at great price: considerable energy is invested in maintaining intrapersonal and interpersonal separation, energy that might otherwise be used in the service of self-actualization. These leaders set ambitious goals for their group—no less than addressing and ameliorating the toxic effects of the highly competitive American culture.

As the goal of the group shifted from education in a traditional sense to personal change, the names of the group shifted from T-group (training in human relations) or sensitivity training group (training in interpersonal sensitivity), to ones more consonant with the basic thrust of the group. Several labels were advanced: "personal growth" or "human potential" or "human development" groups. Carl Rogers suggested the term "encounter group," which stressed the basic authentic encounter between members and between leader and members and between the disparate parts of each member. His term had the most staying power and became the most popular name for the "let it all hang out" experiential group prevalent in the 1960s and 1970s.

The third force in psychology (third after Freudian analysis and Watsonian-Skinnerian behaviorism), which emphasized a holistic, humanistic concept of the person, provided impetus and form to the encounter group from yet another direction. Psychologists such as A. Maslow, G. Allport, E. Fromm, R. May, F. Perls, C. Rogers, and J. Bugenthal (and the existential philosophers behind them—Nietzsche, Sartre, Tillich, Jaspers, Heidegger, and Husserl), rebelled strongly against the mechanistic model of behaviorism, the determinism and reductionism of analytic theory. Where, they asked, is the person? Where is consciousness, will, decision, responsibility, and a recognition and concern for the basic and tragic dimensions of existence?

All of these influences resulted in groups with a much broader, and vaguer, goal—nothing less than "total enhancement of the individual." Time in the group was set aside for reflective silence, for listening to music or poetry. Members were encouraged to give voice to their deepest concerns—to reexamine these basic life values and the discrepancies between them and their lifestyles, to encounter their many false selves; to explore the long-buried parts of themselves (the softer, feminine parts in the case of men, for example).

Collision with the field of psychotherapy was inevitable. Encounter groups claimed that they offered therapy for normals, yet also that "normality" was a sham, that *everyone* was a patient. The disease? A dehumanized runaway technocracy. The remedy? A return to grappling with basic problems of the human condition. The vehicle of remedy? The encounter group! In their view the medical model could no longer be applied to mental illness. The differentiation between mental illness and health grew as vague as the distinction between treatment and education. Encounter group leaders claimed that patienthood is ubiquitous, that therapy is too good to be limited to the sick, and that one need not be sick to get better.

The Role of the Leader

Despite the encroachment of encounter groups on the domain of psychotherapy, there were many striking differences in the basic role of group therapist and encounter group leader. At the time of the emergence of the encounter group, many group therapists assumed entirely different rules of conduct from the other members. They merely transferred their individual therapy psychoanalytic style to the group arena and remained deliberately enigmatic and mystifying. Rarely transparent, they took care to disclose only a professional front, with the result that members often regarded the therapist's statements and actions as powerful and sagacious, regardless of their content.

Encounter group leaders had a very different code of conduct. They were more flexible, experimental, more self-disclosing, and they earned prestige as a result of their contributions. The group members regarded encounter group leaders far more realistically and similar to themselves except for their superior skill and knowledge in a specialized area. Furthermore, the leaders sought to transmit not only knowledge but also skills, expecting the group members to learn methods of diagnosing and resolving interpersonal problems. Often they explicitly behaved as teachers—for example, explicating some point of theory or introducing some group exercise, verbal or nonverbal, as an experiment for the group to study. It is interesting, incidentally, to note the reemergence of flexibility and the experimental attitude displayed by contemporary therapy group leaders in the construction of cognitive-behavioral group formats addressing a wide number of special problems and populations.

THE EFFECTIVENESS OF THE ENCOUNTER GROUP

In its early days the social psychologists involved with T-groups painstakingly researched their process and outcome. Many of these studies still stand as paradigms of imaginative, sophisticated research.

The most extensive controlled research inquiry into the effectiveness of groups that purport to change behavior and personality was conducted by Lieberman, Yalom, and Miles in 1973. This project has much relevance to group therapy, and since I draw from its findings often in this book I will describe the methodology and results briefly. (The design and method are complex, and I refer interested, research-minded readers to the previous edition's version of this chapter at www.yalom.com or, for a complete description, to the monograph on the study, *Encounter Groups: First Facts.*)[7]

The Participants

We offered an experiential group as an accredited course at Stanford University. Two hundred ten participants were randomly assigned to one of eighteen groups, each of which met for a total of thirty hours over a twelve-week period. Sixty-nine subjects, similar to the participants but who did not have a group experience, were used as a control population and completed all the outcome research instruments.

The Leaders

Since a major aim of the study was to investigate the effect of leader technique on outcome, we sought to diversify leader style by employing leaders from several ideological schools. We selected experienced and expert leaders from ten such schools that were currently popular:

1. Traditional T-groups
2. Encounter groups (personal growth group)

3. Gestalt groups
4. Sensory awareness groups (Esalen group)
5. Transactional analytic (TA) groups
6. Psychodrama groups
7. Synanon groups
8. Psychoanalytically oriented experiential groups
9. Marathon groups
10. Encounter-tapes (leaderless) groups

There were a total of eighteen groups. Of the 210 subjects who started in the eighteen groups, 40 (19 percent) dropped out before attending half the meetings, and 170 finished the thirty-hour group experience.

What Did We Measure?

We were most interested in an intensive examination of outcome as well as the relationship between outcome, leader technique, and group process variables. To evaluate outcome, an extensive psychological battery of instruments was administered to each subject three times—before beginning the group, immediately after completing it, and six months after completion.[8]

To measure leader style, teams of trained raters observed all meetings and coded all behavior of the leader in real time. All statements by the leaders were also coded by analyzing tape recordings and written transcripts of the meetings. Participants also supplied observations of the leaders through questionnaires. Process data was collected by the observers and from questionnaires filled out by participants at the end of each meeting.

Results: What Did We Find?

First, the participants rated the groups very highly. At the termination of the group, the 170 subjects who completed the groups considered them "pleasant" (65 percent), "constructive" (78 percent), and "a good learning experience" (61 percent). Over 90 percent felt that encounter groups should be a regular part of the elective college curriculum. Six months later, the enthusiasm had waned, but the overall evaluation was still positive.

So much for testimony. What of the overall, more objective battery of assessment measures? Each participant's outcome (judged from all assessment measures) was rated and placed in one of six categories: high learner, moderate changer, unchanged, negative changer, casualty (significant, enduring, psychological decompensation that was due to being in the group), and dropout. The results for all 206 experimental subjects and for the sixty-nine control subjects are summarized in Table 16.1. ("Short post" is at termination of group and "long post" is at six-month follow-up.)

TABLE 16.1 Index of Change for All Participants Who Began Study

	Casualties	Negative Changer	Dropouts	Unchanged	Moderate Changer	High Learner	Total
Short Post							
Participants	16 (8%)	17 (8%)	27 (38%)	78 (38%)	40 (20%)	28 (14%)	206
Controls		16 (23%)		41 (60%)	9 (13%)	3 (4%)	69
Long Post							
Participants	16 (10%)	13 (8%)	27 (17%)	52 (33%)	37 (23%)	15 (9%)	160
Controls		7 (15%)		32 (68%)	5 (11%)	3 (6%)	47

TABLE 16.2 Index of Change for Those Who Completed Group (N = 179 Short Post, 133 Long Post)

	Casualties	Negative Changer	Unchanged	Moderate Changer	High Learner
Short Post	09%	10%	44%	22%	16%
Long Post	12%	10%	39%	28%	11%

SOURCE: Morton A. Lieberman, Irvin D. Yalom, and Matthew B. Miles, *Encounter Groups: First Facts* (New York: Basic Books, 1973).

Table 16.1 indicates that approximately one-third of the participants at the termination of the group and at six-month follow-up had undergone moderate or considerable positive change. The control population showed much less change, either negative or positive. *The encounter group thus clearly influenced change, but for both better and worse.* Maintenance of change was high: of those who changed positively, 75 percent maintained their change for at least six months.

To put it in a critical fashion, one might say that Table 16.1 indicates that, of all subjects who began a thirty-hour encounter group led by an acknowledged expert, approximately two-thirds found it an unrewarding experience (either dropout, casualty, negative change, or unchanged).

Viewing the results more generously, one might put it this way. The group experience was a college course. No one expects that students who drop out will profit. Let us therefore eliminate the dropouts from the data (see table 16.2). With the dropouts eliminated, it appears that *39 percent of all students taking a three-month college course underwent some significant positive personal change that persisted for at least six months.* Not bad for a twelve-week, thirty-hour course! (And of course this perspective on the results has significance in the contemporary setting of group therapy, where managed care has mandated briefer therapy groups.)

However, even if we consider the goblet one-third full rather than two-thirds empty, it is difficult to escape the conclusion that, in this project, encounter groups did not appear to be a highly potent agent of change. *Furthermore, a significant risk factor was involved: 16 (8 percent) of the 210 subjects suffered psychological injury that produced sequelae still present six months after the end of the group.*

Still, caution must be exercised in the interpretation of the results. It would do violence to the data to conclude that encounter groups per se are ineffective or even dangerous. First, it is difficult to gauge the degree to which we can generalize these findings to populations other than an undergraduate college student sample. But, even more important, we must take note that *these are all massed results*: the data are handled as though all subjects were in one encounter group. There was no standard encounter group experience; there were eighteen different groups, each with a distinct culture, each offering a different experience, and each with very different outcomes. In some groups, almost every member underwent some positive change with no one suffering injury; in other groups, not a single member benefited, and one was fortunate to remain unchanged.

The next obvious question—and one highly relevant to psychotherapy—is: *Which type of leader had the best, and which the worst, results?* The T-group leader, the gestalt, the transactional analytic leader, the psychodrama leader, and so on? However, we soon learned that the question posed in this form was not meaningful. The behavior of the leaders when carefully rated by observers varied greatly and did not conform to our pregroup expectations. *The ideological school to which a leader belonged told us little about that leader's actual behavior.* We found that the behavior of the leader of one school—for example, gestalt therapy, resembled the behavior of the other gestalt therapy leader no more closely than that of any of the other seventeen leaders. In other words, the leaders' behavior is not predictable from their membership in a particular ideological school. *Yet the effectiveness of a group was, in large part, a function of its leader's behavior.*

How, then, to answer the question, "Which is the more effective leadership style?" Ideological schools—what leaders *say* they do—is of little value. What is needed is a more accurate, empirically derived method of describing leader behavior. We performed a factor analysis of a large number of leader behavior variables (as rated by observers) and derived four important basic leadership functions:

1. *Emotional activation* (challenging, confronting, modeling by personal risk-taking and high self-disclosure)
2. *Caring* (offering support, affection, praise, protection, warmth, acceptance, genuineness, concern)
3. *Meaning attribution* (explaining, clarifying, interpreting, providing a cognitive framework for change; translating feelings and experiences into ideas)
4. *Executive function* (setting limits, rules, norms, goals; managing time; pacing, stopping, interceding, suggesting procedures)

These four leadership functions (emotional activation, caring, meaning attribution, executive function) have great relevance to the group therapy leadership. Moreover, they had a clear and striking relationship to outcome. *Caring and meaning attribution had a linear relationship to positive outcome*: in other words, *the higher the caring and the higher the meaning attribution, the higher the positive outcome.*

The other two functions, *emotional stimulation and executive function, had a curvilinear relationship to outcome*—the rule of the golden mean applied: in other words, *too much or too little of this leader behavior resulted in lower positive outcome.*

Let's look at leader emotional stimulation: *too little* leader emotional stimulation resulted in an unenergetic, devitalized group; *too much* stimulation (especially with insufficient meaning attribution) resulted in a highly emotionally charged climate with the leader pressing for more emotional interaction than the members could integrate.

Now consider leader *executive function: too little* executive function— a laissez-faire style—resulted in a bewildered, floundering group; too *much* executive function resulted in a highly structured, authoritarian, arrhythmic group that failed to develop a sense of member autonomy or a freely flowing interactional sequence.

The most successful leaders, then—and this has great relevance for therapy—were those whose style was moderate in amount of stimulation and in expression of executive function and high in caring and meaning attribution. Both caring and meaning attribution seemed necessary: neither alone was sufficient to ensure success.

These findings from encounter groups strongly corroborate the functions of the group therapist as discussed in chapter 5. Both emotional stimulation and cognitive structuring are essential. Carl Rogers's factors of empathy, genuineness, and unconditional positive regard thus seem incomplete; we must add the cognitive function of the leader. The research does not tell us *what kind of meaning attribution is essential.* Several ideological explanatory vocabularies (for example, interpersonal, psychoanalytic, transactional analytic, gestalt, Rogerian, and so on) seemed useful. What seems important is *the process of explanation,* which, in several ways, enabled participants to integrate their experience, to generalize from it, and to transport it into other life situations.

The importance of meaning attribution received powerful support from another source. When members were asked at the end of each session to report the most significant event of the session and the reason for its significance, we found that those members who gained from the experience were far more likely to report incidents involving cognitive integration. (Even so revered an activity as self-disclosure bore little relationship to change unless it was accompanied by intellectual insight.) The pervasiveness and strength of this finding was impressive as well as unexpected in that encounter groups had a fundamental anti-intellectual ethos.

The study had some other conclusions of considerable relevance to the change process in experiential groups. When outcome (on both group and individual level) was correlated with the course of events during the life of a group, findings emerged suggesting that a number of widely accepted experiential group maxims needed to be reformulated, for example:

1. *Feelings not thought* should be altered to *feelings, only with thought*.
2. *Let it all hang out* is best revised to *let more of it hang out than usual, if it feels right in the group, and if you can give some thought to what it means*. In this study, self-disclosure or emotional expressiveness (of either positive or negative feelings) was not in itself sufficient for change.
3. *Getting out the anger is essential* is best revised to *getting out the anger may be okay, but keeping it out there steadily is not*. Excessive expression of anger was counterproductive: it was not associated with a high level of learning, and it generally increased risk of negative outcome.
4. *There is no group, only persons* should be revised to *group processes make a difference in learning, whether or not the leader pays attention to them*. Learning was strongly influenced by such group properties as cohesiveness, climate, norms, and the group role occupied by a particular member.
5. *High yield requires high risk* should be changed to *the risk in encounter groups is considerable and unrelated to positive gain*. The high-risk groups, those that produced many casualties, did not at the same time produce high learners. The productive groups were safe ones. The high-yield, high-risk group is, according to our study, a myth.
6. *You may not know what you've learned now, but later, when you put it all together, you'll come to appreciate how much you've learned* should be revised to *bloom now, don't count on later*. It is often thought that individuals may be shaken up during a group experience but that later, after the group is over, they integrate the experience they had in the group and come out stronger than ever. In our project, individuals who had a negative outcome at the termination of the group never moved to the positive side of the ledger at follow-up six months later.

THE RELATIONSHIP BETWEEN THE ENCOUNTER GROUP AND THE THERAPY GROUP

Having traced the development of the encounter group to the moment of collision with the field of group psychotherapy, I now turn to the evolution of the therapy group in order to clarify the interchange between the two disciplines.

The Evolution of Group Therapy

The history of group therapy has been too thoroughly described in other texts to warrant repetition here.[9] A rapid sweep will reveal the basic trends. Joseph Hersey Pratt, a Boston internist, is generally acknowledged to be the father of contemporary group therapy. Pratt treated many patients with advanced tuberculosis, and, recognizing the relationship between psychological health and the physical course of tuberculosis, Pratt undertook to treat the person rather than the disease. In 1905, he designed a treatment regimen that included home visits, diary keeping by patients, and weekly meetings of a tuberculosis class of approximately twenty-five patients. At these classes, the diaries were inspected, weight gains were recorded publicly on a blackboard, and testimonials were given by successful patients. A degree of cohesiveness and mutual support developed that appeared helpful in combating the depression and isolation so common among patients with tuberculosis.

During the 1920s and 1930s, several psychiatrists experimented with group methods. In Europe, Adler used group methods because of his awareness of the social nature of human problems and his desire to provide psychotherapeutic help to the working classes.[10] Lazell, in 1921, met with groups of patients with schizophrenia in St. Elizabeths Hospital in Washington, D.C., and delivered lectures on schizophrenia.[11] Marsh, a few years later, used groups for a wide range of clinical problems, including psychosis, psychoneurosis, psychophysiological disorders, and stammering.[12] He employed a variety of techniques, including didactic methods such as lectures and homework assignments as well as exercises designed to promote considerable interaction; for example, members were asked to treat one another; or all were asked to discuss such topics as one's earliest memory, ingredients of one's inferiority complex, night dreams, and daydreams. In the 1930s, Wender used analytic group methods with hospitalized nonpsychotic patients, and Burrows and Schilder applied these techniques to the treatment of psychoneurotic outpatients. Slavson, who worked with groups of disturbed children and young adolescents, exerted considerable influence in the field through his teaching and writing at a time when group therapy was not yet considered an effective therapeutic approach. Moreno, who first used the term group therapy, employed group methods before 1920 but has been primarily identified with psychodrama, which he introduced into America in 1925.[13]

These tentative beginnings in the use of group therapy were vastly accelerated by the Second World War, when the enormous numbers of military psychiatric patients and the scarcity of trained psychotherapists made individual therapy impractical and catalyzed the search for more economic modes of treatment.

During the 1950s, the main thrust of group therapy was directed toward using groups in different clinical settings and with different types of clinical problems. Theoreticians—Freudian, Sullivanian, Horneyan, Rogerian—explored the application of their conceptual framework to group therapy theory and practice.

The T-group and the therapy group thus arose from different disciplines; and for many years, the two disciplines, each generating its own body of theory and technique, continued as two parallel streams of knowledge, even though a few leaders straddled both fields and, in different settings, led both T-groups and therapy groups. The T-group maintained a deep commitment to research and continued to identify with the fields of social psychology, education, and organizational development.

Therapy Group and Encounter Group: First Interchanges

In the 1960s, there was some constructive interchange between the group therapy and the sensitivity training fields. Many mental health professionals participated in some form of encounter group during their training and subsequently led encounter groups or applied encounter techniques to their psychotherapeutic endeavors. Clinical researchers learned a great deal from the T-group research methods; T-groups were commonly used in the training of group therapists[14] and in the treatment program of chronically hospitalized patients.[15] Some clinicians referred their individual therapy patients to a T-group for opening-up (just as, later, in the 1980s, some clinicians referred their patients to large group awareness training programs, such as est and Lifespring).[16]

But later, as the T-group evolved into the flamboyant encounter group that claimed to offer "group therapy for normals" and claimed that "patienthood is ubiquitous," an acrimonious relationship developed between the two fields. Disagreements arose about territorial issues and the true differences in the goals of encounter and therapy groups.

Encounter group leaders grew even more expansive and insisted that their group participants had a therapeutic experience and that in reality there was no difference between personal growth and psychotherapy (in the language of the time, between "mind expansion" and "head shrinking"). Furthermore, it became evident that there was much overlap: there was much similarity between those seeking psychotherapy and those seeking encounter experiences. Thus, many encounter group leaders concluded that they were, indeed, practicing psychotherapy—a superior, more efficient type of psychotherapy—and advertised their services accordingly.

The traditional mental health field was alarmed. Not only were psychotherapists threatened by the encroachment on their territory, but they also considered encounter groups reckless and potentially harmful to participants. They expressed concerns about the lack of responsibility of the encounter group leaders, their lack of clinical training, and their unethical advertising that suggested that months, even years of therapy could be condensed into a single intensive weekend. Polarization increased, and soon mental health professionals in many areas launched campaigns urging their local governments to pass legislation to regulate encounter group practice, to keep it out of schools, and to hold leaders legally responsible for untoward effects.

In part the vigorous response of the mental health profession was an irrational reaction, but it was also appropriate to certain excesses in some factions of the encounter field. These excesses issued from a crash-program mentality, successful in such ventures as space exploration and industrialization, but a reductio ad absurdum in human relations ventures. If something is good, more must be better. If self-disclosure is good in groups, then total, immediate, indiscriminate self-disclosure in the nude must be better. If involvement is good, then prolonged, continuous, marathon involvement must be better. If expression of feeling is good, then hitting, touching, feeling, kissing, and fornicating must be better. If a group experience is good, then it is good for everyone—in all stages of the life cycle, in all life situations. These excesses were often offensive to the public taste and could, as research has indicated, be dangerous to some participants.

Since that period of acrimony and polarization decades ago, the established fields of therapy and the usurping encounter group field are no longer the same. Although the encounter group movement with all its excesses, grandiosity, and extravagant claims has come and gone,* it has nonetheless influenced contemporary group therapy. The inventiveness, research attitude and expertise, sophisticated leadership, and training technology of the pioneer encounter group leaders have left an indelible mark on our field.

---

*This is not to say that the encounter ethos suddenly vanished. Many aspects of the encounter movement linger. For one thing, it was transformed and commercialized in the large group awareness training enterprises like est and Lifespring (versions of which are still viable in various parts of the world) and is much in evidence in such programs as the widespread Judeo-Christian National Marriage Encounter programs.

Chapter 17

TRAINING THE
GROUP THERAPIST

Group therapy is a curious plant in the garden of psychotherapy. It is hardy: the best available research has established that group therapy is effective, as robust as individual therapy.[1] Yet it needs constant tending; its perennial fate is to be periodically choked by the same old weeds: "superficial," "dangerous," "second-rate—to be used only when individual therapy is unavailable or unaffordable."

Clients and many mental health professionals continue to underrate and to fear group therapy, and unfortunately those very same attitudes adversely influence group therapy training programs. Group therapy has not often been accorded academic prestige. The same situation prevails in clinics and hospital administration hierarchies: rarely does the individual who is most invested in group therapy enjoy a position of professional authority.

Why? Perhaps because group therapy cannot cleanse itself of the anti-intellectual taint of the encounter group movement, or because of the intrinsic methodological obstacles to rigorous, truly meaningful research. Perhaps it is because we therapists share the client's wish to be the special and singular object of attention that individual therapy promises. Perhaps many of us prefer to avoid the anxiety inherent in role of the group leader—greater public exposure of oneself as a therapist, less sense of control, fear of being overwhelmed by the group, more clinical material to synthesize. Perhaps it is because groups evoke for us unpleasant personal memories of earlier peer group experiences.[2]

Attempts to renew interest in group therapy have always worked—but only for brief periods. An initial wave of renewed enthusiasm for group therapy is followed by neglect, and soon all the old weeds crowd in once again. The moment demands a whole new generation of well-trained gardeners, and it behooves us to pay careful attention to the education of beginning group therapists and to our own continuing professional development.

In this chapter, I present my views about group therapy training, not only in specific recommendations for a training curriculum but also in the form of general considerations concerning an underlying philosophy of training. The approach to therapy described in this book is based on both clinical experience and an appraisal of the best available research evidence. Similarly, in the educational process, a clinical and a research orientation are closely interrelated: the acquisition of an inquiring attitude to one's own work and to the work of others is necessary in the development of the mature therapist.

Many training programs for mental health professionals are based on the individual therapy model and either do not provide group therapy training or offer it as an elective part of the program. Despite clear acknowledgment that the practice of group therapy will continue to grow, recent surveys show that most academic training programs fall short in the actual provision of group training. In fact, it is not unusual for students to be given excellent intensive individual therapy supervision and then, early in their program, to be asked to lead therapy groups with no specialized guidance whatsoever. Many program directors apparently expect, naively, that students will be able somehow to translate their individual therapy training into group therapy skills without meaningful group experiential or clinical exposure. This not only provides inadequate leadership but causes students to devalue the group therapy enterprise.[3] It is essential that mental health training programs appreciate the need for rigorous, well-organized group training programs and offer programs that match the needs of trainees. Both the American Group Psychotherapy Association (AGPA) and the American Counseling Association have established training standards for group therapy certification that can serve as a template for training. For example, the AGPA's National Registry of Certified Group Psychotherapists requires a minimum of 12 hours of didactic training, 300 hours of group therapy leadership, and 75 hours of group therapy supervision with a group therapist who has met the standards of certification.[4]

The crisis in medical economics and the growth of managed health care force us to recognize that one-to-one psychotherapy cannot possibly suffice to meet the pressing mental health needs of the public. Managed care leaders also forecast rapid growth in the use of group therapy, particularly in structured and time-limited groups.[5] It is abundantly clear that, as time passes, we will rely on group approaches ever more heavily. I believe that any psychotherapy training program that does not acknowledge this and does not expect students to become as fully proficient in group as in individual therapy is failing to meet its responsibilities to the field.

Every program has its own unique needs and resources. While I cannot hope to offer a blueprint for a universal training program, I shall, in the following section, discuss the four major components that I consider essential to a comprehensive training program beyond the didactic: (1) observation of experienced group therapists at work, (2) close clinical supervision of students' maiden groups, (3) a personal group experience, and (4) personal psychotherapeutic work.

OBSERVATION OF EXPERIENCED CLINICIANS

Student therapists derive enormous benefit from watching an experienced group practitioner at work.† It is exceedingly uncommon for students to observe a senior clinician doing individual therapy. The more public nature of group therapy makes it often the only form of psychotherapy that trainees will ever be able to observe directly. At first, experienced clinicians may feel considerable discomfort while being observed; but once they have taken the plunge, the process becomes comfortable as well as rewarding for all parties: students, therapists, and group members.

The format of observation depends, of course, on the physical facilities. I prefer having my students observe my group work through a one-way mirror, but if students' schedules do not permit them to be present for a ninety-minute group and a postgroup discussion, I videotape the meeting and replay segments in a shorter seminar with the students. This procedure requires a greater time investment for the therapist and greater discomfort for the members because of the presence of the camera. If there are only one or two observers, they may sit in the group room without unduly distracting the members, but I strongly recommend that they sit silently outside the group circle and decline to respond to questions that group members may pose to them.

Regardless of the format used, the group members must be fully informed about the presence of observers and their purpose. I remind clients that observation is necessary for training, that I was trained in that fashion, and that their willingness to permit observers will ultimately be beneficial to clients the student observers will treat in the future. I add another point: the observations of the students offered to me in our postgroup discussion are frequently of value to the process of therapy. There are formats (to be described shortly) in which clients attend the postgroup observer-therapist discussion and generally profit considerably from the discussion.

The total length of students' observation time is generally determined by service and training rotations. If there is sufficient program flexibility, I would suggest that observation continue for at least six to ten sessions, which generally provides a sufficient period of time for changes to occur in group development, in interactional patterns, and in perceivable intrapersonal growth. If their schedules preclude regular and consistent attendance, I distribute a detailed summary of the group to the students before the next meeting (see chapter 14).

A postmeeting discussion is an absolute necessity in training, and there is no better time for the group leader/teacher to meet with student observers than immediately after the meeting. I prefer to meet for thirty to forty-five minutes, and I use the time in a variety of ways: obtaining the students' observations, answering their questions about underlying reasons for my interventions, and using the clinical material as a springboard for discussion of fundamental principles of group therapy. Other instructors prefer to delay the discussion and assign the students the task of writing a description of the meeting, focusing primarily on process (that is, the interpersonal relationships among the members of the group and group dynamics). The students may be asked to exchange their summaries and meet later in the week for an analysis of the meeting.[6] Although some introductory didactic sessions are useful, I find that much of the material presented in this book can be best discussed with students around appropriate clinical material that arises over several sessions of an observed group.[7] Theory becomes so much more alive when it is immediately relevant.

The relationship between observers, the group, and the group therapists is important. There will be times when an inordinate amount of carping ("Why didn't you . . . ?") creates discomfort for the therapists and impairs their efficiency. Not infrequently, observers complain of boredom, and therapists may feel some pressure to increase the group's entertainment quotient. My experience is that, in general, *boredom is inversely related to experience*; as students gain in experience and sophistication, they come increasingly to appreciate the many subtle, fascinating layers underlying every transaction. The observation group has a process of its own as well. Observers may identify with the therapist, or with certain characteristics of the clients, which, if explored in the debriefing session, may provide an opportunity to explore empathy, countertransference, and projective identification. At times, observers may express the wish that they were in the group as participants and develop strong attachments to group members. In every instance, observers should be held to the same standard of professionalism regarding confidentiality and ethical conduct as are the therapists.[8]

Group members respond differently to being observed by students. Like any group event, the different responses are grist for the therapeutic mill. If all members face the same situation (that is, being observed by students), why do some respond with anger, others with suspicion, and still others with pleasure, even exhilaration? Why such different responses to a common stimulus? The answer, of course, is that *each member has a different inner world,* and the differing responses facilitation examination of each inner world.

Nonetheless, for the majority of clients, traditional observation is an intrusion. Sometimes the observers may serve as a lightning rod for anxiety arising from other concerns. For example, one group that had been regularly observed suddenly became preoccupied with the observers and grew convinced that they were mocking and ridiculing the members. One group member reported encountering a person in the washroom before the group, whom he was convinced was an observer, and this person smirked at him. The group members demanded that the observers be brought into the group room to account for themselves. The power of the group's reaction was intense and caused me to wonder if there had been some breach of trust. As we continued to examine where this heat was coming from, it became more apparent that the group was in fact projecting onto the observers their apprehension about impending changes in the group—two senior members of the group had left and two new additions to the group were imminent. The real issue for the group was whether the new additions would value the group or deride the process and the members.

Though the most a leader can generally expect from clients is a grudging acceptance and dimming awareness of the observers' presence, there are methods of turning the students' observation to therapeutic advantage. I remind the group that the observers' perspectives are valuable to me as the leader and, if appropriate, I cite some helpful comments observers made after the previous meeting. I also let the group know that I often incorporate some of the observers' comments into the written summary.

Another, more daring, strategy is to invite the group members to be present at the observers' postmeeting discussion. In chapter 15, I discussed a model of an inpatient group that regularly included a ten-minute observers' discussion that the group members observed.[9] I have used a similar format for outpatient groups: I invite members and observers to switch rooms at the end of a meeting so that the clients observe through the one-way mirror the observers' and co-therapists' postgroup discussion. My only proviso is that the entire group elect to attend: if only some members attend, the process may be divisive and retard the development of cohesiveness. A significant time commitment is required: forty-five minutes of postgroup discussion after a ninety-minute group therapy session make for a long afternoon or evening.

This format has interesting implications for teaching. It teaches students how to be constructively transparent, and it conveys a sense of respect for the client as a full ally in the therapeutic process. It also demystifies therapy: it is a statement that therapy is a potent, rational, collaborative process requiring no part of Dostoevsky's Grand Inquisitor's triumvirate—magic, mystery, and authority.

If clients do observe the postgroup discussion, then there must be an additional teaching seminar just after the observation period or later, perhaps just before the next group meeting. Additional teaching time is required, because the postmeeting discussions that the clients observe differ from the typical postgroup rehash. The postgroup discussion becomes part of the therapy itself as the observers' and therapists' comments evoke feelings from the group members. Hence, in this format less time is available for formal instruction of basic theory or strategic principles. Furthermore, the students tend to be inhibited in their questions and comments, and there is less free-ranging discussion of transference and countertransference. A benefit is that boredom in the observation room absolutely vanishes: students, knowing they will later take part in the meeting, become more engaged in the process.

A useful adjunct teaching tool may be a group videotape especially designed to illustrate important aspects of leader technique and group dynamics. I have produced two videotape programs—one for outpatient groups and one for inpatients—around which group therapy courses may be constructed.[10]

SUPERVISION

A supervised clinical experience is a sine qua non in the education of the group therapist. This book posits a general approach to therapy, delineates broad principles of technique, and, especially when discussing the opening and closing stages of therapy, suggests specific tactics. But the laborious working-through process that constitutes the bulk of therapy cannot be thoroughly depicted in a text. An infinite number of situations arise, each of which may require a rich, imaginative approach. It is precisely at these points that a supervisor makes a valuable and unique contribution to a student therapist's education. Because of its central importance in training, supervision has become a major focus of attention in the psychotherapy literature, although there is a paucity of empirical research on the subject.[11]

What are the characteristics of effective supervision? Supervision first requires the establishment of a *supervisory alliance* that conveys to the student the ambiance and value of the *therapeutic alliance*. Supervision not only conveys technical expertise and theoretical knowledge, it also models the profession's values and ethics. Accordingly, supervisors must strive for congruence: they should treat their students with the same respect and care that the student should provide to clients. If we want our trainees to treat their clients with respect, compassion, and dignity, that is how we must treat our trainees.[12]

The supervisor should focus on the professional and clinical development of the trainee and be alert to any blocks—either from lack of knowledge or from countertransference—that the trainee encounters. A fine balance must be maintained between training and therapy. Alonso suggests that the supervisor should listen like a clinician but speak like a teacher.[13]

The most effective supervisors are able to tune in to the trainee, track the trainee's central concerns, capture the essence of the trainee's narrative, guide the trainee through clinical dilemmas, and demonstrate personal concern and support. Supervision that is unduly critical, shaming, or closed to the trainee's principal concerns will not only fail educationally, it will also dispirit the trainee.[14]

How personal and transparent should the supervisor be? Probably the more the better! By revealing their own experiences and clinical challenges, supervisors reduce the power hierarchy and help the trainee see that there is no shame in not having all the answers. What's more, such a revealing and nondefensive stance will influence the type of clinical material the trainee will bring to supervision.[15]

The neophyte therapist's first group is a highly threatening experience. Even conducting psychoeducational groups, with their clear content and structure, can be inordinately challenging to the neophyte.[16] In a study of neophyte trainees, researchers compared trainees who had positive and those who had negative group therapy training experiences. Both groups reported high degrees of apprehension and frankly unpleasant emotional reactions early in the work. One variable distinguished the two groups: the quality of the supervision. Those with high-quality supervision were far more likely to feel positive about group therapy.[17]

In another study, my colleagues and I examined twelve nonprofessionally trained leaders who led groups in a psychiatric hospital. Half received ongoing supervision as well as an intensive training course in group leadership; the others received neither. Observers who did not know which therapists received supervision rated the therapists at the beginning of their groups and again six months later. The results indicated that not only did the trained therapists improve but the untrained therapists, at the end of six months, *were less skilled than at the beginning*.[18] Sheer experience, apparently, is not enough. Without ongoing supervision and evaluation, *original errors may be reinforced by simple repetition*. Supervision may be even more important for the neophyte group therapist than the budding individual therapist because of the inherent stress in the group leader role: I have had many trainees report anxiety dreams filled with images about being out of control or confronting some threatening group situation just before commencing their first group experience.

In many ways, group therapy supervision is more taxing than individual therapy supervision. For one thing, mastering the cast of characters is in itself a formidable task. Furthermore, there is such an abundance of data that both student and supervisor must often be highly selective in their focus.

A few practical recommendations may be helpful. First, supervision should be well established before the first group, both to attend to the selection and preparation tasks of group leadership and to address therapist apprehension about starting the group. *One supervisory hour per group therapy session* is, in my experience, the optimal ratio. It is wise to hold the supervisory session soon after the group session, preferably the following day. Some supervisors observe the last thirty minutes of each meeting and hold the supervisory session immediately thereafter. At the very least, the supervisor must observe one or two sessions at the beginning of supervision and, if possible, an occasional session throughout the year: it permits the supervisor to affix names to faces and also to sample the affective climate of the group. Videotapes may serve this purpose also (audiotapes, too, though far less satisfactorily).

If much time elapses between the group meeting and the supervisory session, the events of the group fade; in this case students are well advised to make detailed postgroup notes. Therapists develop their own style of note taking. My preference is to record the major themes of each session—generally, from one to three: for example: (1) John's distress at losing his job and the group's efforts to offer support; (2) Sharon's anger at the men in the group; (3) Annabelle's feeling inferior and unaccepted by the group.

Once this basic skeleton is in place, I fill in the other vital data: the transition between themes; each member's contribution to each of the themes; my interventions and feelings about the meeting as a whole and toward each of the members. Other supervisors suggest that students pay special attention to choice points—a series of critical points in the meeting where action is required of the therapist.[19] Still others make use of clients' feedback obtained from questionnaires distributed at the end of a group session.[20]

A ninety-minute group session provides a wealth of material. If trainees present a narrative of the meeting, discuss each member's verbal and nonverbal contribution as well as their own participation, and explore in depth their countertransference and realistically based feelings toward each of the members and toward their co-therapist, there should be more than enough important material to occupy the supervisory hour. If not, if the trainee quickly runs out of material, if the supervisor has to scratch hard to learn the events of the meeting, something has gone seriously wrong in the supervisory process. At such times supervisors would do well to examine their relationship with the trainee(s). Are the students guarded, distrustful, or fearful of exposing themselves to scrutiny? Are they cautious lest the supervisor pressure them to operate in the group in a manner that feels alien or beyond them?

The supervisory session is no less a microcosm than is the therapy group, and the supervisor should be able to obtain much information about the therapist's behavior in a therapy group by attending to the therapist's behavior in supervision. (Sometimes this phenomenon is referred to as the "parallel process" in supervision.)[21]

If students lead groups as co-therapy teams (and, as chapter 14 explains, I recommend that format for neophyte therapists), a process focus in the supervisory hour is particularly rich. It is likely that the relationship of the two co-therapists in the supervisory hour parallels their relationship during the therapy group meetings. Supervisors should attend to such issues as the degree of openness and trust during the supervisory hour. Who reports the events of the meeting? Who defers to whom? Do the co-leaders report two bewilderingly different views of the group? Is there much competition for the supervisor's attention?

The relationship between co-therapists is of crucial importance for the therapy group, and the supervisor may often be maximally effective by focusing attention on this relationship. For example, I recall supervising two residents whose personal relationship was strained. In the supervisory session, each vied for my attention; there was a dysrhythmic quality to the hour, since neither pursued the other's lead but instead brought up different material, or the same material from an entirely different aspect. Supervision was a microcosm of the group: in the therapy sessions they competed intensely with each other to make star interpretations and to enlist members onto their respective teams. They never complemented each other's work by pursuing a theme the other had brought up; instead, each remained silent, waiting for an opportunity to introduce a different line of inquiry. The group paid the price for the therapists' poor working relationship: no good work was done, absenteeism was high, and demoralization evident.

Supervision in this instance focused almost entirely on the co-therapy relationship and took on many of the characteristics of couples therapy, as we examined the therapists' competition and their wish to impress me. One had just transferred from another residency and felt strongly pressed to prove her competence. The other felt that he had made a great mistake in blindly accepting a co-therapist and felt trapped in a dysfunctional relationship. We considered a "divorce"—dissolving the co-therapy team— but decided that such a move would be countertherapeutic. What chance do we have of persuading our clients to work on their relationships if we therapists refuse to do the same? If co-therapists can successfully work on their relationship, there is a double payoff: therapy is served (the group works better with an improved inter-leader relationship), and training is served (trainees learn firsthand some of the basic principles of conflict resolution).

In the ongoing work the supervisor must explore the student's verbal and nonverbal interventions and check that they help establish useful group norms. At the same time, the supervisor must avoid making the student so self-conscious that spontaneity is stunted. Groups are not so fragile that a single statement markedly influences their direction; it is the therapist's overall posture that counts.

Most supervisors will at times tell a supervisee what they themselves would have said at some juncture of the group. It is not uncommon, however, for student therapists to mimic the supervisor's comments at an inappropriate spot in the following group meeting and then begin the next supervisory session with: "I did what you said, but . . ." Thus, when I tell a student what I might have said, I preface my comments: "Don't say this at the next meeting, but here's one way you might have responded . . ." Here too, a delicate balance needs to be maintained. Supervision should rarely be prescriptive and never heavy-handed. But there are times when suggesting a particular approach or intervention is essential and much welcomed.

Many teachers have, to good effect, expanded the supervisory hour into a continuous case seminar for several student therapists, with the group leaders taking turns presenting their group to the entire supervision group. Since it takes time to assimilate data about all the members of a group, I prefer that one group be presented for several weeks before moving on to another. In this format, three to four groups can be followed throughout the year.

There are several benefits to providing group therapy supervision in a group format. For one thing, it may be possible for a skillful supervisor to focus on the interaction and the group dynamics of the supervisory group. The learning opportunities may be further enhanced by asking supervisees to describe and record their experiences in the supervision group. Another benefit of group supervision is the presence of peer support. Furthermore, accounts of colleagues' experiences, conceptualizations, and techniques exposes trainees to a greater range of group therapy phenomena and broadens their empathic awareness. Trainees also have the opportunity to think like a supervisor or consultant, a skill that will be useful at other points in their career.[22] Feedback about one's clinical work is often a delicate process. Supervision groups demand and model metacommunication—ways to communicate authentically, respectfully, and empathically.

A group supervision format may also encourage subsequent participation in a peer supervision group by demonstrating the value of peer supervision, consultation, and support.[23] The supervision group should not, however, transform itself into a personal growth or therapy group—that group experience comes with a substantially different set of norms and expectations.

Some recent supervision innovations have made good use of the Internet to offer supervision to practitioners living in isolated or distant locales. Students and supervisor may begin with a few face-to-face meetings and then continue contact through an electronic bulletin board or a facilitated online supervision group.[24]

A GROUP EXPERIENCE FOR TRAINEES

A personal group experience has become widely accepted as an integral part of training and continuing professional development. Such an experience may offer many types of learning not available elsewhere. You are able to learn at an emotional level what you may previously have known only intellectually. You experience the power of the group—power both to wound and to heal. You learn how important it is to be accepted by the group; what self-disclosure really entails; how difficult it is to reveal your secret world, your fantasies, feelings of vulnerability, hostility, and tenderness. You learn to appreciate your own strengths as well as your weaknesses. You learn about your own preferred role in the group, about your habitual countertransference responses and about group-as-a-whole and system issues that lurk in the background of the meetings. Perhaps most striking of all, you learn about the role of the leader by becoming aware of your own dependency and your own, often unrealistic, appraisal of the leader's power and knowledge.

Even experienced practitioners who are being trained in a new model of group therapy profit greatly when an experiential affective component is added to their didactic training. Personal participation is the most vital way to teach and to learn group process.[25]

Surveys indicate that one-half to two-thirds of group therapy training programs offer some type of personal group experience.[26] Some programs offer a simulated group in which one or two trainees are appointed co-therapists and the rest role-play the group members. The most common model (which will be discussed in detail shortly) is a group composed of other trainees and referred to by any number of terms (T-group, support group, process group, experiential training group, and so on). This group may be short-term, lasting maybe a dozen sessions, or it may consist of an intensive one- or two-day experience; but the model I prefer is a weekly process group that meets for sixty to ninety minutes throughout the entire year.

I have led groups of psychology interns and psychiatric residents for over thirty years and, without exception, have found the use of such groups to be a highly valuable teaching technique. Indeed, many psychotherapy students, when reviewing their entire training program, have rated their group as the single most valuable experience in their curriculum.

A group experience with one's peers has a great deal to recommend it: not only do the members reap the benefits of a group experience but also, if the group is led properly, members may improve relationships and communication within the trainee class and, thus, enrich the entire educational experience. Students always learn a great deal from their peers, and any efforts that potentiate that process increase the value of the program.

Are there also disadvantages to a group experience? One often hears storm warnings about the possible destructive effects of staff or trainee experiential groups. These warnings are, I believe, based on irrational premises: for example, that enormous amounts of destructive hostility would ensue once a group unlocks suppressive floodgates, or that a group would constitute an enormous invasion of privacy as forced confessionals are wrung one by one from each of the hapless trainees. We know now that responsibly led groups that are clear about norms and boundaries facilitate communication and constructive working relationships.

Should Training Groups Be Voluntary?

An experiential group is always more effective if the participants engage voluntarily and view it not only as a training exercise but as an opportunity for personal growth. Indeed, I prefer that trainees begin such a group with an explicit formulation of what they want to obtain from the experience personally as well as professionally. To this end, it is important that the group be introduced and described to the trainees in such a way that they consider it to be consonant with their personal and professional goals. I prefer to frame the group within the students' training career by asking them to project themselves into the field of the future. It is, after all, highly probable that mental health practitioners will spend an increasing amount of their time in groups—as members and leaders of treatment teams. To be effective in this role, clinicians of the future will simply have to know their way around groups. They will have to learn how groups work and how they themselves work in groups.

Once an experiential group is introduced as a regular part of a training program, and once the faculty develops confidence in the group as a valuable training adjunct, there is little difficulty in selling it to incoming trainees. Still, programs differ on whether to make the group optional or mandatory. My experience is that if a group is presented properly, the trainees not only look forward to it with anticipation but experience strong disappointment if for some reason the opportunity for a group experience is withheld.

If a student steadfastly refuses to enter the training group or any other type of experiential group, it is my opinion that some investigation of such resistance is warranted. Occasionally, such a refusal stems from misconceptions about groups in general or is a reflection of some respected senior faculty member's negative bias toward groups. But if the refusal is based on a pervasive dread or distrust of group situations, and if the student does not have the flexibility to work on this resistance in individual therapy, in a supportive training group, or in a bona fide therapy group, I believe it may well be unwise for that student to pursue the career of psychotherapist.

Who Should Lead Student Experiential Groups?

Directors of training programs should select the leader with great care. For one thing, the group experience is an extraordinarily influential event in the students' training career; the leader will often serve as an important role model for the trainees and therefore should have extensive clinical and group experience and the highest possible professional standards. The overriding criteria are, of course, the personal qualities and the skill of the leader: a secondary consideration is the leader's professional discipline (whether it be, for example, in counseling, clinical psychology, social work, or psychiatry).

I believe that a training group model led by a leader skilled in the interactional group therapy model provides the best educational experience.[27] Supporting this view is a study of 434 professionals who participated in two-day American Group Psychotherapy Association training groups. Process-oriented groups that emphasized here-and-now interaction resulted in significantly greater learning about leadership and peer relations than groups that were more didactic or structured. The members felt they profited most from an atmosphere in which leaders supported participants, demonstrated techniques, and facilitated an atmosphere in which members supported one another, revealed personal feelings, took risks, and enjoyed the group.[28]

Another reason the leader should be selected with great care is that it is extremely difficult to lead groups of mental health professionals who will continue to work together throughout their training. The pace is slow; intellectualization is common; and self-disclosure and risk taking are minimal. The chief instrument in psychotherapy is the therapist's own person. Realizing this truth, the neophyte therapist feels doubly vulnerable in self-disclosure: at stake are both personal and professional competence.

Should the Leader be a Staff or a Faculty Member of the Training Program?

A leader who wears two hats (group leader and member of training staff) compounds the problem for the group members who feel restricted by the presence of someone who may in the future play an evaluative role in their careers. Mere reassurance to the group that the leader will maintain strictest confidentiality or neutrality is insufficient to deal with this very real concern of the members.

I have on many occasions been placed in this double role and have approached the problem in various ways but with only limited success. One approach is to confront the problem energetically with the group. I affirm the reality that I *do* have a dual role, and that, although I will attempt in every way to be merely a group leader and will remove myself from any administrative or evaluative duties, I may not be able to free myself from all unconscious vestiges of the second role. I thus address myself uncompromisingly to the dilemma facing the group. But, as the group proceeds, I also address myself to the fact that each member must deal with the "two-hat" problem. Similar dilemmas occur throughout the practice of group therapy and are best embraced rather than avoided or denied.[29] What can we learn through this dilemma? Each member may respond to it very differently: some may so distrust me that they choose to remain hidden in silence; some curry my favor; some trust me completely and participate with full abandon in the group; others persistently challenge me. All of these stances toward a leader reflect basic attitudes toward authority and are good grist for the mill, provided there is at least a modicum of willingness to work.

Another approach I often take when in this "two-hat" position is to be unusually self-disclosing—in effect, to give the members more on me than I have on them. In so doing, I model openness and demonstrate both the universality of human problems and how unlikely it would be for me to adopt a judgmental stance toward them. In other words, leader transparency offered in the service of training lowers the perceived stakes for the participants by normalizing their concerns.

My experience has been that, even using the best techniques, leaders who are also administrators labor under a severe handicap, and their groups are likely to be restricted and guarded. The group becomes a far more effective vehicle for personal growth and training if led by a leader from outside the institution who will play no role in student evaluation. It facilitates the work of a group if, at the outset, the leader makes explicit his or her unwillingness under any circumstances ever to contribute letters of reference—either favorable or unfavorable—for the members. All these issues—group goals, confidentiality, and participation should be made explicit at the beginning of the group experience.

Is the Training Group a Therapy Group?

This is a vexing question. In training groups of professionals, no other issue is so often used in the service of group resistance. It is wise for leaders to present their views about training versus therapy at the outset of the group. I begin by asking that the members make certain commitments to the group. Each member should be aware of the requirements for membership: a willingness to invest oneself emotionally in the group, to disclose feelings about oneself and the other members, and to explore areas in which one would like to make personal changes.

There is a useful distinction to be made between a therapy group and a therapeutic group. *A training group, though it is not a therapy group, is therapeutic in that it offers the opportunity to do therapeutic work.* By no means, though, is each member expected to do extensive therapeutic work.

The basic contract of the group, in fact, its raison d'être, is training, not therapy. To a great extent, these goals overlap: a leader can offer no better group therapy training than that of an effective therapeutic group. Furthermore, every intensive group experience contains within it great therapeutic potential: members cannot engage in effective interaction, cannot fully assume the role of a group member, cannot get feedback about their interpersonal style and their blind spots without some therapeutic spin-off. Yet that is different from a therapy group that assembles for the purpose of accomplishing extensive therapeutic change for each member of the group.

In a therapy group, the intensive group experience, the expression and integration of affect, the recognition of here-and-now process are all essential but secondary considerations to the primary goal of individual therapeutic change. In a training group of mental health professionals, the reverse is true. There will be many times when the T-group leader will seize an opportunity for explication and teaching that a group therapist would seize for deeper emotional exploration.

Leader Technique

The leader of a training group of mental health professionals has a demanding task: he or she not only provides a role model by shaping and conducting an effective group but must also make certain modifications in technique to deal with the specific educational needs of the group members.

The basic approach, however, does not deviate from the guidelines I outlined earlier in this book. For example, the leader is well advised to retain an interactional, here-and-now focus. It is an error, in my opinion, to allow the group to move into a supervisory format where members describe problems they confront in their clinical work: such discussion should be the province of the supervisory hour. Whenever a group is engaged in discourse that can be held equally well in another formal setting, it is failing to use its unique properties and full potential. Instead, members can discuss these work-related problems in more profitable group-relevant ways: for example, they might discuss how it would feel to be the client of a particular member. The group is also an excellent place for two members who happen to work together in therapy groups, or in marital or family therapy, to work on their relationship.

There are many ways for a leader to use the members' professional experience in the service of the group work. For example, I have often made statements to the training group in the following vein: "The group has been very slow moving today. When I inquired, you told me that you felt 'lazy' or that it was too soon after lunch to work. If you were the leader of a group and heard this, what would you make of it? What would you do?" Or: "Not only are John and Stewart refusing to work on their differences but others are lining up behind them. What are the options available to me as a leader today?" In a training group, I am inclined, much more than in a therapy group, to explicate group process. In therapy groups, if there is no therapeutic advantage in clarifying group process, I see no reason to do so. In training groups, there is always the superordinate goal of education.

Often process commentary combined with a view from the leader's seat is particularly useful. For example:

> Let me tell you what I felt today as a group leader. A half hour ago I felt uncomfortable with the massive encouragement and support everyone was giving Tom. This has happened before, and though it was reassuring, I haven't felt it was really helpful to Tom. I was tempted to intervene by inquiring about Tom's tendency to pull this behavior from the group, but I chose not to—partly because I've gotten so much flak lately for being nonsupportive. So I remained silent. I think I made the right choice, since it seems to me that the meeting developed into a very productive one, with some of you getting deeply into your feelings of needing care and support. How do the rest of you see what's happened today?

In a particularly helpful essay, Aveline, an experienced group leader of student groups, suggests that the leader has five main tasks:

1. Containment of anxiety (through exploration of sources of anxiety in the group and provision of anxiety-relieving group structure)
2. Establishment of a therapeutic atmosphere in the group by shaping norms of support, acceptance, and group autonomy
3. Establishing appropriate goals that can be addressed in the time available
4. Moderating the pace so that the group moves neither too fast nor too slow and that members engage in no forced or damaging self-disclosure
5. Ending well[30]

PERSONAL PSYCHOTHERAPY

A training group rarely suffices to provide all the personal self-exploration a student therapist requires. Few would dispute that personal psychotherapy is necessary for the maturation of the group therapist. A substantial number of training programs require a personal therapy experience.[31] A large survey of 318 practicing psychologists indicated that 70 percent had entered therapy during their training—often more than one type of therapy: 63 percent in individual therapy (mean = 100 hours); 24 percent in group therapy (mean = 76 hours); 36 percent in couples therapy (mean = 37 hours). This survey determined that over their lifetime, 18 percent of practicing psychologists never entered therapy.

What factors influenced the decision to enter therapy? Psychologists were more likely to engage in therapy if they had an earlier therapy experience in their training, if they were dynamically oriented in their practice, and if they conducted many hours of therapy during the week.[32] In another survey, over half of psychotherapists entered personal psychotherapy after their training, and over 90 percent reported considerable personal and professional benefit from the experience.[33]

Without doubt, the training environment influences the students' decision to pursue personal therapy. In the past, psychiatry training programs had very high participation rates. Although a few still do, the trend is downward and, regrettably, fewer residents choose to enter therapy.[34]

I consider my personal psychotherapy experience, a five-times-a-week analysis during my entire three-year residency, the most important part of my training as a therapist.[35] I urge every student entering the field not only to seek out personal therapy but to do so more than once during their career—different life stages evoke different issues to be explored. The emergence of personal discomfort is an opportunity for greater self-exploration that will ultimately make us better therapists.[36]

Our knowledge of self plays an instrumental role in every aspect of the therapy. An inability to perceive our countertransference responses, to recognize our personal distortions and blind spots, or to use our own feelings and fantasies in our work will severely limit our effectiveness. If you lack insight into your own motivations, you may, for example, avoid conflict in the group because of your proclivity to mute your feelings; or you may unduly encourage confrontation in a search for aliveness in yourself. You may be overeager to prove yourself or to make consistently brilliant interpretations, and thereby disempower the group. You may fear intimacy and prevent open expression of feelings by premature interpretations—or do the opposite: overemphasize feelings, make too few explanatory comments, and overstimulate clients so that they are left in agitated turmoil. You may so need acceptance that you are unable to challenge the group and, like the members, be swept along by the prevailing group current. You may be so devastated by an attack on yourself and so unclear about your presentation of self as to be unable to distinguish the realistic from the transference aspects of the attack.

Several training programs—for example, the British Group Analytic Institute and the Canadian Group Psychotherapy Association—recommend that their candidates participate as bona fide members in a therapy group led by a senior clinician and composed of nonprofessionals seeking personal therapy.[37] Advocates of such programs point out the many advantages to being a real member of a therapy group. There is less sibling rivalry than in a group of one's peers, less need to perform, less defensiveness, less concern about being judged. The anticipated pitfalls are surmountable. If a trainee attempts to play assistant therapist or in some other way avoids genuine therapeutic engagement, a competent group leader will be able to provide the proper direction.

Experience as a full member of a bona fide therapy group is invaluable, and I encourage any trainee to seek such therapy. Unfortunately, the right group can be hard to find. Advocates of personal group therapy as a part of training hail from large metropolitan areas (London, New York, Toronto, Geneva). But in smaller urban areas, the availability of personal group therapy is limited. There are simply not enough groups that meet the proper criteria—that is, an ongoing high-functioning group led by a senior clinician with an eclectic dynamic approach (who, incidentally, is neither a personal nor professional associate of the trainee).

There is one other method of obtaining both group therapy training and personal psychotherapy. For several years, I led a therapy group for practicing psychotherapists. It is a straightforward therapy group, not a training group. Admission to the group is predicated on the need and the wish for personal therapy, and members are charged standard therapy group fees. Naturally, in the course of their therapy, the members—most but not all of whom are also group therapists—learn a great deal about the group therapy process.

Since every training community has some experienced group therapists, this format makes group therapy available to large numbers of mental health professionals. The composition of the group is generally more compatible for the student group therapist in that there is great homogeneity of ego strength. The group is a stranger group; members are all professionals but do not work together (though I have seen therapists with some informal affiliation—for example, sharing the same office suite—participate without complication in the same group). This eliminates many of the competitive problems that occur in groups of students in the same training program. Members are highly motivated, psychologically minded, and generally verbally active. The highly experienced group therapist will find that such groups are not difficult to lead. Occasionally, members may test, judge, or compete with the leader, but the great majority are there for nononsense work and apply their own knowledge of psychotherapy to help the group become maximally effective.

SUMMARY

The training experiences I have described—observation of an experienced clinician, group therapy supervision, experiential group participation, and personal therapy—constitute, in my view, the minimum essential components of a program to train group therapists. (I assume that the trainee has had (or is in the midst of) training in general clinical areas: interviewing, psychopathology, personality theory, and other forms of psychotherapy.) The sequence of the group therapy training experiences may depend on the structural characteristics of a particular training institute. I recommend that observation, personal therapy, and the experiential group begin very early in the training program, to be followed in a few months by the formation of a group and ongoing supervision. I feel it is wise for trainees to have a clinical experience in which they deal with basic group and interactional dynamics in an open-ended group of nonpsychotic, highly motivated clients before they begin to work with goal-limited groups of highly specialized client populations or with one of the new specialized therapy approaches.

Training is, of course, a lifelong process. It is important that clinicians maintain contact with colleagues, either informally or through professional organizations such as the American Group Psychotherapy Association or the Association for Specialists in Group Work. For growth to continue, continual input is required. Many formats for continued education exist, including reading, working with different co-therapists, teaching, participating in professional workshops, and having informal discussions with colleagues. Postgraduate personal group experiences are a regenerative process for many. The American Group Psychotherapy Association offers a two-day experiential group, led by highly experienced group leaders, at their annual institute, which regularly precedes their annual meeting. Follow-up surveys attest to the value—both professional and personal—of these groups.[38]

Another format is for practicing professionals to form leaderless support groups. Although such groups date back to Freud, until recently there has been little in the literature on support groups of mental health professionals. I can personally attest to their value. For over fifteen years I have profited enormously from membership in a group of eleven therapists of my own age and level of experience that meets for ninety minutes every other week. Several members of the group share the same office suite and over the years had observed, somewhat helplessly, as several colleagues suffered, and sometimes fell victim to, severe personal and professional stress. Their unanimous response to the support group has been: "Why on earth didn't we do this twenty-five years ago?" Such groups not only offer personal and professional support but also remind therapists of the power of the small group and permit a view of the group therapeutic process from the members' seat. Like all groups, they benefit from a clear consensus of expectations, goals, and norms to ensure that they stay on track and are able to address their own group process.[39]

BEYOND TECHNIQUE

The group therapy training program has the task of teaching students not only *how to do* but also *how to learn*. What clinical educators must not convey is a rigid certainty in either our techniques or in our underlying assumptions about therapeutic change: the field is far too complex and pluralistic for disciples of unwavering faith. To this end, I believe it is most important that we teach and model a basic research orientation to continuing education in the field. By research orientation, I refer not to a steel-spectacled chi-square efficiency but instead to an open, self-critical, inquiring attitude toward clinical and research evidence and conclusions—a posture toward experience that is consistent with a sensitive and humanistic clinical approach.

Recent developments in psychotherapy research underscore this principle. For a while there was a fantasy that we could greatly abbreviate clinical training and eliminate variability in therapy outcome by having therapists adhering to a therapy manual. This remains an unrealized fantasy: therapy manualization has not improved clinical outcomes. Ultimately it is the therapist more than the model that produces benefits. Adherence to the nuts and bolts of a psychotherapy manual is a far cry from the skillful, competent delivery of psychotherapy. Many practitioners feel that manuals restrict their natural responsiveness and result in a "herky-jerky" ineffective therapeutic process. Therapist effectiveness has much to do with the capacity to improvise as the context demands it, drawing on both new knowledge and accrued wisdom. Manuals on psychotherapy do not provide that.[40]

We need to help students critically evaluate their own work and maintain sufficient technical and attitudinal flexibility to be responsive to their own observations. Mature therapists continually evolve: they regard each client, each group—indeed, their whole career—as a learning experience. It is equally important to train students to evaluate group therapy research and, if appropriate, to adapt the research conclusions to their clinical work. The inclusion of readings and seminars in clinical research methodology is thus highly desirable. Although only a few clinicians will ever have the time, funding, and institutional backing to engage in large-scale research, many can engage in intensive single-person or single-group research, and all clinicians must evaluate published clinical research. If the group therapy field is to develop coherently, it must embrace responsible, well-executed, relevant, and credible research; otherwise, group therapy will follow its capricious, helter-skelter course, and research will become a futile, effete exercise.

Consider how the student may be introduced to a major research problem: outcome assessment. Seminars may be devoted to a consideration of the voluminous literature on the problems of outcome research. (Excellent recent reviews may serve to anchor these discussions.)[41] In addition to seminars, each student may engage in a research practicum by interviewing clients who have recently terminated group therapy.

Once having engaged even to a limited extent in an assessment of change, the student becomes more sensitive and more constructively critical toward outcome research. The problem, as the student soon recognizes, is that conventional research continues to perpetuate the error of extensive design, of failing to individualize outcome assessment.

Clinicians fail to heed or even to believe research in which outcome is measured by before-and-after changes on standardized instruments—and with good reason. Abundant clinical and research evidence indicates that change means something different to each client. Some clients need to experience less anxiety or hostility; for others, improvement would be accompanied by greater anxiety or hostility. Even self-esteem changes need to be individualized. It has been demonstrated that a high self-esteem score on traditional self-administered questionnaires can reflect either a genuinely healthy regard of self or a defensive posture in which the individual maintains a high self-esteem at the expense of self-awareness.[42] These latter individuals would, as a result of successful treatment, have lower (but more accurate) self-esteem as measured by questionnaires.

Hence, not only must the general strategy of outcome assessment be altered, but also the criteria for outcome must be reformulated. It may be an error to use, in group therapy research, criteria originally designed for individual therapy outcome. I suspect that although group and individual therapies are equivalent in overall effectiveness, each modality may affect different variables and have a different type of outcome. For example, group therapy graduates may become more interpersonally skilled, more inclined to be affiliative in times of stress, more capable of sustaining meaningful relationships, or more empathic, whereas individual therapy clients may be more self-sufficient, introspective, and attuned to inner processes.[43]

For years, group therapists have considered therapy a multidimensional laboratory for living, and it is time to acknowledge this factor in outcome research. As a result of therapy, some clients alter their hierarchy of life values and grow to place more importance on humanistic or aesthetic goals; others may make major decisions that will influence the course of their lives; others may be more interpersonally sensitive and more able to communicate their feelings; still others may become less petty and more elevated in their life concerns; some may have a greater sense of commit-ment to other people or projects; others may experience greater energy; others may come to meaningful terms with their own mortality; and still others may find themselves more adventuresome, more receptive to new concepts and experiences. Complicating matters even more is the fact that many of these changes may be orthogonal to relief of presenting symp-toms or to attainment of greater comfort.[44]

A research orientation demands that, throughout your career as a ther-apist, you remain flexible and responsive to new evidence and that you live with a degree of uncertainty—no small task. Uncertainty that stems from the absence of a definitive treatment system begets anxiety.

Many practitioners seek solace by embracing the Loreleis of orthodox belief systems: they commit themselves to one of the many ideological schools that not only offer a comprehensive system of explanation but also screen out discrepant facts and discount new evidence. This commit-ment usually entails a lengthy apprenticeship and initiation. Once within the system, students find it difficult to get out: first, they have usually un-dergone such a lengthy apprenticeship that abandonment of the school is equivalent to denouncing a part of oneself; and second, it is extremely dif-ficult to abandon a position of certainty for one of uncertainty. Clearly, however, such a position of certainty is antithetical to growth and is par-ticularly stunting to the development of the student therapist.

On the other hand, there are potential dangers in the abrogation of certainty. Anxious and uncertain therapists may be less effective. Deep un-certainty may engender therapeutic nihilism, and the student may resist mastering any organized technique of therapy. Teachers, by personal ex-ample, must offer an alternative model, demonstrating that they believe, in accordance with the best evidence available, that a particular approach is effective, but expect to alter that approach as new information becomes available. Furthermore, the teachers must make clear to their students the pride they derive from being part of a field that attempts to progress and is honest enough to know its own limitations.

Practitioners who lack a research orientation with which to evaluate new developments are in a difficult position. How can they, for example, react to the myriad recent innovations in the field—for example, the proliferation of brief, structured group approaches? Unfortunately, the adoption of a new method is generally a function of the vigor, the per-suasiveness, or the charisma of its proponent, and some new therapeu-tic approaches have been extraordinarily successful in rapidly obtaining both visibility and adherents. Many therapists who do not apply a con-sistent and critical approach to evidence have found themselves either unreasonably unreceptive to all new approaches or swept along with some current fad and then, dissatisfied with its limitations, moving on to yet another.

The critical problem facing group psychotherapy, then, is one of balance. A traditional, conservative sector is less receptive to change than is optimal; the innovative, challenging sector is less receptive to stability than is optimal. The field is swayed by fashion, whereas it should be influenced by evidence. Psychotherapy is a science as well as an art, and there is no place in science for uncritical orthodoxy or for innovation for its own sake. Orthodoxy offers safety for adherents but leads to stagnation; the field becomes insensitive to the zeitgeist and is left behind as the public goes elsewhere. Innovation provides zest and a readily apparent creative outlet for proponents but, if unevaluated, results in a kaleidoscopic field without substance—a field that "rides off madly in all directions."[45]

Appendix

Information and Guidelines
for Participation in Group Therapy

Group therapy has a long, proven record as a highly effective and useful form of psychotherapy. It is as helpful as, and in some cases more helpful than, individual therapy, particularly when social support and learning about interpersonal relationships are important objectives of treatment. The vast majority of individuals who participate in group therapy benefit from it substantially. Although group therapy is generally highly supportive, you may at times find it stressful.

SOME GOALS OF GROUP PSYCHOTHERAPY

Many individuals seeking therapy feel isolated and dissatisfied in their particular life situation. They may have difficulties establishing and maintaining close, mutually gratifying, and meaningful relationships with others. Frequently they are interested in learning more about how they relate to others.
   Group therapy offers an opportunity to:

- Receive and offer support and feedback
- Improve interpersonal relationships and communication
- Experiment with new interpersonal behaviors
- Talk honestly and directly about feelings
- Gain insight and understanding into one's own thoughts, feelings, and behaviors by looking at relationship patterns both inside and outside the group
- Gain understanding of other peoples' thoughts, feelings, and behaviors
- Improve self-confidence, self-image, and self-esteem

- Undergo personal change inside the group with the expectation of carrying that learning over into one's outside life

CONFIDENTIALITY

All statements by participants in psychotherapy must be treated with the utmost respect and confidentiality. It is an essential part of ethical, professional conduct.

a) Therapists

Group therapists are pledged to maintain complete confidentiality except in one situation: when there is an immediate risk of serious harm to a group member or to someone else.

If you are in concurrent individual treatment, we request your permission to communicate with your individual therapist at regular intervals. Your therapists are your allies and it is important for your therapy that they communicate with one another.

b) Group Members

Confidentiality is similarly expected of all group members. Group members must maintain confidentiality to create a safe environment for the work of therapy and to develop trust within the group. Most individuals in therapy prefer to keep the therapy a private place and refrain from any discussions about it with others. If, however, in discussions with friends or family, you wish at some point to refer to your group therapy, you should speak only about your own experience, not about any other member's experience. Never mention any other member's name or say anything that might inadvertently identify any group members.

WHAT DO YOU DO IN THE GROUP? HOW ARE YOU EXPECTED TO BEHAVE?

There will not be a prescribed agenda for each session. Participants are encouraged to talk about any personal or relationship issues relevant to the problems and goals that led them to therapy.

Participants are encouraged to offer support, to ask questions, to wonder about things said or not said, to share associations and thoughts. Much emphasis will be placed on examining the relations between members—that is, the "here-and-now." Members will often be asked to share their impressions of one another—their thoughts, fears, and positive feelings. The more we work in the here-and-now of the group, the more effective we will be.

Disclosure about oneself is necessary for one to profit from group therapy, but members should choose to disclose at their own pace. We never pressure members for confessions.

In order to construct a therapeutic group environment, we ask that members always try to say things to other members in a way that is constructive. Helpful feedback focuses on what is happening in the here-and-now, does not blame, is relevant, and connects the member receiving the feedback with the member offering the feedback. This kind of direct feedback and engagement is novel: rarely in our culture do individuals speak so honestly and directly. Hence, it may at first feel risky, but it may also feel deeply engaging and meaningful.

Direct advice-giving from group members and therapists is not generally useful. Neither are general discussions of such topics as sports or politics helpful unless there is something about a current event that has particular relevance to one's personal or interpersonal issues.

The therapy group is not a place to make friends. Rather, it is a social laboratory—a place in which one acquires the skills to develop meaningful and satisfying relationships. In fact, therapy groups (unlike support or social groups) do not encourage social contact with other members outside the group. Why? Because an outside relationship with another member or members generally impedes therapy!

How is therapy impeded? To explain this we need first to emphasize that your primary task in the therapy group is to explore fully your relationships with each and every member of the group. At first, that may seem puzzling or unrelated to the reasons you sought therapy.

Yet it begins to make sense when you consider the fact that the group is a social microcosm—that is, the problems you experience in your social life will emerge also in your relationships *within* the group. Therefore, by exploring and understanding all aspects of your relationships with other members and then transferring this knowledge to your outside life you begin the process of developing more satisfying relationships.

If, however, you develop a close relationship with another member (or members) outside the group, you may be disinclined to share all your feelings about that relationship *within* the group. Why? Because that friendship may mean so much that you may be reluctant to say anything that might jeopardize it in any way. What happens in a therapy group when openness and honesty are compromised? Therapy grinds to a halt!

Therefore, it is best that members who meet outside the group (by chance or design) share all relevant information with the group. Any type of secrecy about relationships slows down the work of therapy. At times members develop strong feelings toward other members. We encourage that these feelings be discussed, both positive feelings as well as other feelings such as irritation or disappointment. Group members are expected to talk about feelings without acting on their feelings.

Group Therapists

Your group therapists are not going to "run the show." Their role is more that of a participant/facilitator rather than of an instructor. Therapy is most productive when it is a collaborative and a shared enterprise. Keep in mind that the input from other members may often be as important as, or even more important than, the leaders' comments. The therapists may make observations about group interactions and behavior, or about what particular individuals say or do in the group. They might also comment on progress or obstructions within the group.

When you have something to say to the group therapists, we hope that, as much as possible, you do so in the group sessions. However, if there is something urgent you must discuss with the group therapists outside of group, between sessions, this can be arranged. But it is useful to bring up in the next group meeting what was discussed with the therapists. Even relevant material from your individual or couples therapy with another therapist should be shared. We hope that there will be really no issues that you cannot talk about within the group. At the same time, we recognize that trust develops only over time and that some personal disclosures will be made only when you feel sufficiently safe in the group.

INITIAL LENGTH OF
TRIAL PERIOD OR COMMITMENT

Group therapy does not generally show immediate positive benefit to its participants. Because of this fact, participants sometimes find themselves wanting to leave therapy early on if it becomes stressful for them. We ask that you suspend your early judgment of the group's possible benefits and continue to attend and to talk about the stresses involved and your doubts about group therapy.

We ask that you make an initial commitment to attend and participate in your therapy group for at least 12 sessions. By then you will have a clearer sense of the potential helpfulness of the group.

ATTENDANCE AND GROUP COHESION

The group works most effectively if it is cohesive, reliable, and predictable. Regular attendance is a key part of that, so we request that you make it a priority in your schedule. Group therapy progresses best when each member values and respects the commitment and work of each participant. Regular attendance and active participation in the meetings is an important way to demonstrate that respect and valuing. Similarly, arriving on time to each session is important. If you know that you are going to be late or absent, we ask that you call the group therapists as far ahead of time as possible so that they can let the group know at the beginning of the session.

If you know a week or more ahead of time of a necessary lateness or absence, inform the group at an earlier session. We ask that you also inform the group of your vacation plans well ahead of time if possible. The group therapists will do the same.

There may be times when the group is the last place you want to be, because of uncomfortable feelings. These times may in fact be unusually productive opportunities to do the work of psychotherapy. In the same vein, you can anticipate that some of the difficulties that you have experienced in your life will express themselves in the group. Don't be discouraged by this. It is in fact a great opportunity, because it means that you and the group members are tackling the important issues that concern you.

You have decided, by agreeing to participate in group therapy, to begin a process of giving and receiving support and working toward needed changes in your personal and interpersonal life. We look forward to the opportunity of working together with you in this group.

Notes

Additional reference information and suggested readings of relevant articles can be found at www.yalom.com. Where specific references exist at www.yalom.com, a † has been added to the text in this book.

CHAPTER 1

1. C. McRoberts, G. Burlingame, and M. Hoag, "Comparative Efficacy of Individual and Group Psychotherapy: A Meta-Analytic Perspective," *Group Dynamics: Theory, Research, and Practice* 2 (1998): 101–117. M. Smith, G. Glass, and T. Miller, *The Benefits of Psychotherapy* (Baltimore: Johns Hopkins University Press, 1980). L. Tillitski, "A Meta-Analysis of Estimated Effect Sizes for Group Versus Individual Versus Control Treatments," *International Journal of Group Psychotherapy* 40 (1990): 215–24. G. Burlingame, K. MacKenzie, and B. Strauss, "Small-Group Treatment: Evidence for Effectiveness and Mechanisms of Change," in *Bergin and Garfield's Handbook of Psychotherapy and Behavior Change*, 5th ed., ed. M. Lambert (New York: Wiley and Sons, 2004), 647–96.

2. S. Bloch, "Therapeutic Factors in Group Psychotherapy," in *APA Annual Review V* (Washington, D.C.: APA Press, 1986), pp. 679–98. D. Kivlighan, K. Multon, and D. Brossart, "Helpful Impacts in Group Counseling: Development of a Multidimensional Rating System," *Journal of Counseling Psychology* 43 (1996); 347–55.

3. M. Lieberman, I. Yalom, and M. Miles, *Encounter Groups: First Facts* (New York: Basic Books, 1973).

4. H. Feifel and J. Eells, "Patients and Therapists Assess the Same Psychotherapy," *Journal of Consulting and Clinical Psychology* 27 (1963): 310–18.

5. J. Schaffer and S. Dreyer, "Staff and Inpatient Perceptions of Change Mechanisms in Group Therapy," *American Journal of Psychiatry* 139 (1982): 127–28. S. Bloch and J. Reibstein, "Perceptions by Patients and Therapists of Therapeutic Factors in Group Therapy," *British Journal of Psychiatry* 137 (1980): 274–78. R. Cabral and A. Paton, "Evaluation of Group Therapy: Correlations Between Clients' and Observers' Assessments," *British Journal of Psychiatry* 126 (1975): 475–77. C. Glass and D. Arnkoff, "Common and Specific Factors in Client Descriptions and Explanations for Change," *Journal of Integrative and Eclectic Psychotherapy* 7 (1988): 427–40.

6. T. Butler and A. Fuhriman, "Level of Functioning and Length of Time in Treatment Variables Influencing Patients' Therapeutic Experience in Group Psychotherapy," *International Journal of Group Psychotherapy* 33 (1983): 489–504.

7. J. Maxmen, "Group Therapy as Viewed by Hospitalized Patients," *Archives of General Psychiatry* 28 (March 1973): 404–8. T. Butler and A. Fuhriman, "Patient Perspective

on the Curative Process: A Comparison of Day Treatment and Outpatient Psychotherapy Groups," *Small Group Behavior* 11 (1980): 371–88. T. Butler and A. Fuhriman, "Curative Factors in Group Therapy: A Review of the Recent Literature," *Small Group Behavior* 14 (1983): 131–42. M. Leszcz, I. Yalom, and M. Norden, "The Value of Inpatient Group Psychotherapy: Patients' Perceptions," *International Journal of Group Psychotherapy* 35 (1985): 411–35. E. Rynearson and S. Melson, "Short-Term Group Psychotherapy for Patients with Functional Complaints," *Postgraduate Medicine* 76 (1984): 141–50.

8. B. Corder, L. Whiteside, and T. Haizlip, "A Study of Curative Factors in Group Psychotherapy with Adolescents," *International Journal of Group Psychotherapy* 31 (1981): 345–54. N. Macaskill, "Therapeutic Factors in Group Therapy with Borderline Patients," *International Journal of Group Psychotherapy* 32 (1982): 61–73. S. Colijn et al., "A Comparison of Curative Factors in Different Types of Group Psychotherapy," *International Journal of Group Psychotherapy* 41 (1991): 365–78.

9. M. Lieberman and L. Borman, *Self-Help Groups for Coping with Crisis* (San Francisco: Jossey-Bass, 1979). M. Lieberman, "Comparative Analyses of Change Mechanisms in Group," in *Advances in Group Therapy,* ed. R. Dies and K. MacKenzie (New York: International Universities Press, 1983): 191–208. S. Bloch and E. Crouch, Therapeutic Factors in Group Therapy (Oxford: Oxford University Press, 1985), 25–67.

10. K. MacKenzie and V. Tschuschke, "Relatedness, Group Work, and Outcome in Long-Term Inpatient Psychotherapy Groups," *Journal of Psychotherapy Practice and Research* 2 (1993): 147–55. G. Burlingame, "Small-Group Treatment." D. Kivligham, "Helpful Impacts."

11. A. Goldstein, *Therapist-Patient Expectancies in Psychotherapy* (New York: Pergamon Press, 1962). S. Bloch et al., "Patients' Expectations of Therapeutic Improvement and Their Outcomes," *American Journal of Psychiatry* 133 (1976): 1457–59. J. Frank and J. Frank, *Persuasion and Healing: A Comparative Study of Psychotherapy,* 3rd ed. (Baltimore: Johns Hopkins University Press, 1991), 132–54. J. Connelly et al., "Premature Termination in Group Psychotherapy: Pretherapy and Early Therapy Predictors," *International Journal of Group Psychotherapy* 36 (1986): 145–52. A. Rabin et al., "Factors Influencing Continuation," *Behavioral Therapy* 23 (1992): 695–98. H. Hoberman et al., "Group Treatment of Depression: Individual Predictors of Outcome," *Journal of Consulting and Clinical Psychology* 56 (1988): 393–98. M. Pearson and A. Girling, "The Value of the Claybury Selection Battery in Predicting Benefit from Group Therapy," *British Journal of Psychiatry* 157 (1990): 384–88. W. Piper, "Client Variables," in *Handbook of Group Psychotherapy,* ed. A. Fuhriman and G. Burlingame (New York: Wiley, 1994): 83–113.

12. M. Seligman, "The Effectiveness of Psychotherapy: The Consumer Reports Study," *American Psychologist* 50 (1995): 965–74.

13. A. Leuchter, I. Cook, E. Witte, M. Morgan, and M. Abrams, "Changes in Brain Function of Depressed Subjects During Treatment with Placebo," *American Journal of Psychiatry* 159 (2002): 122–29.

14. D. Spiegel and C. Classen, *Group Therapy for Cancer Patients* (New York: Basic Books, 2000). M. Leszcz and P. Goodwin, "The Rationale and Foundations of Group Psychotherapy for Women with Metastatic Breast Cancer," *International Journal of Group Psychotherapy* 48 (1998): 245–74.

15. Goldstein, *Therapist-Patient Expectancies,* 35–53. Kaul and Bednar, "Experiential Group Research," 229–63. E. Uhlenhuth and D. Duncan, "Some Determinants of Change in Psychoneurotic Patients," *Archives of General Psychiatry* 18 (1968): 532–40. Frank and Frank, *Persuasion and Healing.*

16. Lieberman and Borman, *Self-Help Groups.*

17. K. Lorig et al., "Evidence Suggesting That a Chronic Disease Self-Management Program Can Improve Health Status While Reducing Hospitalization: A Randomized Trial," *Medical Care* 37 (1999): 5–14.

18. F. Fawzy, N. Fawzy, and J. Wheeler, "A Post-Hoc Comparison of the Efficiency of a Psychoeducational Intervention for Melanoma Patients Delivered in Group Versus Individual Formats: An Analysis of Data from Two Studies," *Psycho-Oncology* 5 (1996): 81–89. A. Bandura, *Self-Efficacy: The Exercise of Control* (New York: Freeman, 1997).

19. J. Moreno, "Group Treatment for Eating Disorders," in Fuhriman and Burlingame, *Handbook of Group Psychotherapy:* 416–457.

20. S. Gold-Steinberg and M. Buttenheim, "'Telling One's Story' in an Incest Survivors' Group," *International Journal of Group Psychotherapy* 43 (1993): 173–89. F. Mennen and D. Meadow, "Process to Recovery: In Support of Long-Term Groups for Sexual Abuse Survivors," *International Journal of Group Psychotherapy* 43 (1993): 29–44. M. Schadler, "Brief Group Therapy with Adult Survivors of Incest," in *Focal Group Therapy,* ed. M. McKay and K. Paleg (Oakland, Calif.: New Harbinger Publications, 1992), 292–322.

21. J. Kelly, "Group Therapy Approaches for Patients with HIV and AIDS," *International Journal of Group Psychotherapy* 48 (1998): 145–62. C. Rose, L. Sekula, and E. Rubenstein, "Group Interventions for Widowed Survivors of Suicide," *Suicide and Life-Threatening Behavior* 31 (2001): 428–41.

22. P. Tsui and G. Schultz, "Ethnic Factors in Group Process," *American Journal of Orthopsychiatry* 58 (1988): 136–42.

23. N. Hansen, F. Pepitone-Arreola-Rockwell, and A. Greene, "Multicultural Competence: Criteria and Case Examples," *Professional Psychology: Research and Practice* 31 (2000): 652–60. G. Nagayama Hall, "Psychotherapy Research with Ethnic Minorities: Empirical, Ethical, and Conceptual Issues," *Journal of Consulting and Clinical Psychology* 69 (2001): 502–10.

24. M. Jones, "Group Treatment with Particular Reference to Group Projection Methods," *American Journal of Psychiatry* 101 (1944): 292–99.

25. L. Marsh, "Group Therapy and the Psychiatric Clinic," *Journal of Nervous and Mental Diseases* 82 (1935): 381–90.

26. M. Galanter, "Zealous Self-Help Groups as Adjuncts to Psychiatric Treatment: A Study of Recovery, Inc.," *American Journal of Psychiatry* 143 (1988): 1248–53. M. Galanter, "Cults and Zealous Self-Help Movements," *American Journal of Psychiatry* 145 (1990): 543–51. C. Gartner, "A Self-Help Organization for Nervous and Former Mental Patients—Recovery, Inc., Chicago," *Hospital and Community Psychiatry* 42 (1991): 1055–56.

27. P. Murray, "Recovery, Inc., as an Adjunct to Treatment in an Era of Managed Care," *Psychiatric Services* 47 (1996): 1378–81.

28. A. Low, *Mental Health Through Will Training* (Boston: Christopher Publishing House, 1950).

29. Lieberman and Borman, *Self-Help Groups,* 194–234. G. Goodman and M. Jacobs, "The Self-Help Mutual Support Group," in Fuhriman and Burlingame, *Handbook of Group Psychotherapy:* 484–526. D. Salem, E. Seidman, and J. Rappaport, "Community Treatment of the Mentally Ill: The Promise of Mutual Help Organizations," *Social Work* 33 (1988): 403–8. Lieberman and Borman, *Self-Help Groups.*

30. H. Fensterheim and B. Wiegand, "Group Treatment of the Hyperventilation Syndrome," *International Journal of Group Psychotherapy* 41 (1991): 399–404. R. McNally, "Psychological Approaches to Panic Disorder: A Review," *Psychological Bulletin* 108 (1990): 403–19.

31. S. Tenzer, "Fat Acceptance Therapy: A Non-Dieting Group Approach to Physical Wellness, Insight and Self-Acceptance," *Women and Therapy* 8 (1989): 39–47.

32. Moreno, "Group Treatment for Eating Disorders." J. Mitchell et al., "A Comparison Study of Antidepressants and Structured Intensive Group Therapy in the Treatment of Bulimia Nervosa," *Archives of General Psychiatry* 47 (1990): 149–57. J. Laube, "Why Group for Bulimia?" *International Journal of Group Psychotherapy* 40 (1990): 169–88. D.

Franko, "The Use of a Group Meal in the Brief Group Therapy of Bulimia Nervosa," *International Journal of Group Psychotherapy* 43 (1993): 237–42.

33. M. Kalb, "The Effects of Biography on the Divorce Adjustment Process," *Sexual and Marital Therapy* 2 (1987): 53–64. D. Grenvold and G. Welch, "Structured Short-Term Group Treatment of Postdivorce Adjustment," *International Journal of Group Psychotherapy* 29 (1979): 347–58.

34. S. Drob and H. Bernard, "Time-Limited Group Treatment of Genital Herpes," *International Journal of Group Psychotherapy* 36 (1986): 133–44.

35. D. Ornish, *Dr. Dean Ornish's Program for Reversing Heart Disease* (New York: Random House, 1990). R. Allen and S. Scheidt, "Group Psychotherapy for Patients with Coronary Heart Disease," *International Journal of Group Psychotherapy* 48 (1998): 187–214.

36. B. Mara and M. Winton, "Sexual Abuse Intervention: A Support Group for Parents Who Have a Sexually Abused Child," *International Journal of Group Psychotherapy* 40 (1990): 63–78.

37. T. Poynter, "An Evaluation of a Group Program for Male Perpetrators of Domestic Violence," *Australian Journal of Marriage and Family* 12 (1991): 64–76. J. Edelson and R. Gruznski, "Treating Men Who Batter," *Journal of Social Service Research* 12 (1988): 3–22. B. Wallace and A. Nosko, "Working with Shame in the Group Treatment of Male Batterers," *International Journal of Group Psychotherapy* 43 (1993): 45–61.

38. I. Yalom and S. Vinogradov, "Bereavement Groups: Techniques and Themes," *International Journal of Group Psychotherapy* 38 (1988): 419–46.

39. S. Levine et al., "Group Psychotherapy for HIV-Seropositive Patients with Major Depression," *American Journal of Psychotherapy* 55 (1991): 413–25. G. Tunnell, "Complication in Group Psychotherapy with AIDS Patients," *International Journal of Group Psychotherapy* 41 (1991): 481–98. A. Beckett and J. Rutan, "Treating Persons with ARC and AIDS in Group Psychotherapy," *International Journal of Group Psychotherapy* 40 (1990): 19–30. Kelly, "Group Therapy Approaches for Patients with HIV and AIDS."

40. S. Price, A. Heinrich, and J. Golden, "Structured Group Treatment of Couples Experiencing Sexual Dysfunction," *Journal of Sex and Marital Therapy* 6 (1981): 247–57.

41. L. Gallese and E. Treuting, "Help for Rape Victims Through Group Therapy," *Journal of Psychosocial Nursing and Mental Health Services* 19 (1981): 20–21.

42. R. Kris and H. Kramer, "Efficacy of Group Therapy with Postmastectomy Self-Perception, Body Image, and Sexuality," *Journal of Sex Research* 23 (1986): 438–51.

43. E. Herman and S. Baptiste, "Pain Control: Mastery Through Group Experience," *Pain* 10 (1981): 79–86.

44. S. Abbey and S. Farrow, "Group Therapy and Organ Transplantation," *International Journal of Group Psychotherapy* 48 (1998): 163–86.

45. Z. Segal, J. Williams, and J. Teasdale, *Mindfulness-Based Cognitive Therapy for Depression* (New York: Guilford Press, 2002).

46. J. Kabat-Zinn, *Full Catastrophe Living: Using the Wisdom of Your Body and Mind to Face Stress, Pain, and Illness* (New York: Dell, 1990). Segal et al., *Mindfulness-Based Cognitive Therapy.*

47. V. Helgeson, S. Cohen, R. Schulz, and J. Yasko, "Education and Peer Discussion Group Interventions and Adjustment to Breast Cancer," *Archives of General Psychiatry* 56 (1999): 340–47.

48. I. Yalom, P. Houts, G. Newell, and K. Rand, "Preparation of Patients for Group Therapy: A Controlled Study," *Archives of General Psychiatry* 17 (1967): 416–27.

49. F. Fromm-Reichman, *Principles of Intensive Psychotherapy* (Chicago: University of Chicago Press, 1950).

50. J. Ledoux and J. Gorman, "A Call to Action: Overcoming Anxiety Through Active Coping," *American Journal of Psychiatry* 158 (2001): 1953–55.

51. J. Frank et al., "Behavioral Patterns in Early Meetings of Therapy Groups," *American Journal of Psychiatry* 108 (1952): 771–78. C. Peters and H. Grunebaum, "It Could Be Worse: Effective Group Therapy with the Help-Rejecting Complainer," *International Journal of Group Psychotherapy* 27 (1977): 471–80. E. Berne, *Games People Play* (New York: Grove Press, 1964).

52. J. Rubin and K. Locasio, "A Model for Communication Skills Group Using Structured Exercises and Audiovisual Equipment," *International Journal of Group Psychotherapy* 35 (1985): 569–84.

53. J. Flowers, "The Differential Outcome Effects of Simple Advice, Alternatives, and Instructions in Group Psychotherapy," *International Journal of Group Psychotherapy* 29 (1979): 305–15.

54. W. Beardslee, E. Wright, P. Rothberg, P. Salt, and E. Versage, "Response of Families to Two Preventive Intervention Strategies: Long-Term Differences in Behavior and Attitude Change," *Journal of the American Academy of Child and Adolescent Psychiatry* 35 (1996): 774–82.

55. S. Holmes and D. Kivlighan, "Comparison of Therapeutic Factors in Group and Individual Treatment Processes," *Journal of Counseling Psychology* 47 (2000): 478–84.

56. Frank and Frank, *Persuasion and Healing.*

57. V. Frankl, *The Will to Meaning* (Cleveland: World Publishing, 1969).

58. S. Folkman, S. Greer, "Promoting Psychological Well-being in the Face of Serious Illness: When Theory, Research and Practice Inform Each Other," *Psycho-Oncology* 9 (2000): 11–19.

59. L. Ormont, "The Role of the Leader in Resolving Resistances to Intimacy in the Group Setting," *International Journal of Group Psychotherapy* 38 (1988): 29–45.

60. D. Goleman, *Emotional Intelligence* (New York: Bantam Books, 1995).

61. S. Barlow et al., "Leader Communication Style: Effects on Members of Small Groups," *Small Group Behavior* 13 (1982): 513–81.

62. S. Borgers, "Uses and Effects of Modeling by the Therapist in Group Therapy," *Journal for Specialists in Group Work* 8 (1983): 133–39.

63. E. Kuipers et al., "London–East Anglia Randomized Controlled Trial of Cognitive-Behaviour Therapy for Psychosis: I. Effects of the Treatment Phase," *British Journal of Psychiatry* 171 (1997): 319–27.

64. A. Bandura, E. Blanchard, and B. Ritter, "The Relative Efficacy of Desensitization and Modeling Approaches for Inducing Behavioral, Affective, and Attitudinal Changes," *Journal of Personality and Social Psychology* 13 (1969): 173–99. A. Bandura, D. Ross, and S. Ross, "Vicarious Reinforcements and Imitative Learning," *Journal of Abnormal and Social Psychology* 67 (1963): 601–7.

65. J. Moreno, "Psychodramatic Shock Therapy," *Sociometry* 2 (1939): 1–30.

66. S. Colijin et al., "A Comparison of Curative Ractors in Different Types of Group Therapy," *International Journal of Group Therapy* 41 (1991): 365–78.

CHAPTER 2

1. R. Baumeister and M. Leary, "The Need to Belong: Desire for Interpersonal Attachments as a Fundamental Human Motivation," *Psychology Bulletin* 117 (1995): 497–529.

2. J. Bowlby, *Attachment and Loss*, vol. 3, *Loss: Sadness and Depression* (New York: Basic Books, 1980).

3. D. Winnicott, *Through Pediatrics to Psychoanalysis* (London: Hogarth Press, 1978; orig. published 1952).

4. S. Mitchell, *Relational Concepts in Psychoanalysis* (Cambridge, Mass.: Harvard University Press, 1988).

5. W. James, *The Principles of Psychology,* vol. 1 (New York: Henry Holt, 1890), 293.

6. L. Syme, *Social Support and Health* (Orlando, Fla.: Academic Press, 1985). J. Hartog, J. Audy, and Y. Cohen, eds., *The Anatomy of Loneliness* (New York: International Universities Press, 1980). J. Lynch, *The Broken Heart: The Medical Consequences of Loneliness* (New York: Basic Books, 1977).

7. J. House, K. Landis, and D. Umberson, "Social Relationships and Health," *Science* 241 (1988): 540–45.

8. E. Maunsell, J. Brisson, and L. Deschenes, "Social Support and Survival Among Women with Breast Cancer," *Cancer* 76 (1995): 631–37. M. Price et al., "The Role of Psychosocial Factors in the Development of Breast Carcinoma, Part II: Life Event Stressors, Social Support, Defense Style, and Emotional Control and Their Interactions," *Cancer* 91 (2001): 686–97. J. Leserman et al., "Impact of Stressful Life Events, Depression, Social Support, Coping, and Cortisol on Progression to AIDS," *American Journal of Psychiatry* 157 (2000): 1221–28.

9. V. Schermer, "Contributions of Object Relations Theory and Self Psychology to Relational Psychology, Group Psychotherapy," *International Journal of Group Psychotherapy* 50 (2000): 199–212.

10. S. Mitchell, *Hope and Dread in Psychoanalysis* (New York: Basic Books, 1993).

11. H. Sullivan, *The Interpersonal Theory of Psychiatry* (New York: Norton, 1953). H. Sullivan, *Conceptions of Modern Psychiatry* (New York: Norton, 1940).

12. D. Kiesler, *Contemporary Interpersonal Theory and Research* (New York: Wiley, 1996).

13. P. Mullahy, "Harry Stack Sullivan," in *Comprehensive Textbook of Psychiatry,* ed. H. Kaplan, A. Freedman, and B. Sadock (Baltimore: Williams & Wilkins, 1980): 152–55. P. Mullahy, *The Contributions of Harry Stack Sullivan* (New York: Hermitage House, 1952).

14. J. McCullough Jr., *Treatment for Chronic Depression: Cognitive Behavioral Analysis System of Psychotherapy (CBASP)* (New York: Guilford Press, 2000). D. Hellerstein et al., "Adding Group Psychotherapy to Medication Treatment in Dysthymia: A Randomized Prospective Pilot Study," *Journal of Psychotherapy Practice and Research* 10 (2002): 93–103. J. Safran and Z. Segal, *Interpersonal Process in Cognitive Therapy* (New York: Basic Books, 1990).

15. D. Kiesler, *Contemporary Interpersonal Theory.*

16. Mullahy, *Contributions,* 22.

17. H. Grunebaum and L. Solomon, "Peer Relationships, Self-Esteem, and the Self," *International Journal of Group Psychotherapy* 37 (1987): 475–513.

18. M. Leszcz, "Integrated Group Psychotherapy for the Treatment of Depression in the Elderly," *Group* 21 (1997): 89–113.

19. P. Fonagy, "The Process of Change and the Change of Processes: What Can Change in a 'Good Analysis'," keynote address to the spring meeting of Division 39 of the American Psychological Association, New York, April 16, 1999.

20. Bowlby, *Attachment and Loss.*

21. Safran and Segal, *Interpersonal Process.* Kiesler, *Contemporary Interpersonal Theory.*

22. H. Strupp and J. Binder, *Psychotherapy in a New Key* (New York: Basic Books, 1984). R. Giesler and W. Swann, "Striving for Confirmation: The Role of Self-Verification in Depression, in *The Interactional Nature of Depression,* ed. T. Joiner and J. Coyne (Washington, D.C.: American Psychological Association, 1999), 189–217.

23. Kiesler, *Contemporary Interpersonal Theory.* Kiesler describes this interpersonal vicious circle as a maladaptive transaction cycle (MTC). Current research emphasizes interpersonal complementarity—the idea that specific behavior elicits specific responses from others—as the mechanism that initiates and maintains vicious circles of maladaptive interactions. Consider, for example, two dimensions of behavior much used in interpersonal research: agency and affiliation. *Agency* (that is, self definition, assertion and initiative) ranges from domination to subordination. Complementarity in agency means that dominating be-

haviors pull reciprocal counter responses of submission; submissive behavior in turn will reciprocally pull forth dominating forms of responses. *Affiliation* (that is, one's attitude to interpersonal connection) ranges from hostility to friendliness and pulls for similarity and agreement: hostility draws further hostility, and friendliness pulls for friendliness back). Anticipating and understanding specific types of interpersonal pulls informs the group leader about clients' actual and potential maladaptive transactions in therapy. Moreover, this information can be used to help group therapists maintain a therapeutic perspective in the presence of the strong interpersonal pulls affecting others or themselves. Once therapists recognize the interpersonal impact of each client's behavior, they more readily understand their own countertransference and can provide more accurate and useful feedback.

24. Mullahy, *Contributions,* 10.

25. L. Horowitz and J. Vitkis, "The Interpersonal Basis of Psychiatric Symptomatology," *Clinical Psychology Review* 6 (1986): 443–69.

26. Kiesler, *Contemporary Interpersonal Theory.*

27. Sullivan, *Conceptions,* 207.

28. Ibid., 237.

29. B. Grenyer and L. Luborsky, "Dynamic Change in Psychotherapy: Mastery of Interpersonal Conflicts," *Journal of Consulting and Clinical Psychology* 64 (1996): 411–16.

30. S. Hemphill and L. Littlefield, "Evaluation of a Short-Term Group Therapy Program for Children with Behavior Problems and Their Parents," *Behavior Research and Therapy* 39 (2001): 823–41. S. Scott, Q. Spender, M. Doolan, B. Jacobs, and H. Espland, "Multi-Center Controlled Trial of Parenting Groups for Childhood Antisocial Behavior in Clinical Practice," *British Medical Journal* 323 (2001): 194–97.

31. D. Wilfley, K. MacKenzie, V. Ayers, R. Welch, and M. Weissman, *Interpersonal Psychotherapy for Group* (New York: Basic Books, 2000).

32. I. Yalom and C. Greaves, "Group Therapy with the Terminally Ill," *American Journal of Psychiatry* 134 (1977): 396–400.

33. E. Kübler-Ross, *On Death and Dying* (New York: Macmillan, 1969).

34. F. Alexander and T. French, *Psychoanalytic Therapy: Principles and Applications* (New York: Ronald Press, 1946). For a more contemporary psychoanalytic view of the corrective emotional experience, see T. Jacobs, "The Corrective Emotional Experience: Its Place in Current Technique," *Psychoanalytic Inquiry* 10 (1990): 433–545.

35. F. Alexander, "Unexplored Areas in Psychoanalytic Theory and Treatment," in *New Perspectives in Psychoanalysis, Sandor Rado Lectures 1957–1963,* ed. G. Daniels (New York: Grune & Stratton, 1965), 75.

36. P. Fonagy, G. Moran, R. Edgcumbe, H. Kennedy, and M. Target, "The Roles of Mental Representations and Mental Processes in Therapeutic Action," *The Psychoanalytic Study of the Child* 48 (1993): 9–48. J. Weiss, *How Psychotherapy Works: Process and Technique* (New York: Guilford Press, 1993).

37. P. Fretter, W. Bucci, J. Broitman, G. Silberschatz, and J. Curtis, "How the Patient's Plan Relates to the Concept of Transference," *Psychotherapy Research* 4 (1994): 58–72.

38. Alexander, "Unexplored Areas," 79–80.

39. J. Frank and E. Ascher, "The Corrective Emotional Experience in Group Therapy," *American Journal of Psychiatry* 108 (1951): 126–31.

40. J. Breuer and S. Freud, *Studies on Hysteria,* in S. Freud, *The Standard Edition of the Complete Psychological Works of Sigmund Freud,* vol. 2 (London: Hogarth Press, 1955).

41. M. Lieberman, I. Yalom, and M. Miles, *Encounter Groups: First Facts* (New York: Basic Books, 1973).

42. Ibid.

43. A. Alonso and J. Rutan, "Character Change in Group Therapy," *International Journal of Group Psychotherapy,* 43, 4 (1993): 439–51.

44. B. Cohen, "Intersubjectivity and Narcissism in Group Psychotherapy: How Feedback Works," *International Journal of Group Psychotherapy* 50 (2000): 163–79.

45. R. Stolorow, B. Brandschaft, and G. Atwood, *Psychoanalytic Treatment: An Inter-subjective Approach* (Hillsdale, N.J.: Analytic Press, 1987).

46. J. Kleinberg, "Beyond Emotional Intelligence at Work: Adding Insight to Injury Through Group Psychotherapy," *Group* 24 (2000): 261–78.

47. Kiesler, *Contemporary Interpersonal Theory.* J. Muran and J. Safran, "A Relational Approach to Psychotherapy," in *Comprehensive Handbook of Psychotherapy,* ed. F. Kaslow, vol. 1, *Psychodynamic/Object Relations,* ed. J. Magnavita (New York: Wiley, 2002), 253–81.

48. M. Leszcz and J. Malat, "The Interpersonal Model of Group Psychotherapy," in *Praxis der Gruppenpsychotherapie,* ed. V. Tschuschke (Frankfurt: Thieme, 2001), 355–69.

49. N. Jacobson et al., "A Component Analysis of Cognitive-Behavioral Treatment for Depression," *Journal of Consulting and Clinical Psychology* 64 (1996): 295–304.

50. R. Dies, "Group Psychotherapies," in *Essential Psychotherapies: Theory and Practice,* ed. A. Gurman and S. Messer (New York: Guilford Publications, 1998): 488-522. E. Crouch and S. Bloch, "Therapeutic Factors: Interpersonal and Intrapersonal Mechanisms," in *Handbook of Group Psychotherapy,* ed. A. Fuhriman and G. Burlingame (New York: Wiley, 1994), 25–87. R. Dies, "Clinical Implications of Research on Leadership in Short-Term Group Psychotherapy," in *Advances in Group Psychotherapy,* ed. R. Dies and K. MacKenzie (New York: International Universities Press, 1983), 27–79. J. Frank, "Some Values of Conflict in Therapeutic Groups," *Group Psychotherapy* 8 (1955): 142–51. J. Kaye, "Group Interaction and Interpersonal Learning," *Small Group Behavior* 4 (1973): 424–48. A. German and J. Gustafson, "Patients' Perceptions of the Therapeutic Relationship and Group Therapy Outcome," *American Journal of Psychiatry* 133 (1976): 1290–94. J. Hodgson, "Cognitive Versus Behavioral-Interpersonal Approaches to the Group Treatment of Depressed College Students," *Journal of Counseling Psychology* 28 (1981): 243–49.

51. J. Donovan, J. Bennett, and C. McElroy, "The Crisis Group: An Outcome Study," *American Journal of Psychiatry* 136 (1979): 906–10.

52. L. Kohl, D. Rinks, and J. Snarey, "Childhood Development as a Predictor of Adaptation in Adulthood," *Genetic Psychology Monographs* 110 (1984): 97–172. K. Kindler et al., "The Family History Method: Whose Psychiatric History Is Measured?" *American Journal of Psychiatry* 148 (1991): 1501–4. P. Chodoff, "A Critique of the Freudian Theory of Infantile Sexuality," *American Journal of Psychiatry* 123 (1966): 507–18. J. Kagan, "Perspectives on Continuity," in *Constancy and Change in Human Development,* ed. J. Kagan and O. Brim (Cambridge, Mass.: Harvard University Press, 1980). J. Kagan, *The Nature of the Child* (New York: Basic Books, 1984), 99–111.

53. E. Kandel, "A New Intellectual Framework for Psychiatry," *American Journal of Psychiatry* 155 (1998): 457–69.

54. P. Fonagy, H. Kachele, R. Krause, E. Jones, R. Perron, and L. Lopez, *"An Open Door Review of Outcome Studies in Psychoanalysis."* London: International Psychoanalytical Association, 1999.

CHAPTER 3

1. C. McRoberts, G. Burlingame, and M. Hoag, "Comparative Efficacy of Individual and Group Psychotherapy: A Meta-analytic Perspective," *Group Dynamics: Theory, Research, and Practice* 2 (1998): 101–17. W. McDermut, I. Miller, and R. Brown, "The Efficacy of Group Psychotherapy for Depression: A Meta-Analysis and Review of Empirical Research," *Clinical Psychology: Science and Practice* 8 (2001): 98–116. G. Burlingame, K. MacKenzie, and B. Strauss, "Small-Group Treatment: Evidence for Effectiveness and Mechanisms of Change," in *Bergin and Garfield's Handbook of Psychotherapy and Behavior Change,* 5th ed., ed. M. Lambert (New York: Wiley, 2004), 647–96. L. Luborsky, P. Crits-Christoph, J. Mintz, and A. Auerbach, *Who Will Benefit from Psychotherapy?* (New York:

Basic Books, 1988). H. Bachrach, R. Galantzer-Levy, A. Skolnikoff, and S. Waldron, "On the Efficacy of Psychoanalysis," *Journal of the American Psychoanalytic Association* 39 (1991): 871–916. L. Luborsky, L. Diguer, E. Luborsky, B. Singer, D. Dickter, and K. Schmidt, "The Efficacy of Dynamic Psychotherapy: Is It True That Everyone Has Won and All Must Have Prizes?" *Psychodynamic Treatment Research: A Handbook for Clinical Practice* (New York: Basic Books, 1993): 497–518. M. Lambert and A. Bergin, "The Effectiveness of Psychotherapy," in *Handbook of Psychotherapy and Behavioral Change: An Empirical Analysis,* 4th ed., ed. S. Garfield and A. Bergin (New York: Wiley, 1994), 143–89. M. Smith, G. Glass, and T. Miller, *The Benefits of Psychotherapy* (Baltimore: Johns Hopkins University Press, 1980). A. Bergin and M. Lambert, "The Evaluation of Therapeutic Outcomes," in *Handbook of Psychotherapy and Behavioral Change: An Empirical Analysis,* 2nd ed., ed. S. Garfield and A. Bergin (New York: Wiley, 1978), 139–83. R. Bednar and T. Kaul, "Experiential Group Research: Can the Canon Fire?" in Garfield and Bergin, *Handbook of Psychotherapy and Behavioral Change,* 4th ed., 631–63. C. Tillitski, "A Meta-Analysis of Estimated Effect Sizes for Group Versus Individual Versus Control Treatments," *International Journal of Group Psychotherapy* 40 (1990): 215–24. R. Toseland and M. Siporin, "When to Recommend Group Therapy: A Review of the Clinical and Research Literature," *International Journal of Group Psychotherapy* 36 (1986): 171–201.

2. W. McFarlane et al., "Multiple-Family Groups in Psychoeducation in the Treatment of Schizophrenia," *Archives of General Psychiatry* 52 (1996): 679–87. M. Galanter and D. Brook, "Network Therapy for Addiction: Bringing Family and Peer Support into Office Practice," *International Journal of Group Psychotherapy* 51 (2001): 101–23. F. Fawzy, N. Fawzy, and J. Wheeler, "A Post-Hoc Comparison of the Efficiency of a Psychoeducational Intervention for Melanoma Patients Delivered in Group Versus Individual Formats: An Analysis of Data from Two Studies," *Psycho-Oncology* 5 (1996): 81–89.

3. H. Strupp, S. Hadley, and B. Gomes-Schwartz, *Psychotherapy for Better or Worse: The Problem of Negative Effects* (New York: Jason Aronson, 1977). Lambert and Bergin, "Effectiveness of Psychotherapy," 176–80. Luborsky et al. raise a dissenting voice: In their study they found little evidence of negative psychotherapy effects. See *Who Will Benefit from Psychotherapy?* M. Lambert and B. Ogles, "The Efficacy and Effectiveness of Psychotherapy," in *Bergin and Garfield's Handbook of Psychotherapy and Behavior Change,* 5th ed., ed. M. Lambert (New York: Wiley, 2004): 139–93.

4. D. Martin, J. Garske, and M. Davis, "Relation of the Therapeutic Alliance with Outcome and Other Variables: A Meta-Analytic Review," *Journal of Consulting and Clinical Psychology* 68 (2000): 438–50. A. Horvath, L. Gaston, and L. Luborsky, "The Therapeutic Alliance and Its Measures," in *Dynamic Psychotherapy Research,* ed. N. Miller, L. Luborsky, and J. Docherty (New York: Basic Books, 1993): 297–373. L. Gaston, "The Concept of the Alliance and Its Role in Psychotherapy: Theoretical and Empirical Considerations," *Psychiatry* 27 (1990): 143–53.

5. J. Krupnick et al., "The Role of the Therapeutic Alliance in Psychotherapy and Pharmacotherapy Outcome: Findings in the National Institute of Mental Health Collaborative Research Program," *Journal of Consulting and Clinical Psychology* 64 (1996): 532–39. D. Orlinsky and K. Howard, "The Relation of Process to Outcome in Psychotherapy," in Garfield and Bergin, *Handbook of Psychotherapy and Behavioral Change,* 4th ed., 308–76. H. Strupp, R. Fox, and K. Lessler, *Patients View Their Psychotherapy* (Baltimore: Johns Hopkins University Press, 1969). P. Martin and A. Sterne, "Post-Hospital Adjustment as Related to Therapists' In-Therapy Behavior," *Psychotherapy: Theory, Research, and Practice* 13 (1976): 267–73. P. Buckley et al., "Psychodynamic Variables as Predictors of Psychotherapy Outcome," *American Journal of Psychiatry* 141 (1984): 742–48.

6. W. Meissner, "The Concept of the Therapeutic Alliance," *Journal of the American Psychoanalytic Association* 40 (1992): 1059–87. "Therapeutic alliance" is a term first used by Zetsel to describe the client's capacity to collaborate with her psychoanalyst in the tasks of psychoanalysis. The client's objectivity and commitment to explore and work

through the thoughts and feelings generated in the treatment are key aspects in this early definition. Contemporary views of the therapeutic alliance define it more specifically as the understanding shared between the client and therapist regarding the therapy's goals and the therapy's tasks, along with the mutuality of trust, respect, and positive regard that characterize a successful therapy experience. (Bordin; Safran and Muran) Wolfe and Goldfried view the therapeutic alliance as "the quintessential integrative variable." It lies at the heart of every effective mental health treatment, regardless of model or therapist orientation. E. Zetsel, "The Concept of the Transference," in *The Capacity for Emotional Growth* (New York: International Universities Press, 1956), 168–81. E. Bordin, "The Generalizability of the Psychoanalytic Concept of the Therapeutic Alliance," *Psychotherapy: Theory, Research, and Practice* 16 (1979): 252–60. J. Safran and J. Muran, *Negotiating the Therapeutic Alliance: A Relational Treatment Guide* (New York: Guilford Press, 2003). B. Wolfe and M. Goldfried, "Research on Psychotherapy Integration: Recommendations and Conclusions from an NIMH Workshop," *Journal of Consulting and Clinical Psychology* 56 (1988): 448–51.

7. A. Horvath and B. Symonds, "Relation Between Working Alliance and Outcome in Psychotherapy: A Meta-Analysis," *Journal of Consulting Psychology* 38 (1991): 139–49. F. Fiedler, "A Comparison of Therapeutic Relationships in Psychoanalytic, Non-directive, and Adlerian Therapy," *Journal of Consulting Psychology* 14 (1950): 436–45. M. Lieberman, I. Yalom, and M. Miles, *Encounter Groups: First Facts* (New York: Basic Books, 1973).

8. R. DeRubeis and M. Feeley, "Determinants of Change in Cognitive Therapy for Depression," *Cognitive Therapy and Research* 14 (1990): 469–80. B. Rounsaville et al., "The Relation Between Specific and General Dimension: The Psychotherapy Process in Interpersonal Therapy of Depression," *Journal of Consulting and Clinical Psychology* 55 (1987): 379–84. M. Salvio, L. Beutler, J. Wood, and D. Engle, "The Strength of the Therapeutic Alliance in Three Treatments for Depression," *Psychotherapy Research* 2 (1992): 31–36. N. Rector, D. Zuroff, and Z. Segal, "Cognitive Change and the Therapeutic Alliance: The Role of Technical and Non-technical Factors in Cognitive Therapy," *Psychotherapy* 36 (1999): 320–28.

9. J. Ablon and E. Jones, "Validity of Controlled Clinical Trials of Psychotherapy: Findings from the NIMH Treatment of Depression Collaborative Research Program," *American Journal of Psychiatry* 159 (2002): 775–83.

10. L. Castonguay, M. Goldfried, S. Wiser, P. Raus, and A. Hayes, "Predicting the Effect of Cognitive Therapy for Depression: A Study of Common and Unique Factors," *Journal of Consulting and Clinical Psychology* 65 (1996): 588–98. Rector et al., "Cognitive Change and the Therapeutic Alliance."

11. G. Burlingame, A. Fuhriman, and J. Johnson, "Cohesion in Group Psychotherapy," in *A Guide to Psychotherapy Relationships that Work*, ed. J. Norcross (Oxford, England: Oxford University Press, 2002). E. Smith, J. Murphy, and S. Coats, "Attachment to Groups: Theory and Measurement," *Journal of Personality and Social Psychology* 77 (1999): 94–110. D. Forsyth, "The Social Psychology of Groups and Group Psychotherapy: One View of the Next Century," *Group* 24 (2000): 147–55.

12. Bednar and Kaul, "Experiential Group Research."

13. S. Bloch and E. Crouch, *Therapeutic Factors in Group Psychotherapy* (New York: Oxford University Press, 1985), 99–103. N. Evans and P. Jarvis, "Group Cohesion: A Review and Reevaluation," *Small Group Behavior* 2 (1980): 359–70. S. Drescher, G. Burlingame, and A. Fuhriman, "Cohesion: An Odyssey in Empirical Understanding," *Small Group Behavior* 16 (1985): 3–30. G. Burlingame, J. Kircher, and S. Taylor, "Methodological Considerations in Group Therapy Research: Past, Present, and Future Practices," in *Handbook of Group Psychotherapy*, ed. A. Fuhriman and G. Burlingame (New York: Wiley, 1994): 41–82. G. Burlingame, J. Johnson, and K. MacKenzie, "We Know It When We See It, But Can We Measure? Therapeutic Relationship in Group," presented at the annual meeting of the American Group Psychotherapy Association, New Orleans, 2002.

14. D. Cartwright and A. Zander, eds., *Group Dynamics: Research and Theory* (Evanston, Ill.: Row, Peterson, 1962), 74.

15. J. Frank, "Some Determinants, Manifestations, and Effects of Cohesion in Therapy Groups," *International Journal of Group Psychotherapy* 7 (1957): 53–62.

16. Bloch and Crouch, "Therapeutic Factors."

17. Researchers either have had to depend on members' subjective ratings of attraction to the group or critical incidents or, more recently, have striven for greater precision by relying entirely on raters' evaluations of global climate or such variables as fragmentation versus cohesiveness, withdrawal versus involvement, mistrust versus trust, disruption versus cooperation, abusiveness versus expressed caring, unfocused versus focused. See S. Budman et al., "Preliminary Findings on a New Instrument to Measure Cohesion in Group Psychotherapy," *International Journal of Group Psychotherapy* 37 (1987): 75–94.

18. D. Kivlighan and D. Mullison, "Participants' Perceptions of Therapeutic Factors in Group Counseling," *Small Group Behavior* 19 (1988): 452–68. L. Braaten, "The Different Patterns of Group Climate: Critical Incidents in High and Low Cohesion Sessions of Group Psychotherapy," *International Journal of Group Psychotherapy* 40 (1990): 477–93.

19. D. Kivlighan and R. Lilly, "Developmental Changes in Group Climate as They Relate to Therapeutic Gain," *Group Dynamics: Theory, Research, and Practice* 1 (1997): 208–21. L. Castonguay, A. Pincus, W. Agras, and C. Hines, "The Role of Emotion in Group Cognitive-Behavioral Therapy for Binge Eating Disorder: When Things Have to Feel Worse Before They Get Better," *Psychotherapy Research* 8 (1998): 225–38.

20. R. MacKenzie and V. Tschuschke, "Relatedness, Group Work, and Outcome in Long-Term Inpatient Psychotherapy Groups," *Journal of Psychotherapy Practice and Research* 2 (1993): 147–56.

21. G. Tasca, C. Flynn, and H. Bissada, "Comparison of Group Climate in an Eating Disorders Partial Hospital Group and a Psychiatric Partial Hospital Group," *International Journal of Group Psychotherapy* 52 (2002): 419–30.

22. R. Segalla, "Hatred in Group Therapy: A Rewarding Challenge," *Group* 25 (2001): 121–32.

23. A. Roarck and H. Sharah, "Factors Related to Group Cohesiveness," *Small Group Behavior* 20 (1989): 62–69.

24. Frank, "Some Determinants." C. Marmarosh and J. Corazzini, "Putting the Group in Your Pocket: Using Collective Identity to Enhance Personal and Collective Self-Esteem," *Group Dynamics: Theory, Research, and Practice* 1 (1997): 65–74.

25. H. Grunebaum and L. Solomon, "Peer Relationships, Self-Esteem, and the Self," *International Journal of Group Psychotherapy* 37 (1987): 475–513.

26. Frank, "Some Determinants." Braaten, "The Different Patterns of Group Climate."

27. K. Dion, "Group Cohesion: From 'Field of Forces' to Multidimensional Construct," *Group Dynamics: Theory, Research, and Practice* 4 (2000): 7–26.

28. K. MacKenzie, "The Clinical Application of a Group Measure," in *Advances in Group Psychotherapy: Integrating Research and Practice*, ed. R. Dies and K. MacKenzie (New York: International Universities Press, 1983), 159–70. Tasca et al., "Comparison of Group Climate."

29. E. Marziali, H. Munroe-Blum, and L. McCleary, "The Contribution of Group Cohesion and Group Alliance to the Outcome of Group Psychotherapy," *International Journal of Group Psychotherapy* 47 (1997): 475–99. J. Gillaspy, A. Wright, C. Campbell, S. Stokes, and B. Adinoff, "Group Alliance and Cohesion as Predictors of Drug and Alcohol Abuse Treatment Outcomes," *Psychotherapy Research* 12 (2002): 213–29. G. Burlingame and colleagues have completed a comprehensive review of the current group relationship measures, describing the strengths and limitations of the available rating measures. See Burlingame et al., "We Know It When We See It."

30. H. Spitz, *Group Psychotherapy and Managed Mental Health Care: A Clinical Guide for Providers* (New York: Brunner Mazel, 1996). H. Spitz, "Group Psychotherapy of

Substance Abuse in the Era of Managed Mental Health Care," *International Journal of Group Psychotherapy* 51 (2001): 21–41.

31. H. Dickoff and M. Lakin, "Patients' Views of Group Psychotherapy: Retrospections and Interpretations," *International Journal of Group Psychotherapy* 13 (1963): 61–73. Twenty-eight patients who had been in either clinic or private outpatient groups were studied. The chief limitation of this exploratory inquiry is that the group therapy experience was of brief duration (the mean number of meetings attended was eleven).

32. I. Yalom, *The Theory and Practice of Group Psychotherapy*, 1st ed. (New York: Basic Books, 1970).

33. R. Cabral, J. Best, and A. Paton, "Patients' and Observers' Assessments of Process and Outcome in Group Therapy," *American Journal of Psychiatry* 132 (1975): 1052–54.

34. F. Kapp et al., "Group Participation and Self-Perceived Personality Change," *Journal of Nervous Mental Disorders* 139 (1964): 255–65.

35. I. Yalom et al., "Prediction of Improvement in Group Therapy," *Archives of General Psychiatry* 17 (1967): 159–68. Three measures of outcome (symptoms, functioning, and relationships) were assessed both in a psychiatric interview by a team of raters and in a self-assessment scale.

36. Cohesiveness was measured by a postgroup questionnaire filled out by each client at the seventh and the twelfth meetings, with each question answered on a 5-point scale:

 1. How often do you think your group should meet?
 2. How well do you like the group you are in?
 3. If most of the members of your group decided to dissolve the group by leaving, would you like an opportunity to dissuade them?
 4. Do you feel that working with the group you are in will enable you to attain most of your goals in therapy?
 5. If you could replace members of your group with other ideal group members, how many would you exchange (exclusive of group therapists)?
 6. To what degree do you feel that you are included by the group in the group's activities?
 7. How do you feel about your participation in, and contribution to, the group work?
 8. What do you feel about the length of the group meeting?
 9. How do you feel about the group therapist(s)?
 10. Are you ashamed of being in group therapy?
 11. Compared with other therapy groups, how well would you imagine your group works together?

37. I. Falloon, "Interpersonal Variables in Behavioral Group Therapy," *British Journal of Medical Psychology* 54 (1981): 133–41.

38. J. Clark and S. Culbert, "Mutually Therapeutic Perception and Self-Awareness in a T-Group," *Journal of Applied Behavioral Science* 1 (1965): 180–94.

39. Outcome was measured by a well-validated rating scale (designed by A. Walker, R. Rablen, and C. Rogers, "Development of a Scale to Measure Process Changes in Psychotherapy," *Journal of Clinical Psychology* 16 [1960]: 79–85) that measured change in one's ability to relate to others, to construe one's experience, to approach one's affective life, and to confront and cope with one's chief problem areas. Samples of each member's speech were independently rated on this scale by trained naive judges from taped excerpts early and late in the course of the group. Intermember relationships were measured by the Barrett-Lennard Relationship Inventory (G. Barrett-Lennard, "Dimensions of Therapist Response as Causal Factors in Therapeutic Change," *Psychological Monographs* 76, [43, Whole No. 562] [1962]), which provided a measure of how each member viewed each other member (and the therapist) in terms of "unconditional, positive regard, empathic understanding, and congruence."

40. Lieberman, Yalom, and Miles, *Encounter Groups*.

41. First, a critical incident questionnaire was used to ask each member, after each meeting, to describe the most significant event of that meeting. All events pertaining to group attraction, communion, belongingness, and so on were tabulated. Second, a cohesiveness questionnaire similar to the one described earlier (Yalom et al., "Prediction of Improvement") was administered early and late in the course of the group.

42. J. Hurley, "Affiliativeness and Outcome in Interpersonal Groups: Member and Leader Perspectives," *Psychotherapy* 26 (1989): 520–23.

43. MacKenzie and Tschuschke, "Relatedness, Group Work, and Outcome."

44. Budman et al., "Preliminary Findings on a New Instrument." Although this scale is based on the assumption that cohesiveness is multidimensional, results of a well-designed study of time-limited (fifteen sessions) therapy groups in fact supported cohesiveness as a single factor. Furthermore, an attempt to distinguish cohesiveness from alliance was also unsuccessful. The authors suggest that it may be especially critical for group leaders to attempt to develop a strong working alliance between group members during the first half hour of each group. S. Budman, S. Soldz, A. Demby, M. Feldstein, T. Springer, and M. Davis, "Cohesion, Alliance, and Outcome in Group Psychotherapy, *Psychiatry* 52 (1989): 339–50.

45. Marziali et al., "The Contribution of Group Cohesion."

46. Budman et al., "Preliminary Findings on a New Instrument."

47. D. Hope, R. Heimberg, H. Juster, and C. Turk, *Managing Social Anxiety: A Cognitive-Behavioral Therapy Approach* (San Antonio: Psychological Corp., 2001).

48. S. Woody and R. Adesky, "Therapeutic Alliance, Group Cohesion, and Homework Compliance During Cognitive-Behavioral Group Treatment of Social Phobia," *Behavior Therapy* 33 (2002): 5–27.

49. H. Sexton, "Exploring a Psychotherapeutic Change Sequence: Relating Process to Intersessional and Posttreatment Outcome," *Journal of Consulting and Clinical Psychology* 61 (1993): 128–36.

50. K. MacKenzie, R. Dies, E. Coche, J. Rutan, and W. Stone, "An Analysis of AGPA Institute Groups," *International Journal of Group Psychotherapy* 37 (1987): 55–74.

51. V. Tschuschke and R. Dies, "Intensive Analysis of Therapeutic Factors and Outcome in Long-Term Inpatient Groups," *International Journal of Group Psychotherapy* 44 (1994): 185–208.

52. Horvath and Symonds, "Relation Between Working Alliance and Outcome." Martin et al., "Relation of the Therapeutic Alliance with Outcome."

53. C. Rogers, "A Theory of Therapy, Personality, and Interpersonal Relationships," in *Psychology: A Study of a Science,* vol. 3, ed. S. Koch (New York: McGraw-Hill, 1959), 184–256.

54. F. Nietzsche, *Thus Spoke Zarathrusta*, trans. R. Hollingsdale (New York: Penguin Books, 1969).

55. K. Horney, *Neurosis and Human Growth* (New York: Norton, 1950), 15.

56. J. Weiss, *How Psychotherapy Works: Process and Technique* (New York: Guilford Press, 1993).

57. Rector et al., "Cognitive Change and the Therapeutic Alliance."

58. C. Truax, "The Process of Group Therapy: Relationships Between Hypothesized Therapeutic Conditions and Intrapersonal Exploration," *Psychological Monographs* 75 (5111 [1961]).

59. A. Walker, R. Rablen, and C. Rogers, "Development of a Scale to Measure Process Changes in Psychotherapy," *Journal of Clinical Psychology* 16 (1960): 79–85.

60. Roarck and Sharah, "Factors Related to Group Cohesiveness." Tschuschke and Dies, "Intensive Analysis."

61. A. Bandura, *Social Foundations of Thought and Action* (Englewood Cliffs, N.J.: Prentice Hall, 1986).

62. C. Rogers, personal communication, April 1967.

63. C. Rogers, "The Process of the Basic Encounter Group," unpublished mimeograph, Western Behavioral Science Institute, La Jolla, Calif., 1966.

64. P. Schlachet, "The Once and Future Group: Vicissitudes of Belonging," *Group* 24 (2000): 123–32.

65. I. Rubin, "The Reduction of Prejudice Through Laboratory Training," *Journal of Applied Behavioral Science* 3 (1967): 29–50. E. Fromm, *The Art of Loving* (New York: Bantam Books, 1956).

66. M. Leszcz, E. Feigenbaum, J. Sadavoy, and A. Robinson, "A Men's Group: Psychotherapy with Elderly Males," *International Journal of Group Psychotherapy* 35 (1985): 177–96.

67. D. Miller, "The Study of Social Relationships: Situation, Identity, and Social Interaction," in Koch, *Psychology: A Study of a Science* 3 (1983): 639–737.

68. H. Sullivan, *Conceptions of Modern Psychiatry* (London: Tavistock, 1955), 22.

69. Smith et al., "Attachment to Groups."

70. Miller, "Study of Social Relationships," 696.

71. E. Murray, "A Content Analysis for Study in Psychotherapy," *Psychological Monographs* 70 (13 [1956]).

72. R. DeRubeis and M. Feeley, "Determinants of Change in Cognitive Therapy for Depression," *Cognitive Therapy and Research* 14 (1990): 469–80. Rounsaville et al., "The Relation Between Specific and General Dimensions." J. Safran and L. Wallner, "The Relative Predictive Validity of Two Therapeutic Alliance Measures in Cognitive Therapy," *Psychological Assessment* 3 (1991): 188–95. Rector et al., "Cognitive Change."

73. Weiss, *How Psychotherapy Works*. P. Fretter, W. Bucci, J. Broitman, G. Silberschatz, and J. T. Curtis, "How the Patient's Plan Relates to the Concept of Transference," *Psychotherapy Research* 4 (1994): 58–72.

74. D. Lundgren and D. Miller, "Identity and Behavioral Change in Training Groups," *Human Relations Training News* 9 (Spring 1965).

75. Yalom et al., "Prediction of Improvement."

76. Before beginning therapy, the patients completed a modified Jourard self-disclosure questionnaire (S. Jourard, "Self-Disclosure Patterns in British and American College Females," *Journal of Social Psychology* 54 [1961]: 315–20). Individuals who had previously disclosed much of themselves (relevant to the other group members) to close friends or to groups of individuals were destined to become popular in their groups. Hurley demonstrated, in a ten-week counseling group, that popularity was correlated with self-disclosure in the group as well as prior to group therapy (S. Hurley, "Self-Disclosure in Small Counseling Groups," Ph.D. diss., Michigan State University, 1967).

77. Measured by the FIRO-B questionnaire (see chapter 10).

78. J. Connelly et al., "Premature Termination in Group Psychotherapy: Pretherapy and Early Therapy Predictors," *International Journal of Group Psychotherapy* 36 (1986): 145–52.

79. Ibid.

80. P. Costa and R. McCrae, *Revised NEO Personality Inventory and Five-Factor Inventory Professional Manual* (Odessa, Fla.: Psychological Assessment Services, 1992). The NEO-PI assesses five personality dimensions: extraversion, agreeableness, conscientiousness, neuroticism, and openness to experience.

81. C. Anderson, O. John, D. Keltner, and A. Kring, "Who Attains Social Status? Effects of Personality and Physical Attractiveness in Social Groups," *Journal of Personality and Social Psychology* 81 (2001): 116–32.

82. R. Depue, "A Neurobiological Framework for the Structure of Personality and Emotion: Implications for Personality Disorders," in *Major Theories of Personality Disorders*, ed. J. Clarkin and M. Lenzenweger (New York: Guilford Press, 1996), 342–90.

83. Lieberman, Yalom, and Miles, *Encounter Groups*.

84. G. Homans, *The Human Group* (New York: Harcourt, Brace, 1950).

85. Anderson et al., "Who Attains Social Status?"

86. Yalom et al., "Prediction of Improvement." I. Yalom, "A Study of Group Therapy Drop-Outs," *Archives of General Psychiatry* 14 (1966): 393–414.

87. E. Nash et al., "Some Factors Related to Patients Remaining in Group Psychotherapy," *International Journal of Group Psychotherapy* 7 (1957): 264–75.

88. Yalom, "A Study of Group Therapy Drop-Outs."

89. I. Yalom and K. Rand, "Compatibility and Cohesiveness in Therapy Groups," *Archives of General Psychiatry* 13 (1966): 267–76. P. Sagi, D. Olmstead, and F. Atalsek, "Predicting Maintenance of Membership in Small Groups," *Journal of Abnormal Social Psychology* 51 (1955): 308–11. In this study of twenty-three college student organizations, a significant correlation was noted between attendance and group cohesiveness. Yalom and Rand, "Compatibility and Cohesiveness." This study of cohesiveness, among forty members of five therapy groups found that the members who experienced little cohesion terminated within the first twelve meetings. Yalom et al., "Prediction of Improvement." J. Connelly et al., "Premature Termination." This study of sixty-six clients revealed that the twenty-two dropouts had less cohesiveness—they were less engaged, they perceived the group as less compatible and less supportive, and they were viewed less positively by other members. H. Roback and M. Smith, "Patient Attrition in Dynamically Oriented Treatment Groups," *American Journal of Psychiatry* 144 (1987): 165–77. Dropouts in this study reported that they felt less mutual understanding within the group. H. Roback, "Adverse Outcomes in Group Psychotherapy: Risk Factors, Prevention, and Research Directions," *Journal of Psychotherapy Practice and Research* 9 (2000): 113–22.

90. Lieberman, Yalom, and Miles, *Encounter Groups.*

91. I. Yalom, J. Tinklenberg, and M. Gilula, "Curative Factors in Group Therapy," unpublished study, Department of Psychiatry, Stanford University, 1968.

92. Braaten, "The Different Patterns of Group Climate." K. MacKenzie, "Time-Limited Theory and Technique," in *Group Therapy in Clinical Practice,* ed. A. Alonso and H. Swiller (Washington, D.C.: American Psychiatric Press, 1993).

93. M. Sherif et al., *Intergroup Conflict and Cooperation: The Robbers' Cave Experiment* (Norman: University of Oklahoma Book Exchange, 1961).

94. R. Baumeister and M. Leary, "The Need to Belong: Desire for Interpersonal attachments as a Fundamental Human Motivation," *Psychology Bulletin* 117 (1995): 497–529.

95. P. Evanson and R. Bednar, "Effects of Specific Cognitive and Behavioral Structure on Early Group Behavior and Atmosphere," *Journal of Counseling Psychology* 77 (1978): 258–62. F. Lee and R. Bednar, "Effects of Group Structure and Risk-Taking Disposition on Group Behavior, Attitudes, and Atmosphere," *Journal of Counseling Psychology* 24 (1977): 191–99. J. Stokes, "Toward an Understanding of Cohesion in Personal Change Groups," *International Journal of Group Psychotherapy* 33 (1983): 449–67.

96. A. Cota, C. Evans, K. Dion, L. Kilik, and R. Longman, "The Structure of Group Cohesion," *Personality and Social Psychology Bulletin* 21 (1995): 572–80. N. Evans and P. Jarvis, "Group Cohesion: A Review and Evaluation," *Small Group Behavior* 11 (1980): 357–70. S. Budge, "Group Cohesiveness Reexamined," *Group* 5 (1981): 10–18. Bednar and Kaul, "Experiential Group Research." E. Crouch, S. Bloch, and J. Wanless, "Therapeutic Factors: Intrapersonal and Interpersonal Mechanisms," in *Handbook of Group Psychotherapy,* ed. A. Fuhriman and G. Burlingame (New York: Wiley, 1994): 269–317.

97. Castonguay et al., "The Role of Emotion."

98. J. Frank, "Some Values of Conflict in Therapeutic Groups," *Group Psychotherapy* 8 (1955): 142–151.

99. I. Yalom *The Schopenhauer Cure,* (New York: HarperCollins, 2005) 175ff.

100. A study by Pepitone and Reichling offers experimental corroboration. Paid college students were divided into thirteen high-cohesion and thirteen low-cohesion laboratory task groups. Cohesion was created in the usual experimental manner: members of high-cohesion groups were told before their first meeting that their group had been composed

of individuals who had been carefully matched from psychological questionnaires to ensure maximum compatibility. The members of low-cohesion groups were given the opposite treatment and were told the matching was unsuccessful and they would probably not get along well together. The groups, while waiting for the experiment to begin, were systematically insulted by a member of the research team. After he had left, the members of the high-cohesive groups were significantly more able to express open and intense hostility about the authority figure (A. Pepitone and G. Reichling, "Group Cohesiveness and the Expression of Hostility," *Human Relations* 8 [1955]: 327–37).

101. S. Schiedlinger, "On Scapegoating in Group Psychotherapy," *International Journal of Group Psychotherapy* 32 (1982): 131–43.

102. T. Postmes, R. Spears, and S. Cihangir, "Quality of Decision Making and Group Norms," *Journal of Personality and Social Psychology* 80 (2001): 918–30.

103. I. Janis, *Groupthink: Psychological Studies of Policy Decisions and Fiascoes,* 2d ed. (Boston: Houghton Muffin, 1982), 9.

104. Postmes et al., "Quality of Decision Making."

105. G. Hodson and R. Sorrentino, "Groupthink and Uncertainty Orientation: Personality Differences in Reactivity to the Group Situation," *Group Dynamics: Theory, Research, and Practice* 1 (1997): 144–55.

106. These findings are strongly correlative—that is, cohesion and the reported group variables increase together at the same time. Although this does not establish a clear cause-and-effect relationship, it underscores the important relationship between cohesion and a large number of desired outcomes. Research on the therapeutic alliance in individual psychotherapy is relevant: there is a strong, enduring positive relationship between therapeutic alliance and outcome. This is a genuine finding; it is not an artifact of clients who endorse therapy strongly because of early change in their target symptoms. See Martin et al., "Relation of the Therapeutic Alliance with Outcome."

107. A. Goldstein, K. Heller, and L. Sechrest, *Psychotherapy and the Psychology of Behavior Change* (New York: Wiley, 1966).

108. Cartwright and Zander, "Group Cohesiveness: Introduction," in *Group Dynamics,* 69–74.

109. K. Back, "Influence Through Social Communication," *Journal of Abnormal Social Psychology* 46 (1951): 398–405.

110. G. Rasmussen and A. Zander, "Group Membership and Self-Evaluation," *Human Relations* 7 (1954): 239–51.

111. S. Seashore, "Group Cohesiveness in the Industrial Work Group," Monograph, Ann Arbor, Mich., Institute for Social Research, 1954.

112. Rasmussen and Zander, "Group Membership and Self-Evaluation." Goldstein et al., *Psychology of Behavior Change,* 329.

113. R. Kirschner, R. Dies, and R. Brown, "Effects of Experiential Manipulation of Self-Disclosure on Group Cohesiveness," *Journal of Consulting and Clinical Psychology* 46 (1978): 1171–77.

114. S. Schachter, "Deviation, Rejection, and Communication," *Journal of Abnormal Social Psychology* 46 (1951): 190–207. A. Zander and A. Havelin, "Social Comparison and Intergroup Attraction," cited in Cartwright and Zander, *Group Dynamics,* 94. A. Rich, "An Experimental Study of the Nature of Communication to a Deviate in High and Low Cohesive Groups," *Dissertation Abstracts* 29 (1968): 1976.

115. Goldstein et al., *Psychology of Behavior Change.* Schachter, "Deviation, Rejection, and Communication." These findings stem from experimentally composed groups and situations. As an illustration of the methodology used in these studies, consider an experiment by Schachter, who organized groups of paid volunteers to discuss a social problem—the correctional treatment of a juvenile delinquent with a long history of recidivism. In the manner described previously, several groups of low and high cohesiveness were formed, and paid confederates were introduced into each group who deliberately as-

sumed an extreme position on the topic under discussion. The content of the discussion, sociometric data, and other postgroup questionnaires were analyzed to determine, for example, the intensity of the efforts to influence the deviant and the degree of rejection of the deviant.

116. A. Fuerher and C. Keys, "Group Development in Self-Help Groups for College Students," *Small Group Behavior* 19 (1988): 325–41.

CHAPTER 4

1. B. Brown, T. Hedinger, G. Mieling, "A Homogeneous Group Approach to Social Skills Training for Individuals with Learning Disabilities," *Journal for Specialists in Group Work* 20 (1995): 98–107. D. Randall, "Curative Factor Rankings for Female Incest Survivor Groups: A Summary of Three Studies," *Journal of Specialists in Group Work* 20 (1995): 232–39. K. Card and L. Schmider, "Group Work with Members Who Have Hearing Impairments," *Journal for Specialists in Group Work* 20 (1995): 83–90. K. Kobak, A. Rock, and J. Greist, "Group Behavior Therapy for Obsessive-Compulsive Disorder," *Journal of Specialists in Group Work* 20 (1995): 26–32. G. Price, P. Dinas, C. Dunn, and C. Winterowd, "Group Work with Clients Experiencing Grieving: Moving from Theory to Practice," *Journal of Specialists in Group Work* 20 (1995): 159–67. J. DeLucia-Waack, "Multiculturalism Is Inherent in All Group Work," *Journal for Specialists in Group Work* 21 (1996): 218–23. J. McLeod and A. Ryan, "Therapeutic Factors Experienced by Members of an Outpatient Therapy Group for Older Women," *British Journal of Guidance and Counseling* 21 (1993): 64–72. I. Johnson, T. Torres, V. Coleman, and M. Smith, "Issues and Strategies in Leading Culturally Diverse Counseling Groups," *Journal for Specialists in Group Work* 20 (1995): 143–50. S. Bloch and E. Crouch, *Therapeutic Factors in Group Psychotherapy* (New York: Oxford University Press, 1985). E. Crouch, S. Bloch, and J. Wanless, "Therapeutic Factors: Intrapersonal and Interpersonal Mechanisms," in *Handbook of Group Psychotherapy,* ed. A. Fuhriman and G. Burlingame (New York: Wiley, 1994): 269–312. R. Rugel, "Addictions Treatment in Groups: A Review of Therapeutic Factors," *Small Group Research* 22 (1991): 475–91. W. Fawcett Hill, "Further Consideration of Therapeutic Mechanisms in Group Therapy," *Small Group Behavior* 6 (1975): 421–29. A. Fuhriman and T. Butler, "Curative Factors in Group Therapy: A Review of the Recent Literature," *Small Group Behavior* 14 (1983): 131–42. K. MacKenzie, "Therapeutic Factors in Group Psychotherapy: A Contemporary View," *Group* 11 (1987): 26–34. S. Bloch, R. Crouch, and J. Reibstein, "Therapeutic Factors in Group Psychotherapy," *Archives of General Psychiatry* 38 (1981): 519–26.

2. An alternative method of assessing therapeutic factors is the "critical incident" approach used by my colleagues and me in a large encounter group study (M. Lieberman, I. Yalom, and M. Miles, *Encounter Groups: First Facts* [New York: Basic Books, 1973]) and by Bloch and Crouch *(Therapeutic Factors in Group Psychotherapy).* In this method, clients are asked to recall the most critical event of the therapy session, and the responses are then coded by trained raters into appropriate categories. The following are examples of studies using critical incident methodology:R. Cabral, J. Best, and A. Paton, "Patients' and Observers' Assessments of Process and Outcome in Group Therapy: A Follow-up Study," *American Journal of Psychiatry* 132 (1975): 1052–54. R. Cabral and A. Paton, "Evaluation of Group Therapy: Correlations Between Clients' and Observers' Assessments," *British Journal of Psychiatry* 126 (1975): 475–77. S. Bloch and J. Reibstein, "Perceptions by Patients and Therapists of Therapeutic Factors in Group Psychotherapy," *British Journal of Psychiatry* 137 (1980): 274–78. D. Kivlighan and D. Mullison, "Participants' Perception of Therapeutic Factors in Group Counseling: The Role of Interpersonal Style and Stage of Group Development," *Small Group Behavior* 19 (1988): 452–68. D. Kivlighan and D. Goldfine, "Endorsement of Therapeutic Factors as a Function of Stage of Group Development and Participant Interpersonal Attitudes," *Journal of Counseling*

Psychology 38 (1991): 150–58. G. Mushet, G. Whalan, and R. Power, "In-patients' Views of the Helpful Aspects of Group Psychotherapy: Impact of Therapeutic Style and Treatment Setting," *British Journal of Medical Psychology* 62 (1989): 135–41.

3. K. Lese, R. McNair-Semands, "The Therapeutic Factor Inventory Development of a Scale," *Group* 24 (2000): 303–17.

4. R. Bednar and T. Kaul, "Experiential Group Research: Can the Canon Fire?" in *Handbook of Psychotherapy and Behavioral Change: An Empirical Analysis,* 4th ed., ed. S. Garfield and A. Bergin (New York: Wiley, 1994): 631–63.

5. H. Roback, "Experimental Comparison of Outcome in Insight and Non-Insight-Oriented Therapy Groups," *Journal of Consulting Psychology* 38 (1972): 411–17. J. Lomont et al., "Group Assertion Training and Group Insight Therapies," *Psychological Reports* 25 (1969): 463–70. S. Abramowitz and C. Abramowitz, "Psychological-Mindedness and Benefit from Insight-Oriented Group Therapy," *Archives of General Psychiatry* 30 (1974): 610–15. S. Abramowitz and C. Jackson, "Comparative Effectiveness of There-and-Then Versus Here-and-Now Therapist Interpretations in Group Psychotherapy," *Journal of Counseling Psychology* 21 (1974): 288–94.

6. W. Piper, A. Joyce, M. McCallum, and H. Azim, "Interpretive and Supportive Forms of Psychotherapy and Patient Personality Variables," *Journal of Consulting and Clinical Psychology* 66 (1998): 558–67. R. Wing and R. Jeffery, "Benefits of Recruiting Participants with Friends and Increasing Social Support for Weight Loss and Maintenance," *Journal of Consulting and Clinical Psychology* 67 (1999): 132–38.

7. B. Berzon, C. Pious, and R. Parson, "The Therapeutic Event in Group Psychotherapy: A Study of Subjective Reports by Group Members," *Journal of Individual Psychology* 19 (1963): 204–12. H. Dickoff and M. Lakin, "Patients' Views of Group Psychotherapy: Retrospections and Interpretations," *International Journal of Group Psychotherapy* 13 (1963): 61–73.

8. J. Reddon, L. Payne, and K. Starzyk, "Therapeutic Factors in Group Treatment Evaluated by Sex Offenders: A Consumers Report," *Journal of Offender Rehabilitation* 28 (1999): 91–101. A. Nerenberg, "The Value of Group Psychotherapy for Sexual Addicts," *Sexual Addiction and Compulsivity* 7 (2000): 197–200). R. Morgan and C. Winterowd, "Interpersonal Process-Oriented Group Psychotherapy with Offender Populations," *International Journal of Offender Therapy and Comparative Criminology* 46 (2002): 466–82.

9. K. Lese and R. McNair-Semands, "The Therapeutic Factors Inventory: Development of a Scale," *Group* 24 (2000): 303–17. I. Yalom, J. Tinklenberg, and M. Gilula, "Curative Factors in Group Therapy," unpublished study, Department of Psychiatry, Stanford University, 1968.

10. Spurred by the large data pool of the NIMH Treatment of Depression Collaborative Research Program, individual psychotherapy researchers have used a method similar to the Q-sort discussed in detail in this chapter: they developed a 100-item scale, the Psychotherapy Process Q Set (PQS), which is completed by trained raters evaluating session recordings at sessions 4 and 12 of a sixteen-session treatment. The PQS evaluates the therapy, therapist, and therapy relationship on a range of process criteria. Analysis of the 100 items produces a core of therapeutic factors. Successful therapies, both interpersonal therapy and cognitive-behavioral therapy, were similar in that in both treatments created a relationship in which clients developed a positive sense of self and very strong positive regard for their therapist (J. Ablon and E. Jones, "Psychotherapy Process in the National Institute of Mental Health Treatment of Depression Collaborative Research Program," *Journal of Consulting and Clinical Psychology* 67 (1999): 64–75). Lese and McNair-Semands ("The Therapeutic Factors Inventory") developed the group therapy Therapeutic Factors Inventory (TFI), a self-report instrument. The TFI, which builds on the original therapeutic factor Q-sort, demonstrates promise as a research tool with empirically acceptable levels of internal consistency and test-retest reliability.

11. Yalom et al., "Curative Factors in Group Therapy."

12. There were four checks to ensure that our sample was a successfully treated one: (1) the therapists' evaluation; (2) length of treatment (previous research in the same clinic demonstrated that group members who remained in therapy for that length of time had an extremely high rate of improvement [I. Yalom et al., "Prediction of Improvement in Group Therapy," *Archives of General Psychiatry* 17 (1967): 158–68]); (3) the investigators' independent interview ratings of improvement on a 13-point scale in four areas: symptoms, functioning, interpersonal relationships, and self-concept; and (4) the members' self-rating on the same scale.

13. S Freeman and J. Hurley, "Perceptions of Helpfulness and Behavior in Groups," *Group* 4 (1980): 51–58. M. Rohrbaugh and B. Bartels, "Participants' Perceptions of 'Curative Factors' in Therapy and Growth Groups," *Small Group Behavior* 6 (1975): 430–56. B. Corder, L. Whiteside, and T. Haizlip, "A Study of Curative Factors in Group Psychotherapy with Adolescents," *International Journal of Group Psychotherapy* 31 (1981): 345–54. P. Sullivan and S. Sawilowsky, "Yalom Factor Research: Threats to Internal Validity," presented at the American Group Psychotherapy Convention, San Diego, Calif., February 1993. M. Stone, C. Lewis, and A. Beck, "The Structure of Yalom's Curative Factor Scale," presented at the American Psychological Association Convention, Washington, D.C., 1992.

14. The number in each of the seven piles thus approaches a normal distribution curve and facilitates statistical assessment. For more about the Q-sort technique, see J. Block, *The Q-Sort Method in Personality Assessment and Psychiatric Research* (Springfield, Ill.: Charles C. Thomas, 1961).

15. Freedman and Hurley ("Perceptions of Helpfulness") studied twenty-eight subjects in three fifty-hour sensitivity-training groups. Seven of the ten items selected as most helpful by these subjects were among the ten I listed. The subjects in Freedman and Hurley's study placed three new items (21, 23, and 24 in table 4.1) into the top ten. These items are all interpersonal output items, and it is entirely consistent that members of a sensitivity group that explicitly focused on modifying interpersonal behavior should value these items. B. Corder, L. Whiteside, and T. Haizlip ("A Study of Curative Factors in Group Psychotherapy") studied sixteen adolescents from four different groups in different clinical settings, both outpatient and inpatient. The youths did not highly value the adults' top ranked item (insight), but their next four highest items were identical to those the adults had chosen. Overall, they valued the therapeutic factors of universality and cohesiveness more highly than did adults. R. Marcovitz and J. Smith ("Patients' Perceptions of Curative Factors in Short-Term Group Psychotherapy," *International Journal of Group Psychotherapy* 33 [1983]: 21–37) studied thirty high-functioning inpatients who attended group psychotherapy in a psychiatric hospital. Only three of the top ten items in their study corresponded to our results, but their method was different: they asked patients to rate items from 1 to 60, rather than the Q-sort technique of sorting into piles from most helpful to least helpful. Their subjects' top selected item was item 60 *(Ultimately taking responsibility for my own life)*. When condensed into the rankings of overall therapeutic factors, their results were quite similar to ours, with five of the top six factors the same; their subjects ranked altruism third, notably higher than the outpatient sample did. M. Rohrbaugh and B. Bartels ("Participants' Perceptions of 'Curative Factors'") studied seventy-two individuals in both psychiatric settings and growth groups. Their results were also consistent with our original Q-sort study: interpersonal learning (both input and output), catharsis, cohesiveness, and insight were the most valued factors, and guidance, family reenactment, and identification were least valued.

16. M. Weiner, "Genetic Versus Interpersonal Insight," *International Journal of Group Psychotherapy* 24 (1974): 230–37. Rohrbaugh and Bartels, "Participants' Perceptions." T. Butler and A. Fuhriman, "Patient Perspective on the Curative Process: A Comparison of Day Treatment and Outpatient Psychotherapy Groups," *Small Group Behavior* 11 (1980): 371–88. T. Butler and A. Fuhriman, "Level of Functioning and Length of Time in Treatment: Variables Influencing Patients' Therapeutic Experience in Group Therapy," *International*

Journal of Group Psychotherapy 33 (1983): 489–504. L. Long and C. Cope, "Curative Factors in a Male Felony Offender Group," *Small Group Behavior* 11 (1980): 389–98. Kivlighan and Mullison, "Participants' Perception of Therapeutic Factors." S. Colijn, E. Hoencamp, H. Snijders, M. Van Der Spek, and H. Duivenvoorden, "A Comparison of Curative Factors in Different Types of Group Psychotherapy," *International Journal of Group Psychotherapy* 41 (1991): 365–78. V. Brabender, E. Albrecht, J. Sillitti, J. Cooper, and E. Kramer, "A Study of Curative Factors in Short-Term Group Therapy," *Hospital and Community Psychiatry* 34 (1993): 643–44. M. Hobbs, S. Birtchnall, A. Harte, and H. Lacey, "Therapeutic Factors in Short-Term Group Therapy for Women with Bulimia," *International Journal of Eating Disorders* 8 (1989): 623–33. R. Kapur, K. Miller, and G. Mitchell, "Therapeutic Factors Within Inpatient and Outpatient Psychotherapy Groups," *British Journal of Psychiatry* 152 (1988): 229–33. I. Wheeler, K. O'Malley, M. Waldo, and J. Murphy, "Participants' Perception of Therapeutic Factors in Groups for Incest Survivors," *Journal for Specialists in Group Work* 17 (1992): 89–95. Many of these studies (and the personal-growth therapeutic factor studies and inpatient group studies discussed later) do not use the sixty-item Q-sort but use instead an abbreviated instrument based on it. Generally, the instrument consists of twelve statements, each describing one of the therapeutic factors, which patients are asked to rank-order. Some studies use the critical incident method described in note 2. In the Lieberman, Yalom, and Miles encounter group study *(Encounter Groups)*, the most important factors involved expression of a feeling (both positive and negative) to another person, attainment of insight, vicarious therapy, and responding with strong positive and/or negative feelings. In the Bloch and Reibstein study ("Perceptions by Patients and Therapists"), the most valued factors were self-understanding, self-disclosure (which includes some elements of catharsis and interpersonal learning on other tests), and learning from interpersonal actions. Although the structure of the categories is different, the findings of these projects are consistent with the studies of the therapeutic factor in the abbreviated Q-sort.

17. Lieberman, Yalom, and Miles, *Encounter Groups*. S. Freedman and J. Hurley, "Maslow's Needs: Individuals' Perceptions of Helpful Factors in Growth Groups," *Small Group Behavior* 10 (1979): 355–67. Freedman and Hurley, "Perceptions of Helpfulness." Kivlighan and Goldfine, "Endorsement of Therapeutic Factors."

18. MacKenzie, "Therapeutic Factors in Group Psychotherapy."

19. Stone et al., "The Structure of Yalom's Curative Factor Scale."

20. S. Holmes and D. Kivlighan, "Comparison of Therapeutic Factors in Group and Individual Treatment Process," *Journal of Counseling Psychology* 47 (2000): 478–84.

21. A. Fuhriman and G. Burlingame, "Consistency of Matter: A Comparison Analysis of Individual and Group Process Variables," *Counseling Psychologist* 18 (1990): 6–63. Holmes and Kivlighan, "Comparison of Therapeutic Factors."

22. J. Breuer and S. Freud, *Studies on Hysteria* (New York: Basic Books, 2000).

23. Lieberman, Yalom, and Miles, *Encounter Groups*.

24. Bloch and Crouch suggest "purifying" the factor of catharsis. They separate out the acquisition of the skill of being emotionally expressive and include it in another therapeutic factor, "learning from interpersonal action." Furthermore, they split off the expression of bothersome ideas into a separate category, "self-disclosure." Cleared of these, catharsis is left with only "emotional release," which I think has the advantage of greater consistency yet becomes separated from any clinical reality, since emotional expression in the group cannot help but have far-reaching interpersonal ramifications. See Crouch, Bloch and Wauless, "Therapeutic Factors: Intrapersonal and Interpersonal Mechanisms."

25. Freedman and Hurley, "Perceptions of Helpfulness."

26. M. McCallum, W. Piper, and H. Morin, "Affect and Outcome in Short-Term Group Therapy for Loss," *International Journal of Group Psychotherapy* 43 (1993): 303–19.

27. A. Stanton et al., "Emotionally Expressive Coping Predicts Psychological and Physical Adjustment to Breast Cancer," *Journal of Consulting and Clinical Psychology* 68 (2000): 875–72.

28. J. Bower, M. Kemeny, S. Taylor, and J. Fahey, "Cognitive Processing, Discovery of Meaning, CD4 Decline, and AIDS-Related Mortality Among Bereaved HIV-Seropositive Men," *Journal of Consulting and Clinical Psychology* 66 (1998): 979–86.

29. Rohrbaugh and Bartels, "Participants' Perceptions."

30. J. Flowers and C. Booraem, "The Frequency and Effect on Outcome of Different Types of Interpretation in Psychodynamic and Cognitive-Behavioral Group Psychotherapy," *International Journal of Group Psychotherapy* 40: 203–14.

31. A. Maslow, "The Need to Know and the Fear of Knowing," *Journal of General Psychology* 68 (1963): 111–25.

32. J. Weiss, *How Psychotherapy Works: Process and Technique* (New York: Guilford Press, 1993).

33. A. Maslow, *Motivation and Personality* (New York: Harper, 1954).

34. D. Hellerstein, R. Rosenthal, H. Pinsker, L. Samstag, J. Muran, and A. Winston, "A Randomized Prospective Study Comparing Supportive and Dynamic Therapies: Outcome and Alliance," *Journal of Psychotherapy Practice and Research* 7 (1998): 261–71.

35. Maslow, "The Need to Know."

36. R. White, "Motivation Reconsidered: The Concept of Competence," *Psychological Review* 66 (1959): 297–333.

37. Dibner exposed forty psychiatric patients to a psychiatric interview after dividing them into two experimental conditions. Half were prepared for the interview and given cues about how they should, in a general way, conduct themselves; the other half were given no such cues (a high-ambiguity situation). During the interview, the subjects in the high-ambiguity situation experienced far greater anxiety as measured by subjective, objective, and physiological techniques (A. Dibner, "Ambiguity and Anxiety," *Journal of Abnormal Social Psychology* 56 [1958]: 165–74).

38. L. Postman and J. Brunner, "Perception Under Stress," *Psychological Review* 55 (1948): 314–23.

39. S. Korchin et al., "Experience of Perceptual Distortion as a Source of Anxiety," *Archives of Neurology and Psychiatry* 80 (1958): 98–113.

40. Maslow, "The Need to Know."

41. B. McEwen, "Protective and Damaging Effects of Stress Mediators," *New England Journal of Medicine* 38 (1998): 171–79. B. McEwen and T. Seeman, "Protective and Damaging Effects of Mediators of Stress: Elaborating and Testing the Concepts of Allostasis and Allostatic Load," *Annals of the New York Academy of Sciences* 896 (1999): 30–47.

42. F. Fawzy, N. Fawzy, and J. Wheeler, "A Post-Hoc Comparison of the Efficiency of a Psychoeducational Intervention for Melanoma Patients Delivered in Group Versus Individual Formats: An Analysis of Data from Two Studies," *Psycho-Oncology* 5 (1996): 81–89. K. Lorig et al., "Evidence Suggesting That a Chronic Disease Self-Management Program Can Improve Health Status While Reducing Hospitalization: A Randomized Trial," *Medical Care* 37 (1999): 5–14.

43. F. Wright, "Being Seen, Moved, Disrupted, and Reconfigured: Group Leadership from a Relational Perspective," *International Journal of Group Psychotherapy* 54 (2004): 235–50.

44. J. Ablon and E. Jones, "Psychotherapy Process in the National Institute of Mental Health Treatment of Depression Collaborative Research Program," *Journal of Consulting and Clinical Psychology* 67 (1999): 64–75. D. Rosenthal, "Changes in Some Moral Values Following Psychotherapy," *Journal of Consulting Psychology* 19 (1955): 431–36.

45. Colijn et al., "A Comparison of Curative Factors."

46. D. Randall, "Curative Factor Ratings for Female Incest Survivor Groups: A Summary of Three Studies," *Journal for Specialists in Group Work* 20 (1995): 232–39.

47. Reddon et al., "Therapeutic Factors in Group Treatment.

48. M. Leszcz, I. Yalom, and M. Norden, "The Value of Inpatient Group Psychotherapy and Therapeutic Process: Patients' Perceptions," *International Journal of Group*

Psychotherapy 35 (1985): 331–54. R. Rugal and D. Barry, "Overcoming Denial Through the Group," *Small Group Research* 21 (1990): 45–58. G. Steinfeld and J. Mabli, "Perceived Curative Factors in Group Therapy by Residents of a Therapeutic Community," *Criminal Justice and Behavior* 1 (1974): 278–88. Butler and Fuhriman, "Patient Perspective on the Curative Process." J. Schaffer and S. Dreyer, "Staff and Inpatient Perceptions of Change Mechanisms in Group Psychotherapy," *American Journal of Psychiatry* 139 (1982): 127–28. Kapur et al., "Therapeutic Factors Within Inpatient and Outpatient Psychotherapy Groups." J. MacDevitt and C. Sanislow, "Curative Factors in Offenders' Groups," *Small Group Behavior* 18 (1987): 72–81.

49. M. Leszcz and P. Goodwin, "The Rationale and Foundations of Group Psychotherapy for Women with Metastatic Breast Cancer," *International Journal of Group Psychotherapy* 48 (1998): 245–74. M. Greenstein and W. Breitbart, "Cancer and the Experience of Meaning: A Group Psychotherapy Program for People with Cancer," *American Journal of Psychotherapy* 54 (2000): 486–500. D. Spiegel and C. Classen, *Group Therapy for Cancer Patients* (New York: Basic Books, 2000).

50. McLeod and Ryan, "Therapeutic Factors Experienced by Members."

51. L. Lovett and J. Lovett, "Group Therapeutic Factors on an Alcohol In-patient Unit," *British Journal of Psychiatry* 159 (1991): 365–70.

52. R. Morgan, S. Ferrell, and C. Winterowd, "Therapist Perceptions of Important Therapeutic Factors in Psychotherapy of Therapy Groups for Male Inmates in State Correctional Facilities," *Small Group Research* 30 (1999): 712–29.

53. J. Prochaska and J. Norcross, "Contemporary Psychotherapists: A National Survey of Characteristics, Practices, Orientations, and Attitudes," *Psychotherapy: Theory, Research, and Practice* 20 (1983): 161–73.

54. R. Dies, "Models of Group Therapy: Sifting Through Confusion," *International Journal of Group Psychotherapy* 42 (1992): 1–17.

55. It is noteworthy that my book, *The Gift of Therapy,* (New York: HarperCollins, 2002) which offers eighty-five existential tips for therapy had a wide readership stemming from all the various therapy ideological schools.

56. S. Mitchell, *Hope and Dread in Psychoanalysis* (New York: Basic Books, 1993). S. Mitchell and M. Black, *Freud and Beyond: A History of Modern Psychoanalytic Thought* (New York: Basic Books, 1995).

57. E. Jones, *The Life and Work of Sigmund Freud,* vol. 1 (New York: Basic Books, 1953), 40.

58. I. Yalom, *Existential Psychotherapy* (New York: Basic Books, 1980).

59. I. Yalom, *Love's Executioner* (New York: Basic Books, 1989).

60. I. Yalom, *When Nietzsche Wept* (New York: Basic Books, 1992).

61. I. Yalom, *The Gift of Therapy* (New York: HarperCollins, 2002).

62. I. Yalom, *Momma and the Meaning of Life* (New York: Basic Books, 1999).

63. I. Yalom, *The Schopenhauer Cure* (New York: HarperCollins, 2005).

64. R. Tedeschi, L. Calhoun, "The Posttraumatic Growth Inventory: Measuring the Positive Legacy of Trauma," *Journal of Traumatic Stress* 9 (1996): 455–71.

65. M. Antoni et al., "Cognitive-Behavioral Stress Management Intervention Decreases Prevalence of Depression and Enhances Benefit Finding Among Women Under Treatment for Early-Stage Breast Cancer," *Health Psychology* 20 (2001): 20–32.

66. D. Cruess et al., "Cognitive-Behavioral Stress Management Reduces Serum Cortisol by Enhancing Benefit Finding Among Women Treated for Early Stage Breast Cancer," *Psychosomatic Medicine* 62 (2000): 304–8.

67. I. Yalom and C. Greaves, "Group Therapy with the Terminally Ill," *American Journal of Psychiatry* 134 (1977): 396–400. Bower et al., "Cognitive Processing, Discovery of Meaning, CD4 Decline." P. Goodwin et al., "The Effect of Group Psychosocial Support on Survival in Metastatic Breast Cancer," *New England Journal of Medicine* 345 (2001): 1719–26.

68. E. Fromm, *Escape from Freedom* (New York: Henry Holt, 1995).

69. M. Heidegger, *Being and Time* (New York: Harper & Row, 1962), 210–24.

70. J. Sartre, *Being and Nothingness,* trans. Hazel Barnes (New York: Philosophical Library, 1956), 633.

71. K. Jaspers, cited in J. Choron, *Death and Western Thought* (New York: Collier Books, 1963), 226.

72. Yalom and Greaves, "Group Therapy with the Terminally Ill."

73. Bower et al., "Cognitive Processing, Discovery of Meaning, CD4 Decline."

74. F. Nietzsche, *Twilight of the Idols* (London: Penguin Books, 1968), 33. Yalom, *The Gift of Therapy.*

75. D. Spiegel, J. Bloom, and I. Yalom, "Group Support for Patients with Metastatic Cancer," *Archives of General Psychiatry* 38 (May 1981): 527–34. I. Yalom, *Existential Psychotherapy* (New York: Basic Books, 1980), 36–37.

76. A. Schopenhauer, in *Complete Essays of Schopenhauer,* trans. T. Saunders, Book 5 (New York: Wiley, 1942), 18.

77. In a widely cited report, R. Corsini and B. Rosenberg ("Mechanisms of Group Psychotherapy: Processes and Dynamics," *Journal of Abnormal Social Psychology* 51 [1955]: 406–11) abstracted the therapeutic factors from 300 pre-1955 group therapy articles; 175 factors were clustered into nine major categories, which show considerable overlap with the factors I have described. Their categories, and my analogous categories in parentheses, are:

1. Acceptance (group cohesiveness)
2. Universalization (universality)
3. Reality testing (includes elements of recapitulation of the primary family and of interpersonal learning)
4. Altruism
5. Transference (includes elements of interpersonal learning, group cohesiveness, and imitative behavior)
6. Spectator therapy (imitative behavior)
7. Interaction (includes elements of interpersonal learning and cohesiveness)
8. Intellectualization (includes elements of imparting information)
9. Ventilation (catharsis)

W. Hill, in 1957, interviewed nineteen group therapists and offered these therapeutic factors: catharsis, feelings of belongingness, spectator therapy, insight, peer agency (that is, universality), and socialization (W. Hill, "Analysis of Interviews of Group Therapists' Papers," *Provo Papers* 1 [1957], and "Further Consideration of Therapeutic Mechanisms in Group Therapy," *Small Group Behavior* 6 [1975]: 421–29).

78. Fiedler's study, described in chapter 3, indicates that experts, regardless of their school of conviction, closely resemble one another in the nature of their relationship with patients (F. Fiedler, "A Comparison of Therapeutic Relationships in Psychoanalytic, Nondirective, and Adlerian Therapy," *Journal of Consulting Psychology* 14 (1950): 436–45. Truax and Carkhuff's work, also discussed in chapter 3 (C. Truax and R. Carkhuff, *Toward Effective Counseling and Psychotherapy* [Chicago: Aldine, 1967]), and the Ablon and Jones analysis of the NIMH depression trial provide further evidence that effective therapists operate similarly in that they establish a warm, accepting, understanding relationship with their clients (Ablon and Jones, "Psychotherapy Process in the National Institute of Mental Health," and J. Ablon and E. Jones, "Validity of Controlled Clinical Trials of Psychotherapy: Findings from the NIMH Treatment of Depression Collaborative Research Program," *American Journal of Psychiatry* 159 [2002]: 775–83). Strupp, Fox, and Lessler, in a study of 166 patients in individual therapy, reached a similar conclusion: successful patients underscored the fact that their therapists were attentive, warm, respectful, and, above all, human (H. Strupp, R. Fox, and K. Lessler, *Patients View Their Psychotherapy* (Baltimore: Johns Hopkins University Press, 1969). A comprehensive

review of the rapidly accumulating research in this area reveals that therapist qualities of acceptance, nonpossessive warmth, and positive regard are strongly associated with successful outcomes. See H. Conte, R. Ratto, K. Clutz, and T. Karasu, "Determinants of Outpatients' Satisfactions with Therapists: Relation to Outcome," *Journal of Psychotherapy Practice and Research* 4 (1995): 43–51; L. Alexander, J. Barber, L. Luborsky, P. Crits-Christoph, and A. Auerbach, "On What Bases Do Patients Choose Their Therapists," *Journal of Psychotherapy Practice and Research* 2 (1993): 135–46; S. Garfield, "Research on Client Variables in Psychotherapy," in *Handbook of Psychotherapy and Behavior Change,* 4th ed., ed. A. Bergin and S. Garfield (New York: Wiley, 1994), 190–228; M. Lambert, "The Individual Therapist's Contribution to Psychotherapy Process and Outcome," *Clinical Psychology Review* 9 (1989): 469–85; S. Butler, L. Flather, and H. Strupp, "Countertransference and Qualities of the Psychotherapist," in *Psychodynamic Treatment Research: A Handbook for Clinical Practice,* ed. N. Miller, L. Luborsky, J. Barber, and J. Docherty (New York: Basic Books, 1993), 342–60; and S. Van Wagoner, C. Gelso, T. Hayes, and R. Diemer, "Countertransference and the Reputedly Excellent Therapist," *Psychotherapy* 28 (1991): 411–21. Furthermore, as reviewed in chapter 3, the link between a positive therapeutic bond and favorable outcome is one of the most consistent and certain findings in all of psychotherapy research. These conclusions regarding therapist contributions to successful psychotherapy are so well established that they have been incorporated in professional practice psychotherapy guidelines (K. MacKenzie et al., "Guidelines for the Psychotherapies in Comprehensive Psychiatric Care: A Discussion Paper," *Canadian Journal of Psychiatry* 44 (suppl 1)(1999): 4S–17S).

79. Schaffer and Dreyer, "Staff and Inpatient Perceptions."

80. Lovett and Lovett, "Group Therapeutic Factors."

81. M. Lee, L. Cohen, S. Hadley, and F. Goodwin, "Cognitive Behavioral Group Therapy with Medication for Depressed Gay Men with AIDS or Symptomatic HIV Infection," *Psychiatric Services* 58 (1999): 948–52.

82. R. Morgan and C. Winterowd, "Interpersonal Process-Oriented Group Psychotherapy with Offender Populations," *International Journal of Offender Therapy and Comparative Criminology* 46 (2002): 466–82. Morgan et al., "Therapist Perceptions of Important Therapeutic Factors." J. MacDevitt and C. Sanislow, "Curative Factors in Offenders' Groups," *Small Group Behavior* 18 (1987): 72–81.

83. D. Randall, "Curative Factor Rankings for Female Incest Survivor Groups: A Summary of Three Studies," *Journal of Specialists in Group Work* 20 (1995): 232–39.

84. H. Feifel and J. Eells, "Patients and Therapists Assess the Same Psychotherapy," *Journal of Consulting Psychology* 27 (1963): 310–18.

85. I. Yalom and G. Elkin, *Every Day Gets a Little Closer: A Twice-Told Therapy* (New York: Basic Books, 1975; reissued 1992).

86. D. Orlinsky, K. Grawe, and B. Parks, "Process and Outcome in Psychotherapy," in *Handbook of Psychotherapy and Behavioral Change: An Empirical Analysis,* 4th ed., ed. S. Garfield and A. Bergin (New York: Wiley, 1994): 270–370. D. Martin, J. Garske, and M. Davis, "Relation of the Therapeutic Alliance with Outcome and Other Variables: A Meta-Analytic Review," *Journal of Consulting and Clinical Psychology* 68 (2000): 438–50.

87. Colijn et al., "A Comparison of Curative Factors." M. Kahn, P. Webster, and M. Storck, "Curative Factors in Two Types of Inpatient Psychotherapy Groups," *International Journal of Group Psychotherapy* 36 (1986): 579–85. Kapur et al., "Therapeutic Factors Within Inpatient and Outpatient Psychotherapy Groups." V. Tschuschke and R. Dies, "Intensive Analysis of Therapeutic and Outcome in Long-Term Inpatient Groups," *International Journal of Group Psychotherapy* 44 (1994): 185–208. J. Maxmen and N. Hannover, "Group Therapy as Viewed by Hospitalized Patients," *Archives of General Psychiatry* 28 (1973): 404–8. Steinfeld and Mabli, "Perceived Curative Factors." Butler and Fuhriman, "Patient Perspective on the Curative Process." N. Macaskill, "Therapeutic Factors in Group Therapy with Borderline Patients," *International Journal of Group*

Psychotherapy 32 (1982): 61–73. Leszcz et al., "The Value of Inpatient Group Psychotherapy." Marcovitz and Smith, "Patients' Perceptions of Curative Factors." Schaffer and Dreyer, "Staff and Inpatient Perceptions."Mushet et al., "In-patients' Views of the Helpful Aspects."

88. Marcovitz and Smith, "Patients' Perceptions of Curative Factors."

89. J. Falk-Kessler, C. Momich, and S. Perel, "Therapeutic Factors in Occupational Therapy Groups," *American Journal of Occupational Therapy* 45 (1991): 59–66.

90. P. Kellerman, "Participants' Perceptions of Therapeutic Factors in Psychodrama," *Journal of Group Psychotherapy, Psychodrama, and Sociometry* 38 (1985): 123–32.

91. M. Lieberman and L. Borman, *Self-Help Groups for Coping with Crisis* (San Francisco: Jossey-Bass, 1979), 202–5.

92. S. Horowitz, S. Passik, and M. Malkin, "In Sickness and in Health: A Group Intervention for Spouses Caring for Patients with Brain Tumors," *Journal of Psychosocial Oncology* 14 (1996): 43–56.

93. P. Chadwick, S. Sambrooke, S. Rasch, and E. Davies, "Challenging the Omnipotence of Voices: Group Cognitive Behavior Therapy for Voices," *Behavior Research and Therapy* 38 (2000): 993–1003.

94. E. Pence and M. Paymar, *Power and Control: Tactics of Men Who Batter*, rev. ed. (Duluth: Minnesota Program Development, 1990).

95. F. Mishna, "In Their Own Words: Therapeutic Factors for Adolescents Who Have Learning Disabilities," *International Journal of Group Psychotherapy* 46 (1996): 265–72.

96. McLeod and Ryan, "Therapeutic Factors Experienced by Members."

97. H. Riess, "Integrative Time-Limited Group Therapy for Bulimia Nervosa," *International Journal of Group Psychotherapy* 52 (2002): 1–26.

98. Kivlighan, Goldfine, "Endorsement of Therapeutic Factor."

99. Tschuschke and Dies, "Intensive Analysis of Therapeutic Factors and Outcome."V. Tschuchke, K. MacKenzie, B. Nasser, and G. Janke, "Self-Disclosure, Feedback, and Outcome in Long-Term Inpatient Psychotherapy Groups," *Journal of Psychotherapy Practice and Research* 5 (1996): 35–44.

100. Fuhriman and Butler, "Curative Factors in Group Therapy."

101. Kivlighan and Mullison, "Participants' Perception of Therapeutic Factors."

102. Kivlighan and Goldfine, "Endorsement of Therapeutic Factors."

103. J. Schwartz and M. Waldo, "Therapeutic Factors in Spouse-Abuse Group Treatment," *Journal for Specialists in Group Work* 24 (1999): 197–207.

104. Mushet et al., "In-patients' Views of the Helpful Aspects."

105. Yalom et al., "Curative Factors in Group Therapy."

106. Lieberman, Yalom, and Miles, *Encounter Groups*.

107. Butler and Fuhriman, "Level of Functioning and Length of Time in Treatment."

108. Leszcz et al., "The Value of Inpatient Group Psychotherapy."

109. Encounter group "high learners" valued vicarious learning: they had the ability to learn from the work of others (Lieberman, Yalom, and Miles, *Encounter Groups*). Clients who are dominant interpersonally discount interpersonal feedback and altruism and are less open to group influence, and clients who are overly responsible appear to discount cohesion and value altruism, suggesting that they feel burdened by others' needs yet compelled to help (R. MacNair-Semands and K. Lese, "Interpersonal Problem and the Perception of Therapeutic Factors in Group Therapy," *Small Group Research* 31 [2002]: 158–79). High self/other acceptors tended to value deeper insight into their interpersonal relations and into their family structure, whereas low self/other acceptors placed more value on universality and advice/guidance from members and leaders. Highly affiliative students in time-limited counseling groups gained more through self-understanding, whereas the nonaffiliative members benefited more from interpersonal learning, self-disclosure, and altruism (Kivlighan and Mullison, "Participants' Perception of Therapeutic Factors"; Kivlighan and Goldfine, "Endorsement of Therapeutic Factors").

CHAPTER 5

1. T. Postmes, R. Spears, S. Cihangir, "Quality of Decision Making and Group Norms." *Journal of Personality and Social Psychology*, 80(2001): 918–30.

2. D. Shapiro and L. Birk, "Group Therapy in Experimental Perspective," *International Journal of Group Psychotherapy* 17 (1967): 211–24.

3. E. Coche, R. Dies, and K. Goettelman, "Process Variables Mediating Change in Intensive Group Therapy Training," *International Journal of Group Psychotherapy* 41 (1991): 379–97.

4. D. Kivlighan, J. Tarrant, "Does Group Climate Mediate the Group Leadership–Group Member Outcome Relationship? A Test of Yalom's Hypothesis About Leadership Priorities," *Group Dynamics: Theory, Research, and Practice* 3 (2001): 220–34.

5. D. Strassberg, H. Roback, K. Anchor, S. Abramowitz, "Self-Disclosure in Group Therapy with Schizophrenics," *Archives of General Psychiatry* 32 (1975): 1259–61.

6. Shapiro and Birk, "Group Therapy in Experimental Perspective." See also R. Nye, *The Legacy of B. F. Skinner* (Pacific Grove, Calif.: Brooks Cole, 1992).

7. I. Goldfarb, "A Behavioral Analytic Interpretation of the Therapeutic Relationship," *Psychological Record* 42 (1992): 341–54. R. Kohlenberg, "Functional Analytic Psychotherapy," in *Psychotherapists in Clinical Practice: Cognitive and Behavioral Perspectives,* ed. N. Jacobson (New York: Guilford Press, 1987), 388–443. D. Powell, "Spontaneous Insights and the Process of Behavior Therapy: Cases in Support of Integrative Psychotherapy," *Psychiatric Annals* 18 (1988): 288–94.

8. R. Heckel, S. Wiggins, and H. Salzberg, "Conditioning Against Silences in Group Therapy," *Journal of Clinical Psychology* 18 (1962): 216–17.

9. M. Dinoff et al., "Conditioning the Verbal Behavior of a Psychiatric Population in a Group Therapy–Like Situation," *Journal of Clinical Psychology* 16 (1960): 371–72.

10. G. Burlingame, A. Fuhriman, and J. Johnson, "Cohesion in Group Psychotherapy," in *A Guide to Psychotherapy Relationships That Work,* ed. J. Norcross (Oxford, England: Oxford University Press, 2002).

11. A. Bandura, "Modelling Approaches to the Modification of Phobic Disorders," presented at the Ciba Foundation Symposium, "The Role of Learning in Psychotherapy," London, May 1968. A. Bandura, J. Grusec, and F. Menlove, "Vicarious Extinction of Avoidance Behavior," *Journal of Personality and Social Psychology* 5 (1967): 16–23.

12. A. Bandura, D. Ross, and J. Ross, "Imitation of Film Mediated Aggressive Models," *Journal of Abnormal and Social Psychology* 66 (1963): 3–11.

13. J. McCullough, *Treatment for Chronic Depression: Cognitive Behavioral Analysis System of Psychotherapy* (CBASP) (New York: Guilford Press, 2000).

14. D. Morran, R. Stockton, J. Cline, and C. Teed, "Facilitating Feedback Exchange in Groups: Leader Interventions," *Journal for Specialists in Group Work* 23 (1998): 257–60.

15. A. Schwartz and H. Hawkins, "Patient Models and Affect Statements in Group Therapy," presented at the American Psychological Association Meetings, Chicago, September 1965.

16. A. Goldstein et al., "The Use of Planted Patients in Group Psychotherapy," *American Journal of Psychotherapy* 21 (1967): 767–74.

17. L. Murphy, M. Leszcz, A. Collings, and J. Salvendy, "The Experience of the Neophyte Group Therapist," *International Journal of Group Psychotherapy*, 46 (1996): 543–52.

18. I. Yalom, *The Schopenhauer Cure* (New York: HarperCollins, 2005), 213.

19. I. Yalom, *Existential Psychotherapy* (New York: Basic Books, 1980), 178–87.

20. I. Yalom, *The Schopenhauer Cure* (New York: HarperCollins, 2005), 214–20.

21. S. Gold-Steinberg and M. Buttenheim, "'Telling One's Story' in an Incest Survivors Group," *International Journal of Group Psychotherapy* 43 (1993): 173–89.

CHAPTER 6

1. L. Mangione and R. Forti, "The Use of the Here and Now in Short-Term Group Psychotherapy," in *Innovation in Clinical Practice: A Source Book*, ed. L. VandeCreeke and T. Jackson (Sarasota: Professional Resources Press, 2001), 241–56.

2. R. Dies, "Models of Group Therapy: Sifting Through Confusion," *International Journal of Group Psychotherapy* 42 (1992): 1–17.

3. J. Flowers and C. Booraem, "The Effects of Different Types of Interpretation on Outcome in Group Therapy," *Group* 14 (1990): 81–88. This small (N = 24 clients), intensive study also indicated that here-and-now interpretations that focused on patterns of behavior were most effective in producing positive outcomes, followed by interpretations of impact of behavior on others, and then by historical interpretations. Interpretations of motivation were often countertherapeutic.

4. N. Brown, "Conceptualizing process," *International Journal of Group Psychotherapy* 53 (2003): 225–47. M. Ettin, "From Identified Patient to Identifiable Group: The Alchemy of the Group as a Whole," *International Journal of Group Psychotherapy* 50 (2000): 137–62.

5. M. Miles, "On Naming the Here-and-Now," unpublished essay, Columbia University, 1970.

6. B. Cohen, M. Ettin, and J. Fidler, "Conceptions of Leadership: The 'Analytic Stance' of the Group Psychotherapist," *Group Dynamics: Theory, Research and Practice* 2 (1998): 118–31.

7. Y. Agazarian, "Contemporary Theories of Group Psychotherapy: A Systems Approach," *International Journal of Group Psychotherapy* 42 (1992): 177–202.

8. D. Morran, R. Stockton, J. Cline, C. Teed, "Facilitating Feedback Exchange in Groups: Leader Interventions," *Journal for Specialists in Group Work* 23 (1998): 257–60.

9. J. McCullough, *Treatment for Chronic Depression: Cognitive Behavioral Analysis System of Psychotherapy (CBASP)* (New York: Guilford Press, 2000). S. Knox, S. Hess, D. Petersen, and C. Hill, "A Qualitative Analysis of Client Perceptions of the Effects of Helpful Therapist Self-Disclosure in Long-Term Therapy," *Journal of Counseling Psychology* 44 (1997): 274–83. M. Barrett and J. Berman, "Is Psychotherapy More Effective When Therapists Disclose Information About Themselves?" *Journal of Consulting Clinical Psychology* 69 (2001): 597–603.

10. M. Lieberman, I. Yalom, and M. Miles, *Encounter Groups: First Facts* (New York: Basic Books, 1973). Group research offers corroborative evidence. In one group project, the activating techniques (structured exercises) of sixteen different leaders were studied and correlated with outcome. There were two important relevant findings: (1) the more structured exercises the leader used, the *more competent* did members (at the end of the thirty-hour group) *deem the leader to be;* (2) the more structured exercises used by the leader, the *less* positive were the results (measured at a six-month follow-up). In other words, members desire leaders who lead, who offer considerable structure and guidance. They equate a large number of structured exercises with competence. Yet this is a confusion of form and substance: having too much structure or too many activating techniques is counterproductive.

11. L. Ormont, "The Leader's Role in Resolving Resistances to Intimacy in the Group Setting," *International Journal of Group Psychotherapy* 38 (1988): 29–47.

12. D. Kiesler, "Therapist Countertransference: In Search of Common Themes and Empirical Referents," *Journal of Clinical Psychology/In Session* 57 (2001): 1023–63.

13. D. Marcus and W. Holahan, "Interpersonal Perception in Group Therapy: A Social Relations Analysis," *Journal of Consulting and Clinical Psychology* 62 (1994): 776–82.

14. G. Brown and G. Burlingame, "Pushing the Quality Envelope: A New Outcome Management System," *Psychiatric Services* 52 (2001): 925–34.

15. M. Leszcz, "Geriatric Group Therapy," in *Comprehensive Textbook of Geriatric Psychiatry*, 3rd ed., ed. J. Sadavoy, L. Jarvik, G. Grossberg, and B. Myers (New York: Norton, 2004), 1023–54.

16. Kiesler "Therapist Countertransference."

17. S. Foulkes and E. Anthony, *Group Psychotherapy: The Psychoanalytic Approach*, 2nd ed. (Baltimore: Penguin, 1965), 153.

18. Ormont, "The Leader's Role in Resolving Resistances."

19. D. Martin, J. Garske, and M. Davis, "Relation of the Therapeutic Alliance with Outcome and Other Variables: A Meta-Analytic Review," *Journal of Consulting and Clinical Psychology* 68 (2000): 438–50.

20. D. Kiesler, *Contemporary Interpersonal Theory and Research* (New York: Wiley, 1996). McCullough, *Treatment for Chronic Depression*. J. Muran and J. Safran, "A Relational Approach to Psychotherapy," in *Comprehensive Handbook of Psychotherapy*, ed. F. Kaslow, vol. 1, *Psychodynamic/Object Relations*, ed. J. Magnavita (New York: Wiley, 2002), 253–81. S. Stuart and M. Robertson, *Interpersonal Psychotherapy: A Clinical Guide* (London: Arnold Press, 2003).

21. L. Murphy, M. Leszcz, A. Collings, and J. Salvendy, "The Experience of the Neophyte Group Therapist," *International Journal of Group Psychotherapy* 46 (1996): 543–52.

22. Interpreting motivations tends to be unhelpful. Flowers and Booraem have demonstrated that here-and-now comments (about patterns of behavior or impact of behavior) were positively correlated with group therapy outcome, whereas motivational interpretations were correlated with negative outcome (Flowers and Booraem, "The Effects of Different Types of Interpretation").

23. M. Keller et al. "A Comparison of Nefazodone, Cognitive Behavioral-Analysis System of Psychotherapy, and Their Combination for the Treatment of Chronic Depression," *New England Journal of Medicine* 342 (2000): 1462–70.

24. O. Rank, *Will Therapy and Truth and Reality* (New York: Knopf, 1950). R. May, *Love and Will* (New York: Norton, 1969). S. Arieti, *The Will to Be Human* (New York: Quadrangle Books, 1972). L. Farber, *The Ways of the Will* (New York: Basic Books, 1966). A. Wheelis, "Will and Psychoanalysis," *Journal of the Psychoanalytic Association* 4 (1956): 285–303. I. Yalom, *Existential Psychotherapy* (New York: Basic Books, 1980).

25. Yalom, *Existential Psychotherapy*, 286–350.

26. Farber, *Ways of the Will*.

27. Psychological treatments for addictions and eating disorders have particularly benefited from an appreciation of the role of the client's will in the process of change. Several research teams have employed five stages of motivation and then match therapy interventions to the client's stage of motivation or "change readiness." The five stages are:

   1. The precontemplation stage (no recognition that a problem exists)
   2. The contemplation stage (some recognition of the problem but with ambivalence about doing something about it)
   3. The preparation stage (a desire to change but a lack of knowledge about how to do so)
   4. The action stage (actual behavioral shifts)
   5. The maintenance stage (consolidating gains and preventing regression or relapse)

J. Prochaska, C. DiClemente, and J. Norcross, "In Search of How People Change: Applications to Addictive Behaviors," *American Psychologist* 47 (1992): 1102–14. R. Feld, D. Woodside, A. Kaplan, M. Olmstead, J. Carter, "Pre-treatment of Motivational Enhancement Therapy for Eating Disorders," *International Journal of Eating Disorders* 29 (2001): 393–400. W. Miller and S. Rollnick, *Motivational Interviewing: Preparing People To Change Addictive Behavior* (New York: Guilford Press, 2002).

28. T. Aquinas, quoted in P. Edwards, ed., *The Encyclopedia of Philosophy*, vol. 7 (New York: Free Press, 1967), 112.

29. Keep in mind that explanatory systems benefit therapists as well as clients: It provides therapists with focus, stability, confidence and tenacity. B. Wampold, *The Great Psychotherapy Debate: Models, Methods and Findings* (Mahwah, N.J.: Erlbaum, 2001). G. Burlingame, K. MacKenzie, and B. Strauss, "Small-Group Treatment: Evidence for Effectiveness and Mechanisms of Change," in *Bergin and Garfield's Handbook of Psychotherapy and Behavior Change*, 5th ed., ed. M. Lambert (New York: Wiley and Sons, 2004), 647–96.

30. J. Frank and J. Frank, *Persuasion and Healing: A Comparative Study of Psychotherapy*, 3rd ed. (Baltimore: Johns Hopkins University Press, 1991), 21–51.

31. D. Spence, *Narrative Truth and Historical Truth* (New York: Norton, 1982).

32. Sandra Blakeslee, "Brain-Updating Machinery May Explain False Memories," *New York Times*, September 19, 2000.

33. See Dies, "Models of Group Therapy."

34. B. Slife and J. Lanyon, "Accounting for the Power of the Here and Now: A Theoretical Revolution," *International Journal of Group Psychotherapy* 35 (1991): 225–38.

35. J. S. Rutan and W. M. Stone, *Psychodynamic Group Psychotherapy*, 3rd ed. (New York: Guilford Press, 2001).

36. J. Lichtenberg, F. Lachmann, and J. Fossaghe, *Self and Motivational Systems* (Hillsdale, N.J.: Analytic Press, 1992). J. Sandler and A. Sandler, "The Past Unconscious, the Present Unconscious, and Interpretation of Transference," *Psychoanalytic Inquiry* 4 (1984): 367–99.

37. Frank and Frank, *Persuasion and Healing*.

38. J. Weiss, *How Psychotherapy Works: Process and Technique* (New York: Guilford Press, 1993).

39. C. Rycroft, *Psychoanalysis Observed* (London: Constable, 1966), 18.

40. W. Bion, *Experiences in Groups and Other Papers* (New York: Basic Books, 1959). For more information about Bion's contributions, see an earler edition of this text or go to my Web site, www.yalom.com.

41. M. Nitsun, "The Future of the Group," *International Journal of Group Therapy* 50 (2000): 455-472.

42. M. Klein, cited in J. Strachey, "The Nature of the Therapeutic Action of Psychoanalysis," *International Journal of Psychoanalysis* 15 (1934): 127–59.

CHAPTER 7

1. J. Breuer and S. Freud, *Studies on Hysteria*, in S. Freud, *The Standard Edition of the Complete Psychological Works of Sigmund Freud* [hereafter *Standard Edition*], vol. 2 (London: Hogarth Press, 1955): 253–305.

2. S. Freud, *Five Lectures on Psycho-Analysis*, in *Standard Edition*, vol. 11 (London: Hogarth Press, 1957): 3–62.

3. In contemporary psychotherapy the client's schema describes the core beliefs the client holds about both himself and his relationship with his interpersonal world, along with the interpersonal behaviors that arise from these beliefs and cognitions. The schema also encompasses the client's usual way of perceiving his environment and processing information. See J. Safran and Z. Segal, *Interpersonal Process in Cognitive Therapy* (New York: Basic Books, 1990).

4. N. Miller, L. Luborsky, J. Barber, and J. Docherty, *Psychodynamic Treatment Research* (New York: Basic Books, 1993).

5. J. Marmor, "The Future of Psychoanalytic Therapy," *American Journal of Psychiatry* 130 (1973): 1197–1202.

6. S. Mitchell, *Hope and Dread in Psychoanalysis* (New York: Basic Books, 1993), 25.

7. V. Schermer, "Contributions of Object Relations Theory and Self Psychology to Relational Psychology and Group Psychotherapy," *International Journal of Group Psychotherapy*

50 (2000): 199–212. F. Wright, "The Use of Self in Group Leadership: A Relational Perspective," *International Journal of Group Psychotherapy* 50 (2000): 181–98. F. Wright, "Introduction to the Special Section on Contemporary Theoretical Developments and the Implications for Group Psychotherapy," *International Journal of Group Psychotherapy* 51 (2001): 445–48.

8. P. Cohen, "The Practice of Modern Group Psychotherapy: Working with Past Trauma in the Present," *International Journal of Group Psychotherapy* 51 (2001): 489–503.

9. M. Khan, "Outrageous, Complaining, and Authenticity," *Contemporary Psychoanalysis* 22 (1986): 629–50.

10. O. Kernberg, "Love in the Analytic Setting," *Journal of the American Psychoanalytic Association* 42 (1994): 1137–58.

11. R. Greenson, *The Technique and Practice of Psychoanalysis* (New York: International Universities Press, 1967).

12. A. Cooper, cited in G. Gabbard, *Psychodynamic Psychiatry in Clinical Practice* (Washington, D.C.: American Psychiatric Press, 1987).

13. M. West and J. Livesley, "Therapist Transparency and the Frame for Group Therapy," *International Journal of Psychoanalysis* 36 (1986): 5–20.

14. L. Horwitz, "Discussion of 'Group as a Whole'," *International Journal of Group Psychotherapy* 45 (1995): 143–48.

15. H. Durkin and H. Glatzer, "Transference Neurosis in Group Psychotherapy: The Concept and the Reality," *International Journal of Group Psychotherapy* 47 (1997): 183–99. Reprinted from: H. Durkin and H. Glatzer, "Transference Neurosis in Group Psychotherapy: The Concept and the Reality," in *Group Therapy 1973: An Overview,* ed. L. Wolberg and E. Schwartz (New York: Intercontinental Book Corp., 1973). P. Kauff, "Transference and Regression in and Beyond Analytic Group Psychotherapy: Revisiting Some Timeless Thoughts," *International Journal of Group Psychotherapy* 47 (1997): 201–10.

16. S. Freud, *Group Psychology and the Analysis of the Ego,* in *Standard Edition,* vol. 18 (London: Hogarth Press, 1955): 62–143.

17. G. Gabbard, "Advances in Psychoanalytic Therapy," presented to the Department of Psychiatry, University of Toronto, May 13, 1998.

18. S. Freud, *Group Psychology and the Analysis of the Ego.*

19. E. Fromm, *Escape from Freedom* (New York: Holt, Rinehart and Winston, 1941), 21.

20. L. Horwitz, "Narcissistic Leadership in Psychotherapy Groups," *International Journal of Group Psychotherapy* 50 (2000): 219–35. M. Leszcz, "Reflections on the Abuse of Power, Control, and Status in Group Therapy and Group Therapy Training," *International Journal of Group Psychotherapy* 54 (2004): 389–400. I. Harwood, "Distinguishing Between the Facilitating and Self-Serving Charismatic Group Leader," *Group* 27 (2004): 121–29.

21. S. Scheidlinger, "Freud's Group Psychology Revisited: An Opportunity Missed," *Psychoanalytic Psychology* 20 (2003): 389–92. Scheidlinger underscores that Freud relished his power as the leader of the psychoanalytic study group. He was relentlessly authoritarian and demanded total acceptance of his theories. Scheidlinger comments that Freud could have made an even larger contribution to group psychology and group psychotherapy had he not abandoned his work in this area because of a falling out with Trigant Burrow. Burrow, a former associate of Freud and early president of the American Psychoanalytic Association developed a model of group analysis that Freud felt challenged some of his own ideas. He ended his relationship with Burrow and gave no further thought in writing to groups.

22. L. Tolstoy, *War and Peace* (New York: Modern Library, Random House, 1931; orig. published 1865–69), 231.

23. Ibid., 245.

24. M. Nitsun, "The Future of the Group," *International Journal of Group Psychotherapy* 50 (2000): 455–72.

25. M. Levy, "A Helpful Way to Conceptualize and Understand Re-Enactments," *Journal of Psychotherapy Practice and Research* 7 (1998): 227–38.

26. S. Freud, *The Future of an Illusion,* in *Standard Edition,* vol. 21 (London: Hogarth Press, 1961), 1–56.

27. G. Thorne, *When It Was Dark,* cited by S. Freud in *Group Psychology and the Analysis of the Ego.*

28. S. Knox, S. Hess, D. Petersen, and C. Hill, "A Qualitative Analysis of Client Perceptions of the Effects of Helpful Therapist Self-Disclosure in Long-Term Therapy," *Journal of Counseling Psychology* 44 (1997): 274–83. B. Cohen and V. Schermer, "Therapist Self-Disclosure in Group Psychotherapy from an Intersubjective and Self-Psychological Standpoint," *Group* 25 (2001): 41–57.

29. R. Dies, "Models of Group Therapy: Sifting Through Confusion," *International Journal of Group Psychotherapy* 42 (1992): 1–17.

30. I. Yalom, *Inpatient Group Psychotherapy* (New York: Basic Books, 1983). E. Berne, "Staff Patient Conferences," *American Journal of Psychiatry* 125 (1968): 286–88.

31. A. Rachman, *Sandor Ferenczi, The Psychotherapist of Tenderness and Passion* (New York: Jason Aronson, 1996).

32. J. Rutan, "Sandor Ferenczi's Contributions to Psychodynamic Group Therapy," *International Journal of Group Psychotherapy* 53 (2003): 375–84.

33. S. Ferenczi, quoted in *Interpersonal Analysis: The Selected Papers of Clara M. Thompson,* ed. M. Green (New York: Basic Books, 1964), 70. For a brief period, Ferenczi conducted the ultimate experiment in therapist transparency: mutual analysis. He and the analysand alternated roles: one hour he analyzed the client, and the next hour the client analyzed him. Eventually he dropped this impractical format, but he was not convinced that the transparency impeded therapy (S. Ferenczi, *The Clinical Diaries of S. Ferenczi* [Cambridge, Mass.: Harvard University Press, 1993]).

34. S. Foulkes, "A Memorandum on Group Therapy," *British Military Memorandum,* ADM, July, 1945.

35. I. Yalom, *Love's Executioner* (New York: Basic Books, 1990). I. Yalom, *Lying on the Couch* (New York: Basic Books, 1996). I. Yalom, *Momma and the Meaning of Life* (New York: Basic Books, 1999). I. Yalom, *When Nietzsche Wept* (New York: Basic Books, 1992).

36. I. Yalom, *The Schopenhauer Cure* (New York: HarperCollins, 2005).

37. D. Fromm, G. Dickey, J. Shaefer, "Group Modification of Affective Verbalization: Reinforcements and Therapist Style Effects," *Journal of Clinical Psychology* 39 (1983): 893–900. R. Dies, "Therapist Variables in Group Psychotherapy Research," in *Handbook of Group Psychotherapy,* ed. A. Fuhriman and G. Burlingame (New York: Wiley, 1994): 114–54. R. Dies, "Research in Group Psychotherapy: Overview and Clinical Applications," in *Group Therapy in Clinical Practice,* ed. A. Alonso and H. Swiller (Washington, D.C.: American Psychiatric Press, 1993): 473–518.

38. M. Nichols and R. Schwartz, *Family Therapy: Concepts and Methods* (Needham Heights, Mass.: Allyn and Bacon, 1991), 265.

39. S. Wiser and M. Goldfried, "Therapist Interventions and Client Emotional Experiencing in Expert Psychodynamic-Interpersonal and Cognitive-Behavioral Therapies," *Journal of Consulting and Clinical Psychology* 66 (1998): 634–40. T. Eels, "What Do We Know About Master Therapists?" *Journal of Psychotherapy Practice and Research* 67 (1999): 314–17.

40. F. Wright, "Being Seen, Moved, Disrupted, and Reconfigured: Group Leadership from a Relational Perspective," *International Journal of Group Psychotherapy* 54 (2004): 235–50.

41. S. Foreman, "The Significance of Turning Passive into Active in Control Mastery Theory," *Journal of Psychotherapy Practice and Research* 5 (1996): 106–21.

42. S. Knox, S. Hess, D. Peterson, and C. Hill, "A Qualitative Analysis of Client Perceptions of the Effects of Helpful Therapist Self-Disclosure in Long-Term Therapy," *Journal of Counseling Psychology* 49 (1997): 274–83.

43. M. Allan, "An Investigation of Therapist and Patient Self-Help Disclosure in Outpatient Therapy Groups," *Dissertation Abstracts International* 41 (1980), no. 8021155.

44. H. Conte, R. Ratto, K. Clutz, and T. Karasu, "Determinants of Outpatients' Satisfactions with Therapists: Relation to Outcome," *Journal of Psychotherapy Practice and Research* 4 (1995): 43–51.

45. S. Wilkinson and G. Gabbard, "Therapeutic Self-Disclosure with Borderline Patients," *Journal of Psychotherapy Practice and Research* 2 (1993): 282–95.

46. K. Ullman, "Unwitting Exposure of the Therapist Transferential and Countertransferential Dilemmas," *Journal of Psychotherapy Practice and Research* 10 (2001): 14–21.

47. T. Gutheil and G. Gabbard, "The Concepts of Boundaries in Clinical Practice: Theoretical and Risk-Management Dimensions," *American Journal of Psychiatry* 150 (1993): 188–96.

48. T. Gutheil and G. Gabbard, "Misuses and Misunderstandings of Boundary Theory in Clinical and Regulatory Settings," *American Journal of Psychiatry* 155 (1998): 409–14. A. Elfant, "Group Psychotherapist Self-Disclosure: Why, When, and How?" presented at the annual meeting of the American Group Psychotherapy Association, New Orleans, February 21, 2003.

49. Self-disclosure was carried to extreme in the time-extended marathon groups popular in the 1970s (see chapter 10), which met from twenty-four to forty-eight consecutive hours and placed paramount emphasis on total self-disclosure of the group as well as the group leader. The sheer physical fatigue wore down defenses and abetted maximal disclosure. Then there is the ultimate in self-disclosure: group therapy in the nude. In the late 1960s and early 1970s, the mass media (for example, *Time* magazine) gave considerable coverage to nude marathons in Southern California (*Time,* February 23, 1968, 42). Many of the wilder innovations in therapy have sprung from Southern California. It brings to mind Saul Bellow's fanciful notion in *Seize the Day* (New York: Viking Press, 1956) of someone tilting a large, flat map of the United States and observing that "everything that wasn't bolted or screwed down slid into Southern California."

50. D. Kivlighan and J. Tarrant, "Does Group Climate Mediate the Group Leadership-Group Member Outcome Relationship? A Test of Yalom's Hypothesis About Leadership Priorities," *Group Dynamics: Theory, Research and Practice* 3 (2001): 220–34.

51. M. Parloff, "Discussion of Accelerated Interaction: A Time-Limited Approach Based on the Brief Intensive Group," *International Journal of Group Psychotherapy* 28 (1968): 239–44.

52. Ferenczi, quoted in M. Green, *Interpersonal Analysis*.

53. R. Dies, "Leadership in Short-Term Groups," in *Advances in Group Psychotherapy,* ed. R. Dies and R. MacKenzie (New York: International Universities Press, 1983), 27–78. R. Dies, "Group Therapist Transparency: A Critique of Theory and Research," *International Journal of Group Psychotherapy* 27 (1977): 177–200. R. Dies and L. Cohen, "Content Considerations in Group Therapist Self-Disclosure," *International Journal of Group Psychotherapy* 26 (1976): 71–88.

54. S. McNary and R. Dies, "Co-Therapist Modeling in Group Psychotherapy: Fact or Fantasy," *Group* 17 (1993): 131–42.

55. E. O'Neill, *The Iceman Cometh* (New York: Random House, 1957).

56. H. Ibsen, *The Wild Duck* (New York: Avon Press, 1965; orig. published 1884).

57. V. Frankl, personal communication, 1975.

CHAPTER 8

1. W. Piper, M. McCallum, A. Joyce, J. Rosie, and J. Ogrodniczuk, "Patient Personality and Time-Limited Group Psychotherapy for Complicated Grief," *International Journal of*

Group Psychotherapy 51 (2001): 525–52. R. Kadden, M. Litt, N. Cooney, E. Kabela, H. Getter, "Prospective Matching of Alcoholic Clients to Cognitive-Behavioral or Interactional Group Therapy," *Journal of Studies on Alcohol* May (2001): 359–69.

2. G. Burlingame, A. Fuhriman, and J. Mosier, "The Differential Effectiveness of Group Psychotherapy: A Meta-Analytic Perspective," *Group Dynamics: Theory, Research, and Practice* 7 (2003): 3–12. G. Burlingame, K. MacKenzie, and B. Strauss, "Small-Group Treatment: Evidence for Effectiveness and Mechanism of Change," in *Bergin and Garfield's Handbook of Psychotherapy and Behavior Change*, 5th ed., ed. M. Lambert (New York: Wiley, 2004), 647–96.

3. R. Toseland and M. Siporin, "When to Recommend Group Treatment: A Review of the Clinical and the Research Literature," *International Journal of Group Psychotherapy* 36 (1986): 171–201.

4. C. McRoberts, G. Burlingame, and M. Hoag, "Comparative Efficacy of Individual and Group Psychotherapy: A Meta-Analytic Perspective," *Group Dynamics: Theory, Research, and Practice* 2 (1998): 101–17.

5. K. MacKenzie, "Where Is Here and When Is Now? The Adaptational Challenge of Mental Health Reform for Group Psychotherapy," *International Journal of Group Psychotherapy* 44 (1994): 407–28. M. Parloff and R. Dies, "Group Psychotherapy Outcome Research," *International Journal of Group Psychotherapy* 27 (1977): 281–322. W. Piper and A. Joyce, "A Consideration of Factors Influencing the Utilization of Time-Limited, Short-Term Group Therapy," *International Journal of Group Psychotherapy* 46 (1996): 311–28.

6. K. Graham, H. Annis, P. Brett, P. Venesoen, and R. Clifton, "A Controlled Field Trial of Group Versus Individual Cognitive-Behavioral Training for Relapse Prevention," *Addiction* 91 (1996): 1127–39.

7. D. Renjilian, M. Peri, A. Nezu, W. McKelvey, R. Shermer, and S. Anton, "Individual Versus Group Therapy for Obesity: Effects of Matching Participants to the Treatment Preferences," *Journal of Consulting Clinical Psychology* 69 (2001): 717–21.

8. F. Fawzy, N. Fawzy, and J. Wheeler, "A Post-Hoc Comparison of the Efficiency of a Psychoeducational Intervention for Melanoma Patients Delivered in Group Versus Individual Formats: An Analysis of Data from Two Studies," *Psycho-Oncology* 5 (1996): 81–89.

9. E. Westbury and L. Tutty, "The Efficacy of Group Treatment for Survivors of Childhood Abuse," *Child Abuse and Neglect* 23 (1999): 31–44.

10. K. MacKenzie, "Where Is Here and When Is Now? The Adaptational Challenge of Mental Health Reform for Group Psychotherapy," *International Journal of Group Psychotherapy* 44 (1994): 407–28.

11. S. Holmes and D. Kivlighan, "Comparison of Therapeutic Factors in Group and Individual Treatment Processes," *Journal of Counseling Psychology* 47 (2000): 478–84.

12. G. Gazda, "Discussion of When to Recommend Group Treatment: A Review of the Clinical and the Research Literature," *International Journal of Group Psychotherapy* 36 (1986): 203–6. F. de Carufel and W. Piper, "Group Psychotherapy or Individual Psychotherapy: Patient Characteristics As Predictive Factors," *International Journal of Group Psychotherapy* 38 (1988): 169–88.

13. E. Nash et al., "Some Factors Related to Patients Remaining in Group Psychotherapy," *International Journal of Group Psychotherapy* 7 (1957): 264–75. J. Johnson, *Group Psychotherapy: A Practical Approach* (New York: McGraw-Hill, 1963). E. Fried, "Basic Concepts in Group Therapy," in *Comprehensive Group Therapy*, ed. H. Kaplan and B. Sadock (Baltimore: Williams & Wilkins, 1971), 50–51.

14. L. Horwitz, "Indications and Contraindications for Group Psychotherapy," *Bulletin of the Menninger Clinic* 40 (1976): 505–7.

15. S. Slavson, "Criteria for Selection and Rejection of Patients for Various Kinds of Group Therapy," *International Journal of Group Psychotherapy* 5 (1955): 3–30. S. Adrian, "A Systematic Approach to Selecting Group Participants," *Journal of Psychiatric Nursing* 18 (1980): 37–41.

16. Nash et al., "Some Factors." Johnson, Group Psychotherapy. Fried, "Basic Concepts." R. MacNair-Semands, "Predicting Attendance and Expectations for Group Therapy," *Group Dynamics: Theory, Research, and Practice* 6 (2002): 219–28.

17. M. Weiner, "Group Therapy in a Public Sector Psychiatric Clinic," *International Journal of Group Psychotherapy* 38 (1988): 355–65. M. Rosenbaum and E. Hartley, "A Summary Review of Current Practices of Ninety-Two Group Therapists," *International Journal of Group Psychotherapy* 12 (1962): 194–98. W. Friedman, "Referring Patients for Group Therapy: Some Guidelines," *Hospital and Community Psychiatry* 27 (1976): 121–23. A. Frances, J. Clarkin, and J. Marachi, "Selection Criteria for Outpatient Group Psychotherapy," *Hospital and Community Psychiatry* 31 (1980): 245–49. M. Woods and J. Melnick, "A Review of Group Therapy Selection Criteria," *Small Group Behavior* 10 (1979): 155–75.

18. R. Morgan and C. Winterowd, "Interpersonal Process-Oriented Group Psychotherapy with Offender Populations," *International Journal of Offender Therapy and Comparative Criminology* 46 (2002): 466–82. Toseland and Siporin, "When to Recommend Group Treatment." I. Yalom, "Group Therapy of Incarcerated Sexual Deviants," *Journal of Nervous Mental Disorders* 132 (1961): 158–70.

19. Friedman, "Referring Patients." Woods and Melnick, "Group Therapy Selection Criteria." Frances, Clarkin, and Marachi, "Selection Criteria." Horwitz, "Indications and Contraindications."

20. Horwitz, "Indications and Contraindications." Friedman, "Referring Patients." H. Grunebaum and W. Kates, "Whom to Refer for Group Psychotherapy," *American Journal of Psychiatry* 134 (1977): 130–33.

21. M. Linehan, "Dialectical Behavior Therapy for Borderline Personality Disorder: A Cognitive Behavioral Approach to Parasuicide," *Journal of Personality Disorders* 1 (1987): 328–33. M. Linehan, "Naturalistic Follow-Up of a Behavioral Treatment for Chronically Parasuicidal Borderline Patients," *Archives of General Psychiatry* 50 (1993): 971–74. E. Marziali and H. Munroe-Blum, *Interpersonal Group Psychotherapy for Borderline Personality Disorder* (New York: Basic Books, 1994).

22. I. Yalom, "A Study of Group Therapy Dropouts," *Archives of General Psychiatry* 14 (1966): 393–414.

23. M. Wierzbicki and G. Pekarik, "A Meta-Analysis of Psychotherapy Dropouts," *Professional Psychology: Research and Practice* 24 (1993): 190–95.

24. W. Stone and J. Rutan, "Duration of Treatment in Group Psychotherapy," *International Journal of Group Psychotherapy* 34 (1984): 93–109. M. Leszcz, "Guidelines for the Practice of Group Psychotherapy," in *Guidelines and Standards for the Psychotherapies,* ed. P. Cameron, J. Ennis and J. Deadman (Toronto: University of Toronto Press, 1998), 199–227. H. Roback, "Adverse Outcomes in Group Psychotherapy: Risk Factors, Prevention, and Research Directions," *Journal of Psychotherapy Practice and Research* 9 (2000): 113–22.

25. M. Lieberman, I. Yalom, and M. Miles, *Encounter Groups: First Facts* (New York: Basic Books, 1972).

26. M. Seligman, "The Effectiveness of Psychotherapy: The Consumer Reports Study," *American Psychologist* 50 (1995): 965–74.

27. W. Piper, A. Joyce, J. Rosie, and H. Azim, "Psychological Mindedness, Work and Outcome in Day Treatment," *International Journal of Group Psychotherapy* 44 (1994): 291–311; M. McCallum, W. Piper, and A. Joyce, "Dropping Out from Short-Term Group Therapy," *Psychotherapy* 29 (1992): 206–13. In a study of 109 patients with prolonged or pathological grief in brief (twelve-week), analytically oriented group therapy, the 33 dropouts were found to be significantly less psychologically minded than continuers. They also tended to have greater psychiatric symptomatology and greater intensity of target symptoms. S. Rosenzweig and R. Folman, "Patient and Therapist Variables Affecting Premature Termination in Group Psychotherapy," *Psychotherapy: Theory, Research and Prac-*

tice 11 (1974): 76–79. In a study of thirteen dropouts from V.A. outpatient clinic groups a battery of psychological tests did *not* distinguish between the continuers and the dropouts, but the therapists' pretherapy judgments about their ability to empathize with the clients, their clients' ability to form a therapeutic relationship, and the therapists' overall liking of a client were significantly predictive of premature termination. B. Kotkov and A. Meadow, "Rorschach Criteria for Continuing Group Psychotherapy," *International Journal of Group Psychotherapy* 2 (1952): 324–31. A study of Veterans Administration ambulatory groups found that dropouts had less capacity to withstand stress, less desire for empathy, less ability to achieve emotional rapport, a lower Wechsler verbal scale IQ, and came from a lower socioeconomic class. (Many other studies have reported that dropouts [from any psychotherapeutic format] are disproportionately high among the lower socioeconomic class.) R. Klein and R. Carroll, "Patient Characteristics and Attendance Patterns in Outpatient Group Therapy," *International Journal of Group Psychotherapy* 36 (1986): 115–32; H. Roback and M. Smith, "Patient Attrition in Dynamically Oriented Treatment Groups," *American Journal of Psychiatry* 144 (1987): 426–43; L. Gliedman et al., "Incentives for Treatment Related to Remaining or Improving in Psychotherapy," *American Journal of Psychotherapy* 11 (1957): 589–98. M. Grotjahn, "Learning from Dropout Patients: A Clinical View of Patients who Discontinued Group Psychotherapy," *International Journal of Group Psychotherapy* 22 (1972): 306–19. Grotjahn studied his long-term analytic groups and noted that, over a six-year period, forty-three group members (35 percent) dropped out within the first twelve months of therapy. He felt that, in retrospect, approximately 40 percent of the dropouts were predictable and fell into three categories: (1) clients with diagnoses of manifest or threatening psychotic breakdowns; (2) clients who used the group for crisis resolution and dropped out when the emergency had passed; (3) highly schizoid, sensitive, isolated individuals who needed more careful, intensive preparation for group therapy. Nash et al., "Some Factors." Nash and his co-workers studied thirty group therapy clients in a university outpatient clinic. The seventeen dropouts (three or fewer meetings) differed significantly from the thirteen continuers in several respects: they were more socially ineffective, experienced their illness as progressive and urgent or were high deniers who terminated therapy as their denial crumbled in the face of confrontation by the group. R. MacNair and J. Corazzini, "Clinical Factors Influencing Group Therapy Dropout," *Psychotherapy: Theory, Research, Practice and Training* 31 (1994): 352–61. MacNair and colleagues also studied two large groupings of clients treated at a university counseling service in 16 session interactional interpersonal group therapy. This study of 155 and 310 clients respectively over several years employed The Group Therapy Questionnaire (GTQ) to evaluate the group members. Dropouts and poor attenders could be predicted by the following characteristics: anger, hostility and argumentativeness; social inhibition; substance abuse; and somatization. In contrast, prior experience in some form of psychotherapy was a protective variable. (R. MacNair-Semands, "Predicting Attendance and Expectations for Group Therapy," *Group Dynamics: Theory, Research and Practice* 6 [2002]: 219–28.) This latter finding echoes an earlier report that demonstrated that dropouts were much more likely to be individuals for whom group therapy was their first experience in psychotherapy. W. Stone and J. Rutan, "Duration of Treatment in Group Psychotherapy," *International Journal of Group Psychotherapy* 34 (1984): 93–109. G. Tasca et al., "Treatment Completion and Outcome in a Partial Hospitalization Program: Interaction Among Patient Variables," *Psychotherapy Research* 9 (1999): 232–47. Tasca and colleagues studied 102 clients in an intensive group therapy day hospital program and reported that dropouts were predicted by the combined presence of reduced psychological-mindedness and chronicity of problems. High degrees of psychological-mindedness offset the negative impact of illness chronicity on treatment completion. M. McCallum, W. Piper, J. Ogrodniczuk, and A. Joyce, "Early Process and Dropping Out from Group Therapy for Complicated Grief," *Group Dynamics: Theory, Research and Practice* 6 (2002): 243–54. Dropout rates for 139 clients participating in 12 session group therapy for complicated grief were 23% (regardless whether they were in an interpretive or a supportive model of group therapy). Dropouts experienced far less positive emotion in the early sessions and were less compatible with, and less important to the group. The therapists reported they had less emotional investment in these clients from the outset of therapy. The phenomenon of very early therapist divestment and antipathy to the clients who ultimately drop out has been reported by others as well. (L. Lothstein, "The Group Psychotherapy Dropout Phenomenon Revisited," *American Journal of Psychiatry* 135 [1978]: 1492–95; O. Stiwne, "Group Psychotherapy with Borderline Patients: Contrasting Remainers and Dropouts," *Group* 18 [1994]: 37–45. T. Oei and T. Kazmierczak, "Factors Associated with Dropout in a Group Cognitive Behavior Therapy for Mood Disorders," *Behavior, Research and Therapy* 35 [1997]: 1025–30.) In a study of 131 clients in CBT groups for depression, 63 clients (48%) dropped out prematurely. Pretherapy variables, including degree of depression did not predict dropouts. In contrast however, lack of participation in the group activities and exercises was predictive. Race and ethnicity are also important considerations. A number of recent studies have shown that visible minorities may terminate prematurely, feeling a lack of universality, comfort and familiarity within the group. (S. Sue, D. Hu, D. Takevch, and N. Zane, "Community Mental Health Services for Ethnic Minority Groups: A Test of the Cultural Responsiveness Hypothesis," *Journal of Consulting and Clinical Psychology* 59 [1991]: 533–40; K. Organista, "Latinos," in *Cognitive-Behavioral Group Therapy for Specific Problems and Populations,* ed. J. White and A. Freeman [Washington, D.C.: American Psychiatric Press, 2000], 281–303; H. Chang and D. Sunders, "Predictors of Attrition in Two Types of Group Programs for Men Who Batter," *Journal of Family Violence* 17 [2002]: 273–92.) Clients' negative expectations built upon negative experiences in society also play an important role. (C. Taft, C. Murphy, J. Elliott, and T. Morrel, "Attendance Enhancing Procedures in Group Counseling for Domestic Abusers," *Journal of Counseling Psychology* 48 [2001]: 51–60.)

28. Notes for Table 8.1:

[a] R. Klein and R. Carroll, "Patient Characteristics and Attendance Patterns in Outpatient Group Psychotherapy," *International Journal of Group Psychotherapy* 36 (1986): 115–32.

[b] M. McCallum and W. Piper, "A Controlled Study for Effectiveness and Patient Suitability for Short-Term Group Psychotherapy," *International Journal of Group Psychotherapy* 40 (1990): 431–52.

[c] M. McCallum, W. Piper, and A. Joyce, "Dropping Out from Short-Term Group Therapy," *Psychotherapy* 29 (1992): 206–13.

[d] Nash et al., "Some Factors."

[e] B. Kotkov, "The Effects of Individual Psychotherapy on Group Attendance," *International Journal of Group Psychotherapy* 5 (1955): 280–85.

[f] S. Rosenzweig and R. Folman, "Patient and Therapist Variable Affecting Premature Termination in Group Psychotherapy," *Psychotherapy: Theory, Research and Practice* 11 (1974): 76–79.

[g] Yalom, "Group Therapy Dropouts."

[h] E. Berne, "Group Attendance: Clinical and Theoretical Considerations," *International Journal of Group Psychotherapy* 5 (1955): 392–403.

[i] Johnson, *Group Psychotherapy.*

[j] M. Grotjahn, "Learning from Dropout Patients: A Clinical View of Patients Who Discontinued Group Psychotherapy," *International Journal of Group Psychotherapy* 22 (1972): 306–19.

[k] L. Koran and R. Costell, "Early Termination from Group Psychotherapy," *International Journal of Group Psychotherapy* 24 (1973): 346–59.

[l] S. Budman, A. Demby, and M. Randall, "Short-Term Group Psychotherapy: Who Succeeds, Who Fails," *Group* 4 (1980): 3–16.

[m] M. Weiner, "Outcome of Psychoanalytically Oriented Group Therapy," *Group* 8 (1984): 3–12.

n W. Piper, E. Debbane, J. Blenvenu et al., "A Comparative Study of Four Forms of Psychotherapy," *Journal of Consulting and Clinical Psychology* 52 (1984): 268–79.

o W. Stone and S. Rutan, "Duration of Treatment in Group Psychotherapy," *International Journal of Group Psychotherapy* 34 (1984): 93–109.

p K. Christiansen, K. Valbak, and A. Weeke, "Premature Termination in Analytic Group Therapy," *Nordisk-Psykiatrisk-Tidsskrift* 45 (1991): 377–82.

q R. MacNair and J. Corazzini, "Clinical Factors Influencing Group Therapy Dropouts," *Psychotherapy: Theory, Research, Practice and Training* 31 (1994): 352-61.

r M. McCallum, W. Piper, J. Ogrodniczuk, and A. Joyce, "Early Process and Dropping Out."

s T. Oei and T. Kazmierczak, "Factors Associated with Dropout in a Group Cognitive Behavior Therapy for Mood Disorders," *Behaviour Research and Therapy* 35 (1997): 1025-30.

29. Yalom, "Group Therapy Dropouts."

30. W. Piper, M. McCallum, and H. Azim, *Adaption to Loss Through Short-Term Group Psychotherapy* (New York: Guilford Press, 1992).

31. McCallum et al., "Early Process and Dropping Out."

32. W. Stone, "Group Psychotherapy with the Chronically Mentally Ill," in *Comprehensive Group Psychotherapy*, eds. M. Kaplan and B. Sadock. (Baltimore: Williams and Wilkins, 1993), 419–29.

33. M. Horowitz, "The Recall of Interrupted Group Tasks: An Experimental Study of Individual Motivation in Relation to Group Goals," In *Group Dynamics: Research and Theory*, ed. D. Cartwright and A. Zander (New York: Row, Peterson, 1962), 370–94.

34. L. Coch and J. French Jr., "Overcoming Resistance to Change," in Cartwright and Zander, *Group Dynamics,* 31–41. E. Stotland, "Determinants of Attraction to Groups," *Journal of Social Psychology* 49 (1959): 71–80.

35. D. Lundgren and D. Miller, "Identity and Behavioral Changes in Training Groups," *Human Relations Training News* (Spring 1965).

36. Lieberman, Yalom, Miles, *Encounter Groups*, p. 324.

37. I. Yalom and P. Houts, unpublished data, 1966.

38. S. Schachter, "Deviation, Rejection, and Communication," in Cartwright and Zander, *Group Dynamics,* 260–85.

39. H. Leavitt, "Group Structure and Process: Some Effects of Certain Communication Patterns on Group Performance," in *Readings in Social Psychology,* eds. E. Maccoby, T. Newcomb, E. Hartley (New York: Holt, Rinehart & Winston, 1958), 175–83.

40. J. Jackson, "Reference Group Processes in a Formal Organization," in Cartwright and Zander, *Group Dynamics,* 120–40.

41. L. Festinger, S. Schachter, and K. Back, "The Operation of Group Standards," in Cartwright and Zander, *Group Dynamics,* 241–59.

42. C. Anderson, O. John, D. Kelter, and A. Kring, "Who Attains Social Status? Effects of Personality and Physical Attractiveness in Social Groups," *Journal of Personality and Social Psychology* 8 (2001): 116–32.

43. M. Sherif, "Group Influences Upon the Formation of Norms and Attitudes," in Maccoby et al., *Readings in Social Psychology,* 219–32.

44. S. Asch, "Interpersonal Influence: Effects of Group Pressure Upon the Modification and Distortion of Judgments," in Maccoby et al., *Readings in Social Psychology,* 175–83.

45. P. Leiderman, "Attention and Verbalization: Differentiated Responsivity of Cardiovascular and Electrodermo Systems," *Journal of Psychosomatic Research* 15 (1971): 323–28.

46. Lieberman, Yalom, and Miles, *Encounter Groups*.

47. Schachter, "Deviation, Rejection, and Communication."

48. McCallum et al., "Early Process and Dropping Out."

49. R. Harrison and B. Lubin, "Personal Style, Group Composition, and Learning— Part I," *Journal of Applied Behavioral Science* 1 (1965): 286–94.

50. Similar findings were reported in the NIMH trial of the treatment of depression. Clients with poor interpersonal functioning could not utilize interpersonal therapy effectively. (S. Sotsky et al., "Patient Predictors of Response to Psychotherapy and Pharmacotherapy: Findings in the NIMH Treatment of Depression Collaborative Research Program," *American Journal of Psychiatry* 148 (1991): 997–1008.)

51. R. Lee, M. Draper, and S. Lee, "Social Connectedness, Dysfunctional Interpersonal Behaviors, and Psychological Distress: Testing a Mediator Model," *Journal of Counseling Psychology* 48 (2001): 310–18.

52. Clients do well with intensive psychotherapies if they have mature relationship capacities (measured by the Quality of Object Relations Scale (QOR) (H. Azim et al., "The Quality of Object Relations Scale," *Bulletin of the Menninger Clinic* 55 (1991): 323–43). Clients with less mature QOR scores do poorly with intensive therapy, often experiencing interpretations as hurtful criticisms. These clients do much better with the more supportive therapies. (A. Joyce, M. McCallum, W. Piper, and J. Ogrodniczuk, "Role Behavior Expectancies and Alliance Change in Short-Term Individual Psychotherapy," *Journal of Psychotherapy Practice and Research* 9 (2000): 213–25.) Higher psychological-mindedness, not surprisingly, is a general predictor of positive outcome for all psychotherapies. (Joyce et al., ibid; Piper et al., "Patient Personality and Time-Limited Group.")

53. M. Pines, "The Self as a Group: The Group as a Self," in *Self-Experiences in Group: Objective and Self-Psychological Pathways to Human Understanding*, ed. I. Harwood and M. Pines (Philadelphia: Taylor & Francis, 1998): 24–29. A. Gray, "Difficult Terminations in Group Therapy: A Self-Psychologically Informed Perspective," *Group* 25 (2001): 27–39.

54. M. Leszcz, "Group Psychotherapy of the Characterologically Difficult Patient," *International Journal of Group Psychotherapy* 39 (1989): 311–35.

55. Nash et al., "Some Factors."

56. H. Bernard and S. Drob, "Premature Termination: A Clinical Study," *Group* 13 (1989): 11–22.

57. M. Seligman, "The Effectiveness of Psychotherapy."

58. L. Bellak, "On Some Limitations of Dyadic Psychotherapy and the Role of the Group Modalities," *International Journal of Group Psychotherapy* 30 (1980): 7–21. J. Rutan and A. Alonso, "Group Therapy, Individual Therapy, or Both?" *International Journal of Group Psychotherapy* 32 (1982): 267–82.

59. Grunebaum and Kates, "Whom to Refer."

60. Frances, Clarkin, and Marachi, "Selection Criteria," 245.

61. H. Swiller, "Alexithymia: Treatment Utilizing Combined Individual and Group Psychotherapy," *International Journal of Group Psychotherapy* 38 (1988): 47–61.

62. L. Horowitz and J. Vitkis, "The Interpersonal Basis of Psychiatric Symptomatology," *Clinical Psychology Review* 6 (1986): 443–69.

63. P. Crits-Christoph and M. Connolly, "Patient Pretreatment Predictors of Outcome," in *Psychodynamic Treatment Research*, ed. N. Miller, L. Luborsky, J. Barber, and J. Docherty (New York: Basic Books, 1993), 185.

64. I. Yalom, P. Houts, S. Zimerberg, and K. Rand, "Predictions of Improvement in Group Therapy," *Archives of General Psychiatry* 17 (1967): 159–68.

65. The forty clients studied were adult, middle class, well educated, psychologically sophisticated outpatients who suffered from neurotic or characterological problems. Outcome was evaluated by a team of raters who, on the basis of a structured interview, evaluated (with excellent reliability) change in symptoms, functioning, and relationships. The clients also independently rated their own outcome, using the same scale. Psychological-mindedness was measured by subscale of the California Personality Inventory and by the therapists after an initial screening interview. The therapists rated each client on a seven-point scale after the initial interview for how well they thought he or she would do in therapy. Previous self-disclosure was measured by a modification of the Jourard Self-Disclosure Questionnaire (S. Jourard, "Self-Disclosure Patterns in British and American

College Females," *Journal of Social Psychology* 54 (1961): 315–20). The clients' attraction to group therapy and their general popularity in the group were measured by a group cohesiveness questionnaire and a sociometric questionnaire.

66. C. Anderson, "Who Attains Social Status?"

67. Using a comprehensive personality inventory researchers found, unsurprisingly, that the Extraversion factor (exemplified by individuals who are energetic, sociable, assertive, and display positive emotionality) is strongly associated with popularity. (R. McCrae and R. Costa, "The NEO Personality Inventory: Using the Five-Factor Model in Counseling," *Journal of Counseling and Development* 69 (1991): 367–72.) These individuals draw others to them because their ready and warm responsiveness rewards and encourages overtures for engagement. (R. Depue, "A Neurobiological Framework for the Structure of Personality and Emotion: Implications for Personality Disorders," in *Major Theories of Personality Disorders*, ed. J. Clarkin and M. Lenzenweger [New York: Guilford Press, 1996], 342–90.)

68. Lieberman, Yalom, and Miles, *Encounter Groups*.

69. J. Melnick and G. Rose, "Expectancy and Risk-Taking Propensity," *Small Group Behavior* 10 (1979): 389–401. Scales: Jackson Risk-Taking inventory and the Hill Interactional Matrix. Sociometric assessment: Depth of Involvement Scale (Evensen and Bednar), Moos and Humphrey Group Environment Scale.

70. J. Frank and J. Frank, *Persuasion and Healing: A Comparative Study of Psychotherapy*, 3rd ed. (Baltimore: Johns Hopkins University Press, 1991), pp. 132–53. W. Piper, "Client Variables," in *Handbook of Group Psychotherapy*, ed. A. Fuhriman and G. Burlingame (New York: Wiley, 1994): 83–113.

71. Joyce et al., "Role Behavior Expectancies and Alliance Change." J. Rooney and R. Hanson, "Predicting Attrition from Treatment Programs for Abusive Men," *Journal of Family Violence* 16 (2001): 131–49.

72. Lothstein, "The Group Psychotherapy Dropout Phenomenon." McCallum et al., "Early Process and Dropping Out."

73. J. Frank, "Some Determinants, Manifestations, and Effects of Cohesiveness in Therapy Groups," *International Journal of Group Psychotherapy* 7 (1957): 53–63.

74. Oei and Kazmierczak, "Factors Associated with Dropout."

75. The amount of "group work" accomplished (as reported by the client, comembers, and the group therapist) predicts outcome. (Piper et al., "Psychological Mindedness, Work, and Outcome.") Piper and colleagues define "group work" in clear terms: "to work in therapy means that you are trying to explain a problem that you are facing by exploring your own contributions to it." It involves taking responsibility for one's role in one's difficulties and helping other members do the same. (M. McCallum, W. Piper, and J. O'Kelly, "Predicting Patient Benefit from a Group-Oriented Evening Treatment Program," *International Journal of Group Psychotherapy* 47 (1997): 291–314, 300.)

76. M. Parloff, "Therapist-Patient Relationships and Outcome of Psychotherapy," *Journal of Consulting Psychology* 25 (1961): 29–38.

77. R. Heslin and D. Dunphy, "Three Dimensions of Member Satisfaction in Small Groups," *Human Relations* 17 (1964): 99–112.

78. Frank, "Some Determinants."E. Ends and C. Page, "Group Psychotherapy and Psychological Changes," *Psychological Monographs* 73 (1959): 480.

CHAPTER 9

1. D. Waltman and D. Zimpfer, "Composition, Structure, and the Duration of Treatment," *Small Group Behavior* 19 (1988): 171–84.

2. P. Costa and R. McCrae, "Revised NEO Personality Inventory (NEO PI-R) and NEO Five-Factor Inventory (NEO-FFI)," *Professional Manual* (Odessa, Fla.: Psychological Assessment Resources, 1992).

3. M. First et al., "DSM-IV and Behavioral Assessment," *Behavioral Assessment* 14 (1992): 297–306. J. Shedler and D. Westen, "Refining Personality Disorder Diagnosis: Integrating Science and Practice," *American Journal of Psychiatry* 161 (2004): 1350–65. The chief architect of the DSM, Robert Spitzer, chronicles the challenges of developing the DSM in an interview with Alix Spiegel in the January 3, 2005, issue of *The New Yorker*.

4. P. Crits-Christoph and M. Connolly Gibbon, "Review of W. Piper, A. Joyce, M. Mc-Callum, H. Azim, and J. Ogrodniczuk, *Interpersonal and Supportive Psychotherapies: Matching Therapy and Patient Personality*," *Psychotherapy Research* 13 (2003): 117–19.

5. W. Piper, "Client Variables," in *Handbook of Group Psychotherapy*, ed. A. Fuhriman and G. Burlingame (New York: Wiley, 1994): 83–113.

6. W. Piper and M. Marrache, "Selecting Suitable Patients: Pretraining for Group Therapy as a Method for Group Selection," *Small Group Behavior* 12 (1981): 459–74. Group behavior was measured by the Hill Interaction Matrix, W. Hill, *Hill Interactional Matrix* (Los Angeles: Youth Studies Center, University of Southern California, 1965).

7. As DSM-IV-TR states, "A common misconception is that a classification of mental disorders classifies people, when actually what are being classified are disorders that people have" (*Diagnostic and Statistical Manual of Mental Disorders*, 4th ed., rev. American Psychiatric Association, 2000, xxxi).

8. A. Camus, *The Fall* (New York: Knopf, 1956).

9. J. Deer and A. Silver, "Predicting Participation and Behavior in Group Therapy from Test Protocols," *Journal of Clinical Psychology* 18 (1962): 322–25. C. Zimet, "Character Defense Preference and Group Therapy Interaction," *Archives of General Psychiatry* 3 (1960): 168–75. E. Borgatta and A. Esclenbach, "Factor Analysis of Rorschach Variable and Behavior Observation," *Psychological Reports* 3 (1955): 129–36.

10. T. Miller, "The Psychotherapeutic Utility of the Five-Factor Model of Personality: A Clinician's Experience," *Journal of Personality Assessment* 57 (1991): 415–33.

11. K. Menninger, M. Mayman, and P. Pruyser, *The Vital Balance* (New York: Viking Press, 1963).

12. M. Seligman, "The Effectiveness of Psychotherapy: The Consumer Reports Study," *American Psychologist* 50 (1995): 965–74.

13. L. Beutler, "Predictors of Differential Response to Cognitive, Experiential, and Self-Directed Psychotherapeutic Procedures," *Journal of Consulting and Clinical Psychology* 59 (1991): 333–40.

14. H. Hoberman, P. Lewinson, and M. Tilson, "Group Treatment of Depression: Individual Predictors of Outcome," *Journal of Consulting and Clinical Psychology* 56 (1988): 393–98.

15. S. Joure et al., "Differential Change Among Sensitivity-Training Participants as a Function of Dogmatism," *Journal of Psychology* 80 (1972): 151–56.

16. R. Harrison and B. Lubin, "Personal Style, Group Composition, and Learning: Part 2," *Journal of Applied Behavioral Science* 1 (1965): 294–301.

17. C. Crews and J. Melnick, "The Use of Initial and Delayed Structure in Facilitating Group Development," *Journal of Consulting Psychology* 23 (1976): 92–98.

18. P. Kilmann and R. Howell, "The Effects of Structure of Marathon Group Therapy and Locus of Control on Therapeutic Outcome," *Journal of Consulting and Clinical Psychology* 42 (1974): 912.

19. R. Robinson, "The Relationship of Dimension of Interpersonal Trust with Group Cohesiveness, Group Status, and Immediate Outcome in Short-Term Group Counseling," *Dissertation Abstracts* 40 (1980): 5016-B.

20. J. Melnick and G. Rose, "Expectancy and Risk-Taking Propensity: Predictors of Group Performance," *Small Group Behavior* 10 (1979): 389–401. Melnick and Rose demonstrated, in a well-designed experiment involving five undergraduate student experiential groups, that social risk-taking propensity was significantly predictive of therapeutically appropriate self-disclosure, risk-taking behavior, and high verbal activity in the group sessions.

21. K. Horney, *Neurosis and Human Growth* (New York: Norton, 1950).

22. J. Bowlby, *Attachment and Loss*, vol. 1, *Attachment* (New York: Basic Books, 1969); vol. 2, *Separation* (1973); vol. 3, *Loss* (1980). C. George, N. Kaplan, and M. Main, *Adult Attachment Interview*, 3rd ed. Unpublished manuscript, University of California at Berkeley, 1996. J. Cassidy ad J. Mohr, "Unsolvable Fear, Trauma, and Psychopathology: Theory, Research, and Clinical Considerations Related to Disorganized Attachment Across the Life Span," *Clinical Psychology: Science and Practice* 8 (2001): 275–98.

23. R. Maunder and J. Hunter, "An Integrated Approach to the Formulation and Psychotherapy of Medically Unexplained Symptoms: Meaning and Attachment-Based Intervention," *American Journal of Psychotherapy* 58 (2004): 17–33. E. Chen and B. Mallinckrodt, "Attachment, Group Attraction, and Self-Other Agreement in Interpersonal Circumplex Problems and Perceptions of Group Members," *Group Dynamics: Therapy, Research and Practice* 6 (2002): 311–24.

24. C. Tyrrell, M. Dozier, G. Teague, and R. Fallot, "Effective Treatment Relationships for Persons with Serious Psychiatric Disorders: The Importance of Attachment States of Mind," *Journal of Consulting and Clinical Psychology* 67 (1999): 725–33. E. Smith, J. Murphy, and S. Coats, "Attachment and Group Theory and Measurement," *Journal of Personality and Social Psychology* 77 (1999): 94–110.

25. L. Horwitz, S. Rosenberg, B. Baer, G. Ureno, and V. Villasenor, "Inventory of Interpersonal Problems: Psychometric Properties and Clinical Applications," *Journal of Consulting and Clinical Psychology* 56 (1988): 885–92. K. MacKenzie and A. Grabovac, "Interpersonal Psychotherapy Group (IPT-G) for Depression," *Journal of Psychotherapy Practice and Research* 10 (2001): 46–51.

26. Contemporary interpersonal circumplex methodology is built on Leary's original interpersonal circle (T. Leary, *Interpersonal Diagnosis of Personality* [New York: Ronald Press, 1957]) and bears some similarity to Schutz's FIRO (Fundamental Interpersonal Relations Inventory) *FIRO-B: Interpersonal Underworld* (Palo Alto, Calif.: Science and Behavior Books, 1966). See M. Gutman and J. Balakrishnan, "Circular Measurement Redux: The Analytical Interpretation of Interpersonal Circle Profile," *Clinical Psychology Science and Practice* 5 (1998): 344–60. This approach provides a visual schema of the individual's interpersonal style that synthesizes two key interpersonal dimensions: affiliation (ranging from hostile to friendly) and agency or control (ranging from dominant to submissive). Individuals can be described along the lines of hostile, hostile-dominant, hostile-submissive, hostile or friendly, friendly-dominant, friendly-submissive, submissive, respectively.

27. Chen and Mallinckrodt, "Attachment, Group Attraction, and Self-Other Agreement." R. MacNair-Semands and K. Lese, "Interpersonal Problems and the Perception of Therapeutic Factors in Group Therapy," *Small Group Research* 31 (2000): 158–74.

28. J. Ogrodniczuk, W. Piper, A. Joyce, M. McCallum, and J. Rosie, "NEO–Five Factor Personality Traits as Predictors of Response to Two Forms of Group Psychotherapy," *International Journal of Group Psychotherapy* 53 (2003): 417–43.

29. P. Costa and R. McCrae, "Normal Personality Assessment in Clinical Practice: The NEO Personality Inventory," *Psychological Assessment* 4 (1992): 5–13. The NEO Personality Inventory (NEO-PI) and its shorter version, the NEO-FFI, are self-report inventories that are easy to administer, reliable, and well validated across cultures. Five personality variables are evaluated: Neuroticism (distress, vulnerability to stress and propensity for shame); Extraversion (verbal, eager to engage, and enthusiastic); Conscientiousness (hard working, committed, able to delay gratification); Openness (embraces the novel and unfamiliar with creativity and imagination); and Agreeableness (trusting, cooperative, altruistic).

30. W. Piper, A. Joyce, J. Rosie, and H. Azim, "Psychological Mindedness, Work and Outcome in Day Treatment," *International Journal of Group Psychotherapy* 44 (1994): 291–311. M. McCallum, W. Piper, and J. Kelly, "Predicting Patient Benefit from a Group-Oriented Evening Treatment Program," *International Journal of Group Psychotherapy* 47

(1997): 291–314. W. Piper, A. Joyce, M. McCallum, H. Azim, and J. Ogrodniczuk, *Interpersonal and Supportive Psychotherapies: Matching Therapy and Patient Personality* (Washington, D.C.: American Psychological Association, 2001). W. Piper, J. Ogrodniczuk, M. McCallum, A. Joyce, and J. Rosie, "Expression of Affect as a Mediator of the Relationship Between Quality of Object Relations and Group Therapy Outcome for Patients with Complicated Grief," *Journal of Consulting and Clinical Psychology* 71 (2003): 664–71. M. McCallum, W. Piper, J. Ogrodniczuk, and A. Joyce, "Relationships Among Psychological Mindedness, Alexithymia, and Outcome in Four Forms of Short-Term Psychotherapy," *Psychology and Psychotherapy: Theory, Research, and Practice* 76 (2003): 133–44.

31. Piper, Joyce, Rosie, and Azim, "Psychological Mindedness."

32. W. Piper et al., "Expression of Affect as a Mediator." McCallum et al., "Relationships Among Psychological Mindedness, Alexithymia, and Outcome." M. McCallum, W. Piper, and J. Kelly, "Predicting Patient Benefit from a Group-Oriented Evening Treatment Program," *International Journal of Group Psychotherapy* 47 (1997): 291–314.

33. Piper et al., "Expression of Affect as a Mediator." J. Ogrodniczuk, W. Piper, M. McCallum, A. Joyce, and J. Rosie, "Interpersonal Predictors of Group Therapy Outcome for Complicated Grief," *International Journal of Group Psychotherapy* 52 (2002): 511–35.

34. S. Sotsky et al., "Patient Predictors of Response to Psychotherapy and Pharmacotherapy: Findings in the NIMH Treatment of Depression Collaborative Research Program," *American Journal of Psychiatry* 148 (1991): 997–1008. S. Blatt, D. Quinlan, P. Pilkonis, and M. Shea, "Impact of Perfectionism and Need for Approval on the Brief Treatment of Depression: The National Institute of Mental Health Treatment of Depression Collaborative Research Program Revisited," *Journal of Consulting and Clinical Psychology* 63 (1995): 125–32.

35. A. Goldstein, K. Heller, and L. Sechrest, *Psychotherapy and the Psychology of Behavior Change* (New York: Wiley, 1966), 329.

36. R. Moos and S. Clemes, "A Multivariate Study of the Patient-Therapist System," *Journal of Consulting Psychology* 31 (1967): 119–30. C. Zimet, "Character Defense Preference and Group Therapy Interaction," *Archives of General Psychiatry* 3 (1960): 168–75. F. Giedt, "Predicting Suitability for Group Therapy," *American Journal of Psychotherapy* 15 (1961): 582–91.

37. Moos and Clemes, "A Multivariate Study."

38. G. McEvoy and R. Beatty, "Assessment Centers and Subordinate Appraisals of Managers: A Seven-Year Examination of Predictive Validity," *Personnel Psychology* 42 (1989): 37–52. H. Fields, "The Group Interview Test: Its Strength," *Public Personnel Review* 11 (1950): 39–46. Z. Shechtman, "A Group Assessment Procedure as a Predictor of On-the-Job Performance of Teachers," *Journal of Applied Psychology* 77 (1992): 383–87. R. Baker, "Knowing What You're Looking For: An Outcome-Based Approach to Hiring," *Leadership Abstracts* 13 (2000), Worldwide Web Edition.

39. E. Borgatta and R. Bales, "Interaction of Individuals in Reconstituted Groups," *Sociometry* 16 (1953): 302–20.

40. E. Borgatta and R. Bales, "Task and Accumulation of Experience as Factors in the Interaction of Small Groups," *Sociometry* 16 (1953): 239–52. B. Bass, *Leadership, Psychology, and Organizational Behavior* (New York: Harper & Row, 1960).

41. V. Cerbin, "Individual Behavior in Social Situations: Its Relation to Anxiety, Neuroticism, and Group Solidarity," *Journal of Experimental Psychology* 51 (1956): 161–68.

42. Ibid.

43. R. Cattell, D. Saunders, and G. Stice, "The Dimensions of Syntality in Small Groups," *Journal of Social Psychology* 28 (1948): 57–78.

44. S. Foulkes and E. Anthony, *Group Psychotherapy: The Psychoanalytic Approach* (Harmondsworth, England: Penguin, 1957). G. Bach, *Intensive Group Therapy* (New York: Ronald Press, 1954).

45. W. Stone, M. Parloff, and J. Frank, "The Use of Diagnostic Groups in a Group Therapy Program," *International Journal of Group Psychotherapy* 4 (1954): 274–84.

46. W. Stone and E. Klein, "The Waiting-List Group," *International Journal of Group Psychotherapy* 49 (1999): 417–28.

47. E. Klein, W. Stone, D. Reynolds, and J. Hartman, "A Systems Analysis of the Effectiveness of Waiting List Group Therapy," *International Journal of Group Psychotherapy* 51 (2001): 417–23.

48. W. Piper and M. Marrache, "Selecting Suitable Patients: Pretraining for Group Therapy as a Method for Group Selection," *Small Group Behavior* 12 (1981): 459–74.

49. J. Connelly and W. Piper, "An Analysis of Pretraining Work Behavior as a Composition Variable in Group Psychotherapy," *International Journal of Group Psychotherapy* 39 (1989): 173–89.

50. H. Sullivan, *The Psychiatric Interview* (New York: Norton, 1954).

51. G. Klerman, M. Weissman, B. Rounsaville, and E. Chevron, *Interpersonal Psychotherapy of Depression* (New York: Basic Books, 1984). McCullough, *Treatment for Chronic Depression*.

52. F. Powdermaker and J. Frank, *Group Psychotherapy* (Cambridge, Mass.: Harvard University Press, 1953), 553–64.

53. This framework is a central component of a number of contemporary psychotherapy approaches. It may be alternately identified as the client's "plan" (J. Weiss, *How Psychotherapy Works: Process and Technique* [New York: Guilford Press, 1993]) or "cognitive-interpersonal schema" (J. Safran and Z. Segal, *Interpersonal Process in Cognitive Therapy* [New York: Basic Books, 1990]). M. Leszcz and J. Malat, "The Interpersonal Model of Group Psychotherapy," in *Praxis der Gruppenpsychotherapie*, ed. V. Tschuschke (Frankfurt: Thieme, 2001), 355–69. D. Kiesler, *Contemporary Interpersonal Theory and Research* (New York: Wiley, 1996).

54. G. Burlingame, A. Fuhriman, and J. Johnson, "Cohesion in Group Psychotherapy," in *A Guide to Psychotherapy Relationships and Work*, ed. J. Norcross (Oxford, England: Oxford University Press, 2002): 71–88.

55. M. Nitsun, "The Future of the Group," *International Journal of Group Psychotherapy* 50 (2000): 455–72.

56. M. Lieberman, I. Yalom, and M. Miles, *Encounter Groups: First Facts* (New York: Basic Books, 1972).

57. A. Francis, J. Clarkin, and J. Morachi, "Selection Criteria for Outpatient Group Psychotherapy," *Hospital and Community Psychiatry* 31 (1980): 245–250. J. Best, P. Jones, and A. Paton, "The Psychotherapeutic Value of a More Homogeneous Group Composition," *International Journal of Social Psychiatry* 27 (1981): 43–46. J. Melnick and M. Woods, "Analysis of Group Composition Research and Theory for Psychotherapeutic and Growth Oriented Groups," *Journal of Applied Behavioral Science* 12 (1976): 493–513.

58. G. Burlingame, A. Fuhriman, and J. Johnson, "Cohesion in Group Psychotherapy."

59. M. Siebert and W. Dorfman, "Group Composition and Its Impact on Effective Group Treatment of HIV and AIDS Patients," *Journal of Developmental and Physical Disabilities* 7 (1995): 317–34.

60. M. Esplen et al., "A Multi-Centre Phase II Study of Supportive-Expressive Group Therapy for Women with BRCA1 and BRCA2 Mutations," *Cancer* (2004): 2237–2342.

61. Foulkes and Anthony, *Group Psychotherapy*, 94.

62. I. Yalom et al., "Prediction of Improvement in Group Therapy," *Archives of General Psychiatry* 17 (1967): 159–68. I. Yalom et al., "Preparation of Patients for Group Therapy: A Controlled Study," *Archives of General Psychiatry* 17 (1967): 416–27. A. Sklar et al., "Time-Extended Group Therapy: A Controlled Study," *Comparative Group Studies* (1970): 373–86. I. Yalom and K. Rand, "Compatibility and Cohesiveness in Therapy Groups," *Archives of General Psychiatry* 13 (1966): 267–76.

63. F. Rabinowitz, "Group Therapy for Men," in *The New Handbook of Psychotherapy and Counseling with Men: A Comprehensive Guide to Settings, Problems, and Treatment Approaches,* vol. 2, ed. G. Brooks and G. Good (San Francisco: Jossey-Bass, 2001), 603–21. L. Holmes, "Women in Groups and Women's Groups," *International Journal of Group Psychotherapy* 52 (2002): 171–88.

64. Ibid. F. Wright and L. Gould, "Research on Gender-Linked Aspects of Group Behaviors: Implications for Group Psychotherapy," in *Women and Group Psychotherapy: Theory and Practice,* ed. B. DeChant (New York: Guilford Press, 1996), 333–50. J. Ogrodniczuk, W. Piper, and A. Joyce, "Differences in Men's and Women's Responses to Short-Term Group Psychotherapy," *Psychotherapy Research* 14 (2004): 231–43.

65. T. Newcomb, "The Prediction of Interpersonal Attraction," *American Psychology* 11 (1956): 575–86.

66. M. Lieberman, "The Relationship of Group Climate to Individual Change," Ph.D. diss., University of Chicago, 1958.

67. C. Fairbairn et al., "Psychotherapy and Bulimia Nervosa," *Archives of General Psychiatry* 50 (1993): 419–28. D. Wilfley et al., "Group Cognitive-Behavioral Therapy and Group Interpersonal Psychotherapy for the Nonpurging Bulimic Individual: A Controlled Comparison," *Journal of Consulting and Clinical Psychology* 61 (1993): 296–305.

CHAPTER 10

1. N. Taylor, G. Burlingame, K. Kristensen, A. Fuhriman, J. Johansen, and D. Dahl, "A Survey of Mental Health Care Providers' and Managed Care Organization Attitudes Toward Familiarity With, and Use of Group Interventions," *International Journal of Group Psychotherapy* 51 (2001): 243–63. S. Rosenberg and C. Zimet, "Brief Group Treatment and Managed Health Care," *International Journal of Group Psychotherapy* 45 (1995): 367–79. P. Cox, F. Ilfeld, B. Ilfeld, and C. Brennan, "Group Therapy Program Development: Clinician-Administrator Collaborations in New Practice Settings," *International Journal of Group Psychotherapy* 50 (2000): 3–24.

2. S. Green and S. Bloch, "Working in a Flawed Mental Health Care System: An Ethical Challenge," *American Journal of Psychiatry* 158 (2001): 1378–83.

3. K. Long, L. Pendleton, B. Winter, "Effects of Therapist Termination on Group Process" *International Journal of Group Psychotherapy*, 38 (1988): 211–22.

4. B. Donovan, A. Padin-Rivera, and S. Kowaliw, "Transcend: Initial Outcomes from a Post-Traumatic Stress Disorder/Substance Abuse Treatment Program," *Journal of Traumatic Stress* 14 (2001): 757–72. S. Lash, G. Petersen, E. O'Connor, and L. Lahmann, "Social Reinforcement of Substance Abuse Aftercare Group Therapy Attendance," *Journal of Substance Abuse Treatment* 20 (2001): 3–8. M. Leszcz, "Geriatric Group Psychotherapy," in *Comprehensive Textbook of Geriatric Psychiatry,* ed. J. Sadavoy, L. Jarvik, G. Grossberg, and B. Meyers (New York: Norton, 2004), 1023–54.

5. K. MacKenzie, "Time-Limited Group Psychotherapy," *International Journal of Group Psychotherapy* 46 (1996): 41–60.

6. S. Budman, *Treating Time Effectively* (New York: Guilford Press, 1994).

7. R. Weigel, "The Marathon Encounter Group: Vision or Reality: Exhuming the Body for a Last Look," *Consulting Psychology Journal: Practice and Research* 54 (2002): 186–298.

8. F. Stoller, "Accelerated Interaction: A Time-Limited Approach Based on the Brief Intensive Group," *International Journal of Group Psychotherapy* 18 (1968): 220–35.

9. G. Bach, "Marathon Group Dynamics," *Psychological Reports* 20 (1967): 1147–58.

10. A. Rachman, "Marathon Group Psychotherapy," *Journal of Group Psychoanalysis and Process* 2 (1969): 57–74.

11. F. Stoller, "Marathon Group Therapy," in *Innovations to Group Psychotherapy,* ed. G. Gazda (Springfield, Ill.: Charles C. Thomas, 1968), 71.

12. G. Bach and F. Stoller, "The Marathon Group," cited in N. Dinges and R. Weigel, "The Marathon Group: A Review of Practice and Research," *Comparative Group Studies* 2 (1971): 339–458.

13. M. Gendron, "Effectiveness of the Intensive Group Process–Retreat Model in the Treatment of Bulimia," *Group* 16 (1992): 69–78.

14. C. Edmonds, G. Lockwood, and A. Cunningham, "Psychological Response to Long-Term Group Therapy: A Randomized Trial with Metastatic Breast Cancer Patients," *Psycho-Oncology* 8 (1999): 74–91. Weigel, "The Marathon Encounter."

15. S. Asch, "Effects of Group Pressure upon the Modification and Distortion of Judgments," in *Group Dynamics: Research and Theory*, ed. D. Cartwright and A. Zander (New York: Harper and Row, 1960): 189–201.

16. T. Loomis, "Marathon vs. Spaced Groups: Skin Conductance and the Effects of Time Distribution on Encounter Group Learning," *Small Group Behavior* 19 (1988): 516–27.

17. C. Winnick and A. Levine, "Marathon Therapy: Treating Rape Survivors in a Therapeutic Community," *Journal of Psychoactive Drugs* 24 (1992): 49–56.

18. R. Page, B. Richmond, and M. de La Serna, "Marathon Group Counseling with Illicit Drug Abusers: Effects on Self-Perceptions," *Small Group Behavior* 14 (1987): 483–97. N. Dinges and R. Weigel, "The Marathon Group: A Review of Practice and Research," *Comparative Group Studies* 2 (1971): 220–35. P. Kilmann and W. Sotile, "The Marathon Encounter Group: A Review of the Outcome Literature," *Psychological Bulletin* 83 (1976): 827–50.

19. A. Sklar et al., "Time-Extended Group Therapy: A Controlled Study," *Comparative Group Studies* 1 (1970): 373–86.

20. Thus, during their first sixteen meetings, each group had one six-hour session and fifteen meetings of conventional length (ninety minutes). Tape recordings of the second, sixth, tenth, twelfth, and sixteenth meetings were analyzed to classify the verbal interaction. Postgroup questionnaires measuring members' involvement with the group and with each other were obtained at these same meetings. The Hill Interaction Matrix method of scoring interaction was used. The middle thirty minutes of the meeting were systematically evaluated by two trained raters who were naive about the design of the study. (The six-hour meeting itself was not analyzed, since we were interested primarily in studying its effect on the subsequent course of therapy.) (W. Hill, *HIM: Hill Interaction Matrix* [Los Angeles: Youth Study Center, University of Southern California, 1965].)

21. B. Jones reports similar findings in a study of three ongoing therapy groups, two of which had weekend marathons (B. Jones, "The Effect of a Marathon Experience upon Ongoing Group Therapy," *Dissertation Abstracts* [1977]: 3887-B).

22. I. Yalom et al., "The Impact of a Weekend Group Experience on Individual Therapy," *Archives of General Psychiatry* 34 (1977): 399–415.

23. I. Yalom et al., ibid.

24. Taylor et al., "A Survey of Mental Health Care Providers."

25. M. Koss and J. Butchner, "Research on Brief Therapy," in *Handbook of Psychotherapy and Behavioral Change: An Empirical Analysis*, 3rd ed., ed. S. Garfield and A. Bergin (New York: Wiley, 1986), 626.

26. K. MacKenzie, "Where Is Here and When Is Now? The Adaptational Challenges of Mental Health Reform for Group Psychotherapy," *International Journal of Group Psychotherapy* 44 (1994): 407–20. D. Wilfley, K. MacKenzie, R. Welch, V. Ayres, and M. Weissman, *Interpersonal Psychotherapy for Group* (New York: Basic Books, 2000).

27. S. Budman and A. Gurman, *Theory and Practice of Brief Therapy* (New York: Guilford Press, 1988), 248.

28. S. Budman, *Treating Time Effectively*.

29. K. Howard, S. Kopta, and M. Krause, "The Dose-Effect Relationship in Psychotherapy," *American Psychologist* 41 (1986): 159–64.

30. S. Kopta, K. Howard, J. Lowry, and L. Beutler, "Patterns of Symptomatic Recovery in Time-Limited Psychotherapy," *Journal of Consulting Clinical Psychology* 62 (1994): 1009–16. S. Kadera, M. Lambert, and A. Andrew, "How Much Therapy Is Really Enough? A Session-By-Session Analysis of the Psychotherapy Dose-Effect Relationship," *Journal of Psychotherapy Practice and Research* 5 (1996): 132–51.

31. N. Doidge, B. Simon, L. Gillies, and R. Ruskin, "Characteristics of Psychoanalytic Patients Under a Nationalized Health Plan: DSM-III-R Diagnoses, Previous Treatment, and Childhood Trauma," *American Journal of Psychiatry* 151 (1994): 586–90.

32. R. Klein, "Short-Term Group Psychotherapy," in *Comprehensive Group Psychotherapy*, ed. H. Kaplan and B. Sadock (Baltimore: Williams & Wilkins, 1993), 257–70. K. MacKenzie, "Time-Limited Group Psychotherapy."

33. S. Budman, S. Cooley, A. Demby, G. Koppenaal, J. Koslof, and T. Powers, "A Model of Time-Effective Group Psychotherapy for Patients with Personality Disorders," *International Journal of Group Psychotherapy* 46 (1996): 315–24. K. MacKenzie, "Where Is Here and When Is Now?" K. MacKenzie, *Time-Managed Group Psychotherapy: Effective Clinical Applications* (Washington, D.C.: American Psychiatric Press, 1997).

34. Budman and Gurman, *Theory and Practice of Brief Therapy.*

35. J. Mann and R. Goldman, *A Casebook in Time-limited Psychotherapy* (Washington, D.C.: American Psychiatric Press, 1987).

36. Budman and Gurman, *Theory and Practice of Brief Therapy.*

37. Wilfley et al., *Interpersonal Psychotherapy for Group.*

38. In an HMO setting, Budman employs the pregroup individual session primarily for screening and reframing the patient's problems to facilitate the client's working in a brief time frame. Much of the group preparation is held in a large-group (approximately twelve patients) ninety-minute workshop that is both didactic and experiential. This preparatory model has also proved highly effective in reducing dropouts. (Budman and Gurman, *Theory and Practice.*)

39. K. MacKenzie, "Time-Limited Group Psychotherapy." K. MacKenzie, *Time-Managed Group Psychotherapy.* K. MacKenzie and A. Grabovac, "Interpersonal Psychotherapy Group (IPT-G) for Depression," *Journal of Psychotherapy Practice and Research* 10 (2001): 46–51. S. Budman, P. Simeone, R. Reilly, and A. Demby, "Progress in Short-Term and Time-Limited Group Psychotherapy: Evidence and Implications," in *Handbook of Group Psychotherapy,* ed. A. Fuhriman and G. Burlingame (New York: Wiley, 1994): 319–39.

40. M. Esplen et al., "A Supportive-Expressive Group Intervention for Women with a Family History of Breast Cancer: Results of a Phase II Study," *Psycho-Oncology* 9 (2000): 243–52.

41. J. Hardy and C. Lewis, "Bridging the Gap Between Long- and Short-Term Therapy: A Viable Model," *Group* 16 (1992): 5–17.

42. W. McDermut, I. Miller, and R. Brown, "The Efficacy of Group Psychotherapy for Depression: A Meta-Analysis and a Review of Empirical Research," *Clinical Psychology: Science and Practice* 8 (2001): 98–104.

43. MacKenzie and Grabovac, "Interpersonal Psychotherapy Group." A. Ravindran et al., "Treatment of Primary Dysthymia with Group Cognitive Therapy and Pharmacotherapy: Clinical Symptoms and Functional Impairments," *American Journal of Psychiatry* 156 (1999): 1608–17.

44. W. Piper, M. McCallum, and A. Hassan, *Adaptation to Loss Through Short-Term Group Psychotherapy* (New York: Guilford Press, 1992).

45. W. Piper, M. McCallum, A. Joyce, J. Rosie, and J. Ogrodniczuk, "Patient Personality and Time-Limited Group Psychotherapy for Complicated Grief," *International Journal of Group Psychotherapy* 51 (2001): 525–52.

46. E. Marziali and H. Munroe-Blum, *Interpersonal Group Psychotherapy for Borderline Personality Disorder* (New York: Basic Books, 1994).

47. A. Sherman et al., "Group Interventions for Patients with Cancer and HIV Disease, Part I: Effects on Psychosocial and Functional Outcomes at Different Phases of Illness," *International Journal of Group Psychotherapy* 54 (2004): 29–82.

48. W. Piper, E. Debbane, J. Bienvenue, and J. Garant, "A Comparative Study of Four Forms of Psychotherapy," *Journal of Consulting and Clinical Psychology* 52 (1984): 268–79.

49. S. Budman et al., "Comparative Outcome in Time-Limited Individual and Group Psychotherapy," *International Journal of Group Psychotherapy* 38 (1988): 63–86.

50. M. Koss and J. Shiang, "Research in Brief Psychotherapy," in *Handbook of Psychotherapy and Behavioral Change: An Empirical Analysis,* 4th ed., ed. S. Garfield and A. Bergin (New York: Wiley, 1994): 664–700.

51. I. Elkin, "Perspectives on the NIMH Collaborative Treatment of Depression Study," presented at Mount Sinai Hospital, Toronto, Ontario, Canada, April 1995.

52. . Fulkerson, D. Hawkins, and A. Alden, "Psychotherapy Groups of Insufficient Size," *International Journal of Group Psychotherapy* 31 (1981): 73–81.

53. J. White and M. Keenan, "Stress Control: A Pilot Study of Large Group Therapy for Generalized Anxiety Disorder," *Behavioral Psychotherapy* 18 (1990): 143–46.

54. T. Oei, M. Llamas, and L. Evans, "Does Concurrent Drug Intake Affect the Long-Term Outlook of Group Cognitive Behavior Therapy in Panic Disorder with or Without Agoraphobia?" *Behavior Research and Therapy* 35 (1997): 851–57.

55. A. Cunningham, C. Edmonds, and D. Williams, "Delivering a Very Brief Psychoeducational Program to Cancer Patients and Family Members in a Large Group Format," *Psycho-Oncology* 8 (1999): 177–82.

56. A. Cunningham, "Adjuvant Psychological Therapy for Cancer Patients: Putting It on the Same Footing as Adjunctive Medical Therapies," *Psycho-Oncology* 9 (2000): 367–71.

57. G. Castore, "Number of Verbal Interrelationships as a Determinant of Group Size," *Journal of Abnormal Social Psychology* 64 (1962): 456–57.

58. A. Hare, *Handbook of Small Group Research* (New York: Free Press of Glencoe, 1962), 224–45.

59. L. Carter et al., "The Behavior of Leaders and Other Group Members," *Journal of Abnormal Social Psychology* 46 (1958): 256–60.

60. A. Marc, "A Study of Interaction and Consensus in Different Sized Groups," *American Social Review* 17 (1952): 261–67.

61. Y. Slocum, "A Survey of Expectations About Group Therapy Among Clinical and Nonclinical Populations," *International Journal of Group Psychotherapy* 37 (1987): 39–54.

62. M. Bowden, "Anti-Group Attitudes and Assessment for Psychotherapy," *Psychoanalytic Psychotherapy* 16 (2002): 246–58. M. Nitsun, "The Future of the Group," *International Journal of Group Psychotherapy* 50 (2000): 455–72.

63. M. Bowden, ibid.

64. H. Bernard, "Patterns and Determinants of Attitudes of Psychiatric Residents Toward Group Therapy," *Group* 15 (1991): 131–40.

65. S. Sue, "In Search of Cultural Competence in Psychotherapy Counseling," *American Psychologist* 53 (1998): 440–48. M. LaRoche and A. Maxie, "Ten Considerations in Addressing Cultural Differences in Psychotherapy," *Professional Psychology: Research and Practice* 34 (2003): 180–86.

66. B. Meyer, J. Krupnick, S. Simmens, P. Pilkonis, M. Egan, and S. Sotsky, "Treatment Expectancies, Patient Alliance, and Outcome: Further Analysis from the NIMH Treatment of Depression Collaborative Research Program," *Journal of Consulting and Clinical Psychology* 70 (2002): 1051–55. C. Carver and M. Schriver, *On the Self-Regulation of Bulimia* (New York: Cambridge University Press, 1998).

67. M. Connolly Gibbon, P. Crits-Christoph, C. de la Cruz, J. Barber, L. Siqueland, and M. Gladis, "Pretreatment Expectations, Interpersonal Functioning, and Symptoms in the

Prediction of the Therapeutic Alliance Across Supportive-Expressive Psychotherapy and Cognitive Therapy," *Psychotherapy Research* 13 (2003): 59–76.

68. H. Roback, R. Moor, F. Bloch, and M. Shelton, "Confidentiality in Group Psychotherapy: Empirical Finds and the Law," *International Journal of Group Psychotherapy* 46 (1996): 117–35. H. Roback, E. Ochoa, F. Bloch, and S. Purdon, "Guarding Confidentiality in Clinical Groups: The Therapist's Dilemma," *International Journal of Group Psychotherapy* 42 (1992): 426–31.

69. J. Beahrs and T. Gutheil, "Informed Consent in Psychotherapy," *American Journal of Psychiatry* 158 (2001): 4–10.

70. R. Crandall, "The Assimilation of Newcomers into Groups," *Small Group Behavior* 9 (1978): 331–36.

71. E. Gauron and E. Rawlings, "A Procedure for Orienting New Members to Group Psychotherapy," *Small Group Behavior* 6 (1975): 293–307.

72. W. Piper, "Pretraining for Group Psychotherapy: A Cognitive-Experiential Approach," *Archives of General Psychiatry* 36 (1979): 1250–56. W. Piper et al., "Preparation of Patients: A Study of Group Pretraining for Group Psychotherapy," *International Journal of Group Psychotherapy* 32 (1982): 309–25. S. Budman et al., "Experiential Pre-Group Preparation and Screening," *Group* 5 (1981): 19–26.

73. S. Budman et al., "Experiential Pre-group Preparation and Screening," *Group* 5 (1981): 19–26. S. Budman, S. Cooley, A. Demby, G. Koppenaal, J. Koslof, and T. Powers, "A Model of Time-Effective Group Psychotherapy for Patients with Personality Disorders," *International Journal of Group Psychotherapy* 46 (1996): 315–24.

74. J. Connelly and W. Piper, "An Analysis of Pretraining Work Behavior as a Composition Variable in Group Psychotherapy," *International Journal of Group Psychotherapy* 39 (1989): 173–89.

75. R. Kadden, M. Litt, N. Cooney, and D. Busher, "Relationship Between Role-Play Measures of Coping Skills and Alcoholism Treatment Outcome," *Addiction Behavior* 17 (1992): 425–37.

76. W. Piper et al., "Preparation of Patients: A Study of Group Pretraining for Group Psychotherapy," *International Journal of Group Psychotherapy* 32 (1982): 309–25.

77. J. Prochaska, C. DiClemente, and J. Norcross, "In Search of How People Change: Applications to Addictive Behaviors," *American Psychologist* 47 (1992): 1102–14.

78. R. Feld, D. Woodside, A. Kaplan, M. Olmstead, and J. Carter, "Pre-Treatment Motivational Enhancement Therapy for Eating Disorders: A Pilot Study," *International Journal of Eating Disorders* 29 (2001): 393–400. G. O'Reilly, T. Morrison, D. Sheerin, A. Carr, "A Group-Based Module for Adolescents to Improve Motivation to Change Sexually Abusive Behavior," *Child Abuse Review* 10 (2001): 150–69. W. Miller and S. Rollnick, *Motivational Interviewing: Preparing People to Change Addictive Behavior* (New York: Guilford Press, 2002).

79. I. Yalom et al., "Preparation of Patients for Group Therapy," *Archives of General Psychiatry* 17 (1967): 416–27.

80. The interaction of the groups was measured by scoring each statement during the meeting on the a sixteen-cell matrix (W. Hill, *HIM: Hill Interaction Matrix* [Los Angeles: Youth Study Center, University of Southern California, 1965]). Scoring was performed by a team of raters naive to the experimental design. Faith in therapy was tested by postgroup patient-administered questionnaires.

81. D. Meadow, "Preparation of Individuals for Participation in a Treatment Group: Development and Empirical Testing of a Model," *International Journal of Group Psychotherapy* 38 (1988): 367–85. R. Bednar and T. Kaul, "Experiential Group Research: Can the Canon Fire?" in *Handbook of Psychotherapy and Behavioral Change: An Empirical Analysis,* 4th ed., ed. S. Garfield and A. Bergin (New York: Wiley, 1994): 631–63. G. Burlingame, A. Fuhriman, and J. Mosier, "The Differential Effectiveness of Group Psychotherapy: A Meta-Analytic Perspective," *Group Dynamics: Theory, Research, and Practice* 7 (2003): 3–12.

82. M. Wogan et al., "Influencing Interaction and Outcomes in Group Psychotherapy," *Small Group Behavior* 8 (1977): 25–46.

83. W. Piper and E. Perrault, "Pretherapy Training for Group Members," *International Journal of Group Psychotherapy* 39 (1989): 17–34. Piper et al., "Preparation of Patients." W. Piper and J. Ogrodniczuk, "Pregroup Training," in *Praxis der Gruppenpsychotherapie*, ed. V. Tschuschke (Frankfurt: Thieme, 2001): 74–78. Connelly and Piper, "An Analysis of Pretraining Work Behavior." S. Budman and M. Bennet, "Short-Term Group Psychotherapy," in *Comprehensive Group Psychotherapy*, 2nd ed., ed. H. Kaplan and B. Sadock (Baltimore: Williams & Wilkins, 1983), 138–44. D. France and J. Dugo, "Pretherapy Orientation as Preparation for Open Psychotherapy Groups," *Psychotherapy* 22 (1985): 256–61.

84. J. Heitler, "Clinical Impressions of an Experimental Attempt to Prepare Lower-Class Patients for Expressive Group Psychotherapy," *International Journal of Group Psychotherapy* 29 (1974): 308–22. K. Palmer, R. Baker, and T. Miker, "The Effects of Pretraining on Group Psychotherapy for Incest-Related Issues," *International Journal of Group Psychotherapy* 47 (1997): 71–89.

85. W. Piper and J. Ogrodniczuk, "Pregroup Training."

86. E. Werth, "A Comparison of Pretraining Models for Encounter Group Therapy," *Dissertation Abstracts* 40 (1979).

87. G. Silver, "Systematic Presentation of Pre-therapy Information in Group Psychotherapy: Its Relationship to Attitude and Behavioral Change," *Dissertation Abstracts* (1976): 4481-B.

88. Piper et al., "Preparation of Patients." L. Annis and D. Perry, "Self-Disclosure in Unsupervised Groups: Effects of Videotaped Models," *Small Group Behavior* 9 (1978): 102–8. J. Samuel, "The Individual and Comparative Effects of a Pre-group Preparation Upon Two Different Therapy Groups," *Dissertation Abstracts International* 41 (1980): 1919-B. S. Barnett, "The Effect of Preparatory Training in Communication Skills on Group Therapy with Lower Socioeconomic Class Alcoholics," *Dissertation Abstracts International* 41 (1981): 2744-B.

89. Barnett, ibid. P. Pilkonis et al, "Training Complex Social Skills for Use in a Psychotherapy Group: A Case Study," *International Journal of Group Psychotherapy* 30 (1980): 347–56.

90. Pilkonis et al., ibid.

91. T. Zarle and S. Willis, "A Pre-Group Training Technique for Encounter Group Stress," *Journal of Counseling Psychology* 22 (1975): 49–53.

92. T. Curran, "Increasing Motivation to Change in Group Treatment," *Small Group Behavior* 9 (1978): 337–48.

93. J. Steuer et al., "Cognitive Behavior and Psychodynamic Group Psychotherapy in Treatment of Geriatric Depression," *Journal of Consulting and Clinical Psychology* 52 (1984): 180–89.

94. O. Farrell, T. Cutter, and F. Floyd, "Evaluating Marital Therapy for Male Alcoholics," *Behavior Therapy* 16 (1985): 147–67.

95. Curran, "Increasing Motivation to Change."

96. M. Cartwright, "Brief Reports: A Preparatory Method for Group Counseling," *Journal of Counseling Psychology* 23 (1976): 75–77.

97. A. Hare, "A Study of Interaction and Consensus in Different Sized Groups," *American Social Review* 17 (1952): 261–67.

98. C. Taft, C. Murphy, J. Elliott, and T. Morrel, "Attendance Enhancing Procedures in Group Counseling for Domestic Abusers," *Journal of Counseling Psychology* 48 (2001): 51–60.

99. Piper and Ogrodniczuk, "Pregroup Training."

100. I. Gradolph, "The Task-Approach of Groups of Single-Type and Mixed-Type Valency Compositions," in *Emotional Dynamics and Group Culture*, ed. D. Stock and H.

Thelen (New York: New York University Press, 1958), 127–30. D. Stock and W. Hill, "Intersubgroup Dynamics as a Factor in Group Growth," *Emotional Dynamics and Group Culture,* ed. D. Stock and H. Thelen (New York: New York University Press, 1958), 207–21.

101. Piper (Piper & Perrault 1989) suggests that clients tend to drop out of therapy groups if they receive no pretherapy preparation because of excessive anxiety: that is, they did not have the opportunity to extinguish anxiety by experiencing controlled modulation of anxiety in the presence of experienced leaders. R. Curtis, "Self-Organizing Processes, Anxiety, and Change," *Journal of Psychotherapy Integration* 2 (1992): 295–319.

102. R. White, "Motivation Reconsidered: The Concept of Competence," *Psychological Review* 66 (1959): 297–333.

103. B. Rauer and J. Reitsema, "The Effects of Varied Clarity of Group Goal and Group Path Upon the Individual and His Relation to His Group," *Human Relations* 10 (1957): 29–45. A. Cohen, "Situational Structure, Self-Esteem, and Threat-Oriented Reactions to Power," in *Studies in Social Power,* ed. D. Cartwright (Ann Arbor, Mich.: Research Center for Group Dynamics, 1959), 35–52. A. Goldstein, K. Heller, and L. Sechrest, *Psychotherapy and the Psychology of Behavior Change* (New York: Wiley, 1966), 405.

104. Goldstein et al., ibid., 329. E. Murray, "A Content Analysis for Study in Psychotherapy," *Psychological Monographs* 70 (1956).

105. Beahrs and Gutheil, "Informed Consent."

106. American Psychological Association, *Ethical Principles of Psychologists and the Code of Conduct* (Washington, D.C.: American Psychological Association, 1992).

107. American Psychiatric Association, *The Principles of Medical Ethics with Annotations Especially Applicable to Psychiatry* (Washington, D.C.: American Psychiatric Association, 1998), 24.

108. E. Aronson and J. Mills, "The Effect of Severity of Initiation on Liking for a Group," *Journal of Abnormal Social Psychology* 59 (1959): 177–81. R. Cialdini, "Harnessing the Science of Persuasion," *Harvard Business Review* 79 (2001): 72–79.

CHAPTER 11

1. B. Tuckman, "Developmental Sequences in Small Groups," *Psychological Bulletin* 63 (1965): 384–99. Tuckman's third stage—"norming"—refers to the development of group cohesion. His fourth stage—"performing"—refers to the emergence of insight and functional role-relatedness.

2. K. MacKenzie, "Clinical Application of Group Development Ideas," *Group Dynamics: Theory, Research and Practice* 1 (1997): 275–87. Y. Agazarian and S. Gantt, "Phases of Group Development: Systems-centered Hypotheses and Their Implications for Research and Practice," *Group Dynamics: Theory, Research and Practice* 7 (2003): 238–52. S. Wheelan, B. Davidson and F. Tilin, "Group Development Across Time: Reality or Illusion?" *Small Group Research* 34 (2003): 223–45. G. Burlingame, K. MacKenzie, B. Strauss, "Small-Group Treatment: Evidence for Effectiveness and Mechanisms of Change," in Bergin and Garfield's *Handbook of Psychotherapy and Behavior Change*, 5th ed., ed. M. Lambert (New York: John Wiley & Sons Ltd., 2004), 647–96.

3. D. Kivlighan and D. Mullison, "Participants' Perception of Therapeutic Factors in Group Counseling: The Role of Interpersonal Style and Stage of Group Development," *Small Group Behavior* 19 (1988): 452–68. D. Kivlighan and R. Lilly, "Developmental Changes in Group Climate as They Relate to Therapeutic Gain," *Group Dynamics: Theory, Research, and Practice* 1 (1997): 208–21.

4. S. Wheelan, "Group Development and the Practice of Group Psychotherapy," *Group Dynamics: Theory, Research, and Practice* 1 (1997): 288–93. S. Wheelan, D. Murphy, E. Tsumura, and S. Fried-Kline, "Member Perceptions of Internal Group Dynamics and Productivity," *Small Group Research* 29 (1998): 371–93. Wheelan and Hochberger developed and validated the Group Development Questionnaire (GDQ) as a measure of group de-

velopment in work and task groups. The GDQ, a self-report measure, consists of a series of questions that fall into four domains: (1) dependency/inclusion; (2) counterdependence/flight; (3) trust/structure; and (4) work/productivity. The GDQ has not been applied to psychotherapy groups to date, but it holds promise in this regard (S. Wheelan and J. Hochberger, "Validation Studies of the Group Development Questionnaire," *Small Group Research* 27 [1996]: 143–70).

5. L. Murphy, M. Leszcz, A. Collings, and J. Salvendy, "Some Observations on the Subjective Experience of Neophyte Group Therapy Trainees," *International Journal of Group Psychotherapy* 46 (1996): 543–52.

6. R. Kamm, "Group Dynamics and Athletic Success," presented at the annual meeting of the American Group Psychotherapy Association, New York City, February, 27, 2004.

7. C. Kieffer, "Phases of Group Development: A View from Self-Psychology," *Group* 25 (2002): 91–105.

8. P. Flores, "Addiction as an Attachment Disorder: Implications for Group Therapy," *International Journal of Group Psychotherapy* 51 (2001): 63–82.

9. M. Ettin, "From Identified Patient to Identifiable Group: The Alchemy of the Group as a Whole," *International Journal of Group Psychotherapy* 50 (2000): 137–62. Kieffer, "Phases of Group Development."

10. I. Harwood, "Distinguishing Between the Facilitating and Self-Serving Charismatic Group Leader," *Group* 27 (2003): 121–29.

11. S. Freud, *Group Psychology and the Analysis of the Ego*, in Standard Edition, vol. 18 (London: Hogarth Press, 1955), 67–143.

12. C. Rich and F. Pitts Jr., "Suicide by Psychiatrists: A Study of Medical Specialists Among 18,730 Consecutive Physician Deaths During a Five-Year Period, 1967–72," *Journal of Clinical Psychiatry* 41 (1980): 261–63. E. Frank, H. Biola, and C. Burnett, "Mortality Rates Among U.S. Physicians," *American Journal of Preventive Medicine* 19 (2000): 155–59.

13. J. Ogrodniczuk and W. Piper, "The Effect of Group Climate on Outcome in Two Forms of Short-Term Group Therapy," *Group Dynamics: Theory, Research and Practice* 7 (1): 64–76.

14. W. Schutz, *The Interpersonal Underworld* (Palo Alto, Calif.: Science and Behavior Books, 1966), 24. K. Roy MacKenzie and W. John Livesley, "A Developmental Model for Brief Group Therapy," in *Advances in Group Therapy*, ed. R. Dies and K. Roy MacKenzie (New York: International Universities Press, 1983), 101–16. Tuckman, "Developmental Sequences in Small Groups."

15. G. Bach, *Intensive Group Psychotherapy* (New York: Ronald Press, 1954), 95.

16. P. Slater, *Microcosm* (New York: Wiley, 1966).

17. S. Freud, *Totem and Taboo*, in S. Freud, *Standard Edition of the Complete Psychological Works of Sigmund Freud*, vol. 13 (London: Hogarth Press, 1953), 1–161.

18. S. Freud, *Group Psychology and the Analysis of the Ego*, in S. Freud, *Standard Edition*, vol. 18 (London: Hogarth Press, 1955), 123.

19. W. Bennis, "Patterns and Vicissitudes in T-Group Development," in *T-Group Theory and Laboratory Method: Innovation in Re-Education*, ed. L. Bradford, J. Gibb, and K. Benne (New York: Wiley, 1964), 248–78.

20. T. Mills, personal communication, April 1968.

21. Tuckman, "Developmental Sequences in Small Groups." I. Harwood, "Distinguishing Between the Facilitating and Self-Serving Charismatic Group Leader," *Group* 27 (2003): 121–29.

22. Murphy et al., "Some Observations on the Subjective Experience."

23. N. Harpaz, "Failures in Group Psychotherapy: The Therapist Variable," *International Journal of Group Psychotherapy* 44 (1994): 3–19. M. Leszcz, "Discussion of Failures in Group Psychotherapy: The Therapist Variable," *International Journal of Group Psychotherapy* 44 (1994): 25–31.

24. S. Scheidlinger, "Presidential Address: On Scapegoating in Group Psychotherapy," *International Journal of Group Psychotherapy* 32 (1982): 131–43. A. Clark, "Scapegoating: Dynamics and Interventions in Group Counseling," *Journal of Counseling and Development* 80 (2002): 271–76.

25. E. Schein and W. Bennis, *Personal and Organizational Change Through Group Methods* (New York: Wiley, 1965), 275.

26. S. Hayes, "Acceptance, Mindfulness and Science," *Clinical Psychology: Science and Practice* 9 (2002): 101–06. A. Wells, "GAD, Metacognition, and Mindfulness: An Information Processing Analysis," *Clinical Psychology: Science and Practice* 9 (2002): 95–100.

27. Bennis, "Patterns and Vicissitudes."

28. F. Taylor, "The Therapeutic Factors of Group-Analytic Treatment," *Journal of Mental Science* 96 (1950): 976–97.

29. R. Shellow, J. Ward, and S. Rubenfeld, "Group Therapy and the Institutionalized Delinquent," *International Journal of Group Psychotherapy* 8 (1958): 265–75.

30. D. Whitaker and M. Lieberman, *Psychotherapy Through the Group Process* (New York: Atherton Press, 1964). M. Grotjahn, "The Process of Maturation in Group Psychotherapy and in the Group Therapist," *Psychiatry* 13 (1950): 63–67. MacKenzie and Livesley, "A Developmental Model."

31. J. Abrahams, "Group Psychotherapy: Implications for Direction and Supervision of Mentally Ill Patients," in *Mental Health in Nursing*, ed. T. Muller (Washington, D.C.: Catholic University Press, 1949), 77–83.

32. J. Thorpe and B. Smith, "Phases in Group Development in Treatment of Drug Addicts," *International Journal of Group Psychotherapy* 3 (1953): 66–78.

33. A. Beck and L. Peters, "The Research Evidence for Distributed Leadership in Therapy Groups," *International Journal of Group Psychotherapy* 31 (1981): 43–71. R. Josselson, "The Space Between in Group Psychotherapy: A Multidimensional Model of Relationships," *Group* 27 (2003): 203–19.

34. Schutz, *The Interpersonal Underworld,* 170.

35. I. Janis, *Groupthink: Psychological Studies of Policy Decisions and Fiascoes*, 2nd ed. (Boston: Houghton Mifflin, 1982). G. Hodson and R. Sorrentino, "Groupthink and Uncertainty Orientation: Personality Differences in Reactivity to the Group Situation," *Group Dynamics: Theory, Research, and Practice* 1 (1997): 144–55.

36. G. Burlingame, K. MacKenzie, B. Strauss, "Small-Group Treatment."

37. S. Drescher, G. Burlingame, and A. Fuhriman, "An Odyssey in Empirical Understanding," *Small Group Behavior* 16 (1985): 3–30.

38. I. Altman, A. Vinsel, and B. Brown, cited in K. MacKenzie, "Group Development," in *Handbook of Group Psychotherapy*, ed. A. Fuhriman and G. Burlingame (New York: Wiley, 1994), 223–68.

39. D. Barker, "The Behavioral Analysis of Interpersonal Intimacy in Group Development," *Small Group Research* 22 (1991): 76–91.

40. D. Kivlighan and R. Lilly, "Developmental Changes in Group Climate." L. Castonguay, A. Pincers, W. Agrees, C. Hines, "The Role of Emotion in Group Cognitive-Behavioral Therapy for Binge Eating Disorder: When Things Have to Feel Worse Before They Get Better," *Psychotherapy Research* 8 (1998): 225–38.

41. D. Hamburg, personal communication, 1978.

42. M. Nitsun, *The Anti-Group: Destructive Forces in the Group and Their Creative Potential* (London: Routledge, 1996). M. Nitsun, "The Future of the Group," *International Journal of Group Psychotherapy* 50 (2000): 455–72.

43. B. Rasmussen, "Joining Group Psychotherapy: Developmental Considerations," *International Journal of Group Psychotherapy* 49 (1999): 513–28.

44. D. Jung and J. Sasik, "Effects of Group Characteristics on Work Group Performance: A Longitudinal Investigation," *Group Dynamics: Theory, Research and Practice* 3 (1999): 279–90.

45. I. Yalom, "A Study of Group Therapy Dropouts," *Archives of General Psychiatry* 14 (1966): 393–414.

46. A. Beck describes a similar set of behavior for clients she terms "scapegoat leaders" (Beck and Peters, "The Research Evidence for Distributed Leadership").

47. D. Kiesler, *Contemporary Interpersonal Theory and Research* (New York: J. Wiley & Sons Ltd., 1996).

48. A. Rice, *Learning for Leadership* (London: Tavistock Publications, 1965).

49. W. Henry, H. Strupp, S. Butler, T. Schacht, and J. Binder, "Effects of Training in Time-Limited Dynamic Psychotherapy: Changes in Therapist Behavior," *Journal of Consulting and Clinical Psychology* 61 (1993): 434–40. J. Waltz, M. Addis, K. Koerner, and N. Jacobson, "Testing the Integrity of a Psychotherapy Protocol: Assessment of Adherence and Competence," *Journal of Consulting and Clinical Psychology* 61 (1993): 620–30. W. Piper, J. Ogrodniczuk, "Therapy Manuals and the Dilemma of Dynamically Oriented Therapists and Researchers," *American Journal of Psychotherapy* 53 (1999): 467–82.

50. I. Yalom, P. Houts, S. Zimerberg, and K. Rand, "Predictions of Improvement in Group Therapy: An Exploratory Study," *Archives of General Psychiatry* 17 (1967): 159–68.

51. L. Lothstein, "The Group Psychotherapy Dropout Phenomenon Revisited," *American Journal of Psychiatry* 135 (1978): 1492–95.

52. W. Stone, M. Blase, and J. Bozzuto, "Late Dropouts from Group Therapy," *American Journal of Psychotherapy* 34 (1980): 401–13.

53. W. Stone and S. Rutan, "Duration of Treatment in Group Psychotherapy," *International Journal of Group Psychotherapy* 34 (1984): 101–17. R. MacNair and J. Corazzini, "Clinical Factors Influencing Group Therapy Dropout," *Psychotherapy: Theory, Research, Practice and Training* 31 (1994): 352–61.

54. S. Budman, A. Demby, and M. Randall, "Short-Term Group Psychotherapy: Who Succeeds, Who Fails," *Group* 4 (1980): 3–16. H. Roback and M. Smith, "Patient Attrition in Dynamically Oriented Treatment Groups," *American Journal of Psychiatry* 144 (1987): 426–43. W. Piper et al., "A Comparative Study of Four Forms of Psychotherapy," *Journal of Consulting and Clinical Psychology* 52 (1984): 268–79. M. McCallum, W. Piper, and A. Joyce, "Dropping Out from Short-Term Therapy," *Psychotherapy* 29 (1992): 206–15.

55. R. Tolman and G. Bhosley, "A Comparison of Two Types of Pregroup Preparation for Men Who Batter," *Journal of Social Services Research* 13 (1990): 33–44. S. Stosny, "Shadows of the Heart: A Dramatic Video for the Treatment Resistance of Spouse Abuse," *Social Work* 39 (1994): 686–94.

56. C. Taft, C. Murphy, J. Elliott, and T. Morrel, "Attendance-Enhancing Procedures in Group Counseling for Domestic Abusers," *Journal of Counseling Psychology* 48 (2001): 51–60.

57. Stone et al., "Late Dropouts."

58. W. Piper, M. McCallum, A. Joyce, J. Rosie, and J. Ogrodniczuk, "Patient Personality and Time-Limited Group Psychotherapy for Complicated Grief," *International Journal of Group Psychotherapy* 51 (2001): 525–52.

59. Yalom, "A Study of Group Therapy Dropouts."

60. Lothstein, "The Group Psychotherapy Dropout Phenomenon Revisited."

61. H. Bernard, "Guidelines to Minimize Premature Terminations," *International Journal of Group Psychotherapy* 39 (1989): 523–29. H. Roback, "Adverse Outcomes in Group Psychotherapy: Risk Factors, Prevention and Research Directions," *Journal of Psychotherapy, Practice, and Research*, 9 (2000): 113–22.

62. Yalom, "A Study of Group Therapy Dropouts."

63. M. McCallum, W. Piper, J. Ogrodniczuk, and A. Joyce, "Early Process and Dropping Out from Short-term Group Therapy for Complicated Grief," *Group Dynamics: Theory, Practice and Research* 6 (2002): 243–54. L. Samstag, S. Batchelder, J. Muran, J. Safran, A. Winston, "Early Identification of Treatment Failures in Short-Term Psychotherapy," *Journal of Psychotherapy Practice and Research* 7 (1998): 126–43.

64. J. Weinberg, "On Adding Insight to Injury," *Gerontologist* 16 (1976): 4–10.

65. M. Leszcz and P. Goodwin, "The Rationale and Foundations of Group Psychotherapy for Women with Metastatic Breast Cancer," *International Journal of Group Psychotherapy* 48 (1998): 245–73.

66. S. Foulkes and E. Anthony, *Group Psychotherapy: The Psychoanalytic Approach* (Harmondsworth, England: Penguin, 1957).

67. L. Rosenthal, "The New Member: 'Infanticide' in Group Psychotherapy," *International Journal of Group Psychotherapy* 42 (1992): 277–86.

68. B. Rasmussen, "Joining Group Psychotherapy." E. Shapiro and R. Ginzberg, "The Persistently Neglected Sibling Relationship and Its Applicability to Group Therapy," *International Journal of Group Psychotherapy* 51 (2001): 327–41.

69. R. Crandall, "The Assimilation of Newcomers into Groups," *Small Group Behavior* 9 (1978): 331–37.

CHAPTER 12

1. K. MacKenzie, *Time-Managed Group Psychotherapy: Effective Clinical Applications* (Washington, D.C.: American Psychiatric Press, 1997). A. Berman and H. Weinberg, "The Advanced-Stage Group," *International Journal of Group Psychotherapy* 48 (1998): 498–518.

2. J. Silverstein, "Acting Out in Group Therapy: Avoiding Authority Struggles," *International Journal of Group Psychotherapy* 47 (1997): 31–45.

3. R. White and R. Lippit, "Leader Behavior and Member Reaction in Three 'Social Climates,'" in *Group Dynamics: Research and Theory*, ed. D. Cartwright and A. Zander (New York: Row, Peterson, 1962), 527–53.

4. G. Hodson, R. Sorrentino, "Groupthink and Uncertainty Orientation: Personality Differences in Reactivity to the Group Situation," *Group Dynamics* 2 (1997): 144–55.

5. I. Yalom, "A Study of Group Therapy Dropouts," *Archives of General Psychiatry* 14 (1966): 393–414.

6. S. Freud, *Group Psychology and the Analysis of the Ego,* in S. Freud, *Standard Edition of the Complete Psychological Works of Sigmund Freud,* vol. 18 (London: Hogarth Press, 1955), 69–143. I. Yalom, "Group Psychology and the Analysis of the Ego: A Review," *International Journal of Group Psychotherapy* 24 (1974): 67–82.

7. I. Yalom and P. Houts, unpublished data, 1965.

8. Y. Agazarian, "Contemporary Theories of Group Psychotherapy: A Systems Approach to the Group-as-a-Whole," *International Journal of Group Psychotherapy* 42 (1992): 177–204. G. Burlingame, R. MacKenzie, B. Strauss, "Small-Group Treatment: Evidence for Effectiveness and Mechanisms of Change," in *Bergin and Garfield's Handbook of Psychotherapy and Behavior Change,* 5th Ed., ed. M. Lambert (New York: Wiley & Sons, 2004), 647–96.

9. M. Dubner, "Envy in the Group Therapy Process," *International Journal of Group Psychotherapy* 48 (1998): 519–31.

10. J. Kelly Moreno, "Group Treatment for Eating Disorders," in *Handbook of Group Psychotherapy*, ed. A. Fuhriman and G. Burlingame (New York: Wiley, 1994): 416–57. J. Bohanske and R. Lemberg, "An Intensive Group Process Retreat Model for the Treatment of Bulimia," *Group* 11 (1987): 228–37.

11. I. Yalom and C. Greaves, "Group Therapy with the Terminally Ill," *American Journal of Psychiatry* 134 (1977): 396–400. M. Leszcz and P. Goodwin, "The Rationale and Foundations of Group Psychotherapy for Women with Metastatic Breast Cancer," *International Journal of Group Psychotherapy* 48 (1998): 245–73.

12. A. Camus, *The Fall* (New York: Vintage, 1956), 58.

13. Ibid., 68.

14. Ibid., 63.

15. L. Ormont, "Developing Emotional Insulation," *International Journal of Group Psychotherapy* 44 (1994): 361–75. L. Ormont, "Meeting Maturational Needs in the Group Setting," *International Journal of Group Psychotherapy* 51 (2001): 343–59.

16. B. Buchele, "Etiology and Management of Anger in Groups: A Psychodynamic View," *International Journal of Group Psychotherapy* 45 (1995): 275–85. A. Alonso, "Discussant Comments for Special Section on Anger and Aggression in Groups," *International Journal of Group Psychotherapy* 45 (1995): 331–39.

17. My discussion of conflict in the therapy group draws much from essays by Jerome Frank and Carl Rogers. J. Frank, "Some Values of Conflict in Therapeutic Groups," *Group Psychotherapy* 8 (1955): 142–51. C. Rogers, "Dealing with Psychological Tensions," *Journal of Applied Behavioral Science* 1 (1965): 6–24.

18. S. Foulkes and E. Anthony, *Group Psychotherapy: The Psychoanalytic Approach* (Harmondsworth, England: Penguin, 1957).

19. Frank, "Some Values of Conflict."

20. F. Dostoevsky, "The Double," in *Great Short Works of Fyodor Dostoevsky*, ed. R. Hingley (New York: Harper & Row, 1968).

21. L. Horwitz, "Projective Identification in Dyads and Groups," *International Journal of Group Psychotherapy* 33 (1983): 254–79.

22. W. Goldstein, "Clarification of Projective Identification," *American Journal of Psychiatry* 148 (1991): 153–61. T. Ogden, *Projective Identification and Psychotherapeutic Technique* (New York: Jason Aronson, 1982).

23. L. Horwitz, "Projective Identification in Dyads."

24. M. Livingston and L. Livingston, "Conflict and Aggression in Group Psychotherapy: A Self Psychological Vantage Point," *International Journal of Group Psychotherapy* 48 (1998): 381–91. J. Gans and R. Weber, "The Detection of Shame in Group Psychotherapy: Uncovering the Hidden Emotion," *International Journal of Group Psychotherapy* 50 (2000): 381–96. W. Stone, "Frustration, Anger, and the Significance of Alter-Ego Transference in Group Psychotherapy," *International Journal of Group Psychotherapy* 45 (1995): 287–302.

25. J. Gans, "Hostility in Group Therapy," *International Journal of Group Psychotherapy* 39 (1989): 499–517. M. Dubner, "Envy in the Group Therapy Process."

26. A. Clark, "Scapegoating: Dynamics and Intervention in Group Counselling," *Journal of Counseling and Development* 80 (2002): 271–76. B. Cohen and V. Schermer, "On Scapegoating in Therapy Groups: A Social Constructivist and Intersubjective Outlook," *International Journal of Group Psychotherapy* 52 (2002): 89–109.

27. R. Giesler and W. Swann, "Striving for Confirmation: The Role of Self-Verification in Depression," in *The Interactional Nature of Depression,* ed. T. Joiner and J. Coyne (Washington, D.C.: American Psychological Association, 1999), 189–217.

28. Terence, *The Self-Tormentor,* trans. Betty Radice (New York: Penguin, 1965).

29. P. Fonagy, "Multiple Voices Versus Meta-Cognition: An Attachment Theory Perspective," *Journal of Psychotherapy Integration* 7 (1997): 181–94. A. Wells, "GAD, Metacognition, and Mindfulness: An Information Processing Analysis," *Clinical Psychology* 9 (2002): 95–100. M. Leszcz, "Group Psychotherapy of the Characterologically Difficult Patient," *International Journal of Group Psychotherapy* 39 (1989): 311–35.

30. D. Winnicott, *Maturational Processes and the Facilitating Environment* (London: Hogarth Press, 1965).

31. L. Ormont, "The Leader's Role in Dealing with Aggression in Groups," *International Journal of Group Psychotherapy* 34 (1984): 553–72.

32. E. Berne, *Games People Play* (New York: Grove Press, 1964).

33. M. Leszcz and J. Malat, "The Interpersonal Model of Group Psychotherapy," in *Praxis der Gruppenpsychotherapie*, ed. V. Tschuschke (Frankfurt: Thieme, 2001), 355–69.

34. M. Livingston, "Vulnerability, Tenderness and the Experiences of Self-Object Relationship: A Self Psychological View of Deepening Curative Process in Group Psychotherapy," *International Journal of Group Psychotherapy* 49 (1999): 19–40.

35. V. Tschuschke and R. Dies, "Intensive Analysis of Therapeutic Factors and Outcome in Long-Term In-Patient Groups," *International Journal of Group Psychotherapy* 44 (1994): 185–208. G. Burlingame, R. MacKenzie, B. Strauss, "Small-Group Treatment."

36. V. Tschuschke and R. Dies, "Intensive Analysis of Therapeutic Factors and Outcome in Long-Term In-Patient Groups," *International Journal of Group Psychotherapy* 44 (1994): 185–208. G. Burlingame, A. Fuhriman, and L. Johnson, "Cohesion in Group Therapy," in *A Guide to Psychotherapy Relationships That Work,* ed. J. Norcross (Oxford, England: Oxford University Press, 2002), 71–88.

37. I. Yalom et al., "Predictions of Improvement in Group Therapy: An Exploratory Study," *Archives of General Psychiatry* 17 (1967): 159–68.

38. S. Hurley, "Self-Disclosure in Small Counseling Groups," Ph.D. diss., Michigan State University, 1967.

39. M. Worthy, A. Gary, and G. Kahn, "Self-Disclosure as an Exchange Process," *Journal of Personality and Social Psychology* 13 (1969): 59–63.

40. S. Bloch and E. Crouch, *Therapeutic Factors in Group Psychotherapy* (New York: Oxford University Press, 1985). S. Bloch and E. Crouch, "Therapeutic Factors: Intrapersonal and Interpersonal Mechanisms," in *Handbook of Group Psychotherapy,* ed. A. Fuhriman and G. Burlingame (New York: Wiley, 1994): 269–318. W. Query, "Self-Disclosure as a Variable in Group Psychotherapy," *International Journal of Group Psychotherapy* 14 (1964): 107–15. D. Johnson and L. Ridener, "Self-Disclosure, Participation, and Perceived Cohesiveness in Small Group Interaction," *Psychological Reports* 35 (1974): 361–63.

41. P. Cozby, "Self-Disclosure, Reciprocity, and Liking," *Sociometry* 35 (1972): 151–60.

42. N. Brown, "Conceptualizing Process," *International Journal of Group Psychotherapy* 53 (2003): 225–44.

43. C. Truax and R. Carkhuff, "Client and Therapist Transparency in the Psychotherapeutic Encounter," *Journal of Consulting Psychology* 12 (1965): 3–9.

44. H. Peres, "An Investigation of Non-Directive Group Therapy," *Journal of Consulting Psychology* 11 (1947): 159–72.

45. M. Lieberman, I. Yalom, and M. Miles, *Encounter Groups: First Facts* (New York: Basic Books, 1973).

46. S. Wiser and M. Goldfried, "Therapist Interventions and Client Emotional Experiencing in Expert Psychodynamic – Interpersonal and Cognitive-Behavioral Therapies," *Journal of Consulting and Clinical Psychology* 66 (1998): 634–40. J. Ablon and E. Jones, "Psychotherapy Process in the National Institute of Mental Health Treatment of Depression Collaborative Research Program," *Journal of Consulting and Clinical Psychology* 67 (1999): 64–75. B. Cohen and V. Schermer, "Therapist Self-Disclosure."

47. R. Slavin, "The Significance of Here-and-Now Disclosure in Promoting Cohesion in Group Psychotherapy," *Group* 17 (1993): 143–50.

48. S. Mitchell, *Hope and Dread in Psychoanalysis* (New York: Basic Books, 1993).

49. D. Medeiros and A. Richards, "Sharing Secrets: Where Psychotherapy and Education Meet," in *Studies in Humanistic Psychology,* ed. C. Aanstoos (Carollton: West Georgia College Studies in the Social Sciences, vol. 29, 1991).

50. L. Vosen, "The Relationship Between Self-Disclosure and Self-Esteem," Ph.D. diss., University of California at Los Angeles, 1966, cited in Culbert, *Interpersonal Process of Self-Disclosure: It Takes Two to See One* (Washington, D.C.: NTL Institute for Applied Behavioral Science, 1967).

51. Culbert, *Interpersonal Process.*

52. J. Sternbach, "Self-Disclosure with All-Male Groups," *International Journal of Group Psychotherapy* 53 (2003): 61–81. S. Bergman, *Men's Psychological Development: A Relational Perspective* (Wellesley, Mass.: The Stone Center, 1991).

53. E. Goffman, *The Presentation of Self in Everyday Life* (Garden City, N.Y.: Doubleday Anchor Books, 1959). S. Jourard and P. Lasakow, "Some Factors in Self-Disclosure," *Journal of Abnormal Social Psychology* 56 (1950): 91–98.

54. D. Strassberg and his colleagues studied eighteen patients with chronic schizophrenic for ten weeks in inpatient group therapy and concluded that high self-disclosing patients made less therapeutic progress than their counterparts who revealed less personal material (D. Strassberg et al., "Self-Disclosure in Group Therapy with Schizophrenics," *Archives of General Psychiatry* 32 [1975]: 1259–61.)

55. A. Maslow, unpublished mimeographed material, 1962.

56. I. Yalom, See *The Schopenhauer Cure*, pp. 237ff.

57. N. Fieldsteel, "The Process of Termination in Long-term Psychoanalytic Group Therapy," *International Journal of Group Psychotherapy* 46 (1996): 25–39. R. Klein, "Introduction to Special Section on Termination and Group Therapy," *International Journal of Group Psychotherapy* 46 (1996): 1–4.

58. J. Pedder, "Termination Reconsidered," *International Journal of Psychoanalysis* 69 (1988): 495–505.

59. I. Yalom, *Existential Psychotherapy* (New York: Basic Books, 1980).

60. M. Seligman, "The Effectiveness of Psychotherapy: The Consumer Reports Study," *American Psychologist* 50 (1995): 965–74.

61. S. Kopta, K. Howard, J. Lowry, and L. Beutler, "Patterns of Symptomatic Recovery in Time-Unlimited Psychotherapy," *Journal of Clinical and Consulting Psychology* 62 (1994): 1009–16. S. Kadera, M. Lambert, A. Andrews, "How Much Therapy Is Really Enough: A Session-by-Session Analysis of the Psychotherapy Dose-Effect Relationship," *Journal of Psychotherapy Practice and Research* 5 (1996): 132–51.

62. S. Freud, *Analysis Terminable and Interminable*, in S. Freud, *Standard Edition of the Complete Psychological Works of Sigmund Freud*, vol. 23 (London: Hogarth Press, 1968), 211–53.

63. Pedder, "Termination Reconsidered." B. Grenyer and L. Luborsky, "Dynamic Change in Psychotherapy: Mastery of Interpersonal Conflicts," *Journal of Consulting and Clinical Psychology* 64 (1996): 411–16.

64. V. Schermer and R. Klein, "Termination in Group Psychotherapy from the Perspectives of Contemporary Object Relations Theory and Self Psychology," *International Journal of Group Psychotherapy* 46 (1996): 99–115.

65. Scott Rutan, personal communication, 1983.

66. Leszcz, "Group Psychotherapy of the Characterologically Difficult Patient." M. Leszcz, "Group Psychotherapy of the Borderline Patient," in *Handbook of Borderline Disorders*, ed. D. Silver and M. Rosenbluth (Madison, Conn.: International Universities Press, 1992), 435–69.

67. J. Rutan and W. Stone, "Termination in Group Psychotherapy," in *Psychodynamic Group Therapy* (New York: Guilford Press, 1993): 239–54. E. Shapiro and R. Ginzberg, "Parting Gifts: Termination Rituals in Group Psychotherapy," *International Journal of Group Psychotherapy* 52 (2002): 317–36.

68. D. Nathanson, "The Nature of Therapeutic Impasse."

69. K. Long, L. Pendleton, and B. Winters, "Effects of Therapist Termination on Group Process," *International Journal of Group Psychotherapy* 38 (1988): 211–22.

70. E. Counselman and R. Weber, "Changing the Guard: New Leadership for an Established Group," *International Journal of Group Psychotherapy* 52 (2002): 373–86.

CHAPTER 13

1. F. Wright, "Discussion of Difficult Patients," *International Journal of Group Psychotherapy* 48 (1998): 339–48. J. Gans and A. Alonso, "Difficult Patients: Their Construction in Group Therapy," *International Journal of Group Psychotherapy* 48 (1998): 311–26. P. Cohen, "The Practice of Modern Group Psychotherapy: Working with Post Trauma in the Present," *International Journal of Group Psychotherapy* 51 (2001): 489–503.

2. R. Dies, "Models of Group Psychotherapy: Shifting Through Confusion," *International Journal of Group Psychotherapy* 42 (1992): 1–17.

3. S. Scheidlinger, "Group Dynamics and Group Psychotherapy Revisited Four Decades Later," *International Journal of Group Psychotherapy* 47 (1997): 141–59.

4. I. Yalom and P. Houts, unpublished data, 1965.

5. L. Ormont, "Cultivating the Observing Ego in the Group Setting," *International Journal of Group Psychotherapy* 45 (1995): 489–502. L. Ormont, "Meeting Maturational Needs in the Group Setting," *International Journal of Group Psychotherapy* 51 (2001): 343–59.

6. M. Lieberman, I. Yalom, and M. Miles, *Encounter Groups: First Facts* (New York: Basic Books, 1973).

7. D. Lundgren and D. Miller, "Identity and Behavioral Changes in Training Groups," *Human Relations Training News* (spring 1965).

8. R. Coyne and R. Silver, "Direct, Vicarious, and Vicarious-Process Experiences," *Small Group Behavior* 11 (1980): 419–29. R. Rosner, L. Beutler, and R. Daldrup, "Vicarious Emotional Experience and Emotional Expression in Group Psychotherapy," *Journal of Counseling Psychology* 56 (2000): 1–10.

9. V. Tschuschke and R. Dies, "Intensive Analysis of Therapeutic Factors and Outcome in Long-Term Inpatient Groups," *International Journal of Group Psychotherapy* (1994): 185–208. V. Tschuschke, K. MacKenzie, B. Haaser, and G. Janke, "Self-Disclosure, Feedback, and Outcome in Long-Term Inpatient Psychotherapy Groups," *Journal of Psychotherapy Practice and Research* 5 (1996): 35–44.

10. J. Gans and E. Counselman, "Silence in Group Psychotherapy: A Powerful Communication," *International Journal of Group Psychotherapy* 50 (2000): 71–86. J. Rutan, "Growth Through Shame and Humiliation," *International Journal of Group Psychotherapy* 50 (2000): 511–16.

11. L. Ormont, "The Craft of Bridging," *International Journal of Group Psychotherapy* 40 (1990): 3–17.

12. M. Leszcz and J. Malat, "The Interpersonal Model of Group Psychotherapy," in *Praxis der Gruppenpsychotherapie,* ed. V. Tschuschke (Frankfurt: Thieme, 2001), 355–69. S. Cohen, "Working with Resistance to Experiencing and Expressing Emotions in Group Therapy," *International Journal of Group Psychotherapy* 47 (1997): 443–58.

13. M. McCallum, W. Piper, J. Ogrodniczuk, and A. Joyce, "Relationships Among Psychological Mindedness, Alexithymia and Outcome in Four Forms of Short-Term Psychotherapy," *Psychology and Psychotherapy: Theory, Research and Practice* 76 (2003): 133–44. G. Taylor, R. Bagby, D. Ryan, J. Parker, K. Dooday, and P. Keefe, "Criterion Validity of the Toronto Alexithymia Scale," *Psychosomatic Medicine* 50 (1988): 500–09.

14. H. Swiller, "Alexithymia: Treatment Utilizing Combined Individual and Group Psychotherapy," *International Journal of Group Psychotherapy* 38 (1988): 47–61. M. Beresnevaite, "Exploring the Benefits of Group Psychotherapy in Reducing Alexithymia in Coronary Heart Disease Patients: A Preliminary Study," *Psychotherapy and Psychosomatics* 69 (2000): 117–22.

15. P. Sifneos, "The Prevalence of 'Alexithymic' Characteristics in Psychosomatic Patients," *Psychotherapy and Psychosomatics* 22 (1973): 255–62.

16. Beresnevaite, "Exploring the Benefits of Group Psychotherapy." The researchers in this study employed a sixteen-session integrative model of group therapy, combining the active identification of subjective feelings, role play, empathy exercises, and stress reduction in the treatment of patients with heart disease. The groups produced significant reductions in alexithymia ratings and improvements in cardiac functioning that were sustained over a two-year period.

17. W. Shields, "Hope and the Inclination to Be Troublesome: Winnicott and the Treatment of Character Disorder in Group Therapy," *International Journal of Group Psychotherapy* 50 (2000): 87–103.

18. J. Kirman, "Working with Anger in Group: A Modern Analytic Approach," *International Journal of Group Psychotherapy* 45 (1995): 303–29. D. Kiesler, "Therapist Countertransference: In Search of Common Themes and Empirical Referents," *In Session: Psychotherapy in Practice* 57 (2001): 1053–63. G. Gabbard, "A Contemporary Psychoanalytic Model of Countertransference," *In Session: Psychotherapy in Practice* 57 (2001): 983–91. J. Hayes, "Countertransference in Group Psychotherapy: Waking a Sleeping Dog," *International Journal of Group Psychotherapy* 45 (1995): 521–35.

19. J. Frank et al., "Behavioral Patterns in Early Meetings of Therapeutic Groups," *American Journal of Psychiatry* 108 (1952): 771–78.

20. E. Shapiro, "Dealing with Masochistic Behavior in Group Therapy from the Perspective of the Self," *Group* 25 (2002): 107–20. R. Maunder and J. Hunter, "An Integrated Approach to the Formulation and Psychotherapy of Medically Unexplained Symptoms: Meaning- and Attachment-Based Intervention," *American Journal of Psychotherapy* 58 (2004): 17–33. M. Berger and M. Rosenbaum, "Notes on Help-Rejecting Complainers," *International Journal of Group Psychotherapy* 17 (1967): 357–70. S. Brody, "Syndrome of the Treatment-Rejecting Patient," *Psychoanalytic Review* 51 (1964): 75–84. C. Peters and H. Grunebaum, "It Could Be Worse: Effective Group Psychotherapy with the Help-Rejecting Complainers," *International Journal of Group Psychotherapy* 27 (1977): 471–80.

21. Maunder and Hunter, "An Integrated Approach."

22. E. Shapiro, "Dealing with Masochistic Behavior in Group Therapy from the Perspective of the Self," *Group* 25 (2002): 107–20. Maunder and Hunter, "An Integrated Approach." S. Foreman, "The Significance of Turning Passive into Active in Control Mastery: Theory," *Journal of Psychotherapy Practice and Research* 5 (1996): 106–21. Both self psychological and attachment paradigms converge here. From an attachment perspective, the client relates in a preoccupied and insecure attachment pattern. The preoccupation with the caregiver is rooted in the wish to connect. Complaining is intended to create closeness by pulling the caregiver near. Simultaneously the client's past experience of inconsistent, unreliable caregiving fuels his vigilance for any evidence that he will be eventually abandoned. Accepting help and being sated fuels the dread of this very abandonment.

23. Do not neglect to consider the real meaning of the help-rejecting complainer's complaint. Some clinicians propose that there may be a hidden positive or adaptive value to the unrelenting complaints that needs to be understood.

24. Frank et al., "Behavioral Patterns in Early Meetings." E. Berne, *Games People Play* (New York: Grove Press, 1964). Peters and Grunebaum, "It Could Be Worse."

25. Wright, "Discussion of Difficult Patients." R. Jacobs and D. Campbell, "The Perpetuation of an Arbitrary Tradition Through Several Generations of a Laboratory Microculture," *Journal of Abnormal and Social Psychology* 62 (1961): 649–58.

26. R. Moos and I. Yalom, "Medical Students' Attitudes Toward Psychiatry and Psychiatrists," *Mental Hygiene* 50 (1966): 246–56.

27. L. Coch and J. French, "Overcoming Resistance to Change," *Human Relations* 1 (1948): 512–32.

28. N. Kanas, "Group Psychotherapy with Bipolar Patients: A Review and Synthesis," *International Journal of Group Psychotherapy* 43 (1993): 321–35. F. Volkmar et al., "Group Therapy in the Management of Manic-Depressive Illness," *American Journal of Psychotherapy* 35 (1981): 226–33. I. Patelis-Siotis et al., "Group Cognitive-Behavioral Therapy for Bipolar Disorder: A Feasibility and Effectiveness Study," *Journal of Affective Disorders* 65 (2001): 145–53. M. Sajatovic, M. Davies, and D. Hrouda, "Enhancement of Treatment Adherence Among Patients with Bipolar Disorder," *Psychiatric Services* 55 (2004): 264–69. R. Weiss, L. Najavits, and S. Greenfield, "A Relapse Prevention Group for Patients with Bipolar and Substance Use Disorders," *Journal of Substance Abuse Treatment* 16 (1999): 47–54. F. Colom et al., "A Randomized Trial on the Efficacy of Group Psychoeducation in the Prophylaxis of Recurrences in Bipolar Patients Whose Disease Is in Remission," *Archives of General Psychiatry* 60 (2003): 402–7.

29. M. Leszcz, "Group Psychotherapy of the Characterologically Difficult Patient," *International Journal of Group Psychotherapy* 39 (1989): 311–35. L. Ormont, "The Role of the Leader in Managing the Preoedipal Patient in the Group Setting," *International Journal of Group Psychotherapy* 39 (1989): 147–71. R. Klein, J. Orleans, and C. Soule, "The Axis II Group: Treating Severely Characterologically Disturbed Patients," *International Journal of Group Psychotherapy* 41 (1991): 97–115. D. Silver, "Psychotherapy of the Characterologically Difficult Patient," *Canadian Journal of Psychiatry* 28 (1983): 513–21.

30. J. Shedler and D. Westen, "Refining Personality Disorder Diagnosis: Integrating Science and Practice," *American Journal of Psychiatry* 161 (2004): 1350–65.

31. Gans and Alonso, "Difficult Patients."

32. M. Leszcz, "Group Psychotherapy of the Borderline Patient," in *Handbook of Borderline Disorders*, ed. D. Silver and M. Rosenbluth (Madison, Conn.: International Universities Press, 1992), 435–70. E. Marziali and H. Monroe-Blum, *Interpersonal Group Psychotherapy for Borderline Personality Disorder* (New York: Basic Books, 1994). S. Budman, A. Demby, S. Soldz, and J. Merry, "Time-Limited Group Psychotherapy for Patients with Personality Disorders: Outcomes and Dropouts," *International Journal of Group Psychotherapy* 46 (1996): 357–77. S. Budman, S. Cooley, A. Demby, G. Koppenaal, J. Koslof, and T. Powers, "A Model of Time-Effective Group Psychotherapy for Patients with Personality Disorders: A Clinical Model," *International Journal of Group Psychotherapy* 46 (1996): 329–55. A. Bateman and P. Fonagy, "Treatment of Borderline Personality Disorder with Psychoanalytically Oriented Partial Hospitalization: An 18-Month Follow-Up," *American Journal of Psychiatry* 158 (2001): 36–42. W. Piper and J. Rosie, "Group Treatment of Personality Disorders: The Power of the Group in the Intensive Treatment of Personality Disorders," *In Session: Psychotherapy in Practice* 4 (1998): 19–34. W. Piper, J. Rosie, A. Joyce, and H. Azim, *Time-Limited Day Treatment for Personality Disorders: Integration of Research and Practice in a Group Program* (Washington, D.C.: American Psychological Association, 1996). M. Chiesa and P. Fonagy, "Psychosocial Treatment for Severe Personality Disorder: 36-Month Follow-Up," *British Journal of Psychiatry* 183 (2003): 356–62.

33. J. Herman, *Trauma and Recovery* (New York: Harper Collins, 1992). M. Zanarin, F. Frankenburg, E. Dubo, A. Sickel, A. Trikha, and A. Levin, "Axis I Comorbidity of Borderline Personality Disorder," *American Journal of Psychiatry* 155 (1998): 1733–39. J. Ogrodniczuk, W. Piper, A. Joyce, and M. McCallum, "Using DSM Axis IV Formulation to Predict Outcome in Short-Term Individual Psychotherapy," *Journal of Personality Disorders* 15 (2001): 110–22. C. Zlotnick et al., "Clinical Features and Impairment in Women with Borderline Personality Disorder (BPD) with Posttraumatic Stress Disorder (PTSD), BPD Without PTSD, and Other Personality Disorders with PTSD," *Journal of Nervous and Mental Diseases* 191 (2003): 706–13.

34. M. Leszcz, "Group Therapy," in *Treatment of Psychiatric Disorders,* vol. 3, ed. J. Gunderson (Washington, D.C.: American Psychiatric Press, 1990), 2667–78.

35. J. Sartre, *The Age of Reason,* trans. Eric Sutton (New York: Knopf, 1952), 144.

36. American Psychiatric Association, *Diagnostic and Statistical Manual of Mental Disorders,* 4th ed. Text Rev. (Washington, D.C.: American Psychiatric Association, 2000).

37. O. Kernberg, "An Ego Psychology Object Relations Theory of the Structure and Treatment of Pathologic Narcissism: An Overview," *Psychiatric Clinics of North America* 12 (1989): 723–29. O. Kernberg, *Borderline Conditions and Pathological Narcissism* (New York: Jason Aronson, 1975).

38. J. Perry, "Problems and Considerations in the Valid Assessment of Personality Disorders," *American Journal of Psychiatry* 149 (1992): 1645–53. G. Mellsop et al., "The Reliability of Axis II of DSM-III," *American Journal of Psychiatry* 139 (1982): 1360–61.

39. Kernberg, "An Ego Psychology Object Relations Theory." Kernberg, *Borderline Conditions and Pathological Narcissism.* H. Kohut, *The Analysis of the Self* (New York:

International Universities Press, 1971). H. Kohut, *The Restoration of the Self* (New York: International Universities Press, 1977).

40. J. Gunderson, *Borderline Personality Disorder: A Clinical Guide* (Washington, D.C.: American Psychiatric Press, 2001). Piper and Rosie, "Group Treatment of Personality Disorders." Leszcz, "Group Psychotherapy of the Borderline Patient." Marziali and Monroe-Blum, *Interpersonal Group Psychotherapy for Borderline Personality Disorder.* Bateman and Fonagy, "Treatment of Borderline Personality Disorder." American Psychiatric Association, "Practice Guideline for the Treatment of Patients with Borderline Personality Disorder," *American Journal of Psychiatry* 158 (suppl 11 2001): 1–52.

41. L. Horwitz, "Group Psychotherapy for Borderline and Narcissistic Patients," *Bulletin of the Menninger Clinic* 44 (1980): 181–200. N. Wong, "Clinical Considerations in Group Treatment of Narcissistic Disorders," *International Journal of Group Psychotherapy* 29 (1979): 325–45. R. Kretsch, Y. Goren, and A. Wasserman, "Change Patterns of Borderline Patients in Individual and Group Therapy," *International Journal of Group Psychotherapy* 37 (1987): 95–112. Klein et al., "The Axis II Group." J. Grobman, "The Borderline Patient in Group Psychotherapy: A Case Report," *International Journal of Group Psychotherapy* 30 (1980): 299–318. B. Finn and S. Shakir, "Intensive Group Psychotherapy of Borderline Patients," *Group* 14 (1990): 99–110. K. O'Leary et al., "Homogeneous Group Therapy of Borderline Personality Disorder," *Group* 15 (1991): 56–64. S. Shakir, personal communication, February 1994. M. Leszcz, I. Yalom, and M. Norden, "The Value of Inpatient Group Psychotherapy: Patients' Perceptions," *International Journal of Group Psychotherapy* 35 (1985): 411–33. I. Yalom, *Inpatient Group Psychotherapy* (New York: Basic Books, 1983). N. Macaskill, "The Narcissistic Core as a Focus in the Group Therapy of the Borderline Patient," *British Journal of Medical Psychology* 53 (1980): 137–43. S. Budman, A. Demby, S. Soldz, and J. Merry, "Time-Limited Group Psychotherapy for Patients with Personality Disorders: Outcomes and Dropouts," *International Journal of Group Psychotherapy* 46 (1996): 357–77.

42. M. Leszcz, "Group Psychotherapy of the Borderline Patient."

43. Klein et al., "The Axis II Group."

44. M. Bond, E. Banon, and M. Grenier, "Differential Effects of Interventions on the Therapeutic Alliance with Patients with Borderline Personality Disorders," *Journal of Psychotherapy Practice and Research* 7 (1998): 301–18.

45. K. Heffernan and M. Cloitre, "A Comparison of Posttraumatic Stress Disorder with and Without Borderline Personality Disorder Among Women with a History of Childhood Sexual Abuse: Etiological and Clinical Characteristics," *Journal of Nervous and Mental Diseases* 188 (2000): 589–95. M. Cloitre and K. Koenen, "The Impact of Borderline Personality Disorder on Process Group Outcomes Among Women with Posttraumatic Stress Disorder Related to Childhood Abuse," *International Journal of Group Psychotherapy* 51 (2001): 379–98.

46. Leszcz, "Group Psychotherapy of the Characterologically Difficult Patient." Horwitz, "Group Psychotherapy for Borderline and Narcissistic Patients." Wong, "Clinical Considerations in Group Treatment of Narcissistic Disorders." N. Wong, "Combined Group and Individual Treatment of Borderline and Narcissistic Patients," *International Journal of Group Psychotherapy* 30 (1980): 389–403. Klein et al., "The Axis II Group."

47. J. Kosseff, "The Unanchored Self: Clinical Vignettes of Change in Narcissistic and Borderline Patients in Groups: Introduction," *International Journal of Group Psychotherapy* 30 (1980): 387–88.

48. Shedler and Westen, "Refining Personality Disorder Diagnosis."

49. American Psychiatric Association, *Diagnostic and Statistical Manual of Mental Disorders*, 4th ed., 661.

50. Kernberg, "An Ego Psychology Object Relations Theory." Kernberg, *Borderline Conditions and Pathological Narcissism.*

51. M. Livingston and L. Livingston, "Conflict and Aggression in Group Psychotherapy: A Self Psychological Vantage Point," *International Journal of Psychotherapy* 48 (1998): 381–91. J. Horner, "A Characterological Contraindication for Group Psychotherapy," *Journal of American Academy of Psychoanalysis* 3 (1975): 301–05.

52. The tasks of therapy may be facilitated by theoretical frames of reference such as a self psychological framework or an intersubjective framework. Both approaches sharpen our focus on the subjective experience of the narcissistically vulnerable client. Leszcz, "Group Psychotherapy of the Characterologically Difficult Patient." Livingston and Livingston, "Conflict and Aggression in Group Psychotherapy." M. Baker and H. Baker, "Self-Psychological Contributions to the Theory and Practice of Group Psychotherapy," in *Group Therapy in Clinical Practice,* ed. A. Alonso and H. Swiller (Washington, D.C.: American Psychiatric Press, 1993), 49–68. I. Harwood, "Distinguishing Between the Facilitating and the Self-Serving Charismatic Group Leader," *Group* 27 (2003): 121–29. W. Stone, "Self Psychology and the Higher Mental Functioning Hypothesis: Contemporary Theories," *Group Analysis* 29 (1996): 169–81. D. Brandchaft and R. Stolorow, "The Difficult Patient: Intersubjective Perspective," in *Borderline and Narcissistic Patients in Therapy,* ed. N. Slavinsky-Holy (Madison, Conn.: International Universities Press, 1988), 243–66.

53. M. Pines, "Group Analytic Therapy of the Borderline Patient," *Group Analysis* 11 (1978): 115–26.

CHAPTER 14

1. E. Paykel, "Psychotherapy, Medication Combinations, and Compliance." *Journal of Clinical Psychiatry* 56 (1995): 24–30. D. Greben, "Integrative Dimensions of Psychotherapy Training," *Canadian Journal of Psychiatry* 49 (2004): 238–48.

2. H. Bernard and S. Drob, "The Experience of Patients in Conjoint Individual and Group Therapy," *International Journal of Group Psychotherapy* 35 (1985): 129–46. K. Porter, "Combined Individual and Group Psychotherapy: A Review of the Literature, 1965–1978," *International Journal of Group Psychotherapy* 30 (1980): 107–14.

3. K. Schwartz, "Concurrent Group and Individual Psychotherapy in a Psychiatric Day Hospital for Depressed Elderly," *International Journal of Group Psychotherapy* 54 (2004): 177–201.

4. B. Roller and V. Nelson, "Group Psychotherapy Treatment of Borderline Personalities," *International Journal of Group Psychotherapy* 49 (1999): 369–85. F. DeZuleta and P. Mark, "Attachment and Contained Splitting: A Combined Approach of Group and Individual Therapy to the Treatment of Patients from Borderline Personality Disorder," *Group Analysis* 33 (2000): 486–500. E. Fried, "Combined Group and Individual Therapy with Passive Narcissistic Patients," *International Journal of Group Psychotherapy* 5 (1955): 194.

5. K. Chard, T. Weaver, and P. Resick, "Adapting Cognitive Processing Therapy for Child Sexual Abuse Survivors," *Cognitive and Behavioral Practice* 4 (1997): 31–52. N. Lutwack, "Shame, Women, and Group Psychotherapy," *Group* 22 (1998): 129–43.

6. L. Ormont, "Principles and Practice of Conjoint Psychoanalytic Treatment," *American Journal of Psychiatry* 138 (1981): 69–73.

7. J. Rutan and A. Alonso, "Group Therapy, Individual Therapy, or Both?" *International Journal of Group Psychotherapy* 32 (1982): 267–82. K. Porter, "Combined Individual and Group Psychotherapy," in *Group Therapy in Clinical Practice,* ed. A. Alonso and H. Swiller (Washington, D.C.: American Psychiatric Association Press, 1993), 309–41.

8. Ormont, "Principles and Practice of Conjoint Psychoanalytic Treatment." M. Leszcz, "Group Psychotherapy of the Borderline Patient," in *Handbook of Borderline Disorders,* ed. D. Silver and M. Rosenbluth (Madison, Conn.: International Universities Press, 1992), 435–69. J. Schacter, "Concurrent Individual and Individual In-a-Group Psychoanalytic Psychotherapy," *Journal of the American Psychoanalytic Association* 36 (1988): 455–71.

9. J. Gans, "Broaching and Exploring the Question of Combined Group and Individual Therapy," *International Journal of Group Psychotherapy* 40 (1990): 123–37.

10. K. Ulman, "The Ghost in the Group Room: Countertransferential Pressures Associated with Conjoint Individual and Group Psychotherapy," *International Journal of Group Psychotherapy* 52 (2002): 387–407. K. Porter, "Combined Individual and Group Psychotherapy," in *Group Therapy in Clinical Practice,* ed. A. Alonso and H. Swiller (Washington, D.C.: American Psychiatric Press, 1993): 309–41.

11. K. Porter, "Combined Individual and Group Psychotherapy." S. Lipsius, "Combined Individual and Group Psychotherapy: Guidelines at the Interface," *International Journal of Group Psychotherapy* 41 (1991): 313–27. H. Swiller, "Alexithymia: Treatment Using Combined Individual and Group Psychotherapy," *International Journal of Group Psychotherapy* 37 (1988): 47–61. J. Rutan and A. Alonso, "Common Dilemmas in Combined Individual and Group Treatment," *Group* 14 (1990): 5–12.

12. E. Amaranto and S. Bender, "Individual Psychotherapy as an Adjunct to Group Psychotherapy," *International Journal of Group Psychotherapy* 40 (1990): 91–101. S. Budman, personal communication, 1993.

13. J. Rutan and W. Stone, "Duration of Treatment in Group Psychotherapy," *International Journal of Group Psychotherapy* 34 (1984): 93–109. A study comparing conjoint and combined group therapy for patients with eating disorders found that the combined format was far more effective at preventing dropouts. (More than three times as many patients dropped out of conjoint groups.) K. Scheuble et al., "Premature Termination: A Risk in Eating Disorder Groups," *Group* (1987): 85–93.

14. R. Matano and I. Yalom, "Approaches to Chemical Dependency: Chemical Dependency and Interactive Group Therapy: A Synthesis," *International Journal of Group Psychotherapy* 41 (1991): 269–93. M. Freimuth, "Integrating Group Psychotherapy and 12-Step Work: A Collaborative Approach," *International Journal of Group Psychotherapy* 50 (2000): 297–314.

15. E. Khantzian, "Reflection on Group Treatments as Corrective Experiences in Addictive Vulnerability," *International Journal of Group Psychotherapy* 51 (2001): 11–20.

16. P. Flores, "Addition as an Attachment Disorder: Implications for Group Therapy," *International Journal of Group Psychotherapy* 51 (2001): 63–82. M. Litt, R. Kadden, N. Cooney, and E. Kabela, "Coping Skills and Treatment Outcomes in Cognitive-Behavioral and Interactional Group Therapy for Alcoholism," *Journal of Consulting and Clinical Psychology* 71 (2003): 118–28.

17. Project MATCH Research Group, "Matching Alcoholism Treatments to Client Heterogeneity: Project MATCH Post-Treatment Drinking Outcomes," *Journal of Studies in Alcohol* 58 (1997): 7–29. Stephanie Brown, personal communication, 2004. M. Seligman, "The Effectiveness of Psychotherapy: The Consumer Reports Study," *American Psychologist* 50 (1995): 965–74.

18. P. Ouimette, R. Moos, and J. Finney, "Influence of Outpatient Treatment and 12-Step Group Involvement on One Year Substance Abuse Treatment Outcomes," *Journal of Studies on Alcohol* 59 (1998): 513–22. S. Lash, G. Petersen, E. O'Connor, and L. Lahmann, "Social Reinforcement of Substance Abuse After Care Group Therapy Attendants," *Journal of Substance Abuse Treatment* 20 (2001): 3–8.

19. Matano and Yalom, "Approaches to Chemical Dependency." Freimuth, "Integrating Group Psychotherapy and 12-Step Work."

20. Matano and Yalom, "Approaches to Chemical Dependency."

21. Research studies of therapists' preferences demonstrate that 75–90 percent prefer the cotherapy mode (I. Paulson, J. Burroughs, and C. Gelb, "Co-Therapy: What Is the Crux of the Relationship?" *International Journal of Group Psychotherapy* 26 [1976]: 213–24). R. Dies, J. Mallet, and F. Johnson, "Openness in the Co-Leader Relationship: Its Effect on Group Process and Outcome," *Small Group Behavior* 10 (1979): 523–46. H.

Rabin, "How Does Co-Therapy Compare with Regular Group Therapy?" *American Journal of Psychotherapy* 21 (1967): 244–55.

22. C. Hendrix, D. Fournier, and K. Briggs, "Impact of Co-Therapy Teams on Client Outcomes and Therapist Training in Marriage and Family Therapy," *Contemporary Family Therapy: An International Journal* 23 (2001): 63–82.

23. H. Rabin, "How Does Co-therapy Compare." H. Spitz and S. Kopp, "Multiple Psychotherapy," *Psychiatric Quarterly Supplement* 31 (1957): 295–331. Paulson et al., "Co-Therapy: What Is the Crux." Dies et al., "Openness in the Co-leader Relationship." R. Dick, K. Lessler, and J. Whiteside, "A Developmental Framework for Co-Therapy," *International Journal of Group Psychotherapy* 30 (1980): 273–85.

24. M. Leszcz and P. Goodwin, "The Rationale and Foundations of Group Psychotherapy for Women with Metastatic Breast Cancer," *International Journal of Group Psychotherapy* 48 (1998): 245–74.

25. I. Harwood, "Creative Use of Gender in a Co-Therapy Group Composition When Addressing Early Attachment, Trauma, and Cross-Cultural Issues," *Psychoanalytic Inquiry* 23 (2003): 697–712. L. Livingston, "Transferences Toward the Co-Therapist Couple: Dyadic Relationships and Self-Object Needs," *Group* 25 (2001): 59–72.

26. B. Roller and V. Nelson, *The Art of Co-Therapy: How Therapists Work Together* (New York: Guilford Press, 1991). R. Dies, "Current Practice in the Training of Group Therapists," *International Journal of Group Psychotherapy* 30 (1980): 169–85.

27. I. Yalom, J. Tinklenberg, and M. Gilula, unpublished data, Department of Psychiatry, Stanford University, 1967.

28. S. McNary and R. Dies, "Co-Therapist Modeling in Group Psychotherapy: Fact or Fiction?" *Group* 15 (1993): 131–42.

29. J. Haley, *Problem Solving Therapy*, 2nd ed. (San Francisco: Jossey-Bass, 1987).

30. B. Roller and V. Nelson, "Cotherapy," in *Comprehensive Group Psychotherapy*, ed. H. Kaplan and B. Sadock (Baltimore: Williams & Wilkins, 1993), 304–12.

31. Paulson et al., "Co-therapy: What Is the Crux."

32. Roller and Nelson, "Cotherapy."

33. L. Murphy, M. Leszcz, A. Collins, and J. Salvendy, "Some Observations on the Subjective Experience of Neophyte Group Therapy Trainees," *International Journal of Group Psychotherapy* (1996): 543–52.

34. A model for co-therapy development has been described that identifies 9 stages: forming a contract about the work; forming an identity as a team; developing mutuality and respect; developing closeness; defining strengths and limitations; exploring possibilities; supporting self confrontation; implementing change; closing or re-organizing. (J. Dugo and A. Beck, "Significance and Complexity of Early Phases in the Development of the Co-Therapy Relationship," *Group Dynamics: Theory, Research, and Practice* 1 (1997): 294–305. S. Wheelan, "Co-Therapists and the Creation of a Functional Psychotherapy Group: A Group Dynamics Perspective," *Group Dynamics: Theory, Research, and Practice* 1 (1997): 306–10.

35. R. Desmond and M. Seligman, "A Review of Research on Leaderless Groups," *Small Group Behavior* 8 (1977): 3–24.

36. Rutan and Stone, *Psychodynamic Group Psychotherapy* 3rd ed. (New York: Guilford, 2000).

37. Yalom, Tinklenberg, and Gilula, unpublished data.

38. D. Derr and D. Zampfer, "Dreams in Group Therapy: A Review of Models," *International Journal of Group Psychotherapy* 46 (1996): 501–15.

39. M. Livingston, "Self-Psychology, Dreams, and Group Psychotherapy: Working in the Play Space," *Group* 25 (2001): 15–26.

40. J. Pawlik et al., "The Use of Dreams in a Small Analytic Group," *Group Analysis* 23 (1990): 163–71. C. Kieffer, "Using Dream Interpretation to Resolve Group Developmental Impasses," *Group* 20 (1996): 273–85.

41. M. Alpert, "Videotaping Psychotherapy," *The Journal of Psychotherapy Practice and Research* 5 (1996): 93–105.

42. M. Berger, ed., *Videotape Techniques in Psychiatric Training and Treatment* (New York: Brunner/Mazel, 1978). D. Skafte, "Video in Groups: Implications for a Social Theory of Self," *International Journal of Group Psychotherapy* 37 (1987): 389–402.

43. D. Miller, "The Effects of Immediate and Delayed Audio and Videotaped Feedback on Group Counseling," *Comparative Group Studies* 1 (1970): 19–47. M. Robinson, "A Study of the Effects of Focused Videotaped Feedback in Group Counseling," *Comparative Group Studies* 1 (1970): 47–77.

44. M. Berger, "Use of Videotape in Group Psychotherapy," in *Comprehensive Group Psychotherapy*, ed. H. Kaplan and B. Sadock (Baltimore: Williams & Wilkins, 1993): 355–62.

45. N. Mayades and D. O'Brien, "The Use of Videotape in Group Therapy," in *Videotape Techniques in Psychiatric Training and Treatment,* ed. M. Berger (New York: Brunner/Mazel, 1978), 216–29.

46. M. Ravensborg, "Debunking Video Magic," *International Journal of Group Psychotherapy* 38 (1988): 521–22.

47. M. Berger, "The Use of Video Tape with Psychotherapy Groups in a Community Mental Health Program."

48. J. Rubin and K. Locascio, "A Model for Communicational Skills Group Using Structured Exercises and Audiovisual Equipment," *International Journal of Group Psychotherapy* 35 (1985): 569–84.

49. M. Alpert, "Videotaping Psychotherapy," *Journal of Psychotherapy Practice and Research* 5 (1996): 93–105.

50. C. Classen et al., "Effectiveness of a Training Program for Enhancing Therapists' Understanding of the Supportive-Expressive Treatment Model for Breast Cancer Groups," *Journal of Psychotherapy Practice and Research* 6 (1997): 211–18.

51. J. Waltz, M. Addis, K. Koerner, and N. Jacobson, "Testing the Integrity of a Psychotherapy Protocol: Assessment of Adherence and Competence," *Journal of Consulting Clinical Psychology* 61 (1994): 620–30. P. Goodwin et al., "Lessons Learned from Enrollment in the BEST Study: A Multicenter Randomized Trial of Group Psychosocial Support in Metastatic Breast Cancer," *Journal of Clinical Epidemiology* 53 (2000): 47–55.

52. I. Yalom, S. Brown, and S. Bloch, "The Written Summary as a Group Psychotherapy Technique," *Archives of General Psychiatry* 32 (1975): 605–13.

53. R. Beck, "The Written Summary in Group Psychotherapy Revisited," *Group* 13 (1989): 102–11. M. Aveline, "The Use of Written Reports in a Brief Group Psychotherapy Training," *International Journal of Group Psychotherapy* 36 (1986): 477–82.

54. It is noteworthy as well that the last ten to twenty years has marked an explosion in narrative approaches in medicine and psychological treatments in which clients and/or caregivers write about their emotional experience and reactions to illness, trauma, and the provision of treatment. Such writing results in significant benefits that include not only subjective reports of psychological wellbeing but also objective measures of medical health and illness. (M. White and D. Epston, *Narrative Means to Therapeutic Ends*, [New York: Norton, 1990].) R. Lieb and S. Kanofsky, "Toward a Constructivist Control Mastery Theory: An Integration with Narrative Therapy," *Psychotherapy: Theory, Research, Practice, Training* 40 (2003): 187–202. There are also reports of therapists writing letters to clients delineating obstacles to therapy during the course of the treatment or shortly after termination. (B. Laub and S. Hoffmann, "Dialectical Letters: An Integration of Dialectical Cotherapy and Narrative Therapy," *Psychotherapy: Theory, Research, Practice, Training* 39 [2002]: 177–83.)

55. M. Chen, J. Noosbond, and M. Bruce, "Therapeutic Document in Group Counseling: An Active Change Agent," *Journal of Counseling and Development* 76 (1998): 404–11.

56. S. Brown and I. Yalom, "Interactional Group Therapy with Alcoholics," *Journal of Studies on Alcohol* 38 (1977): 426–56.

57. H. Spitz, *Group Psychotherapy and Managed Mental Health Care: A Clinical Guide for Providers* (New York: Brunner/Mazel, 1996), 159–69. M. Leszcz, "Recommendations for Psychotherapy Documentation," Guidelines of the University of Toronto, Department of Psychiatry, Psychotherapy Program, 2001.

58. M. Leszcz, "Group Therapy," in *Comprehensive Review of Geriatric Psychiatry*, 3rd Edition, J. Sadavoy, L. Jarvik, G. Grossberg, and B. Meyers, eds. (New York: Norton, 2004) 1023–54. I. Yalom, *Inpatient Group Psychotherapy* (New York: Basic Books, 1983). B. van der Kolk, "The Body Keeps the Score: Approaches to the Psychobiology of Post Traumatic Stress Disorder," in *Traumatic Stress, the Effects of Overwhelming Experience on Mind, Body and Society*, ed. B. van der Kolk, A.C. McFarlane, and L. Weisaeth (New York: Guilford Press, 1996), 214–41.

59. J. Kabat-Zinn, *Wherever You Go, There You Are: Mindfulness Meditation in Everyday Life* (New York: Hyperion, 1994). Z. Segal, M. Williams, J. Teasdale, *Mindfulness-Based Cognitive Therapy for Depression: a New Approach to Preventing Relapse* (New York: Guilford Press, 2001).

60. P. Finkelstein, B. Wenegrat, and I. Yalom, "Large Group Awareness Training," *Annual Review of Psychology* 33 (1982):515–39.

61. F. Perls, *The Gestalt Approach and Eyewitness to Therapy* (Ben Lomond, Calif.: Science and Behavior Books, 1974). F. Perls, *Gestalt Therapy Verbatim* (Moab, Utah: Real People Press, 1969). F. Perls, *Ego, Hunger, and Aggression* (New York: Vintage Books, 1969).

62. R. Harmon, "Recent Developments in Gestalt Group Therapy," *International Journal of Group Psychotherapy* 34 (1984): 473–83. R. Feder and R. Ronall, *Beyond the Hot Seat: Gestalt Approaches to Group* (New York: Brunner/Mazel, 1980). D. Greve, "Gestalt Group Psychotherapy," in *Comprehensive Group Psychotherapy*, ed. H. Kaplan and B. Sadock (Baltimore: Williams & Wilkins, 1993), 228–35. C. Naranjo, *Gestalt Therapy: The Attitude and Practice of an Atheoretical Experimentalism* (Nevada City, Nev.: Gateways/IDHHB Publishing, 1993). S. Ginger and A. Ginger, "Gestalt Therapy Groups: Why?" *Gestalt* 4 (2000). J. Earley, "A Practical Guide to Fostering Interpersonal Norms in a Gestalt Group," *Gestalt Review* 4 (2000): 138–51.

63. M. Lieberman, I. Yalom, M. Miles, *Encounter Groups: First Facts* (New York: Basic Books, 1973).

63. Ibid.

CHAPTER 15

1. Neither space limitations nor the rapidly growing numbers of specialized groups permit a comprehensive list and bibliography in this text. Computer literature searches are so accessible and efficient that the reader may easily obtain a recent bibliography of any specialized group.

2. P. Cox, F. Ilfeld Jr., B. Squire Ilfeld, and C. Brennan, "Group Therapy Program Development: Clinician-Administrator Collaboration in New Practice Settings," *International Journal of Group Psychotherapy* 50 (2000): 3–24. E. Lonergan, "Discussion of 'Group Therapy Program Development'," *International Journal of Group Psychotherapy* 50 (2000): 43–45. G. Burlingame, D. Earnshaw, M. Hoag, S. Barlow, "A Systematic Program to Enhance Clinician Group Skills in an Inpatient Psychiatric Hospital," *International Journal of Group Psychotherapy* 52 (2002): 555–87.

3. J. Salvendy, "Brief Group Therapy at Retirement," *Group* 13 (1989): 43–57. H. Nobler, "It's Never Too Late to Change: A Group Therapy Experience for Older Women," *Group* 16 (1992): 146–55.

4. M. Leszcz, "Group Therapy," in *Comprehensive Review of Geriatric Psychiatry*, 3rd ed., ed. J. Sadavoy, L. Jarvik, G. Grossberg, and B. Meyers (New York: Norton, 2004), 1023–54.

5. R. Klein and V. Schermer, "Introduction and Overview: Creating a Healing Matrix," in *Group Psychotherapy for Psychological Trauma,* ed. R. Klein and V. Schermer (New York: Guilford Press, 2000), 3–46. J. Herman, *Trauma and Recovery,* rev. ed. (New York: Basic Books, 1997). H. Lubin, M. Loris, J. Burt, and D. Johnson, "Efficacy of Psychoeducational Group Therapy in Reducing Symptoms of Posttraumatic Stress Disorder Among Multiply Traumatized Women," *American Journal of Psychiatry* 155 (1998): 1172–77. M. Robertson, P. Rushton, D. Bartrum, and R. Ray, "Group-Based Interpersonal Psychotherapy for Posttraumatic Stress Disorder: Theoretical and Clinical Aspects," *International Journal of Group Psychotherapy* 54 (2004): 145–75.

6. A. McKarrick et al., "National Trends in the Use of Psychotherapy in Psychiatric Inpatient Settings," *Hospital Community Psychiatry* 39 (1988): 835–41.

7. In the following discussion, I draw heavily from my book *Inpatient Group Psychotherapy* (New York: Basic Books, 1983), where interested readers may find more in-depth discussion. Although this model was developed for the inpatient ward, it has been modified and adapted to many other settings, including partial hospitalization groups and intensive two- to three-week programs for substance abusers. (In chapter 10, I discussed a particularly common major group therapy modification: the time-limited, brief, closed therapy group.)

8. M. Leszcz, I. Yalom, and M. Norden, "The Value of Inpatient Group Psychotherapy: Patients' Perceptions," *International Journal of Group Psychotherapy* 35 (1985): 411–35. Yalom, *Inpatient Group Psychotherapy,* 313–35.

9. M. Echternacht, "Fluid Group: Concept and Clinical Application in the Therapeutic Milieu," *Journal of the American Psychiatric Nurses Association* 7 (2001): 39–44.

10. S. Green and S. Bloch, "Working in a Flawed Mental Health Care System: An Ethical Challenge," *American Journal of Psychiatry* 158 (2001): 1378–83.

11. B. Rosen et al., "Clinical Effectiveness of 'Short' Versus 'Long' Psychiatric Hospitalization," *Archives of General Psychiatry* 33 (1976): 1316–22.

12. A. Alden et al., "Group Aftercare for Chronic Schizophrenics," *Journal of Clinical Psychiatry* 40 (1979): 249–52. R. Prince et al., "Group Aftercare: Impact on a Statewide Program," *Diseases of the Nervous System* 77 (1977): 793–96. J. Claghorn et al., "Group Therapy and Maintenance Therapy of Schizophrenics," *Archives of General Psychiatry* 31 (1974): 361–65. M. Herz et al., "Individual Versus Group Aftercare Treatment," *American Journal of Psychiatry* 131 (1974): 808–12. C. O'Brien et al., "Group Versus Individual Psychotherapy with Schizophrenics: A Controlled Outcome Study," *Archives of General Psychiatry* 27 (1972): 474–78. L. Mosher and S. Smith, "Psychosocial Treatment: Individual, Group, Family, and Community Support Approaches," *Schizophrenia Bulletin* 6 (1980): 10–41.

13. Leszcz et al., "The Value of Inpatient Group Psychotherapy." Yalom, *Inpatient Group Psychotherapy,* 313–35.

14. Yalom, *Inpatient Group Psychotherapy,* 34. B. Corder, R. Corder, and A. Hendricks, "An Experimental Study of the Effects of Paired Patient Meetings on the Group Therapy Process," *International Journal of Group Psychotherapy* 21 (1971): 310–18. J. Otteson, "Curative Caring: The Use of Buddy Groups with Chronic Schizophrenics," *Journal of Consulting and Clinical Psychology* 47 (1979): 649–51.

15. A number of effective clinical models have been described, each predicated upon a different conceptual frame such as psychoeducation, problem-solving, psychoanalytic, cognitive-behavioral. V. Brabender and A. Fallow, *Models of Inpatient Group Psychotherapy* (Washington, D.C.: American Psychological Association, 1993).

16. C. Williams-Barnard and A. Lindell, "Therapeutic Use of 'Prizing' and Its Effect on Self-Concept of Elderly Clients in Nursing Homes and Group Homes," *Issues in Mental Health Nursing* 13 (1992): 1–17.

17. W. Stone, "Self Psychology and the Higher Mental Functioning Hypothesis: Contemporary Theories," *Group Analysis* 29 (1996): 169–81.

18. Yalom, *Inpatient Group Psychotherapy,* 134.

19. Leszcz et al., "The Value of Inpatient Group Psychotherapy."

20. M. Leszcz, "Inpatient Group Therapy," in *APA Annual Update V* (Washington, D.C.: American Psychiatric Associative Press, 1986): 729–43.

21. Leszcz et al, "The Value of Inpatient Group."

22. I. Yalom, M. Lieberman, and M. Miles, *Encounter Groups: First Facts* (New York: Basic Books, 1973).

23. For an excellent example of departures from and modifications of my model, see W. Froberg and B. Slife, "Overcoming Obstacles to the Implementation of Yalom's Model of Inpatient Group Psychotherapy," *International Journal of Group Psychotherapy* 37 (1987): 371–88.

24. Froberg and Slife, "Overcoming Obstacles to the Implementation of Yalom's Model."

25. Leszcz et al., "The Value of Inpatient Group Psychotherapy." Yalom, *Inpatient Group Psychotherapy,* 262.

26. A. Cunningham, "Adjuvant Psychological Therapy for Cancer Patients: Putting It on the Same Footing as Adjunctive Medical Therapies," *Psycho-Oncology* 9 (2000): 367–71. M. Leszcz, "Gruppenpsychotherapie fur brustkrebspatientinnen," *Psychotheraput* 49 (2004): 314–30. K. Lorig et al., "Evidence Suggesting That a Chronic Disease Self-Management Program Can Improve Health Status While Reducing Hospitalization," *Medical Care* 37 (1999): 5–14.

27. J. Kelly, "Group Psychotherapy for Persons with HIV and AIDS-Related Illnesses," *International Journal of Group Psychotherapy* 48 (1998): 143–62. S. Abbey and S. Farrow, "Group Therapy and Organ Transplantation," *International Journal of Group Psychotherapy* 48 (1998): 163–85. R. Allan and S. Scheidt, "Group Psychotherapy for Patients with Coronary Heart Disease," *International Journal of Group Psychotherapy* 48 (1998): 187–214. B. Toner et al., "Cognitive-Behavioral Group Therapy for Patients with Irritable Bowel Syndrome," *International Journal of Group Psychotherapy* 48 (1998): 215–43. M. Leszcz and P. Goodwin, "The Rationale and Foundations of Group Psychotherapy for Women with Metastatic Breast Cancer," *International Journal of Group Psychotherapy* 48 (1998): 245–73. J. Spira, *Group Therapy for Medically Ill Patients* (New York: Guilford Press, 1997). The ENRICHD Investigators, "Enhancing Recovery in Coronary Heart Disease (ENRICHD) Study Intervention: Rationale and Design," *Psychosomatic Medicine* 63 (2001): 747–55. L. Paparella, "Group Psychotherapy and Parkinson's Disease: When Members and Therapist Share the Diagnosis," *International Journal of Group Psychotherapy* 54 (2004): 401–9. A. Sherman et al., "Group Interventions for Patients with Cancer and HIV Disease: Part I. Effects on Psychosocial and Functional Outcomes at Different Phases of Illness," *International Journal of Group Psychotherapy* 54 (2004): 29–82. A. Sherman et al., "Group Interventions for Patients with Cancer and HIV Disease: Part II. Effects on Immune, Endocrine, and Disease Outcomes at Different Phases of Illness," *International Journal of Group Psychotherapy* 54 (2004): 203–33. A. Sherman et al., "Group Interventions for Patients with Cancer and HIV Disease: Part III. Moderating Variables and Mechanisms of Action," *International Journal of Group Psychotherapy* 54 (2004): 347–87.

28. Sherman et al., "Group Interventions for Patients with Cancer and HIV Disease: Part I."

29. The ENRICHD Investigators, "Enhancing Recovery in Coronary Heart Disease." Allan and Scheidt, "Group Psychotherapy for Patients with Coronary Heart Disease."

30. Sherman et al., "Group Interventions for Patients with Cancer and HIV Disease: Part I." Spira, *Group Therapy for Medically Ill Patients.*

31. M. Hewitt, N. Breen, and S. Devesa, "Cancer Prevalence and Survivorship Issues: Analyses of the 1992 National Health Interview Survey," *Journal of the National Cancer Institute* 91 (1999): 1480–86.

32. M. Esplen, B. Toner, J. Hunter, G. Glendon, K. Butler, and B. Field, "A Group Therapy Approach to Facilitate Integration of Risk Information for Women at Risk for Breast Cancer," *Canadian Journal of Psychiatry: Psychosomatics Edition* 43 (1998): 375–80. M. Esplen et al., "A Multi-Centre Phase II Study of Supportive-Expressive Group Therapy for Women with BRCA1 and BRCA2 Mutations," *Cancer* 101 (2004): 2327–40.

33. M. Stuber, S. Gonzalez, H. Benjamino, and M. Golart, "Fighting for Recovery," *Journal of Psychotherapy Practice and Research* 4 (1995): 286–96. M. Figueiredo, E. Fries, and K. Ingram, "The Role of Disclosure Patterns and Unsupportive Social Interactions in the Well-Being of Breast Cancer Patients," *Psycho-Oncology* 13 (2004): 96–105.

34. L. Fallowfield, S. Ford, and S. Lewis, "No News Is Not Good News: Information Preferences of Patients with Cancer," *Psycho-Oncology* 4 (1995): 197–202. M. Slevin, et al., "Emotional Support for Cancer Patients: What Do Patients Really Want?" *British Journal of Cancer* 74 (1996): 1275–79.

35. I. Yalom, *Existential Psychotherapy* (New York: Basic Books, 1980).

36. L. Baider, "Psychological Intervention with Couples After Mastectomy," *Support Care Cancer* 3 (1995): 239–43. B. Bultz, M. Speca, P. Brasher, P. Geggie, and S. Page, "A Randomized Controlled Trial of a Brief Psychoeducational Support Group for Partners of Early Stage Breast Cancer Patients," *Psycho-Oncology* 9 (2000): 303–13.

37. Leszcz, "Group Therapy."

38. S. Folkman and S. Greer, "Promoting Psychological Well-Being in the Face of Serious Illness: When Theory, Research, and Practice Inform Each Other," *Psycho-Oncology* 9 [2000]: 11–19.) Not surprisingly, integrating these coping dimensions creates particularly powerful interventions as noted by R. Lazarus, "Toward Better Research on Stress and Coping," *American Psychologist* 55 (2000): 665–73.

39. D. Kissane et al., "Cognitive-Existential Group Psychotherapy for Women with Primary Breast Cancer: A Randomized Controlled Trial," *Psycho-Oncology* 12 (2003): 532–46. V. Helgeson, S. Cohen, R. Schulz, and J. Yasko, "Education and Peer Discussion Group Interventions and Adjustment to Breast Cancer," *Archives of General Psychiatry* 56 (1999): 340–47. D. Scaturo, "Fundamental Clinical Dilemmas in Contemporary Group Psychotherapy," *Group Analysis* 37 (2004): 201–17.

40. F. Fawzy and N. Fawzy, "A Post-Hoc Comparison of the Efficiency of a Psychoeducational Intervention for Melanoma Patients Delivered in Group Versus Individual Formats: An Analysis of Data from Two Studies," *Psycho-Oncology* 5 (1996): 81–89.

41. I. Yalom, *Gift of Therapy* (New York: HarperCollins, 2003), 6–10.

42. SEGT addresses the following main areas: (1) medical illness and treatment; (2) cognitive and behavioral coping skills for the illness and treatment; (3) family and social network issues; (4) relationships with health care providers; (5) life values and priorities; (6) self-image; (7) death and dying; and (8) group functioning regarding task and engagement. Each group ends with a stress reduction exercise of relaxation and guided imagery. D. Spiegel and J. Spira, *Supportive Expressive Group Therapy: A Treatment Manual of Psychosocial Interventions for Women with Recurrent Breast Cancer* (Stanford: Psychosocial Treatment Laboratories, 1991). Leszcz and Goodwin, "The Rationale and Foundations." D. Spiegel and C. Classen, *Group Therapy for Cancer Patients: A Research-Based Handbook of Psychosocial Care* (New York: Basic Books, 2000).

43. C. Classen et al., "Effectiveness of a Training Program for Enhancing Therapists' Understanding of the Supportive-Expressive Treatment Model for Breast Cancer Groups," *Journal of Psychotherapy Practice and Research* 6 (1997): 211–18. D. Spiegel et al., "Group Psychotherapy for Recently Diagnosed Breast Cancer Patients: A Multicenter Feasibility Study," *Psycho-Oncology* 8 (1999): 482–93. P. Goodwin et al., "Lessons Learned from Enrollment in the BEST Study: A Multicenter, Randomized Trial of Group Psychosocial Support in Metastatic Breast Cancer," *Journal of Clinical Epidemiology* 53 (2000): 47–55.

44. Spiegel et al., "Group Psychotherapy for Recently Diagnosed." M. Esplen et al., "A Supportive-Expressive Group Intervention for Women with a Family History of Breast Cancer: Results of a Phase II Study," *Psycho-Oncology* 9 (2000): 243–52.

45. I. Yalom and C. Greaves, "Group Therapy with the Terminally Ill," *American Journal of Psychiatry* 134 (1977): 396–400. D. Spiegel, J. Bloom, and I. Yalom, "Group Support for Patients with Metastatic Cancer," *Archives of General Psychiatry* 38 (1981): 527–33. D. Spiegel and M. Glafkides, "Effects of Group Confrontation with Death and Dying," *International Journal of Group Psychotherapy* 33 (1983): 433–37. F. Fawzy et al., "Malignant Melanoma: Effects of an Early Structured Psychiatric Intervention, Coping, and Affective State on Recurrence and Survival 6 Years Later," *Archives of General Psychiatry* 50 (1993): 681–89. T. Kuchler et al., "Impact of Psychotherapeutic Support on Gastrointestinal Cancer Patients Undergoing Surgery: Survival Results of a Trial," *Hepatogastroenterology* 46 (1999): 322–35. S. Edelman, J. Lemon, D. Bell, and A. Kidman, "Effects of Group CBT on the Survival Time of Patients with Metastatic Breast Cancer," *Psycho-Oncology* 8 (1999): 474–81. A. Ilnyckj, J. Farber, M. Cheang, and B. Weinerman, "A Randomized Controlled Trial of Psychotherapeutic Intervention in Cancer Patients," *Annals of the Royal College of Physicians and Surgeons of Canada* 27 (1994): 93–96. Kissane et al., "Cognitive-Existential Group Psychotherapy."

46. Spiegel notes that contemporary trials may not demonstrate a survival effect because the baseline of psychosocial care provided for all patients with cancer (including the control sample) has improved significantly over the past ten to twenty years, a welcome advance emerging from the recognition that state of mind affects state of body (D. Spiegel, "Mind Matters: Group Therapy and Survival in Breast Cancer," *New England Journal of Medicine* 345 (2001): 1767–68. D. Spiegel, J. Bloom, H. Kraemer, and E. Gottheil, "Effect of Psychosocial Treatment on Survival of Patients with Metastatic Breast Cancer," *Lancet* 8669 (1989): 888–91. A. Cunningham et al., "A Randomized Controlled Trial of the Effects of Group Psychological Therapy on Survival in Women with Metastatic Breast Cancer," *Psycho-Oncology* 7 (1998): 508–17. P. Goodwin et al., "The Effect of Group Psychosocial Support on Survival in Metastatic Breast Cancer," *New England Journal of Medicine* 345 (2001): 1719–26.

47. C. Classen et al., "Supportive-Expressive Group Therapy and Distress in Patients with Metastatic Breast Cancer: A Randomized Clinical Intervention Trial," *Archives of General Psychiatry* 58 (2001): 494–501. Spiegel et al., "Group Psychotherapy for Recently Diagnosed."

48. A. Beck, *Cognitive Therapy and the Emotional Disorders* (New York: International Universities Press, 1976). G. Klerman, M. Weissman, B. Rounsaville, and E. Chevron, *Interpersonal Psychotherapy of Depression* (New York: Basic Books, 1984).

49. Leszcz, "Gruppenpsychotherapie fur brustkrebspatientinnen."

50. M. Lieberman, I. Yalom, and M. Miles, *Encounter Groups: First Facts* (New York: Basic Books, 1973).

51. N. Morrison, "Group Cognitive Therapy: Treatment of Choice or Sub-Optimal Option?" *Behavioural and Cognitive Psychotherapy* 29 (2001): 311–32.

52. J. White, "Introduction," in *Cognitive-Behavioral Group Therapy for Specific Problems and Populations*, ed. J. White and A. Freeman (Washington, D.C.: American Psychological Association, 2000), 3–25.

53. Beck, *Cognitive Therapy and the Emotional Disorders*.

54. J. Safran and Z. Segal, *Interpersonal Process in Cognitive Therapy* (New York: Basic Books, 1990).

55. T. Oei and L. Sullivan, "Cognitive Changes Following Recovery from Depression in a Group Cognitive-Behaviour Therapy Program," *Australian and New Zealand Journal of Psychiatry* 33 (1999): 407–15.

56. M. Enns, B. Coz, and S. Pidlubny, "Group Cognitive Behaviour Therapy for Residual Depression: Effectiveness and Predictors of Response," *Cognitive Behaviour Therapy* 31 (2002): 31–40.

57. A. Ravindran et al., "Treatment of Primary Dysthymia with Group Cognitive Therapy and Pharmacotherapy: Clinical Symptoms and Functional Impairments," *American Journal of Psychiatry* 156 (1999): 1608–17.

58. S. Ma and J. Teasdale, "Mindfulness-Based Cognitive Therapy for Depression: Replication and Exploration of Differential Relapse Prevention Effects," *Journal of Consulting Clinical Psychology* 72 (2004): 31–40.

59. C. Kutter, E. Wolf, and V. McKeever, "Predictors of Veterans' Participation in Cognitive-Behavioral Group Treatment for PTSD," *Journal of Traumatic Stress* 17 (2004): 157–62. D. Sorenson, "Healing Traumatizing Provider Interaction Among Women Through Short-Term Group Therapy," *Archives of Psychiatric Nursing* 17 (2003): 259–69.

60. C. Wiseman, S. Sunday, F. Klapper, M. Klein, and K. Halmi, "Short-Term Group CBT Versus Psycho-Education on an Inpatient Eating Disorder Unit," *Eating Disorders* 10 (2002): 313–20. N. Leung, G. Waller, and G. Thomas, "Outcome of Group Cognitive-Behavior Therapy for Bulimia Nervosa: The Role of Core Beliefs," *Behaviour Research and Therapy* 38 (2000): 145–56.

61. C. Dopke, R. Lehner, and A. Wells, "Cognitive-Behavioral Group Therapy for Insomnia in Individuals with Serious Mental Illnesses: A Preliminary Evaluation," *Psychiatric Rehabilitation Journal* 3 (2004): 235–42.

62. J. Lidbeck, "Group Therapy for Somatization Disorders in Primary Care," *Acta Psychiatrica Scandinavia* 107 (2003): 449–56.

63. C. Taft, C. Murphy, P. Musser, and N. Remington, "Personality, Interpersonal, and Motivational Predictors of the Working Alliance in Group Cognitive-Behavioral Therapy for Partner Violent Men," *Journal of Consulting Clinical Psychology* 72 (2004): 349–54.

64. W. Rief, S. Trenkamp, C. Auer, and M. Fichter, "Cognitive Behaviour in Panic Disorder and Comorbid Major Depression," *Psychotherapy and Psychosomatics* 69 (2000): 70–78.

65. A. Volpato Cordioli et al., "Cognitive-Behavioral Group Therapy in Obsessive-Compulsive Disorder: A Randomized Clinical Trial," *Psychotherapy and Psychosomatics* 72 (2003): 211–16.

66. A. Page and G. Hooke, "Outcomes for Depressed and Anxious Inpatients Discharged Before or After Group Cognitive Behaviour Therapy: A Naturalistic Comparison," *Journal of Nervous and Mental Disease* 191 (2003): 653–59. M. Dugas et al., "Group Cognitive-Behavioral Therapy for Generalized Anxiety Disorder: Treatment Outcome and Long-Term Follow-Up," *Journal of Consulting and Clinical Psychology* 71 (2003): 821–25.

67. R. Heimberg et al., "Cognitive Behavioural Group Therapy vs. Phenelzine Therapy for Social Phobia: 12-Week Outcome," *Archives of General Psychiatry* 55 (1998): 1133–41.

68. R. Siddle, F. Jones, and F. Awenat, "Group Cognitive Behaviour Therapy for Anger: A Pilot Study," *Behavioural and Cognitive Psychotherapy* 31 (2003): 69–83.

69. L. Johns, W. Sellwood, J. McGovern, and G. Haddock, "Battling Boredom: Group Cognitive Behaviour Therapy for Negative Symptoms of Schizophrenia," *Behavioural and Cognitive Psychotherapy* 30 (2002): 341–46. P. Chadwick, S. Sambrooke, S. Rasch, and E. Davies, "Challenging the Omnipotence of Voices: Group Cognitive Behaviour Therapy for Voices," *Behaviour Research and Therapy* 38 (2000): 993–1003.

70. P. Schnurr et al., "Randomized Trial of Trauma-Focused Group Therapy for Post-Traumatic Stress Disorder: Results from a Department of Veterans Affairs Cooperative Study," *Archives of General Psychiatry* 60 (2003): 481–89.

71. White, "Introduction," in White and Freeman, eds.

72. Heimberg et al., "Cognitive Behavioral Group Therapy vs. Phenelzine."

73. Safran and Segal, *Interpersonal Process in Cognitive Therapy*.

74. White, "Introduction," in White and Freeman, eds.

75. Heimberg et al., "Cognitive Behavioral Group Therapy vs. Phenelzine."

76. Klerman et al., *Interpersonal Psychotherapy of Depression*.

77. D. Wilfley, K. MacKenzie, R. Welch, V. Ayers, and M. Weissman, *Interpersonal Psychotherapy for Group* (New York: Basic Books, 2000).

78. D. Wilfley et al., "Group Cognitive-Behavioral Therapy and Group Interpersonal Psychotherapy for the Nonpurging Bulimic Individual: A Controlled Comparison," *Journal of Consulting and Clinical Psychology* 61 (1993): 296–305. K. MacKenzie and A. Grabovac, "Interpersonal Psychotherapy Group (IPT-G) for Depression," *Journal of Psychotherapy Practice and Research* 10 (2001): 46–51. C. Klier, M. Muzik, K. Rosenblum, and G. Lenz, "Interpersonal Psychotherapy Adapted for the Group Setting in the Treatment of Postpartum Depression," *Journal of Psychotherapy Practice and Research* 10 (2001): 124–31. H. Verdeli et al., "Adapting Group Interpersonal Psychotherapy (IPT-G-U) for a Developing Country: Experience in Uganda," *World Psychiatry* (June 2003): 114–20. P. Ravitz, "The Interpersonal Fulcrum: Interpersonal Therapy for Treatment of Depression," *CPA Bulletin* 36 (2203): 15–19. Robertson et al., "Group-Based Interpersonal Psychotherapy."

79. Y. Levkovitz et al., "Group Interpersonal Psychotherapy for Patients with Major Depression Disorder: Pilot Study," *Journal of Affective Disorders* 60 (2000): 191–95.

80. H. Verdeli et al., "Adapting Group Interpersonal Psychotherapy." P. Bolton et al., "Group Interpersonal Psychotherapy for Depression in Rural Uganda: A Randomized Controlled Trial," *JAMA* 289 (2003): 3117–24.

81. MacKenzie and Grabovac, "Interpersonal Psychotherapy Group."

82. R. Kessler, K. Mickelson, and S. Zhao, "Patterns and Correlations of Self-Help Group Membership in the United States," *Social Policy* 27 (1997): 27–47.

83. F. Riessman and E. Banks, "A Marriage of Opposites: Self-Help and the Health Care System," *American Psychologist* 56 (2001): 173–74. K. Davison, J. Pennebaker, and S. Dickerson, "Who Talks? The Social Psychology of Support Groups," *American Psychologist* 55 (2000): 205–17. J. Kelly, "Self-Help for Substance-Use Disorders: History, Effectiveness, Knowledge Gaps, and Research Opportunities," *Clinical Psychology Review* 23 (2003): 639–63. L. Adamsen, "From Victim to Agent: The Clinical and Social Significance of Self-Help Group Participation for People with Life-Threatening Diseases," *Scandinavian Journal of Caring Sciences* (Special Issue: The Challenging Complexity of Cancer Care Research) 16 (2002): 224–31. S. Barlow, G. Burlingame, R. Nebeker, and E. Anderson, "Meta-Analysis of Medical Self-Help Groups," *International Journal of Group Psychotherapy* 50 (2000): 53–69.

84. Riessman and Banks, "A Marriage of Opposites." Davison et al., "Who Talks?"

85. An unpublished study by a Turkish colleague comparing the therapeutic factors of AA and a professional therapy group (N = 44 patients) revealed that interpersonal learning input and output were ranked significantly higher by the therapy group, whereas universality, cohesiveness, and instillation of hope were chosen by the AA members (Cem Atbasoglu, personal communication, 1994).

86. Ibid.

87. S. Cheung and S. Sun, "Helping Processes in a Mutual Aid Organization for Persons with Emotional Disturbance," *International Journal of Group Psychotherapy* 51 (2001): 295–308. Riessman and Banks, "A Marriage of Opposites." Davison et al., "Who Talks?" M. Salzer, J. Rappaport, and L. Segre, "Professional Appraisal of Professionally Led and Self-Help Groups," *American Journal of Orthopsychiatry* 69 (1999): 536–40.

88. L. Roberts, D. Salem, J. Rappaport, P. Toro, D. Luke, and E. Seidman, "Giving and Receiving Help: Interactional Transactions in Mutual-Help Meetings and Psychosocial Adjustment of Members," *American Journal of Community Psychology* 27 (1999): 841–68. K. Prior and M. Bond, "The Roles of Self-Efficacy and Abnormal Illness Behaviour in Osteoarthritis Self-Management," *Psychology, Health, and Medicine* 9 (2004): 177–92.

89. Davison et al., "Who Talks?"

90. Kelly, "Self-Help for Substance-Use Disorders."

91. J. Tonigan, R. Toscova, and W. Miller, "Meta-Analysis of the Literature on Alcoholics Anonymous: Sample and Study Characteristics Moderate Findings," *Journal of Studies on Alcohol* 57 (1996): 65–72.

92. M. Lieberman and L. Snowden, "Problems in Assessing Prevalence and Membership Characteristics of Self-Help Group Participants," *Journal of Applied Behavioral Science* 29 (1993): 166–80. B. Carlsen, "Professional Support of Self-Help Groups: A Support Group Project for Chronic Fatigue Syndrome Patients," *British Journal of Guidance and Counselling* 31 (2003): 289–303.

93. Data are from PEW Internet and America Life Project (www.pewinternet.org), July 16, 2003.

94. J. Alleman, "Online Counseling: The Internet and Mental Health Treatment," *Psychotherapy: Theory, Research, Practice, Training* 39 (2002): 199–209. M. White and S. Dorman, "Receiving Social Support Online: Implications for Health Education," *Health Education Research* 16 (2001): 693–707. M. Lieberman, M. Golant, A. Winzelberg, and F. McTavish, "Comparisons Between Professionally Directed and Self-Directed Internet Groups for Women with Breast Cancer," *International Journal of Self-Help and Self Care* 2 (2004): 219–35.

95. S. Hopss, M. Pepin, and J. Boisvert, "The Effectiveness of Cognitive-Behavioral Group Therapy for Loneliness via Inter-Relay-Chat Among People with Physical Disabilities," *Psychotherapy: Theory, Research, Practice, Training* 40 (2003): 136–47. J. Walther, "Computer-Mediated Communication: Impersonal, Interpersonal, and Hyperpersonal Interaction," *Communication Research* 23 (1996): 3–43. Alleman, "Online Counseling." White and Dorman, "Receiving Social Support Online."

96. V. Waldron, M. Lavitt, and K. Douglas, "The Nature and Prevention of Harm in Technology-Mediated Self-Help Settings: Three Exemplars," *Journal of Technology in Human Services* 17 (2000): 267–93. White and Dorman, "Receiving Social Support Online." R. Kraut, M. Patterson, V. Lundmark, S. Kiesler, T. Mukopadhyay, and S. Scherlis, "Internet Paradox: A Social Technology that Reduces Social Involvement and Psychological Well-Being," *American Psychologist* 53 (1998): 1017–31.

97. H. Weinberg, "Community Unconscious on the Internet," *Group Analysis* 35 (2002): 165–83.

98. Alleman, "Online Counseling." A. Ragusea and L. VandeCreek, "Suggestions for the Ethical Practice of Online Psychotherapy," *Psychotherapy: Theory, Research, Practice, Training* 40 (2003): 94–102.

99. Hopss et al., "The Effectiveness of Cognitive-Behavioral Group Therapy."

100. K. Luce, A. Winzelberg, and M. Zabinski, "Internet-Delivered Psychological Interventions for Body Image Dissatisfaction and Disordered Eating," *Psychotherapy: Theory, Research, Practice, Training* 40 (2003): 148–54.

101. D. Tate, R. Wing, and R. Winett, "Using Internet Technology to Deliver a Behavioral Weight Loss Program," *JAMA* 285 (2001): 1172–77. A. Celio and A. Winzelberg, "Improving Compliance in On-line, Structured Self-Help Programs: Evaluation of an Eating Disorder Prevention Program," *Journal of Psychiatric Practice* 8 (2002): 14–20.

102. M. Zabinski et al., "Reducing Risk Factors for Eating Disorders: Targeting At-Risk Women with a Computerized Psychoeducational Program," *Journal of Eating Disorders* 29 (2001): 401–8. M. Zabinski, D. Wilfley, K. Calfas, A. Winzelberg, and C. Taylor, "An Interactive, Computerized Psychoeducational Intervention for Women at Risk of Developing an Eating Disorder," presented at the 23rd annual meeting of the Society for Behavioral Medicine, Washington, D.C., 2002.

103. T. Houston, L. Cooper, and D. Ford, "Internet Support Groups for Depression: A 1-Year Prospective Cohort Study," *American Journal of Psychiatry* 159 (2002): 2062–68.

104. Ibid., 2066.

105. White and Dorman, "Receiving Social Support Online." D. Gustafson et al., "Development and Pilot Evaluation of a Computer-Based Support System for Women with

Breast Cancer," *Journal of Psychosocial Oncology* 11 (1993): 69–93. D. Gustafson et al., "Impact of a Patient-Centered, Computer-Based Health Information/Support System," *American Journal of Preventive Medicine* 16 (1999): 1–9

106. Winzelberg et al., "Evaluation of an Internet Support Group."

107. M. Lieberman et al., "Electronic Support Groups for Breast Carcinoma: A Clinical Trial of Effectiveness," *Cancer* 97 (2003): 920–25.

108. M. Lieberman, personal communication, 2004.

109. Lieberman et al., "Comparisons Between Professionally Directed and Self-Directed Internet Groups."

CHAPTER 16

1. H. Coffey, personal communication, 1967. A. Bavelas, personal communication, 1967. A. Marrow, "Events Leading to the Establishment of the National Training Laboratories," *Journal of Applied Behavioral Science* 3 (1967): 144–50. L. Bradford, "Biography of an Institution," *Journal of Applied Behavioral Science* 3 (1967): 127–44. K. Benne, "History of the T-Group in the Laboratory Setting," in *T-Group Theory and Laboratory Method*, ed. L. Bradford, J. Gibb, and K. Benne (New York: Wiley, 1964), 80–135.

2. Benne, "History of the T-Group."

3. E. Schein and W. Bennis, *Personal and Organizational Change Through Group Methods* (New York: Wiley, 1965), 41.

4. Ibid., 43.

5. J. Luft, *Group Processes: An Introduction to Group Dynamics* (Palo Alto, Calif.: National Press, 1966).

6. I. Wechsler, F. Messarik, and R. Tannenbaum, "The Self in Process: A Sensitive Training Emphasis," in *Issues in Training,* ed. I. Wechsler and E. Schein (Washington, D.C.: National Education Association, National Training Laboratories, 1962), 33–46.

7. M. Lieberman, I. Yalom, and M. Miles, *Encounter Groups: First Facts* (New York: Basic Books, 1973). M. Lieberman, I. Yalom, and M. Miles, "The Group Experience Project: A Comparison of Ten Encounter Technologies," in *Encounter,* ed. L. Blank, M. Gottsegen, and G. Gottsegen (New York: Macmillan, 1971). M. Lieberman, I. Yalom, and M. Miles, "The Impact of Encounter Groups on Participants: Some Preliminary Findings," *Journal of Applied Behavioral Sciences* 8 (1972): 119–70.

8. These self-administered instruments attempted to measure any possible changes encounter groups might effect—for example, in self-esteem, self-ideal discrepancy, interpersonal attitudes and behavior life values, defense mechanisms, emotional expressivity, values, friendship patterns, and major life decisions. Much third-party outcome assessment was collected—evaluations by leaders, by other group members, and by a network of each subject's personal acquaintances. *The assessment outcome was strikingly similar to that of a psychotherapy project but with one important difference: since the subjects were not clients but ostensibly healthy individuals seeking growth, no assessment of target symptoms or chief complaints was made.*

9. M. Ettin, "By the Crowd They Have Been Broken, By the Crowd They Shall Be Healed: The Advent of Group Psychotherapy," *International Journal of Group Psychotherapy* 38 (1988): 139–67. M. Ettin, "Come on, Jack, Tell Us About Yourself: The Growth Spurt of Group Psychotherapy," *International Journal of Group Psychotherapy* 39 (1989): 35–59. S. Scheidlinger, "History of Group Psychotherapy," in *Comprehensive Group Psychotherapy,* ed. H. Kaplan and B. Sadock (Baltimore: Williams & Wilkins, 1993), 2–10.

10. M. Rosenbaum and M. Berger, *Group Psychotherapy and Group Function* (New York: Basic Books, 1963).

11. E. Lazell, "The Group Treatment of Dementia Praecox," *Psychoanalytic Review* 8 (1921): 168–79.

12. L. Marsh, "Group Therapy and the Psychiatric Clinic," *Journal of Nervous and Mental Disorders* 32 (1935): 381–92.

13. L. Wender, "Current Trends in Group Psychotherapy," *American Journal of Psychotherapy* 3 (1951): 381–404. T. Burrows, "The Group Method of Analysis," *Psychoanalytic Review* 19 (1927): 268–80. P. Schilder, "Results and Problems of Group Psychotherapy in Severe Neurosis," *Mental Hygiene* 23 (1939): 87–98. S. Slavson, "Group Therapy," *Mental Hygiene* 24 (1940): 36–49. J. Moreno, *Who Shall Survive?* (New York: Beacon House, 1953).

14. L. Horwitz, "Training Groups for Psychiatric Residents," *International Journal of Group Psychotherapy* 17 (1967): 421–35. L. Horwitz, "Transference in Training Groups and Therapy Groups," *International Journal of Group Psychotherapy* 14 (1964): 202–13. S. Kaplan, "Therapy Groups and Training Groups: Similarities and Differences," *International Journal of Group Psychotherapy* 17 (1967): 473–504.

15. R. Morton, "The Patient Training Laboratory: An Adaptation of the Instrumented Training Laboratory," in *Personal and Organizational Change Through Group Methods,* ed. E. Schein and W. Bennis (New York: Wiley, 1965), 114–52.

16. J. Simon, "An Evaluation of est as an Adjunct to Group Psychotherapy in the Treatment of Severe Alcoholism," *Biosciences Communications* 135 (1977): 141–48. J. Simon, "Observations on 67 Patients Who Took Erhard Seminars Training," *American Journal of Psychiatry* 135 (1978): 686–91.

CHAPTER 17

1. C. McRoberts, G. Burlingame, and M. Hoag, "Comparative Efficacy of Individual and Group Psychotherapy: A Meta-Analytic Perspective," *Group Dynamics* 2 (1998): 101–17. G. Burlingame, K. MacKenzie, and B. Strauss, "Small-Group Treatment: Evidence for Effectiveness and Mechanisms of Change," in *Bergin and Garfield's Handbook of Psychotherapy and Behavior Change*, 5th ed., ed. M. Lambert (New York: Wiley, 2004), 647–96.

2. I. Yalom, "Problems of Neophyte Group Therapists," *International Journal of Social Psychiatry* 7 (1996): 52–59. L. Murphy, M. Leszcz, A. Collings, and J. Salvendy, "Some Observations on the Subjective Experience of Neophyte Group Therapy Trainees," *International Journal of Group Psychotherapy* (1996): 543–52. R. Billow, "The Therapist's Anxiety and Resistance to Group Therapy," *International Journal of Group Psychotherapy* 51 (2001): 225–42. S. Scheidlinger, "Response to 'The Therapist's Anxiety and Resistance to Group Psychotherapy,'" *International Journal of Group Psychotherapy* 52 (2002): 295–97.

3. S. Feiner, "Course Design: An Integration of Didactic and Experiential Approaches to Graduate Training of Group Therapy," *International Journal of Group Psychotherapy* 48 (1998): 439–60. A. Fuhriman and G. Burlingame, "Group Psychotherapy Training and Effectiveness," *International Journal of Group Psychotherapy* 5 (2001): 399–416. H. Markus and A. Abernethy, "Joining with Resistance: Addressing Reluctance to Engage in Group Therapy Training," *International Journal of Group Psychotherapy* 51 (2001): 191–204. H. Markus and D. King, "A Survey of Group Psychotherapy Training During Predoctoral Psychology Internship," *Professional Psychology, Research, and Practice* 34 (2003): 203–9.

4. American Group Psychotherapy Association, "Guidelines for Certification: Group Psychotherapy Credentials." Available at www.agpa.org.

5. N. Taylor, G. Burlingame, K. Kristensen, A. Fuhriman, J. Johansen, and D. Dahl, "A Survey of Mental Health Care Provider's and Managed Care Organization Attitudes Toward, Familiarity With, and Use of Group Interventions," *International Journal of Group Psychotherapy* 51 (2001): 243–63.

6. B. Schwartz, "An Eclectic Group Therapy Course for Graduate Students in Professional Psychology," *Psychotherapy: Theory, Research, and Practice* 18 (1981): 417–23.

7. Although didactic courses are among the *least* effective methods of teaching, over 90 percent of psychiatric residency teaching programs use them. E. Pinney, "Group Psychotherapy Training in Psychiatric Residency Programs," *Journal of Psychiatric Education* 10 (1986): 106.

8. J. Gans, J. Rutan, and E. Lape, "The Demonstration Group: A Tool for Observing Group Process and Leadership Style," *International Journal of Group Psychotherapy* 52 (2002): 233–52.

9. See I. Yalom, *Inpatient Group Psychotherapy* (New York: Basic Books, 1983), 259–73, for a full discussion of this format.

10. To order, go to psychotherapy.net/ and click on "videotapes." V. Brabender, "Videotape Resources for Group Psychotherapists: A 5-Year Retrospective," *International Journal of Group Psychotherapy* 52 (2002): 253–63. Brabender (2002) has completed a detailed summary of currently available video tape training resources. A particularly effective approach in training that is often used in clinical trials is an intensive workshop in which trainees watch videotape segments of group therapy—led well and poorly. Trainees then discuss how they understand what they observed; what worked and why; what failed and why; what alternative approaches could be used?

11. H. Bernard, "Introduction to Special Issue on Group Supervision of Group Psychotherapy," *International Journal of Group Psychotherapy* 49 (1999): 153–57.

12. Murphy et al., "Some Observations on the Subjective Experience." J. Kleinberg, "The Supervisory Alliance and the Training of Psychodynamic Group Psychotherapists," *International Journal of Group Psychotherapy* 49 (1999): 159–79. S. Shanfield, V. Hetherly, and D. Matthews, "Excellent Supervision: The Residents' Perspective," *Journal of Psychotherapy Practice and Research* 10 (2001): 23–27. M. Bowers Jr., "Supervision in Psychiatry and the Transmission of Values," *Academic Psychiatry* 23 (1999): 42–45. M. Leszcz, "Reflections on the Abuse of Power, Control, and Status in Group Therapy and Group Therapy Training," *International Journal of Group Psychotherapy* 54 (2004): 389–400.

13. A. Alonso, "On Being Skilled and Deskilled as a Psychotherapy Supervisor," *Journal of Psychotherapy Practice and Research* 9 (2000): 55–61.

14. M. Leszcz and L. Murphy, "Supervision of Group Psychotherapy," in *Clinical Perspectives on Psychotherapy Supervision*, ed. S. Greben and R. Ruskin (Washington, D.C.: American Psychiatric Press, 1994), 99–120. Shanfield et al., "Excellent Supervision."

15. M. Hantoot, "Lying in Psychotherapy Supervision: Why Residents Say One Thing and Do Another," *Academic Psychiatry* 24 (2000): 179–87.

16. G. Burlingame et al., "A Systematic Program to Enhance Clinician Group Skills in an Inpatient Psychiatric Hospital," *International Journal of Group Psychotherapy* 52 (2002): 555–87.

17. Murphy et al., "Some Observations on the Subjective Experience."

18. G. Ebersole, P. Leiderman, and I. Yalom, "Training the Nonprofessional Group Therapist," *Journal of Nervous and Mental Disorders* 149 (1969): 294–302.

19. L. Tauber, "Choice Point Analysis: Formulation, Strategy, Intervention, and Result in Group Process Therapy and Supervision," *International Journal of Group Psychotherapy* 28 (1978): 163–83.

20. H. Roback, "Use of Patient Feedback to Improve the Quality of Group Therapy Training," *International Journal of Group Psychotherapy* 26 (1976): 243–47.

21. J. Elizur, "'Stuckness' in Live Supervision: Expanding the Therapist's Style," *Journal of Family Therapy* 12 (1990): 267–80. V. Alpher, "Interdependence and Parallel Processes: A Case Study of Structural Analysis of Social Behavior in Supervision and Short-Term Dynamic Psychotherapy," *Psychotherapy* 28 (1991): 218–31.

22. A. Alonso, "Training for Group Psychotherapy," in *Group Therapy and Clinical Practice,* ed. A. Alonso and H. Swiller (Washington, D.C.: American Psychiatric Press, 1993), 521–32. Leszcz and Murphy, "Supervision of Group Psychotherapy."

23. D. Altfeld, "An Experiential Group Model for Psychotherapy Supervision," *International Journal of Group Psychotherapy* 49 (1999): 237–54. E. Counselman and R. Weber, "Organizing and Maintaining Peer Supervision Groups," *International Journal of Group Psychotherapy* 54 (2004): 125–43.

24. D. Janoff and J. Schoenholtz-Read, "Group Supervision Meets Technology: A Model for Computer-Mediated Group Training at a Distance," *International Journal of Group Psychotherapy* 49 (1999): 255–72.

25. C. Classen et al., "Effectiveness of a Training Program for Enhancing Therapists' Understanding of the Supportive-Expressive Treatment Model for Breast Cancer Groups," *Journal of Psychotherapy Practice and Research* 6 (1997): 211–18. H. Verdeli et al., "Adapting Group Interpersonal Psychotherapy for a Developing Country: Experience In Rural Uganda," *World Psychiatry* 2 (2002): 114–20. S. Feiner, "Course Design: An Integration of Didactic and Experiential Approaches to Graduate Training of Group Therapy," *International Journal of Group Psychotherapy* 48 (1998): 439–60.

26. Pinney, "Group Psychotherapy Training in Psychiatric Residency Programs." J. Gans, J. Rutan, and N. Wilcox, "T-Groups (Training Groups) in Psychiatric Residency Programs: Facts and Possible Implications," *International Journal of Group Psychotherapy* 45 (1995): 169–83. V. Nathan and S. Poulsen, "Group-Analytic Training Groups for Psychology Students: A Qualitative Study," *Group Analysis* 37 (2004): 163–77.

27. M. Aveline, "Principles of Leadership in Brief Training Groups for Mental Health Professionals," *International Journal of Group Psychotherapy* 43 (1993): 107–29.

28. E. Coche, F. Dies, and K. Goettelmann, "Process Variables Mediating Change in Intensive Group Therapy Training," *International Journal of Group Psychotherapy* 41 (1991): 379–98. V. Tschuschke and L. Greene, "Group Therapists' Training: What Predicts Learning?" *International Journal of Group Psychotherapy* 52 (2002): 463–82.

29. D. Scaturo, "Fundamental Clinical Dilemmas in Contemporary Group Psychotherapy," *Group Analysis* 37 (2004): 201–17.

30. Aveline, "Principles of Leadership in Brief Training Groups."

31. C. Mace, "Personal Therapy in Psychiatric Training," *Psychiatric Bulletin* 25 (2001): 3–4.

32. J. Guy et al., "Personal Therapy for Psychotherapists Before and After Entering Professional Practice," *Professional Psychology: Research and Practice* 19 (1988): 474–76.

33. J. Norcross, "Personal Therapy for Therapists: One Solution, 96th annual meeting of the American Psychological Association: The Hazards of the Psychotherapeutic Practice for the Clinician (1988, Atlanta, Georgia)," *Psychotherapy in Private Practice* 8 (1990): 45–59. J. Prochaska and J. Norcross, "Contemporary Psychotherapists: A National Survey of Characteristics, Practices, Orientations, and Attitudes," *Psychotherapy: Theory, Research, and Practice* 20 (1983): 161–73.

34. D. Weintraub, L. Dixon, E. Kohlhepp, and J. Woolery, "Residents in Personal Psychotherapy: A Longitudinal Cross-Sectional Perspective," *Academic Psychiatry* 23 (1999): 14–19.

35. I. Yalom, *The Gift of Therapy* (New York: HarperCollins, 2003).

36. N. Elman and L. Forrest, "Psychotherapy in the Remediation of Psychology Trainees: Exploratory Interviews with Training Directors," *Professional Psychology: Research and Practice* 35 (2004): 123–30. L. Beutler et al., "Therapist Variables," in *Bergin and Garfield's Handbook of Psychotherapy and Behavior Change*, 5th ed., ed. M. Lambert (New York: Wiley, 2004), 647–96. The research in this area is problematic. There is substantial evidence that therapist psychological well-being is associated with better clinical outcomes but personal psychotherapy is not. Perhaps the best explanation for these findings is that engaging in personal psychotherapy by itself is not synonymous with psychological well-being. Many practitioners may have long struggled personally and not yet achieved what they need from their personal psychotherapy. Even so, personal psychotherapy makes therapists more resilient in the face of the demands of the clinical work.

37. The Canadian Group Psychotherapy Association, as of 1986, required ninety hours of personal experience in either a bona fide therapy group or a prolonged experiential workshop with other professionals (Kent Mahoney, personal communication, 1994). J. Salvendy, "Group Therapy Trainees as Bona Fide Members in Patient Groups," in *Group and Family Therapy,* ed. L. Wolberg and M. Aronson (New York: Brunner/Mazel, 1983). R. Alnoes and B. Sigrell, "Evaluation of the Outcome of Training Groups Using an Analytic Group Psychotherapy Technique," *Psychotherapy and Psychosomatics* 25 (1975): 268–75. R. Dies, "Attitudes Toward the Training of Group Psychotherapists," *Small Group Behavior* 5 (1974): 65–79. H. Mullan and M. Rosenbaum, *Group Psychotherapy* (New York: Free Press, 1978), 115–73. M. Pines, "Group Psychotherapy: Frame of Reference for Training," in *Psychotherapy: Research and Training,* ed. W. DeMoor, W. Wijingaarden, and H. Wijngaarden (Amsterdam: Elsevier/North Holland Biomedical Press, 1980), 233–44. J. Salvendy, "Group Psychotherapy Training: A Quest for Standards," *Canadian Journal of Psychiatry* 25 (1980): 394–402. R. Battegay, "The Value of Analytic Self-Experiencing Groups in the Training of Psychotherapists," *International Journal of Group Psychotherapy* 33 (1983): 199–213.

38. Coche et al., "Process Variables Mediating Change."

39. Counselman and Weber, "Organizing and Maintaining Peer Supervision Groups."

40. E. Bein et al., "The Effects of Training in Time-Limited Dynamic Psychotherapy: Changes in Therapeutic Outcome," *Psychotherapy Research* 10 (2000): 119–32. B. Wampold, *The Great Psychotherapy Debate: Models, Methods, and Findings* (Mahwah, N.J.: Erlbaum, 2001). I. Elkin, "A Major Dilemma in Psychotherapy Outcome Research: Disentangling Therapists from Therapies," *Clinical Psychology: Science and Practice* 6 (1999): 10–32. S. Miller and J. Binder, "The Effects of Manual-Based Training on Treatment Fidelity and Outcome: A Review of the Literature on Adult Individual Psychotherapy," *Psychotherapy: Theory, Research, Practice, Training* 39 (2002): 184–98.

41. Burlingame et al., "Small-Group Treatment."

42. E. Silber and J. Tippet, "Self-Esteem: Clinical Assessment and Validation," *Psychological Reports* 16 (1965): 1017–71.

43. S. Holmes and D. Kivlighan, "Comparison of Therapeutic Factors in Group and Individual Treatment Processes," *Journal of Counseling Psychology* 47 (2000): 478–84.

44. M. Lieberman and I. Yalom, "Brief Psychotherapy for the Spousally Bereaved: A Controlled Study," *International Journal of Group Psychiatry* 42 (1992): 117–33.

45. S. Leacock, "Gertrude the Governess or Simple 17," *A Treasury of the Best Works of Stephen Leacock* (New York: Dodd, Mead, 1954).

Index

AA. *See* Alcoholics Anonymous
AA serenity prayer, 477
Absenteeism, 392; of group members, 167–68, 325–32; meaning of, 328; value of, 329
Acceleration of interaction, 164
Acceptance, 54, 58, 117, 147; among juveniles, 57; enhanced by group, 66; group, 62; importance of, 57; by others, 56; universal need for, 26; valued by group members, 61
Activating procedures, 163–64; curvilinear nature of, 164
Active coping, 11
Actualizing tendency, 62
Acute inpatient therapy groups: acute inpatient hospitalization *v.*, 484–85; alleviating hospital-related anxiety in, 487; altruism in, 487; clinical setting for, 481–84; formulation of goals in, 484–87; maladaptive interpersonal behavior in, 486; modes of structure in, 494–98; modification of technique for, 487–94; working model for higher-level group, 498–506. *See also* Inpatient groups
Adaptive social skills, augmented by group popularity, 69
Adaptive spiral, 113; facilitated by therapist, 49; through imitative behavior, 96; in therapy groups, 49
Addition of new members to group: group response to, 338–40; therapeutic guidelines for, 340–43; timing of, 337–38
Adult Survivors of Incest, 9
Advice-giving, 12
Advice-seeking, interpersonal pathology and, 12
Affect, 48; borderline clients and, 418; critical incident and, 29; expression of, 510; illness and, 31; modeled by therapist, 334
Affiliation, 56
Affiliativeness, 60
Agreeableness, 264

Ahistorical focus, 98
Alcohol treatment groups, 479; existential factors and, 99, 107; as twelve-step groups, 440–41. *See also* Alcoholics Anonymous (AA); Twelve-step groups
Alcoholics Anonymous (AA), 5, 518; direct advice used by, 12; here-and-now focus in, 141; higher power and, 441; large-group format of, 293; therapeutic factors and, 109. *See also* Twelve-step groups
Alcoholism, 43, 234, 375, 381
Alexander, Franz, 27
Alexithymia, 400–401
Alienation, 30
Allport, G., 531
Aloneness, 102
Altruism, 1, 13–15, 81–82, 98, 107, 109–11; in AA, 14; in acute inpatient therapy groups, 487; in medical illness groups, 509; in systems of healing, 14
Alzheimer's caregiver groups, moving to leaderless format, 390
Ambiguity, decreased by self-knowledge, 95
Ambulatory groups, 282–83; written summaries for, 304
American Counseling Association, 521
American Group Psychotherapy Association, 391, 544; experiential groups, 89; training groups, 61, 555
American Psychiatric Association, 308
American Psychological Association, 521
American Self-Help Clearinghouse, 518
Analysis of resistance, 472–73
Analysis Terminable and Interminable (Freud), 190
Analytic movement, 470
Analytic theory, 531
Anamnestic technique, 192
Anger: expression of, 28–29; group, 394; in leaderless meetings, 449; prejudice as source of, 368; scapegoating and, 367;